GO
YIA

Saint

Saint

ADRIENNE YOUNG

TITAN BOOKS

Saint

Print edition ISBN: 9781803362717

E-book edition ISBN: 9781803360065

Published by Titan Books

A division of Titan Publishing Group Ltd.

144 Southwark Street, London SE1 0UP

www.titanbooks.com

First Titan edition: January 2023

10 9 8 7 6 5 4 3 2 1

A CIP catalogue record for this title is available from the British Library.

Printed and bound by CPI Group (UK) Ltd, Croydon CR0 4YY.

FOR KRISTIN,

THE VERY FIRST SOUL I EVER TRUSTED WITH MY
IMAGINATION. THIS ONE'S FOR YOU.

JOHN B!

Saint

ISOLDE

There was a blue door with a black lantern on Forsyth Street.

Behind it was a man who could make me disappear.

My hand dragged over the uneven brick wall as I paced up the walk, the heels of my boots a sharp clip in the night. Rain still dripped from the edges of the rooftops, beading down the single-pane windows, and the damask silk of my skirts was heavy with the damp.

North End's intricate tangle of alleys and streets unfurled into the wet corners of a city that had just seen a storm. It was a labyrinth I didn't know. Bastian was my home, but I'd never been to North End, not even with my father. A girl like me had no reason to. I was the daughter of a merchant who'd lived every day of her life to please her mother, even if I'd left that version of me back at Azimuth House. But there was no betrayal like the one I carried in my pocket. Now, I was no more than a traitor.

"Blue door. Black lantern," I whispered to myself again.

My eyes skipped over the buildings and I squinted, trying to make out their shapes and colors in the dark. The helmsman of the *Craven* was a man I'd seen many times at my mother's house and on her ships, but he'd kept his distance from me like most of her traders did. No one wanted to touch the flame that burned at the center of my mother's hands. She protected her precious things.

But the helmsman had been my father's friend. So, when I'd pulled him behind the gauze curtains that looked out over the candlelit gala and whispered to him that I needed to leave the city, he'd told me how. I could hardly pick out his deep voice over the sound of the music, and now I wondered if I'd heard him right at all.

North End. Look for the blue door with the black lantern on Forsyth Street.

That warm light at my mother's gala was still alive around me, as if it were clinging to my edges as I slipped through the dark. But I could feel it bleeding from me, like the slow smear of ink in water. Threads of color that stretched until they disappeared. The glint of the gold wallpaper of my mother's study. My father's portrait looking down at me. The way the midnight's song had filled the room until my ears were ringing with it.

In a matter of seconds, that world had come crashing

down with only three words spoken from Holland's lips: *a necessary sacrifice.*

It had taken me the length of a breath to decide to open the gem case. To walk out that door. And I was never, ever going back.

I wiped the tear from my numb cheek, walking faster as the street curved deeper into the borough. When the glossy blue door of the row house finally appeared, it was easy to spot. The paint looked fresh, almost wet, and the black lantern that hung over the threshold was fitted with not one flame, but two, illuminating the alcove that sat hollow at the top of the steps.

I glanced over my shoulder before I climbed them, knocking softly with a trembling hand. It was the middle of the night, but if what I'd heard about North End was true, it wouldn't be so unusual to have a visitor at this hour. The work on these streets was done in shadow, out of view of the guilds and the harbor watch and the Trade Council. I suspected that was why the helmsman of the *Craven* had sent me there.

I raised my fist to knock again before the door's lock turned and it opened, revealing the face of a girl not much older than me. One long braid was pinned over the crown of her head and the color of her simple frock matched it, made notable only by the bright silver chain of a pocket watch tucked into her belt. Her dark, owlish eyes raked over my gown before they shot to the street behind me.

"I think you knocked on the wrong door." There was a

cutting edge to her voice that hardened the soft curves of her face.

My hands clenched tighter in my skirts, a bead of sweat sliding down my spine, and the hair beginning to unravel from its pins blew across my cheek as another rain-soaked gust of wind swallowed the street.

"I'm looking for Simon," I said.

The name the helmsman of the *Craven* had given me seemed to surprise her, but the look on her face quickly turned into curiosity. She studied me another moment, the set of her mouth steady as her gaze tightened on my face. She was looking for something there, I realized, and once she found it, she let the door swing open.

I glanced once more at the empty street before I stepped over the threshold, into the amber light that filled the narrow hallway. The floorboards popped beneath the soles of my boots, the windows of the house rattling in the wind, but the sound buzzing in my chest was a different one. Gemstone.

The hum hovered between the walls in a chorus that reverberated in my bones. It was everywhere, coming from all around me.

There was a moment, a fleeting one, when I wanted to reach for the door before it closed and run from that feeling that had haunted me since the day my mother first realized what I was. But as quickly as the thought came, it was gone again. There was no going back. Not now.

The door's heavy bolt slid into place and the girl turned to face me. There was a beat of silence that made me think that she, too, was reconsidering whether she should have let me inside.

Her chin lifted. "Follow me."

The fabric of my thick skirts brushed along the walls of the cramped hallway, making me feel like it was growing narrower by the second. The familiar sounds of garnet and emerald and diamond caught my ear, interlaced with a dozen others, but they didn't belong here. The tiny, run-down row house wasn't the home of someone who wore a merchant's ring from the Gem Guild, which would deem the trade inventory under this roof a legitimate one. North End was famous for its criminals, and they'd made my mother's life very difficult over the last few years. I could only hope that meant this was the last place she'd come looking for me.

The hall came to an end, and I followed the girl down a winding staircase, catching sight of her face only briefly as she looked back at me. "You're lucky you didn't have those jewels and that ridiculous frock ripped off of you in the street."

The words weren't laced with a threat or even any kind of reproach. In fact, she sounded as if she was genuinely marveling at the fact that I'd made it there in one piece. And she was probably right. I'd walked all the way from the merchants' district, keeping to the alleys so I wouldn't be spotted. My mother would have already noticed I was gone, and that wasn't entirely unusual. But when she saw what I'd taken with me, she'd have the whole city combing the streets and the harbor.

The girl opened another door and we entered a large, dark cellar lit only by a small fireplace tucked into one corner. The walls were almost entirely hidden by stacks of closed crates that reached to the ceiling, marked with port seals I recognized. They stretched from the Unnamed Sea to the Narrows.

It took me a moment to spot the man sitting at the long wooden table on the other side of the room. Simon, I hoped. He looked up from a stack of parchment, eyes struggling to focus on me. His light brown hair was a wild sweep across his forehead, the buttons of his shirt half undone.

"She's looking for you." The girl's fingers slipped from the door handle as she watched me.

I finally let go of my skirts, wiping my slick palms against the smooth fabric. "You're Simon?"

"I am." The man's voice was measured, as unreadable as his face, but I saw his gaze pause on the pearl-and-sapphire earrings that still hung from my ears.

"My name is—"

"I know who you are," he interrupted. "The question is, what are you doing here?"

I hadn't planned to give him my real name, but the fact that he knew my face woke a sinking feeling in the center of my chest. I'd been raised among the likes of the guild, but I'd lived most of my days with my mother's ship crews. This man was neither. And I was sure I'd never seen him before.

"I was told you can get me out of the city," I said.

His hands moved from the parchment, folding it on the table before him, and his attention drifted back to the girl in the doorway. It was only a moment before it found me again.

"If you want to leave Bastian, all you have to do is walk down to the harbor and pay for passage."

"No. I can't." I swallowed, thinking of Holland. She saw every manifest. Every inventory list. The harbor master himself answered to her. "I need to . . . disappear."

Simon finally stood, letting the stool scrape against the uneven floor behind him. The sound made me shift on my feet. When he came around the table to face me, I took an involuntary step backward.

"To where?"

"Ceros," I answered, hands twisting into the fabric of my skirts again.

It would take no time at all for Holland to find me in Nimsmire or Sagsay Holm. There wasn't a single port in the Unnamed Sea she didn't have eyes on. And if I was going to cut her the only place she could feel, I had to get to the Narrows.

"Who sent you here?" he asked.

"The helmsman of the *Craven*."

Simon seemed to consider that a moment. He paced the floor, arms crossed over his chest, but beside me, the girl looked wary. They weren't fools. If they knew who I was then they knew who I was running from, and no one in their right mind would go against my mother. But this man and Holland were probably already on opposite sides of a line.

"Won't take her long to look through the passenger lists," he thought aloud, and I was grateful he didn't call Holland by name. "And there's only one way to leave Bastian—the sea."

"A crew, then," I said.

"Crew?" One of his eyebrows lifted. "You want to crew on a ship headed to the Narrows?"

"If you know who I am, then you know I'm a dredger."

He stopped his pacing then, staring at me. Holland's dredger daughter was a source of entertainment for the guilds. Freediving the coral reefs that snaked through the Unnamed Sea to excavate gemstone wasn't exactly a refined trade. But it wasn't just the dredging my mother used me for, and that was the reason her empire had stretched the entire coast of the Unnamed Sea. In a way, I'd raised and fed the dragon that had all but devoured me.

My father hadn't been so lucky. He'd had the sense to keep my gift as a gem sage a family matter. It was only in the last few years that it had become all but impossible to do. And his worry for me had eventually become his end.

"Put me on a crew. As long as they're going to Ceros, I don't care which one."

I had no intention of diving for anyone ever again. Not unless it was my own pockets I was filling with coin. But I needed a ship. One my mother wouldn't look twice at.

Simon's head tilted to one side, considering it. "Not the worst idea." He pulled a fresh sheet of parchment from the stack on the table. "There's a ship in the harbor that's scheduled to leave at dawn. It's called the *Luna*."

I exhaled, so heavy with relief that I felt as if I might fall through the floor.

He kept his back to me and took his time, dipping the quill into the inkpot between lines of words and sanding the ink. When he was finished, he folded the parchment carefully and sealed it with a deep violet wax the color of opaque amethyst.

"You're sure?" The girl's quiet voice was heavy as she eyed Simon. I'd almost forgotten she was standing there.

He answered with only a brief glance in her direction before he gestured to me.

"Those should do it."

It took a moment for me to realize he was talking about the earrings he'd been inspecting when I walked through the door. I hesitated before I reached up, unclasping each one and dropping them into his hand. They were worth over a hundred coppers each, but I'd expected to pay more.

He tucked them into the pocket of his vest, jerking his chin toward the door, where the young woman was still patiently waiting.

"Get her something to wear, Eden." He handed her the parchment. "And have the seamstress cut up that frock. The silk should fetch something."

She vanished without another word, leaving us alone in the dark cellar.

Simon leaned into the edge of the table, watching me as her steps faded up the staircase. It was only then I could feel just how far I was from the protective reach and scrutinizing gaze of my mother. And instead of that knowledge bringing me fear, there was only fury burning inside of me.

"Looks like fate is smiling on me tonight," he said, almost to himself.

My hand slipped into my pocket, finding the small purse that held the midnight stone. It was the only thing that had the power to pierce Holland's iron skin. The only thing I'd ever seen put a flash of terror in her eyes, bright behind that look of hunger.

Simon's attention seemed to narrow on me the moment I thought it. "What exactly is it you're you running from, Isolde?"

I didn't like hearing my name on a stranger's tongue, but there was more than one answer to that question. My mother. Her empire. Her blood that ran through my veins. It wasn't the first time I'd wanted to escape, but when I heard those words leave her mouth, the cold had wrapped around my heart and squeezed until I couldn't breathe.

A necessary sacrifice.

It had been almost a year since my father died on Yuri's Constellation, the system of reefs I'd grown up diving. The helmsman who'd run the dive for my mother arrived at the harbor with the news. A terrible accident, he'd called it. A sudden turn of tide in an unexpected storm.

It wasn't until the night of the gala, almost a year later, as I stood in my mother's study listening to her hushed words entangled with the voice of the Unnamed Sea's Gem Guild master, that I understood. She'd called my father a necessary sacrifice.

The pieces clicked together one at a time until the picture formed in my mind. It took only minutes to find the ship logs. To find no mention of the storm that had swallowed my father and my heart in a single moment.

He'd wanted to leave Bastian with me. To take me away from my mother's growing shadows. I would have followed him anywhere, but Holland had made sure I had no one to follow. No one but her.

My hand squeezed the purse of gemstone in my pocket so hard that my knuckles ached. I wasn't just going to set fire to everything she'd built. I was going to throw her into the flames too.

Simon took a step toward me. "I said, what are you running from?"

My eyes lifted to meet his, the midnight burning like a hot ember in the center of my palm. "A monster."

ONE

SAINT

My father told me once that the only fools who sailed the Narrows were the dead and the dying. Sometimes, I think I'm both.

I leaned into the railing of the *Riven* with both hands, watching the lanterns in the harbor flicker to life one by one in the distance. Water dripped from the sails overhead and the meager crew on the deck was still white-faced from the swells we'd carved down only an hour before we spotted land.

Behind them, Clove stood at the helm, the spokes light in his fingers as it spun. His stained shirt was rolled up to his elbows, and most of his blond hair was now unraveled from its knot, blowing across his face as we turned into the wind.

We'd chosen Dern for two reasons. The first was because there was little cause for anyone to come here, other than the traders from the Unnamed Sea who bought grain from the crofters for less than it cost to grow it. The second was because Rosamund was the only shipwright willing to risk taking the coin off two fishermen's sons from Cragsmouth who had no legitimate way to explain where they got it.

There was an explanation, of course. Just not one I was willing to give.

The fading daylight painted the sails over our heads a brilliant amber and the intricately stitched canvas glistened with droplets of rain. They were more patchwork than anything these days, having been repaired by the sailmaker so many times that he'd flat-out refused to take a needle to them again.

He wasn't the only one who thought I was mad, tempting the sea demons by sailing the rickety old ship into deep waters. But I'd come out the other side of enough black, tangled clouds to stop asking whether a storm would kill me. The sea had had her chance enough times. She'd never taken it.

I unfolded my hand, eyeing the fresh cut across my palm beside a stack of healed scars. It was still raw and red from the last port we'd left, stinging as the skin stretched.

"Take us in," I murmured to Clove, ducking into the narrow passage behind him.

His voice called out the orders to our sorry excuse for a crew as I pushed into the sorry excuse for a helmsman's quarters. The cramped room smelled like mold and years-old mullein smoke seeping from the damp wood, but it had been my home for the last two and a half years and it had stayed afloat, which was more than most bastards got.

I hadn't had oil for the lantern in weeks—another luxury we couldn't afford—so when the sun went down it was damn near impossible to see anything. I felt my way along the bulkhead to the chest against the wall and lifted the lid. The stiff hinges creaked as the trunk opened and I reached inside. I didn't bother hiding copper on this ship because there wasn't anyone stupid enough to steal from me. That was where the stories they told about us had served us well.

My reflection appeared on the round, cracked mirror beside the window as I stood. Blue eyes stared back at me, set beneath thick, dark brows. The angles of my face were deeper than usual, and my jaw was shadowed with scruff. But there wasn't a single coin in our coffers that hadn't already been spent. The lowest on the list was a full belly or a clean shave or lanterns we could actually light. I wouldn't have any of those things until well after Rosamund was paid.

I took the long, cylindrical map case from the wall and pulled the strap over my head so that the case rested against my back. Then I raked one hand through my almost-black hair, tucking it behind one ear and pulling up the collar of my jacket. The purse was heavy in my palm as I stowed it in my pocket, and the ship creaked perilously around me as it began to slow. I wasn't sure how many more voyages across the Narrows the *Riven* could take, but I wouldn't have to find out either.

I caught my own gaze in the mirror for a moment more, brushing off the shoulders of my jacket. I didn't look anything like the Saltbloods who sailed their fancy ships from the Unnamed Sea and plucked what little the Narrows had from our starving hands. Even so, in a month's time, we'd be hocking the *Riven* to whoever wanted the scrap iron and salvageable wood. Then we'd be sailing from Dern under a real trader's crest.

Clove was already waiting beside the ladder when I came back out onto the deck. He leaned into the railing, eyeing Julian as he tied off the lines of the foremast with a hard set to his mouth. The young deckhand's fingers faltered under Clove's gaze, and he pulled at its length, starting again. There was no impressing the *Riven*'s navigator, and with a helmsman who steered them into storms that were the stuff of nightmares, the crew we picked up at each port never lasted long. A few times, they'd disappeared without even waiting to collect the coin they were owed.

It was just as well. There was no shortage of bastards in the Narrows who thought they were willing to die for copper. I usually got at least a few crossings out of them before they realized they weren't.

"Ready?" Clove pulled on his cap as the deckhand finished, swinging one leg over the railing.

"Ready."

I followed him down to the dock, where the harbor master was already waiting. Gerik studied the ship with a scrutinizing gaze, his lip curled under his pointed nose. The

Riven was nothing much to look at, but I'd stopped being ashamed of her a long time ago.

"You know, every time you leave, I'm sure it's the last time I'll see this ship," Gerik muttered, scratching at a page in his log with a feathered quill. His gaze lifted to the crate of rye being lowered from the railing behind us.

"Messages?" I asked, eyeing the opening of his jacket, where a stack of folded parchment was tucked against his chest.

"No," he answered.

I clenched my teeth, the weight on my chest pressing just a little heavier. Every time we made port, I was sure the summons to the Trade Council would be waiting.

"I guess that means you still don't have that license you keep promising?"

"I don't."

Gerik's eyes squinted. "Then why are you unloading rye on my dock?"

I reached into my vest for the smaller purse of coin I'd known I would need. Now that the Narrows had its own legitimate Trade Council, every helmsman who sailed its waters was vying for a license to compete with the Saltbloods. Us included. But it took copper to get a license—a lot of it— and the only way to get that much coin was to trade *without* a license first and hope that everyone kept their mouths shut.

Gerik could be paid to look the other way, but he could also be paid to snitch. So far, we'd been lucky.

"It's coming," I grunted, handing the purse over.

"Says you and every other fool with a ship." He took it, immediately turning on his heel. "We'll see, won't we?"

"Bastard," Clove muttered.

He hated Gerik even more than I did. He hated most people, in fact. We'd grown up on the wide-bellied fishing boats in Cragsmouth and we'd each pulled the other from churning waters more times than I could count, but that wasn't the reason he was the only soul in the Narrows I trusted. Anyone could throw a drowning man a line. Finding someone who would catch hold of you before you fell overboard in the first place was harder, if not impossible.

I pulled the watch from my pocket, tilting it toward the lantern light. "Need to make this quick."

Clove scanned the docks around us as I started toward the stairs, and a moment later, his footsteps sounded behind me. Dern was no more than a cluster of stone buildings along the rocky shore. It was an outpost of sorts that had slowly become a port when the ships from the Unnamed Sea started showing up here for grain, but the village hadn't caught much attention from the new Trade Council in Ceros. Not yet anyway.

I climbed the steps and took the winding path that led up the hill, away from the busy main thoroughfare. Rosamund didn't like being in the mix of things, but the longer our arrangement dragged on, the more likely it was that someone would get wind of what I was up to. It would come out eventually. But controlling *when* was the key.

The shore grew steep as we reached the little cove, where a few piers reached out over the water. One of them had never been repaired after the storm that took its roof a few years ago, but the other two were still standing, and Rosamund's seal adorned both.

I rapped on the door with my fist twice, and the lock turned a moment later. Ros's apprentice, Nash, didn't look happy to see us. He never did.

His eyes dragged over me from head to toe. "Back already?"

I leaned into the doorframe. "She here?"

Nash's lips pursed as he inspected my shirt, and I ignored him. Not all of us had the steady place of an apprenticeship to keep our clothes mended and our hair trimmed. Not all of us wanted one either. I'd sooner find my death in the deep than live under a guild's crooked thumb.

Nash pushed the door open, letting us in, and he locked it behind us. Inside, lantern light washed over the warm, golden-hued hull of a ship.

The *Aster*.

She was a schooner with two masts and a hull that would hold more than enough cargo for us to get our trade off the ground. Most important, she was ours. Or she would be once I handed this purse of coin over.

The last time we'd seen her, the masts hadn't been standing. Now they reached up into the rafters that arched over our heads, where a few silver-feathered pigeons were perched in crumbling straw nests. The ship was set onto braces that stretched out over the open black water below. In a few weeks, she would be lowered into the sea for the first time and we'd be raising the sails.

I met Clove's eyes. There was the faint shadow of a smirk on his lips. He was thinking the same thing. Somehow, we'd pulled this thing off. To be honest, I wasn't even sure how.

"Thought I heard coin jingling," Rosamund's rasping voice called out from the deck above. She peered down at us over the railing of the starboard side before climbing down to the platform.

Nash crossed his arms over his chest, still sneering. "You sure you can handle a ship like this one? I'd hate to see it sail away just to hear it's sunk a week later."

"We do the building, not the sailing, Nash," Rosamund said, jumping down from the ladder with a grunt. "What do you care, as long as you get paid?"

She pulled the straps of her heavy tool belt from her shoulders and loosened the buckle at her waist. When she was free of it, she reached up, kneading the tight muscles at the back of her neck. Rosamund wasn't a slight woman, but the bulky shipwright's gear made her look it.

"All right. Get on with it." She wasn't a gentle woman either.

I reached into my jacket and pulled the purse free, setting it into her open hand. She felt its weight before she passed it to Nash, and he found a seat at the small table against the wall to begin counting right away.

"How many days?" I asked, watching him carefully as he opened the purse.

Rosamund turned the merchant's ring on her finger, thinking. The silver was dinged and bent up from the work

19

she did, but the stone at its center marked her as an approved merchant by the Shipwrights Guild. If Nash was lucky, one day he'd wear one too.

"I'd say we'll have her sea ready by the next full moon, give or take a few days."

Clove took a step toward the edge of the platform and reached up, running a hand over the smooth wood planks that stretched to the bow. There was a rare tenderness in the touch. He'd waited a long time for this. We both had.

"But I gotta say," Ros sighed, "those fools up at the tavern are gettin' more curious by the day."

Clove's gaze slid to meet mine. That was a problem. We weren't the only ones trying to establish a Narrows-born trading operation, and there was no shortage of helmsmen who'd see this ship burn before they let us get ahead of them in that line. We'd managed to keep the *Aster* a secret while it was being built, but if people in Dern found out Rosamund was building a ship for us, that would catch attention. And not just from the helmsmen of the Narrows who stopped here. The Saltbloods didn't want to lose their hold on trade, and one more ship sailing wouldn't do them any favors. We didn't need anyone sniffing around and finding out just how close we were.

Rosamund set her hands on her hips impatiently. "How're we lookin', Nash?"

"So far so good," he grunted, taking his time with each stack of coin.

When I realized he was only halfway through the purse, I pulled the watch from my pocket to check the time again.

It was nearly half past the hour, and I knew what happened when I was late. My next appointment wouldn't wait for me, no matter how long we'd been doing business.

"Go." Clove jerked a chin toward the door. "I'll finish up here and meet you at the tavern for the count."

I nodded, snapping the watch closed and dropping it back into my jacket. I pulled my cap on and started toward the door, but I looked back once more before I pushed out into the rain.

The *Aster* glowed in the lantern light, the gleaming wood as smooth as the morning sea. She wasn't just a ship. She was an idea. She was the thing I'd risked my neck for a hundred times over the last two years and my chance at a trade license, along with a crest of my own. But the *Aster* wasn't just going to change things for me and Clove. She was going to change things for the Narrows.

TWO

SAINT

Three chimneys rose from the mist over the only tavern in Dern, smoke billowing from their narrow, blackened mouths.

In the two years I'd been stopping in the village, I'd never seen the tavern empty. There was no merchant's house here, even though there was a growing trade, and that meant the tavern was the place of business for anyone stopping through, including me.

The roar of voices came tumbling out onto the street as I opened the doors, and the humid warmth of the fire in the stone fireplace at the back hit me like a wall. I was never on dry land long enough to rid my bones of the chill or fully dry the damp from my clothes, but the smell of burning wood reminded me of the days before I'd given my life to the sea.

The door closed behind me and I instinctively rolled my shoulders. I didn't like being closed in by four walls and I didn't like the feeling of solid earth beneath my feet. I preferred the openness of the water, where you could at least see what was coming for you on the horizon.

The barkeeper gave me a nod in greeting when he spotted me, immediately turning toward the wall of bottles behind him and reaching for the one that quite literally had my name on it. Barkeepers made a nice side profit on pouring watered-down rye for patrons once they were a few drinks in, pocketing the excess coin. The first time I'd caught him filling my glass with it, I'd drawn my knife from my belt so quickly that he didn't even have time to stopper it.

I could see that look—the one that flashed in the eyes of the people who'd heard the stories about the helmsman of the *Riven*. In those tales, I'd made a pact with sea demons to spare my ship from storms and offered my own crew as sacrifices to the sea. I was mad. Reckless. Just asking to meet my death out on the water.

The barkeeper hadn't tried cutting my rye again, and I doubted he would since I kept him stocked with Sowan's best bottle. I couldn't blame him for trying, but Clove and I weren't just two kids from a fishing village who'd washed up in the harbor. And I counted on him to make sure I didn't look cheap in front of my guest.

I leaned on the counter with both hands, waiting as he pulled the bottle from its place on the wall. He set it down, followed by two small green glasses.

"Your luck never ceases to amaze me, Saint." He grunted. "Just missed a hell of a storm."

I smirked to myself. We hadn't missed it. And luck had nothing to do with it. "Our room ready?"

He gave me a nod and I lifted the map case from my shoulder, handing it to him. One of the kitchen maids was already climbing the stairs with it when I picked up the bottle and the glasses, heading for the row of wooden booths that lined the wall.

The toe of a shined leather boot stuck out from under one of the tables and when I rounded the high back of the seat, Henrik Roth didn't even bother looking up from his ledger.

His mouth moved silently around the numbers he was writing along the right-hand column of the open page as I slid into the seat across from him. His pocket watch was open on the table, the second hand quietly ticking around the face. I waited for him to finish before I set the two glasses between us.

Henrik dropped the quill, looking up. He was only four or five years older than me, but something about the look in his eyes always made me forget that. His light brown hair had the slightest tinge of red and it was somehow always freshly cut and expertly combed, as if whatever ship he came in on had a barber on board. His tailored jacket and spotless white shirt made him stand out among the grimy traders that filled the tavern, but I'd always gotten the impression that he liked it that way. He was the most smartly dressed criminal I'd ever met.

"Could smell you as soon as you came through the door." He sat back, giving me a wry grin. "You're more fish guts than human these days."

I unstopped the bottle, pouring his rye before I poured my own. "You're probably right about that." I set it down and picked up my glass.

Henrik followed, lifting his to meet mine at the center of the table, and they clinked before we shot them back in one swallow. The taste burned in the back of my throat, warming my belly as Henrik took it upon himself to pour the second round.

"When are you going to tell me where you get this stuff?" He lifted one eyebrow.

I swirled the rye in my glass. The bottles Clove and I sold illegally at each port had no maker's mark, and that was intentional. If we were caught selling it, I didn't want it falling back on the crofter who made it. But I also didn't want anyone knowing where it came from because when we finally had our license, we'd be the only ones trading the stuff.

"I'll tell you where the rye comes from if you tell me how you get those gem fakes to weigh out," I said.

Henrik smiled at that, his brown eyes sparkling. The Roths had built their business on gem fakes that were more than convincing, but the real mystery was how they'd been able to get their stones to pass the scales. According to the accounts I'd heard in the Narrows taverns, it had been more than thirty years since the Roths' fakes had first started appearing in the merchant's houses, and no one had been able to crack it. Not even the few gem sages who were left.

Between our rye and Henrik's stones, we'd started a risky but mutually beneficial enterprise in the Narrows. Almost two years in, Clove and I had finally been able to fund the build of the *Aster* and our petition for a license in one sweep.

Henrik reached into his vest, producing a small blue velvet pouch and setting it down in front of me. I finished my glass before opening it and pouring the faceted crimson pieces into my palm. Their faces caught the lantern light, sparkling, and the sight made me swallow hard. It was the largest haul we'd ever traded for him, and if I played it right, it could be the last. Now that the *Aster* and our trade license was paid for, the coin we cut from this deal would go to launch our first official route through the Narrows. It was the kind of coin that spilled blood. Ours, if we weren't careful.

"Red beryl, ranging from about a quarter to a third of a carat each. The cuts are clean and the color is some of the best I've done. These'll pass anyone's inspection as long as you steer clear of a gem sage."

"Lucky for you those aren't so easy to find these days," I said, holding one of the stones up to the light.

The ratio of real to fake was at least one to three, but I wouldn't be able tell them apart if my life depended on it. Even the gem merchants' most sophisticated gem lamps rarely detected them.

"I'm definitely not complaining."

I poured the stones back into the pouch, cinching it closed and tucking it into my jacket before I pulled my final purse of coin free. Henrik didn't even bother counting it. We'd traded enough times for him to know I was good for it, and I knew him well enough now to understand that if I crossed the Roths, I'd pay with my life.

"Happy to be rid of them. Most of the gem sages in Bastian are gone. Sagsay Holm too."

"Where are they headed?"

Henrik shrugged. "Don't know. Don't care. But my job is getting a lot easier without them."

There was a time when gem sages had been in high demand in both Bastian and Ceros for their unparalleled skills with the gems. But when they started out-earning the merchants who relied upon them, there were bounties put out and no shortage of people who were willing to collect that coin. People like the Roths, whose business relied on the production and trade of fakes, had benefited.

"I've heard there are merchants in the Narrows paying top dollar to have a gem sage smuggled in. I'd be careful," he said.

That didn't surprise me. Now that the Narrows had a Trade Council, there wasn't a single guild member who wasn't trying to climb up in the world to try their hand at beating out the merchants of the Unnamed Sea. If they had to buy gem sages to do it, they would.

"Thanks for the tip."

Henrik leaned on the table with both elbows. "You lose business, I lose business."

He met my eyes, making sure I understood that it wasn't charity. It was a warning. If he didn't bring in the coin he was supposed to, his father, Felix Roth, would deal with him. That was what made getting mixed up with the Roths so dangerous. Everyone had something to lose.

Henrik was the only one involved in this arrangement who knew where the gems were going. I sold them in Sowan to a merchant named Lander who collected a percentage for bleeding them into the gem trade in Bastian, but he had no idea where they came from or how they'd gotten into the Narrows in the first place. I was just the first link in the chain.

"Anything else I should know?" I asked.

"Nothing of consequence."

He turned his empty glass on the table, the look in his eyes sharpening. The ease that had been in his demeanor, I realized, was suddenly gone. "Anything *I* should know?"

"No."

"That's funny. I could have sworn I heard talk of a shipwright here in Dern working on a new schooner for an unknown Narrows-born helmsman."

I met his eyes, taking every care not to react. He was onto me. But I couldn't risk giving him any information he didn't already have. "Something you want to ask me, Henrik?"

"You know the stories they tell about you, don't you?" His head tilted to one side. "About a kid from nowhere who sails into storms that would make a seasoned trader piss his trousers. That you're pious. Superstitious. A believer in the old tales. That a blood pact with sea demons is the only reason you're still breathing."

My fist tightened under the table, where the cut of my own blade striped my palm.

I knew the stories. They were what had given me the name I was known by outside of Cragsmouth—Saint. No one knew Elias, the boy born in a backwater fishing village who'd made a mistake that cost him everything.

"When I first heard about you, I thought to myself, that's one smart bastard, letting the rumors do the work for him while he writes his own story. It's one of the reasons I agreed to work with you. But this little misstep has had me wondering if I made a mistake."

"You didn't."

"Good. Because I don't make mistakes. If you want to trade with a legit license and sail under your own crest on a new ship, that's your business. But as soon as people get wind of it, someone is going make sure you never make it to the next port. And *my* coin will be at the sea bottom with you."

That was exactly the reason we'd been treading lightly.

"No one will get wind of it," I said.

"You sure about that?"

Warm blood pooled in my hand where I'd torn open the cut in my palm.

"Someone in this village has a loose tongue." Henrik leaned in closer. "Might be time for you to cut it out."

My teeth clenched tightly as I nodded. If someone was talking, we had less time than I thought to get that license and raise our crest over the *Aster*. Only then would we have the protection of the Trade Council to keep us from getting a knife in the back.

Henrik picked up his pocket watch and closed his ledger, tucking both inside of his jacket. "See you in three weeks."

He stood and I stared into the back of the booth, waiting until the door of the tavern opened and closed before I poured myself one more glass of rye. I'd known from the beginning that we were playing with fire by working with the Roths, but the risk had paid off. Even if I could feel the careful framework we'd built rattling around me, threatening to come crashing down.

I lifted the glass and tipped my head back, letting the rye burn in my chest. There were a hundred different ways this could still go wrong and no shortage of blades I could find at my throat. By the time we got back out onto the water, I needed to be sure I was rid of at least one of them.

THREE

ISOLDE

Being the only Saltblood on a ship had its advantages until someone left a dead rat in your hammock.

I stood in the dim light of the crew's cabin, staring down into the quilted fabric. It reeked of mildew and rye, but it was the most honest bed I'd ever slept in. Everything I'd had in Bastian was bought with someone else's blood.

I didn't miss the warm fire of my rooms, the fine quilts, or the plush rugs that covered the marble floor at Azimuth House. The only thing I missed was someone who wasn't there anymore.

I fished the poor, lifeless creature out of my hammock by the tail, holding it away from me. The bloodstain it left behind would be of little consequence, but the message was another matter. It was an old custom and I'd seen it on my mother's ships many times.

Dredgers weren't the lowest rung of a crew, but they drew the most suspicion. Accusations of pocketing gems on a dive or selling cache locations to other traders were something that every dredger had to deal with, but they were disadvantages I'd never really suffered because my mother employed every member of the crews I'd been on. Making a move against me meant making a move against the great gem merchant Holland, and that was a risk no one was willing to take.

But I wasn't on the Unnamed Sea anymore. As soon as I'd handed my earrings and my frock over, Simon had taken me down to the docks, where the *Luna* was waiting. I'd known as soon as I met its helmsman that it wouldn't be as easy as simply hitching a ride to the Narrows. But a dead rodent dangling from my fingertips was nothing to the mess I'd left behind in Bastian.

I climbed the steps of the passageway back to the deck and the sunlight hit my face, the wind clearing away the stagnant stench that hovered below. The crew was at work and the navigator, Burke, was at the helm, his eyes following my path as I crossed to the portside railing. We'd been at sea for almost a week and I hadn't earned anyone's favor. I wouldn't unless I started putting coin in the helmsman's purse with a haul of dredged gemstones.

I tossed the rat into the water, turning on my heel to scan the masts above until I spotted Yasmin, the ships' lead bosun. Her long blond hair was tied in a series of knots between her shoulder blades, and she was holding back a smile breaking on her lips. If I had to guess, I would say the rat had been her doing or maybe that of Darin, one of the deckhands who warmed her bed. They had no unwavering loyalty to the *Luna*. In fact, I was certain they were running their own side trades on the ship. The rat had been more about making sure I knew where I stood. Here, I wasn't untouchable the way I'd been in Bastian, and I liked that. I just hoped it didn't get me killed.

"What was that, dredger?" Burke eyed me over the helm.

"Just a bit of fun," I lied, hooking my thumbs into my belt. My hips felt bare without the weight of my dredging tools. I couldn't get used to it.

He jerked his chin to one of the deckhands, signaling for him to take over the wheel, and waved me toward the passage that led to the helmsman's quarters. I let out a long breath, staring at the carved wood trim that adorned the door.

I'd had exactly one crew to choose from when I went to Simon and asked him to put me on a ship out of Bastian. The helmsman of the *Luna* had taken me on without question when he read Simon's letter, and he had only one requirement: that I sign a one-year contract to dredge for him. It was a small price to pay when it wasn't my own name at the bottom of that parchment. I wasn't Isolde anymore. I was Eryss. And I was finished diving for anyone but me.

As soon as we got to Ceros, I'd leave the *Luna* and never look back. There was no recourse against a dredger who'd broken her contract if she didn't actually exist. Not even in the eyes of the new Trade Council.

The work of the crew beat on the upper deck as I ducked into the passage, and I flattened myself against the wall when the stryker came barreling through with a plucked pheasant clutched in each hand. Burke was already relaying the ordeal with the rat to the helmsman when I came through the door, and he didn't look pleased.

Zola's black eyes lifted to me as I stepped inside, but he didn't stand from his chair. He was a peacock with dull feathers, obviously from the Narrows, and I wasn't sure what he'd been doing in the Unnamed Sea in the first place, much less how he'd been allowed to drop anchor there. The only explanation was that he had a scheme of some kind, one that must benefit someone who mattered. But it took guts to waltz into Bastian with no permit. I'd give him that.

"Eryss?" Zola looked to me, waiting for an explanation.

I kept my tone light, careful not to meet his eyes for too long. I didn't like how he was always trying to hold my gaze.

"You know how crews are."

"Yes, I do," he said.

He set down the quill in his hand, abandoning the letter he was writing, and my eyes lingered on the humble quail feather it was crafted from. My mother gifted the loyal merchants and traders who did her bidding a quill made with the glossy, black-tipped feather of a whistling swan—a symbol of repute. A kind of imperious crown for those she deemed worthy of her attention and evidence that you had Holland's power behind you. But this man was just a would-be trader who would not only be unlikely to recognize me, he'd never be important enough to catch my mother's notice.

"I can't afford to lose my new dredger," he continued.

My new dredger.

The words made my teeth grate. The very fact that I was standing here was proof that for the first time in my life, I didn't belong to anyone. But someone like Zola would never understand that. He'd probably only ever belonged to himself.

"Move her up here until we get to Ceros." Zola directed the order to Burke.

My brow pinched. "What?"

"You'll stay here in my quarters until they've had some time to get used to having a Saltblood on board."

Saltblood. The slur was a demeaning one, used to identify people from the Unnamed Sea, where the water was like a bitter brine. Here in the Narrows, the sea was diluted with the fresh water of the rivers that dumped from their shores.

"That's *not* necessary," I said, a little too forcefully. "And I don't care if they get used to me. I can take care of myself."

"You signed a contract. And if someone decides to gut you in the middle of the night, I'll have lost a dredger before we even get to our first dive."

The helmsman had lofty ideas about running dives once the new Narrows Trade Council granted him a trade license. But he was fooling himself. The *Luna* wasn't equipped for gem dives and not a single preparation had been made. I hadn't even seen a tide map among the charts in his quarters. The man had no idea what he was doing.

"I'll sleep in the crew's cabin. Like everyone else." The words came out flat. I wasn't politely declining. I'd rather get stuffed into a trunk in the cargo hold and left for a few days than sleep in Zola's quarters.

His hands splayed on the desk as he pushed himself to standing and the length of his black coat slid from the stool, dropping to his ankles. His gaze was locked on mine as he came around the desk and stopped so close to me that when he looked down into my face, the buttons of his jacket brushed my sleeve.

His silvery eyes were cold as they held mine, and after a moment, they moved, traveling down over my mouth, to my chin.

"I can replace any deckhand or stryker or bosun with a hundred others in Ceros," he said. "But Simon said you're a dredger with uncommon skill. Those aren't easy to come by."

My eyes narrowed on him, my heartbeat ticking up just a little as I searched his eyes for any deeper meaning behind the words. But there was no way Zola could know I was a gem sage. My father had made sure of that.

"I can take care of myself," I said again.

"Fine." His tone soured as he drifted forward another inch, letting his height loom over me, but I didn't budge, keeping my feet planted. He wanted me to be afraid of him, and I was. But I wasn't going to let him see it.

His head finally swiveled to Burke. "Anyone touches her, and they'll lose a limb of their choosing." The words grew spines.

Zola wasn't good at hiding his irritation, clearly bothered that I cared so little for his attentions. But I wasn't going to stroke his ego, even if it got me what I needed. That was a door that was hard to close once it was opened.

Burke didn't look at me, but I could feel his thoughts drifting in my direction. The crew wouldn't be the only ones to suffer if they broke the helmsman's decree. As second in command, Burke would bear a punishment for failing to control them, and the last thing I needed was for him to have a reason to resent me.

Zola dismissed him with a wave of his hand. "Make sure they're ready to make port."

Burke seemed to still be debating whether to protest Zola's order, but he thought better of it, shuffling out and leaving the two of us alone.

"Make port?" I asked, trying to read the open log at the corner of his desk. "I thought we wouldn't be in Ceros for a few more days."

He found his way back around the desk, eyes off me now. "We won't."

"Then where are we stopping?"

"We run routes in the Narrows, just like they do in the Unnamed Sea. We make stops." The sarcasm changed the rhythm of his speech. The poisoned honey that had been there moments ago was gone now and the man the crew feared had returned. The rumors belowdecks were that he'd buried his knife in the chest of his last stryker only weeks before I arrived on the *Luna*.

I bit my tongue, swallowing down the argument that was climbing up my throat. Every day I was on the water was another day someone was looking for Holland's daughter and the fabled gemstone she'd stolen. I needed to get to Ceros before someone found me.

Zola returned his eyes to the parchment in front of him. The wooden rim that skirted his desk was the only thing keeping the contents from sliding when the ship tilted under a gale. I leaned to the left, instinctively countering my own weight.

"If that's all, I have work to do," he said.

He was a creature that needed to feel like he was calling the shots. In more than one way, he reminded me of my mother—wheels always turning. Always plotting and scheming.

I pulled the door shut behind me and came back out onto the deck as the sound of voices lifted over the wind. The horizon was a thick line of blue that encircled us in every direction, a color that deepened before it blended seamlessly into the sea.

Burke stepped past me, walking straight for the bow, and he lifted a hand to shield his eyes from the sunlight. I squinted, trying to see what he was looking at, but it wasn't until the low-hanging clouds cleared that I could make out the dark sliver of coastline far in the distance.

My heart jumped up into my throat when I saw it. Land. Not the red sand or craggy rocks that lined the shores of the Unnamed Sea. We'd officially crossed into the Narrows, the hovel of crofters and fishermen far north of Bastian. Its blue-green waters were haunted by storms that were the stuff of legends. It was also the last place, I hoped, that my mother would think to look for me.

"What city is this?"

Burke laughed through a grunt, leaning into the railing to spit into the water below. "City? There's only one of those in the Narrows, if you want to call it that—Ceros. This is just Dern, a rotting crofter's village. But there's a tavern and more than fish and fowl to eat." He turned back toward the helm, cupping his hands around his mouth. "Bear north six degrees! Get ready to reef the sheets!"

The crew was already moving, finding their places to start the sequence of actions that would take the ship to port. I reached up, feeling the small leather purse beneath my shirt that hung from the long gold chain around my neck.

There was no way to bring my father back or travel through the threads of time to save him. There was no way to tell the younger version of me to take his hand and run, the way I knew he wanted me to.

Leaving my mother would undercut her trade and undermine the power she was quickly amassing in the Unnamed Sea.

There was only one thing she hated more than losing, and that was the idea of losing to the Narrows. When we anchored in Ceros I would go to the Trade Council Chamber. I would ask to see the Gem Guild master who'd never be good enough for Holland. And then I'd hand him the thing that could sink her—the midnight.

The wind picked up, pushing the *Luna* toward shore, and I looked down to the splash of white water cutting around the bilge. I'd never sailed the waters of the Narrows or set foot on its shores. But there was a solid feeling in my gut as I watched the sea race beneath the ship.

I hadn't just left my mother in the Unnamed Sea. I'd left my home. The place I'd taken my first breaths. But I could feel in my bones that these unknown waters were the place I'd take my last.

···

FOUR

···

SAINT

C love sat on an overturned crate, running the sharp edge of his knife around the mouth of the jewel-blue bottle with the same calm, certain look he always had.

This wasn't a job we could do on the ship. The less our ever-changing crew knew, the better. The barkeeper at the tavern, however, owed us a hundred times over and it was in his best interest to let us have the room at the end of the hallway to work in when we came to Dern. Our payment was the unmarked Sowan rye we left behind.

Clove turned the bottle in a circle until the wax seal was broken and then he pried the cork free before handing it to me. Using the rye to trade the gem fakes had been his idea from the start, and the scheme had made us most of the coin we'd used for the *Aster*. But we hadn't counted on the fact that the rye would turn out to be so popular in the taverns, and we'd had to be careful to not let it get out of hand. If we were caught, it could cost us the license we'd been waiting for.

I set the bottle on the table beside the others. This particular crate wouldn't find its way to a tavern or the cabinet of a guild member in Ceros.

I opened the velvet pouch Henrik had given me and poured the red gemstones onto a wooden tray, counting them out in sets of twelve with the tip of my knife. There would be four bottles that would hold a dozen stones each, some of them fake and some of them genuine. The gem merchants in Ceros wouldn't be able to tell the difference unless they had a gem sage in their charge, and even then, they couldn't report it to the Trade Council. Not when they'd purchased them illegitimately in the first place. It was the kind of trade that everyone involved stood to lose from. They also stood to gain a lot of coin.

Looking at the red beryl now, the weight of the risk we were taking settled heavily in the center of my chest. We'd traded small sums many times before, but Felix Roth would sooner gut us than lose a haul this valuable. I wondered what Henrik had done to convince him it was a good idea.

"It's no different than any other deal we've done," Clove said, reading my mind. His fair eyelashes caught the light as he rolled the block of red wax over the flame of the candle on the table.

I dropped the first set of twelve into the open bottle before me. The stones were never traced back to us because, technically, we didn't exist. We weren't traders or merchants and no one knew where the rye came from, so it couldn't be tracked that way. Even so, we were stretching our luck after almost two years of being a courier for the Roths. If Henrik was right and there were rumors about the *Aster,* we were running out of time.

The gems sank down to the bottom of the rye, disappearing in the dark liquid. When I was finished with the last of them, I replaced the corks and leaned forward, letting Clove drip the softened wax in a steady stream over the neck of each bottle. The wax lightened as it cooled on the glass, and he rotated it with a steady hand three times until the cork was resealed.

"So? Who do you think's talking?" Clove blew out the candle, setting both elbows on his knees.

My eyes lifted to meet his. "Gerik?"

"I don't think so. If we disappear, so does the coin we give him," Clove said skeptically.

"Maybe someone else is willing to pay him more."

His mouth flattened. He was likely thinking the same thing I was. Of all the helmsmen in the Narrows trying to set up their own trading operations, Zola was the only one I'd ever worried about. He was brash and quick to take whatever opportunity came his way, lacking the loyalty to these waters that other helmsmen had. That was how he'd ended up the errand boy for a handful of Saltblood traders in Bastian. It was a job I wouldn't do for an entire cargo hold full of coin.

"Zola's not a fool. He knows we're up to something," I said.

He'd been watching us more closely over the last six months and I was sure he knew we'd petitioned for a trade license. But there was no way he expected us to be able to pay for one. Not when we sailed the likes of the *Riven*. I was also sure he'd petitioned for his own license, and as long as he had the coin, he had every chance of getting it.

I'd told myself that more Narrows-born traders could only be a good thing. Without them, the Narrows Trade Council would never stand against the Unnamed Sea. But Zola's allegiances weren't to the Narrows. They were to himself.

Clove lifted the empty crate onto the table and marked the corner of the wood with the remaining wet wax in a straight line. It was the only identifying marker we used to track the gems among the dozens of crates we moved at each port.

"All right. Let's get out of here." I put the last bottle inside and stood, slinging the map case across my back.

Clove stacked one filled crate on top of the other and lifted them against his chest, waiting. The tavern had only gotten busier as the night drew on, but no one was going to look twice at a rye delivery, especially a regularly scheduled one.

I unlocked the door, letting it swing open before I picked up the other two crates and started down the hall. It was an unusually cold night and the fire was already stacked up, making the air feel dry in my throat.

As soon as we made it to the bottom of the stairs, the barkeeper drifted down the counter toward us, turning a clean glass through the towel in his hand. I set down the crates on the stool beside me and held the key to the door up between us.

He tucked it into his pocket. "Three weeks?"

"Three weeks," Clove answered.

"That rye isn't lasting that long these days."

"I'm sure a little water will fix that," Clove said under his breath.

The barkeeper ignored the accusation. He didn't have to admit it for it to be true. There wasn't a barkeeper in the Narrows who didn't do the same thing.

"Rosamund says there's talk about the build she's working on. That true?" I asked.

"What's it to you?"

The barkeeper's tone didn't change, but his grip on the glass tightened just enough for me to notice. The quickest way for him to get a knife in the back was to start repeating the rumors he heard at that counter.

"The less curious people are about what's in that pier, the more likely it is I keep showing up with your rye," I reminded him.

That got his attention. He set the glass on the stack behind him, tossing the rag over his shoulder.

"Who's talking?"

His chin dipped down, his voice lowering. "That fool apprentice Ros has got."

Clove's gaze locked on mine, and he cursed under his breath.

Nash.

"He's been offering to give the details of the build to anyone willing to pay a purse of copper. So far, no one has."

People speculating was one thing. But Nash actually knew what was going on in that pier. And three weeks was too long to wait and see if he found someone who was interested in the information he was selling. We were too close to let it all come apart now.

"Start a new rumor. I don't care what it is, as long as it has nothing to do with me," I said.

The barkeeper gave a reluctant nod in answer. "You got it."

"Saint!"

My name traveled across the tavern, carried on the voice of the last person I wanted to see.

Clove met my eyes and I let out a long, measured breath before I turned to see Zola leaning one shoulder into the wall beside the fire. The *Luna*'s navigator, Burke, was at his side. Zola's long black jacket nearly touched the tops of his new boots and I could see the shine of the brass eyelets gleaming from where I stood. Over the last few months, he'd been coming and going from the Unnamed Sea on almost every round of his route. I'd been sure we would miss him.

"Must have come in early," Clove muttered.

Zola lifted a hand into the air, waving us over, and I hesitated before hauling the crates back up into my arms. We made our way toward them as Burke filled his pipe with mullein, uninterested.

Zola, on the other hand, feigned a smile. It was no secret that he was out for our blood, but there were appearances to be kept up in the Narrows. Especially if you didn't want someone to see your knife coming. We both had a part to play and, up until now, we'd played them very well.

I set the crates down at my feet, taking Zola's extended hand and shaking. "How was Bastian?"

"Productive." Zola's smile widened.

I'd known him a long time. Long enough to recognize when he was playing games. But the thing about Zola was that to him, everything was sport. That made it difficult to pull apart the lies from the truths.

The first time we'd crossed his path, Clove and I were just getting started on what would later become our unofficial route. We'd made a stop in Ceros and, back then, Zola was nothing more than a deckhand who floated from one ship to another. Now, he was running his own unsanctioned trade route while he waited for his license, like the rest of us. We were set to be each other's competition in the Narrows, but Clove and I weren't much of a threat on the *Riven*. There was no doubt in my mind that he would step in if he knew what Rosamund was building over in the pier.

"Headed to Sowan?" he asked, eyes dropping to the crates.

I nodded. "The usual."

"I've told you there's no money in rye, Saint. You should be moving gems. That's all those guild bastards in Ceros care about. Trust me."

"One day," I answered, struggling to conjure up the pretense we usually exchanged.

Zola had built himself a crew and he had enough friends in the guilds to ensure he'd be granted a license, but he was the muck on the boot of every trader from the Unnamed Sea. Especially since he'd started sailing to Bastian. It was a move that had earned him the disdain of every would-be trader from Dern to Ceros and he knew it. He was Narrows-born, but he wasn't one of us.

"You know, that's not the only thing they're paying good coin for. The hull of the *Luna* will be leaking copper for months once I get to Ceros."

This was how these talks usually went. Zola drawing attention to some obscure trade. Me pretending to show interest.

"What have you got yourself into now?"

I took the bait, because that was what I was supposed to do. Whatever he'd dragged back from Bastian had put a genuine glint of light in his eye. And if he was excited enough to brag about it, it might actually be something we should take note of. That was what had worked in my favor with Zola.

He leaned forward, brushing the sleeve of my jacket before he hooked his arm around my shoulders. Clove straightened beside me, hand drifting toward the knife tucked into the back of his belt. But Zola wouldn't make a move here. Not for everyone to see.

"The kind of goods that no one is *making*."

My brow furrowed as I studied him. The rye in his belly was most likely twisting his words. There was a tilt to both his voice and his shoulders that wasn't typically there.

I shoved him off and he laughed, reaching for the bottle and refilling his glass.

"You've never had a sense of humor, Saint."

"Maybe not," I said, checking my watch.

We were set to leave at dawn but there was still work to be done tonight. Work we didn't want anyone noticing.

Zola took his time before he opened his mouth to speak again, but he fell silent when the door to the street opened and his gaze shot past me.

I turned, stopping short when a face I didn't recognize appeared among the dozens of others that filled the tavern.

A black-haired girl with a pair of pale blue eyes rimmed in dark lashes shoved the door closed with one arm. Beneath the other, she had several long, rolled pieces of parchment that looked like maps.

"Not bad to look at either," Zola murmured, a smile curling on his thin lips. "Eryss!" he called out, catching her attention.

It took her a moment to spot him and she hesitated before she made her way toward us, her gaze flitting from Zola to me and Clove and back again as she wove through the tables.

"Finally find someone willing to climb into your bed?" Clove gave Zola a bored look. We didn't have time for this.

But Zola laughed again, clapping Clove awkwardly on the back. "There's no coin to be made in love."

The girl stopped in front of Zola, readjusting the parchments under her arm. Her long, dark hair spilled out of the opening of her jacket, and it wasn't until she pushed her hood back to fall on her shoulders that I realized it wasn't black. It was the darkest shade of red. The kind that looked like threads of fire when the light touched it.

The smooth fabric of her jacket was the color of the moss that clung beneath the railing of the *Riven*, but it was set with shining brass buttons and her boots were worn but not shabby. She didn't have the weathered look everyone else in the tavern did, as if she'd been carved from ivory. She definitely wasn't Narrows-born, and clearly no one had told her that the Saltbloods didn't venture beyond the harbor in Dern. If Zola was going to parade her from port to port, he'd only get her the kind of attention she didn't want.

"My new dredger," Zola said.

Clove's eyes found me from the corner of his gaze. Zola had been saying for years that he was going to start running dives as soon as his license came through. That didn't explain why he was still grinning like a cat.

He took hold of the girl's arm, pulling her beside him, but as soon as his fingers touched her, she yanked free, giving him a taut look. A quick flash of fury darkened his face before he took a step back, as if to show her off. He was saving face, but it was clear he wanted us to see his prize.

He rambled on, recounting the broader details that had brought her to his ship, but when I glanced at the girl from the corner of my eye, she had lifted a hand to the candle on the table beside us, absently flicking her fingertips over the flame dancing on the wick.

"He's not the friendliest helmsman, is he?" Zola turned to meet my eyes again. "Come on. Where are your manners, Saint?"

My jaw clenched as I finally turned to look at her, and I almost immediately wished I hadn't. Freckles scattered over her olive skin, tracing over her cheekbones, along her jaw, down to the opening of her shirt where the hollow of her throat was visible.

She held her hand over the flame for another moment before she lifted it between us, meeting my eyes. She didn't so much as blink. "Eryss," she said, waiting.

Zola worked at opening a fresh bottle of rye as I took her hand and her calloused fingers brushed over mine, sending a pool of heat swirling in my palm. From the candle, I realized. But as soon as I felt it, I pulled my hand from hers, taking a small step backward, and her head tilted as her eyes narrowed on me.

I realized she was still waiting for a response.

"Elias." My name rolled off my tongue so easily that it made my blood run cold for just a moment. Because it wasn't the one I was known by. I hadn't even planned to say it. In fact, I hadn't heard the name spoken aloud in what felt like years.

Her eyes studied my mouth, as if waiting for me to say it again, and the hand that had just been in hers instinctively found my pocket. There was something about her that made the hair on the back of my neck stand on end.

Zola finally had the bottle open, turning back to us. "That's better," he said with an edge of ridicule. "You'll find that this helmsman is the stuff of legends in these waters." Zola took his pipe from his pocket, handing it to Burke to be filled.

He was setting my teeth on edge. I didn't like the confidence I heard in his voice. He was up to something. Something big.

The girl shifted beside me and I turned to see her eyes locked on the crate at my feet. The one marked with the haphazard stripe of red wax. Her lips twisted to one side and I realized the hand she'd held over the candle flame was absently drifting toward the bottles. As if she hadn't even meant to do it.

Clove shot me a look, but I watched her catch herself, her fingers curling into her palm before her eyes snapped up to me. A bloom of red lit in her cheeks, making her gray-blue eyes glow.

Zola's voice was lost to the noise of the tavern as slowly, it clicked together, piece by piece. Maybe this girl was a dredger, like Zola said. But that wasn't all she was. There was only one reason to look twice at that crate of rye. The gems. And the only person who could possibly know they were there was a gem sage.

Henrik's warning echoed in my mind. If Zola was headed to Ceros to collect heavy coin, he was selling something. Or *someone*. He'd been making stops in the Unnamed Sea and keeping whatever he was doing there quiet. Even the harbor masters in the Narrows didn't seem to know what he was running. If he was selling gem sages to merchants in Ceros, he had more powerful friends than I thought.

But if this girl was a gem sage headed to the auction block, it didn't look like she had any idea.

I cleared my throat, tearing my eyes from the dredger. I had bigger concerns than whatever Zola had going, but if he was trading gem sages, he was about to become more than a Narrows-born trader. He could eventually fund an entire fleet with that kind of coin.

"Have a drink with us?" Zola turned his pipe in his hand as he tamped down the mullein leaves.

"Not tonight," I answered, my eyes falling one more time on the girl before I lifted the crates from the floor. Her hand was still clutched in a tight fist, her gaze avoiding mine.

"Let's go." Clove's voice was close now.

I turned, giving the girl my back and falling into step beside him.

"Well? What do you make of that?" he asked, his voice a flat line.

I glanced back once more to the dredger as we pushed through the doors. She was watching me.

"I think Zola's bought into a new kind of trade."

FIVE

ƗSOLDE

The song of the red beryl was still ringing in my ears even after the helmsman disappeared onto the street. Those narrowed blue eyes had left a feeling like fire everywhere they'd landed and I could still feel it now, the ghost of it alive on my skin.

For a moment, I'd been sure he'd seen me. Like his gaze had held some kind of familiarity in them. Some sort of knowing. But as quickly as I'd spotted it, it vanished again.

That stone was one of the first of the gems my father taught me, a low hum that resonated in the air, and the feeling instantly conjured his face in my mind.

I blinked, trying to clear it before it could bring a lump into my throat.

"Slippery bastard," Zola muttered, sinking into the booth against the wall.

My eyes lingered on the door for another moment. Whoever the young helmsman was, he was going to get himself killed moving gems inside bottles of rye. It was clever, sure. But a trade like that only lasted so long before someone got the better of you.

"Sit," Zola ordered.

I pulled my gaze from the door, remembering why I'd come to the tavern in the first place. Burke sat beside him, hunching over the table and puffing on his pipe. The mullein smoke wrapped around me, making my eyes water.

I reluctantly found a seat across from them, setting down the charts I'd been given. They'd only confirmed my suspicions about Zola and the *Luna*. He was in over his head if he thought they were going to launch a dredging operation. There was a reason the Unnamed Sea ruled the gem trade.

A young woman with a blue scarf tied around the crown of her head appeared, plucking up an empty rye bottle before turning her attention to me. "What can I get you?"

"A pot of tea," I said, shooting a glance at Zola.

She gave me a knowing look before turning on her heel. Bleary-eyed men with too-loud voices didn't faze her, but a drunk helmsman was useless to me. Dangerous, even.

Zola drained his glass and wiped the corner of his mouth with the back of his hand. "Have you finished going over the charts?"

"I have."

"And?"

I cleared the table, sliding Zola's glass to the edge so I could unroll the first of the parchments. They were outdated and hard to read, but they were better than nothing. If getting the *Luna* ready to dive would keep his attentions off of me, I would do it. But I'd be gone before Zola ever dropped anchor on a reef.

I set my finger on the diagram of the coral system that snaked down the center of the Narrows, with notations on the bedrock that lay beneath them. There wasn't much reef to speak of except for the ones surrounding a small island and a large cluster in an area marked as Tempest Snare, but there was enough to work with.

"Here," I said. "This is as good a place to start as any."

Burke's eyes instantly cleared of their haze and he sat up straight, clamping his teeth down on his pipe. Beside him, Zola's expression had lost some of its arrogant ease.

"What?" I looked between the two of them.

"No one sails the Snare," Burke answered. "And for good reason."

"What? Why?"

Zola sniffed. "It's a death trap. The shallows stretch for miles and the storms blow you right into them. There are dozens of ships sunk on those reefs. We might as well cut a hole in the bottom of the ship and drop anchor."

"Not even Saint sails those waters." Burke jerked his chin in the direction of the door the young helmsman had disappeared through.

Saint. That was what Zola had called the helmsman with the crates of rye, but he'd given me the name Elias. I didn't know why it surprised me. If the helmsman was anything like Zola, being a liar was the least of his flaws. And to be fair, I hadn't given him my real name either.

"We're not sailing the Snare," Zola said again, more heavily.

The tone of his voice made him sound nervous. Afraid, even.

"Fine." I sighed, turning to the next chart. "Then as far as I can tell, your best bet is going to be carnelian and zircon. Both can be found in shale, and that makes up half of what you've got in these seabeds. The gems are easy to locate and easy to dredge, and you can work the reefs to find out what else is hiding there. Once you've got updated charts, you can build out a more extensive plan. Hire more dredgers, find—"

"We." Zola tapped his ringed finger against his empty glass.

"What?"

"*We.* You keep saying *you.*"

"We," I corrected myself, keeping my eyes on the parchment.

I'd dismissed Zola has a fool when I first stepped onto the *Luna.* A pawn who was likely in over his head doing favors for the likes of Simon in the Unnamed Sea. But this helmsman wasn't as simple as I'd first pegged him. He had designs of his own, and he intended to see them through.

"So, what? We just drop anchor anywhere and start bringing up gems?"

"It's not that simple. There's planning to be done, and the *Luna* will need to be outfitted with the right equipment."

"Good thing I have your expertise, then." Zola draped one arm over the back of his seat. "Get Burke a list of what we need, and he'll get it in Ceros."

I studied Burke's face, but he was distracted by the conversation of the next table, smoke trailing from his wide nostrils. He wouldn't know the first thing about the supplies they'd need for diving and that was of no consequence to me. But dredging was my best bet at making coin after I did what I needed to do in Ceros, and I'd need a belt of tools.

"The tools I'll need to get here."

"Don't trust me?" Burke asked, catching me off guard when I realized that he was still listening.

"Not particularly," I said. He probably didn't know a fine-needle chisel from a toothpick.

One side of Zola's mouth lifted. "I don't buy my bosun's tools and I'm not going to buy yours either."

"You're also not trying to build your trade on your bosun's back."

His eyes began to clear, the lazy posture of his body straightening. "My trade is built on *my* back." His voice took on a tone I hadn't heard before. One that sent a chill up my spine.

My shoulders drew back, my jaw clenching.

"Look, I don't know what you're running from in the

Unnamed Sea, and I don't care. But I do know if there was anywhere else for you to go, you wouldn't have asked Simon to put you on the *Luna*. So stop pretending like you have any cards to play."

That unsettled feeling I'd gotten in his quarters that afternoon returned as I met his eyes. I didn't like what I saw there. He was right. Even if he didn't know who my mother was or why I'd gone to Simon that night, he knew I needed him for something. And he wasn't going to let me forget it.

"It's a game, Eryss." The name I'd signed on his contract sounded hollow in his mouth. "All of it. The guilds, the councils, the traders and their coin."

I knew that better than he did. My father had known it too.

"I suggest you start figuring out how to play."

The woman returned with the pot of tea and two cups hooked on her pinky finger, but as soon as she set them down, Zola reached for the bottle of rye again.

I slid the pot toward me instead, filling one of the cups. Grounds swirled in the bottom like mud painting the porcelain, and I grimaced.

"If you want to disappear in the Narrows," Zola said, lifting his glass to touch my teacup, "then you better start blending in."

"Is that all it takes? Drown myself in the same rye I smuggle my gems in and then I'll be one of you?" It came out more bitter than I wanted it to and I didn't like that it made me sound as if I cared.

But Zola didn't seem as if he'd noticed. The glass in his hand stilled in midair the moment the words left my mouth. And though I wasn't sure why, I was immediately certain I'd done something wrong.

"What did you say?" He set down the glass.

I glanced to Burke across the table. He pulled the pipe from his mouth.

Zola leaned closer, his voice deepening. "Is that what he's doing? Saint? Smuggling gems?"

My eyes darted to the door the blue-eyed helmsman had walked through only minutes ago, that burning trail coming back to life on my skin.

A furious sneer twisted Zola's face and I pinned my gaze to the tea in my cup, taking a sip. I hadn't exactly meant to give the helmsman away, but the bastard was practically begging to be caught. I'd felt the red beryl as soon as I'd entered the tavern. My ear was tuned to even the faintest gemstone. But I was usually better at hiding it.

"And how exactly do you know he's running gems in the rye?"

For a moment, I was sure that Zola had figured me out, and the thought made my stomach drop. I'd tipped my hand more than I should have.

"He had the crate marked. I've seen others do it in Bastian and Sagsay Holm," I lied.

I was skirting far too close to the truth, but Zola seemed to buy it. He was ambitious, even if he wasn't clever or discerning. People like him were no more than mice catching

60

crumbs. People like my mother were the ones feasting at the table. That didn't mean Zola wasn't a threat.

Burke looked between us, uneasy, and Zola's fist hit the table, making me jolt.

"That's how he's staying on the water. Paying a crew. Who knows how many stones he's moved. Of course he's not just trading rye." Zola was talking to himself now, but the sound of his voice trailed off as he drew in a long, steady breath. By the time he let it out, he was his usual, composed self again. "What does Gerik say?" he asked, turning to Burke.

"Nothing. Just that they're running some rye every few weeks. Your typical low-rung trade under the noses of the Trade Council."

It was a gamble to trust a harbor master, but no one else at a port knew more about what was moving in the ships or the merchant's houses.

Zola squinted, staring past me with a singular focus that was unnerving. "He's petitioned for a trade license, and now he's running gems."

"Even if he gets the license, that ship of his will run two or three routes before it's sunk," Burke offered.

Zola had grand ideas of operating his own trade route in the Narrows when his license came through. But all I'd seen him do since I stepped onto his ship was pretend to be anything but Narrows-born. It was my best guess at why he'd taken me on. Maybe to him, running dredging dives like they did in the Unnamed Sea and having Saltbloods on your crew made you one step closer to being one yourself.

"We need to be in Ceros in three days," he said. "Make sure the crew doesn't wander. We'll leave before sundown tomorrow."

Burke nodded.

I picked up my cup again, trying to give my fidgeting hands something to do. Now things were moving in the right direction. I didn't care about their stupid disputes and rivalries. I just needed to get to Ceros.

Zola reached into his vest, pulling a small purse of coin free. He tossed it onto the table in front of me.

I stared at it.

"For the tools."

"I thought you didn't buy tools for your crew."

"I think you've earned it." He got to his feet and Burke followed, leaving me alone at the table.

In a matter of moments, pairs of eyes were finding me from every corner of the room in quick, pointed side glances and sinister stares. The people of Dern didn't like having a Saltblood in their tavern, and they wanted me to know it.

I took the purse and abandoned the tea, buttoning up my jacket before I started toward the door. It wasn't easy for me to admit, but I might have gotten more than I bargained for with this helmsman.

SIX

•◂•

SAINT

The streets of Dern were quiet after dark, but in a village this small, there was no going unnoticed.

I leaned into the brick wall at the corner of the alley, watching the lantern light in a window across the street dance over the cobblestones. The woman inside was spinning wool on a wheel and her shadow was cast onto the wall like one of the stringed-puppet shows performed on the streets of Ceros.

I'd been a boy the first time I saw one. My father had finally let me come with him to the city on his yearly trip to resupply his fishing boat with fresh lines, hooks, and nets. The buildings were taller than any I'd ever seen, and the maze of rope bridges that stretched over the rooftops was like something from a story. But what had most captured my imagination were the ships from the Unnamed Sea that were anchored in the harbor. The towering masts and crisp white canvas painted with trader's crests. The busy work of the crews on the decks.

My father made me wait outside of the merchant's house while he made his purchases, but I climbed up one of the thick, knotted vines that covered the east wall to a window so I could watch as the traders did their business below.

Even as a boy, I'd seen it—the expansive divide between the well-dressed Saltbloods and the Narrows folk selling their goods. I'd heard talk in Cragsmouth about them, but there was no reason for anyone from the Unnamed Sea to come to a village like ours. That was the first time I'd seen a breed like theirs, and by the time we were leaving the harbor, I was imagining a Narrows crest on one of those ships. Now that Ceros had their own Trade Council and the ability to grant a license, I'd be sailing one of them, just like my father wanted.

The soft slap of bare feet on stone echoed up the alley and I tore my eyes from the shadows, watching the darkness. The girl appeared a moment later, her pale face flashing in the moonlight. She tucked herself into my shadow against the wall, looking up at me with wide, dark eyes.

"Up one street, third building on the left. It's the flat on the top floor," she said.

"Did he see you?"

She shook her head, lifting an open hand between us.

I pulled a copper from my vest, holding it up. When she tried to take it, I lifted it higher, out of her reach. "Don't give this to anyone. Use it to get some supper," I said. "Do as I say, and I'll have another errand for you the next time I come to Dern. Understand?"

Her mouth twisted up on one side before she reluctantly nodded, and I pressed the coin into her palm. A girl like that had more worries than half this village. A sibling to feed. A mother to care for. But if she was smart, she'd see me for what I was: a chance. No one else was going to give her one.

Her fingers closed over the coin and she took off, disappearing around the corner.

I'd been hungry enough times to know that urchins like her made the most trustworthy souls at any port, and I'd needed someone who wouldn't be noticed. The next time the *Riven* dropped anchor, the girl would probably be waiting outside the tavern and I'd keep my promise. I wasn't going to change her rotten fortune—that was a task for her alone—but she'd at least get a few hot meals out of me.

I stepped out from the alley and followed the walk to the next street. I counted three buildings before I found the door I was looking for, and I watched the windows above before I opened it. The stairs were narrow, dripping with the last bit of rain that had leaked through the roof. I climbed them with slow, silent steps, passing door after door. Behind them, I could hear voices and the sounds of spoons scraping bowls. A baby whimpering.

The stairs ended at the top floor, where a wood plank door that was once painted red was fixed into the cracked plaster wall. I slipped the knife from the back of my belt, listening. It was quiet inside, which meant he was alone, and that was simpler. Cleaner too, if it came to spilling blood. And it might.

I fit the tip of the blade into the jamb and slid it up, catching the bolt on the other side. It took two tries to get it lifted enough to push the door open, and then the light from the flat spilled out into the hall. Every corner of the tiny room was visible from the doorway. A simple cot, a small writing desk. The room was small and bare, but the evidence of someone living in it was in the patchwork blanket folded over a chair and a few books set neatly on a crudely carved shelf. The sight almost made me want to laugh. Nash liked to make a show of looking down on us when we came to Rosamund's, but his life didn't look so different from mine.

Beside the window, he was bent over the wash bowl, scrubbing his face with both hands before scooping up the water and pulling it through his hair with his fingers. His suspenders hung from his waist and his shirt was untucked, as if he'd just finished his work at the pier. In another few minutes, he'd probably have been headed to the tavern.

I stepped inside, crossing the floor with silent steps, the way my father had taught me to do when we were trapping birds in the fields. I'd always had a weight in my gut on those mornings, a guilt that didn't leave me. But it wasn't there now. It had been a long time since I'd felt it.

Nash stood, flicking his dripping fingers into the bowl, and I stopped behind him as he raked both wet hands through his hair. The moment he caught sight of my reflection in the mirror, he froze.

The slow drip out in the hall was the only sound except for the wind tapping the shutter outside. If he shouted, someone might hear him. Or they might not. In a place like Dern, the likelihood of someone racing up here to help him was slim.

He seemed to be thinking the same thing, his eyes frantic as he ran through his options. When he finally turned to face me, his voice was still riding on bravado. But I could see in his eyes that he was scared shitless. "What the hell are you doing here?" His gaze dropped to my bandaged hand.

I didn't answer. What was the point in that?

The smugness he'd had at the pier was nearly gone now. Here, he was just a fool who'd made an enemy that he was completely unmatched for.

I took a step toward him and he lifted one hand between us, his breaths coming harder than they were seconds ago. "What is this, Saint?"

"I think you know what this is."

His eyes widened and he drew back, closer to the window.

"I know you've been talking. Now we have to figure out what to do about it."

Nash's eyes went to the door behind me, as if someone were going to appear there and get him out of this mess. "Look, I have coin, all right? Just take whatever you want and go."

My hand tightened on the handle of the knife. "It's too late for that."

It really was that uncomplicated. There were actions and reactions in the Narrows. Most of them had set, unavoidable consequences. Nash had known when he started the rumors at the tavern that they would demand an answer. If he didn't know, then he was a dead man anyway. People who didn't follow the rules never lived long.

His eyes darted to the dressing table, where his own knife was sitting beside his watch, but before he could make a move for it I lunged forward, catching him by the throat and shoving him backward. He crashed into the wall, nearly toppling over.

I kept my voice even and calm. "You have two choices: be left here to bleed out on this floor or come with us."

Nash stilled, confusion replacing the panic in his eyes. "Come with you?"

"The *Riven* is always in need of someone who can make repairs. And that will keep you out of the tavern long enough for us to get back to the *Aster* and set sail."

"I'm not going anywhere with you. Getting on that ship is as good as tying a stone around my feet and jumping into the harbor. It won't last another crossing."

That was the thing about the *Riven*. People were always underestimating her.

"All right." I took a step back, turning the knife in my hand so that the blade faced his direction, and Nash's hands flew up, his eyes wide.

"Wait! Wait!"

I paused, giving him the seconds he needed to make the

right choice. And he would. Because Nash was a coward who would probably do anything to keep his throat from being cut.

He gritted his teeth, nostrils flaring. "Fine." He finally met my eyes.

I let him go and his weight slumped against the wall, his white shirt crumpled. "Welcome to the crew of the *Riven*. Happy to have you."

I flung my arm back and brought the butt of the knife down with the full force of my body behind it, slamming it into his temple. His head whipped to the side and he collapsed in a heap, hitting the floor hard.

The risk of him making a scene in the harbor was one I wasn't going to take. There were only so many times Gerik would look the other way, and I didn't have enough coin to pay him for another favor. I needed Nash to come quietly.

I returned the knife to my belt before I took the watch from his dressing table and blew out the candle. Starlight filled the small room as I sank down, throwing his arm over my shoulder so I could haul him up.

There was no one waiting on the stairs or looking out their windows as I stepped out onto the street. If anyone had heard the argument or the sound of Nash's body hitting the floor upstairs, they hadn't deemed it worthy of their curiosity. I had a feeling Nash didn't have a lot of friends in this village. That, or they were just smart enough to mind their own business.

I followed the alleys back the way I'd come and scaled the steep steps of the harbor, keeping to the shadows. Clove was already waiting.

His dark jacket made him melt into the darkness on the steps beneath the lantern that was usually lit this time of night. He'd seen to the harbor master and anyone else who might be lingering on the docks. When I left for Nash's, there'd been just as much chance I'd be carrying a dead body to the *Riven*, and that was a crime that could come back to haunt us when we had our trade license.

When I reached him, Clove tipped his head to one side, peering into Nash's slack face.

"I guess he's coming with us, then?" he said.

"Guess so."

When we reached the slip where the *Riven* was anchored, I let Nash slide from my shoulders, toppling his limp body onto the dock. Above us, the *Riven* was dark.

The ladder was unrolled against the hull of the ship beside a few lines Clove had let down, and we hauled Nash up onto the deck.

With Nash gone, whatever rumors he'd started at the tavern would lose clout, especially once the barkeeper changed the story. But the *Aster* would still be on stilts at the pier for another few weeks, and that was a long time to wait and see if the curiosity died down.

It would be at least a couple of days before anyone realized he was missing, which gave us plenty of time to head to Sowan. If we could stay below notice until then and the summons from the Trade Council came, we'd be sailing from Dern on our first licensed trade route. But we had several purses of coin to make before then.

We dragged Nash down the steps into the passageway and I hooked my hands beneath his arms, waiting as Clove unlocked the cargo hold. Once it was open, I lugged Nash inside and dropped him to the floor. His head rolled to one side, the thin trail of blood already dried on his cheek. He'd have a nasty headache, but he was lucky to have his life. There weren't many helmsmen who'd have given him the choice I had.

Clove snatched a coil of rope from the bulkhead and sank down, binding Nash's hands methodically in a well-tied knot. "It'll be hard to keep the crew from talking about this in Sowan."

"It doesn't matter. By the time the story catches, we'll be in Ceros." With any luck, we'd be holding a license by the time we left.

The faint pop of wood overhead made me look up, and I watched the stripe of light between the slats.

"What is it?" Clove stood.

I ducked my head into the passageway, listening. The ship was quiet, but there was a turn of the air belowdecks I didn't like. As if the *Riven* was unsettled somehow.

I climbed the ladder up to see the deck, where the moonlight washed the wood white. The harbor was still empty, but there was the lingering buzz of a presence still hanging in the air. I lowered myself back down into the passageway, pushing into the crew's cabin. Inside, the empty hammocks gently swung with the rocking of the ship. The deckhands weren't due back until morning.

Clove appeared in the open doorway of the cargo hold. "Do you hear that?"

A soft beat moved over our heads. Not the rhythmic pattern of wind knocking rigging against the mast. Something else. I could barely make it out.

The beat of my heart kicked up slightly as my eyes trailed over the corners of the claustrophobic room. I reached one hand up, touching my fingers to the wooden rafters above us. I could feel it—the faint vibration of footsteps. Someone was on the ship.

"*Shit.*"

I pulled myself through the narrow doorway and tore up the ladder, stumbling as I came back up to the deck and the sound of a splash hit the water on the other side of the jib.

"Hey!" I lunged forward, clawing my way around a stack of coiled rope, but when I slammed into the rail and peered down into the darkness, there was nothing. Only the ripple of moonlight on the water.

My breath fogged in the air as my eyes slid to the knot of rope beside my hand. A line was anchored to the iron rungs at my feet, draping over the side and disappearing into the black water.

Whoever it was, they were already gone.

When I turned back, Clove had already disappeared through the open door of the helmsman's quarters. When I pushed inside, he stood before the desk with a coldness in his eyes.

"What?" I rasped.

"They're gone."

I could barely sift the sound of his deep voice from the wind outside.

"Henrik's gems. All of them."

I paced past him, rounding the desk and wrenching the tarp from the crates against the wall. They were unstacked neatly on the floor, only one crate missing. The one with the red wax mark.

"I haven't left the ship," he said. "I've been right here. Waiting."

I pinched my eyes closed, swallowing down the sickness brewing in my stomach. Whoever had been here had been watching us. As soon as Clove climbed down to the docks, they'd taken their chance.

"One of the crew?" he guessed.

"No."

There wasn't anyone on the crew of the *Riven* who'd been around long enough to pick up on the trade of fakes we'd been running. The only people who knew were me, Clove, Henrik, and Lander, the merchant in Sowan we sold them to.

The answer seemed to come to life in Clove's eyes the moment it settled in my mind.

Zola.

He wasn't smart enough to figure out what we'd been up to, but his new gem sage dredger was. She'd put it together in a matter of moments.

Nearly thirty-six hundred coppers worth of gemstones and fakes were gone. And it didn't matter how friendly I'd become with Henrik Roth. His father would gut me when he found out.

SEVEN

ISOLDE

The smith eyed me as I turned the pick over in my hand, pressing the tip of my finger to the point.

He hadn't taken his attention off of me since I'd walked through the door. The only business the traders and crews of the Unnamed Sea usually did in the Narrows was picking up their inventory and drinking rye on the docks before heading back to Bastian or whatever port they'd hailed from to turn a mountain of profits. A Saltblood coming into his shop for dredging tools might be a first.

This smith, tucked into a back alley of Dern, was worth his salt—I had to give him that. The tools were solid, even if they didn't have any of the frills that my gear in the Unnamed Sea had had.

My mother had given me my last set as a gift after one

of the most lucrative dives we'd ever completed in Yuri's Constellation, and they were the finest dredging tools I'd ever seen. Maybe the finest ever forged, and that was exactly why I'd left them behind. Each tool in the belt had my name engraved in the iron and set with gold, along with the stamp of my mother's crest. At the time, I'd thought the gift was her way of telling me she was proud of me. But I could see now it was just another way of polishing the jewels in her own crown.

The lot of mallets and chisels and files that filled the tiny smith's shop were nothing to look at. The metal was discolored in places where nickel had been melted with the iron, likely because the merchant was cutting corners. It was a flaw that I might not have noticed right away if I couldn't hear the distinct ring of the nickel between my fingertips. Still, he'd managed to use what he had to make something that would withstand its intended purpose. That took an undeniable skill.

I set the pick onto the tray with the others I'd selected. I couldn't have cared less what they looked like. They'd get the job done. Now all I had to do was untangle myself from Zola when we got to Ceros.

The smith hauled the scales onto the counter, setting the first piece into one side. "You'll need a belt too?" he asked, marking the first number down on a scrap piece of parchment.

"Yes."

"Well, take your pick."

His merchant's ring glinted as he pointed to the far window, where a string of leather straps was hanging against the glass. The brass buckles weren't even shined, and the color of the oiled leather ranged from the lightest gold to nearly black. I lifted onto my toes, running my fingertips down a belt that was a warm shade of red. The openings cut for the tools were even on both sides and I'd have to trim its length for it to fit around my hips, but as long as it didn't slip under the weight of the metal, I could make it work.

I unhooked it from the string of others and set it down on the counter as the smith finished the tally. When he turned the parchment toward me, he pointed to the total sum of coppers I owed.

Forty-one. I almost wanted to laugh at the number. Zola had given me fifty coppers for the dredging gear and I'd been sure he was trying to cheat me. A full belt of tools of this quality in the Unnamed Sea would have cost me more than twice that.

I counted the coins from the purse and the smith raked them into a can under the counter without so much as a thank-you. I wouldn't have thanked me either. The ports in the Narrows hated Saltbloods as much as they needed them. It was our coin that flowed through the port of Ceros, and our stones that filled the gem merchants' shops. That copper was what funded the smiths, the shipwrights, the sailmakers, and even the fishermen and crofters. The Unnamed Sea needed the Narrows' cheap grain. The Narrows needed the Unnamed Sea's coin and their trade routes to reach outside of these waters. We were a teetering, precarious construct. A bridge on the verge of collapse. If you removed one piece, they would all come crashing down.

The smith disappeared into the back room and I laid the belt out before me, smoothing the flat of my palm over the length of the rough leather. The smell of the oil used to dye it was pungent in my nose, but that was what would keep it from being ruined from day after day in the water.

I methodically slipped the tools into the openings, arranging them in the order I preferred to reach for them. I'd developed my own system through the years, placing the picks and chisels based on frequency of use rather than their lengths like other dredgers. I could find what I was looking for without so much as glancing down.

When I was finished, I lifted the belt, weighing it in my arms. It was significantly heavier than my old one, but it wouldn't take many dives for my legs to get used to it. And this belt was the only tether I had to a chance at starting over in the Narrows. Whatever came, I could dive. That was what I'd told myself as I stood in my mother's study beneath my father's portrait the night I left. It was the last thought I'd had before I knocked on Simon's door.

I reached up to touch the purse that hung beneath my shirt. That memory wasn't the only thing I'd taken with me. The ringing of the midnight hanging around my neck was a constant reminder of the moment I'd realized it wasn't the sea that had taken my father. It wasn't the reef or the tides or the turn of wind. It was Holland.

My father was a gem sage who gave up the work to dedicate his life to the humble craft of celestial navigation. But when it became clear that I'd inherited the gift, he turned his attention to my training. Every night, we sat on the floor of my bedroom and he meticulously taught me the language of the gems. Their names. Their colors. Their clarity. Most importantly, their song.

I was fourteen when I began working for my mother, traveling to the farthest reaches of the Unnamed Sea on her ships to dive with crews of men and women two and three times my age. More than once, I'd come close to finding my death on those reefs. But my mother was happy as long as I came home with gems. And when I got my first taste of what her approval felt like, that was exactly what I continued to do.

I hoisted the belt over one shoulder and stepped out onto the street, welcoming the weight of it. I'd felt too light without it, but now I had a sense of gravity about me. A distinct feeling of place. I didn't know if I'd ever feel like myself again. That version of Isolde was gone. But the girl who'd only ever felt at home beneath the surface of the water was still there inside of me somewhere.

I made my way back toward the harbor, as promised, where Burke would be waiting. The small strip of shops in this part of the village were filled and the dockworkers were still unloading the inventories that had come in the night before. Smiths, shipwrights, and sailmakers were people that every port needed, no matter how small. With Dern sitting at the farthest you could get down shore before venturing into the waters of the Unnamed Sea, there was no shortage of traders stopping in on their way to and from Ceros. In another few years, I imagined, the port would look very different than it did now.

The top of the *Luna*'s main mast was visible in the harbor as I walked down the hill. The slick cobblestones were still running with gray water from the morning's rain, but the sea looked calm for the trip to Ceros. Zola would be finishing up his rounds with the merchants before we set sail, and he was in a hurry.

I took another step just as a hand shot out from behind the corner of the next building, taking hold of my jacket and wrenching me from the street. The belt slipped from my shoulder and the back of my head hit the stone wall, making me gasp as two stormy blue eyes appeared before me. Eyes that had glistened in the firelight of the tavern the night before.

It was the young helmsman with the crates of rye. The one who'd left the burn of his touch lingering on my skin.

Now his hands tightened on the opening of my jacket, firmly pinning me in place. "You scream, and it'll be the last sound you ever make." His voice was low and steady. Different than it had been when he gave me that name—*Elias*.

I tried to shove him back, but he didn't budge. The unnerving, calm look on his face didn't waver as his chin dipped down so he could look into my eyes. He was so close that I could feel his breath on my cheek.

"What do you want?" I spoke through clenched teeth.

"I want my gems back."

I searched his face as I shrank even more heavily into the wall. The gems. In the rye bottles. Zola hadn't wasted any time making his move, and there was no trace of a question or a guess in the helmsman's voice. He knew that I knew, which meant I hadn't imagined that look he'd given me in the tavern.

"I don't have your gems," I spat.

"Your helmsman does. And you're going to get them back for me."

"I have no idea what Zola does or doesn't have. I'm just his dredger."

A bitter smile appeared on his lips, making his eyes glint. "Is that all you are?"

I went still, my chest rising and falling between us in the silence. The sounds of the village felt far away now.

His hands suddenly loosened and he let me go. But he didn't step back even an inch. He still looked down into my face and the resounding thought that kept circling in my head was that this didn't feel the same as when Zola towered over me, letting his frame swallow mine. It was something else. And there was no doubt in my mind as he met my eyes that he knew. He knew what I was.

"I saw you in the tavern," he breathed. "You're a gem sage. It only took you seconds to figure out what was in those bottles and then you told your helmsman."

I pressed my lips together, my face flashing hot at the sound of him calling Zola *mine*. But I didn't deny the accusation. Something told me it wouldn't do me any favors.

"I hope you at least negotiated a cut."

I hadn't, because I'd never intended to steal the gems. Zola wasn't that kind of businessman, anyway.

"I need them back. Today," he said.

Need. Not want. Despite the smooth expression on his face, I could see in his eyes that there was a shadow of desperation behind the words. I'd been right—this helmsman was in over his head.

My eyes drifted to the street behind him. I could still see the tip of the *Luna*'s main mast against the gray sky. "Or what? You'll tell Zola what I am?"

He finally took a step back, putting more space between us, and I almost moved forward. As if the air had the same pull as water. But I didn't move. Slowly, the look on his face changed into something like amusement. He nearly laughed. "You think he doesn't know?"

My heart was beating harder now, the sound of it loud in my ears. Whatever he was alluding to, I wasn't following.

"That bastard is taking you to Ceros to sell you to the highest bidder. And not as a dredger. As a gem sage." His voice didn't lower when he said it and the words echoed around us in the alley, making me swallow hard.

"You're lying," I said, more unsteadily than I'd meant to.

"Am I? Zola can get twenty times the copper for you than he can from a gem haul. Enough to launch a trade route."

I could feel the blood draining from my face, my fingertips going cold, and I almost wished he would move closer again so I could feel the heat that hovered around him.

The way he looked at me, patiently waiting for me to put it together, made the sick feeling inside of me churn. Part of me, even if it was a small part, believed him.

"Why would you tell me that, *Elias*?" I said, using the false name he'd given me. I wanted to feel as if I had some kind of balance to the scales. Zola was a liar, yes. But so was he.

He moved closer again, setting his hands on the stone behind me to frame me in his arms, and I immediately regretted that I'd silently willed him to do so. The collar of his shirt was unbuttoned beneath the opening of his jacket, revealing an expanse of sun-darkened skin.

"You just cost me a lot of copper. Now you're going to fix your mistake. If you don't, I'll make sure that Zola isn't the only one who knows your secret. And you'll have half the helmsmen in the Narrows trying to sell you to the gem merchants in Ceros."

He met my eyes for another breath before he dropped his arms and the cold instantly came rushing back, making gooseflesh rise on my skin.

"I'm raising anchor at sundown. And I want those gems back by the time I set sail." He blinked once before he turned on his heel, the tail of his dull blue jacket flicking around the corner as he disappeared.

I finally let out the breath I was holding, my weight collapsing into the wall. Slowly, I slid down the brick until I was crouched in the shadow of the building. Beside me, the dredging belt was half submerged in a puddle of water, painting the leather a darker red.

The helmsman was lying. He had to be. If Zola knew what I was, then he had no need of me as a dredger. But there were stories bleeding into every corner of the Unnamed Sea about gem sages being snatched up. Disappearing. It was the reason my father had wanted us to leave Bastian. To never look back.

Traders smuggling gem sages to merchants who were willing to pay were things I'd never had to worry about because of my family. Because of Holland. But I wasn't her daughter anymore. I'd cut that thread between us the moment I opened that gem case and took the midnight.

And that was the thing. Here, in the Narrows, I was no one.

EIGHT

ISOLDE

Burke was waiting on the dock when I reached the harbor, his usually slanted mouth set in a straight line. Behind him, the *Luna* was readying to set sail, the deckhands climbing the masts to do their routine checks. As soon as Zola returned, we'd be raising anchor.

I reached up, rubbing the spot on the back of my head that had hit the brick wall. It was aching, but the pain was nothing to what the helmsman from the tavern had said. I could still feel his weight pressing into me, the smell of him thick in my lungs, and his words felt like a tightening rope around my ribs.

I'd taken the place on the *Luna*'s crew without thinking twice. I'd signed a name that didn't belong to me, knowing I'd slip away in Ceros before Zola ever even knew I was gone. But if Zola knew I was a gem sage, it wasn't a far leap for me to believe that he had other plans for me in Ceros. And it wouldn't be so easy to disappear.

Burke's eyes scanned the crowd spilling down from the street, and when they finally landed on me, his eyebrows raised in annoyance. I let myself be pulled into the stream of people headed to the ships, my grip tightening on the dredging belt that hung over my shoulder.

I'd been caught up in rivalries before, always between my mother and someone else, and I was used to being used. She'd paraded me around, flashing me like a diamond ring to the guild and her fellow merchants in Bastian. Now that I thought about it, it had felt the same way last night in the tavern with Zola.

"What took so long?" Burke growled, taking hold of the ladder when I reached him.

"Smith had other customers."

Whether he believed me, I couldn't tell. He flung a hand toward the ship, waiting for me to climb, and I pulled myself up the ropes, feeling the solid ground of the docks vanish beneath me. Burke was always gruff, but he was agitated in a way that made me uneasy. If they'd taken the gems last night, and it was likely they had, he'd be eager to get the ship out of the harbor.

I'd lived at least half my life on the sea, my feet always finding their way to the water. But as I stepped back onto the *Luna*, I was missing the feeling of safety it had once given me.

In the Unnamed Sea, the stories about the disappearing gem sages had seemed like folklore, a ghost story told over glasses of cava and cups of tea. But something about Saint's words rang too true. There was more to them than a feud between two helmsmen.

If Saint was right and Zola was going to sell me to a merchant in Ceros, I would have little chance to get out of this mess once we got out on the water. The thought put a stone in my throat. I didn't want to imagine what lay at the end of that fate. A room with a locked door. A lonely death. Years dictated by the amount of coin I could earn some guild member in Ceros. I'd lived at least one of those lives already.

But I also didn't doubt that Saint was telling me what I needed to hear in order to get what he wanted—his gems. The way I saw it, I had two choices. If I trusted Zola, I risked the possibility that he was going to hand me over to a merchant. And not every story like that ended with being a prisoner in some guild member's workshop. There were also rumors about merchants willing to pay just so they could cut a gem sage's throat. The fewer of us there were, the more power and coin the Gem Guild had.

If I trusted Saint, I might save my own neck, but I'd also make an enemy of Zola and give up my only passage to Ceros. All of this—leaving Bastian and Holland and everything else—would have been for nothing.

The problem was, I didn't trust anyone. And once the *Luna* set sail, the decision would be made for me.

The deck was crawling with crew when we came over the railing and Burke immediately got to work, taking his log from his jacket. Once he checked the coordinates and Zola returned, we'd be setting sail.

I eyed the cracked door beside the helmsman's quarters in the passageway, where the coin master worked from morning to night. I didn't have any friends on the *Luna* or favors to call in, but if the answers I needed were here on the ship, that was where they'd be. The coin master would already be at work in his tiny office, updating the ledgers with the trade they'd done in Dern before they went on to Zola to be checked.

The door of the cabin creaked as I gently pushed it open and the man only half looked up, lifting his quill from the parchment. His curling black hair was stuck under his cap, still wet from the morning rain.

"What is it?" There was a flinch in his eyes. I was the last person he'd expected at the door of his little stall.

I jerked my chin toward the deck, sounding as detatched as possible. "Harbor master's looking for you."

His brow wrinkled. "Harbor master?"

"Something about docking payment?"

He let out a heavy breath, pinching his eyes closed. "You've got to be kidding."

"Says we can't go until it's paid."

"The man couldn't keep a ledger if his life depended on it," he muttered, getting to his feet.

He reached down, giving the chest on the floor a firm yank to be sure it was locked, and the ledger fell closed before he tucked it into his jacket. No coin master with any sense left a ledger unattended. If it wasn't with him, it was with Zola. But that wasn't what I was after.

He wedged himself around the table in the cramped room, turning sideways to slip out the door. I started down the passageway behind him, following until he was climbing down to the dock. As soon as he was out of sight, I stopped short, scanning the deck. Burke was already unpacking the sextant, but there was still no sign of Zola in the harbor.

I turned into the passageway and slipped back inside the coin master's cabin, letting the door fall closed behind me. The wall was fit with a series of locked cabinets behind iron grates that held the copper the *Luna* kept on hand. From what I'd been able to gather in the last couple of weeks, the chest bolted to the floor was the same. But the coin master didn't only keep the ledgers. He also handled the correspondence and contracts that ran the *Luna*'s operations.

The deep shelf that stuck out over the desk kept them within reach. I thumbed through their edges quickly, my eyes flitting over dozens of pages of folded and filed parchment. An array of handwriting penned in different inks covered their faces, their broken wax seals stamped with the insignias of ports and merchants. For someone who couldn't even call himself a trader in the eyes of the Trade Council, Zola had certainly gotten his hands into a lot of business.

He'd steered clear of my mother, it seemed. There wasn't a single parchment that bore her seal, and that was no surprise. She had no need of a low-level helmsman from the Narrows to do her bidding when she had the whole of the Unnamed Sea lining up to do it.

But there was *one* parchment that caught my eye.

My fingers stopped on a broken wax seal that was the color of amethyst. The same deep violet I'd seen Simon use in North End.

I slipped it out from between the others and unfolded it carefully. It was the same one given to Zola when I came to the docks that night. But it had been sealed and only now could I see that it was a contract, stamped with a merchant's seal I didn't recognize. The terms were written out above the signatures.

TRANSPORT AGREEMENT

Courier: *The Luna*
Recipient: *Oliver Durant*
Route: *Bastian to Ceros*
Cargo: *26 bolts Nimsmire silk*

Payment of 8,000 coppers upon procurement,
15,000 upon October 12th delivery

I stopped, reading the numbers again. The sum was high, much too high for Nimsmire silks. And twenty-six bolts was a quantity no single merchant had need of. Especially in the Narrows.

Signed,
Simon Fuerst

Simon Fuerst. I blinked.

Simon. *Blue door, black lantern.*

The question was already spinning in my head like the eddies that churned over the coral reefs before a storm.

I know who you are.

When he'd said it, I'd thought only of my name. My parentage. But what if that wasn't all Simon knew about me?

My finger moved over the words as I read them again, still telling myself that it didn't prove anything. Simon had sent me to Zola, but that didn't mean Saint was right.

My gaze narrowed on the date. October 12th. That was four days from now. A cold prick crept up my fingers and over the tops of my hands as I refolded the parchment and returned it to its place. Zola was determined to be in Ceros in three days' time.

The cargo hold was full of goods he was transporting and there was no reason to believe there weren't twenty-six bolts of Nimsmire silk somewhere among the crates. Unless . . .

I sank down onto the stool, shifting the parchment on the desk until I found it—the record of the ship's master inventory. That was one log that never left this room.

My finger trailed down the list quickly as I read, picking up from before the last stop in Bastian. It looked to be the only port in the Unnamed Sea they'd stopped at.

Silver ingots, crystal glasses, reams of parchment, even a crate of handmade horn buttons. But no silks. There wasn't a single mention of them in the last several pages of the log.

My eyes trailed to the wall that the coin master's cabin shared with the *Luna*'s helmsman's quarters.

It wasn't proof that Saint was telling the truth, but it lined up with what he'd said. Maybe Zola had no intention of having me run dives and turn over hauls for the rising gem merchants of the Narrows.

Maybe he was running a delivery service instead.

NINE

ISOLDE

The sharp ping of an adze reverberated in the wooden slats beneath my feet, a sign that Yasmin was at work belowdecks. She wasn't a friend by any stretch, but I also knew she had no affection for Zola. Everyone, however, had an affection for copper.

A deckhand shouldered past me in the narrow passageway as I followed the sound of Yasmin's tools around the corner. She was crouched beneath the door of the cargo hold with a set of new hinges at her feet. The lantern over her head swung as a wave hit the side of the ship and the adze slipped from her fingers. I caught myself on the wall beside her, leaning into the rock of the vessel before I lost my balance.

"What do you want, dredger?" She only half

acknowledged me with a sideways glance as she picked up the adze.

I waited for another pair of footsteps to disappear up the stairs. "I have a question, and I can pay for the answer," I said, keeping my voice low.

She gave me an indifferent frown, opening her hand.

I fished a copper from my belt and held it between us. "How often does this ship go to Bastian?"

"What kind of question is that?"

"Just tell me."

"I don't know. It's not exactly a set schedule. Once a month maybe. Why?"

"What do you usually pick up there?"

"I'm the bosun. I keep the ship floating to and from a port. I don't keep tabs on inventory once we get there."

I leveled my gaze at her. "We both know that you're not just a bosun. You're running a side trade on this ship, which means you know exactly what's on it."

When her eyes lifted again, the icy expression I expected them to hold wasn't there. She was entertained, if anything. "Well, look who's been paying attention. Thought you were just another cushy Saltblood brat looking for adventure."

"Maybe I am."

"I doubt that." She glanced down the passageway. "If you're wanting to be cut in, you can forget it. I have enough hands begging for coin."

"I don't care about what you're skimming. I care how you're doing it. What does he pick up in Bastian?"

"Metals, mostly. Silver-cast tea sets, gold-plated cutlery, stuff like that. Things the guild members in Ceros request to make them feel like their tin scales are a little shinier."

"What about silks?"

"For the Narrows?" She half laughed, plucking the coin from my fingers. "No. No silks."

I leaned into the doorframe, my eyes moving over the contents of the cargo hold behind her. It wasn't even half full, but what was there was contained within barrels and crates. I didn't see the seal of Nimsmire stamped on any of them.

"Do you ever stop in Nimsmire?"

Her eyebrow arched up as she crossed her arms over her chest and I sighed, pulling out another coin.

"No. Never been that far north." She took it. "Any other questions you'd like to bleed copper for?"

Zola clearly had powerful friends in Ceros if he'd gotten away with unsanctioned trade for this long. If he was running under-the-table trades for guild members, that would explain it. It was the same in Bastian. The merchants who made and upheld the laws were the first to break them, and maybe the new Trade Council of the Narrows was no different. They also had something to prove.

There was more going on here than Zola had let on. I was sure of that. I started back up the passageway, stopping short when Yasmin's words finally settled in the back of my mind.

I turned to face her again. "What did you mean . . . *another*?"

Yasmin's irritation was at the surface now. "What?"

"You said I was just *another* Saltblood brat."

"Yeah?"

"What did you mean by that? Have you had others on the *Luna* before?"

"Sure. A few times."

It wasn't until that moment that I could see the threads coming together. I took a step in her direction. "Where do they come from?"

She shrugged. "Bastian. We usually pick up at least one stray there."

"And then?"

"And then they get off in Ceros."

There was numb feeling hovering beneath the surface of my thoughts. A coldness blooming inside of me. Zola wasn't running errands for guild members. He was selling to them. He was going to Bastian to courier gem sages.

That was what Simon had meant the night I knocked on his door, when he said that fate was smiling on him. I was an entire crate of coin that would make it back to his coffers.

My eyes followed the beam of light coming from the stairs that led to the deck, where it was pooling on the floor. Zola was building a fortune. There was no telling how many gem sages he'd handed over in Ceros.

I reached inside my shirt, pulling at the chain around my neck until it was over my head. Yasmin's eyes narrowed on me as I untied the small leather purse from its length and stuffed it into the pocket of my jacket. The gold chain glistened, tangled in my fingers as I made a fist.

She studied my face. "That's a lot more than a coin's worth."

"It's yours if you get me into the helmsman's quarters. Worth at least sixty-five coppers. Maybe seventy."

Yasmin dropped the adze into the loop on her belt, taking the chain from me. She ran the links through her fingertips, inspecting them. "You have a death wish?"

"Maybe."

A smile broke on her lips as she plucked a hooked pick from the back of her belt. "You get caught and I'll deny I helped you. And there isn't a bastard on this ship who won't back me on that."

I nodded. "Understood."

She looked up and down the passageway, sighing. "All right. Come on."

I followed her back up the steps, keeping a few paces behind her when we came up onto the deck. Burke was still at the bow, taking wind measurements before he finalized the course, and any minute, Zola would be climbing the ladder and the deckhands would be raising anchor. I had minutes. Seconds, maybe.

Darin was on the upper deck loosening the lines of the main sail as we passed beneath him and Yasmin caught his eyes, gesturing to Burke. He looked at her with a question he didn't ask aloud before he nodded and immediately retied the rope and made his way down the mast to the deck. When he placed himself before the helm, I realized he was keeping watch. They'd probably done this dozens of times.

Yasmin took hold of the long blond braid over her shoulder and let it fall to her waist as she pressed herself into the opening of the door. I gave her my back, keeping an eye on the opening of the passageway, and I tightened the dredging belt around my waist, tugging at the knot. The sound of metal scraping the wood sounded for a moment before it fell quiet again. The hinges creaked softly and then she was walking past me, bumping my shoulder with hers. She didn't look back as she took the steps belowdecks and disappeared again.

I wet my lips, swallowing hard before I stepped backward toward the door. I didn't breathe as my hand reached for the handle, and a chill crept up my spine. The door swung open and I slipped inside, letting it close with a soft click.

The crate of rye I'd seen in the tavern was behind the desk, and to anyone else it would look like something Zola had picked up as his personal supply. It was only twelve unmarked bottles, but even from across the room, I could feel the buzz of the red beryl dancing over my skin.

I pulled the knife from my belt and touched each bottle with my fingertips, lifting the ones that reverberated with gemstone and setting them on the floor beside me. There were four in all. I picked up the first one, cutting at the fresh wax in an arc until I could pry it up. Then I wedged the cork free before starting on the next. When I had them all opened, I searched the room for the chamber pot. Every cabin had one, and Zola's was tucked beneath his bed. To my luck, it had recently been cleaned.

I tipped the first bottle over my cupped hand, pouring slowly. The cold amber liquid ran through my trembling fingers and when the first stone landed in my palm, I exhaled. One after the other, they came tumbling out until the facets of twelve stones cast a spray of red glitter over the ceiling and the walls around me. I picked up the next bottle, doing the same.

The rye sloshed in the chamber pot when another wave rocked the ship, and as I picked up the third bottle, Burke's gruff voice rang out.

"Raise anchor!"

I jolted, dropping the bottle, and it rolled across the floorboards beneath the bed, spilling as it went. If Burke was raising the anchor, he'd spotted Zola. The ship was about to leave.

I cursed, scrambling after the bottle and when I got back up on my knees, I poured it out faster. Too fast. One of the gems fell through my fingers. I abandoned the last bottle, slipping it back into the crate.

More orders were called out and the footsteps of the crew beat on the upper deck as I pushed the chamber pot back to its place and got to my feet. I pulled the leather purse from my pocket and opened it, my heart racing as I dumped the red beryl inside with the midnight. As soon as it was cinched closed, I bolted toward the window.

The shadows of bodies on the ship moved over the green water below and I climbed up, swinging my legs through the opening. Behind me, the iron door handle lifted, and I clasped my fingers around the purse tightly before I jumped.

I fell through the air, hitting the rough water and plunging beneath its surface. A flurry of white bubbles rushed up around me, tracing over my feet, my legs, my hands, my hair. I let the weight of my belt pull me deep, and the belly of the ship grew smaller overhead as the first bit of air slipped through my lips. I dropped more than twenty-five feet before my feet touched the soft, sandy bottom, making pain swell in my ears until the ache filled my skull.

I waited, watching the surface above. The sound of the red beryl amplified in the water around me, along with the other stone in my purse, and my fingers curled tighter around it as I pressed it to my chest.

It had begun with gems, I thought, my knuckles throbbing the tighter my fingers curled. And it didn't matter how far from my mother I sailed. It would end with them too.

TEN

SAINT

"She's not coming."

Clove stood at the foremast behind me, leaning into it with one shoulder. His eyes were fixed on the harbor's entrance, where the trickle of people leaving the merchant's house was thinning by the minute.

I looked down at my watch again before studying the water below. The orange light was skipping over the surface and the shadows of the crews up on the ships moved over the docks. It was nearly sundown and the dredger hadn't shown, just like Clove said she wouldn't.

"Then why aren't they leaving?" I said, thinking aloud.

I turned to glance at the *Luna*, floating a few slips down. According to Gerik, Zola had been scheduled to set sail well before nightfall, but the sails were still rolled up tight and the anchor hadn't been raised.

Clove uncrossed his arms, coming to stand beside me. His silence had been growing heavier by the hour and though it was like him to worry, this was different. This time, we weren't just gambling with the *Aster* or a trade license. We were gambling with our lives.

"I cut the crew by more than half. Kept Julian and Mateo," he said. "We need to get on the water if we don't want to pay for another night to dock."

The crew, we could do without, for a while, anyway. We couldn't afford to feed them and we didn't need more eyes on us than was necessary. Not when we had Nash locked in the belly of the ship.

"Managed to convince some dockworkers to mix up some of the inventory coming out of the merchant's house. Wool was the best I could do."

"All right," I murmured, eyes still fixed on the *Luna*.

I didn't like stealing from crofters, but at least they'd been paid already. The Saltbloods would be the ones with the coin deficit, and that was nothing more than justice.

"And these." He pulled a fistful of silver and gold from his vest, the result of a collection of grabs he'd done coming to and from the tavern. Rings, bracelets, a pocket watch. Even a pair of spectacles. It was a talent of his that had kept us fed when the ledger was less than kind.

I nodded.

"We need to decide how to handle this," Clove said. "Henrik."

I tucked my watch into my jacket, the sinking feeling returning to my chest. Henrik was a problem we couldn't afford to have. When he found out that we'd lost his gems, he wouldn't be happy. His father, Felix, on the other hand, would gut us in front of the harbor master and not think twice.

"Any ideas?" I said.

Clove shook his head. "Not any that will be quick enough. We have to have that coin by the time we get back to Dern. That's only three weeks to scrape together the copper we need to pay him."

I set my elbows onto the railing, staring out at the horizon. The minute Henrik got wind of this, there would be hell to pay. Our usual rounds wouldn't touch what we owed him, and it would only put us even deeper with Emilia, the rye crofter who supplied us. We didn't even have the option of running. Not until Rosamund was finished with the *Aster*.

I had no doubt that Zola was the one who'd taken the rye. He'd been after us for months, poking around and trying to sniff out what we were up to. But he had three times the crew and three times the ship we did. I'd be dead before I stepped a single foot on the *Luna*. And he knew it. Which was why I'd bet on the dredger. But I'd bet wrong.

We'd known the risks of running such a tight trade and investing so much coin into the *Aster*'s build. There was no give when we lost copper or fell short. By the time the Roths were finished with us, it wouldn't matter if I was holding a trade license or standing on a brand-new ship. I was a dead man.

"We'll have to trade as much rye as we can. Maybe swipe some more inventory in Sowan or make a deal in Ceros that will hold us over. If we have something to give Henrik when we get back to Dern, it's better than nothing."

It would be a hungry and sleepless few weeks, but we might be able to come out the other end with our lives. If we were lucky.

Clove's mouth flattened. What I really meant by *make a deal* was take on a debt to someone. Something we'd sworn since the beginning that we would never do.

"Or we disappear for a while. Until we can pay."

"There's no disappearing in the Narrows. Not for us."

It was true. There were already too many stories about the two foolhardy boys who sailed a sinking ship into hell-born storms. And the Trade Council had its eye on us now that we'd applied for a license.

"We could go to Cragsmouth," he said.

My eyes cut to his, my shoulders going rigid. "No."

That was something else we'd sworn we'd never do. There were too many ghosts waiting for us there. I didn't think of it as home anymore. Not since our fathers died. And I wasn't sure the people in Cragsmouth would give us safe harbor, anyway. I had too much blood on my hands.

"May not have a choice."

I knew what Clove was thinking. He'd never wanted to get mixed up with Henrik. Anyone in their right mind wouldn't. But I'd known the stakes when I took the first batch of gems from the Roths, and until now, they'd played in our favor. The law was clear—only gem merchants who'd been given a ring from the Gem Guild could buy and sell gems. Traders could take them from one port to the other. But we were neither. And working with a notorious fake-gem maker from Bastian was another matter altogether.

"I'll deal with it," I tried to reassure him. I was reassuring myself too.

I watched my reflection ripple on the water below for another moment before I finally started across the deck. We'd make it to Sowan with a skeleton crew and Emilia would be waiting with a new inventory of rye. But the copper to pay for it was gone. That was a puzzle I'd solve when we got there.

I pushed into the helmsman's quarters and shut the door, leaning into it heavily as I stared into the dark. I took three long breaths before I finally crossed the small room. My hand hovered over the handle of the drawer that held the ledger for a beat and when I pulled it open, I flipped it to the last page that was covered in my writing. The numbers were dismal. Impossible. They had been for months. But this was a sum that would sink us.

I picked up the quill, my hand freezing in midair when I spotted a small leather purse at the corner of the desk beside the inkpot. One I'd never seen before. And it hadn't been there that morning.

A prickle ran over my skin as I dropped the quill and picked it up, letting it roll into the center of my palm. It didn't have the feel of copper inside.

I unraveled the ties, tilting the opening toward the last bit of light coming through the window, and the shine of red lit within it. Gemstone.

A long, heavy exhale escaped my lips and I swallowed hard, feeling suddenly unsteady.

"It's not all of them." A soft voice sounded behind me and I shot up from the stool, turning with the gems clasped tightly in my hand.

Zola's dredger was crouched in the corner, her clothes wet and her hair drying in thick waves over her shoulder. She looked like she was somehow painted into the shadows of the room.

"How the hell did you get in here?"

Her eyes went to the window on the other side of the cabin in an unspoken answer. The shutter was closed over a trail of wet footprints drying on the floor.

"It's not all of them," she said again, standing slowly. A belt of dredging tools was draped over the chest beside her. "I was only able to get three of the bottles."

She stepped into the small bit of light cast through the room, her gray eyes flashing more blue. There was a flush to her skin that hadn't been there that morning. A warmth beneath her cheeks.

"That wasn't the deal."

I didn't like how she met my eyes so directly. I wasn't

used to that anymore. Everywhere we went, Clove and I were given a wide berth, but either this dredger didn't know anything about us or she just didn't care.

"I don't remember making a deal," she said. "A *deal* would imply I was offered something in return."

"Look around, dredger. I have nothing to give."

Still, her gaze didn't leave my face. The feel of it traveled from my eyes to my chin. "They're good fakes. Some of the best I've seen."

The words sounded like a question. But if she was hoping to find out who the maker was, she was a fool.

"I'd say thank you, but you haven't done me any favors." I closed the purse and tossed it onto the desk. "How exactly are you planning to pay for the ones you lost?"

"I can't."

"Then why are you still standing in my quarters?"

Her mouth twisted.

"Let me guess. Zola wasn't the upstanding chap you thought he was."

She stared at me, that deep silence returning.

"Then I'd get a new crew if I were you. And fast. I'm sure one of those Saltblood helmsmen headed back to Bastian will take you."

She surprised me by taking a step in my direction, and the cabin immediately felt smaller around me. There was something about her that filled up the space. She was like a thick, curling smoke in the air. "I can't," she said again.

"Why?"

"It's complicated."

The harbor bell rang out in the distance, signaling a ship out of the bay, and the muscle in her jaw ticked before she reached up, opening the shutter just enough to peer out.

"He's not going to leave. Not with his precious cargo missing," I said. "He'll tear this village apart until he finds you."

Her fingers slipped from the shutter and she folded herself back into the shadow of the wall, watching me. "Maybe there will be nothing to find."

"You can't be serious."

"I gave you back the gems. Now I need to get out of here."

"You said yourself that it wasn't a deal. And you didn't even pay in full."

"I need to get to Ceros."

It was only then that I could see beneath the hardness on her face. She was scared. Terrified, even. And I still had that feeling when I looked at her—like the eerie quiet that fell over a ship before lightning struck.

"Saint!" Clove's voice sounded on the deck, making both of us still.

The dredger's eyes widened before she pressed herself to the wall. Across the cabin, the door opened and Clove appeared in the glow of lantern light on the deck. It took him all of three seconds to read the look on my face. In the next breath, his eyes found her.

"You're kidding." The faintest trace of mirth laced the words.

"Seems the dredger showed up after all."

"The gems? She has them?"

"*Some* of them." I shot her an irritated look.

The low beat of steady pounding reverberated in the floorboards of the cabin from the cargo hold below, and the girl looked between us warily.

"Shut him up before someone on the docks hears him," I muttered.

Clove's gaze lingered on the dredger for another moment before he took two steps backward, toward the door. I followed him out, closing it behind me.

He took the stairs belowdecks, stopping halfway down. When he looked up at me, it was with a look I knew well. "So?"

My eyes lifted to the closed door of my helmsman quarters in the passageway as I reached for the knife in the back of my belt. I closed my hand over the blade before pulling it through my fist and then I lifted it into the air, over the railing. A steady stream of blood dripped into the water below.

"Raise anchor. Set course for Sowan."

Clove let out a long breath. "You sure about that?"

I met his eyes reluctantly. He always saw more than I wanted him to. "No."

He was so still for a moment that I was almost sure he would argue. But instead, he gave me a nod and climbed down the ladder.

If we did this, things would be different. The rivalry with Zola had been beneath the surface until now. This would change everything.

I glanced up to the raised sails of the *Riven*. She was half cloaked in fog, making her look more like a ghost than a ship. And maybe she was. I'd seen enough strange things at sea to believe it. The *Riven* had lost her soul a long time ago. So had we.

ELEVEN

SAINT

The sun disappeared over the horizon, the light striping the surface of the water in one long pillar of gold before it began to fade. It was crisp and clear, wavering on the surface, but the sight gave me an uneasy feeling. The sea was too quiet, and that could only mean one thing—that she was readying for something. There was a distant whisper I could hear on the wind, an echo from miles away. A storm was coming. It always was.

The adder stones jingled in the open window, where they were strung on a thin stretch of twine. It was an old helmsman's trick to ward away the eyes of the sea demons, and I'd paid a few Waterside strays in Ceros to collect them for me in the early hours before dawn the day Clove and I first set sail. I'd stood up on the rocks, watching their lanterns bob on the black sand below, and I'd given them a copper each before I hung the stones up.

I knew better than to ignore the traditions. I'd learned the hard way what happened when you did. And though my piety and consecration of the old ways sent myths about me trailing through the Narrows, there was one that only Clove knew. The black sea. The open mouth of the wave. Wide eyes looking up at me from beneath the water as they disappeared. There were some sins you paid for your whole life. I knew that now.

The light cast an orange glow in the cabin as I dipped the finest-tipped quill into the pot of blue ink and tapped along its rim. I'd managed to get a pint of oil for the lanterns to last us until we got to Emilia's croft by promising the barkeeper at the tavern in Dern two extra bottles of rye on our next stop. If I caught Emilia in a good mood when we reached Sowan, maybe she would see us off with more.

Before me, the map I'd spent the last year working on was unrolled across the desk. The thick parchment was unmarked, every edge still sharp. It was the only thing on the ship that wasn't tattered or half rotted with damp, and in another month or two, it would be complete.

The Narrows.

What lay before me was the first accurate rendition of the entire mercurial shoreline that crept in from the Unnamed Sea into spidering veins of water that spilled in from the rivers. I was no mapmaker. My father had been the one with that talent, even if he'd never properly used it, but I knew how to mimic him. Every careful brushstroke, etch, and symbol.

No one had ever made a complete map of the Narrows. Ceros had its share of charts, but not the whole of the waters. And why would they? Every helmsman worth their salt had its shape and depth and width carved on their bones. Had its waters running through their veins. But to the outside world, the Narrows was more of an idea than a place. A reputation. In a way, I figured, we didn't really exist until we were recorded with parchment and ink. Until we were, we'd never be seen as a people standing on our own.

The map archived every angle, every degree, every depth in careful detail. I set the heel of my hand onto the edge, letting the breath ease out of my lungs before the tip of the quill touched down. I dragged it in a stack of straight lines, shadowing an arch of reef that snaked east and opened to a circular well that plunged forty feet deep. The water there was crystal clear, and on sunny days, you could see the gold glittering on the sand below.

I picked up the quill and set it onto the linen beside me, unfolding my fingers to stretch the sore muscles in my hand. My father had been a much better artist than I was, but he'd made me practice every night, painstakingly drawing the fishing routes on scrap parchment that would later feed the fire.

Mind the ink, Elias.

I could still hear his voice, hovering in the darkness around me.

I picked up the bowl of sand and sprinkled it over the map to dry the ink and it scattered, covering the work I'd just done. When it was dry, I carefully rolled up the parchment, returning it to the waxed-leather cylinder case and fitting the lid on tight.

The trip to Emilia's was usually an easy one. Those were the nights on our route when we had coin in our coffers and gems in our rye. It was the leg back to Dern that had our bellies growling and our hull light. But this time we were sailing with shadows following us. Zola. Henrik's gems. Rosamund's missing apprentice.

Mateo stood at the helm, eyes on the black sky as I came from the passageway, which meant that Julian was asleep below. The *Riven* was too much ship to be handled by only four sets of hands, especially if any of us wanted more than two hours of sleep. But if Julian and Mateo were curious about what had made us dump the rest of the crew in Dern, they hadn't shown it. Maybe that was why Clove had kept them over the others.

Clove was waiting on the upper deck when I came up the steps, his boots propped up on a coil of rope and his hands folded behind his head. He'd been waiting.

"Where is she?" I asked.

"Down in the crew's cabin. Sleeping, I think." He sniffed.

I hadn't seen the dredger since I'd sent her belowdecks, but she hadn't left my mind for even a moment. I was a believer in signs, and the sea gave plenty of them. But there had been no warning when I caught sight of her in the tavern and that heavy feeling sank deep in my chest. There was no accounting for the fact that it hadn't left me either.

I rubbed one hand over my face, feeling the grit that covered my skin. "And Nash?"

"We can let him out in the morning. He has nowhere to go."

A rumbling wind growled over the water and my eyes went to the expanse of darkness that surrounded the ship.

"Too late now," Clove said, dropping his feet from the ropes and setting his elbows onto his knees as he looked up at me. His hands were folded before him.

"I know what you're thinking."

"Do you?"

"That it was a mistake to leave Dern with her on board."

"And I'm right."

My hand dropped from the collar of my shirt. Clove never minced words or told me only what I wanted to hear. He wasn't afraid of me either. But I'd harbored a hope that in this, he wouldn't be against me.

"Could have told me that before we raised anchor."

"Wouldn't have done any good." He smirked. "We do need to talk about it though."

"About what?"

"Zola," he said simply. "As soon as he finds out about this, we're his enemies. Forever."

"We were already enemies."

"Not that kind."

That, I did understand. There was an understanding between Zola and me. We needed each other if we were going to establish trade in the Narrows among the helmsmen born on our shores. But we also couldn't let each other pull too far ahead. It was an alliance that was doomed to turn deadly.

"Then it's already done," I said. "It was done the minute we left Dern."

Clove gave me a knowing look.

"What?" I sat on the crank beside him.

"Even with the gems she brought back, we'll still owe."

I'd already added that up. No matter what, we'd still be short of what Henrik would be expecting, and that was including every single coin we had. It was better than having nothing to give him, but it wouldn't be enough.

"We have less than three weeks to come up with the rest." He didn't sound like he believed we could do it.

"How?"

He stared at me. "We have the rye."

"We don't have it yet."

Emilia wouldn't be happy when we showed up unable to pay for the last haul of crates she'd given us. She would be even less amused when I asked her for more.

"She'll do it," I said.

"I don't know." Clove's head tilted to one side.

"Emilia needs us like we need her. She'll do it."

"Even if we sell every bottle she has, it will only be enough for Henrik. There won't be anything else."

The coin from this trade would have been the seed money that would launch our trade under our new license. Now we'd have to get it some other way. But there was also the matter of hiring crew for the *Aster* and everything else we'd need to outfit the vessel. When we got back to Dern, we'd have a ship, but nothing else. Not even a way to sail it.

The wind howled, a low groan rattling the ship around us, and my teeth clenched, every muscle in my body tensing.

"Storm?" Clove asked.

I shook my head. "No. Not tonight." The sound of my voice trailed off.

This wasn't the hum that bubbled beneath the water before the sky started churning. It was more than that. Something I hadn't felt in a long time. And I couldn't pretend that I didn't know it was about the girl sleeping in the crew's cabin.

"We'll get rid of her," I said, swallowing. "In Sowan."

One blond eyebrow arched beneath the sweep of hair on Clove's forehead and a mischievous look I recognized resurfaced in his expression. Sometimes I forgot that version of Clove still lived inside of him. The one I'd known before we left Cragsmouth. Before we both watched as our fathers were swallowed by the sea.

"What?"

"Am I really the only one who is putting this together?"

I stared at him.

"We leave that gem sage in Sowan, and Zola will track her down. It's plain to anyone who looks at her she isn't Narrows-born. Her clothes. The way she talks. She doesn't exactly blend in. And when he finds her, he's taking her to Ceros."

Still, I said nothing. I knew where he was going with this.

"So, if Zola's expecting a crate of coin when he delivers her, we might as well sink the *Aster* before we ever set sail," he said. "We've clawed our way onto even ground with that bastard. For the first time, we're on equal footing. But if Zola gets a fortune to launch his trade route . . ." He didn't bother finishing.

I knew Clove was right. Zola wouldn't just have the advantage over us in starting our trade, he'd also be able to buy the loyalty of harbor masters and merchants at every port. His first priority would be to make sure that our trade never got off the ground. In fact, I wouldn't be surprised if he had designs on eventually making sure we ended up at the bottom of the sea.

"She isn't just a gem sage. She's a dredger, Saint."

"I know she's a dredger."

His eyes cut to the stairs that led down to the main deck. "Last I checked, we don't have one of those."

"You just said that you think it was a mistake to bring her on the ship. Now you want to take her on as crew?"

"I do think it was a mistake. But it might have also been a stroke of luck. If we've dug a grave with Zola anyway, we might as well keep her out of his hands. If we don't, we'll lose any chance we had to beat him."

I stared at the crack running along the boards under my feet, a black crevice paved with tar. The clock was ticking down. On us. On this ship. It was a desperate ache in my chest that had lived there for years. I was good at plotting and strategizing and making do. But I was also tired of waiting for it all to pay off.

Another rumble of thunder sounded in the dark and Clove let out a long breath. "Go get some sleep. I'll wake you in a few hours."

I didn't argue. I was so tired that I could feel my weight threatening to fall through the deck. I pulled myself to my feet and Clove set his head back, crossing his arms over his chest as he watched the fog.

The ship was quiet as I came down the steps. Even when we had an actual crew aboard, we weren't the kind of ship that sang songs or played dice after the sun went down. We weren't the kind that enjoyed each other's company either. On the *Riven*, we existed for one purpose—to get to the next port alive.

Every waking moment sailing that ship had been with the idea that one day, we would be rid of her. We'd cut her bones up and feed them to the vultures, and then we'd say our thanks before boarding the *Aster* and bidding the *Riven* farewell. She'd been good to us, but the ship was an open, gaping mouth. It was only a matter of time before she devoured us. I knew that.

I ducked out into the passageway, closing the door of my quarters behind me, and I stared into the shadows as a cloud passed over the moon. The cabin filled with darkness, and a swift cold bled into its corners around me. I had that hollow feeling inside of me now—one I knew well. The sea didn't forget our sins. She just let us pay for them in different increments of blood.

I pulled the shirt over my head and kicked off my boots, sitting at the edge of the cot and raking my hands over my face. Across the cramped room, the mirror was lit with moonlight, and the shape of me moved over the glass. Sometimes, I thought I looked like him. Or at least, the version of him that I could remember. It had only been six years since my father died, but it felt like longer. I'd become a man without him. I'd become a lot of things.

TWELVE

ISOLDE

The grand estate my mother called Azimuth House in the merchants' district had never been a home to me. Waking on a ship was the only time I didn't have that split second of confusion about where I was. The sounds, smells, and gentle rock of the hammock were where I belonged. I'd always thought it was because of my father's love of the sea. That maybe I had more of his blood running in my veins than my mother's. I liked that idea. I hoped it was true.

Beside me, the other four hammocks strung up in the crew's cabin were empty. Aside from the helmsman and the navigator, the *Riven* was sailing with only two deckhands. It wasn't a large ship by any stretch, but they were tempting fate by having so few on a vessel that was in such bad shape.

I sat up, letting my weight tip forward until the toes of my boots hit the floor. It was slick with a thin layer of moisture, the humid air thick in the room around me. My clothes were damp with it. That was a bad sign too—an indication that the seal of the hull was compromised.

"Take one more step and I'll cut his throat!"

I froze at the sound of the voice, my eyes finding the open door, where the narrow passage belowdecks was washed with the sunlight spilling down the hatch.

"I mean it!"

I climbed out of the hammock and pulled my knife free, following the trail of light with slow steps. The crude ladder that rose up from the floor to the hatch was missing its bottom rung, but when I lifted onto my toes I could see the main deck, where the noise was coming from.

The navigator stood near the bow, eyes fixed on an auburn-haired man with his back pressed to the railing. In one hand, the man had a knife. In the other, he had the twisted shirt of a young deckhand with a busted face, pinning him against the foremast.

"I told you to let him *out*, Julian, not let him take hostages." The navigator glared at the cowering deckhand to his right.

The young man he'd called Julian had wide eyes, his chest rising and falling in panicked breath. "I'm—I'm sorry, Clove—I—"

Clove. I didn't remember Zola saying the name at the tavern.

"Where exactly do you plan to go, Nash?" Clove didn't bother letting the deckhand finish, looking utterly bored by the scene playing out before him.

The red-haired man shot a look out to the water, jaw clenching. "You can't keep me as a prisoner. You can't just—"

"This is my ship, and I can do whatever I'd like on it."

The helmsman's voice came from the other side of the mast, forcing me to step up onto the lowest rung so I could see him. When my eyes finally landed on his face, I swallowed hard. He was missing the shirt and jacket he usually wore, the roped muscles of his arms, back, and chest moving under his olive skin as he leaned one hand into the railing. He looked as if the commotion had caught him mid-dress, and he, too, appeared more annoyed than concerned for the deckhand who had a knife at his throat.

"You had a choice, Nash," he continued, "now you can live with it."

The deckhand with Nash's knife to his throat pinched his eyes closed, whimpering.

I climbed up the ladder, coming onto the deck as the helmsman took a step toward them.

"I'll make you a deal," he said. "When we're out to sea, you're free to move about the ship. And you'll do whatever work is requested if you want to be fed. When we make port, you return to the cargo hold. If you follow these rules, you can walk off the ship when we get back to Dern and we'll be even. If you don't . . ."

Nash's face flushed a furious crimson.

"You kill him, and we'll turn that knife on you. Even if you make it over that railing, you'll drown before you reach land."

Nash seemed to weigh his options and it only took moments for him to realize he didn't have any. He lowered the knife, shoving the deckhand to the ground.

The young man scrambled back to his feet, a look of terror still distorting his face. The helmsman didn't even wait to see if he was all right before he turned back into the passageway, disappearing without another word.

"You all right, kid?" Clove offered him a hand, pulling him up to his feet.

But he didn't answer, reaching up to wipe blood from his lip.

Clove clapped him on the back. "Get the bosun's tools from below. Nash has work to do."

Nash glared in answer, but the deckhand still looked like he was going to vomit, edging away from Nash as he slipped behind the main mast. It was only then that anyone seemed to notice me.

Clove looked me up and down before he breezed past me to the helm, where his log was lying open on the deck. It looked as if he'd dropped it there. He snatched it up and headed for the ladder that led to the cargo hold.

"What did you do to end up on this death wish of a ship?"

The question was coming from Nash, who'd had the knife in his hand only moments ago. He leaned into the railing, arms crossed over his chest as he watched me.

My grip tightened on my own knife as I squared my shoulders to him. "Just needed passage," I answered.

But he wasn't buying it. He smirked, the tilt of his lips changing his face. The fury that had been there a moment ago was only a simmer now. He'd accepted his fate. "Sure. And I just needed a change of scenery."

I couldn't tell now if he was the kind of person who would hold a blade to the deckhand's face for show, or if he'd meant it. He gave me his back, turning out to the water, and the wind pushed his curling hair to one side. His clothes weren't ones that I'd seen helmsmen and their crews wear. He looked more like a tradesman.

"Dredger!"

The helmsman's voice sounded in the passageway and my eyes trailed to the open door of his quarters across the deck.

I followed the sound, letting my shoulder touch the wall and leaning forward just enough to see through the crack above the door's hinge before my shadow crossed the threshold. He stood behind the desk, pulling a fresh shirt over his head before he rolled up each of the sleeves.

When he was finished, he retied the bandage that was wrapped around his hand.

"You going to just stand out there?"

His eyes suddenly flicked up, finding mine through the crack in the door, and I lifted my chin as I pushed the door all the way open. His gaze traveled from my boots to the top of my head, as if he was trying to measure me against the girl he'd found in his quarters the night before.

The corners of the small room were now visible in the daylight. It was bare and simple, stocked with only the most necessary items, including my dredging belt that he'd draped over the chair beside the desk. But it was the string of adder stones in the window that held my attention. A superstition that I recognized from the old sea myths.

He picked up the quill on the desk and returned it to its inkpot. It was fit with a worn little heron feather that needed replacing and the sight of it was a reminder that here, I was still safely hidden away from my mother's eye. From her whistling swan feather quills and the fools who did her bidding.

He stared at me for a moment before he reached into the drawer for the purse of gems and carefully dumped them into a wooden tray, pushing them toward me.

I stared at him.

"Well?" he said, the word heavy and impatient.

"Well what?"

"What do we have here?"

I hesitated before I took a step forward and lowered myself to the stool across from him. My fingers hovered over the stones before I gently sifted the real red beryl from the others, pushing them to one side of the tray.

"Which are the fakes?"

I placed a finger in front of the larger group. In all, there were eleven real gems and twenty-four fakes.

He scratched at the scruff on his jaw, eyeing them. He was unreadable, his face like stone as he picked up the quill.

He dipped it in the inkpot before opening the ledger and turning the page. "I didn't do myself any favors by leaving Dern with you. Is there anything I should know before I arrive in Sowan with you on my ship?"

If he only knew just how important that question was. There was plenty for him to know. Zola wouldn't be the only one looking for me or what I held in my pocket. But he was already keeping the most precious of my secrets.

I pulled my gaze from the red beryl, finding his face again. The straight line of his thick, dark brows made his blue eyes look like polished sea glass.

"I'm just a dredger."

"I think we've established that you're not just a dredger. And if you want to keep anyone else from finding out, you'd better be more careful. I marked you as a gem sage almost the second I met you."

He fell quiet, studying me again. The calm in his face was unsettling, but most unnerving was the fact that I believed him. I'd felt it in the tavern that night, the way he'd looked right into me.

The expression in his eyes shifted so slightly I thought maybe I imagined it, but it ignited a warmth in the air that hadn't been there moments ago.

Now *I* was studying *him*.

"What?" he asked, as if trying to unearth my thoughts.

I considered just how honest I could be. "How do I know you're not planning to sell me when we get to Ceros like Zola was going to?"

127

"I don't trade people."

"Then what was that out on the deck?" I asked flatly.

"A shipwright's apprentice who couldn't keep his mouth shut," he answered. "Trust me, it's a problem I didn't ask for."

So I'd been right. Nash wasn't a sailor. He was a guild hopeful.

The helmsman leaned into the desk with both hands, meeting my eyes directly again, and a flick of heat raced over my skin, the buzz of something alive waking in the air.

"If you're thinking about cutting loose in Sowan, that's a death sentence. It's a small village and you draw too much attention. He'll find you."

"What do you care?"

That question seemed to catch him off guard, but he recovered quickly. "If he gets what he wants, I don't get what I want."

It was that simple. Those were the clearly defined rules that hadn't changed once I crossed into the Narrows. It was every man for himself. And I was no different. I'd been thinking the same thing when I left Bastian.

Zola didn't have the power that someone like my mother did, but he was a proud man. He wouldn't forget what I'd done, and the Narrows was a small world. Our paths would cross again, and when they did, I needed to hold the upper hand.

"And if he starts telling people what I am?"

"He won't risk it. Not when he's this close to getting a trade license. It's too likely you'll be traced back to the *Luna* and if that happens, things won't go well with him and the Council."

It sounded like he was saying that as long I was on the *Riven*, I was safe. But nothing felt safe anymore.

"How did you end up on that ship?"

"A man named Simon." I gave the answer more easily than I'd meant to. I wasn't even sure if it was information I should keep to myself. "I asked for a way out of the city and he gave me one. I didn't know about the gem sages."

He stared at the corner of his desk in an absent way, like he was thinking. Sifting through line after line of numbers and possible outcomes. But he spoke none of it aloud.

"What's your name?" he asked suddenly. "The real one. The one you were born with."

He didn't blink, watching the war on my face as I contemplated lying again.

"You trusted me with your life when you got on this ship. But you don't trust me with your name?"

It wasn't that. The thing that made me want to bite my tongue was that I *did* trust him. I had absolutely no reason to, but I did. And I didn't like that feeling.

"Isolde."

This time, the truth of it was in the tone of my voice. The familiar way the word sounded on my lips. Even I could hear it.

"What's yours?" I asked.

"I already told you." He met my eyes again in that open way that made me feel like the ship was threatening to give way around me.

Elias.

The name he'd given me in the tavern. But I hadn't heard a single person call him that, which meant that somewhere along the way, he'd picked up another. The one I'd heard Zola call him by—Saint. That name held an emptiness to it, like a gem with no song. But it also felt safer. Elias was something hallowed, and that made a string of silent questions dance on my tongue.

I wanted to ask, but instead I held his gaze in an excruciating silence until, finally, his eyes fell back to the ledger.

With that, I was dismissed.

I picked up my dredging belt from the chair, setting it on my shoulder, and opened the door. But before it closed, I peered through the crack, finding Saint again. He leaned over the desk, running one hand through his hair as he wrote. His bandaged hand was bleeding through the wrapping, but he didn't seem to notice.

I pushed outside and welcomed the sting of the wind as it hit my face. I breathed it in deeply, trying to rid my lungs of the tight feeling I'd had as I stood in Saint's quarters.

That look on his face was as beautiful as it was cold, and I didn't like that I'd had to force myself to tear my eyes from his. I didn't know if it was this ship or the sea or the strange look of the sky that made my blood hum in my veins. I hoped it was.

I hoped it was anything but him.

THIRTEEN

SAINT

The wooden crates creaked, threatening to pop at the joints as the pulley lifted them from the *Riven*, and Ward, Sowan's harbor master, guided the load onto the dock. Clove stood beside him, watching over his shoulder as he logged the inventory. Six crates of wool we had no claim to, but the coin from its sale would keep us sailing until we got back to Dern.

The look on Ward's face as he scratched the numbers onto the page wasn't a friendly one. He'd been much harder to keep in line than Gerik, and his patience was wearing thin. Where Gerik was all gruff talk and empty threats, Ward was genuinely unpredictable. It was a quality that worried me.

Doing favors and making friends didn't serve anyone in the Narrows. There was always a bag of copper heavy enough to sway alliances, and Zola's coffers had only grown in the months since the Trade Council was instated. If this wasn't our last unsanctioned stop in Sowan, I wasn't sure we'd be able to risk a return. Not when we had a gem sage on our ship.

Nash had stowed himself in the cargo hold, as agreed, and the two deckhands we'd brought from Dern were perched on the jib, watching the busy, narrow street that overlooked the harbor. We didn't have the coin to pay someone on the docks to keep watch of the *Riven,* so there they would stay.

Isolde came up to the deck with her jacket buttoned up beneath her chin, and I couldn't help but think the name suited her in a strange kind of way. It had felt both new and familiar as she said it.

Her eyes skimmed the ships in the harbor and I watched as her gaze stopped on a carrack four slips down. She drew her bottom lip between her teeth and reached up, tucking the length of her dark red hair into her jacket.

"How long will we be here?" She looked nervous. Skittish, even.

"Just a night," I answered, dropping the map case over my shoulder. "Long enough to offload those gems and pick up more rye from the crofter."

"How do you know the merchant won't spot the fakes?"

"He doesn't need to. He knows what he's buying."

Her expression twisted into confusion. "Then why would he buy them?"

My gaze narrowed on her skeptically. She wasn't Narrows-born, but she was a dredger. And that usually came with a wealth of knowledge in working with traders, their crews, and the merchants they sold to. It was a world that went hand in hand with illicit trade, making it hard to believe she didn't know how any of this worked.

The last crate came over the side and once it touched down, I swung myself over the railing, catching the ladder with my boots.

I climbed down and Isolde hesitated before she followed, jumping from the last rung and landing on both feet beside me. Ward was already glaring at me from the top of his spectacles, but I was eyeing the stack of parchment tucked behind his ledger.

"Messages?" This time, I was almost afraid of the answer.

"No," Ward said, only half paying attention.

My hands curled into fists in my pockets, my eyes meeting Clove's. It had been almost three months since we'd submitted the petition for our trade license and the longer we went without it, the longer we sailed without the Trade Council's protection. We'd never needed it more than we did now.

Ward was far more concerned about the next crate of wool being lowered from the *Riven*. His crooked brow slanted even higher than usual.

"Since when do you transport wool?"

"Since now." Clove's words were an impatient warning.

There were plenty of people Ward could snitch to. The only thing we had going for us besides a bribe was the fact that Clove and I stood an entire head taller than him. Ward had the good sense to be afraid of us. That was all.

Ward's eyes traveled to Isolde, who stood behind me, and I didn't like the way they narrowed. There was no getting around the fact that she drew the eye. She was beautiful and she very clearly did not belong with us. But the more she piqued curiosity, the more likely it was to get back to Zola.

Clove took a step toward him, drawing his gaze from Isolde. "Are you going to have it taken to the merchant's house or do I need to find someone myself?"

Ward met Clove's cold stare, hand tightening around the quill, before he shot a glance up the dock. A shrill whistle cut into the air as his head tipped back, and two men jogged up the slip.

"Merchant's house," he ordered, pushing past them without another word.

"I'll deal with this. You get to Lander's." Clove's head tilted in Isolde's direction. "Probably shouldn't take her into the merchant's house."

I nodded, studying the crates of wool as the men lifted the first one on its side, sliding it onto the wheeled platform. We'd scraped Dern's port seal from the wood, but it wouldn't take much for someone to put together that the crates were stolen. I could only hope that Clove found a merchant who needed a deal.

"Go," Clove pressed. "I've got it."

I hooked one hand into the strap of the map case stretching across my chest and reluctantly turned on my heel, leaving him behind. If anyone could get out of a scrape, it was Clove. But he was also very good at getting into them.

Isolde followed as I started up the dock and her boots were beside mine in seconds as she put herself between me and the railing, keeping her head down.

From the corner of my eye, I could see her instinctively reach for her pocket, hand curling around whatever was there. But it was the way she walked that caught my attention. It wasn't just the fact that she was closer to me than she'd been since Dern, when I'd pulled her into the alley. It was the way she kept one shoulder turned away from the docks, her eyes cast down. Like she didn't want to be seen.

My gaze drifted over the ships to our right. Sowan was a much bigger harbor than Dern and there were ships from every port in the Narrows and several from the Unnamed Sea. I wondered, not for the first time, what exactly Isolde had left behind there.

The winding road that snaked through the village was crowded with doors open to the cool breeze coming in from the water and the stream of people coming and going from the harbor. I followed it up until the cobblestone path narrowed and curved into a broken vein of shops. Lander's was the only one that was shut up tight, the windows dark.

I stopped in front of the door, lifting a fist to tap the round beveled glass with my knuckles.

"This is it?" Isolde looked skeptical.

"Not impressed?" I muttered.

I'd never been to the Unnamed Sea, but if their traders had taught me anything, it was that they prized presentation over everything else. Usually, it was just a shell of pretense that got them what they wanted. People in the Narrows were used to bending beneath them.

"You can wait out here if you're worried about getting your hands dirty."

I didn't know why I'd said it. Lander didn't need, nor did he deserve my defense, but the look on her face stoked a fire in me. I wouldn't let her look down on him either.

"That's not what I meant," she whispered.

I turned to look at her. "Then what *did* you mean?"

Her chin tipped up so she could meet my eyes, and she didn't shrink beneath me. She squared her shoulders, licking her lips before her mouth opened to speak. But before the words left her tongue, the door opened.

Lander stood on the other side, a glazed look in his eye and his shirt only half buttoned. He hadn't even bothered to comb his hair.

"You're late," he said flatly.

Isolde's eyes slid to me, an almost-smirk on her lips, as if the picture of the man before us had been exactly the point she was trying to make.

I ignored the jab. Lander disappeared inside without extending an invitation for us to follow, and Isolde stared into the empty doorway before I stepped over the threshold. She stuck close as I pushed into the shop, one eye on the window that looked out over the street. She still had that look in her eyes. Like she was waiting for a face she knew to appear there.

"Who's this?" Lander followed her with a suspicious, unfocused gaze.

"My new dredger," I answered, lifting the strap of the map case over my head and setting it on the counter. I pulled the purse of stones from inside my jacket.

Isolde's eyes cut to me again, but this time, a tension hung in the air. She didn't like being claimed, I realized.

"Not every day you find crew so nice to look at." Lander pulled the scale onto the counter. Beside it, the tray and the ledger were already waiting.

When he looked up, catching sight of my face, he gave a nervous laugh. "Come on. Just a bit of fun."

Beside me, Isolde wasn't laughing. But she didn't look surprised either.

"All right, what have we got?" He set both hands on the counter, waiting.

I could smell the rye on his breath. The slick look of his skin and damp hair at his temples gave him away for a night of drinking at the tavern. I'd found Lander in this state more and more lately, and there were hardly any signs of business in his shop. The shelves were dusty, the candles unburned. My guess was he was spending all his coin on drink, and if that was the case, he was becoming unreliable. I couldn't have that.

"Red beryl." I let the purse fall open and the stones came tumbling out onto the tray, their facets like glistening drops of blood in the pale light.

The corners of Lander's mouth turned down, his chin jutting out. He was impressed. And he should have been.

They were the most valuable gems we'd ever moved. The fact that we were missing half of them was something he would have no way of knowing, and that worked in my favor. The arrangement was to pay the standard rate of a gem by carat, and it was as simple as that.

He'd pay me the sum that I'd take to Henrik before he gave me my cut, and then Lander would sell them to a few merchants in Ceros who thought they were getting the finest Bastian stones from some Saltblood's side trade. They were buying below their value if the gems were legitimate, but they weren't. In the end, the merchants would pay four times their worth.

The low murmur of Lander's voice broke the silence as he counted to himself, and Isolde's eyes finally found mine, though I could no longer read the look that lay there. She could hear the gems. Feel them, in a way. But we stood in a shop filled with everything from silver to onyx and, if that was true, she didn't show it.

"That makes . . ." Lander murmured, his hand shaking slightly on the quill. The sheen of sweat at his temple had now pearled into a single drop, trailing along his jaw, to his chin. It fell onto the wooden counter between his fingers. "Seven and a quarter."

"Seven and a quarter," I repeated.

The corner of Isolde's mouth twitched.

"That's right." Lander tapped the page of the ledger with his finger, reaching for the trunk he kept under the shelf. I waited for him to fit the key into the lock.

"That's funny," I said.

"What is?"

"When I weighed them this morning, there were nearly nine and a half carats."

Lander's lazy grin returned as he pulled two large purses of coin free. "Your scale must have been off. That happens with the movement of a ship, you know. Must be time to get it checked."

When I said nothing, he gestured to the stones.

"You can see it for yourself. It says the weight right there."

The brass basket that held the gems was still slightly swaying, the dial that sat in the center a smooth white face with a steel needle that read seven and a quarter.

"It's wrong," I said, the careful tenor of my voice unbroken.

I'd learned a long time ago that it never did much good to lose your temper. In the end, that was just noise. Only when it was quiet could you clearly detect the tells of a liar. The faint hitch of their breath. The shift of their eyes.

"We've been doing business a long time now, Lander." I studied the scale. "So I don't know why you'd choose now to cross me."

Again, the too-quick laughter. The drop of one shoulder as he bent closer. "Saint." He set both hands on the counter between us. "I—"

My hand hooked the handle of my knife before another word could leave his mouth and I lifted its weight into the air before letting my fingers loosen and skim its hilt. By the time I had clasped it in my palm, Lander was already straightening. Already tilting his weight backward.

I caught his wrist, pinning it in place as I drove the knife straight down. I didn't even feel the tip of the blade press into his skin. Between the bones. It slid through muscle and veins until the steel found the solid wooden countertop beneath his palm and the sound of the metal ringing was followed by Lander's strangled cry.

Isolde screamed, one hand flying to her mouth as her eyes widened.

"Saint!" Lander's face twisted, the open gape of his mouth making my name sound misshapen as he gulped for air. "Saint!"

"What are you doing?" Isolde's voice was hoarse. The hand that was pressed to her mouth was now just hovering in the air between us. She was so pale she looked like she was going to faint.

"Check it."

"Wh-What?" she stammered.

"The scale," I said softly. "Check it."

Isolde stood frozen for several breaths before she moved forward, steps halting and jerking like she was struggling to move her feet. Her hands fumbled over the scale until she had hold of the dial.

I let go of the knife, moving my other hand from the counter before the blood that was pooling there could touch my fingers. Isolde sniffed, twisting the back of the dial open until it dislodged, and she bit down onto her bottom lip, looking up at me before she turned the tray so I could see.

Two small iron pellets had been wedged into the mechanism to create more resistance against the needle. I'd seen it done before in Cragsmouth, when my father had his catches weighed for sale. He hadn't drawn his knife on anyone for it, but he should have.

"I'm sorry." Lander gulped, choking. "I'm sorry! I just needed a little—"

"I don't care what you need," I said, reaching around him, into the trunk. "I expect to be dealt with fairly. And if I'm not"—I lifted another purse of coin from inside—"you will be made to wish you had. Next time it won't be a hand."

I counted out the purses for the exact amount, not taking more than I was owed. I wouldn't steal from a Narrows-born, even if he was a cheat. Not unless I had to.

Down the counter, Isolde was staring at me, her chest still rising and falling in rushed breath. I tucked the purses into my jacket one at a time, rebuttoning it before I reached for the handle of my knife.

"Saint." A voice like melted honey filled the cold air of the shop, making all three of us look to the open door behind us.

There, Emilia had a hip propped against the doorframe, her arms crossed over her chest. Her long blond waves fell over one shoulder as her head tipped to one side.

"Expected you this morning." Her brown eyes glinted as they moved from me to the knife pinning Lander to the counter. It was encircled by a shining pool of blood.

"We were delayed," I said.

Emilia's attention went to Isolde and it lingered there for a moment before she hooked her thumbs into her belt.

"Come on. Supper's waiting." She took a step backward out of the shop and the sunlight hit her fair face before she started up the street without us.

I reached for the knife, gripping the handle and yanking it free, sending another sharp cry from Lander's lips. He clutched his hand to his chest, falling into the counter, and Isolde almost stumbled backward, catching herself on the back of a chair.

I dragged the blade over the thick wool of my trousers, turning it twice. When I slid it back into my belt, I looked up to see Isolde watching me, a horrified expression on her face.

"Well?" I said, taking the map case from the counter and slinging it back over my shoulder. "You coming?"

FOURTEEN

ISOLDE

Saint didn't so much as look in my direction as I followed him up the hill in the opposite direction we'd come from the harbor. His dark hair was damp with mist, the collar of his gray-blue coat pulled up to hide the bottom half of his face. But his gaze was on the ground as he walked.

We'd left the merchant's shop with the sound of Lander's moaning at our backs, and the pathetic sound echoed between the stone walls, carried off by the wind. I still had a sick feeling curled in my throat, my hands colder than they should have been.

He hadn't even blinked. Hadn't hesitated for even a second when he drew that knife and drove it down into the man's hand. In broad daylight, with the shop door open, and no one had even come running.

The woman who'd appeared in the doorway of Lander's shop was waiting at the top of the hill, her wavy gold hair drifting in the wind that was rolling in from the water at our back. Her trousers were tied at her middle, a flowing white shirt rippling around her slender frame.

A large wooden market cart was stopped beside her, where the buildings in Sowan began to thin, giving way to an expanse of sprawling hills. They looked like an unrolled painting behind her, yellows and greens in swirling patterns beneath an almost-blue sky. She waited patiently, running a hand over the snout of one of the two dove-gray mules rigged to the cart.

A white-haired man with a bony frame that jutted out from beneath his thin white shirt sat at the front of the cart, leads in hand. He didn't look strong enough to control the beasts or even clear-eyed enough to see the road.

"Saint." The old man's face brightened at the sight of the helmsman, mouth stretching in a smile that revealed a gap between his front teeth.

"Perrie." Saint made his own attempt at a smile, but it was more in his eyes than anything. His face was always set, eyes always watching from beneath his rigid brow like he was bracing for something.

"We were bringing the grain down to the merchant's house and saw the *Riven* in the harbor. Figured we'd save you the walk." Again, the woman's eyes roamed over my face. "I'm Emilia."

I gave her a polite nod.

But Emilia's attention had already skipped to Saint, waiting for an explanation.

"Dredger" was his only reply.

He didn't say *my* this time. I hadn't liked the sound of it in Lander's shop.

"Hope that's true. I don't trust anyone who doesn't have callouses on their hands." Emilia didn't look satisfied with that answer. "If you're taking on crew now, things must be going well."

Saint's face was unreadable, giving nothing away. The words couldn't be further from the truth. He pulled himself up into the cart, finding a seat in the back, and Emilia followed, taking the open place on the bench beside the old man.

"Join us," she said, looking out over the hills in the distance. "It's the only decent meal you'll get for a while yet if you're sailing with this lot."

Saint leaned his back into the railing, waiting, as if to see what I'd do after that display at the merchant's shop. This felt like some kind of test.

I glanced back to the village, where the road bent and disappeared before Lander's could be seen. My hands took hold of the cart's side, tightening, before I lifted myself from the ground and climbed in.

The slap of the leads was followed by the jolt of the wheels before I'd even sat, and the cart pulled off the cobblestones onto the dirt road that curved like an *S* into the hills. Beyond the top of one in the distance, I could see two soft, trailing wisps of smoke. We were headed in their direction.

I hooked one arm into the wooden slat beside me as we rocked from side to side, feeling the chill of Saint's gaze before I finally looked at him.

"What?" His cold eyes bored into mine, which I was beginning to mark as a rare thing.

I swallowed. "You didn't have to hurt him like that."

"Oh, darling." It was Emilia who answered, her back still to us. "Yes, he did."

Darling.

The word reeked of my mother's voice, making my mouth twist to one side.

I'd been no stranger to ruthlessness. I'd seen it many different ways, and it was usually at Holland's order. But things in the Unnamed Sea were done behind closed doors and in shadows. And my mother's hands were never dirty with them.

I'd been young when I began to understand what she was. I was ten years old when my father sat me down in the solarium for a cup of tea and told me what I needed to know about my mother—that she would always choose the trade. Over me. Over him. Over everything. That trust was something that only he and I would have. If I'd listened to him, *really* listened, I thought, he might still be here.

He hadn't said the words with any kind of malice or resentment. There wasn't even a hint of sadness. But he'd wanted me to know. It wasn't until a few years later that I began to understand what he meant.

We came over the last hill before the sun touched the horizon, but the warm light changed the land into sweeps of violet and blue. The chimney smoke drew closer until I followed one of their trails to a small stone house set atop one of the bluffs. Once the clouds cleared and the orange light deepened, I could see what lay beyond it—miles and miles of golden hills rippling beneath the sea wind.

Rye.

I sat up, studying the ridge that overlooked the road. More than one crofter had appeared, watching us from their perches, and a few lifted hands into the air as we passed.

The croft was a well-kept one. Beyond the house, four large barns were erected in a semicircle. One of their doors was pulled open, where I could see a heavy cart of rye stalks disappearing. The cottages that dotted the hillside looked like a constellation of stars. A croft this large likely had a harvest big enough to support at least two or three dozen people to plant and pick and thrush.

The rye was the reason the traders of the Unnamed Sea had first begun to sail in the Narrows. As our cities grew, so did our need for grain. When our own crofters ran out of fertile land, we came looking for more.

Saint's business with the croft seemed to have more to do with the bottles of drink than the sacks of grain they were made from. I had to admit, it was smart. Crofters weren't permitted to sell their crop to anyone without a license, and that had always been the traders from the Unnamed Sea. But there were no clear rules on the sale and transport of the rye drink that filled the taverns in the Narrows. They were outside of the law, but just barely.

Perrie clicked his tongue, pulling back on the leads, and the cart came to a slow stop at the foot of a zigzagging stretch of steps carved into the earth. They led up to the stone house, now drenched in fire-gold sunlight.

Saint stood, waiting for me to jump down before he followed.

"A nice harvest coming in," Emilia said, climbing the steps first and looking out to the barns at our left. "Should be in the barrels in another month. Maybe two."

"And the ones that are already resting?"

"Three or four. They're coming along nicely. I'll take you out to see once you've eaten and the color comes back into your cheeks." She smirked.

She reached out, touching his elbow in a gesture that was familiar. Close. Saint seemed to exist with an invisible space around him, but in an instant, this woman reached through it.

Perrie lifted the latch on the door and it swung wide, releasing the thick smell of baked bread and roasting potatoes into the chilled air around us. My mouth watered, making me instinctively swallow. I hadn't eaten anything that smelled this good since I'd left home.

There was that word again. *Home.*

Saint pushed into the doorway behind him, and Emilia waited at the door, stepping aside for me to enter. But that studying look was still in her eyes, as if she were trying to puzzle something out.

"Thanks," I said, ducking inside.

A long wooden table was set in the center of the space, a kitchen on one end and a row of three tidy cots on the other. Everything from pots to tools to shelves stacked with jars lined the walls and every inch of floor was taken by chairs, needlework baskets and stacked wood before the hearth.

Candles burned in every corner of the rectangular room and lanterns were hung from the rafters overhead, washing the beams that lined the ceiling of the house in light. The last of the sun was still streaming through the windows, but it would be gone in minutes.

A young woman stood over a steaming pot bubbling on a wood stove in the kitchen, stirring with one hand on her hip. When she spotted me, she looked surprised. "Hi there."

"Hello." I bit down hard after the word left my mouth. It sounded too formal, and my accent was becoming more noticeable to my own ears.

She caught Emilia's gaze, amused. "I'm Tansy." She gave Saint a look-over next. "Saint, you look half starved, as always."

He didn't answer, sinking down into one of the chairs at the end of the table. Bowls and plates made of a red clay were set out neatly before short glasses. At the center of the table were two bottles of rye. They looked like the same ones Saint carried on his ship.

The warmth of the fire touched my cold hands, making me curl my fingers into my palms. The house was a home in every sense of the word, but not like any I'd ever known. It was the kind I saw sketched into the pages of fairy tales my father used to read to me. Mice that lived in tiny cottages filled with firelight or fairies that dwelled in star-shaped hovels by the sea. The memory immediately made me swallow hard, a sting lighting behind my eyes.

Tansy made her way around the table, scooping heaping ladles of stew into the bowls, and I took the seat across from Saint. Emilia sat beside him, unbuttoning the collar of her shirt and pulling it open to the air. She was beautiful and rough, the sun baked into her skin and hair like a glaze.

She looked amused when she caught me staring at her. "Bread, Tansy."

The girl scurried back into the small kitchen before returning with a floured loaf. As soon as she set it down, hands were reaching for it.

"And where's Clove?" Perrie asked.

"Made a stop at the merchant's house. He'll be here."

"The merchant's house," Emilia said, as if to herself. "Does that mean you've got that license you haven't shut up about for the last year?"

"Not exactly."

"Hmm." She reached for her knife, dipping it into the plate of butter. "I see. Pretty risky trading in the merchant's house without one, don't you think?"

I watched the look that passed between them. I didn't know what kind of person found fault with unsanctioned trade but didn't blink an eye at pinning a man's hand to a counter with a blade. This woman was a creature cut from the same cloth as Saint and Clove. Riddles with unspoken rules not easily solved.

"It's coming."

"I see." Emilia didn't look convinced. In fact, it almost seemed like she was intentionally provoking him.

Saint didn't seem bothered by it. "Any day now."

"You've been saying that for months. I have a warehouse full of rye I could sell to any of those bastard traders in Sowan. But I'm sitting on it for you."

"Manners, Emilia," Perrie chided.

She arched an eyebrow at me. "An uncle who thinks he's my father," she muttered.

Perrie only smiled wider.

She leveled her gaze at him before it drifted to me again. "And where did they find you?"

Tansy sat down beside me, hiking up her skirts to cross her legs. She looked delighted by the interrogation, a thin smile playing on her lips.

"Dern," I answered, filling my spoon with the broth. I resisted the urge to sip it from the edge, instead putting the whole spoon in my mouth like the people in the tavern did.

Emilia frowned. "Dern, huh? How'd you come by that Saltblood accent then?"

"I'm from Bastian." I answered the question she was really asking, which I should have done in the first place. She didn't strike me as someone who accepted half truths.

"Trading at the merchant's house, taking on Saltbloods . . ." Emilia's eyes cut back to Saint. "You've been busy."

"Any decent crew has a dredger," he said, not looking at me.

"Oh, you're a *decent* crew now." Emilia stifled a laugh.

Tansy, on the other hand, didn't even try to hide it. But the sound was lost to a mouth full of stew, and Perrie followed.

It wasn't what I'd expected when Saint said that he was stopping to meet the rye crofter. This wasn't just business around this table. It was history. Friendship, even.

The knock of boots sounded on the steps outside and every face turned to the door before it opened to the night air. Clove appeared against the dark sky, blond hair swept to one side. His arm was cradled around the small frame of a curly-headed girl no bigger than five or six years old.

"Found him!" she chirped.

"Started without me, I see." Clove smiled, tipping the girl forward so she could peer at Emilia from beneath her curls.

They were too similar not to share blood, but too far apart in age to be sisters. Emilia was the girl's mother, I realized.

"There she is." Tansy's tone was a reproach. "I called for you over an hour ago." She pulled the girl from Clove's arms, but the girl was sliding down as quickly as Clove handed her over, and then she was crawling into Saint's lap.

He barely acknowledged her, pulling one arm from the table so that she could curl into him. There was no rigid set to his mouth now. No attempt to put more space between them. He looked as if she'd sat there a hundred times.

He reached into his jacket, producing a small iridescent shell, and her eyes widened before she plucked it from his fingers. The smile buried on his lips was visible for half a second before it disappeared again.

Emilia pulled out a chair for Clove beside her, and he was taking a bite of bread before he'd even settled into the seat. His blond scruff was like gold dust in the candlelight, making him look younger than his time on the sea painted him.

"Was wondering if those traders in the merchant's house had eaten you for supper."

The comment wasn't an innocent one. She was probing. Wanting to know what exactly they'd been trading. Even if there was history between them, it was clear there were still secrets.

The little girl's bare feet dangled under the table, her toes tapping my leg as Saint shifted. When I looked up, her wide green eyes were trailing over me as she chewed a too-big bite of stew. A dribble of broth dripped down her chin.

"I'm Hazel," she said, wiping it with the back of her hand.

I followed the smear of dirt on her cheek to where it disappeared into her hairline, smiling. She was a wild creature. A character that would fit into one of my father's bedtime stories.

"Isolde," Saint said quietly, giving her my name.

It was timid almost, as if he were trying the name out in his own voice for the first time. The curve of the word was soft and gentle, like those hills the sun had fallen behind. The sound of it made me bite down on my bottom lip.

The talk moved from news in Dern to news in Sowan, and discussion about rye barrels I didn't know how to decode. But across from me, Hazel's attention slowly narrowed, growing more acute by the second. Her eyes were focused, her brow wrinkling as she absently turned the piece of bread in her hand.

I set my elbows onto the table, watching her.

"What is it?" she asked softly.

"What is what?"

Her lips pursed before she set down the bread, and her gaze fell to my pocket.

"The stone," she whispered.

I stilled, suddenly feeling like the midnight in my pocket weighed a hundred pounds. But the strings of the small purse were tucked in. She couldn't see it.

She could *feel* it.

My eyes flitted from one face at the table to the next, gooseflesh racing over my skin. But they were lost in conversation. All of them but Saint.

"Leave it, Hazel," he said lowly.

She picked up her bread, shoulders hunching like a scolded puppy's, but every few seconds, her head involuntarily turned back in the stone's direction. As if it were a magnet drawing her gaze.

I said nothing, not wanting to draw any attention to the stone in my pocket. If Saint had stabbed a man for red beryl, I didn't want to know what he'd do for something as priceless as the midnight. But he didn't seem to be curious about what Hazel had said, and something told me that was because he didn't want *me* paying any attention to the fact that she'd just sniffed the stone out with no reasonable explanation.

Emilia's chair scraped against the floor and she stood, tossing her napkin onto her empty plate. The others didn't even look up, carrying on with Clove about something to do with the next harvest. But Emilia caught eyes with Saint and he mirrored her without a word, shifting Hazel from his lap so he could get to his feet.

He followed her to the door and pulled it closed behind him, the cuff of his shirt shifting beneath his jacket sleeve just enough for me to see the fabric painted a bright red. I bristled, remembering the way the blood had pooled on the counter in the merchant's shop.

Looking at him now, I couldn't tell the difference between the Saint that had stabbed the screaming man and the one who sat across the table, the ghost of a smile on his lips and the gleam of firelight in his eyes.

Maybe there was no difference at all.

FIFTEEN

SAINT

There were false memories tied to the sound of the rye. They woke every time we came here.

Cragsmouth was a scant fishing village north of Dern where the cliffs crumbled down into the sea like a black wall. There was no rye growing there, but there were vast grasslands that rolled up into the hills. And they had the same sound as the croft, like rushing water.

Fishing had been the work of my father and his father before him, but I'd known from the time I was young that I wanted to sail one of the trading ships that crossed our paths when we were pulling in the nets.

My father had wanted it for me too.

Emilia reached out, touching the tops of the stalks as we made our way up the path toward the barn. She was a rye crofter by blood, growing in the same fields her grandmother had planted, but where her family had traditionally only sold the grain in bags at Sowan's merchant's house to traders from the Unnamed Sea, Emilia was the first to start distilling some of it in barrels.

The harvest had already begun and the rows were still filled with workers bent beneath bundles on their backs against the last moments of a brilliant sunset. Some of it would be packed into crates for the traders from the Unnamed Sea or sent by ship to Ceros. The rest would make its way into the barrels. In the end, if things went my way, both Emilia and I would hold its coin.

"You don't look so good, Elias," she said, plucking one of the rye stalks as she passed and crushing it in her palm.

"Thanks." I let the bite of sarcasm touch the word.

"I'm worried about you."

"Don't be."

I followed her around the corner of the first wood-plank building, to the door that faced the fields. She hooked one hand into the iron ring, looking up at me.

"What?" she said.

"You need to be careful." I lowered my voice. "With Hazel."

The set of her mouth faltered for just a moment before it recovered. I'd warned her that the Narrows was crawling with rumors about gem sages going missing. I had one of them on my ship. And all it would take was one disloyal crofter running their mouth at the tavern to tip someone off about Hazel.

Emilia rolled the grain between her fingertips, falling quiet for a moment. I knew she was worried, even if she pretended not to be.

"And you need to be careful with that dredger," she said, changing the subject.

I didn't take the bait. "I'm serious."

"So am I."

"We have new crew on the ship almost every time we come through Sowan."

"You never bring them here," she said, lower.

"I told you. She's just a dredger."

Emilia let it go. She didn't often show any kind of curiosity about the inner workings of our crew, but I'd seen her eyes focus on Isolde more than once since she'd shown up at Lander's.

"How's the rye coming?"

She grinned. "It's coming."

She pulled the door open. Inside, dozens of barrels were stacked on iron racks, all of them missing the mark of the crofter who'd made them. That had been part of our agreement from the beginning. Partly to protect Emilia, but I also didn't want anyone to know where to find the goods I was selling. Not until everyone knew they had to come to me to get them.

She took one of the tin cups hanging on the wall before making her way to a barrel at the back. The spigot gurgled as she pulled down the handle and the red-amber liquid came rushing out. The smell of it was already in the air before she handed it to me.

"Probably the best batch yet," she said, nodding for me to drink. "I've got four dozen crates waiting to be loaded up for you."

I lifted the cup, taking a sniff before I poured the rye into my mouth. The burn traveled over my tongue, down my throat, before pooling in my belly. The taste of wood and fire smoke lit in my nose. She was right. It was good.

If I'd told my father that I'd be trading rye when I finally got my own ship, he would have laughed at me. He'd never have believed it. Growing up, rye was the home brew that the fishermen drank to help drain the cold from their bodies after days on the water. Back then, it was only ale the taverns wanted. But the more people traveled from port to port, the more they were asking the barkeepers for rye. Now, even the Saltbloods were drinking it.

"When can I put my name on it?" she asked, lifting an eyebrow.

"Soon."

I handed her the cup and she stood there, waiting. "You know, you usually pay me before you eat at my table." Her eyes dropped to the swell of coin purses in my jacket. "You going to tell me what's wrong or should I just assume the worst?"

I drew in a deep breath, running one hand through my hair. I'd dreaded this exact moment since I lost the gems because I could feel the sand shifting beneath us. If we were going to have goods to trade on the *Aster* and keep our route, we needed Emilia. But Clove was right. She wouldn't like being put in this position.

"We're short on this run," I said, trying to smooth out the edges of the words so that they didn't carry the scrape I felt as they climbed up my throat.

"What do you mean *short*?"

"It happens sometimes." I looked over her head, to the barrels.

But Emilia wasn't buying into my calm. "Tell me."

It had taken six months to convince her to partner with us, but Clove and I hadn't shared everything with her about our work. She didn't know about Henrik or the fakes. If she did, she would have never agreed to sell us the rye. Emilia knew exactly what we needed her to. That was all.

"Just a bad trade," I said, giving her at least part of the truth.

"You really expect me to believe this has nothing to do with that girl?"

I studied her. "What?"

"After two years of dragging the rattiest crews I've ever seen across the Narrows, you show up here with a girl who looks like she was grown in a glasshouse and for the first time, you have no coin. I'm thinking those two things aren't a coincidence."

I leaned into the barrel beside us. I wasn't going to lie to her. She was too smart for that. But I also wasn't sure just how much trouble the dredger had landed me in and I wasn't going to pretend I did.

"What's really going on, Elias?"

I sighed, the weight of that name making it hard to look

at her. She was one of the few people I'd known before it was erased. "We need crates to sell in Ceros and Dern, but I can't pay you for it. Not yet."

"Rye you can't pay for," she clarified. "That's all you need, huh?"

I nodded.

Emilia scoffed.

"You know we'll pay you."

"I don't know anything." Her tone shifted, her green eyes darkening. "I made a deal with you, Saint. When no one else would. You wouldn't be on the water right now if it weren't for me."

"I know that."

"And if you can't keep your end of that deal, then I'm not going to keep mine."

I straightened, waiting for her to finish the threat. It wasn't a veiled one. I'd been the one to put those ideas into her head about selling the rye, but now, she had the means to do it without me. She knew that the moment traders started getting their licenses in the Narrows, they would line up outside her door. For the first time, she had the upper hand between us, and she wanted me to know she would use it.

"The minute we start doing each other favors, we're done for. You know that, don't you?" she said.

I did. I could feel her patience wearing thin. It had been for a long time. And she was right.

"The next time I see you, I'll have the license."

"Like I haven't heard that a hundred times."

"I mean it." I sounded desperate now, younger.

For the first time in a long time, I could feel that hardness cracking around me. Emilia had it too. We'd needed it. But now we were both just trying to keep our heads above water in a rising sea. The Narrows was changing and we both wanted our stake.

Her expression softened and she sighed, reaching up to hook her fingers in my folded arms. "We're friends, Saint. A rare thing in a world like this one. That's the only reason I'm going to pretend that when you take that rye, you've paid for it."

An ache rose in my throat. I was ashamed of how relieved the words made me.

"Figure I owe you for one thing or another."

We'd known each other for nearly three years, and in that time, we *had* become friends. But we'd been other things to each other too. After Hazel's father, Victor, died, I'd spent more than one night in Emilia's bed, and the ghost of it was in the way she touched me now. But we'd never had anything more than loneliness between us.

"And Perrie?" I asked, shooting a glance toward the open door of the barn.

"He doesn't need to know. No one does."

I nodded.

"But this is the only time, Saint."

I didn't miss that she'd stopped calling me Elias. That was what had gotten her into this mess in the first place.

We took the path back down to the house, the stones

now invisible in the dark. The stars were stretched across the moonless sky over the lantern light of the cottages on the hill. Emilia pulled the pipe from her vest and filled it with mullein, lighting it in an amber glow and the air filled with the sweet smell of the smoke.

"It's not just for me, you know," she said, her face half lit by the candlelight coming through the window. Her gaze moved down the table, landing on Hazel. She was sitting in my empty seat, finishing my bowl of stew. "It's for her."

I knew what she meant. Copper was protection. Emilia had managed to keep her father's farm going after he was gone. Even after she'd lost Victor. The croft was turning out grain at a rate that it never had before, and the truth was, she was good at this. But if she wanted the kind of power that would make people afraid to cross her, she needed more than Saltblood traders vying for her harvest.

Across the table, Isolde was the only thing in the house that didn't belong. She didn't look like she belonged anywhere, really. There was a carefulness to the way she spoke and moved, like she had learned to walk on glass. But she wasn't afraid. I was still trying to figure out what exactly that meant.

She set her elbows on the table, taking small bites of the stew and wiping the corner of her mouth with the linen napkin in her lap. It was those little things that gave away that she was a Saltblood. It was also clear she knew how to do a job. She acted like a well-bred girl, but in her two days on the *Riven,* she'd shown she could crew like anyone else. As far as I could tell, she was a highborn gem sage turned dredger who'd maybe fallen from grace. But nothing about that made any sense.

"Promise me your trouble won't come to my door." Emilia said suddenly.

I turned my face, finding her eyes in the dark. There was no humor in them now. No sly meaning. She was asking, as a friend.

"I promise."

SIXTEEN

ISOLDE

Emilia knotted the leads around the driver's bench before she jumped down from the cart, landing a head shorter than Saint on the ground. Her hair was barely bound up by the wrap around her head, making her look even more like Hazel than she had the night before.

I'd noticed almost right away that Saint seemed antsy on land, and so was I. I'd spent the dark hours on solid ground for the first time since I'd left Bastian, and already, we were headed back out to sea.

Tansy had had to scoop Hazel up to keep her from stowing away on the cart as we pulled away from the stone crofter's cottage at daybreak. The little girl was a gem sage, that much I knew. But I'd lain awake in the night, Saint's deep, even breaths only feet away as I watched the starlight paint the air a silvery blue, wondering what would become of her. The sages in Bastian had all gone, along with their apprentices, and there were people in every port with theories about where. With no one to teach her, I doubted she'd ever learn to use the gift, and maybe that was a good thing.

Hazel had been born into a different world than me or my father. She was probably safer on the rye croft than she would be anywhere else.

The rye jostled in the crates as Clove and Perrie unloaded the last of them, and the men from the docks were already hauling them to the *Riven* down the harbor. But as Emilia watched them, there was a wariness in her eyes.

Saint watched her over the back of the cart for a long moment. Whatever had transpired between them last night, it had changed the feel of the house and altered the easy way they were with each other. He'd been different when he returned from the barn. Quieter, if that was possible. But there was something lighter about him too.

I slid the crock of stew Tansy had given us from the back of the cart and propped it on my hip when Saint gave Emilia a nod as goodbye. She watched him go, taking the steps down into the harbor, but she caught me by the arm before I could follow him.

She reached for my hand, turning it palm up to the sky and brushing a thumb over the lines that covered the rough skin. Along the base of each finger, the pad of my thumb, years-old callouses had been formed by my work on the reefs.

Satisfied, Emilia let me go, pulling her arms back into her cloak. "Keep an eye on those two, dredger."

I smirked, expecting her to do the same, but she didn't. This girl who seemed all wit and cutting tongue wasn't joking. She was serious.

"I mean it." She took a step closer.

The way she looked at me was with the protective eye of a mother or a sister. This wasn't a selfish merchant's concern for the trader carrying her goods or a backhanded way of looking out for herself. She cared about them—Saint and Clove.

"They'll deny it until they're two breaths from death, but they need a keeper," she said.

I wanted to tell her I was no keeper. That I was just trying to figure out how to keep myself. But I'd likely never cross paths with the woman again and I couldn't see what good it would do either of us.

"I'm just taking passage to Ceros." I told her the truth.

The smirk did surface on her lips, then. "So, not a dredger after all."

"I am."

"Well," She pointed a finger at the *Riven*. "There's a ship, or at least, what's left of one. And the beginnings of a crew."

I watched the fog move over the *Riven*, Clove's shape rippling across the deck. "I think my days of diving to fill the purses of traders and merchants are over."

Emilia clicked her tongue. "That one's a got a different kind of affliction, I'm afraid." When she looked past me, her eyes found Saint. He stood on the docks, supervising as the crates of rye were rigged to pulleys.

She turned back to the cart and I watched her untie the leads, hands fidgeting with the crock of stew as I tried to decide whether to say the thing that had been stirring in me since the night before. "It—"

Emilia stopped, looking over her shoulder at me.

"It'll be easier to hide in a year or two," I breathed.

Emilia cocked her head to one side. "What will?"

"Hazel."

As soon as I said her daughter's name, Emilia stilled.

"She'll get better at hiding it. Better at not reacting to the gems when she feels them."

She let go of the leads, her boot finding the ground again. Her eyes searched mine, as if trying to unearth any threat that may lay there.

"It's worse indoors. Louder, and harder to ignore. The merchant's house in particular is difficult. I wouldn't take her there."

The humor she'd had seconds before was gone and for a moment, I wondered if she was considering drawing her knife. But she was silent, waiting for me to continue.

"It would help if someone taught her."

"You offering?" she asked, her tone full of knowing.

I shook my head. "Like I said, I'm just going to Ceros."

I remembered what it was like, to be surrounded by something in the air that only I could feel. The constant buzz and hum, the way it was almost never just quiet. But

I'd had my father. Hazel had a mother who seemed more than capable of protecting her, but that wasn't the same as having a teacher. Emilia reached a hand between us and I took it, shaking.

"Thank you," she whispered.

Perrie came back up the steps of the harbor, latching the back of the cart closed, and my fingers slipped from Emilia's before she climbed back up to the driver's bench.

"Don't drown out there, dredger," she called over her shoulder.

I smiled, pulling up my hood. I started down the stairs and up the dock until I reached the *Riven*. Then I climbed the ladder, dropping myself onto the deck. Clove was high up on the main mast, untying the lines on the sail, and on the upper deck, Saint latched the opening of the hold, his dark hair falling into his face as he heaved the iron lever into place.

"Where are the deckhands?" I looked up at Clove.

"Looks like life on the *Riven* was a little much for Julian and Mateo."

"They left?" I said, confused.

"Not the first time crew's disappeared at port." He climbed down, jumping from the pegs and landing beside me.

"Who's going to crew the ship?"

"We are," he answered.

I glared at him. The *we* he was talking about clearly included me.

"I don't work for free," I said.

"Well, it's a good thing we've paid you in advance with a hot meal and a warm bed at Emilia's." He winked at me.

So, that was how they were going to play this. A game of trading favors.

I held up the crock between us. When he realized what I wanted, he huffed, producing the key from his pocket and starting toward the hatch. We climbed down into the dank passageway that led to the cargo hold and Clove lifted the lock from the bolt, fitting the key inside. The deckhands had abandoned their posts, but they hadn't bothered to let Nash out before they left.

I supposed he deserved that after threatening to cut Mateo's throat.

When the door swung open, Nash was sitting atop a closed barrel, arms crossed over his chest.

"Took you long enough."

"What the . . ." Clove growled, eyeing the empty bottle of rye on the floor. The entire cargo hold reeked of it.

"Man's gotta eat something," Nash muttered, sliding down.

When he saw the crock in my hands, he brightened.

I handed it over and he pried open the lid, giving the stew a sniff. "No bread?"

I glared at him.

"Well, there's at least one civilized creature on this ship." He fished a carrot from the broth and popped it into his mouth. "That's something."

"You just got a promotion," Clove said, turning on his heel and ducking out.

Nash stopped mid-chew, eyeing me.

"The deckhands are gone." I answered his unspoken question.

He cradled the crock in one arm, following after Clove. "Wait a minute."

But Clove was already back on deck, headed for the anchor crank. "I'm not asking."

Nash looked to Saint, who was coming down the stairs from the upper deck. "So, what? You're expanding into slave labor now?"

Saint ignored him. "Just get us out of here." He pulled off his jacket, going to the railing. In one movement, he pulled the knife from his hand and pressed it to his palm. I flinched when I saw the bright shine of blood bead against the steel, but Saint didn't look fazed. Once the blood was flowing, he flicked it into the water below.

I was the only one who seemed to even notice. Behind me, Nash had already climbed up onto the anchor crank, loosening his trousers. In the next breath, he was relieving himself over the side of the ship.

I pinched my eyes closed, grimacing.

Saint had the bleeding fist pressed against his chest, pulling a cloth from his back pocket as a steady stream of blood dripped from between his fingers. Once it was wrapped, he climbed the foremast himself, not waiting to order someone else to do it.

His hair blew to one side as the wind caught him, the hard shape of his arms surfacing under the skin as he rose higher. I tried not to trace the outline of him against the gray sky. It wasn't until I spotted the bloodstain on his sleeve again that I pulled my eyes away.

"Riven!" Ward was coming up the dock with a limp that sagged one shoulder, waving a hand in the air overhead.

"Now what?" Clove muttered, locking the anchor back into place. He went to the railing, leaning into it with both hands as Ward turned onto the slip.

"Looks like that luck of yours finally came in!" Ward lifted a sealed parchment into the air.

Clove's eyes shot up to Saint and I watched as every muscle in Saint's body tightened, all at once, the fog curling before his lips the only evidence that he was still breathing. Slowly, his gaze dropped to Clove, and something boyish lit in his eyes. Something untouched.

The expression was mirrored on Clove's face as he pushed off the crank, untying the ladder again. It rolled down with a slap against the hull and then he was climbing, his flaxen hair disappearing over the portside. When he had the parchment in hand, his thumb brushed over the red wax seal that was pressed to a thin green ribbon. It looked like a summons to the Trade Council.

The wind picked up, reddening the curves of Saint's face, and he climbed back down the foremast. When his boots hit the deck, he didn't move, as if he were afraid that at any moment both the navigator and the parchment would vanish.

An evil grin stretched across Clove's lips as he handed it over, and I didn't know if it was the wind or a slight tremble in Saint's hands that shook the letter as he opened it. His eyes skipped over the words frantically as he raked his hair back from his face.

"So?" Clove paced before the helm, waiting.

But Saint said nothing, lifting his gaze just long enough to find Clove's. They stared at each other, wordless, and then Clove closed the distance between them in two steps, surprising me as he wrapped his arms around Saint, drawing his tall frame to him.

Saint's white-knuckled hands clenched into Clove's shirt and he let out a heavy breath before he let him go. The face he wore was one I'd never seen, the blue of his eyes as deep as the water that surrounded the ship.

"Set course for Ceros," Saint said. "Shove off."

Clove took hold of the pegs on the main mast, not waiting even a beat before he began the climb. A moment later, the sails were unrolling over our heads. The tone of his voice was lighter than I'd ever heard it. "It's about damn time."

SEVENTEEN

SAINT

I didn't sleep on nights I could feel a storm coming.

The ropes creaked around me as I tightened the fastenings at the corner of the sail, leaning back into the lines at the top of the main mast. The heels of my boots were wedged into the joint of the boom, suspending me in midair over the deck far below.

It was pitch black, the air like ink around me, but far in the distance, a tiny flicker of white light had my hackles up. I couldn't see the wall of clouds drifting toward the ship, but I could feel them. Like a silent giant creeping over the water.

The sea was restless. The shapes of the waves weren't the smooth calm we'd seen that morning. I watched as their peaks sharpened and danced, a sinking feeling settling in my chest. No, the sea wouldn't sleep tonight. Neither would I.

Another frayed knot of lightning tangled in the sky, spidering down until it touched the horizon. I guessed we had an hour before it was on top of us. Maybe less.

The ring of grommets on the foremast behind me pulled my gaze from the distant storm and I looked back to see Clove fitting himself into the rigging. Once he was balanced, he pulled on his leather gloves and got to work, wedging an iron rod into one of the knots so he could retie it.

It was a job we wouldn't have entrusted to the deckhands, even if they'd stayed. No one knew the weak joints of this ship like Clove and I did. Put your life in the hands of a vessel enough times, and you developed an intuition about those things.

This was the point when most helmsmen would break from their coordinates and head to the nearest port. But I wasn't most helmsmen. With Zola making his way toward Ceros and the clock ticking on my next meeting with Henrik, we didn't have time to spare.

"Was going to let you sleep a while longer," I said. "It's going to be a long night."

Clove unraveled the rope, letting it fall slack into the air. "You know I don't like to miss the fun."

Really, he just didn't like me out of his sight when a storm was bearing down on us. We both knew just how quickly your fate could change in those moments. How, in a blink, the sea's hands could reach up and take what it wanted.

"You checked the deck when you boarded the ship at port." I didn't ask it like a question but that was what it was.

"I did."

I knew he did, but I needed to hear him say it. I'd checked it myself too. I always did.

A gust of wind hit us, and I glanced again in the direction of the storm. The air was bitterly cold, a sharp contrast to the warm, balmy breeze that had been pushing us to Ceros. But I wasn't sure why that made me nervous.

My hands moved faster over the ropes and I ran my thumb along the stitched seams of the sails, checking them for gaps or loosened threads. Not that it would do any good, anyway. The wind didn't need a foothold. If it wanted one, it would take it.

"You know, I'm still trying to figure out exactly what you're thinking," Clove said, still working at the knots.

"About what?"

"How we're going to pay Emilia back."

My hands stilled on the sail as I finished checking the last seam and I pulled myself up to stand. "We'll sell the rye and see if we can pick up something else to trade in Ceros. It might take a few routes, but once we've made another trade for Henrik—"

"Last I checked, you stabbed our buyer. So, who's going to pay for these gems?"

I climbed down, finding the cleats with my hands in the dark until I was lowering myself onto the deck. "We'll find a new buyer."

Clove fell quiet as he looked at me.

I paced to the bow, passing beneath him, and when I

reached the jib, I checked the stays. "I'm too tired to play games, Clove. Just say what you want to say."

"We have the coin we paid for the petition."

When I didn't answer, Clove jumped down, coming to stand next to me so that he could reach the lines on the other side.

"We could take back the copper."

"We're not giving up the license," I said, the words heavy and final. I couldn't believe he was even suggesting it.

"We wouldn't be giving it up. We can resubmit the petition after we've built the coin back up and settled accounts."

I shook my head. "No. We're not giving it up. Not now."

"Saint—" Clove said lowly.

"No!" I hit jib with the flat of my palm, the word burning my throat.

Clove let his grip slide from the stays, turning to face me.

"I have to do this." I swallowed. "I *have* to."

He looked at me then with an expression I could hardly bear. One that didn't break away or dissolve into his usual brash humor. He held my gaze for a long moment before he said it. "They're gone, Saint. There's no undoing it."

"It's not just for them. You know that."

I had a debt to pay. It was no secret between us that I was to blame for that day on the water when we both watched as our fathers were swept into the sea. It was the reason the people of Cragsmouth had turned their backs on me. The reason we'd left.

But *this*. I couldn't fix what I'd done, but this license was something I *could* do. It's what they'd wanted. What we'd wanted. And after everything, I'd promised myself I'd see Clove and me sail under our own crest, or I'd die trying.

He exhaled, a sound that bordered too close to sympathy. "All right."

My teeth unclenched, my muscles relaxing a little. I knew it didn't make sense. That it was reckless. But losing the license was a risk I couldn't take. Not after everything we'd been through.

"You give any more thought to what I said about the dredger?" Clove said, finally breaking the uncomfortable silence between us.

"Keeping her on?"

He nodded.

"I have."

"And?"

"If she wants a place, she can have it."

Clove grinned to himself, but he didn't say anything. He didn't have to. The dredger had gotten under my skin and I wasn't sure how to remedy that. I wasn't totally sure I wanted to.

The odds of her accepting a place on our crew were slim. She'd be able to find a helmsman in Ceros who would take her on without knowing anything about what she was, much less what happened in Dern. But it was only a matter of time before Zola caught up with her, and I didn't know if she really understood that.

"It's not your problem," Clove said, reading my mind.

I met his eyes for only a moment, releasing the lines of the jib before my gaze traveled over the deck to the hatch, where Isolde was sleeping in the crew's cabin.

He should have been right. The only problem either of us had was each other. That was how we'd always done things and that way of life had kept us both alive. But something about it didn't feel true anymore.

EIGHTEEN

ISOLDE

"Isolde."

My name drifted in the darkness, soft and close, but the sound was muddled by something else. The slosh of water. The slip of wind in the passageway. I turned my face into the damp fabric of the hammock, pulling a deep breath into my chest.

"Isolde."

I opened my eyes and Saint's silhouette hovered over me in the dark crew's cabin. For a moment, his voice filled the air, the murky threads of thought spinning in my mind.

"Storm," he said. "We need you on the deck."

I blinked, finding my feet beneath me as I sat up, and tried to shake the lingering sleep from my mind. I was still between worlds, wondering if I'd heard him right. Wondering if he was even really there, close enough to reach out and touch.

"Are we headed to port, then?" I asked.

"No," he answered, waiting for me to stand.

I did, arms lifting around me to keep my balance as the floor shifted under my boots and I realized the ship was tilting against a swell. Across the small room, the door hit the wall before it righted again.

But if we weren't headed to port, then we were going to ride it out.

I blinked again, waiting for some kind of explanation, but Saint didn't offer one. He kicked the trunk in the corner, checking to see that it was secured before he caught the door with his hand and held it open for me. "Come on."

It was only when I stepped into the passageway that I smelled the rain. The sweet, earth-churned scent lit in my nose, climbing down into my lungs. With it, the flash of light coming from the deck, the movement of the ship, it all came into focus, waking me up.

I followed Saint's shape in the dark and the ship rocked again as the wind barreled into the portside. I caught myself with both hands pressed to the walls before I reached the ladder. Behind us, the doors to the cargo hold and the supply room were shut and locked, and before I'd even made it out of the hull, I could hear Nash cursing.

I turned my face from the wind and rain as I pulled myself up, ducking beneath the overhang where Saint was waiting. His clothes were already wet through, his skin pale in the darkness.

"We still have time!" Nash shouted from the bow, giving the coil of rope in his hands a firm yank. "We can make it to shore!"

"No, we can't" was Saint's only answer.

A trail of fresh blood dripped from his wrist, almost wiped clean by the spray of seawater in the air. At some point since I'd gone to bed, the wound in his hand had torn back open. Looking at the sea now, I wasn't sure how I'd even managed to stay asleep belowdecks. But the darkest of the sky wasn't behind us, or even overhead. This was just the beginning of the storm, and it was an angry one.

My eyes fixed on the feeble sails at the top of the masts. Every time the lightning flashed, it illuminated the tattered labyrinth of seams. My stomach dropped at the sight. But beside Saint, Clove was showing no trace of concern. He looked at ease, like the helmsman.

"Nash is right," I said. "We should head for shore."

Another flash of lightning lit one side of Saint's expressionless face. He'd already given his answer. He wouldn't give it again.

I looked between him and Clove, searching for any hint of fear in their eyes. But this was what the helmsman of the *Riven* and his navigator were known for. There was no telling how many storms they'd sailed through to earn their reputations. And they had no intention of turning toward land.

"All right." I met Saint's gaze. "What do you need me to do?"

For a moment, I thought I could see the smallest tug of a smile on his lips. Maybe even a look of approval in his eyes.

"Into the wind, Clove," he said.

Clove nodded, unlocking the helm and turning the wheel until the air was sweeping from bow to stern. It whipped around me, the rain hitting the glass of the helmsman's quarters' windows like tiny stones.

"Storm sails." Saint was talking to me now.

I moved for the main mast without question and climbed just high enough to reach the small, stowed sails tacked below the open ones. They'd give us more control in the unpredictable winds and keep us from veering too far off course. But once they were open, they'd be almost impossible to get closed again.

Saint came up the other side of the mast, reefing the sheets as I untied the storm sail and hooked one arm into the rigging, letting myself swing out into the air as it filled. There was a short jolt in the frame of the ship as the triangular sail took shape, and I was relieved to see it was in better repair than the ones we'd been sailing with.

All around us, the darkness felt like it was moving, and I tried not to think about how small the *Riven* was beneath the crests of the black waves. The only ships I'd been on in a storm were beasts compared to this one, with the finest construction and rigging copper could buy. But the *Riven* felt like a box of matches floating on the surface of the water. The thought made my stomach roll with nausea.

Saint dropped himself onto the deck beside me and I followed him to the foremast. He waited for me to take hold of the pegs and I lifted myself until one boot left the deck.

"Could get used to this," he said, pulling at the knots over his head.

My fingers loosened on the iron rods until my boot touched back down. Saint was watching me from the top of his gaze now with a look that felt like it was measuring me. Taking stock of my reaction.

Used to this. I didn't know what that meant. Used to having a dredger? Another set of hands? Or used to *me*?

I opened my mouth to ask, but before I'd gotten a single word out, Saint's hands froze on the knots. Slowly, his eyes lifted over my head and the prick in the air turned sharp, the wind suddenly quieting.

A feeling like fire beneath my jacket crept across the surface of my skin and my hands slipped from the pegs, my fingertips numb.

The *Riven* creaked and my weight pulled forward, toward the bow. The feeling was disorienting without being able to see the horizon. It was almost as if the ship were dragging in the opposite direction it had been moving only seconds ago.

Saint stepped away from the foremast and his hair blew across his forehead as he turned his ear to the water. Like he was listening.

"Brace," he said, the hollow word moving over the ship in the silence.

My brow pulled. "What?"

Clove jammed the lock into place at the helm, immediately reaching for the railing of the steps that led to the upper deck. But I was still searching the mist, trying to see whatever Saint did.

Gray light painted the world silver, casting eerie shadows over the ship. When I spotted movement in the distance, I took a step toward the railing, my eyes focusing. The clouds were rolling toward us like a flood of smoke.

But the sound that cut through the air wasn't wind. The ship rumbled with the vibration of it. And every second, it grew louder.

It wasn't clouds. It was *water*.

"Brace!"

The word tore from Saint's throat again and his arms came around me, driving us backward toward the main mast. He pinned me against it, crushing his weight into me, and the sound of the sea towering over us turned into a sickening growl. It was seconds from crashing down.

His face was so close that his cheek brushed mine as he wrapped his fists into the lines behind me. I was wedged tightly between his body and the mast.

He looked me in the eye. "Breathe." The word was soft.

He curled himself around me, and I frantically gulped in a chest full of air before the squall broke over the ship. And then we were gone. The world turned black, the crush of the water scraping over the *Riven* and trying to peel us from the deck. I held on to Saint as it pried at my hands. Pulled my feet from beneath me. The world tipped and turned as the cascade washed over the ship and I buried my face in his chest, my eyes pinched closed.

It wasn't until I heard his gasp for breath against my ear that I realized we weren't underwater anymore. The churning was gone, the clouds visible again.

I willed myself to unclamp my fingers from where they were tangled in Saint's shirt. He was still holding on to me.

"All right?" His words were half broken between breaths.

I nodded, unable to speak. Because we shouldn't have still been standing. The ship shouldn't have even been afloat.

At the bow, Nash's eyes were wide and terrified as he looked up to the sky. He'd pinned himself beneath the foot of the jib. Miraculously, he hadn't been swept away.

Saint's arms slid from where they held me, and then he was pushing toward the helm. "Clove!"

"Here!" Clove launched himself from the stairs to the upper deck, headed in our direction. His blond hair was stuck to his face, his shirt pasted to him like wet parchment.

Saint shot another glance to the sea. All around us, the water was churning again. This was no ordinary storm. Judging by the direction of the wind, the squall shouldn't have even come from the other direction. And it wasn't over. Not yet.

"There are two," I said without thinking. "Two storms."

It was the only explanation. If we'd had the advantage of daylight, we'd have seen it, but in the dark we were blind.

As if the same thought had just occurred to him, Saint

pulled the knife from his belt, reaching for the line of the storm sail I'd just tied. He didn't even try to free it. It was no use. Instead, he took the rope in one hand and started sawing.

As soon as Clove saw what Saint was doing, he crouched down, turning the ends of the lever below the wheel to check the lock. The helm was still holding.

"Wait . . . what are we . . . ?" Nash pulled himself along the railing, panicked now.

"We're going to lie a-hull," Saint answered.

Nash's mouth dropped open. "*What?*"

Lying a-hull was a last resort in a storm like this. A whispered prayer. In another ship, maybe we'd be able to manage with the storm sails, but there was no way to know which direction the next squall would come from. The *Riven* was barely holding together as it was. It wouldn't be able to take the resistance of the water's push and pull.

"Get that anchor freed!" Saint shouted, still sawing through the last threads of rope.

Ahead, Nash hadn't moved, his white-knuckled hands curled around the railing. Rain dripped from his chin in a steady stream.

Water burned in my throat, my eyes, as I turned in a circle, trying to keep my bearings. It still felt like the sky was beneath my feet. The *Riven* swayed again, the masts tipping before it righted, and I crouched down when I began to slide, letting gravity take me toward the anchor crank.

I slammed into it hard, knocking the wind from my lungs, and I wheezed as I reached for the lever. My wet, cold hands slipped from the metal and I jammed it forward, trying to get it to budge. But there was no slack. No tension either.

I hauled myself up and peered over the side. "Shit." I exhaled. The loop of line that reached the hinges was missing.

The slide of the wet ropes sounded overhead and I glanced up to see Clove and Saint heaving the weight of the sails up between gusts to tie them down. But if we didn't have the anchor, there was nothing keeping the next wave from rolling us.

I climbed over, fitting an arm around the railing so that I could lower myself down.

"What are you doing?" Saint's voice was faraway, pulled out to sea by the wind.

Below, the surface of the black water looked like the jagged cut of the onyx or obsidian that covered my mother's jeweled fingers. Like the moment I touched it, it would cut me open.

I didn't think. When I was within reach, I swung my leg, kicking at the latch with the heel of my boot.

Lightning flashed again and there were a few seconds of blood-chilling quiet before the sound exploded in my ears. The high-pitched ring that followed washed out the storm around me. All I could see was the anchor. My boot desperately reaching for it.

I swung my leg again and again, each time draining the dwindling strength in my arms. It took six tries, but it freed with a screech, and the anchor flew out into the air, nearly hitting me. I clung desperately to the railing, trying to lift myself back up, but every muscle was jumping under my skin. I couldn't feel my hands anymore.

I grunted, my teeth bared as I fought against my own weight, and then I was suddenly being pulled. Saint's face appeared over the side of the ship, his ice-blue eyes finding me. But they were missing the calm that usually lived there.

I took hold of his forearm and he grabbed hold of mine, and then Clove was reaching over, yanking me up by the belt. Together, they lifted me back over the railing until my boots were hitting the deck beside theirs. As soon as I felt the ship beneath me, the sick feeling inside of me was climbing up my throat.

I swallowed it down, letting myself slip from Saint's grasp before I sank low to the crank. This time, the handle gave under my weight with the sound of scraping metal. The rope rippled as it raced through the feed, and the anchor lowered, splashing into the water below. A few seconds later, the *Riven* steadied just slightly.

Clove glanced over his shoulder, eyes studying the clouds. "We can't stay out here."

"Go." Saint lowered to his haunches, locking the crank, and Clove pulled me along to the passageway.

We ducked inside the helmsman's quarters, taking a river of water with us. Nash had already wedged himself into a corner, his arms crossed over his chest. He was trembling all over.

The sea dripped from my clothes, my hands, my hair, and I curled my fingers into my palms tightly, trying to make the warmth come back into them. Like it was the only thing that would convince me I was still breathing.

As soon as Saint was inside, the door was closed and he walked straight toward the desk. He pushed the parchment out of the way, sliding one of the maps free. I watched as he rolled it up with steady fingers, taking great care not to get it wet. When he was finished, he snatched the leather cylinder case from the hook on the wall and slipped it inside, securing the lid.

An unsettling silence fell over the cabin as he dropped it over one shoulder, letting the strap stretch across his chest. Whatever it was, he wasn't going to let it go down with the ship.

Almost in unison, Saint and Clove stepped on the heels of their boots, pulling their feet free.

Of course, I thought, the feeling of sickness coiling in my belly again. In case we had to swim.

"Take them off," Saint said, looking at my own boots.

I obeyed, letting them fall to the floor, and Nash reluctantly followed, the blood draining from his face. If he was a shipwright's apprentice, he wasn't used to being out on the water. Certainly not in a storm.

If the *Riven* went down, there was no saving us. As soon as I thought it, it was almost like a weight lifted off of me. A relief in knowing that I had no idea what was going to happen. My life had been lived according to a very specific plan. From the moment my mother knew what I was, every day had a purpose—find gems. Make coin. But the moment

I crossed into the Narrows, the plan for my life had been wiped from my mother's ledgers. And I could feel that open nothingness that stretched before me now more than ever, as the ship groaned against the breaking waves.

At any moment, I could take my last breath. That single truth felt like an infinite space inside of me. Where anything could happen.

I looked up from my boots, catching Saint's eyes on me. They ran over my face slowly, as if he were trying to read my thoughts. Or maybe he was remembering, like I was, what he'd said moments before that wave came down on the ship.

Could get used to this.

I was glad now that I hadn't had the chance to ask for his meaning. Because if it had anything to do with the feeling that flooded my veins when his arms wrapped around me, when his cheek touched mine and his hands gripped me tight, I was almost sure I didn't want to know.

NINETEEN

ISOLDE

I'd never been happier to see the sunrise.

We'd spent the better part of the night in Saint's quarters as the storms tore through the sea, but the race of my heart didn't stop when the howling did. Those storms were still inside of me.

I'd slept in fits and starts, unnerved by the creaks and groans of the *Riven* as if, at any moment, the hull would breach and drown us all. I wasn't the only one who thought so. Every time the ship moaned, Nash shifted in his hammock, his eyes finding mine in the dark. It was nothing short of a miracle that we were still afloat, but we were. And I had no explanation for it.

I stood at the bow, watching the pale green water of the Narrows race beneath the ship. There was no mistaking the difference in the color. The Unnamed Sea was a dark, inky blue that was like the richest hue of sapphire. As soon as we'd crossed into the Narrows on the *Luna,* I'd noticed the slow bleed of it to a shade of turquoise. The air was different too, missing the weight of the salt that laced the water I was used to.

Storms like those we'd seen last night were rare in the Unnamed Sea, and my mother's helmsmen would sooner abandon an unfinished dive than draw her wrath by risking my life by riding one out. I was more precious to her than a single haul of gems, but not because she loved me. I was irreplaceable to Holland because of what I could give her.

I reached into my pocket, finding the only thing I'd taken with me when I left the Unnamed Sea. The purse was heavy in my palm and I pressed the tip of my finger to the sharp point of the midnight I could feel through the soft leather.

The closest I'd ever come to seeing the eye of a real storm was a few years ago, when I was on Fable's Skerry. The little rocky island off the shore of Bastian was home to nothing except the largest lighthouse in the Unnamed Sea. And over time, it became the only refuge I had from my mother. On days when she had business in the city, I'd sneak away and barter with the fishermen to be ferried across the bay, then I'd spend hours lying on the sunny rocks and diving in the skerry's sea caves. There were no people. No dive maps or routes to plan or ledgers to balance. Just me and the seabirds.

I'd been diving the skerry alone for years with no idea that there was anything there to find. Beneath the surface, the sea bottom was only rock and sand and swarms of silver fish. But all that time, the midnight was there. Just waiting.

I glanced over my shoulder to the deck. Clove stood at the helm, letting the wheel tilt just slightly, his eyes on the white clouds that striped the sky.

I cinched the little bag open and let the stone fall into my hand. The glossy black surface was cut into perfect facets and when I raised it to the light, I could see the glow of violet inside. I still remembered the exact moment, more than fifty feet beneath the surface of the water, when I heard it. The soft, lulling chime that was a stranger to me. A gem song I didn't know.

I'd suspected almost immediately that it was important. But I didn't know just how much of my world it would change. And when my mother told me that I was to be the one to name it, I chose *midnight*, the only word I could think of to describe its haunting sound.

The heavy thud of something on the deck made me flinch, and I closed my fingers into a fist over the stone. Behind me, Nash had dropped the bag of bosun's tools at his feet. He was missing his shirt, his skin already slick with sweat despite the cool morning, and his wet hair was curling on top of his head.

"Like trying to plug a hole. It'll just keep widening," he murmured, crouching down over the bag to fish out a long iron bolt.

He turned it over in his hand, shaking his head as he inspected it. The piece of metal looked like it had been salvaged from a ship built fifty years ago that had spent half that time underwater.

I slipped the midnight back into the purse and returned it to my pocket, coming to stand over him. "How much longer do you think this ship has?"

"Weeks? Days? Hours? Minutes, for all I know." He picked up the adze, fitting the bolt to the end of the rod jammed into the anchor crank. A high-pitched ping rang out as he tapped it, gently nudging it forward. "But they won't be sailing this thing for long."

"What do you mean?"

He smirked. "Not a chance. The reason I'm stuck on this death trap is because I talked."

I glanced to the open door of the helmsman's quarters. Saint told me that Nash was a shipwright's apprentice who hadn't kept his mouth shut. But about what?

They couldn't be planning to sail the *Riven* under their new trader's crest. No one in their right mind would risk hauling an expensive inventory in a vessel like this one. But maybe Saint *wasn't* in his right mind. They didn't have the coin to buy a new ship. If they did, they wouldn't have been in such dire straits after I'd gotten their gems stolen.

Unless they'd already spent it.

"They have a ship, don't they?" I guessed, keeping my voice low.

Nash's hand nearly slipped from the adze before he cleared his throat, tapping again in a steady rhythm. "Like I said, I've learned my lesson."

The click of the helm's lock made me turn in time to see Clove climbing down the ladder into the passageway. I watched his blond hair disappear behind the ledge.

They were a curious pair. Nothing like the helmsmen and navigators I'd sailed with before. These two spoke a language that only they knew, reading each other's minds without so much as sharing a glance. They seemed more like brothers than anything, but there was no trace of that in looking at them.

"What was that thing Saint did with the knife back in Sowan? Why did he cut his hand like that?"

Nash wiped a drip of sweat from his chin, looking up at me. "You've never heard those stories?"

I shook my head.

"You're definitely not from the Narrows, then." He dropped the adze, rising to his feet and reaching for the waterskin hanging from the mast behind me. "It's a pact with the sea demons. Something the old sailors used to do."

"What do you mean, a *pact*?"

He shrugged. "Like an agreement. That's why the bastard's ship hasn't sunk. There's a reason people are afraid of him. They're scared they'll cross those demons and draw their eye."

"People really believe that?"

"Most do." He took another drink, replacing the lid. "Others think he's just mad."

I half laughed. "Which do you believe?"

His eyes traveled to the sails stretched over our heads. I

expected him to laugh too, but he didn't. "If you'd asked me yesterday, I'd have said it was all bullshit."

I hesitated. "And now?"

"Can you think of another reason we're still breathing after last night?"

I could only guess that the rumors about Saint and the *Riven* had been born of a hundred other stories just like them. A mad helmsman and a cursed ship, tempting death with the favor of the sea demons. After what I'd seen last night, I couldn't be completely sure that it wasn't true.

Nash passed me the waterskin, lowering down onto his haunches and getting back to work. I'd heard people joke about the backward ways of the Narrows. The archaic manner of living and lack of advancement. We had our own legends and myths in the Unnamed Sea. But no one put any stock in them. Not anymore.

I paced across the deck and into the passageway, peering into the helmsman's quarters. But where I thought I would see Saint sitting at his desk, it was empty.

I hooked one hand on the doorframe, slipping inside, and that scent that followed him hovered between the walls. It was the smell of the sea. Not of the sun-warmed shallows or the surf foaming on the sand. It was the scent of deep water, something I could never describe with words but that I would know anywhere.

The chime of the adder stones clinked in the open window, the only embellishment to the threadbare cabin. The *Riven* was anything but impressive, but even in the helmsman's quarters, Saint wasn't pretending it was. That was one of the first things I'd marked as a difference between him and Zola.

I caught one of the stones in the palm of my hand, rubbing my thumb over its face. My mother would laugh at the simple superstition. She'd mocked the crew members of her ships that followed such rules, but that didn't keep them from practicing the rituals out at sea.

I took a step toward the desk, where a frayed edge of torn white linen was hanging from the smallest drawer. I opened it, peering inside. There were at least a dozen strips folded on top of one another. The same ones Saint always had wrapped around his hand.

The ledger sitting on top of the parchment had been left open and the handwriting that covered the page wasn't careful or practiced. It was hurried. Sloppy, even. But the numbers were legible in the right-hand column. I followed them with my finger.

Ship repairs. Salted pork. Crates of rye.

Nothing about the wool I'd seen them unload in Sowan or the gems I'd stolen back from Zola. If this ship had an off-the-books trade inventory, it was a lean one. They had to be making most of their coin in smuggled fakes. But the sums were almost nonexistent, coming down to nearly zero every few weeks before they shot up again and began ticking down.

That explained the desperation I'd seen in Saint's eyes when he grabbed me in the alley in Dern. At any given moment, this operation was only a breath away from coming apart.

The largest and most recent amount listed as a payment was to a Rosamund in Dern, but there was no notation of what goods it was for. This two-man crew didn't look like much to contend with, but they sure had a lot of secrets. Maybe that was why Zola was so fixated on them.

Beside the desk, the cylinder case Saint had strapped over his chest the night before had been returned to its hook. I reached up, taking it from the wall and prying the lid open. Inside, creamy white parchment was curled up tightly.

I watched the door for any sign of him before I slid it free, unrolling it over the desk.

It was a map. A beautiful one.

I shifted the parchment into the light coming from the window, letting it move over the colors and bring them alive. The scripted writing at the top was done in an expert hand, a flawless calligraphy.

The Narrows

Every inch of the shoreline was drawn in a precise, detailed rendering. It wasn't complete yet, but I'd never seen a map of the Narrows before. Not like this. Even the ones that Zola had given me were just crude charts with rough estimations and no attempt at accurate distance.

The hue of blue paint used for the sea darkened with what I assumed was depth, and the tangle of reefs set in its center was labeled Tempest Snare. I remembered it from the charts Zola had shown me. The graveyard of ships that the sea claimed for its own.

I eyed the inkpots in the tray to the left of the desk. The brushes and quills. The purse of fine sand used to dry the parchment. They were mapmakers' tools.

Saint was making a map of the Narrows. This was *his* work.

"I thought you Saltbloods were all manners and decorum." His voice cut the silence, making my eyes snap up to the door.

I let the edge of the map go and it curled, rolling in on itself as I saw Saint standing in the passageway, watching me. As if that threshold were some kind of boundary between us.

"It's rude to go through someone's things without permission," he said.

If that was all the reproach he would give me, I'd be lucky. But something in him had softened since we'd left Sowan. Like the edges of him had been worn down.

I gestured to the inkpots. "It's good work. Very good."

He reluctantly stepped inside, ducking beneath the beam overhead before coming around the desk. He took up the map, rolling it carefully.

"Where did you learn how to do that?"

"My father."

The tenderness in his voice when he answered made me still, and though there wasn't even the slightest hesitation on his lips, he didn't look at me when he said it.

"He was a mapmaker?"

"A fisherman."

He didn't offer anything more, and I didn't press. I'd never heard of a simple fisherman who had a skill like that.

He returned the map to its case, reaching over me to hang it back on the wall, and I found myself inhaling deeper the closer he was to me. I could feel the warmth of sunlight coming off of his skin and the memory of him last night in the storm, holding onto me as the squall crashed down onto the *Riven*, resurfaced.

I let my gaze fall to his chest. His hands. The meager strip of cloth that was usually tied there was gone, but the blood that had seeped through his fingers was still dried over the knuckles.

"Why do you do it?" I asked. "The storms."

He didn't answer my question this time. Instead, he turned his attention to the desk, closing the ledger.

"I thought we were going to die last night," I pressed.

"Well, we didn't."

"We could have."

"Anyone could die at any time."

I wasn't sure if he meant that as a reason. It was just as likely that he had nothing to live for. I glanced again to the map case on the wall. The notice from the Trade Council that still sat on the desk. The ledger. For someone with a death wish, he sure had a lot of plans.

He fell quiet again. I was beginning to understand that silence was his preferred method of communication. He dealt in the unspoken moments. The quiet in-betweens. But there was something about the helmsman that reminded me of gemstone. Like even when he wasn't speaking, I could still hear, or feel, something in the center of my chest.

"It's smart, you know," I said, eyes flitting to the ledger again. "Saving up the coin in small trades and paying a little at a time. Makes everyone believe you're just scraping by."

Saint nearly laughed, surprising me. "We *are* scraping by."

I stared at him, deciding whether I wanted him to know just how many pieces I'd fit together. "But this isn't the ship that will bear that new trader's crest, is it?"

At that, he paused, and his eyes met mine for just a moment. But again, he said nothing.

"So, you have the license. Or you will once we get to Ceros. And you have the ship. Now you just need the inventory."

"Well done, dredger. You've discovered the secret endeavor of every trader who ever lived: coin."

I shook my head. "A helmsman who's in it for the copper doesn't spend years making a map like that," I said. "That's something else."

Saint looked uncomfortable now.

"You see a future for the Narrows, don't you?"

His chin lifted. In defiance? Self-preservation? I wasn't sure, but I'd definitely hit a nerve.

"You think it's foolish."

"I don't," I said, my voice a whisper, and the way he looked at me made me shift on my feet.

It wasn't foolish. It was terrifying.

He was like this room, this ship—honest. Not pretending. I didn't know what to do with that. Because what I was coming to realize was that I believed every word that came from his mouth. Worse, I suspected I could believe in *him*. This vision of his.

I could feel that endless well within me, the capacity I had to fall in love with this trader and his dreams. But I'd spent too many years giving myself up for the glimmering ambitions of others. I couldn't do that anymore.

"Don't worry," I said, my voice hoarse in an attempt at another laugh, "I think you may have convinced the world of your indifference."

"Maybe. I think people believe what they want to believe," he said.

"Maybe," I echoed.

"What should I believe about you?"

He was asking without asking. He wanted to know. But I couldn't make myself say it.

"When I met you in Dern, you didn't even tell me your real name."

"I didn't know you."

"You still don't," he said, more seriously. "And I still don't know who you really are. Or what you're doing in the Narrows."

There was that hard line again.

"But it doesn't matter to me why you came here. Everyone has secrets."

I pressed my tongue to the roof of my mouth. It was true, but not all secrets carried the same weight. The same risks.

"I need a dredger if I'm going to run a crew." He let the words hang in the air between us. "And from what I saw last night, you can handle yourself on a ship."

I blinked. "Are you giving me a formal offer?"

"We can't pay you. Not for a while yet."

We. The distinction of power between him and Clove was no more than a blur.

"But we can feed you. Make sure you don't get your throat cut. I think those are pretty good terms."

He was right. They were good. I could go looking for a place on another ship, but standing before me was the devil I knew. And if they'd planned to trade me as a gem sage, they'd already have me locked in the cargo hold like Nash.

"Why me?" I asked. "You can find a dredger at any port."

"You're a gem sage, and that's an advantage no other helmsman in the Narrows will have."

My throat constricted, making it difficult to swallow. That was the anchor of it. He wanted to use me. And he wasn't trying to hide it.

"You also don't have a past here. All pasts are good for is making allegiances and enemies. You have neither in these waters."

"Except Zola."

"He's a *common* enemy. Zola won't be able to touch you once we have a license and he's bound by the Trade Council. Signing a contract with a crew is the best protection you can get if you're going to stay in the Narrows."

I'd already signed one as Eryss, I thought. For the next

year, that version of me was contracted to the *Luna*. But Eryss didn't exist. Not really. And the contract could only be enforced by the Trade Council if the trader had a crest.

I'd never intended to stay on this ship or any other. When I'd said I wanted to disappear, I'd meant it. I just had one thing I had to do first.

Again, I let my eyes fall to Saint's unwrapped hand, following the streaks of blood dried dark on his skin.

The more I could feel that thing in the air between us, the more convinced I was that not staying on the *Riven* was for the best. So, why couldn't I say no to him? Why couldn't I just say I didn't want it?

I opened the little drawer of the desk and took a strip of linen from inside. When I held my hand out for his, he didn't move, eyes following the line of my arm down to my wrist. It took a full five seconds for him to make up his mind and, slowly, he set his hand into mine.

His warm skin filled my palm as I opened his fingers, and I bit down onto my lip when I saw it.

The soft spiderweb of lines that should have covered the center of his hand was gone, hidden by a stack of scars that looked like long, thin needles.

I wrapped the fresh cloth over the new cut, gently pressing it. He didn't so much as wince, and I wondered if he could even feel it anymore.

His eyelashes just barely moved as he watched my fingers tie the knot. When I was finished, his hand slowly turned over in mine. Before I realized what he was doing, his rough fingertips were moving over my knuckles, like he was tracing the feel of my bones beneath the skin.

He was touching me. On purpose. With a curious kind of intent. As if he hadn't been sure what would happen if he did.

My heart skipped, beat over beat, tumbling in my chest until I'd stopped breathing. The sinking feeling tugging between my ribs forced me to inhale and I pulled my hand from his before I let myself do something that couldn't be taken back.

"I have to think about it," I said hoarsely.

Saint slid his hand into his pocket, as if to cage it there. A moment later, he nodded.

"There's something I have to do in Ceros. I'll give you my answer after."

It was a coward's move. I knew that. But better to disappear without a word than to look into those eyes and say no to him.

I held his gaze for as long as I could bear to, but there was an intensity there that made me forget to breathe again.

"I have work to do," he finally said, his voice dragging in his throat.

I stepped around the desk, not looking back until I was through the door, my eyes finding him just before it closed. But he hadn't moved, his stare pinned to the desk.

I could see that he knew. I'd seen it the moment the lie left my mouth. There wouldn't be an answer, because when I stepped off the *Riven* tomorrow, I was never coming back.

TWENTY

SAINT

I never should have touched her. That was a mistake.

Only a day after I watched Isolde wrap the bandage around my palm, the *Riven* was drifting into Ceros's harbor. But the passing hours on the small ship had felt more like weeks, that silence she'd left in my cabin worse than the roar of the storm that had almost killed us.

But it hadn't been enough to drown out the single thought that had been replaying in my head over and over.

I never should have touched her.

I wasn't even sure how it had happened. One moment her slim, calloused fingers were waking a fire on my skin, and the next, I was holding her hand in mine. The night and morning since had been spent watching the crack of light beneath my door, half hoping she would come back and also praying she wouldn't.

I pinched the bridge of my nose, willing myself to put it out of my mind. The question I'd asked. The answer she'd given. In the end, it would have been better to wake and find her gone than to imagine that she'd stay. But nothing was worse than admitting I wanted her to.

The sprawling hills and bridges of the city came into view, stretching along the shore in a congested maze. The harbor reflected its chaos. Almost every slip was filled with ships of every kind, most of them from the Unnamed Sea. They'd make their stops to do business with the city's merchants and the new Trade Council before they headed back to Bastian or Nimsmire or Sagsay Holm.

The first time I'd seen this city, I was perched at the top of the mast on my father's fishing boat. But this was the last time I'd stand on these docks without any power in my hands. In truth, he'd been the one to put it there. Long before he died.

I remembered the light in his eyes as the boat floated past those ships, their trading crests flying proudly over the bows. When I'd asked him if one day he'd have a ship like that, he said, *Ah, that's not a future for me, son. It's for you.*

And it wasn't just the dream of it or the grandness of the idea. It was what the idea meant. That one day, when Narrows-born traders were sailing with crests, there wouldn't just be a new horizon. There would be a new world.

Clove jumped down from the ladder of the *Riven* to land beside me on the dock. The last time we'd stood here was three weeks ago, and everything had been different.

"You take care of the docking fee?" He pulled on his cap.

"Yeah," I answered. "Harbor master said the price is going up for anyone with a license."

Clove scoffed. I wouldn't expect any less from the harbor master, finding a way to use the Trade Council's business to squeeze more coin into his purse. He wouldn't be the only one.

"Word must be getting around," Clove said.

I nodded.

There'd been talk about the Trade Council issuing licenses from the moment they were instated, but they'd gone about granting them to every trader from the Unnamed Sea with established business first. They claimed it was part of their plan to legitimize the Narrows, while also not letting the business of the merchants in Ceros suffer. But in the process, they'd kept the Narrows-born crews from doing legal trade, and anyone with eyes could see the guilds just wanted to keep their copper intact.

Now, almost a year after they first took their seats, the Trade Council was finally getting to the job they'd been commissioned for.

Nash came down the ladder next, nearly strangling himself in the ropes before he slipped from the last rung. When he finally had his feet under him, he wobbled, catching himself on the dock post.

Clove laughed, along with a couple of dockworkers in the next slip who were watching Nash struggle to stand up straight.

It was a dead giveaway that he didn't sail. Losing your sense of gravity was a common reaction to solid ground for someone who wasn't used to being on a ship for an extended period of time. The bastard hadn't been at sea for even a week.

"You pull anything, and you'll lose your passage back to Dern," I reminded him.

"Got it," he answered, clearing his throat.

With the deckhands gone, we weren't going to leave him behind on the ship. If he had any sense, he'd behave and get a free ride home. We both knew he didn't have anything to trade with another helmsman.

"That's not all you'll lose," Clove warned.

"I said, I got it." Nash glared at him, trying to comb his unruly hair back with his hand. I'd never seen him so disheveled. Even after a full day's work in Rosamund's pier he'd always looked like he was about to go to tea with a guild member. There were more and more people in the Narrows just like him, trying to put on the airs they thought would eventually carry them into high society. What they didn't understand was that there was no high society in the Narrows. There never would be.

The sunlight flickered overhead and I looked up to see Isolde peering over the side of the *Riven*. Her face was hidden in the shadow, but her hands curled around the railing before she lifted herself onto the ladder. It wasn't until she was climbing down that I saw the belt of dredging tools draped over her shoulder.

I met her eyes when she dropped to the dock. She'd have

no need of that belt in the city. No reason to take it off the ship if she planned to return. That was all the answer she needed to give me.

There was a look on her face that almost resembled guilt. Almost. But she had nothing to be sorry for. I knew firsthand what it meant to carve your own path. I wasn't going to stand in the way of anyone else doing the same.

"You're just going to leave the ship?" she asked, glancing up to the *Riven*. There was almost something protective in her voice and that made me bristle.

"No one wants it," I said, the words more revealing than I meant them to be.

Her eyes searched my face, making it clear that she'd caught my meaning. What I was really saying was that *she* didn't want it. Honestly, I couldn't blame her.

I started up the dock, pressing into the crowd that was headed for the city. Clove wove in and out of the bodies behind me, glancing back to keep an eye on Isolde and Nash. Again, Isolde had her jacket pulled up, one shoulder turned away from the ships as she passed. Her face was cast toward the ground.

I wasn't imagining it. She was trying not to be seen. The question was why, this far from home, she had reason to fear being recognized.

The very little I'd learned about Isolde didn't add up. Why was she so comfortable on the ship if she'd been grown in a glasshouse, as Emilia put it? The dredging didn't seem to be an act. She wasn't playing a part, but how had she taken up such a brutal job if was highborn? Even if she had fallen from grace, there were other cities in the Unnamed Sea to disappear into. Ones bigger than Ceros. So, why had she come to the Narrows at all?

They were questions I'd never have the answers to, I reminded myself. And really, it was better that way. Emilia had every right to be worried, even if I'd brushed her off. I'd managed in the last two years to do the thing no one thought I could. I'd built something from nothing and I'd kept myself free of ties and obligations, with the exception of Clove. But this dredger was like a fever beneath my skin and whatever she was running from, I couldn't afford it finding me.

When we reached the stairs that led up out of the harbor, we followed the river of people to the right and climbed until the bridges were in view. The trail of simple, unpolished buildings followed the curve of the cobblestones beneath the walking bridges suspended over their roofs. From here, it was impossible to see the expanse of the city like you did from the water. The closer you got to it, the more it swallowed you up, until all you could make out was the street ahead. That was the way the city felt too. Like one wrong turn would be the end of you.

No one had thought Ceros would become much of anything when they first built the docks here. It was just an easy place to land with deep enough water to accommodate ships. But once the Saltbloods started coming, the city started growing, and it wasn't exactly something you could pick up and move when you ran out of room. The more crowded the streets became, the more bridges were built. Now, they were suspended over the entire city like a spider's web.

I reached the top of the stairs and looked back, finding Isolde in the sea of faces below. She'd stopped, eyes wandering over the view behind me. There was a shadow of hesitation there. Something reluctant.

When she caught me watching her, she started again, finding her way up the last few steps. Clove was right behind her, brow cinching when she didn't follow him onto the street.

"I have something to take care of. I'll meet you at the tavern," she said, not looking at me.

She didn't even bother asking for the tavern's name to keep up the pretense. There were a dozen in this city.

"Griff's," Clove said. "Near the south side."

She nodded. "Thanks."

But her feet didn't move.

Wherever she was going, she wasn't coming back, and she must have had her reasons for keeping that to herself.

I waited, watching her war over something to say in her mind. I didn't want a thank-you or a goodbye. I wouldn't give either of those things to her. But I also wasn't going to stand there and wait for her to make a fool of us both. So, I'd save her the trouble.

I looked at her one more time, tracing the shape of her face, her jaw, the curve of her throat. I etched it into my mind to keep for no other reason than I felt like I had to. And then I turned and walked away.

Clove followed closely at my side, keeping his eyes on the street ahead. "Think we'll see her again?" he asked.

"No," I answered, "I don't."

TWENTY-ONE

ᏇSOLDE

I don't know why I lied.

I watched Saint disappear into the crowd, the color of his coat snuffed out. Just like that, he was gone. A pinprick on the narrow timeline of my life.

There'd been a moment as I stood on the ship, watching him and Clove from the railing, that I'd imagined myself standing beside them. Maybe because they were alone in the world, like I was. Or maybe because I just didn't *want* to be alone. But eventually, there would come a time when they'd have a choice between me and the copper. And at heart, they were just traders. I knew where that road led. Saint had all but admitted it.

I stood there another moment, watching the sea of people pour down the street, before I forced myself to walk in the opposite direction. With every step, I could feel it. That endless well. Its depths. But the only thing I could do now was to keep walking.

The road widened as soon as I was a few steps from the archway, and shadows danced on the ground, casting the shops in shade. I looked up, almost dizzy as I took in the sheer height of the bridges striping the sky. They rocked and bounced, the knock of boots on the wooden planks like little drums over the city. Below, people filed up the ladders and followed them in every direction, like a fishing net cast over the rooftops.

"Excuse me." I reached out, gently catching a woman by the arm as she shouldered past me.

The open clamshells in the basket she carried clinked like pieces of glass as she stopped. "Yes, dear?" But as soon as her eyes took me in, they narrowed.

"I'm looking for the Trade Council Chamber."

Her mouth twisted. "The what?"

"The chamber," I said again, "the place the Trade Council meets?"

"Ah, those fools," she hissed. "Don't suppose you could leave them to work for their own people, now could you? You Saltbloods never saw a thing you didn't think you could take."

She opened a hand in front of me, her jaw set.

I stared at it.

"Well?"

She was waiting on coin, I realized. I reached into my belt and pressed a copper into her hand without giving her an argument. She wasn't wrong about the traders from the Unnamed Sea or the Trade Council, and it was no secret that these people had no love for us. We'd sailed into these waters with more copper than they had ever had need of. Then we *made* them need it by increasing the demand for their grain without raising the price we were willing to pay. These shores had fed the whole of the Unnamed Sea and now that they were standing on their own two feet, our traders looked for any opportunity to knock them back down. My mother included. But if I did what I'd come to do, her fingers might finally lose their reach in the Narrows.

The woman inspected the coin before she propped her basket on her hip and pointed an elbow toward the ladder at the end of the street. "Follow that bridge toward the building with the four towers."

She shoved into my arm as she continued on, muttering a curse under her breath.

I made my way toward the ladder, waiting my turn before I climbed up out of the still, warm air and into the sea breeze. The wood planks beneath my feet swayed just slightly with the movement as I walked, and I kept one hand to the rope walls, scanning the rooftops in the distance. The building with the four towers was easy to spot, just east, and the higher the bridge rose, the more of the path I could see that would take me there.

Ceros was nothing to Bastian. It didn't look that much different from Sowan, except for its enormous size. No shining marble buildings or painted glass windows. No red cobblestones or smithed iron signs. Bastian was a glistening jewel, a beautiful place. But its heart had gone rotten a long time ago.

I took the nearest ladder down when I was only a few streets from the chamber and the heat that seemed to collect in the streets found me again, making me open up the neck of my jacket and let my hair fall down my back.

A few turns following the northwest spire of the building, and I was there, standing in the open market that snaked through the veins of the alleys behind it. The chamber looked more like a well-dressed pier except for the towers that stood at each corner. The sand-colored brick was set into a simple pattern, stretching across the walls and breaking at a few large windows that looked out over the street like wide, open eyes.

I stood there staring at it for a long while before I finally started walking.

I'd made the decision that night in my mother's house as I stood there in my expensive gown, a glass of cava bubbling in my hand. We'd stood behind the heavy velvet curtain that opened to the hall and the gleam of candlelight reflected off the gem case holding the midnight, lighting my mother's eye.

It will change everything, she'd said.

I'd known then that I was finished.

I'd given her the one thing she needed to curl her fingers around the world. And now I would place it in the hands of her enemy.

I climbed the stone steps to the wide wooden door of the chamber and pulled the brass handle until it opened. It was quiet inside, a stark contrast to the noise of the street, and I stepped into the dim light, where a long hall stretched before me. Brilliant blue paper covered the walls behind large, gold-framed portraits on either side. Beneath each one, a name was engraved on a brass placard that noted their guild. I felt small beneath the faces that were painted there, the same feeling I had in my mother's house. I didn't like it.

It was too familiar a scene. The men and women who filled the portraits were the likes of the guilds, even if they weren't quite as bright and shiny as the high society in Bastian. Tailored suits and lace-trimmed frocks floated past me, and my hands tightened on the dredging belt. They weren't Saltbloods, but they sure looked like them.

Below the gilded frames, a space on the marble was being cleared where the trader's crests would be hung. Before I could imagine Saint's crest among them, I kept walking. But I stopped short when my eyes caught sight of a placard that bore a name I recognized—Oliver Durant. The name I'd seen on the courier agreement with Zola and Simon.

My chin tipped up as I studied the rich colors of the portrait. The man's wide face was set with a large nose beneath a severe brow. The dark curling beard matched the head of hair beneath his fine hat, and one hand was set on the grip of a gold-handled cane.

So, this was the man who'd planned to buy me. A gem merchant, like Saint predicted. An upstanding member of the guild. Maybe these bastards weren't so different from the ones I'd grown up with, after all.

I took a small step forward, looking him in the eye. I didn't want to guess at what his plans for me had been. Lock me up in the back of a shop somewhere in this teeming city? Tie a stone around my feet and drop me in the harbor to be rid of one more gem sage who could spot the fakes he was trading? I was glad that I'd never have to find out. I had Saint to thank for that.

I closed my eyes, trying to scrub the helmsman's name from my mind. I didn't want to think about the *Riven* or what his face had looked like when I stood at the bottom of those steps. I didn't want to remember that scent, like the deepest sea.

I put one foot in front of the other until the hall came to a stop at a circular vestibule with four bronze-plated doors set into the curved wall. When I found the one I was looking for, I raised a fist and knocked.

POST OF EDGAR MORANTON, GEM GUILD MASTER

It was simple. My mother hated the Narrows. She always had. But that hatred had grown into something else entirely when talk of a Trade Council in Ceros began to fester. She'd been wedged out of her own license to trade at their ports and giving the Narrows its own authority didn't bode well for her prospects.

And if there was anyone who would ensure she was never given power in these waters, it would be the Gem Guild master. He wouldn't want her stones fetching more coin than his.

The door opened and a young man's face appeared. He was near my own age, if I had to guess. Maybe an apprentice, or a clerk of some kind. He could even be an heir.

"May I help you?" His narrow face was set with small, dark eyes.

My gaze found the bright beam of sunlight casting through the room behind him. "I'm looking for the Gem Guild master."

"Regarding?"

"A sale."

The young man's brow pulled, his hand already moving toward the door again. "A sale?"

"The sale of a gemstone."

"I'm not sure you—"

"It's all right, son. Let her in," a quiet voice came from inside.

The young man hesitated before he let the door swing open, revealing a large office lit with a circle of windows set into the high ceiling. One of the towers I'd spotted from the bridges, I presumed.

"What is it I can help you with?" The man behind the desk was already standing, abandoning his quill.

His combed hair was tucked behind one ear, his face clean-shaven over the high collar of his suit. He was an entire head taller than me, his broad shoulders nearly the width of the bookcase behind him. In the Unnamed Sea, the seats of the Trade Council were filled with some of the oldest guild members. Men and women who'd climbed the ranks to the honor of being called *master*. But this man was younger than my own father would be if he were still alive.

The thought made me swallow hard.

"Well, you're far from home, aren't you?" he said, looking me over.

I still wasn't sure exactly what it was that gave me away so quickly. The fabric of my clothes? The laces in my boots? Eventually, I'd have to figure out how to scrub myself of those clues.

"Just stopping in Ceros for the night with my crew," I said, giving him the explanation he'd probably already come up with himself.

He gestured to the tool belt. "A dredger, I see."

I nodded.

"And this is regarding a sale, you said?" He was politely masking his impatience now.

"I have something I'd like to offer you. A rare and valuable stone."

He frowned. "I'm sure there are plenty of merchants down at the merchant's house who would be interested."

This man's days of trading in a booth were long gone. They probably had been for some time. A single sale was a waste of his time when he likely had a whole warehouse of gems down at the water. No, this was a man who dealt in the kinds of trades that tipped power balances. That was why I was here, after all.

"This isn't any ordinary gemstone," I said, a pit sinking in my stomach.

That got his attention.

"All right, why don't you take a seat?" He took a gem lamp from the shelf behind him and set it beside the small tray on the desk. "Who did you say you crew for?"

"The *Reverence*," I said, giving him the first name that flitted through my mind. It was a small vessel out of Nimsmire that I wasn't even sure held a license to trade in Ceros, but by the time he checked it out, I'd be gone.

I reached into my pocket, finding the little purse and pulling it free. The midnight sang inside, the feel of it pulsating between my fingers. I'd had that song with me so long now that it would strange to be without it.

"Well, let's see it, then," he said, tugging on the glittering gold chain around his neck until the monocle fell from his vest pocket. He fit it to his eye.

I pulled open the purse strings and the light coming through the window glinted on the smooth face of the stone inside. The sound of the midnight grew louder in my ears, humming in my blood.

My mother was right. It *would* change everything. Just not in the way she thought.

"I'm afraid I'm in a bit of a hurry, dear."

The stone rolled into my hand and the man's eyes narrowed, curiosity pursing his lips. If he was experienced enough to be the Gem Guild master, it would take him all of three seconds to realize this wasn't onyx or obsidian. There was a strange nature to the black color. A sheer, liquid-like quality.

I let the midnight move under the light until flashes of violet ignited beneath the gem's surface. But when I looked up to meet the guild master's eyes, my vision was pulled to the shelf fixed to the wall behind him.

I don't know what it was that snagged my attention. Maybe the shift of a bending shadow or the sparkle of the crystal glasses. But when my eyes fixed on something I recognized, a sick, horrifying feeling bloomed deep in my gut.

An open wooden box displaying a quill was set into the glass case. And fit into the gold nib was a single black-tipped feather. The feather of a whistling swan.

A sharp prick ran over my skin as the guild master's voice sounded again. But I couldn't hear him anymore. My mother's presence was suddenly filling the room, swirling in the air around us. I could smell the sweet scent that she dabbed at her wrists. Hear the tinkling of the jewels around her neck.

I'd thought I'd gone as far from her as I could. That I'd traveled the sea to find the place she didn't exist. But this man sitting in the chamber of the Narrows Trade Council was just another hand of Holland.

I'd known long before I learned the truth about my father that the people who'd been gifted that quill were special to my mother. They weren't just associates or business partners. They were loyal. Devoted to her. And the rumors about what they'd done in her name were the most wicked of her sins.

There was no shortage of her stewards in the Unnamed Sea, so why wouldn't she have them in the Narrows too? It made sense. All part of her plan. Only, I'd been too foolish to see it.

"I'm . . . I'm sorry." I stood, hand clamping so hard over the stone that the pain of it shot up my wrist to my elbow. "I have to go."

The Gem Guild master got to his feet, catching the monocle in his palm. "I'm sorry?"

I took a step backward toward the door, and then another. "I—"

But the words disintegrated before they could take shape and then I was in the hallway. Walking. I stuffed the midnight back into the purse, pulling my hood up and sliding the tool belt from my shoulder so I could roll it up tightly and stuff it into my jacket. When I heard footsteps behind me, I picked up my pace.

"Wait!" a voice echoed.

The portraits of the gem merchants flitted past me on either side and I paced toward the light at the end of the hallway, their eyes bearing down on me.

"I said wait!"

I glanced back at the door of the Gem Guild master's office. He was already flanked by two traders in green jackets, their gold buttons shining as they started toward me.

I pushed into the door to the street with both hands, letting it swing out, and as soon as my feet hit the cobblestones, I was running. The door flew open again behind me and the two traders were running now, the Gem Guild master on their heels.

The market ahead was already filling with a crowd and I looked for an opening, slipping into the stream of people. Voices and boots folded around me, letting me disappear, and when I heard the sound of a creaky wheel, I followed it until I spotted a cart. It came to a stop on the side of the street and I snaked my way toward it, not daring to look back. I came around the railing to lift myself in the bed, then slid myself backward until I was wedged between two barrels that smelled like salted fish. I pressed my body between them, making myself as small as possible.

"Where the hell did she go?" A gruff voice sounded on the other side of the barrel and I filled my lungs with air, holding it.

The corner of a green jacket flashed past the cart, and then another.

"Get down to the harbor. Find her." The Gem Guild master's smooth tone was easy to pick out. So close I could reach out and touch him. *Now.*

The cart jerked forward, moving again, and I let out the breath I was holding. A single hot tear slipped down my cheek and I curled tighter into myself as my hand found the stone in my pocket. The pain in my throat grew until I couldn't swallow. Until my teeth were clenched so tight that my jaw ached.

My father's face found me, his kind eyes moving left to right over his parchment as he sat quietly at his candlelit desk. His fingers tapping at the corner. His gray-streaked hair like threads of silver.

But the vision was replaced by the looming ghost of Holland. Like everything else. It wasn't just that my mother's shadow stretched all the way to the Narrows or that she'd followed me in an endless stream of memories. Her blood ran in my veins. And no matter how far I ran, I realized, I'd never, ever be rid of her.

TWENTY-TWO

SAINT

Griff's Tavern sat on the steepest slope of the city, its windows overlooking the harbor. But as my eyes scanned the crests on the sails of the ships that were docked there, I could only think about the day when none of them would be from the Unnamed Sea.

There were many who thought the idea of the Narrows standing on its own was nothing more than a fantasy. But that was before the streets of Ceros stretched long, following the jagged shore, and the number of piers on the water multiplied. Before we had a Trade Council of our own and merchants to contend with the ones in Bastian. I could feel it changing. Like the patterns that shifted with every wave that broke on the sand.

Maybe I'd never see it in my lifetime, but maybe I would.

Either way, today was where it would truly begin.

"Ready?"

Clove's voice made me blink, coming back to myself, and I turned to see him standing in the doorway. He'd shaved his face, making him look a little like his age for once. We were still young, I remembered. But I hadn't felt that way in a long time.

I nodded, grabbing my jacket from the chair beside the bed and stepping over Nash. He was tucked against the wall at the foot of the two beds, still snoring.

Isolde hadn't showed, and I hadn't expected her to. When we came up from the tavern late last night, a part of me had fleetingly remembered how she'd been curled up in the shadows of my quarters the day I found her on the *Riven*. But as my eyes followed the candlelight sweeping the room, illuminating its shadows, she wasn't there.

My mind would stop drifting to her, I told myself. I would forget the way I'd felt when I'd looked into her eyes in the alley in Dern or when I touched her without thinking on the *Riven*. These things would fade. Drift into the past. No matter how untrue, it was easy to believe when a whole future stretched before me.

The tavern was empty when we came down the creaking steps, but Griff was already at work behind the bar, scrubbing the glasses he'd soon be filling with ale and rye. Morning light pooled on the wood floor, finding the shadows of the empty room, but the embers in the fireplace were still glowing. The sharp scent of woodsmoke was powerful enough to mask the stale, sweet stench of spilled rye.

"Tea?" Griff croaked, hands covered in a froth of white suds. His round middle was cinched by the tie of his apron, his bald head missing the hat he usually wore.

He still looked at Clove and me like the kids our fathers had dragged in behind them, and that was likely why he kept giving us a room even when we couldn't pay for it. But I kept the best of the rye set aside for him every time we picked up from Emilia, the way my father would have wanted.

"No, thanks." I buttoned my jacket up to my chin, answering for both of us.

My stomach was already in knots and a pot of black tea would have me vomiting before I even made it to the Trade Council. I hadn't even been able to eat the bread Griff's wife, Daya, sent up at daybreak.

"Suit yourself." He went back to work, but there was a smile on his lips as he stacked the next glass. It looked a lot like pride. "Better get going, then."

It had been at least an hour since the harbor bell had rung, and the Trade Council would be in session. The last time I'd been there I was emptying my pockets of every coin we had to pay the fee for the license petition. Coin we'd never have been able to save without Griff.

He was the one who'd helped us find the *Riven*, which at times I'd questioned was a favor at all. Some unfortunate soul had won it gambling in the tavern, with no idea that it wouldn't pass muster as a real ship. They'd been only too happy to sell it to us for next to nothing, probably guilt-ridden that they were sending us to our deaths. But here we were, about to claim our own trade license.

I'd never thanked Griff for what he'd done for us. Not directly. But that look in his eye as we pushed out onto the street made me think that maybe I didn't have to.

Clove fell into step beside me, making me feel more grounded. The city was awake, the shopfronts open and carts headed to market. The smell of spice and bread and drying herbs was in the air, bleeding into the sea winds under the maze of bridges suspended overhead.

The sunlight flitted over us as we passed beneath them, painting shapes on the dirt beneath our feet. I didn't know what our fathers would think if they could see us now. Walking the streets of Ceros alone. Headed to the Trade Council to accept a license that granted us the freedom to sail port to port and build our own trade.

My father had dreamed it for me. So had Clove's. But I wondered if they ever really believed it. I hadn't. Not for a long time.

Clove caught my eyes, as if he was thinking the same thing, a nervous grin changing his face. We'd waited for this moment for the last three years. And now it was here.

The home of the new Trade Council was one of the oldest buildings in Ceros, marked by four towers that had once been set with telescopes to watch every inch of the horizon for ships and storms. Its stone walls were bleached by the sun and though it had looked like a giant when I stood before it as a boy, it felt significantly smaller now.

It had been dressed up with newly cast windows and polished hinges and handles on the arched, stained doors. At their center, the port seal of Ceros was burned into the resurfaced wood. That was new too.

We stood there, shoulder to shoulder, with the bustle of one of the city's markets at our backs. We'd walk in as urchins. We'd walk out as traders. I tried to wrap my mind around that.

"You did it," Clove said, his smile growing wider.

There was no protest in him now like there had been the other night, when he tried to convince me to forfeit the license for the petition fee. I was grateful for that.

"I told you I would."

I had. I'd promised him. It wouldn't absolve me of my sins, but it was something.

The door opened and the air chilled by the shadowed marble inside cooled my skin. I hesitated before I stepped over the threshold, one calloused hand dragging along the fine papered wall. A shimmer of gold rippled in its veins as the door shut slowly, snuffing out the sunlight.

Silver candlesticks were fixed overhead in an even line every few paces and the wicks were lit, giving the hall an eerie glow. It was as if, all of a sudden, we weren't in the Narrows anymore. I didn't like that feeling.

I followed the walkway to its end, stopping before the long dais that served as a partition between us and the hall behind it. Its face was covered in a mosaic tile that depicted rolling waves. The woman who stood on the other side looked up from her spectacles with disinterest. Her red velvet jacket was rimmed in a brilliant purple, her fingers covered in gold rings.

She cleared her throat as her gaze raked over us. "May I help you, sirs?"

Sirs. I half expected Clove to start laughing, but he managed to keep quiet.

I pulled the message from my jacket, handing it over, and the woman set down her quill. Her scrutinizing gaze didn't leave us until she had the parchment opened before her.

"Mm." Her eyes snapped up. "It seems congratulations are in order." She gave us a genuine smile and pulled off her spectacles, folding them carefully in her hands. "Wait here."

She stepped down from the dais and her polished shoes clapped on the floor as she made her way into the narrow hall. Beneath the soaring windows on the opposite wall, two men and two women sat at a carved wooden table the length of the room.

The sound of voices echoed and Clove looked to me again before his eyes lifted to the crystal chandelier hanging over us. "Guess they decided to play the part," he muttered.

"Looks like it," I said.

There was humor in it, but not the kind I found entertaining. The Narrows resented the Unnamed Sea not only because of what they'd done in our waters, but also because of their way of life. It had taken years to build the guilds into something that could one day be the seeds of the Trade Council, and now that we were here, they were just trying to turn Ceros into Bastian.

"This way." The woman reappeared, waving us forward, and we followed her through the opening and into the long rectangular room. At one end, a grand fireplace was stacked with a roaring fire, the seals of the guilds pressed into the hearth by the expert hand of a smith.

The four guild masters sat behind the table, glittering in their fine coats and frocks. The backs of their chairs reached up far past their heads, making them look like miniature thrones. They were, in a way.

Gold inkpots were fixed on the table before them, where an array of parchment was stacked in varying heights. One of the women wore a stone around her neck so large that it looked like it could be a lantern's flame.

There wasn't one among them who hadn't grown up on those streets outside or ones like them. Yet, here they were, pretending to be Saltbloods. I bit the inside of my cheek when a bitter smirk pulled at my lips.

The man sitting at the end of the table had my summons open in his hands. His white mustache moved as he smiled up at me. "Ah. Elias, is it?"

"That's right," I answered, finding my feet beneath me again. That name didn't feel familiar like it once had.

"I'm Faros, master of the Shipwrights Guild. This is Corinne, Smiths Guild. And here we have Edgar, Gem Guild, and Irva, Sailmakers Guild."

Each of them nodded as he spoke their names and his voice echoed around us, cut only by the sound of the fire. Its warm glow bled through the room, casting it in a dreamlike light.

"It's an honor to meet you, son." The woman Faros had called Irva smiled, and despite her calling me *son,* her tone wasn't maternal. Her eyes moved from my face, down my chest in a way I recognized. "You're one of the first Narrows-born helmsmen we've had the honor to grant a trade license. And you won't be the last."

"Hear! Hear!" Edgar tapped the table beside his parchment with the knuckles of one hand.

The clip of footsteps echoed again and the woman from the dais returned with a triangular package wrapped in brown paper cradled in her arms. She set it beside Irva before disappearing, but not without one more glance back at us.

Faros clasped his hands before him. "It says here you have a ship. The *Aster.*"

"We do. She's being finished as we speak and will be sea ready by the time we get back to Dern."

"That's good. Don't want our traders sailing in rags, now do we?"

His mouth tilted in a playful grin, as if I were in on the joke. Like we were the same. He had no idea how wrong he was about that.

"And have you a crew?"

"This is my navigator," I answered, giving him only half an answer. Clove was crew, but that was all I had of one.

"Well, I'm sure once you're settled on the *Aster,* you'll have your pick of the rest."

Irva made a sound that resembled an agreement. She took up the paper-wrapped package and got to her feet, coming around the table. When she stopped before me, she held it out between us. "You'll need to fly that crest if you want the harbor masters to know who's coming." She winked.

I took the package in my hands, realizing by the weight that it was a sail. A clean, white, unstitched sail that bore the symbol we'd be known by for the rest of our lives.

Faros came around the table next, and the others stood, chairs scraping over the marble floor. Irva stepped aside, hands clasped behind her back, and Faros lifted a rolled parchment tied in a red satin ribbon into the air. I swallowed hard, trying to keep my hand steady as I took it from him.

"Well, go ahead," he said.

I pulled at the ribbon and it unraveled, letting the parchment unroll in my fingers. The tight feeling in my throat was now a painful lump.

The lavish scrolling letters curved across the top of the parchment in glossy black ink. Beneath it, the crest I'd had the smith make for us was etched onto the page. A curling wave arched over a single triangular sail.

By the power of the
Trade Council of the Narrows

This certifies that the bearer of this crest is hereby licensed to
trade goods at ports Ceros, Dern, and Sowan

Helmsman: Elias Redgrave

TWENTY-THREE

SAINT

Griff had the rye ready to open when we returned. One of the finest bottles he kept in the back under Daya's watchful eye.

The tavern was filled to the brim, the sound of a fiddle playing somewhere beyond the crowd that stretched from the door to the counter. It was a busy night. The harbor was full, the taverns were full, and we weren't the only ones celebrating. The rumor making its way door-to-door in Ceros was that the Trade Council had granted four trade licenses by the time the sun went down. There were four ships, four crests, four helmsmen to contend with the Unnamed Sea. And by the time the sun rose tomorrow, we'd be going port to port stealing the contracts of the Saltbloods and writing new ones. With our own people.

Daya set down a fresh loaf of bread in the center of the table, careful not to spill the pitcher of ale in her other hand. I could finally stomach it now that I had the license in my possession and we were already on our second pot of tea. Clove reached for the plate, tearing the loaf in two and leaving the other half for me. He slathered a mound of butter over its top before taking a bite that could choke him.

"Can't wait to see the look on Gerik's face." He took another bite before he'd even swallowed.

The harbor master in Dern would probably have the license checked for forgery before he'd let himself believe it was real. Not that I could blame him. We'd lied through our teeth for years to build what we had, and trust wasn't something people in the Narrows gave easily. Luckily, we didn't need it. Trading contracts were the only thing that mattered, and harbor masters had little sway over them.

A few tables over, Nash was watching us. He lifted his cup of tea into the air, giving me an impressed tilt of the head. Even he had to admit we'd been right. Two boys adrift from the shores of Cragsmouth had done the impossible. And I didn't care how many Saltbloods had filled their pockets with our coin along the way. I was going to get every single one back.

"You think Zola's got one of those licenses?" Clove asked.

"More than likely," I guessed. "If he doesn't already, he will soon."

He had too many friends, too many favors exchanged, to keep him from the table. I hoped a new license was distraction enough to keep him from trying to track down the gem sage he'd lost. But whoever he'd struck the deal with wouldn't forget so easily.

I set my elbows on the table, turning my hand over. The bandage Isolde had tied around my palm was gone now, but there was something still lingering where she'd touched me. Like the heat of a candle's flame held too close.

"He's going to have quite a shock next time we're in Dern and we set sail on the *Aster*."

I closed my hand into a fist, making the healing cut on my palm sting. "Yes, he is."

Clove was all business now, focused. "The rye won't keep us going forever. It'll be steady, but not enough to build with. There'll be other crofters who want to sign contracts. Potatoes, barley, cheese—anything that'll stand the length of the route without spoiling. Emilia can help us with that."

"And gems?" I asked, studying him. Our agreement with Henrik wouldn't be easy to get out of.

"I think running gems is the easiest way to get a knife in our back, even if they're legitimate stones."

He was right. No matter how you looked at it, the coin of both the Unnamed Sea and the Narrows ran on gemstones. But there was no denying that it was much more profitable than crates of apples or cabbage.

"Crofters it is," I said.

He looked relieved, and I couldn't pretend I didn't know why. Clove was the sensible one. The steady set of feet who could be patient and wait for his prize. I was the hungry one who was never satisfied, and that had gotten us into trouble. It had also cost us almost everything.

"Saint?" Clove interrupted my thoughts, making me look up from my plate.

His gaze was fixed across the room, eyebrows arched up and mouth still full. I turned in my chair, searching the tavern until I saw it. Between the men standing at the next booth, a flash of a dark red braid appeared and then disappeared, sneaking from beneath the hood of a jacket.

When she turned, her face came into view.

Isolde.

The sleeve of her jacket was streaked with mud and the way she stood there was with a weight. Not the tall, sure posture she usually had. She looked as if she were being pressed into the floor. She tucked the loose strand of hair behind her ear as her eyes scanned the tavern. They were a duller blue, like the light had gone out of them a little. When they found us, I could see a moment of relief in them. Or something else.

"Well, look at that," Clove murmured.

But when I looked at him, he wasn't watching Isolde anymore. He was watching me.

She pushed through the crowd, making her way toward us, and I returned my eyes to my plate, breathing through the tight feeling that had returned to my chest. I'd been sure we'd never see her again. I'd also hoped with every breath that I was wrong.

"This day is just getting better and better." Clove slid over in the booth, making room for her beside him.

She stopped at the corner of the table, one hand hooked into the dredging belt on her shoulder like she was waiting for permission. From me.

"Do what you need to do?" I asked, not looking up at her.

"Not really," she said.

Clove lifted a hand in the air until he had Daya's attention and then he pointed to his teacup. She gave him a nod before ducking into the kitchens.

"Well?" He gestured to the seat beside him, and I could feel her look to me again. When I didn't protest, she took it.

"Filled that dredger position yet?" She said it with the slightest edge of humor, trying to make light of the tension that stretched across the table.

If she was looking for some kind of reassurance that she was wanted here, she wasn't going to find it. I'd made her the offer and I wasn't going to take it back. She'd shown up, so I finally had her answer.

"We have now," Clove said.

Still, Isolde's eyes were on me. But I didn't meet them. There was a threshold being crossed here and I wasn't sure I knew where it would take me. I wasn't sure I even wanted to know.

Daya reappeared with a fresh teacup and saucer, letting her eyes slide from me to Clove as she set it down before Isolde. Unlike Emilia, Daya knew how to hold her tongue. But that one look held everything she wasn't saying—that seeing the two of us sharing a table with a face she'd never seen before was more than a little strange.

Clove slid the teapot toward Isolde as Daya shuffled away.

"Is that it?" Isolde said, eyeing the rolled parchment on the table beside him.

"That's it," he echoed.

Isolde poured the tea, but she didn't touch it. "Congratulations." The word was small. There had been a shift in her, and not just in the way she'd looked when she walked through the door. The undertow of anger she always carried was missing now, replaced by something else I couldn't put my finger on.

Clove tapped her with his elbow. "Don't know how I feel about having a Saltblood on the crew though."

She almost smiled then. Almost. I was beginning to be able to predict that look before it hit her face. I was beginning to get used to the feeling I had when I saw it.

"Figured I'd trade one rotten bastard for two," she quipped, finally picking up her tea.

She held the cup like one of *them,* but that edge in her voice was Narrows through and through. I wondered, for the first time, if she'd simply been born on the wrong shore.

"May I?" She set a finger on the wrapped triangular parcel that sat beside my plate. The sail that Irva had given me with the license.

I nodded.

Clove draped one arm over the back of the booth so he could see over her shoulder. She tore one corner of the paper before peeling it down and the crisp white canvas almost glowed in the dim light. I watched as she carefully unwrapped it, letting the fabric fall open in her lap until she could see the entire crest. A wave curling over a triangular sail.

The tip of her finger traced it, her brow pulling. "It looks like—" Her words stopped, then started again. "It looks like it's sinking."

"It is," I said.

Clove didn't look at me, but I could see his posture change. I hadn't shown it to him after I had the smith render it, but it was the crest I'd submitted to the Council with our petition. And it held a meaning that only he and I knew.

"Isn't it bad luck?" Isolde asked.

I shook my head once. "We're not unlucky bastards."

"Not anymore," Clove murmured, making Isolde turn her head to look at him. But he smoothed it over, a gruff smile tilting his head to one side. "The sun's down." His eyes darted to the window. "Time to switch to rye."

"Since when do you need the sun to go down to drink rye?" I asked.

Clove got to his feet. "True."

Isolde stared at the crest for another moment before she refolded the sail and wrapped it, tucking it into the seat beside her.

"Griff!" Clove made his way to the bar.

"Your tea's gone cold," Isolde said, crossing her arms on the table.

I stared down into the cup. The grounds had pooled in the bottom, making it look black as tar. But I didn't know what her observation meant. A way to ask me if there was something wrong, maybe. It was the same question I wanted to ask her. But I wouldn't.

"So, you changed your mind." I chanced a glance in her direction, but my gaze only made it as high as her shoulder.

Her spine straightened, her chin dipping down as she looked over the table. "If I'm going to join a crew, better one that isn't trying to sell me to a gem merchant."

"Zola knows what you are. That problem isn't going to go away."

"Then the better question might be why you decided to take me on. And don't give me the answer you gave me on the *Riven*. Giving safe harbor to a runaway gem sage isn't exactly the smartest way to launch a trade route."

The reason was one I hadn't been completely able to work out myself. Clove was right that keeping her out of Zola's hands would only help us, and it was also true that we needed a dredger on the crew. But I wasn't foolish enough to lie to myself about the fact that I didn't *want* her to go.

Before I could answer, the door to the street was flung open, followed by a sudden hush that rippled over the room, and we both turned.

A flicker of brilliant green moved through the crowd. The shining buttons that adorned the jackets were draped over the shoulders of two men who couldn't look more out of place. Saltblood traders.

They didn't usually venture this far into Ceros. Not even for rye. There were taverns closer to the harbor for that. These bastards were asking for a fight just by walking through that door.

The uncomfortable silence waned as they made their way to the bar, where Griff was handing over three rye glasses to Clove. The men searched the faces around them, scanning the crowd like they were looking for something, and Clove's blue eyes sharpened in the firelight as he watched them from the corner of his gaze. I didn't like the smirk at the corner of his mouth.

Across the table, Isolde sank lower in the booth, pulling her hair to one side and tucking it into her jacket. The pupils in her gray eyes widened, making her irises almost disappear as her gaze followed the men. She was biting down on her bottom lip hard enough to draw blood.

"Whatever this is," I said, keeping my voice low as I tipped a chin toward the traders, "I need to know about it."

I waited for her to nod before I stood, giving my back to the tavern so that she was out of their line of sight, and I reached into my pocket for the key to our room.

"Upstairs. Third door on the left."

She slid out of the booth silently, taking the key, but her fingers closed over mine for just a moment before she slipped through the tables by the fire. A few seconds later, she was disappearing up the steps to the room.

At the bar, the two men were too busy talking to Griff to notice, but from behind them, Clove's eyes met mine. He picked up the bottle of rye Griff had set down, that coy grin making the angle of his jaw sharpen.

I exhaled, shaking my head once. *Don't*. I mouthed the word.

But I could see the moment I said it that it was already too late.

Clove took a step forward, dipping to one side to catch the shoulder of the first man, knocking into him.

"Shit," I muttered, already walking.

Clove rocked back, as if he'd lost his balance, lifting the hand that held the open bottle of rye between them. "Pardon me." He brushed the embroidered fabric of the man's sleeve with the back of his hand, rye sloshing everywhere.

"What the—" The man's hands flew up between them, taking Clove by the shirt.

"Apologies!" Clove's voice rang out, getting the attention of everyone in the room. "Apologies, sir. Please, let me help you." He dropped the green glasses and they shattered at his feet as he reached between them, pouring half the bottle of rye into the man's collar in the process.

"A shame." He could barely keep from laughing. "It's such a fine jacket."

Any attempt at pretense was gone now and the man's face lit red, his nostrils flaring.

I shoved a chair aside, picking up my pace.

Three steps. Two.

The man's fist reared back, his other hand pinning Clove in place, and the fist came down hard across Clove's cheek. A spray of blood spattered the smooth wall beside him as the room erupted in shouting. But when Clove's face lifted to the light again, his eyes were clear, a smile breaking over his lips.

I reached them as the man raised his fist again, taking him by the jacket and wrenching him backward. "He's drunk," I lied. "Leave it."

But the trader wasn't buying it. Anyone looking at Clove knew exactly what had happened. And there wasn't a soul in the tavern who wasn't amused.

The man drew a gold-hilted knife from his belt, raising it between us, and by the time I saw it, Clove was already barreling forward again. The other man plowed toward us and my back hit the wall hard as I launched out of reach of the blade.

The tavern's patrons were all on their feet now, climbing onto chairs and into booths to watch the fight, and the man looked back long enough for me to take hold of his throat, driving him toward the counter. Behind me, Clove was swinging at the man's crewmate, catching him in the gut with a fist.

By the time I saw the lantern light glinting on the trader's blade from the corner of my eye, it was too late. I let my weight fall back into him as I turned, hoping the knife would catch my side instead of finding its way between my ribs to my lung. But just when I expected to feel the landing of the blow, the man's knees buckled, his face going slack before he fell to the ground.

Behind him, Nash stood with the broken bottle of rye he'd just hit the man with clutched in his hand. His eyes were wide, as if he were just as surprised at what he'd done as I was. But the look of shock turned into one of glee as he looked up at me, panting.

"Thanks." I exhaled.

The bottle slipped from Nash's fingers. "You're welcome," he answered between gulps of air.

I took the trader by the collar and I hadn't made it more than a foot from the bar before the other man was being hauled to the door by several sets of hands. I followed them, towing the bastard behind me. I could taste blood in my mouth and smell it in the air. A streak of it was smeared across the floor, beneath my boots.

I dragged him with both hands over it until we were outside, and then I dropped him on the wet cobblestones. When I looked up, Clove was beside me.

"Get on before these fools decide to have fun with you." Griff's voice was at my back. "These boys got a crest today. Don't think the Trade Council will take it lightly if they show up dead the next morning."

Through the doors, the whole of the tavern was still watching.

The traders looked to one another in a silent exchange before the man at my feet stood. He looked me square in the eye before he spit on the ground. Now I was the one smiling, my heart still racing in my chest in a way that made the blood rush through my veins. I couldn't pretend I didn't like it as much as Clove did. The difference now was that we had the protection of the Trade Council between us and Saltbloods.

They disappeared around the corner and I gazed up at

the window of our room that looked out over the street. A hand clutched the curtain, but Isolde was draped in the dark.

"Come on." Griff stepped aside, waiting for us to go in before he followed and closed the doors.

The crowd in the tavern parted, making way for us, and Griff appeared at the counter uncorking that bottle of rye he'd had waiting. Daya brushed off the shoulders of Nash's jacket as he sat before signaling to the two men on the stools beside him to move. They obeyed, picking up their glasses and pressing against the wall.

"Today has just been full of surprises," Clove said, giving Nash an appraising look.

The apprentice blinked a few times, looking a little shaken. "Can't exactly get home if you two end up gutted in an alley somewhere."

Clove's eyebrows raised. "Didn't know you had it in you. Hard to believe you've ever gotten blood on that pretty jacket of yours."

"First time for everything."

Griff surveyed the three of us as I wiped the blood from my lip, both hands perched on the bar in front of him. He shook his head in silence as he reached for the stack of green glasses, plucking three from the top.

The tavern went back to its business, conversations picking up where they left off, pitchers of ale being poured. Griff filled the glasses with rye before securing the cork and moving to the next person standing at the counter. No one even bothered to wipe the blood from the floor.

Nash returned to his table in front of the fire after one drink and I set the gold-hilted knife in front of me, picking up my own glass. "You're a stupid bastard," I said, shooting Clove a look before I took it in one swallow.

He shrugged. His arm was bleeding through his shirt where the tip of a knife blade had grazed his skin. He reached into his pocket, pulling a fist of gold chain and two brass buttons free. All items he'd had the wherewithal to pickpocket in the fight. He dropped them beside the knife.

"They started it."

"Pretty sure you did."

Clove tipped his head back, pouring the rye into his mouth and then victoriously slamming the glass down. "No." He exhaled. "It started the first time those bastards dropped anchor in our waters." He lifted his glass to mine, clinking the rims. "And we, my friend, are going to finish it."

TWENTY-FOUR

ℑSOLDE

It took only minutes for the commotion down in the tavern to return to a calm hum after the traders were hauled out. It was a sight that would have made the hair stand up on the back of my mother's neck, a bunch of Narrows-born urchins throwing traders from the Unnamed Sea out into the muddy street like the contents of a slop bucket.

It was what she'd feared. What the guilds and the entire Trade Council in Bastian had feared. That one day, the Narrows would stand on its own. And when that day came, there would be a war for the waters that had once been ripe for the taking.

Saint was right in his suspicion that things were changing. But which direction the wind would blow remained to be seen. I'd never felt truly beaten by my mother until that moment in the Gem Guild master's post when my eyes landed on that quill. I'd never felt the full weight of her power before. The only thing I could compare it to was that night of the storm on the *Riven*. How small I'd felt. How insignificant.

I knew firsthand what kind of power the coin of the Unnamed Sea produced. I suspected that the Narrows had only seen a glimpse of it. But when helmsmen started losing contracts to Narrows-born traders and had to break that news to the merchants in Bastian, there would be hell to pay. And behind every door there were traces of Holland. There always would be.

The room Saint had let from the barkeeper wasn't unlike his cabin on the *Riven*. It was plain, with no embellishments to be seen. Two small cots were draped with mismatched quilts and what looked to be another makeshift bed on the floor was wedged against one wall.

Hanging over one of the cot posts was the map case from the *Riven*, its cap still tightly in place. The only thing in Saint's quarters that he hadn't been willing to let go down with the ship. The only thing he took when he left it at port. That single map held a vision for the Narrows that was real. Heart-achingly real. He could see it—bustling ports and thriving merchant's houses. Trading ships with cargo holds filled to the brim and guilds that had something to negotiate with.

I'd thought when I left Bastian with the midnight that I had leverage against my mother that no one else had. But I'd been wrong. Her influence didn't just reside in her gem trade or the single piece of midnight I'd put into her hands. It was in her dream of conquering the shores beyond her own. Her teeth-bared hunger for control. All my life I'd seen the ill-fortuned adversaries that rose against her, the schemes and plotting in hopes of taking her down. But she'd never met her match. Not like she would when the dream Saint had encased in the ink of that map came to life.

And it would. I'd see to that myself.

This myth-born trader from nowhere was an enemy she didn't even know existed. And he probably could not care less about Holland, the great gem merchant of the Unnamed Sea. He wasn't trying to take anything from anyone or play tricks. He was just trying to make something he could keep.

I let my eyes raise to the small mirror that hung on the wall over the wash bowl. It reflected my shape back at me, the details of my face appearing as I stepped into the moonlight coming from the window. I slid the knife from my belt slowly, winding my braid around my knuckles until it was pulled tight in my fist.

There was no beating Holland with a single trade. No making her pay for what she'd done. Not when she owned every chest of coin from Ceros to Bastian. But I realized in that moment that fate had landed me on the ship of the one person who just might be able to make my mother's worst nightmares come true.

I pressed the edge of the knife to my braid and met my own eyes as I began to saw back and forth. There was an emptiness there in my expression that I wasn't used to seeing. A void of some kind. But instead of scaring me, I thought for the first time that maybe I could fill that space with whatever I wanted to.

The blade made it through my braid and I stood there, hands heavy at my sides. My hair fell at an angle, its ends hitting my jaw on one side of my face and almost touching my shoulder on the other. Holland would say that I looked like an urchin. The thought made me smile.

The door opened behind me and I went rigid when I saw Saint's reflection in the mirror. The light from the hall was a warm honey hue compared to the moonlight. His gaze fell from mine in the mirror to my hands that still clutched the severed braid and the knife before he stepped inside.

The room felt even smaller with him in it. His jacket was in his hand, his hair swept to one side as if he'd run a hand through it as he came up the stairs from the tavern. But his eyes were still that icy blue that glinted in the darkness.

He shut the door, tossing the jacket onto one of the cots as I slid my knife back into my belt. The braid I set onto the small table that held the wash bowl.

Saint crossed the room with patient steps, stopping on the other side of the mirror and leaning one shoulder against the wall. I could feel his gaze moving from my hair to my belt, where the knife was back in its sheath. I could feel it everywhere.

"Who's looking for you?"

I considered lying. Spinning a different truth than the one that existed. But if Saint was willing to take on Zola for me, I couldn't see him flinching at the thought of a runaway merchant's daughter.

"My mother," I said.

He waited for me to continue, that pensive look on his face unwavering.

"She's a gem merchant. A powerful one."

"Who?"

Again, I weighed the cost of a lie. "Holland."

He didn't like that answer. The set of his mouth flattened, but his eyes didn't leave me. "Why are you running from her?"

I bit down on my bottom lip, remembering the way my blood had run cold in the candlelight that filled my mother's study. The way my father's portrait looked down at me. "Because she killed my father."

That was mostly true. It was the thing that had made me open that case and take the midnight. The thing that had made me go to Simon. But the stone in my pocket, I wasn't ready to talk about that.

Saint's arms crossed over his chest, his brow wrinkling. As if he were trying to work something out.

"She'll have people looking for me," I said. "And she won't let it go."

"Does Zola know?"

I shook my head.

Eventually, she'd find out which ship I'd left on. I had no doubt about that. And that meant Zola was walking a narrow road that led to one place—Holland's retribution.

For a moment, the possibility that Saint and Clove could end up her enemy, too, crossed my mind. The thought made gooseflesh rise on my arms.

"What about you?" I let my eyes drop to his scarred hand, hoping he'd trade one question for another. "What are you running from?"

He untucked the hand from beneath his elbow and turned it over, as if inspecting it. It was a long moment before he finally spoke.

"I was twelve years old. So was Clove." His eyes lifted, finding me in the dark.

I didn't know until he started talking that I hadn't actually expected him to answer. I went still, half afraid he'd fall quiet if I made the slightest move.

"We were going out on the boat to fish with our fathers and their crew and I was the first to the dock that morning. It was only that year they'd let us start coming along with them, and only because they wanted us to learn how to crew. Not on fishing boats. Our fathers wanted us sailing under real trader's crests one day." He paused, trying to find the words. "There were rules. Ones my grandfather and his grandfather before him followed. There was an order to things. A balance between us and the sea. But I'd never believed in them. Not really."

The adder stones that hung in the window of the *Riven* flashed in my mind, followed by the bloodied knife as Saint pulled it through his fist. The drops of blood dripping into the water.

"My father had sent me early to start on the nets because we were fishing a remote reef Clove and I had never been to before. I got to the boat and I saw it right away. A lark. Lying dead on deck. It was right in front of the helm, a sign that we weren't to go out on the water." His voice deepened. "If anyone else on the ship had seen it that morning, we would have never raised anchor. But they didn't."

I suddenly knew what he was going to say before he said it, and a sick feeling twisted in my gut.

"I thought the superstition was just that—a superstition. That it meant nothing. I wanted to go out, so before anyone saw it, I picked it up and threw it into the water. I didn't think twice. And a few hours later, this storm . . . it came out of nowhere. Like it had just risen up from the water instead of falling from the sky. And I knew. I knew exactly what was about to happen." Another pause. "Clove's father locked us in the cargo hold and it went on for hours. We could hear them screaming. Running across the deck. Eventually, the ship rolled. I don't know many times. But when it was finally over, we came up onto the deck and they were gone. All of them."

A tear rolled down my cheek, but I didn't blink. His eyes were still locked on mine, and I didn't want to take that anchor from him. I couldn't tell what he was feeling. He could have told the story a million times, but I had a feeling maybe it had never been spoken aloud. Not like that.

"It took me a few days, but I told Clove the truth. The families of the crew too. The village never forgave me. They turned me out, cut me off. Everyone except for Clove."

It explained a lot. Why Saint and Clove weren't like other crews. Why it was so important to Saint to get that license.

"And now you follow the rules," I said. "That's why you sail in the storms."

He nodded. "I've given my life to the sea. She will never betray me."

He believed it. Completely. I could see that.

"We had a plan: Come to Ceros. Find a ship. Get a trade license." He fell silent, making the emptiness of the room grow heavy.

I knew what he was getting at—*me*. I wasn't a part of that plan.

"If you don't want to take me on, I understand. I can find another crew."

"I do," he answered, more quickly than I'd expected. "*We* do."

I wasn't sure if he amended the statement out of respect for Clove or out of his own survival instinct. There was no denying there was a pull in the air between us, and he wasn't particularly good at hiding it.

I took a step closer to him, studying his face, and his eyes ran over me, wide and open.

"I'm used to being used, Saint." My voice was frailer than I meant it to be. "But I haven't figured out what exactly you want from me."

"Neither have I," he said lowly.

The words caught me so off guard that I almost felt unsteady on my feet, wishing I hadn't closed the space he'd put between us. I felt suddenly like I might cry. From the words or from exhaustion, I wasn't sure. I didn't care. It just felt so good to be told the truth. It felt like the sun after an eternity of night.

He was still looking right at me. Like he was waiting to see what I'd do. "What is this feeling I have?" He spoke again before I could make up my mind. "This thing that makes me not want you to leave?"

I shook my head. "I don't know."

It was an honest answer. I had no idea why he felt like a breath I'd forgotten to take. Like a weight on my chest I couldn't move.

"Just . . . don't," he said.

"Don't what?"

"Leave."

I didn't know what to make of this version of Saint. The one who was asking me not to go instead of dancing around it like he wasn't sure what he wanted. The one who didn't seem to care if he was showing me every crack in his armor.

His hand lifted from his arm, moving toward me in the dark, and I willed myself to stay still. My heart raced as I waited for his touch to find my face, his thumb tracing over my bottom lip before he tipped my chin up toward him. His fingertips pressed into the soft skin below my jaw where my pulse was racing, and the silence in the room was broken by the sound of my breath.

But Saint looked calm, at ease in the shadows, and not the least bit unnerved by the fact that he was touching me. Again.

That at any moment, he was going to kiss me. Like he'd just made up his mind and that was it. That was all there was.

It was so dark that I almost couldn't tell how close he was until his lips touched mine, and the flood of waiting for it filled every inch of me with a buzzing heat. He opened his mouth, his breath featherlight on my skin, and his hand slid to the back of my neck, leaving a searing burn on my cheek.

He kissed me carefully, like he was being sure to remember the way it felt. And when I deepened the kiss, he followed, pressing his body against mine.

Something shifted into place inside of me. Some off-kilter piece of my soul that had fractured that day in Bastian. I didn't know what we were doing. Where it could possibly lead. But this—he and I—we fit, somehow.

Footsteps on the stairs made him pull away from me, and his fingers slipped from my hair, leaving me breathing so hard that my head was light with it. When the door opened, Saint was already across the room, and Nash appeared with Daya on his heels. She had one hand to his back, like she was guiding him through the doorway.

"Can't hold his rye, that's for sure," she quipped, not even looking up as she set down a stack of folded linens on one of the cots. "Figured you'd need a fresh bed." She finally shot me a glance, wiping her hands on her apron. "Need anything else?" The question was meant for Saint.

"No," he answered.

Nash shuffled to the pile of quilts on the floor, collapsing before he'd even taken off his boots. He rolled over, facing the wall as Daya left, and Clove appeared, pulling the shirt over his head as the door closed. The arm of the light cloth was soaked with blood, but Clove didn't look the least bit concerned about the stripe of open flesh beneath his shoulder.

The three of us moved around one another in the dark and the sound of boots hitting the floor and belts being hung was the only backdrop to the image still whirling in my mind. The way Saint had looked at me. The way he'd kissed me. Like he was sure about it.

Clove climbed into his cot and when I picked up the linens Daya had left to make up another bed, Saint took them from my hands without a word. He said nothing as he unrolled them on the ground and lay down.

I stood there, looking around the dark room for a moment before I climbed onto the cot, tucking myself into the quilts. I closed my eyes before I drew the air into my lungs, knowing what scent I'd find there. Deep ocean. *Saint*.

My fingers found my lips, the soft warmth of his mouth still there.

I didn't know what exactly I'd gotten myself into by walking through the door of that tavern. But something about it felt like I'd been waiting for it my entire life. Like every path I could have taken from my mother's study that night led to one place—right here.

◄▼►

TWENTY-FIVE

◄▲►

ℑSOLDE

"H old still," Saint snapped, pinching the bloody needle between his fingers.

The wound on Clove's arm was deep enough to warrant stitches, but he couldn't have looked less concerned.

The tavern was empty again, except for the barkeeper and Daya, whom I'd worked out to be Griff's wife. She'd been kind enough to fetch me some clothes that didn't give away where I was from, and she'd also been the one to insist that Clove's cut needed tending to. But Clove wouldn't let her touch him. Saint was the only one he'd let come near the wound.

She reappeared with a porcelain bowl of warm water and Saint pressed the tip of the needle through the end of the cut, biting the thread before he tied it off. The skin was already red and inflamed, but it didn't look like the blade had reached the bone.

I wondered just how many times he and Clove had stitched each other up. The history between them went back farther and deeper than I could have guessed, and it carried a heaviness that bore more than childhood memories. They were connected in places the eye couldn't see.

I hadn't slept more than an hour or two through the night, lying awake in the dark and replaying that moment in my head over and over again. Saint's hand dragging through my hair. The brush of his lips across mine. Those words he'd spoken—*what is this?*

I still didn't have an answer.

"If your fathers could see you," Griff grunted, dragging the damp rag down the counter as Saint washed Clove's blood from his hands.

Daya tried her best to frown at him, but there was a smile buried beneath it. "They'd be damn proud," she said.

Griff nodded in agreement, as if that was exactly what he was thinking.

"They won't let it go, you know," I said, handing Clove the clean cloth. "Those traders have something to prove now that the Trade Council here is granting licenses."

What I didn't tell them was that I recognized those traders. That they were the same ones who'd chased after me in the market. And more than likely, they'd been there last night looking for me.

Clove pressed the cloth to his arm, wincing. His face was

busted, a cut lip and a bruise forming along his cheek. But it could have been worse. He could have ended up with that knife in his belly.

Daya set one hand on her hip. "Breakfast before you go?"

"Just tea," Saint answered.

"All right." She sighed disapprovingly before trailing back into the kitchen.

Saint took the seat beside mine, not quite as careful to keep the space between us as he'd been before. He didn't have the rigid apprehension I'd expected from him this morning, the hesitancy of someone who regretted their actions. Maybe because I'd said I was staying. Or maybe because he'd put words to the thing that had been unspoken, like letting a wild animal loose from its cage. There was no point in pretending we could put it back.

Clove and Saint had spent the early hours hashing out what came next: sailing to Dern, settling debts, signing contracts. In three weeks' time, we'd be back in Ceros with the *Aster,* and that was when the real trade would begin. But there was still the matter of Henrik's missing coin.

The door to the street scraped over the uneven floor and Griff called out from the kitchen. "Only open to inn guests! Tavern doesn't open for a few hours."

"Then I'll take a room."

I froze when I heard the familiar voice creeping up my spine all the way from across the room.

Zola.

The door fell closed, cutting out the sound of the street,

and I turned on the stool to see him. His tall, lean frame was swallowed by his long black coat and its hem swayed over the floor as he walked toward us. Not with the heavy steps of an angry man, like I might have expected. In fact, he looked like he was at ease.

Saint stood, dropping the rag on the counter and taking a purposeful step to place himself in front of me. He said nothing, but the silence that fell in the tavern spoke for itself. This wasn't the polite call of a friendly rival.

Behind me, my fingertips were already finding the knife in my belt and Clove abandoned the wound, letting the sleeve of his shirt fall back down as he rose from the stool.

I watched over Saint's shoulder as Zola lazily wove through the tables. There was nothing menacing in the look of him, no hint of outrage at seeing me. As if he'd found exactly what he'd come looking for. And there was no sign of Burke, the navigator who never left his side. I wondered if it was possible that Zola had come alone. It didn't seem likely.

"You look surprised to see me." Zola stopped a few paces away, but he wasn't talking to me. He was looking at Saint. "Came in before first light and saw the *Riven* anchored. Thought I'd come find you so we could celebrate."

Clove took a slow, threatening step in his direction, but Zola ignored him. He pulled a rolled parchment tied with a red satin ribbon from his jacket. The same one that Saint had been given from the Trade Council.

"I admit I was a little miffed when I heard you'd received your summons a day before me."

The knife was at my side now, clutched in my fist.

"Also heard that the *Riven* had shown up at port with a new dredger." He shot me a look.

Saint said nothing, but I could imagine his mind was racing with the prospect of someone talking. Not Emilia, surely. So, who?

"Nothing loosens a tongue like a knife through the hand." Zola grinned.

Lander, I realized. The merchant who'd tried to cheat Saint was taking revenge the only way he knew how. The only way he could.

Zola's attention went to Griff, who still stood nervously behind the bar. "Come on, Griff. Not even going to offer me a cup of tea?"

Saint jerked his chin toward the kitchen door, where Daya was watching us through the small window, signaling that it was time for Griff to leave. He disappeared through it a moment later without protest and didn't return.

"Seems I've misplaced some of my inventory," Zola continued. "Just before you left Dern, which one might call quite a coincidence."

"Lot of that goin' around." Clove leveled his gaze at him.

Zola smirked. He wasn't even going to pretend to deny stealing the gems off the *Riven*. "I suppose that can happen when things are off the books."

"What do you want, Zola?" Saint finally spoke, that deep, smooth calm lacing his voice.

Zola pulled out the chair at the table beside him and sat

with his feet flat on the ground, his knees wide. He tapped the license against his knee. "I'd like you to return my dredger," he said.

"Go ahead and ask her. If she wants to go back to the *Luna*, there's nothing stopping her." Still, Saint didn't move from his spot in front of me.

"I'm afraid it's not that simple." He pulled another parchment from his jacket. This one was folded into a small rectangle and when I saw the blot of ink at one corner, I swallowed hard.

A lopsided grin surfaced on Zola's lips. He opened it, holding it in the air. "We have a contract."

Saint's body stilled in front of me, his shoulders drawing down his back as Clove took the three steps to Zola and snatched the document from nis fingers. His eyes skipped over the words written on the parchment before they raised to me. That one look made the last bit of warmth drain from my body.

"It's true," Zola said.

Clove didn't contradict him.

"It's not valid." I stepped forward, taking the contract from Clove and tossing it onto the table.

"It became valid the moment I was given that license. Now every contract I have is governed by the Trade Council and its laws."

I waited for Saint to correct him, but he said nothing. The muscle in his jaw clenched as he watched Zola from the top of his gaze.

"She's either crew or she's inventory. Which is it?" Clove asked.

"Both. For the sake of my coffers, she's inventory. For the sake of the Trade Council's eyes, she's crew."

The contract had just been a way for him to cover his bases, but it was also the thing that would chain me to his ship. If anyone suspected what he was up to, he had a crew's contract to prove I was just a dredger. But when he delivered me to Oliver Durant, he'd need the courier's agreement from Simon in order to get paid. There was no telling how many gem sages Simon had sold that way.

"The name on that contract is Eryss, and she doesn't even exist," I said.

"And would you like to explain that to the Council, or should I?"

Slowly, his point began sinking in, making sense where it hadn't before.

"More than one member of my crew will tell them they know you as Eryss. You can prove them wrong, if you'd like, but the next question they will ask is who you really are."

Somehow, Zola had finally worked it out for himself.

"I put two and two together when the traders in the harbor started asking around for Holland's runaway daughter. I never would have let you on my ship if I'd known I was crossing the single most dangerous merchant in the Unnamed Sea."

I stared at him.

"You've gotten me into quite a mess, Isolde. The least you could do is ensure I get the coin I'm supposed to trade you for."

I could see the smooth exterior of Saint's face cracking slowly. He hadn't expected this. Of course he hadn't.

"She's a thief, you know," Zola continued.

Saint gritted his teeth. "She can't steal what doesn't belong to you. Those gems were mine."

"I'm not talking about the red beryls, Saint." His eyes darted to me. "Don't tell me you haven't told him."

Gooseflesh woke on my skin again, making me shiver. He knew about the midnight too. Somehow, he knew.

"She's a problem you don't need to have. Trust me." Zola sighed. "Hand her back over to me and we'll pretend this never—"

"No," Saint said, not even a beat of hesitation before he cut Zola off.

The sound of him saying it took the breath from my lungs, and it was only then I could admit that I'd been afraid he would agree. That he'd cut his losses as soon as he realized I hadn't been completely honest with him.

"Do you have any idea what she's cost me?" Zola's voice grated.

"I don't care." Saint snatched his jacket from the back of the chair, pulling it on. "There's nothing you can do. You're bound by the same laws that I am now. You lift a hand against me, and the Trade Council will feed that license to the flames."

The way Zola's eyes narrowed told me he knew Saint was right. He couldn't just take me. Not without the Trade Council getting involved.

"You're making a mistake," Zola warned. "I'll have this reported in a matter of hours. And then the Council will be hauling you in for poaching a contracted dredger from my crew."

"We'll see."

Zola sat there motionless for the length of a breath before he stood, his hand curling tightly around the parchment. "You're making trouble for both of us now."

"Maybe."

Zola got to his feet, the bloom of red creeping up from the collar of his jacket. He was angry. Furious.

"That's not all I heard in Sowan." He took his time with the words. "I know about that pretty crofter and her daughter. The one who's selling you the rye. And I know about that ship you've got sitting in a pier in Dern."

The collected demeanor Saint had managed to maintain was gone in an instant. Rage was now rolling off of him in thick waves. It filled the room, palpable in the air. This was getting out of hand. Fast.

"Look—" I said, stepping out from behind Saint.

"Don't . . . say . . . a word." Saint's deep voice made me swallow. He didn't look at me. I wasn't sure he ever would again. "You're not going anywhere near that croft." He turned his attention back to Zola.

"I'm not?"

"No," Clove answered. "Because if you do, we won't just cut your throat and dump you somewhere you won't wash up on shore. We'll sail that ship of yours out into the deepest waters with you and your crew on it." He took another step forward. "And we'll set fire to it before we watch from the *Aster* as each of you chooses which way to die."

A sick feeling bled through me looking between Clove and Saint. They meant it. Every word.

Zola's eyes found me again. "I think you got a little more than you bargained for, didn't you, darling?" He stood, coat swaying around him again.

When I didn't answer, he gave Saint another smile and turned on his heel, pacing back through the tavern. In the next moment, he was gone.

Saint and Clove stood silent, the sound of water dripping somewhere in the tavern the only sound.

"Get that idiot up," Saint grunted, jerking a chin toward the stairs that led to the room where Nash was still sleeping. "And tell Griff nothing. Better to keep him out of it. We'll meet you there."

"Where?" I asked, looking between them.

"You're not really in a position to be asking questions." The cold tenor of Saint's tone made me go rigid. He buttoned up his jacket, staring at the floor between us. "Go."

I obeyed, walking straight for the door and thinking that any minute, Zola would appear on the other side with his knife drawn. But Saint was right. He couldn't touch us. Not yet.

As soon as I stepped onto the street, the door shut behind us and I sucked in a breath. "Saint . . ."

"*Don't.*" The word was so heavy, so final, that it felt like a stone in my chest.

He started up the walk without another word and I followed, staring at the seam of his jacket that ran down the center of his back. His broad shoulders pulled beneath the fabric, rising with each deep breath, as we snaked through the crowds in the opposite direction of the harbor.

We didn't take the bridges. Too easy to be spotted, I guessed. Instead, we zigzagged through the streets until I was so dizzy that nausea roiled in my belly. The alleyways grew narrower with each step until we were dumped into a pocket of buildings crammed so tightly together that the sunlight barely hit the ground beneath our feet.

Faces peered out from dark windows, the stench of rot and refuse thick in the air.

"What is this place?" I whispered, catching a pair of eyes in a darkened window.

He kept walking, not bothering to be sure I kept pace with him.

"Elias," I said, using the name he'd given me in Dern. The one he was born with.

His steps faltered just slightly, slowing. "Somewhere no one comes looking," he answered. "The Pinch."

TWENTY-SIX

SAINT

Daylight was the only reason we were still breathing.

The rain began to fall as the Pinch swallowed us up into its belly and we pushed farther into the tangle of winding veins that made up its suffocating corridors. There were more people living in this pocket of a neighborhood than the whole of North Fyg, each building stacked with flats that held several families whose mothers or fathers worked at the docks or out at sea. It was children, mostly. And they were the most loyal creatures in any village or city.

If Zola had come to the tavern earlier, before the sun rose, I wasn't sure that the threat of the Trade Council's retribution would have kept him from drawing blood. But in the daylight, there were eyes to see your sins. He knew that. And only hours after getting his trade license, he wasn't going to risk it.

The feel of Isolde at my back was like a looming shadow as we walked. I didn't speak because I wasn't sure I had anything to say. Not yet. She'd had the chance to tell me the truth. I'd given her my trust, even if she'd done little to earn it. And as we made the last turn into the dead end of a circular opening of cobblestone, I knew I'd made a huge mistake. The question was, what was I going to do about it?

A blue-painted door was set into the white sandstone, barely hanging on its hinges. There was no need to lock it, other than the fact that a locked door in the Pinch was the only sign that a place had been claimed.

I could feel the eyes of the Pinch watching as I pulled the key from my pocket.

"Saint." Isolde's voice was careful.

"Not here," I said, glancing up to the windows over our heads.

I trusted the kids in the Pinch to keep an eye on this door. But I didn't need them listening.

She fell quiet as I fit the key into the lock and let the door swing open before us. The bare flat was dark, the storm clouds rolling in over the city and snuffing out the sunlight. The sound of the rain dripping came down the stairs from the broken windows on the second floor.

I waited for her to step inside before I followed, locking the door behind us.

The flat was part of a trade we'd made when we first left

Cragsmouth, and one day it would serve as the post for our trading outfit, away from the prying eyes of the merchants and the Saltbloods. No one came to the Pinch unless they had to, and the copper we pressed into palms on these streets ensured that anyone who did come looking wouldn't find this place.

I opened my jacket, letting the air cool my damp skin. It wasn't just the humid rain making me sweat. It was Isolde. That softness that had been there between us that morning was gone now, making me feel like there was a rope tightening around my chest. I'd been the worst kind of fool. And now I was going to pay for it.

I sat on the ledge of the window, crossing one foot over the other before I finally let my eyes land on her. The night before, I hadn't been able to stop myself from touching her, but now I was afraid to even think it.

She stood across the dusty room with her hands tucked into the pockets of her jacket, her newly cut hair falling in a diagonal line around her face. In the shadows it almost looked like the deepest shade of brown, but when the light touched it, it glowed like garnet.

"You need to start talking," I said coldly. "Now."

"I should have told you," she said, the words stumbling into one another. "I know I should have told you."

"Yes, you should have." My words grated, but they didn't sound nearly as angry as I felt. I was even more furious with myself than I was with her. "I wouldn't have let you on the *Riven* if I'd known you had a contract."

"Is that true?" she asked.

I let out a long breath, pinching the bridge of my nose. There was a headache gathering between my eyes. "I don't know," I admitted. "I hope so."

If this was as simple as a crew contract, there would be no question. No hesitation. The laws that governed the Trade Council were clear, and anyone who wanted to keep their license would obey them. But this girl was anything but simple. She was a gem sage. The daughter of a powerful merchant. And she'd given Zola the one thing that ensured he could control her.

"Zola wasn't bluffing. He'll report the broken contract to the Trade Council because he knows you won't tell them who you really are. And no matter where we make port next, there will be a summons waiting."

"So what are we going to do? Just hide here?"

"You have a better idea?" I snapped. "They can't deliver a summons to us if they don't know where we are. Leaving port will only mean we're stranded out there on the water."

She pushed the wet hair back from her face, pressing her palms to her reddened cheeks.

"As soon as I show my face, that summons will find me. And when I go to the Trade Council, they'll demand consequences for poaching you from Zola. Everything I've done, everything I've worked for"—my voice rose—"will be for nothing."

"Then I'll go to them myself. Tell them what Zola was going to do. I'll tell them he's running gem sages and—"

"If you do that, you'll just put blood in the water. You think he's the only trader smuggling gem sages? You might as well go to the merchant's house and put yourself on an auction block."

"Either the Council upholds the law, or they don't. Which is it?"

I let out a heavy breath. "There's a difference between what happens in the Trade Council Chamber and what happens behind closed doors. Guild masters live by their own rules."

She threw her hands up. "What does that even mean? You just make them up as you go?"

You. That was what this was about. The Narrows. Us. The people who lived in this backwater.

I stood up off the window. "Don't do that. Don't act like where you come from is any better."

"I'm not."

"The Unnamed Sea has its own poison. They're the ones who made us into this."

"Into what?"

I shook my head. "You don't understand."

"Then help me to!"

"You can't!" I nearly laughed. "You'll never understand how things work here because you're not *one* of us! You're one of them. All you know how to do is *take.*"

The words were like a blunt blade pressed to the skin. I wasn't sure I even believed them. It was more that I didn't want them to be true. I wanted her to prove me wrong. To tell me whatever she'd left out of the story last night in the tavern. But as we stood there staring at each other in the empty flat, no explanation left her lips. And I wasn't going to ask her for it. Not again.

Isolde's hands fell to her sides heavily. She went quiet, the fire going out of her eyes. "I know you didn't ask for this when you agreed to help me leave Dern or when you offered me a place on this crew. I lied to protect myself and now you're paying the price for that."

I didn't argue with her. "I'm not the only one who could pay," I said, thinking of Emilia and Hazel. Of the promise I'd made that my trouble wouldn't find her door. "If anything happens to them . . ." The darkness of the thought strangled my voice, swallowing my ability to say it out loud.

"What do you want me to do? I'll do it."

My jaw clenched painfully. "I want you to go back in time and not walk into the tavern that night." That, I did mean. With every drop of blood in my veins.

The thrum of the rain was louder now, a distant flash of lightning illuminating her face as the set of her mouth slanted just slightly. Her gray eyes were like glass.

I'd been a ship with a steady course since I left Cragsmouth. I'd known exactly what lay ahead because I'd been willing to do anything to make it happen. But Isolde and whatever she was running from in Bastian was the first thing that had ever made me feel like it was slipping from my fingers. It didn't matter if I had a trade license or a route or a map of the Narrows. What was the point of any of it if there was something that could take it all away from me?

I stood there, waiting for her to say something and also hoping she wouldn't. I didn't want the sound of her voice to conjure that thing in me that had been there in the dark the night before. I didn't want any more reasons to talk myself out of leaving her there in the Pinch and setting sail for Dern, where the *Aster* waited.

I walked past her, to the stairs, and climbed them to the empty second floor, where the windows faced the only small bit of sea visible from this part of the city. I could barely see it now, cloaked in sheets of rain.

That horizon had once felt endless to me. Like a never-ending expanse of possibilities. But our world was shrinking: The Narrows. Our ship. Our crew. Our trade. It was never supposed to be anyone but me and Clove. There was no future outside of the one our fathers had dreamed for us.

Now, Isolde was like a pebble dropped in the shallows, changing the shape of everything on the surface. And the moment I'd kissed her had been a nail in that coffin.

TWENTY-SEVEN

ISOLDE

Nash wasn't happy about trading his cage on the *Riven* for one in the Pinch. He and Clove had arrived by afternoon and Saint's orders were to stay put. If Zola hadn't shown up that morning, we'd be on our way to Dern and Nash would be headed back to the shipwright, his sins absolved. But if Zola had gone to the Trade Council, Saint's enemies were multiplying by the minute.

Hiding out in the Pinch wasn't a solution. It just delayed the inevitable. A summons was coming, but it could only be answered once it was received. And no one was going to come looking in a place like this for a newly licensed helmsman.

The rain kept falling, filling the streets with little rivers that forked and came together in the cracks. Darkness fell before the sun had, the sky hidden away by the storm that descended on the city. A wedge of cheese and loaf of bread Daya had sent with Clove were torn into pieces on the small table, but not even Nash had touched it. No one had a stomach for food when we were waiting for an axe to fall.

Clove sat at the top of the staircase, his knife raking down the length of a piece of wood. The shavings were piled at his feet, his head tilted to one side as he focused. Saint hadn't come down since he'd told me that he wished he had never met me.

I climbed the stairs and sat down a few steps below Clove, pulling my knees up to my chest and hugging them to me. The map case was lying on the floor behind him, along with my dredging belt he'd brought from the tavern.

"Sure made a mess of things, dredger," Clove said, eyes still on his knife. But the words weren't cutting or accusatory. They even had a slight edge of amusement to them.

"I know," I said.

There wasn't much Clove seemed to take seriously, and I wondered if it was his nature or if he'd seen enough of the world to understand just how little control he had over any of it. It was a painful lesson I was beginning to learn.

I leaned forward until I could see through the open doorway behind him, where Saint stood at the window, arms crossed over his chest as he watched the rain. I wasn't sure if he'd even moved from that spot since he came up here.

"What's he doing?" I asked, keeping my voice low.

"He's thinking."

Clove's eyes met mine only for a moment, but they held

his meaning. Saint wasn't just thinking. He was deciding. Deciding what to do with me.

"There's not much to figure out. The Trade Council will require me to return to the *Luna* or they'll take that license they gave you."

"Yes, they will."

I was glad Clove wasn't pretending like there was an answer to this problem. That wouldn't do anyone any good.

"So, what's there to think about?"

"He doesn't like other people making decisions for him. If I had to guess, he's trying to work out how he can still set his own course instead of having it set for him."

"Isn't that what the Trade Council does?"

"I'm not talking about them."

My eyes snapped up to meet his. "Me?"

"You," he said. He dragged the knife down the wood once more before he abandoned it, setting his elbows on his knees. "There aren't enough adder stones in the Narrows to ward off the kind of trouble you'll bring us."

"Not if I go back to the *Luna*."

He shook his head. "It's not the kind of trouble that can come and go, I'm afraid." He smirked. "You're crew."

"I'm not crew."

"You are. And not the kind that disappears at port or finishes out a contract before jumping ship. Somehow, I'm the only one who's figured out that the moment we raised anchor in Dern a decision was being made. One we can't go back on."

"I don't know what you mean."

Clove hesitated, studying me before he spoke again. "It's not just the two of us anymore." He was missing that bitter charm now. He was worried.

"My choices are my own. He's not responsible for what happens to me. Neither are you."

"Maybe. But Saint's good at paying penance, taking the blame. That's his way."

I wished I didn't understand what he meant by that.

Clove picked up the knife again, going back to the wood, and I realized that he wasn't shaping it into anything. He was just keeping his hands busy. Passing the time as he waited for Saint to come away from that window.

I'd figured out pretty quickly that there was more to Saint than the stories about a boy from nowhere who seemed determined to die in a storm. He wasn't the fearless helmsman the Narrows thought he was. In fact, I was sure now that it was fear that drove him into those black clouds.

My eyes fell to the map case on the floor, its worn, smooth leather softened by Saint's hands. He wasn't just afraid of losing everything he'd worked for. He *was* the Narrows. And if it died, he would too.

I got back to my feet, stepping past Clove and picking up the case. Saint didn't turn to look at me as I came through the door. The little room was nothing but dusty floorboards and a pane of cracked glass that looked out over the rooftops. I could see the reflection of his face in it, but his eyes didn't leave that view.

I reached into my pocket for the purse, pulling the cinched strings open. When the gem rolled into my fingers, it felt heavier than it ever had.

"I might not be one of you, but I'm not one of them either," I breathed. "I never was. That's why I came here. Why I can't go back."

I set the midnight down on the windowsill beside him and the dim light caught the glassy edges of the stone. He looked at it, not moving.

"I've been diving for my mother since I was ten years old. For a long time, I didn't care what the gems I was bringing up in those crates meant, as long as she was pleased with me. But the older I got, the more I could see that look in her eyes and the more I couldn't deny that it wasn't the gem sage dredger daughter she wanted. She only loved the coin I could put in her pocket." I swallowed hard. "I found the stone by accident. We weren't even on a dive. And as soon as Holland laid eyes on it, I knew I'd made a mistake. For the first time, I was truly afraid of her and without even deciding to, I lied to her about where it came from."

"What is it?" Saint asked, picking it up carefully.

"Midnight," I answered.

"I've never heard of it."

"Because it doesn't exist. Not yet. It was the haul that was going to make my mother the only god to rule the Unnamed Sea and the Narrows. But I couldn't let that happen. So, I stole it, like Zola said. And I ran."

Understanding lit in Saint's eyes as he turned the gem

over in his hands. "So, she's not looking for you. She's looking for this?"

"Both, I imagine. She's not giving up her gem sage so easily. Not when I've made her rich."

He finally looked at me.

"She killed my father when he tried to protect me from her." Saying it out loud made the pain of it drive deeper inside me. "And I decided the only way to punish her was to take back everything I'd helped her build. I came to Ceros to give this to the Gem Guild master," I said, gesturing to the midnight. "I thought that there would be no better justice than to see her fall beneath the Narrows. But she's always one step ahead of everyone else. And when I went to the chamber, she was already there."

"What do you mean?"

"Her control. Her influence. The Gem Guild master is already in her pocket. And he's probably not the only one."

He didn't look surprised at that.

I drew in a steadying breath. "You said you saw a future for the Narrows."

"I do."

"If you're ever going to see it come true, then you can't be like them."

"I know that."

I let the map case slide from my shoulder and opened it. "You won't beat the Unnamed Sea with gems. They'll always have more—reefs, stones, merchants. But you can use their own power against them."

The parchment slid from the case into my hands, and I unrolled its edge until I could see the sprawling cluster of reef chain he'd painted there. I pointed to it.

"This is how you do it."

I had his attention now. He took one side of the map to hold it open. "Tempest Snare?"

I nodded. "If what Zola said is true, there are dozens of ships wrecked in those reefs, many of them from the Unnamed Sea."

"There are. I've seen them."

"Then there's no telling what lies in their hulls."

Saint's face turned toward me and the memory of him standing that close in the dark the night before came back to life in my mind.

"No one will sail those waters because they're afraid. But if you can map the Narrows, you can map the Snare. And then all you have to do is take what you find."

I could see his mind turning with it, flitting from one thought and possibility to the next.

"Build a trading operation that doesn't rely on the merchants in Ceros. Flood the Narrows with coin and the traders from the Unnamed Sea will begin to lose their grip on the guilds. Once that happens . . ."

"Everything else follows," he finished.

I nodded.

His jaw clenched. "I would need a dredger if we're going to dive Tempest Snare."

"Map it, and when I'm done with my contract on the

Luna, I'll dredge it for you. Every single reef."

He thought about that. "You might not have a choice. If you go back to Zola, he's just going to sell you to Oliver Durant."

"I'll make sure that doesn't happen."

"How?"

I let the map roll closed in my hands. "I can make that bastard more coin dredging than Durant was going to pay him. If I show him that, I can change his mind."

Saint didn't look convinced. I wasn't either, to be honest.

"You'll come back?" he asked.

"If you still want me."

He moved so close that when he looked down into my face, the tip of his nose was inches from mine. "I've wanted you since the minute I saw you. That's the problem, Isolde."

My heartbeat skipped behind my ribs, shortening my breath.

"What do *you* want?" he whispered.

The question made me feel like the rain outside was filling my lungs. This thing between us was like the creaking lines that held the bowing masts of the *Riven.* At any moment, they were going to snap.

I didn't know where we fit together or how. I just knew that we did. Like some tide had carried me from Bastian to that tavern in Dern. Like fate had set me squarely in his path and him in mine. This trader who sailed into storms and spoke to the sea, who'd bound himself to demons, was the first soul who'd ever asked me what I wanted. And the answer was, somehow, so easy to give. I wanted *him*. But it was more than that.

"I want to build something that's not theirs."

"All right," he said. "Then we will."

TWENTY-EIGHT

ᛁSOLDE

"Take us through it."

Saint sat on the edge of the table, facing me and Clove, but they both had their eyes on me.

There was no question that the summons was coming. If the guild masters in Ceros were anything like the ones in the Unnamed Sea, they wouldn't stand for crew poaching. What Saint and Clove did once they *got* the summons was the only question.

"Zola's charge against you will be heard by the Council," I began, "then the summons will be circulated to the harbor masters. Whichever one finds your ship first will collect a payment from the Council in exchange for a report detailing its delivery. From there, you have two days to show at the chamber and face the charge."

Clove's expression was grave, making me feel even more unsettled. He was usually the one making light of a bad situation, but with this, the stakes were too high. It could sink them. "And what will that look like? The charge."

"The Trade Council will hold a formal gathering and invite any guild members who want to attend."

"Why would they want to do that?"

"Lots of reasons. Tracking allegiances and vendettas. Using what they can to get what they want. Recruiting a slighted trader for their own schemes. Covering their tracks. They like to keep tabs on what kind of trouble the traders are getting into and what they can use against other merchants. They can also hold sway over the guild masters who sit on the Trade Council and what they decide."

"I thought the purpose of the Trade Council was to bring order to all of this," Clove muttered. "Sounds like it's just more trouble."

"There's always trouble where there's power to be gained or traded," I said, thinking of my mother.

It was exactly the kind of work she did to climb the rungs of the guilds in the Unnamed Sea. I had no doubt that eventually she'd be sitting on the Trade Council as the Gem Guild master.

"Once the charge has been presented, they'll ask for the evidence against you."

"The contract," Saint thought aloud.

I nodded. "I'll be questioned and asked to explain why I broke the agreement."

"I still don't understand why you can't just tell the truth." Nash's voice drifted down the stairs. I hadn't thought he was listening, but I was beginning to wonder if he always was. "The bastard was going to sell you. Seems justified to me."

"No," Saint said lowly. "The Trade Council's protection doesn't extend beyond the helmsmen who hold their trade licenses to their crews. If we tell them what she is, every crooked trader in Ceros will be lined up behind Zola to sell her to someone else the minute the Council turns its back."

"Better to stay Eryss for now," Clove added.

"We aren't the only ones with leverage, anyway," I said. "Zola knows about your fake gem trade in the rye bottles and who you got those bottles from in the first place. You accuse him of smuggling a gem sage and he'll just make sure they know your hands are dirty too."

"Then what do we do?" Clove asked.

"The Council will demand that I return to the *Luna*."

"And if you don't?"

"They'll take your trade license," I said, not mincing words. That was the bottom line and there was no getting around it. "I'm all but certain they will want to make an example of you. Especially with the Unnamed Sea watching their every move."

Saint and Clove looked at each other. Losing the license wasn't an option.

"As long as I return to the *Luna*, there's nothing to worry about. You'll be dismissed with a fine and you can go back to Dern, get the *Aster*, and set sail."

I kept my voice even. I'd accepted my fate the minute Zola sat down in that chair at Griff's Tavern. I'd signed the contract, even if it wasn't my name. There was no getting around it. And in that moment, I hadn't cared. I'd only wanted to cut my mother's legs from beneath her. But as I stood there in the flat, watching the shadows move over the floor, there was no denying that I hadn't even scratched the surface of her reach. She wasn't a tree I could cut down myself. She was a never-ending web of roots beneath the ground.

"The merchant." Nash's voice broke the silence again, followed by his footsteps on the stairs.

"What merchant?" Saint looked up at him.

"The one who was going to buy you from Zola. What was his name?"

The man's face from the portrait resurfaced in my mind. "Oliver," I answered. "Oliver Durant."

Nash leaned into the wall, crossing one foot over the other. "Then you *do* have something."

"I don't have the courier agreement. It's still on the *Luna*."

"He doesn't know that."

Saint's attention drifted back to me, his mind turning with the thought. It wasn't enough. The Trade Council would require evidence.

"Even if we had it, it's not proof. The order was for Nimsmire silks," I said.

Nash shrugged. "Anyone who digs into the ship's inventory will find out that bastard wasn't carrying silks.

And Simon's name is known in the Narrows for his gem sage business."

A piece of information that would have been helpful before I went to him for help, I thought.

"Might be enough to at least get someone curious. You don't have to report him and risk her being found out. It's enough for him to know you *could* if you wanted to."

"Smashing heads with rye bottles. Scheming against the Trade Council." Clove surveyed Nash with a look that bordered on impressed. "Not so useless after all, are you?"

"Just trying to earn my keep," Nash quipped, giving him a wink.

He was right about the merchant. Having that information was valuable, whether Saint used it now or saved it for a rainy day.

"It still won't change the fact that I'm going back to the *Luna*," I said, making sure it hadn't given Saint any ideas.

"I know," he said.

Clove looked between us. "Guess it's about time I make a trip to the harbor master, then. The summons should already be waiting."

Saint nodded.

There was no point in delaying the inevitable. The longer the Council was looking for Saint, the more suspicious they would be. Especially when his ship was still anchored in Ceros.

"Come on." Clove got to his feet with a groan, jerking his chin toward Nash.

"Me?"

"This city is crawling with Zola's crew. Someone's gotta cover my back."

Nash sighed, snatching his jacket from the hook.

They disappeared out the door a moment later, leaving Saint and me standing in the empty flat alone. His fingers tapped his elbow, his eyes on the cold hearth across the room.

"You don't like being on land, do you?" I asked.

"No."

"Why not?"

He considered his answer, taking his time. "The sea's a lot more honest than people are."

I couldn't argue with that. But I couldn't say the same was true about Saint. He wasn't like other people. The weight of his presence was like a leak on a ship, slowly filling its hollow spaces.

"I meant what I said. I'll come back and help you dredge the Snare."

It wasn't just because I wanted to see my mother fall anymore. It was about the helmsman standing in front of me. It was about that dark gleam in his eyes. The way he said exactly what he meant. If there was a future for the Narrows, he was it. And that was a future for me too.

"I know you will," he said.

I took a step toward him, and this time, I didn't wait for him to kiss me. I lifted up onto my toes and took his face in my hands before I pressed my mouth to his and breathed him in. His arms came around me, fingers finding the skin beneath the hem of my shirt, their warmth flooding into me as they drifted up my back. He kissed me deeper, leaning into me until we were moving backward, across the floor.

He laid me down on the bare cot and I pulled him closer, tugging the shirt over his head so that I could press my hands flat against his ribs, his chest. I said a kind of goodbye that didn't need words or promises or plans.

I couldn't change that night in my mother's study or the path I'd walked to Simon's. I couldn't go back and erase my signature from that contract with Zola. But I could cast my lot alongside Saint's and know that there was something true in it. Because there was. The hum in the air that hovered around us. The calm that settled in my blood when he touched me. The feeling that we were only the beginning of a story that would be told long after we were gone. They were things I could take with me.

A year was nothing if it let me come back to *this*.

TWENTY-NINE

SAINT

The cold that lived in my bones was gone for the first time since I left Cragsmouth.

Isolde slept soundly beside me, despite the fact that she'd face the Trade Council when she woke. She hadn't so much as blinked when she realized there was no way out of it, and I'd half expected her to disappear, slipping out into the night and back to wherever she'd come from. But I was learning that even though she'd left Bastian and her life behind, she wasn't the running kind.

Her hair fell across her cheek, hiding the trail of freckles that crested her cheekbone, and her breath was so soft that I could hardly hear it over the sound of the rain and Nash's snoring upstairs. Even Clove had managed to close his eyes for a rare few hours of uninterrupted sleep. But I hadn't been able to let go of the image of Isolde sleeping beside me, one hand curled against her chest. If she was leaving, I was going to remember it.

The bare cot was draped with a few unraveling quilts and we'd lain there watching the raindrops streak down the window without talking until her breaths pulled long and deep. This girl who'd dropped onto the *Riven* dragging a sea of demons behind her felt like the only unmoving thing. A point on the tilting horizon.

I'd never been given anything, not even from my father. He'd believed in earning. Making myself worthy of something. But I was painfully aware that there was nothing I could do to merit that feeling of warmth at my side. And I wouldn't pretend to.

Carefully, I reached over Isolde's sleeping frame and into the pocket of her jacket for the purse that she kept hidden there. The leather had been worn smooth by her fingers, and the stone's weight was heavy in my hand. I opened it, letting the stone roll into my palm, and I held it to the moonlight. Violet ribbons danced, suspended in the almost-opaque black gem, like a flicker of fire frozen in time.

This one small stone had tipped the balance of Isolde's life until she was tumbling into mine. It was a thing that could build cities or burn them. Make kings or slay them. And I could feel the weight of it the moment she had shown it to me.

There was that thing in me, too. That voice that said that this gem in my hand could mend every unraveling thing—my ship, my debt to Henrik, my trading operation. Bastian, the Trade Council, the Narrows. If there were ever a broken oil lamp just waiting to catch flame, this was it. And I'd never had that kind of power within reach before.

I sat up slowly, letting my arm slip from beneath Isolde's still body. Her face turned to the moonlight as I stood, and my hand closed over the gem tightly until I could feel its points against the tender healing skin of my palm. She'd trusted me with it, but she shouldn't have. Isolde saw the almost-man trying to build a ladder he could climb. She didn't know I'd made that ladder with the bones of the dead.

The door barely creaked as I closed it behind me and stepped out into the alley. The rain was finally beginning to let up and the city was quiet with a calm that only existed in Ceros in the middle of the night. Tomorrow would come with its own worries and problems, but for now, the stars were stretched out across the black skies as brightly as they were on Emilia's croft.

I could feel that warmth I'd left with Isolde pull away from me as I started up the alley, and when a pair of eyes found me in the dark, I pulled a copper from my belt.

As soon as the moonlight hit it, a small boy stepped out from the shadows, his trousers rolled up at the ankles to reveal muddy bare feet. His black hair was wet and curling into ringlets over his eyebrows, as if it had been trimmed just enough for him to see. He blinked once before he looked up at me.

"I want you to sit up in that window." I pointed overhead. "Anyone besides me comes to that door, and I want every bastard in the Pinch to draw their knife."

The boy nodded.

"If you're still there when I get back, I'll have another copper for you."

He snatched the coin from my fingers and scurried away into the black. The sound of his bare feet slapping in the mud disappeared around the corner and I watched the window that looked out over the street until I saw his face appear behind the fogged glass.

I took the bridges toward the merchants' district for the first time. Now that I had a trade license, it wouldn't be the last. There would be deals to strike, contracts to negotiate, and investments to be made if we were going to take the Narrows back, like Clove said. I had a feeling I'd come to know these streets well. Better than I wanted to.

It only took three coppers to find out where the man I was looking for lived. That was the problem with these coin-rich fools. They'd forgotten they had something to fear.

The door of the gray stone house was painted red and set with a brass knocker that was cast in the shape of a ship's helm. On either side, green velvet curtains were pulled closed behind the window glass, but the glow of candlelight seeped between the panels. In another few minutes, the sun would rise over the water, and the house would begin to stir.

I reached up, taking hold of the knocker and rapping three times, more loudly than was necessary in case the bastard wasn't awake yet. The flit of light behind the curtains moved and footsteps shuffled behind the door before it was yanked open. On the other side, a young woman in an apron looked up at me with wide eyes.

"May I"—her gaze raked over me—"help you?"

"I'd like to see the merchant."

"At this hour?"

"He'll want to see me," I said, keeping my hands in my pockets. The stone was still clutched in my fist like a coal fished from the fire.

The woman was wary, and she should have been. She was probably the only person in the house with the sense to be worried.

She stared at me for another moment. "Wait here."

I caught the door with my hand, holding it open. "Tell him it's regarding those silks he's expecting."

When I let go, the bolt locked and the footsteps trailed away, leaving me standing on the street alone. In the distance, the shops of the merchants' district were beginning to show signs of life. The sound of water being poured into the street, a door scraping over the cobblestones. The pale light of morning was creeping into the city by the time the door opened again.

This time, the woman stepped aside to let me in. "May I take your jacket?" she asked, stumbling over the words. I doubted there was decorum for a meeting like this.

"No. I'm not staying long."

Inside, the smell of baking bread and sizzling pork was already in the air. The candles at the top of the stairs were lit, illuminating the shadows of the house as the sun slowly made its way up the sky.

The woman set a hand on the carved wooden banister and began to climb. "Follow me."

I took the steps behind her, eyes roaming over the gilded-framed paintings that hung on the walls. Scenes of the rye fields, the cliffs. Ships in the harbor. It was a version of the Narrows that wouldn't exist much longer if Oliver Durant had his way.

A door at the end of the hallway was open and candlelight reflected on a glass case inside. I stopped in front of the threshold, examining the room. It was a study, the walls fitted with shelves that held books and leather folders and mullein boxes. The wood floor was covered by a handwoven rug edged in gold tassels. Nothing that could have been made here in Ceros, and that was the sum of all I needed to know about the man who sat behind the ornately carved desk.

Oliver Durant.

His wide face was wreathed in a thick beard that was too white for his apparent age. His hair was neatly combed, his tailored vest buttoned closed as if he'd been up and at work on his ledgers before the sun rose. I was sure he had. He set his hands on the arms of his chair, watching me like he was half expecting me to draw my knife.

The woman motioned for me to enter and pulled the door closed behind me. But Oliver didn't take his eyes off me.

"And who the hell are you?"

I crossed the floor with patient steps, taking note of the room's contents. The table against the far wall was set with a gem lamp and several trays of newly cleaned stones. He was a gem merchant who'd decided he had need of a gem sage. Maybe to vet the stones he was buying or to be sure any fakes he traded passed muster. That, or he was like the merchants Henrik talked about, collecting sages to pick them off one by one. The fewer there were, the more power and security men like him held.

"My name is Saint," I said, taking the leather chair on the other side of the desk. I set one foot on the opposite knee, leaning back into it. The soles of my boots were still covered in mud, a detail that Oliver hadn't missed.

His eyes narrowed on me. "Where have I heard that name before?"

I turned the stone over in my pocket again. There was no telling. The merchant's house, the Trade Council, the tavern. I'd lost track of which stories had traveled where. I didn't care either.

"I have a problem, and you're going to fix it," I said.

"I have my own problems, I'm afraid."

"Yes, you do. Because I know about your gem sage trade."

He shifted in his seat, trying to keep his composure. But he was nervous, eyes darting around the room before they landed on me again. "So, you're here to squeeze me dry before you report the contract, is that it?"

"It doesn't serve my purposes for the Trade Council to know about your deal with Simon."

"Then you want me to turn on the courier? The *Luna*?"

"That won't help me either."

"Then what do you want, son?"

"To make a friend in the guild," I answered.

He scoffed, finally releasing his hands from his chair and folding them over the buttons of his vest. "I don't exactly make a habit of befriending people who threaten me."

"I'd reevaluate that if I were you. In another year you'll be begging the favor of traders like me."

Oliver's gaze sharpened, turning curious. "You're a trader."

"I am."

"Is this about a trade contract? Because I've got plenty of those to go around."

"It's about coin. Three hundred and fifty-six coppers, to be exact." It was the exact sum I would owe Henrik when I arrived in Dern.

"Copper," he repeated.

"That's right."

"Why didn't you say so? I've got plenty of that too."

I nodded. "I'll also need you to make sure the *Luna* doesn't secure any trade contracts with the Gem Guild. And I'm making you personally responsible for seeing that this little gem sage trade between the Narrows and the Unnamed Sea goes away. For good."

"I can't possibly—"

"You can. And you will. Or you'll lose that merchant's ring and any chance you had at moving up in the guild."

A tinge of red surfaced beneath his skin, his cheeks flushing over his beard. "How do you suggest I control every merchant in this city?"

"I think you'll figure it out." I set my foot on the ground, leaning forward. "And if you or anyone else touches that gem sage you had couriered from Bastian, I'll cut the tongue from your mouth and feed it to the seabirds. Then I'll tie you to the anchor and drag you over the nearest reef until the flesh is peeled back from your bones enough that no one in the Narrows will recognize you. You'll live the rest of your days in Waterside, begging for the rotten fish the ships can't sell on the docks."

He paled, swallowing hard.

"Do we have an understanding?"

"I believe we do." His voice cracked.

"Good." I got to my feet, taking the time to button my jacket.

Oliver pushed his chair back, pulling open a drawer in the chest behind him and retrieving a purse of coin from inside. He set it on the desk between us. "Is there a designated time frame for this little arrangement?"

"Yes," I said, picking up the purse and tucking it into my pocket. "For as long as it suits me."

I was smart enough to know my leverage would lose its weight with time, but there was no telling how long that would take. By then, I'd have found other ways to make Oliver Durant and the likes of the Gem Guild need me. I was sure of that.

He let out a heavy breath, standing from his chair, and he hesitated before he extended a hand. But I didn't take it. Instead, I turned on my heel, pacing back to the door.

"Happy to make your acquaintance, Mr. Durant." And I meant it.

It wasn't until I reached the stairs that I heard the fist slamming down onto the desk and the curse that followed. His husky voice was no more than a cracked whisper as I slipped back onto the street.

"Urchin *bastard!*"

THIRTY

ISOLDE

The first day of my year on the *Luna* began with birds singing.

I woke in the Pinch with the sunlight streaming through the window. The rain had finally broken during the night and the sea air swept through the city, bringing the sweet scent of a passing storm. I couldn't find it in me to be sad or to dread what was coming. There was too much hope in me for what would come after.

I spent the early hours studying Saint's map of Tempest Snare and making notes for him on a piece of parchment for which routes to try first through the jagged reefs. By the time I came back to him, he and Clove would be ready to dredge and we'd start turning over hauls in Ceros before anyone even knew what we were up to. We would keep them small and parsed out, not too much to draw attention, but in a few years' time, we'd be commissioning a fleet to sail alongside the *Aster*.

Saint came down the steps with one hand raking through his drying hair. His face was washed and his shirt was changed, but he still looked like he was taken right out of one of my father's old books about the sea myths. If he were here now, he'd say that the sea was in the helmsman's eyes.

A trail of mullein smoke drifted past the window, where Clove had a pipe clenched in his teeth. He'd been as quiet as Saint, getting up and dressed quickly before heading outside to wait.

"Ready?" I asked, standing from the stool and setting down the quill.

The map rolled closed in front of me and Saint eyed the notes I was making, turning the parchment so he could read them. He said nothing before his gaze lifted to me and he nodded.

I reached into my pocket and took out the purse of midnight, pressing it into his palm. His fingers closed over mine as the question lit in his eyes.

"Keep it for me?" I asked, swallowing against the lump in my throat.

Saint thought about it for a long moment, his hand still tightly holding mine. He looked unsure. Afraid of it, almost.

"Yeah," he said finally. "Until you come back."

"Thank you."

My voice took on the weight of the words, bending their

shape into something that was hard to say. I wasn't sure what exactly I was thanking him for. I was mostly just glad he existed. That I'd been lucky enough to find him.

His hand tightened on mine before he let it go, and he tucked the midnight into his jacket.

"See ya, dredger." Nash crossed his arms over his chest, watching me from across the room.

Saint had made it clear Nash wasn't invited to the Trade Council Chamber, and he'd looked almost relieved. If he could keep his head on another few days, he'd be back in Dern like the last two weeks had never happened.

He gave me a smile, but it wasn't one of his easy ones. "I'll see you next time you're in Dern?"

"You will." I held out my hand and he shook it. "Keep that mouth of yours shut and you might be able to keep from getting yourself killed."

The smile came more easily at that. "I'll try."

My hand slipped from his and Saint opened the door to the street, where two little boys were watching Clove like birds perched on a tree limb. He ignored them, taking one more drag of his pipe before he dumped it out and crushed the smoldering mullein beneath the heel of his boot.

We started for the bridges without a word, and the trapped dank heat of the Pinch bled away as we climbed the ladder. It was replaced by a brittle cold carried on the wind, a gust I imagined had come all the way from Bastian. I was one of thousands of faces in this city, I thought. I was no one. And I believed for the first time that it could stay that way.

The market was open and busy when we reached the Trade Council Chamber. The city was lost to its rhythms, and I found comfort in that. This summons, this charge against Saint, the contract I'd signed with Zola . . . they were just ripples. A fading light that would be followed by the same dawn that rose in the sky day after day.

I stopped in front of the door, Saint to my left and Clove to my right. "Can I tell you something?" I said, giving Saint a mischievous smile. "I'm glad I walked into the tavern that night."

But Saint didn't return it. He looked down into my face, eyes jumping back and forth on mine. "So am I."

Clove opened the door and the hum of voices came tumbling out. The hall that led to the chamber was empty, but as we made our way past the portraits of the guild members, the crowd came into view. The chamber was filled to the brim, making Saint's steps falter.

My eyes skipped over the long room, finding the Trade Council seated against the opposite wall.

Clove's deep voice was behind us. "It's the first charge brought against a Narrows-born trader. I guess no one wanted to miss that."

He was probably right. Ceros had its own laws and leaders now. The pomp and circumstance of seeing them in action would be a novelty for some time yet. And there wouldn't be a merchant in the city who didn't want to see the guild masters in action.

The voices died down as we wove through the crowd

and the whispers began, filling the corners of the huge room. I kept close to Saint, following behind him with Clove at my back, and when he made it to the center of the chamber, the Trade Council's eyes found him.

Across the tiled floor, Zola was already waiting. His black eyes were focused on me, the sneer on his lips revealing a slice of teeth. He'd done exactly what he said he would do, and the look on his face only confirmed that he knew he'd won.

Lander, the merchant from Sowan, was at his side. He watched Saint warily, cowering with his injured hand tucked into a sling across his chest as if he was afraid Saint would cross the space between the platforms and wrap his hands around his throat. I wouldn't have been surprised if he did.

The Gem Guild master's eyes sharpened on me when I stepped onto the platform beside Saint and he sat up straighter in his chair. He recognized me, and that would bring its own complications.

He surveyed me a moment before he leaned to one side, whispering into the ear of the woman beside him. But her attention stayed on the parchment open before her.

The heavy knock of a gavel bellowed through the room and, slowly, the whispers quieted into a soft murmur. The faces that surrounded us were here for the business of it, but they were also here for sport. The only ones who seemed utterly disinterested were Saint and Clove. But they'd have to learn to play this game eventually, and now was as good a time as any.

"Helmsman of the *Aster*." The man at the end of the table stood. "Please step forward."

For once, Saint obeyed. He lined his boots up with the edge of the platform, jaw ticking.

"A formal charge has been brought against you by the helmsman of the *Luna*, for poaching contracted crew." He pulled a slip of paper free, holding it in the air. "A dredger."

The whispers swelled again as the attention of the crowd found me, and I was instantly grateful that Daya had given me the clothes. For the first time, I blended in with them, no trace of the Unnamed Sea visible from the outside. The inside was a different matter.

"We have a witness here, a Lander . . ." He searched the page in his hands for the name.

"That won't be necessary," Saint said.

Across the room, Lander looked relieved. There was no telling what Zola had offered him to stand up there and speak against Saint. But anyone who looked at him could see he was terrified.

Edgar Moranton, the master of the Gem Guild, spoke next. "Do you have a response to this accusation, then?"

"I do not."

The first man sighed impatiently. "Well, is it true?"

"Yes." Saint's abrupt answer rippled through the room, the deep tenor of his voice hovering in the unnerving silence.

The guild masters who sat the table were all looking at him now. They didn't know this man who measured his words and bartered with their truth. No one did.

"I must say." Edgar fumbled with the parchment in his hands, chancing a look in my direction. "I am disappointed."

"When we said you'd have your pick of crew, this isn't exactly what we meant." The woman at the end folded her hands on the table. The bronze placard before her bore the seal of the Sailmakers Guild.

To that, Saint had no reply.

I stepped forward. "The contract was signed and broken by me and me alone. The helmsman of the *Aster* had no knowledge of it."

Saint stiffened beside me, his eyes finding my boots.

"Unfortunately, you're not the one who will pay for the mistake," the woman said, her words growing heavy. "The helmsman is responsible for his ship and his crew. He's the one who holds the trade license and is subject to the laws of this council."

"I'm prepared to provide restitution," Saint said, steering their attention back to him. He was going to make short work of this, and I was grateful. The longer I stood there, the more I felt the scrutinizing gazes of the merchants around me.

"Good." The man at the other end of the table nodded. "This should be rather simple, then. There will be a fine paid to this council in the amount of—"

"I'd like to purchase the contract," Saint interrupted.

I froze, sure I hadn't heard him right.

The man's fingers slipped from the parchment. "Purchase it?"

"That's right."

He looked down at the contract still unfolded in his hands, reading it over. "That's a lot of coin, son."

"I don't have any coin."

Behind Saint's back, Clove met my eyes, the crease in his brow so severe that it looked like it had been carved there with a knife. He was just as confused as I was.

The master of the Smiths Guild laughed. "Well, what exactly do you plan to purchase it with, then?"

Saint reached into his jacket and pulled a rolled parchment free, holding it at his side. It was tied in a rough twine, but the black ink at the edges of the paper was visible. I didn't recognize it.

It wasn't until I looked back to Clove that I realized the color had completely drained from his face.

"Saint," I whispered.

"A ship." Those two words were like quick strikes of lightning.

My pulse raced, making my head feel light. The platform beneath my feet suddenly seemed to be tilting.

There wasn't a single sound in the room now. That was the last thing anyone could have expected him to say.

"There's a pier in Dern, where a newly constructed schooner is anchored and waiting to set sail," Saint continued. "This is the deed."

The master of the Sailmakers Guild rose to her feet, leaning on the table with both hands. "A ship," she repeated. "For a dredger?"

Saint stared at her, letting his silence answer for him. He

wasn't just careful with his words. He didn't like repeating them either.

Across the room, no one looked more shocked than Zola. He shifted on his feet, his reddened face darkening by the minute.

"Saint," I tried again, keeping my voice low.

I reached for the sleeve of his jacket, but he ignored me, stepping off the platform and making his way to the Council's table. He handed the deed to the master of the Sailmakers Guild and she stared at him for a long moment before she opened it and read the words inked onto the page. When she was finished, her eyes flickered up to Edgar.

"It seems to be genuine," she said.

"This can't be . . ." Zola flung a hand at Saint. "I can't imagine you would allow such a ridiculous—"

"Are you telling us you don't think the worth of a ship covers the cost of a one-year contract with a dredger?" The woman cut him off.

"No, that's not what I'm saying." He spoke through gritted teeth.

"I want to be sure you understand the charge, sir," she began again, looking to Saint. "You've been accused of poaching a fellow trader's contracted dredger, the restitution for which is a fine of eight hundred coppers and the return of the dredger to the ship she's contracted to."

"I understand."

"But you want to purchase the contract instead? With an entire ship?"

"I think it's a fair offer."

"A bit more than fair, I'd say," she said, looking to Zola. "With the *Luna*, the *Aster* is the makings of a fleet. Is there any reason you find this offer deficient?"

"No," he growled.

"Then we have a deal." Saint turned to Zola, who appeared as if he were going to fall off the platform. He extended his hand.

Arguing further would only make the Council wonder what made me so valuable, and Zola wouldn't risk that. I hoped.

He swallowed hard before he stepped down to the floor and took Saint's hand, shaking. The crowd of merchants was already breaking up when the doors at the back of the room opened, and the Trade Council stood, gathering their books and papers.

I stood there, still frozen in place as Saint walked toward us, and then his hand was at my back, guiding me through the room. My breaths were coming too deep now. Too fast. The air was too hot.

It wasn't until the sunlight hit my face that I felt like I could begin putting together what exactly had just happened. "What the hell are you doing?" I whispered. "Go back and tell them you changed your mind. That you're not giving him the *Aster*."

"No" was his only reply.

I looked to Clove, expecting him to agree. But there was a shadow of a smirk on his lips now as he looked between us. He understood something here that I didn't.

"Did you mean it when you said you wanted to build something that's not theirs?" Saint asked, keeping his voice low. He met my eyes, waiting.

I let out a heavy breath. "Yes."

"So did I."

This time when I looked to Clove, he only shrugged. "He's the helmsman." That twinkle lit in his eye again.

"You're mad." I looked between them. "Both of you."

They didn't deny it. How could they?

Something shoved into me hard as a man shouldered past and a pain shot through my arm before I was being spun around. Zola's face was suddenly before me, his hands dragging me by the jacket into the flood of people headed into the market. We were slipping into the alley before I could even get my feet steady beneath me.

As soon as he let go, his fist flew back, coming down across my face. Light exploded around me, the deafening ring in my ears throwing me off-kilter until I tumbled back into the brick wall. I dropped to the ground, pressing a hand to my mouth. The taste of blood was already covering my tongue.

In the next moment, Saint and Clove had pressed through the crowd, Saint's knife drawn as he stalked toward Zola. Clove caught him by the jacket, wrenching him back before he could drive it into Zola's gut.

"Don't." Clove's voice was a resonant warning as he wedged himself between Saint and Zola. I could barely hear his words over the ringing in my ears. "You kill him, and everything you just did in there doesn't matter."

I wiped my lip with the sleeve of my jacket, getting back to my feet unsteadily. "He's right. Let it go."

Nearly every merchant in Ceros had been in that room and if Zola suddenly disappeared, there would be no question about who was responsible. And the Trade Council had no restitution for an offense like that.

Clove held out his hand for the knife and Saint hesitated before he gave it to him. But before Clove's hand had even closed over the handle, Saint was rearing back, his closed fist flying through the air and catching Zola in the jaw.

His head whipped to the side and he fell to one knee, blood dripping from his lip in a steady stream on the dirt beneath his feet. His chest was rising and falling in a panic now, eyes ablaze.

At the mouth of the alley, Lander was watching us with wide eyes, his pathetic hand still clutched to his ribs.

Clove pointed Saint's knife in Zola's direction. "Touch her again and I'll kill you myself. Those laws don't apply to a navigator."

"I won't have to." He spat on the ground, a stream of red trailing his chin as he looked to me. "Your mother has crews combing the Unnamed Sea for you. All I have to do is show up at her door."

A sinking feeling pulled heavy inside of me. His loss with the Trade Council would cost him the coin he'd been promised when he delivered me to Oliver Durant. And it was the kind of sum that paled in comparison to the enemy he'd make of Simon.

"Wonder what she'd give me for the trouble," Zola added.

"I know exactly what she'd give you," I said. "A blade in your chest."

His gaze hardened.

"All *I* have to do is tell her whose ship I left Bastian on."

Zola had built himself a cage with this deal and I could tell by the look in his eye that he knew it. He'd probably never sail the Unnamed Sea again as long as he lived.

Saint helped me to my feet, wiping the blood from my mouth with his thumb before he ran his knuckles softly across my tender cheek. I could already feel it bruising.

"I'm fine," I said, wishing my voice were more convincing.

He stepped aside, waiting for me to pass him before he followed me toward the street. When we reached it, Lander scrambled backward, out of the way, but Saint stopped in front of him when his back hit the wall.

"You owe me a debt," Saint said. "And one day, when you're least expecting it, when you're sure I've forgotten"—he took another step toward Lander, making him grimace—"*that's* when you'll pay it."

THIRTY-ONE

SAINT

The *Riven* had never felt more like home.

The ship creaked, wood popping and masts groaning against the steady winds taking us to Dern. The cargo hold was empty, but not for long. In another week, it would be filled with rye and grain and fishermen's goods. Whatever we could manage to secure in trade to be taken on to Sowan and Ceros.

We'd readied the ship in silence. Even Nash had had the good sense to keep his mouth shut as we raised the new sail over the bow. The trader's crest was supposed to fly over the *Aster,* but there was something that felt right about seeing it catch the wind over the *Riven.* In a way, we'd been born on this ship, Clove and I. It was only right that she take us across the Narrows as traders for the first time.

It wasn't until the shore was out of sight that Isolde found her way to my quarters. She stood at the door as I added Oliver Durant's coin to the ledgers, bringing them back up from the deficit for the first time in weeks.

"Maybe there's still a way to get it back," she said, her voice small.

I set down the quill and closed the ledger, looking up at her. Her hair was tucked behind one ear, its ends brushing her shoulder. I didn't know if I'd seen that look on her face before. Like she was guilty of something.

"It doesn't matter."

"It matters." She gestured to the small cabin that surrounded us. "You *need* a ship."

As if she could hear us, the ship moaned, tilting just a little.

"Not that one," I said.

Isolde's gaze narrowed on me as she stepped into the room. "What does that mean?"

"The *Aster* is a schooner," I said. "Fit for mid-sized inventories crossing the deep water of the Narrows. We need a ship that can navigate the shallows of Tempest Snare."

All at once, she seemed to put it together. "A brigantine," she murmured.

That was exactly what I'd been thinking. Something with a low drag and rigging that could maneuver unpredictable winds. The *Aster* wasn't made for that.

A small laugh escaped her lips. "Of course."

I stood, coming around the desk to stand in front of

her. She was beginning to feel like a permanent fixture in my surroundings. A part of the landscape that made up my life. And I couldn't help feeling like it was rarer than that gemstone in my pocket.

"Besides, I don't want to sail a ship you're not on."

"Then where's my contract?" She smiled.

"I won't sign a contract. Not with you," I said. "If you're here, with me, it's because you want to be. The minute that changes, you're free to go."

She stared at me, and for a moment, I worried that she was really considering whether it was what she wanted.

"So, that's it?" she asked. "No deals or contracts or promises?"

I followed the line of freckles across her cheek, down to her jaw. "There is one promise you have to make me."

She lifted her chin, waiting as I reached into my pocket and pulled the purse she'd given me from inside. When she realized what it was, she looked at it, confused. "What?"

I swallowed, holding it between us. "Don't ever tell me where you got this."

She almost smiled again, as if it were a joke.

"I'm serious, Isolde." My voice deepened. "Promise me you'll never tell me. Ever."

"Why?"

I'd thought through it more ways than one. That stone was the answer to too many problems. It had the ability to wipe the world clean before it destroyed it again. I wasn't the kind of man who could weigh that cost or wield that power.

I'd given up a ship for this girl without thinking twice. I'd give a sea of midnights, if I had to. And something told me that eventually, it might just come to that.

"There are some things I shouldn't be trusted with." I pressed the purse into her hand. "Promise me."

Her eyes met mine for a long, quiet moment before her fingers wove into mine. "All right. I promise."

She lifted up onto her toes and kissed me, arms winding around my neck until she'd rid the air of the cold between us.

This time when I held her, it felt different. Not like before, when I was trying to keep her from slipping away. Now, she was the shore. A place to come back to. And I didn't know if it was the sea that had given her to me or if she was a fate of my own making. There was a part of me that didn't care.

"I wanted you too. The minute I saw you." She whispered my own words against my lips—words I'd once thought could be the end of me.

Now, I was certain they were.

THIRTY-TWO

SAINT

Rosamund's pier felt like a tomb without the *Aster*. The wooden arches that had once bowed over the ship reached up to the high ceilings, where one of the roof sections had been left open to the dimming sky. Strokes of pink and orange swept across the clouds and a few stars were already waking.

Clove, Isolde, and I sat on the edge of the slip, our feet dangling out over the water where the *Aster* had been anchored only a few days ago. Now, it was on its way to Ceros with Burke at the helm. Clove had gone up to the ridge that looked over the harbor to watch them sail it away, but I hadn't had it in me. My blood was nailed into the hull of that ship. My bones had built it. There was a version of myself that would live in its skeleton for as long as it sailed the Narrows. And when it found its end in the deep, it would take that part of me with it.

Clove lifted the rye, refilling our glasses. We'd swiped one of the good bottles from the barkeeper and our only plan between now and morning was to finish it, with the exception of the meeting I had scheduled at the tavern.

"How much?" Clove asked, swallowing the rye down.

He and Isolde had been at it for hours—working out the plans that needed to come together in order for us to start dredging the Snare. Equipment, coin, schedules.

"Another hundred or so," she answered.

Clove hissed, pouring yet another glass.

When I first told Clove about Isolde's idea to dredge Tempest Snare, he'd looked like he was going to be sick. The fishermen from Cragsmouth didn't sail those waters because there were too many dead souls in them. Narrow waterways flowed around half-submerged masts and toothlike coral where a vast stretch of reef had eaten up scores of ships, blown into shallows by erratic, angry storms. There was no telling what kind of hauls were sunk there, and anyone who'd been foolish enough to go looking hadn't come out.

It wouldn't just make us rich. It would fund the first fleet of the Narrows to take on the Saltblood bastards who sucked the blood from its veins.

"Lines and hauling crates aren't free, Clove. And we can't dive without them," she continued.

"Then we'll have the cost of the turnover."

"Not much." She let herself lie back on the wooden planks between us, staring at the rafters overhead. "Most of what we find down there will be in the hulls of sunken ships. Those stones and metals will be clean and cut for the most part."

I hadn't thought of that.

Clove gave me an approving look over her head. We were learning by the day just how much she knew about trade and merchants and the inner workings of the guilds. That was worth tenfold what she could do with the gems.

"When will the map be finished?" Isolde turned her head to look at me.

"Another month. Maybe two."

"There isn't a helmsman or a merchant in the Narrows who won't pay for one."

She was right about that too. "Best not to make it known where it came from. I know a forger in Sowan who can make the copies and sell them."

"A forger?"

Clove tossed the bit of frayed rope he'd been winding around his finger into the water. "They do more than copy contracts and signatures. He's set up for it."

"So, what? You take a cut?"

"Cuts are the safest way to make coin in these waters," I said. I'd learned that the hard way. The minute people could trace a fortune to you, you were a dead man. "Cuts of the maps, cuts of Henrik's hauls, cuts of the rye . . . that's how we'll fund the dives."

They both looked satisfied with that. The plan was a solid one, built in levels that couldn't cave in on one another. That was the only way to build the kind of trade we were undertaking.

"We'll be swimming in copper in ten years' time," Clove murmured.

"But that won't be enough," I said absently. "Not as long as it's gems that run the trade."

Isolde sat back up, shifting to turn and face me. "What do you mean?"

I shook my head. "You were right. Gems aren't the answer. There are more gem merchants in the Unnamed Sea than ships in the Narrows. More reefs to dredge. More guild members. We'll never beat them at it," I thought aloud. "But maybe we don't have to."

Clove was listening now, his eyes sharpening. "What are you thinking?"

I took the bottle from his hand, turning it over so that the label faced me. "What's the one thing you can sell at any port, no matter its size?"

I handed the bottle to Isolde and she set down her glass, taking it from me. "Rye?"

"We're already trading rye," Clove said, still not catching on.

"Not like this, we're not." I pulled the ledger from my jacket, opening it to the last page.

Clove tried to read over my shoulder. "I'm not following."

"The future of the Narrows won't be built on gems or silver or silks. That's not who we are." My mind was racing with it now as I scratched the numbers down. "The Unnamed Sea built their power with gemstones. We'll build ours on rye."

"How? It's just a tavern drink."

"Not anymore." I gestured to the bottle. "In a few years we could be trading this in Bastian."

Isolde's eyes widened at the thought. "You think that could work?"

"I know it can."

"But there's nothing to govern it," Clove interrupted. "The rye crofters don't even have a guild."

"Not yet, they don't." I closed the ledger, handing it to him. "Send a message to Emilia. Tell her to plant every damn field she can in those hills."

"All right." Clove's smile stretched wider. "And Rosamund?"

"Tell her we need the best brigantine she's ever built."

"It'll take at least a year. Maybe more."

"Good. That's about how long we'll need to pay for it."

Clove reopened the ledger, reading the last few entries recorded there. "I'll figure up the first payment."

I pulled the watch from my pocket, checking the time. "I have to go." I got to my feet and Isolde's hand slipped from my knee.

"Rosamund will want a name for the contract, Saint." Clove looked up from the page. "For the ship."

I clicked the watch closed, dropping it into my pocket. "*Lark*," I answered, the word coming out a little more unsteady than I intended. "We'll call her the *Lark*."

That was where it had begun, I thought. That bird lying on the deck. The boy who'd thrown it into the water.

The muscle in Clove's jaw clenched before he gave me a tight nod. I watched him swallow before he repeated after me. "The *Lark*."

THIRTY-THREE

SAINT

The village was nearly dark as I made my way up the street, the harbor bell silent. It would take a few routes before our ship had inventory, but Gerik's eyes had nearly fallen out of his head when he saw me pull that license from my jacket. I was pretty sure I'd caught a gleam of pride in them too.

The *Riven* would hold out, I told myself. She'd stay afloat long enough for another ship to take us to the Snare. And the sea would see to it.

The tavern was nearly empty, still waiting for the evening crowd that would pour in from the merchant's house. But the booth at the back had its usual occupant.

Henrik Roth had both elbows on the table, hands clasped before him as he stared out the window that overlooked the street. The bottle of rye with my name on it was already waiting on the counter and I picked it up, snatching two glasses from the stack.

The fire was blazing despite the warm evening and the doors were propped open, letting the breeze sweep into the tavern. It made the flames on the lanterns bend, casting shadows up the walls.

Henrik didn't look up as I took my seat, his usually combed hair falling from place just enough to land on his brow. There was something different about him. Something unkempt.

I poured the rye, unsure if I even wanted to know what that look meant. Maybe he'd heard what happened to the gems or about the attention we'd gotten in Ceros. He wouldn't be happy about either.

I took the purse of coin from my jacket and set it on the table before I slid his glass toward him.

He finally blinked. "You're late," he said.

"No, you're early."

He almost smiled, in a way that made him look a little more like himself. "You're right."

He swallowed his rye, letting the glass come down hard on the table. I studied him, still trying to sift out that look in his eye.

"Want to count it?" I asked.

"No."

"What are we trading this time?"

"We're not," he said. "I'm wrapping up my business in the Narrows."

I stilled, hand tightening on the bottle. "Wrapping it up? Why?"

"My father's died."

He said it so matter-of-factly that I was almost certain I'd heard him wrong. But Henrik met my eyes, letting the truth of it settle. There was a grief there. One I knew well.

"I'm sorry," I offered.

"I'm needed in Bastian and I'll be focusing my trade there."

I nodded. "Understood."

Henrik was the oldest of the four Roth siblings and I guessed he would be taking his place as the patriarch of the family. That had likely always been the plan.

"It was just a matter of time."

He sounded as if he were trying to reassure himself. Like there was some open wound it might stitch closed if he remembered.

"You'll let me know if there's anything I can do for you."

I studied him, unsure if I'd heard him right. That was a rare, generous offer on his part, but I nodded just the same.

He refilled his own glass, not waiting for me. There was more behind the words than he was saying. A request.

"Is there something you need from me?" I asked.

Henrik stared into his glass, turning it once. "Yes."

I sank back into the booth, unbuttoning my jacket and letting if fall open to the cooler air. I had a feeling I'd need it. "Then I do have something I need from you."

"Name it."

I pulled Isolde's purse from the pocket of my vest, sliding it toward him. He took his time opening it, letting the stone fall into his open hand. When it did, his brow wrinkled.

I watched him study the gem for a few seconds before he lifted it to the light. "What the hell is it?"

"It doesn't matter."

"What do you want me to do with it?"

"Put it in something. Something small that can be carried or worn. Anything that will hide what it is."

"I can do that."

I watched him slip it back into the purse. "No one lays eyes on it except for you," I insisted. *"No one."*

"All right." He tucked it into his jacket, along with the coin.

I poured another round before I asked, "What is it I can do for you in return?"

Henrik wet his lips, his demeanor changing suddenly. I was absolutely sure I'd never seen him that way, as if he were afraid that the air itself couldn't be trusted with whatever he was about to say. "There's a boy in Waterside. A baby."

I stared at him, waiting.

"I want you to make sure he doesn't stay there."

A hundred questions raced through my mind. It was possibly the last thing I'd ever expect him to say.

"How am I going to do that?"

"Keep an eye on him. Look out for him."

The way he didn't meet my eyes told me everything I needed to know. He had a child in Ceros, with one of the women in Waterside. That was what he was doing in the Narrows every few weeks. And now that he was rising through the ranks of the Roth family, he was leaving them behind.

"I can do that."

I wasn't sure I should, but I wasn't going to refuse him. Henrik had taken a chance on me when no one else had. He'd trusted me and taught me how to trade. He'd done it for coin, sure. But I also had a strong suspicion he did it without his father's approval.

"Thank you."

I let another silence fall between us before I stood, leaving the bottle behind for him to finish. He was a man who needed to be alone with his drink. And I could let him have that.

I started toward the door, stopping short before I turned back. "This kid got a name?"

"Yeah," he answered, eyes still fixed on the reflection of light in the glass of rye. He swallowed hard before they lifted to meet mine. "His name is West."

EPILOGUE

ISOLDE

Tempest Snare was where it began. It was fitting that it would end there too.

I pulled the flat-edged chisel from my belt, a stream of bubbles trailing up from my lips. That tight feeling in the center of my chest was like the hands of a clock, slowly twisting tighter, ticking, ticking, ticking.

I had maybe three minutes before I needed to surface, but I wouldn't need that long. Two clean strikes would have the lock of the rusted iron-framed chest freed.

I liked to work the reef alone through the afternoons when the water was warm and the current was calm. The turquoise waters of the Snare were clearer than I'd ever seen them after two straight days of no storms. The sediment had settled so much that it was like looking through glass, everything beneath the surface touched by cascading beams of sunlight.

It was gilded. Otherworldly. And the only place I loved more than the reef was the netting that stretched across the jib of the *Lark,* where Saint and I slept in each other's arms most nights.

I could see the belly of the ship no more than twenty-five feet above, a perfect dark oval on the surface.

The lock broke beneath the weight of the chisel and a cloud of algae erupted in the water, clouding my vision as I opened the trunk. This wreck wasn't as old as some of the others, the wood softened but still intact. Inside, I raked through the disintegrated remains of parchment until my fingers caught hold of what I was looking for. A small coin crate.

The pinch in my lungs surfaced right on cue and I took the crate from the chest, letting it fall into the metal basket at my feet before I gave the rope three tugs. In a matter of seconds, it was lifting away from me.

I kicked off, following it at a steady pace to let my body rise slowly through the changing pressure of the water. When I finally hit the air, a gasp broke from my lips and I blinked until the water cleared my strained vision.

There, leaning on the portside railing of the ship, Saint was watching. He was always watching.

The dark scruff on his face was thick after weeks out at sea, making his blue eyes sparkle. "Was about to come down there and get you."

"You wouldn't last two minutes down there." I smiled, still trying to catch my breath.

I fit one foot into the loop at the end of the line and the crank clicked as I rose from the water, the wind catching me. But I couldn't feel it. I'd been under too long.

Clove was perched on the steps to the upper deck, the quill clenched in his teeth as he silently marked the depths of the trench we were working. It had taken almost two years, but we'd finished mapping almost a dozen veins of the Snare.

Saint reached out for me and when I took hold of him, his brow cinched. He pulled me onto the deck, hands pressing to my shoulder, my throat, my cheek.

"You're cold, love." He said it almost to himself.

"Tea."

Clove said the word almost automatically, rising to his feet and dropping the log on one of the steps as Saint draped the quilt over my shoulders. His arms wrapped tightly around me, hands moving over my skin to bring the warmth back into my limbs.

"Emerald?" I said, trying to keep my voice from shaking with cold. I could hear the gemstone before I'd even opened the crate.

"A lot of it," Saint answered.

The new map he was working on was fixed to the table behind him. He'd specially commissioned the desk from a woodworker in Ceros so that it could be set up beside the railing. That way he could see the surface of the water when

I was diving. I didn't mind. It meant that his face was the first thing I saw every time I came up from below.

I resisted the urge to touch the parchment with my wet hands, but I loved the smell of the ink when he was working. It was almost finished, a detailed rendering of the rugged shoreline west of Sowan. There was no end to the parts of the Narrows that needed mapping and I suspected Saint would spend the better part of his life attempting to complete the job. It was only one of the enterprises he'd begun since we set sail on our first trade route.

Clove reemerged from the passageway with a steaming cup of tea and Saint let me go so that Clove could set it in my hands.

I took a small sip, mostly interested in what the tea's warmth would do for my fingers. "We should head back, leave the rest for next month. There are only so many places we can keep stashing gemstones."

"Emilia's expecting us, anyway," Clove said, picking up the log he'd abandoned. The ink was still staining his fingertips.

We had a system now. Dredge and sell, but not all of it. The rest we found other uses for. Nothing that would draw attention, just enough movement to give the gem merchants in the Narrows an advantage. I imagined the Gem Guild in the Unnamed Sea, baffled by the influx of stones, especially when so many had originally come from their own waters.

That was the irony of it. The tales of the Narrows were different than the ones I'd heard as a child. They weren't just the stories of the traders who sailed these waters or the people who lived on its shores. They were the story of the sea itself. Her love and her anger. Her favor and her cruelty.

Once, a man who ran the gambit shop in Dern told me that the sea gives and she takes. That for every gem dredged from the reefs, she required restitution. And she was patient. She waited to call in her debts.

We'd had no way of knowing just how many ships had sunk on those reefs or how many of them bore crests from the Unnamed Sea. There was a trove of wealth that had been snatched back from Bastian, and no one had thought to come looking for it. Not in the teeth of Tempest Snare.

The wreckage seemed to go on for miles, the poor souls who'd sailed those ships long dead. But the bellies of those vessels still held the jewels and coin that had set up our post in the Pinch and would soon have three new ships under construction in Dern. Nash himself was heading the builds.

It would be slow, and it would be steady, but it was the very fortune Bastian had taken from the sea that was now chipping away at its crumbling, gilded edges.

The stories the gambit told me are true, I thought. *The sea gives.*

Saint believed that she would never betray him. He'd given his heart to her, after all. Like he'd given it to me. But something told me the deep wouldn't share a love like that forever.

One day, she would *take.*

ACKNOWLEDGMENTS

This book was an utter delight to work on. Saint is my favorite character I've written to date, and the fact that readers fell so deeply in love with him in *Fable* and *Namesake* felt like such a gift. For that reason, the first and, frankly, most important acknowledgment has to go to the *Fable* world readers who quite literally gave me no choice but to write this book. I kept each and every one of you in mind as I was writing every single chapter. Thank you from the bottom of my heart for believing in this series. I will never, ever forget it.

Thank you to Kristin Dwyer, whom I'd like to formally congratulate on finally getting her own dedication. Working on this series has felt like the old days, when we'd write in a coffeeshop late at night whispering, "What if . . ." Thank you for being Saint's biggest fan, best advocate, and borderline stalker. He's very grateful.

To my entire team at Wednesday Books, especially my editor, Eileen Rothschild, I am so grateful for the unwavering support you've given the world of the Narrows. This series has been given the room to grow into something beautiful thanks to you.

Thank you, as always, to my agent, Barbara Poelle, who is always game for a hard left turn and never favors the easy road over the adventurous one. This journey would be so very boring without you.

Thank you to my writing community, which keeps me inspired and never doubts me the way I sometimes doubt myself. Especially grateful to Adalyn Grace and Diya Mishra, who played a particularly vital role in the first seedling that would become this book. Thank you for pushing me when I really, really needed it. Thank you also to Jordan Gray for her insightful, intuitive feedback on an early draft of this story and to Natalie Faria, my ride-or-die beta reader.

And of course, the largest piece of my heart is and will always be reserved for my family. You are my fixed point on the horizon. I love you.

ABOUT THE AUTHOR

Adrienne Young is a foodie with a deep love of history and travel and a shameless addiction to coffee. When she's not writing, you can find her on her yoga mat, sipping wine over long dinners or disappearing into her favorite art museums. She lives with her documentary filmmaker husband and their four little wildlings in the Blue Ridge Mountains of North Carolina. She is the author of the *New York Times* bestselling *Sky in the Deep* duology and the *Fable* duology. She posts on Instagram @adrienneyoungbooks.

NAMESAKE

BY ADRIENNE YOUNG

Trader. Fighter. Legend.

With the *Marigold* ship free of her father, Fable and its crew were set to start over. That freedom is short-lived when she becomes a pawn in a notorious thug's scheme. In order to get to her intended destination she must help him to secure a partnership with Holland, a powerful gem trader who is more than she seems.

As Fable descends deeper into a world of betrayal and deception, she learns that the secrets her mother took to her grave are now putting the people Fable cares about in danger. If Fable is going to save them then she must risk everything, including the boy she loves and the home she has finally found.

An exciting, fast-paced ride that will ultimately satisfy those that stepped on board the *Marigold* with Fable last year...There's plenty to love about this sequel: Its relentless pace keeps the story feeling as though something new and dramatic is happening on every page.

– CULTURESS

THE LAST LEGACY

BY ADRIENNE YOUNG

When a letter from her uncle Henrick arrives on Bryn Roth's eighteenth birthday, summoning her back to Bastian, Bryn is eager to prove herself and finally take her place in her long-lost family.

Henrik has plans for Bryn, but she must win everyone's trust if she wants to hold any power in the delicate architecture of the family. It doesn't take long for her to see that the Roths are entangled in shadows. Despite their growing influence in upscale Bastian, their hands are still in the kind of dirty business that got Bryn's parents killed years ago. With a forbidden romance to contend with and dangerous work ahead, the cost of being accepted into the Roths may be more than Bryn can pay.

"This fast-paced tale with a Victorian feeling is filled with an abundance of scandal, high fashion, intrigue, and, of course, romance... the delightfully swoonworthy love story will keep readers engaged and the pages turning eagerly as they hurtle toward the book's satisfying conclusion. An entertaining story of forbidden love, family drama, and elegant couture."
— *Kirkus*

"In this sumptuously rendered historical novel, Young deftly explores concepts of family, loyalty, and growing into one's destiny."
— *Publishers Weekly*

Similar Books Are Available from
www.forgottenbooks.com

RECOLLECTIONS

OF

GEORGE BUTLER

BY

JOSEPHINE E. BUTLER

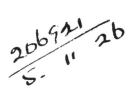

BRISTOL
J. W. ARROWSMITH, 11 QUAY STREET
LONDON
SIMPKIN, MARSHALL, HAMILTON, KENT AND CO, LIMITED

TO

My Children and Grandchildren

I DEDICATE

THESE

RECOLLECTIONS.

RECOLLECTIONS

OF

GEORGE BUTLER.

CHAPTER I.

INTRODUCTORY.—PARENTAGE.—HARROW SCHOOL AT THE BEGIN-
NING OF THE CENTURY.—BRIEF CHARACTER SKETCH OF
DR. GEORGE BUTLER, HEAD MASTER OF HARROW.

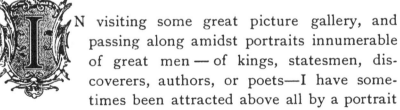

N visiting some great picture gallery, and
passing along amidst portraits innumerable
of great men — of kings, statesmen, dis-
coverers, authors, or poets—I have sometimes been attracted above all by a portrait
without a name, or without the interest attaching to it of
any recorded great exploit, but which nevertheless interests
for its own sake. Something looks forth from those eyes
—something of purity, of sincerity, of goodness—which
draws the beholder to go back again and again to that
portrait, and which gives it a lasting place in the memory
long after many other likenesses of earth's heroes are
more or less forgotten.

2

It is somewhat in this way that I think of a memorial or written likeness of George Butler, if it can but be presented with a simplicity and fidelity worthy of its subject. His character—his single-mindedness, purity, truth, and firmness of attachment to those whom he loved—seem to me worthy to be recorded and to be had in remembrance.

M. Fallot, in the *Revue du Christianisme Pratique*, sketches, in a few words, the character of the revered teacher of his youth, Christophe Dieterlin, whose mortal remains rest beneath the hallowed soil of the Ban de la Roche, in the Vosges, surmounted by a rock of mountain granite—a suitable monument for such a man. When his pupil questioned him concerning prayer, he replied: "The Lord's Prayer is in general sufficient for me. When praying in those words, all my personal pre-occupations become mingled with and lost in the great needs and desires of the whole human race." "He was a Christian," says M. Fallot, "*hors cadre*, refractory to all classification, living outside all parties," a child of Nature and a son of God. These words might with truth be applied to the character of George Butler. It would be difficult to assign him a definite place in any category of persons or parties. He stands apart, *hors cadre*, in his gentleness and simplicity, and in a certain sturdy and immovable independence of character.

The father of the subject of these recollections, Dr. George Butler, who succeeded Dr. Joseph Drury as Head Master of Harrow School in 1805, was born in 1774. He was the son of the Rev. Weeden Butler of Chelsea, whose wife, Anne-Giberne, was of French origin. Mr. Weeden Butler was at one time the amanuensis, and, to the last, the faithful friend of the unfortunate Dr.

Dodd, who was hanged for forgery (committed under circumstances of great temptation). Weeden Butler had taken charge of what had been Dr. Dodd's parish at Pimlico. He showed towards his unhappy friend the most unvarying kindness in his hour of ruin, illustrating a trait characteristic of the family — namely, great tenacity in friendship. Not even so serious a moral lapse could induce him to abandon a person he had once regarded as a friend. He was still found by the side of the ruined and broken-hearted man, to bring hope, not of this world. Dr. Dodd left among his papers some affecting lines, written in prison, in which he speaks of

" Butler, the only faithful found,"

among a crowd of former friends and acquaintances who now shunned him.

Fidelity to friends was, with the subject of these recollections, not only a natural impulse, but a sacred duty. He was fond of the words of "Polonius" in *Hamlet:*

" Those friends thou hast and their adoption tried,
Grapple them to thy soul with hoops of steel;
But do not dull thy palm with entertainment
Of each new hatch'd, unfledgéd comrade."

These words he quoted in the last sermon he ever preached: it was in Winchester Cathedral, and was on the subject of "The Sacredness of Friendship."

Reverently and truly the lines might have been applied to him:

" When once thy hand he taketh,
'Tis clasped in his for ever:
His friend he ne'er forsaketh!"

Dr. George Butler (Head Master of Harrow) entered Sydney College, Cambridge, in 1790. In January, 1794, being then only nineteen years old, he was Senior Wrangler and Senior Smith's Prizeman of his year, Mr. Copley, of Trinity College (afterwards Lord Lyndhurst), being in each case second. In the following year he travelled (principally on foot) through a great part of Germany, where he became acquainted with Klopstock, Schiller, Goethe, and other eminent literary men. On his return to Cambridge he began the study of Law, keeping his terms at Lincoln's Inn, and was on the point of being called to the bar when he was appointed to the Mathematical Lectureship of his College, a circumstance which eventually altered the direction of his life. In 1802 he again went abroad with a pupil, travelling on this occasion through France, Italy, and Sicily. He was subsequently elected a Fellow of his College, was ordained, and shortly after became a select preacher before the University.

Few men could compete with him in versatility of mind and in the variety of his accomplishments. Besides his great mathematical attainments, he was also a distinguished classical scholar, and spoke German, French, and Italian with correctness and fluency. He was practically versed in chemistry and several other branches of physical science; he was a good musician and draughtsman; and he excelled in all athletic exercises, being one of the best skaters, fencers, and swimmers of his time. He was called by his friends a second "admirable Crichton."

He became Head Master of Harrow in the prime of life, at his height of his bodily and mental vigour. He had no easy task before him. Discipline had become lax, and habits of tyranny and tormenting had grown up in the school in the relations between monitors and junior boys.

"There is no incident," says Mr. Percy Thornton, "in Harrow story less familiar to the world than that of the very serious rebellion of 1808. This *emeute* commenced after the Head Master had questioned the legality of certain monitorial innovations, so declared to be by no less a personage than Dr. Parr. Contumacy lapsed into riot and defiance. For several days the paralysis of authority was complete. It would seem that the spirit of the French Revolution had permeated into Harrow; for this strange episode had been ushered in under the names of Liberty and Rebellion!" *

Lord Byron, a pupil at Harrow at the time, was not a good boy. He used his monitorial influence to undermine the authority which it was his duty to support. It is said that, in conjunction with a friend, he tore down the gratings of the hall windows, carrying a pistol in his hand, while gunpowder was placed along a passage where Dr. Butler had to walk. He afterwards made atonement for these follies, desiring (he said in a letter to Dr. Drury) to "frankly acknowledge himself wrong." Mr. Thornton continues: "Dr. Butler seems to have met this crisis with fortitude and tact. Not only did Dr. Goodall of Eton commend Ir. Butler's ruling of the storm, but this commendation was endorsed by George III., who averred that 'no man could have acted better under the circumstances.' "

The *English Illustrated Magazine* (No. 91) has an article on Harrow School, in which the statement occurs: "Byron and Peel were both among the distinguished pupils of George Butler. Lord Byron said later, ' Peel was my form fellow. There were always great hopes of Peel among us all, masters and scholars, and he has not dis-

* *Harrow School and its Surroundings,* p. 219.

appointed them.' · Lord Byron spent many summer
afternoons upon the Peachy tomb in Harrow churchyard,
meditating the tuneful verses which were so caustically
reviewed in *The Edinburgh* when Jeffrey ruled supreme.
It is doubted whether the young poet was a leader among
the boys.   Crippled by a natural infirmity . . . sentimental, and addicted to dreaming on tombstones, he was
not an athlete such as Dr. Merivale imagines a leading
Harrovian must have been.   Mrs. Drury was once heard
to say of him: 'There goes Byron' (Birron she called
him) 'straggling up the hill like a ship in a storm, without
rudder or compass.'"

Dean Merivale, in his *Recollections,* says of Dr. Butler:
" His stature was somewhat below the middle height, but
his limbs were lithe and well set ; his countenance, with
his keen eyes and curved·beak, was full of expression, but
evidently kept under strict control, and his march up to
school at the head of a procession of lagging and, perhaps, unwilling assistants—a custom now, I fear, disused
—was decidedly impressive.   His cropped and powdered
hair and dignified costume gave an idea of more years
than he really numbered. . . . His rule at Harrow was
prosperous, and the affection felt for him by his old pupils
was remarkable."

The march up to school recalls an incident illustrating
the quiet humorousness, even at an early age, of Dr.
Butler's son George.   Too young to be yet a pupil of·
Harrow School, he watched his father from his own door
one morning as he started for school in the dignified
costume above described, which included knee breeches
and cloth gaiters: The doctor, in a fit of absence of
mind, had only put on one gaiter, and so proceeded on
his march.   On returning from school, he said to his

little boy: "You were there, George; did you not see that I had only one gaiter?" "Yes, papa." "Then why did you not tell me?" "Because," answered George, "I thought it would amuse the boys."

In 1818 Dr. Butler married Maria, eldest daughter of John Gray, Esq., of Wembley Park, Middlesex.

After continuing in the arduous office of Head Master of Harrow for twenty-four years, he retired to the Living of Gayton, in Northamptonshire, and devoted himself to the duties of a parish clergyman. In 1836 he became Chancellor of the Diocese; and in 1842 he was appointed by his former pupil, Sir Robert Peel, to the vacant Deanery of Peterborough. In the latter office he continned till his death, discharging its duties to their fullest extent, and preaching constantly in the Cathedral till his health and sight failed. His affection for Harrow School amounted almost to a passion. He maintained with his successors (three of whom he lived to see) a constant and most friendly intercourse. He had the happiness also of living to witness the distinguished honours of his four sons at the Universities.

The following are scattered recollections, written by his daughter Catherine, afterwards wife of Dr. Bowen, Bishop of Sierra Leone, of his life as rector of a rural parish, Gayton, after his retirement from the long Head Mastership at Harrow ·

"Papa's maxim of never leaving till to-morrow what can be done to-day was one secret of his success in many things he attempted. The farmers of Gayton might well despair of getting their way when once he had resolved on carrying out any measure to which they felt opposed. If once they yielded to him under a momentary impression of his eloquent arguments, they had no time left them to retract, for he carried out so swiftly the design agreed upon. Thus it was that he got rid of the old violin, flute, and other rustic musical instruments which had formerly led the congregational music in the church. The performers, in an evil hour for themselves, had quarrelled, one insisting on putting in a long flourish here and another on slackening the pace there, &c. Papa called a vestry meeting, and harangued his audience on the indecent behaviour of the musicians and the bad effect it produced, and obtained their consent to have the musicians discharged and their gallery pulled down. In an hour's time—having engaged the men beforehand to be ready to commence the demolition of the gallery—he gave the farmers the satisfaction of seeing their wishes carried out in grand style.

"He gained much influence in the neighbourhood by his thorough knowledge of agriculture and farming operations. 'The doctor, he knows everything,' they were accustomed to say. When the North-Western Railway was first being laid down, and the company was on the point of building a straight bridge which would have necessitated an awkward bend in the road, papa persuaded them to make a skew bridge, which was done and approved. The bridge was afterwards called 'Butler's Bridge.'

"He never could bear to keep poor people waiting who came to see him, and always said that he felt it his duty to show them quite as much respect as the rich, as we are all equal in the sight of God. He was frequently angry with the servants for sending people away without first telling him.

"The last little festival which took place in his parish at Gayton was almost overwhelming to him. He had been very ill at Peterborough, and had not been at Gayton for some time. There was a striking earnestness in his look and manner which none who saw him will ever forget. He evidently felt he was taking leave of his parishioners. We were all busy preparing for the festivity and left him alone in his library. When we came back we found him just rising from his knees; tears were in his eyes, and he told me how much this day recalled the old times when he was strong and well

"It was in the evening of the only Sunday he spent during this, his last visit to Gayton, that when all the rest of the party were going out for a walk, he asked me to accompany him to the church, as he wished to see it quietly. He was very grave and thoughtful. He sat some minutes without speaking, looking at the family vault, with his hands clasped as if in prayer. At last he said, 'Blessed are the dead that die in the Lord.' We then walked into the vestry and round the church, and then to the Communion table. He stood within the rails and looked down the nave; and then he told me how all his life seemed to come before him again as in a dream: how well he remembered when he first stood there as a young man and formed plans for the good of the people, and how sorry he felt that he had not done more for them. And then he said in a low voice, and with deep fervour, 'God be merciful to me a sinner!' Lastly, he knelt down before the Communion table, and I knelt beside him, holding his hand, which was cold and trembling a good deal. He prayed very fervently for forgiveness for the past and strength for the future, whatever that future might be, concluding by thanking God, in the beautiful Thanksgiving of our General Liturgy, for His great and infinite goodness to him and all of us. He kissed me as we left the church, and the setting sun just then gleaming on his grey hair, I thought of the verse, 'The hoary head is a crown of glory if it be found in the way of righteousness.' Several times after that he talked to me about his daughters who were gone, especially Benigna, but never without strong emotion. He rejoiced in the thought of their present happiness.

"In speaking one day of the various studies in which he had been engaged, he said it was his habit never to begin any fresh study or book without first offering a prayer to God to enable him to use the knowledge gained to His glory, and to grant him success in his work. Even when he came to any hard passage, he would pray for wisdom to understand it, and he often felt his prayer was at once heard. He spoke of his excitement at the time of taking his degree: how anxious he felt to get high rank as a scholar for his father's sake. On the second day of the examination, as he was on the way to the hall, he met one of the examiners, who told him he need not go up again to the hall, for he had done so well that his name was already bracketed apart from all the rest. He said, 'I felt almost choked with joy and gratitude, and hastened to my room and fell on my knees to thank God for His goodness. I thought of my dear father's pleasure when the tidings should reach him.'

"He used to be delighted when any of our brothers gained prizes at school or college; his face beamed at such times. On one occasion, after his health broke down, mamma feared the excitement caused by the good news of his sons' honours would be too much for him. He replied that the news had done him more good than all the medicine in the world, and quoted the line:

'Tears such as tender fathers shed,'

meaning that his were tears of joy. He was very kind to servants, and would never overwork them. He used to quote a saying of his mother's to himself when he was a boy : 'There's trouble enough in the world without giving more, George.' He would even relieve them—we sometimes thought unnecessarily—when riding to North-ampton, by taking parcels, or even a large leather bag, tied to Merlin's saddle, and would come home laden with purchases. He had no notion of its being derogatory to anyone's dignity to carry a parcel. This trait was noticed by the poor people. A poor woman said one day, when her husband had been shy of taking a parcel for her into the town : 'Why, the Dean would think nothing of it ; so it's not for the likes of you to mind it.'

"One Sunday evening, when he was particularly unwell and restless, I read to him Spencer's hymn of Heavenly Love. He was charmed with it, and said : 'You read it with your whole heart, dear, as if you felt it.' His blindness prevented him reading himself. We used to read to him. Sometimes we came to Greek passages which I could not read, as I never learned Greek ; so I set to work and learned the Greek alphabet one day, and practised to myself reading words, and then the next Greek passage I came to I read it off pretty correctly, and he was so pleased. In his later years he enjoyed sitting in the old garden of the Deanery at Peterborough, and listening to the newspaper being read to him. It was a stirring time, politically, then, and there were fine speeches of Sir Robert Peel and others in Parliament which delighted him. He would sit in his bath-chair covered with plaids and basking in the sun, and at the parts where 'cheers' or 'much cheering' came in, I used to give him, at his request, a slight push,

and then he would himself cheer.   He told me one day
that when he was a boy about twelve he was not strong
in health, and his mind was much troubled on religious
subjects.   He got the unhappy notion that he had in
some way put himself outside of the pale of Divine
mercy.   ' I was sitting one day,' he said, ' by the fireside,
when my dear mother came in and talked to me.   She
told me how full of love God is, and how wrong it was
to distrust His mercy ; and she soon convinced me how
completely I had mistaken the whole tenor of the Gospel
offers of salvation.   When she left the room I offered up
a few words of prayer with my whole heart, and soon felt
as if a great burden had been taken from me.' "

A remarkable example is given of Dr. Butler's physical
activity, as well as of the kindness of his heart, in an
incident which occurred in the month of January, 1843,
when he was in his seventieth year.·   He was riding from
Gayton to Northampton ; there was snow on the ground,
and it was an exceedingly frosty day. ·Crossing a bridge
over a canal, he observed something like a woman's dress
moving in the water.   He leapt from his horse, and,
throwing off his coat, plunged into the freezing water,
and rescued from suicide a poor young woman who had
been driven by the unkindness and desertion of a man to
whom she was attached to resolve to drown herself.   He
had considerable difficulty in lifting her out, on account
of the steepness of the sides of the canal.   He succeeded,
however, and conveyed her to a roadside inn, where he
gave directions for everything to be done for her restoration.   He then rode home again, changed his clothes,
and started once more on his errand to Northampton.
The incident excited much public attention on account of
the inclemency of the weather and the Dean's age, as

well as the difficulty of saving anyone in deep water in a canal with steep sides. Several people in the neighbourhood assembled later to vote an address of thanks and appreciation to him, and the Royal Humane Society begged his acceptance of their gold medal. The subsequent history of the young woman was a happy one. The visits and instructions of the Dean resulted in a complete change in her sentiments and character; she regained hope, and was afterwards happily married.

CHAPTER II.

EARLY SCHOOL DAYS.—LIFE AT HARROW.—A YEAR AT TRINITY
COLLEGE, CAMBRIDGE.—MIGRATES TO OXFORD.—RECOLLEC-
TIONS OF HIS FRIENDSHIP WITH GEORGE BUTLER, BY
R. COWLEY POWLES. — GAINS HERTFORD SCHOLARSHIP. —
ELECTED A FELLOW OF HIS COLLEGE WHILE AN UNDER-
GRADUATE.—TAKES HIS DEGREE.—NOTICES OF HIS FRIENDS
AT OXFORD.—BECOMES TUTOR TO LORD HOPETOWN.

GEORGE BUTLER was born at Harrow on the 11th of June, 1819. He was the eldest son of a family of ten: four brothers and six sisters. His first school was Dr. Morris's, a preparatory school for Harrow. He afterwards entered Harrow School. Nothing very re- markable in the way of hard study or distinction can be recorded of him during his school career. When questioned in later life concerning any excellency he attained there, he would answer, reflectively, that he was considered to be extremely good at " shying " stones. He could hit or knock over certain high-up and difficult chimney-pots with wonderful precision, to the envy of other mischievous boys, and I suppose to the annoyance of the owners of the chimney-pots. His father, the Dean of Peterborough, wrote to me in 1852 : " Your references to George's early days make me feel quite young again. He certainly was a nice-looking boy, and had a pretty head of hair ; at least I thought so, and the remembrance of those nursery days is pleasant to me. But oh ! those early experiments in the science of projectiles upon the chimney-pots of the Harrovian neighbours,—why remind me of them, unless you are yourself possessed of the same spirit of mischief?" Sir Thomas Wade, one of George's former Harrow school-fellows, paid us a visit many years afterwards at Liverpool, on the occasion of a prize delivery at the College; and I recollect the two friends sitting side by side in a recess in the window, talking till a late hour in the evening over their Harrow experiences, practical jokes perpetrated, wild adventures in the fields and woods around, humorous relations with masters and pupils, and much boyish mischief. The two venerable men seemed never to weary of these reminiscences. When some one remarked to George Butler, "But you, in your present character as a schoolmaster, punish boys for such tricks," he replied : "Well, they say an old poacher makes the best game-keeper. But I am never hard on boys on account of mere mischief;" and truly he never was : in cases where there was no intended harm or ill-will he was very lenient. Indeed, it was not difficult to discover a lurking sympathy with boys sometimes, whom his position obliged him nevertheless to reprimand more or less seriously, for some spirited or humorous act which transgressed strict discipline. When, on one occasion, an assistant-master gave him his report for the quarter of one of his—George Butler's— own sons, then very young, I recollect his reading the words " too playful in school " with an expression on his face of mixed tenderness and amusement.

Dr. Longley and Dr. Wordsworth were successively headmasters of Harrow while George Butler was at school there. For both he had a sincere attachment, and both continued on terms of warm friendship with him in after years.

Among the prominent figures of that epoch at Harrow there were two whose names were often mentioned in our family with accompanying characteristic anecdotes:— One of them was Henry Drury—"Harry," or "Old Harry," as he was called—who had for many years the largest boarding house and most crowded pupil room of any master there. "It was a sight to see and to remember the massive figure of the ruler of a crowd of boys in his schoolroom, then in the full vigour of his age, striding from end to end of the long room, rolling out awful questions and sonorous recitations, commanding the attention of all, and impressing each with the apprehension that he would be himself the next called up."

Another was Dr. Kennedy, whose generosity, kindness and warmth of heart amply atoned for an occasional outburst of energetic language when strongly moved. Frequently has the story been recounted in our family of the burning down of the head-master's house, in 1838. The lurid glare of the fire was seen, it is said, from London, and sight-seers crowded up from miles around. The only water available was that in the grove pond, and a long line of Harrow schoolboys was organised from there to the fire, to convey buckets from hand to hand. A delightful time for the boys! Dr. Kennedy, full of generous anxiety for the boys who were crowding near the fire, appearing at a window, with flushed and agitated face, cried, "Let the house burn, boys, let it burn, but for God's sake save your precious lives!" After the fire had been pretty well mastered by these prompt efforts and good organisation, "a great clumsy fire engine came lumbering down from Westminster," and poured a volley of water over the ruins, afterwards "taking all the credit to itself (of course) for having put out the fire."

In reference to the freedom in matters of amusement which was allowed under Dr. Christopher Wordsworth, Dr. Longley's successor, George himself * wrote :— "A pack of beagles was kept up for several seasons by a select number of the senior boys. At last Dr. Bloomfield, Bishop of London, who was Visitor of the school, heard, that the Harrow beagles had been seen on a portion of his episcopal manors, and consequently his lordship wrote to the headmaster who was now in office, to remonstrate, and to point out that seven couples of hounds, even so small as beagles, must consume a great deal of food, of which the poor would be glad. Dr. Wordsworth was very good-natured about the matter— so much so, that Tom Smith, a leading member of the hunt, tried to effect a compromise by asking _how many_ beagles they might keep, provided they made a reduction. This was too much for the headmaster, who, with no more than the necessary amount of sternness, replied that they must be given up altogether. And this was the end of that lively little pack."

But school life was not all play for George Butler. He showed an early aptitude for scholarship, gaining among several prizes that for Greek Iambics. Mr. Thomas Butler, a late librarian of the British Museum, wrote: "In ·the many letters of my uncle (Dr. Butler, head master of Harrow) I find occasional mention of one or another of my cousins. In August, 1835, my uncle writes : ' George has come home for the holidays with an excellent character.' At a later date he writes : ' Of George we hear excellent reports, both as to conduct and scholarship.' "

When the holidays came, George travelled to his

family at Gayton and back to Harrow on the top of the coach, which in those days ran between Harrow and Northampton. At Christmas, when the weather was frosty, he used to feel very cold, especially after falling asleep. His physical training was of a rather Spartan character. He recollected to the end of his life those winter drives, when he wore, not a great-coat such as boys have now, but a cape which reached only to the elbows, leaving the lower part of the body exposed to the keen air. His hardy training seemed on the whole to answer, judging from the almost invariable robust health which he enjoyed all his life, until the last few years.

The holidays spent in the pleasant sporting county of Northampton, and in the midst of a large family party, were delightful. His father occasionally took George out with him to try his " 'prentice hand " with a gun in the stubbles, in September. George Butler, the son, was always a good shot, but on one of his first essays his success was of a singular kind. Spying a little brown creature bobbing across a glade between two covers, he took aim, and saw the rabbit, as he took it to be, fall dead. It was a dog however, and on coming up to the scene of the murder, the keeper who accompanied them said : " Well, Master George, you have shot Mrs. So-and-so's dawg ! A prime favourite cove he were ! Never mind, it can't be helped ; chuck him in the bushes." George was sincerely distressed, and gladly consented to accompany his father to Mrs. So-and-so's cottage—a small farmer's wife—to express his remorse, and to apologise. The lady did not however receive the repentant offender at all graciously ; while her husband, coming up at the same moment, said : " It ain't the first time as Master George has been a-shooting what he didn't ought." " Indeed !"

said Dr. Butler, with solemn gravity and alarm. " No ; he saw my missus's sun bonnet hanging on the hedge to dry, and took aim at it and blew it all to pieces."

In the autumn of 1838 George went up to Trinity College, Cambridge. The time he spent there was not profitable, except in the sense in which all experience may be turned to profit, and in the fact that he there made the acquaintance of several men of his own age, some of whom continued to rank among the worthiest of those for whom he retained a life-long friendship. Among these were the late William Lyttleton (of Hagley, Worcestershire) and the present Mr. Justice Denman. The latter wrote to me recently as follows : " Your dear husband came from Harrow, with plenty of Harrow friends at Trinity. I came from Repton with none ; but I made his acquaintance by the accident of his being steerer of the first boat I rowed in, and in common with all the crew, I took a great liking to him at once. He, like myself, seemed to prefer the society of the men who amuse themselves, to that of the exemplary; and he certainly was not then a 'reading man,' in the ordinary meaning of those words. He was in the first class, however, in the Freshmen's May Examination, 1839. When I heard he had given up Cambridge and was going to Oxford, I was *very* sorry; but when I heard that he had so soon got the Hertford Scholarship, I was half amused, and more than half delighted that he had so pulled himself together. I heard long afterwards that he felt, or his father felt, that he had failed in his first start at Cambridge. I suppose he himself was more sensitive than most of us, and joined in the verdict that a fresh start was desirable. But if he had stayed at Cambridge I feel convinced that he would have done what Charles

Kingsley (who was in our year) did, and ultimately been with us in the first class of the Tripos. After he went to Oxford I saw little of him until he was at Liverpool, and then only occasionally; and afterwards (in the way you know) at Winchester. But whenever and wherever we met, he was always the same courteous, modest, gentle, lovable fellow that he was when he steered my first boat —and full of humour without mischief."

During the year he spent at Cambridge, the sense of duty and of responsibility for the use of the opportunities and gifts which he possessed lay dormant within him. Those who loved him best often thanked God, however, as he did himself in later life, that he had escaped the contamination of certain influences which leave a stain upon the soul, and sometimes tend to give a serious warp to the judgment of a man in regard to moral questions. A remarkable native purity of mind, and a loyal and reverent feeling towards women, saved him from associations and actions which, had he ever yielded to them, would have been a bitter memory to such a man as he was. He was however unawakened to the more serious aspects of life; he wasted time and money, and contented himself with the enjoyment of the society of clever and pleasant companions. He was keenly alive to the pleasures of the social side of young university life, and was always attracted by music, art, out-door exercises, and athletics, to the exclusion of the work he was sent to the University to do. It cannot be said, however, that he was indolent, for he was always active, and always busy about something—sometimes joining in the perpetration of practical jokes, or "town and gown rows." All this was very disappointing to his father, to whom it presented a painful contrast with his own early, earnest, and brilliantly successful start in the serious business of life. The stern though affectionate letters which Dr. Butler wrote to his son at this time were not without effect, as the son's subsequent conduct proved. It is instructive to mark how, when once awakened to the mistake he had made, George braced himself to begin afresh; and how, "pulling himself together," as Judge Denman says, he entered with energy and determination upon a wholly different course. This awakening of his moral nature was produced mainly by his reverence for his father, and the sincere sorrow which took possession of his mind for having grieved the heart of that good father, and disappointed the expectations which he had formed of him. Further than this there is little evidence of any deeper motive, or of a sense of direct personal responsibility towards God. These he attained later, while the present "right-about-face," as he called it, set him forward in the direction whence come clearer light and sure guidance.

In the interval between leaving Cambridge and going to Oxford he spent several months in the house of Mr. Augustus Short (afterwards Bishop of Adelaide). Of Mr. Short he retained a grateful recollection to the end of his life. It was while under his roof that he imbibed a true love of work, and learned the enjoyment of overcoming difficulties, and of a steady effort, without pause, towards a definite goal. He wrote, when appointed in 1851 an Examiner in the " Schools " at Oxford : " My work grows upon me in interest. I enjoy reading up my old subjects to prepare for the examination of a really good man, such as some of those we have had. I find my five months' training under Mr. Short invaluable to me. All the work which I did then was systematic and good. Of my college lectures I remember nothing but the mistakes

made by men in construing.   That steady course of
reading was the first good thing I did.   I think of adopt-
ing early hours, getting up at six, dinner at one, a ride or
a walk in the afternoon, then tea, and looking over papers,
so as to completely finish each day's work before going
to bed.   My old tutor (Mr. Short) told me this was
his plan, and it seems a reasonable one—economical
of time and conducive to health.   I shall begin to bathe
in the morning as soon as the weather is less cold."   He
said that at that time (with Mr. Short) he was in "first-
rate condition ; " there was not "a five-barred gate in the
country which he could not jump easily."

One of his life-long and most valued friends, the Rev.
R. Cowley Powles (now Prebendary of Chichester), has
contributed the following recollections of their early
friendship at Oxford, when they were fellow-students at
Exeter College :—

"I first made acquaintance with George Butler in
the winter of 1840, soon after he came into residence
at Exeter College.   He was placed under the same tutor
as I was—the Rev. C. L. Cornish—and shortly after he
entered on residence Mr. Cornish asked me to call on the
new comer.   It was to this that I owe my introduction
to one with whom I was to form one of the closest and
most prized friendships of my life.   Very well do I
remember our first meeting.   I had called on Butler.   He
was not in his room, but he came presently to return the
call.   I was just going out, and opened the door of my
room as he was about to knock.   The half-opened door
intercepting the light from the window prevented my
getting a distinct view of my visitor, but I was struck at
once by the quick, earnest glance of unusually bright eyes,
all the more noticeable because of the shadow in which

he stood. We soon became friendly acquaintances, and, before long, warm friends. We were both disposed to read hard, and to work, especially at classics. Either in the first or second term of our acquaintance, we began to read together subjects not included in our college lectures. Besides other less serious tasks, we read the whole of *Virgil,* and the *Odyssey* each twice over. The reading of the *Odyssey* remains with me as one of the pleasantest of my Oxford memories. We began it in the summer term. Every evening after the boat-races we used to meet in my rooms. I had a study whose window looked into the college garden, and there we set to with our books. Each of us translated a few lines in turn, making out the text as well as we could with lexicons and notes, but not with anything in the nature of a ' crib' to help us. And so we used to go on for two or three hours at a time, never continuing beyond midnight, but often touching closely on the border. The pleasant, cool, summer air, the scent of the acacia blossoms, and the entrancing interest of the glorious poem we were reading for the first time, were all delightful.

" It was in working at the *Odyssey* that I became aware of my companion's powers, especially of the clearness and correctness of his critical insight. In the perplexed passages both of Homer and of Virgil he had a quick discrimination between probable and improbable renderings of the text ; and when we had made our first sifting and came to deal with what we retained, I generally found that his view both as regarded grammatical accuracy and poetic feeling commended itself to my own less competent judgment. He combined in an unusual degree a nice critical faculty for language with true poetic feeling.

" In our amusements at Oxford we were not so much together. George Butler was good at almost all athletic exercises,—I at none. Now and then we rode together. Riding was all that I could manage in the way of physical exercises. On one occasion we had a misadventure, with rather serious consequences. Butler was riding a grey mare of mine, and we wished to have a gallop over a good stretch of turf, separated from the path on which we were riding only by a wire fence about eighteen inches high. Butler put the mare at this, taking for granted that she would step over it. Unfortunately she did not see it, and caught her foot in the wire, falling right over and sending her rider some feet away. He was on his feet in a moment, but deadly pale and evidently in great pain. I scarcely recollect how we managed to get home, but I remember trying to get some brandy for him at a little public-house which we passed. He seemed so faint that I feared without some stimulant he would actually faint. The brandy, so-called, was handed to me. What it was I do not know, but I can recall the wretched stuff now, the colour and thickness of an addled egg. George just took the muddy mixture in his hand, looked at it, and pitched it into the road. It was indeed the only thing to do, but it added to my despair. However, we made our way to the college, and a doctor was sent for, who pronounced the right shoulder to be dislocated, and set it at once.

." On another occasion when riding together, we were nearly having a trouble of another kind. We were trotting across some fields through which there was a right of way. George was then mounted on a famous steeple-chase mare called 'Matilda,' of which I had lately become the owner. He diverged from the path

into a field in order to try the mare's powers at a 'bull-
finch.' Just as he cleared the hedge, the farmer-tenant
and a labourer were seen running towards him with
pitchforks, to cut off his retreat to the path and to exact
a fine for trespassing. Between the field where George
was and this path was a hedge and a broad ditch. To
get back, the rider had to leap the hedge and land on the
bank of the ditch, and then, holding his horse together,
to clear the ditch also. It was done in grand style. The
rider knew what had to be done, and how to do it, and
the horse answered to his handling. I mention this
incident because it shows that my friend was as good
at horsemanship as at racquets, tennis, cricket, skating,
etc.

"It was, I think, in 1841 that Butler got the Hertford
scholarship. I remember meeting him just after his
success had been announced. I was coming back from
a ride, and he stopped me and said: 'I have got the
Hertford.' The announcement was made in his quietest
voice, and with no elation of manner, though his countenance showed how much he was pleased. Never was there
a man with less *brag* about him. In the evening when
talking over the examination he told me with much
amusement that the Examiner had spoken to him of their
surprise that a man who had evidently read so little of
Latin literature should win the Hertford. This illustrates
what was always Butler's way, so long as I knew anything of his way of working, namely—to read thoroughly,
not discursively. It was on this plan that when we had
read through the *Odyssey* and *Virgil*, instead of going on
to other books, we went, at his suggestion, a second time
through these, not now translating every line, but taking
only the more difficult passages and consulting each other

on them, so as to be sure that we knew them, at least as far as our critical faculties enabled us to interpret them. In other work, such as Greek and Latin composition, we gained considerable help from interchanging translations with some Cambridge friends of Butler's—Denman and Penrose—with whom he had made acquaintance at Trinity, and who sent us capital versions of passages, occasionally corrected by Shilleto.

"But it is not of our work together, pleasant and profitable to me as it was, that I most think in recalling our Oxford days; it is of the singular kindness, and even tenderness with which George Butler always treated me. He was naturally of a quick and hasty temper—(nothing in his after life struck me more than the control he had by God's grace gained over his natural irritability); but he bore with my hastiness with infinite patience. I can recall petulant outbursts which he soothed by his sympathy with my provocations, and by his calm considerateness. Not then only but ever afterwards I found his sympathy as keen to make allowances, as his judgment was clear to control and correct. One thing more I should like to add, as showing my dear friend's thoughtful kindness for me. We had decided to stand for Fellowships at Exeter College in the summer of 1842. About three months before the time of competition I met with a terrible accident, which quite incapacitated me for work. As soon as I was sufficiently recovered to leave Oxford I went home. We lived in London at that time. When the time of the examination was coming near, George, who was at his own home at Gayton, wrote to ask me to go thither and stay with him till my return to Oxford. He felt sure I could not regain strength for my work in

London, and he had his father's leave to invite me to the Rectory to pass the intervening ten days, and go up to Oxford together. Those ten days of country air and rest in a most delightful society proved an effectual tonic. We went up to Oxford for the examination, and to our surprise were both elected. Archdeacon Robinson had said 'Good-bye' to us with this exhortation: 'Go up and both win.' We laughed, and said to each other that it was too good to be realised. George thought that I should be elected as the senior, and that it would be thought that he could wait. I thought that he would be elected as the better man. The issue was a delightful realisation of both expectations. Our intercourse as Fellows could not be closer than it had been as Scholars of the same college, but the election served to keep us together and to continue to me the enjoyment of his society till he left Oxford for a tutorship in Durham University.

"I see I have omitted one thing which ought to be mentioned, namely, a *contretemps* which was a vexation to George, and a disappointment to his friends. In 1842, he was in for the Ireland Scholarship, then the most distinguished prize in the University, so far as classical scholarship was concerned. He went in with every prospect of winning it, but owing to a trivial informality in giving in his notice (it was a question of time, not of any greater importance, turning on the point of whether Sunday was to be taken as a day or not), the senior examiner decided that George could not stand, and after he had done two papers he had to retire. But for this we believed he would have added the Ireland to the Hertford Scholarship."

The Rector of Exeter at that time wrote as follows

to George Butler's father, concerning that disappointment :—

"My dear Sir,

"I am afraid you will be much disappointed at hearing that your son has been pronounced inadmissible as a candidate for the Ireland Scholarship, on the ground of his not having given the required notice. He takes the disappointment very well himself, as I should have expected of him, but seems to feel it on your account. I am sure your parental feelings would not allow you to entertain any hard thought of him, but yet I thought it would be satisfactory to you to learn that he is not deserving of any blame in the matter. He took quite as much pains as is usual to inform himself on the point. I do not wish to impeach the justice of the decision of the Trustees, but I think it a stricter construction of the rule than I should have anticipated."

George himself wrote to his father :—

"I write to you in an unexpected position ; viz., that of a rejected candidate for the Ireland. I went to put down my name, when the Warden spoke to me and told me that there were only two days intervening. Therefore I hoped I was exactly within the statutable time. He expressed a doubt as to whether Sunday was reckoned as a day, and referred me to the Provost of Oriel — one of the Trustees of the Scholarship. I went and stated my case to him. He said he would consult his fellow-trustees, and that meanwhile I might go in conditionally. On Monday morning I went in, and no objection was raised. I did my first paper—Latin hexameters—with which I was much pleased. The second paper—Greek translations—I did fairly enough, and thought that I had made a better beginning than last year, when on coming in from my walk about five I found a kind note from Dr. Williams, saying he was sorry to tell me that the Trustees had decided against my being admitted as a candidate. After chapel, the rector spoke to me, and said he thought it a very hard case, but there was nothing to be done. You will probably think I am very much disappointed. I will not deny that I am so. I may 'bear it as a man,' but I must also 'feel it as a man.' Indeed, without such feelings there would be no merit in endurance; not, however, that I wish to make any merit of that. I have received far too many good things from the hand of God to allow me the least pretence for repining. For the rest I shall work through all the allotted papers as they come out, giving myself the regular three hours and no more for each. This done, I shall get one of the Examiners to look over them, and report what he thinks of my performances.

"Your affectionate Son."

He had written at an earlier date to his mother, on the occasion of his getting the Hertford Scholarship :—

"Dearest Mother,

"It is with a heart overflowing with gratitude to God that I sit down to report to you my successful competition for the Hertford Scholarship. There were thirty-six competitors. The favourites were both Eton Newcastle scholars. I imagined my chance a very small one, indeed a blank. After the favour of God, I attribute my success entirely to my living most abstemiously, going early to bed and rising at six, taking a light breakfast and a walk after it, so that my head was clear and in good condition for instant work. This shall be my practice in future, for I have experienced the good effects of it."

To his father he wrote on the same subject :—

"I have heard from the Rector of our College, as well as from Mr. Spranger, that I was '*facile princeps*,'—I quote their words. They recommend . me to enlarge my sphere of reading, which my papers showed to be limited. This, of course, I am fully aware of. I did my papers with all the care that I could bestow on them. I am especially thankful that in this particular case I recovered from the effects of a severe cold in the most singularly rapid way that I ever remember, just in time to go in for the examination. I rejoice in this success on your account more than for any other reason."

It may be mentioned here that previously in this same year, 1842, George Butler had been elected as a Scholar of Exeter College.

His friend James Lonsdale wrote to him after he had taken his degree : " Thank you for your kind letter announcing this good news. I was told that you were the best man in the Schools at this time. I regret the fashion of putting the names in alphabetical order at Exeter College, and not by merit, according to the rule of your old University. I think you have no reason to regret your migration to Oxford, as a College scholarship, a Latin scholarship, and a Fellowship *in one's undergraduate days*, followed by a first class, are no bad things. May you go on prospering as you have begun."

The friendships made by George Butler in early life, and continued through life, must form an important element in the estimate of his character and career.

In 1851, when writing to his future wife, he said : " You know the proverb, ' A man is known by his companions,' and you ask me to tell you something of my friends. I gladly do so ; but the ray of light which will come to you, I fear, will be in a very broken state, as none of the group of friends of whom I was one resembled each other at all closely in character ; in fact there were strong contrasts in that respect amongst us." He then spoke of those whose acquaintance he made first at Exeter College, such as R. C. Powles, J. Anthony Froude, John Duke Coleridge (the present Lord Chief Justice), Seymour, Trithen (a learned German), John Blackett and Matthew Morton (both Northumbrians), the latter a young man of " saintly character," who was afterwards appointed Warden of St. Colomba's College in Ireland, and died young; and later : Max Müller, R. Morier (now Sir Robert), Goldwin Smith, and others.

To his Father, 1841 ·—

" I had last night a nice chat with John Blackett, my old Harrow friend. He is bent on reading hard this term. I mean to do the same, in order doubly to retrieve the honour of Harrow, and not allow Karslake the sole credit in the matter. Karslake is much ' in the mouths of men.' He is a very nice fellow. I see Jowett occasionally, and like him very much. He is very quiet in manner, and does not show off to advantage in a roomful of men, but he is a very agreeable companion. He has made me an exceedingly kind offer, which I think you would like me to accept. He is a member of a debating society called the ' Decade.' I think there are twelve members now. They meet at each other's rooms for discussion on a subject previously announced. Among the members are Jowett himself, Lake (a Fellow of Balliol), Arthur Stanley (son of Bishop Stanley and Fellow of University College), Coleridge, Pritchard, Matthew Arnold (eldest son of Dr. Arnold), Blackett, and a few others. They elect members without their knowledge, and then ask them to join the society, which precludes all canvassing. I am pleased beyond measure at the prospect of getting into such an excellent set, consisting as you may see of the picked men of the University "

· Mr. Froude, writing recently of his friendship with Butler, says :—

" It is difficult to convey briefly the recollections of nearly fifty years of life, and for all that time I may say an unbroken friendship continued between George Butler

and myself. It began on the day when we were elected
Fellows at Exeter together. True, frank, open, faithful,
he was in all his ways. In trouble and in success, in
small things or great, I knew that I could always rely
upon him for advice or help, if I wanted either, or for
sympathy if neither could be of use."

Lord Coleridge also recently wrote :—

" George Butler and I were much together before we
belonged to the same college, as we had the same friends,
the same pursuits and opinions. Amongst our friends,
Seymour (who became my brother-in-law) and Powles
were perhaps the truest and the closest. Then when we
belonged to the same college the ties were drawn tighter,
and we were friends to the last. I thank God for such a
friend."

George wrote again :—

" Trithen was one of my greatest friends. His father
was a Swiss by birth, and a Russian subject. He himself
was one of the most highly-gifted men I ever saw. He
used always to rave against mere book learning, and
would never allow himself to be called a savant, though
he was full of knowledge, ancient and modern. He
valued, as I did, a clear understanding and a sober judgment far more than great acquisitive power (which may
be like a large appetite without a good digestion). He
had a great objection to any display, preferring to deal
lightly with subjects, even though they were weighty;
just as a strong Swiss guide will skip and jump with a
heavy weight of mountaineering apparatus on his back.
He became hopelessly deranged, with no chance of the
balance being restored of his finely-wrought and well-
stored mind. He had been taking part in a trio (he was
an excellent musician), and became rather excited; but

I was not prepared for hearing, as I did a fortnight after, that he was under confinement, from which he was never released."

Of a somewhat different character from most of the friends above-mentioned was Bowen (now Sir George Bowen), who entered the diplomatic service, and is well known as a Colonial Governor. George describes him as "an Irishman, Fellow of Brasenose College, and one of a society called 'The Cosmopolite,' of which I also was a member. Bowen is an excellent, good fellow. Our Cosmopolite society was formed chiefly with a view of cultivating more toleration and more enlarged sympathies than Oxford men generally had. These principles were the bond which united us. Many a pleasant evening have we spent together. Bowen was one of our best members."

In 1843 George Butler took his degree, having obtained a first class.

" I have just got my testamur certified," he wrote to his father : " I have satisfied the Examiner. I was not entirely satisfied with my *vivâ voce* questions. My Examiner in Ethics and I did not understand each other so well as we might.

" It seems strange, after so much labour expended in getting up knotty points, and so much solicitude about the order of historical events, &c., to have all one's knowledge, so laboriously acquired, stewed down into an indefinitely small space. And now I have finished my undergraduate course and am free. I am very thankful that I have had strength given to me to support my labours, at times very severe, for three years without a day's illness. I have continued in good spirits and good health. My impression is that, humanly speaking, nothing can hurt a good constitution with which you do not take liberties, unless it be mental disquietude, which will in spite of oneself arise at times; and it is then that the sympathy of friends, such as you, my dear father have shown to me, is particularly helpful. I cannot tell you the comfort your letters have been to me at times, especially when I was, perhaps, thinking too much of the reward of my labours instead of resting in the faithful prosecution of them, and trusting that the issue, whatever it might be, would be for the best. I do not remember ever having felt so tired as I did after the examination. I had been reading very hard for two or three days. A great deal of this labour I might have spared myself, as the event showed; still I did not feel comfortable in leaving anything to chance which I might secure by diligence, and I went in feeling that though I might not do well in some things, I could not be floored in anything."

In 1851, when revising his classics and philosophy, to qualify himself to be an Examiner in the Schools at Oxford, he wrote:—

"I am working very hard, but I take a good walk every day, and that is something. I am in famous working condition now. I feel just as I used to do when I was reading for my degree. No day was too long for me, and I never got sleepy in the evening. Dining early, eating and drinking very moderately, and taking exercise regularly in all weathers, are very conducive to this. I am beginning to feel as old as I did in 1841. Yes, that was the period of my greatest antiquity. I then went through the owlish phase—read all day, spoke little, ate little, walked much, wrote Latin letters to my friends, and was generally very disagreeable. Ask Emily for particulars."

He kept up his connection very closely with Oxford for four years, making use of the time for various studies and taking pupils or reading parties during the long vacations. He was for some months private tutor to young Lord Hopetoun, part of the time in London and part very pleasantly spent at Hopetoun House, in Scotland, where he received much kindness from the guardian and mother of Lord Hopetoun. On one occasion his naturally irascible temper got the better of him in dealing with his somewhat idle and careless pupil, so much so, that he boxed his ears. Little Lord Hopetoun ran at once to complain to his mother, who sent him back with the message: " Tell Mr. Butler that he has done quite right, and I hope you will be the better for it."

CHAPTER III.

A LONG VACATION READING PARTY AT THE ENGLISH LAKES.—
NOTICES OF J. A. FROUDE, THE ARNOLDS, WORDSWORTH, AND
HARTLEY COLERIDGE.—VISIT TO THE WEST OF IRELAND
WITH MR. FROUDE.—DEATH OF A SISTER.—TAKES A READING
PARTY TO GERMANY IN 1846.—VISITS GERMANY AGAIN IN
1847 WITH PUPILS. RECOLLECTIONS OF THAT·YEAR BY
SPENCER P. BUTLER.—ACCEPTS A TUTORSHIP AT THE
UNIVERSITY OF DURHAM.—MAKES THE ACQUAINTANCE OF
HIS FUTURE WIFE.—CORRESPONDENCE.—DEVELOPMENT OF
CHARACTER.

GEORGE BUTLER gave an account himself in *Longman's Magazine* (October, 1888) of his first long vacation after taking his degree. He went with a reading party, consisting of his younger brother Spencer, and two other pupils, to Grasmere. He wrote:

" I had the advantage of several introductions; viz., to the poet Wordsworth, to Mr. Harrison of Green Bank, Ambleside, and to the Arnolds of Fox How. Hartley Coleridge was an intimate friend of the Greens, at whose house he was staying. Also several Oxford friends had settled here; *i.e.*, Plumptre of University College; Arthur Clough and Theodore Walrond, who were at Patterdale; and Scott of Trinity, Oxford, who was at Grasmere. Mr. Bonamy Price was staying at Ambleside with his brother-in-law, Mr. Edward Rose.

" When my companions arrived we settled down to work,—a morning header or a swim in the lake being a regular institution. I took an early opportunity of calling on Wordsworth. I had made his acquaintance some years previously, when he was on a visit to his nephew, the then Head Master of Harrow. That evening there was no one but the family party. Mrs. Wordsworth and Mrs. Quillinan presided at the tea-table, and a stroll in the garden to see a fine sunset concluded a memorable evening, brightened by the assurance of welcome whenever I was able to visit the Mount.

"Our scheme of hard study allowed for occasional excursions. It is needless to say that we explored all the mountains in the neighbourhood, reserving the higher elevations for more extensive excursions.

"An ascent of Helvellyn was planned; our party was a numerous one. The Arnolds mustered strongly. We were joined by Plumptre, and met on Helvellyn by Clough and Walrond. Near the top Mr. Rose and I had an adventure which might have proved disastrous to one at least of us, and which I shall relate for the sake of warning to younger men and as a tribute to the memory of a friend. Having heard that he was an experienced cragsman, I challenged Mr. Rose to scale the 'Eagle's Crag,' to which he assented. To do this we had to descend a 'screes' or 'shillybed' and then make our way up a steep rock with inconsiderable ledges projecting, and dwarf juniper bushes growing out of the cracks. Out of deference to Mr. Rose's experience and reputation, I asked him to lead, which he did, availing himself of every help which the rocks or juniper bushes afforded. However, I thought it was possible to make the ascent by a more direct way, which accordingly I tried. Before I was two-thirds up, I felt my hold giving way, a juniper bush coming out by the roots. I called out to Rose that I was slipping, and he prepared himself for the worst.

However, fortune in this case favoured the rash. As I was slipping down the face of the rock a sharp, projecting corner caught my shooting-jacket, which had one button fastened ; this checked my descent, and by dint of holding on by the crevices with one hand, and hooking my walking stick, a stout Kendal hazel, over a point of rock above, I managed to retain my position. Fortunately I had been trained at school and college for gymnastics, so that I had no difficulty in drawing myself up by aid of the good hazel till I could get my left hand on to solid rock, after which no difficulty presented itself. But I was in considerable danger, and my brave companion was much relieved to find he had not to help a disabled comrade.

"After some time spent on the mountain top, we raced down to Grasmere, where my brother and I took a second bathe in the lake. There is no danger in going into the water 'hissing hot,' to use a phrase of Arthur Shadwell, that great authority on aquatic sports, including the taking of headers. It helps one to resist the chill of the water, and brings about a speedier reaction, and that glow which is the bather's delight and reward."

Of another day's excursion he wrote to his father, in 1844 : "We had a delightful walk yesterday to Dummail Raise, a hill which commands an excellent panoramic view of the whole lake country. On one side rose Skiddaw and Helvellyn, and on the other Scafell, and its brother Bow Fell, forming, with a conical hill called Great Gable, a magnificent· ridge, which,· lying as it did in broad shadow, reminded me of Shelley's line ·

'And all dark Tempe lay in the shadow of Pelion,'

so completely did it overhang the valley, through which wound a small silver stream.

'The valley or gorge of Borrowdale lay among the

enclosing hills. Beyond it lay Derwentwater and Bassenthwaite Water. In the distance were the Solway Firth and the Cheviot Hills, whilst in the other direction we saw Morecambe Bay and the Lancashire Coast. Between these and the mountains on which we stood lay other lakes: Windermere, looking as blue as any Italian lake one can fancy; Esthwaite, Ribbleswater, part of Grasmere, and lastly Ennerwater Tarns."

The narrative in *Longman's Magazine* continues: "Of minor excursions it is needless to write. Grasmere, with its peaceful lake and wooded hills, is lovely in fine summer weather, when the foliage of the trees is reflected in the calm mirror of the lake. On one occasion the stillness was so perfect that it was impossible to say which image was the clearer, that of the hillside or that which was reflected in the lake. I remember well a moonlight night, when the objects surrounding the lake and its solitary island were seen with wonderful distinctness. I have two sketches made the same evening, after swimming across the lake, representing in grey and white the silvery moonlight, and the hills around the house.

"Hartley Coleridge we saw frequently. He lived in a cottage on Rydal Water, below the Mount, and was the object of great care and attention. His neighbours vied with each other in showing their appreciation of his genius and originality. How he came by his outward garments I cannot say. They were certainly not made for him. He usually wore a long-tailed dress-coat, made for a man half-a-head taller than he was, and a battered straw-hat, better suited for what is called in Northumberland a 'tatie-bogle' than a poet and philosopher. He was little more than five feet in height, with a stoop in his shoulders, long unkempt hair, and bright eyes.

"Great allowance must in all Christian charity be made for Hartley. He inherited a large portion of the genius of his family, without the power of self-restraint. He had been elected probationer Fellow of Oriel, but with strict warning against intemperance. Hartley avoided censure till the evening before his election as full Fellow, and then, alas! succumbed to temptation, and, it is reported, got hopelessly drunk. No further probation was allowed him, and he lost his Fellowship. No doubt he felt bitterly the severity of the sentence. No doubt he suffered acutely at times from self-reproach. His respect for his brother Derwent, who was certainly not his superior in intellect, but who was thoroughly respectable and well-conducted, and who was also remarkably handsome, was very touching. Hartley looked up to him as a superior being, which no doubt he was morally and socially; but the lake dwellers loved poor Hartley, and shewed their regard for him in many ways.

"One day, when Mr. Harrison entertained a large party at Green Bank to 'assist' at a school fête, Mr. Wordsworth was present, and we had the honour of escorting him home. We talked of his literary contemporaries. Of Scott and Southey he spoke with kindly feeling. Not so of Lord Byron. 'He was a man,' he said, 'of the most rancorous disposition, who never cared what pain he inflicted on others so long as he gratified his own vanity. Me, too, he attacked; me, who had never written a word in disparagement of him! He was a man of great natural gifts, which he degraded by his misuse of them.' . It was curious to see how the barbed shaft, sent out by Byron, rankled in the wounded heart of the amiable bard of Rydal Mount. Not having the same ground of personal quarrel, I ventured to put in a word for Byron, as having devoted his time and fortune, and, as it turned out, his life, to the restoration of the liberties of Greece. 'Surely,' I said, 'he was disinterested in this.' But the old man would not admit it. 'It was all owing to a personal vanity.' So we changed the subject of our conversation, and soon arrived at the turning up to Rydal Mount, where we parted.

"I was expecting a visit from my friend and brother Fellow of Exeter College, James Anthony Froude, who was returning from the West of Ireland. When he arrived, we invited Hartley Coleridge to spend a day with us. He accepted the invitation. While walking up to the house with him, I asked him if he could explain why it was that wherever one went, one found legends of the devil, and in most countries a Devil's Bridge. He paused for a moment, saying, as he collected his thoughts : 'It's very curious—very curious indeed ;' then, turning back to me as he entered the door of the house, he said : 'One would think the *devvill* had been Pontifex Maximus.' Some of his best things were said as he walked about the room. He would suddenly pause and look in the face of one of his audience, and pour out his excogitated thoughts —always worth listening to. I regret, however, to say that, whilst Froude and I, though sensible of the ludicrous aspect of the matter, were careful not to show more than interest and sympathy—laughing not at, but with, Hartley Coleridge,—my pupils, being younger, were overpowered with 'unquenchable laughter,' and were fain to retire into the next room.

"We parted, after a memorable evening, with warm assurances of regard. I never saw Hartley again ; but the remembrance of him is green and fresh in my memory. It is very creditable to the natives of Cumberland and

Westmoreland that they should have reverenced the genius and intellect of a man whose moral weaknesses made his life a failure, and that they should have watched over him with an affectionate regard which was very touching.

"The following day my pupils separated, and left Froude and me alone. Our first expedition was to Wastdale Head. Starting from Grasmere about one o'clock, and ascending High Raise, we crossed by the Stake Pass, and made our way over the side of Scawfell—unfortunately, the wrong side, as my remembrance of Flintoff's model made me suspect; and we found ourselves seated on the ridge of Bowfell, looking upon Esk Hawse, which Mr. Wordsworth described to me as the finest instance of crags in the Lake District. There we took some scanty refreshment and commenced our descent into Eskdale. The mountain side was one mass of great boulders. We reached the plain. Eskdale is a wild, waste valley, and it was long before we met a native. Then we asked about the distance to Wastdale Head. He was long in comprehending the question. At last he exclaimed: 'Oh! it's Wauzle Heead ye want to go to. It's a long way to Wauzle Heead.' This he explained as meaning ten or twelve miles. The evening was coming on. We were not sure of our way. So we engaged him to act as our guide. The route lay by Burnmoor Tarn, said to contain pike of antediluvian size. As we were eager to get quarters for the night, we went ahead of our guide, who paid us the compliment of saying: 'Eh! ye be fine travellers. I have never seen such travellers.' We dismissed him when we saw lying before us the head of Wastdale, and our guide pointed out to us the direction of Ritson's house. But then our troubles began again. The road along which we travelled served as a watercourse, and we found ourselves nearly up to our knees in water. So we scrambled up the bank, and made our way across the fields. But it was now dark. The stars came out grandly over our heads, but there was no appearance of a house. We shouted, and our voices came back clear and strong from the hills; but no other human voice replied. It looked as if we were hopelessly benighted. At last Froude thought he saw a light glimmering from the window of a house not very distant, and towards this we made our way, and were rewarded by finding a substantial house, and a cordial reception from Mr. Ritson, the owner—a tall man, with good features, and a friendly independent manner.

" On Monday we started on a final excursion. We were to visit Thirlmere, Buttermere and Crummock. Travelling on foot with a single companion is either very pleasant or much the reverse. Froude was, to me, the most perfect companion imaginable. We had been elected to Fellowships at Exeter College two years previously, and our friendship, begun then, had grown with our growth in years. We both admired natural scenery, and were well matched for walking. We were both fond of the water, and never neglected an opportunity of boating or bathing.

" We walked to Thirlmere, and crossed the bridge. It was a fine picturesque day, and Raven's Crag was seen in all its gloomy grandeur. We walked on by Watendlath to the Grange, Borrowdale, halting for ten minutes over High Lodore, and taking a header in a remarkably clear pool of the Upper Derwent; refreshed by which, we paid a visit to Scott of Trinity, who entertained us hospitably in those lodgings where many a distinguished University man has stayed, for the purpose of quiet study and enjoyment of the scenery. We started again for Buttermere, passing under Honister Crag. The weather was perfect and we did not find the day too long. The following day we wandered along the banks of Buttermere Lake, taking some headers from an inviting rock, covered with heather. I believe we also paid a morning visit to Crummock for the same purpose. Certainly, when we took a boat and rowed from end to end of Crummock for a better view of the mountains and sunset, I at least took a third dip. As years advance our memories do not improve. Yet some events of our lives remain fixed in our minds with remarkable clearness. Some of these I have endeavoured to relate."

Writing in 1888 to George, Mr. Froude said : " The most interesting part of your letter to-day is the promise of your recollections of the Cumberland time. How well and how vividly I remember it all; and how pleasant it will be for you who write, and for me who will read, to have a genuine piece of our human life snatched from forgetfulness, and made fresh and real once more! For some reason or other, perhaps because we were at that age in circumstances which made us both impressionable and made the impressions permanent, those weeks have left a more distinct picture of themselves in my memory than almost any other part of my young life."

A little later he wrote again : " You have brought up as in a photograph the recollections of that summer, and all that we did, said, and thought in it. The features of that walk which are most vivid to myself are the blank, dark hollow of Wastdale, as we looked down into it from the mountains where our guide left us, and scrambled along the watercourse at the bottom, which was the only path we could find, and our unexpected discovery, the next morning, that we were at the top of Scafell, when we thought we were on Stag's Head. Also, I recollect with extreme clearness the beautiful evening on Crummock, before we parted."

In the summer of '45, George went to Ireland with Mr. Froude. They lived almost completely out of doors, an active, healthy life; so that when first one and then the other was attacked by smallpox, the disease took but slight hold of them, and recovery was rapid.

Mr. Froude writes: "We shared each other's tastes and amusements, on mountain and on river bank. We also shared our misfortunes; for he nursed me when I caught smallpox in Ireland, and himself took the fever after me."

He was a very tender nurse; they were in poor quarters, but he made the best of the situation, wrapping his friend Froude in his own plaid when the night was cold, and watching over him with brotherly affection.

The following is a memorandum, which was made some years later, of the illness which attacked the brother tourists:

"On Sunday Froude became feverish, and I had a suspicion of the nature of his malady, which was confirmed by the doctor from Newport, who pronounced that he had smallpox, caught, doubtless, from some of the children whom we saw moving in and out of the fishermen's houses at Oughterard. It was an anxious time. At night he was delirious, and had dreams of strange weird forms coming into his room, but in the day time he was better. On Tuesday morning he begged me to go and get some air; so I went out with my rod, and succeeded in a short time in taking a sixteen-pound salmon in the Long Pool. It was a beautiful fish, and when I exhibited it to Froude his eyes brightened, and, as he declared, he took a turn for the better from that moment.

"A week later I was on the way to Achill Head, having left Froude at a friend's house to recruit. I came to the edge of the cliff, where the view was magnificent. The rocks were so steep that you could drop a pebble, it was said, from a height of 1700 feet into the Atlantic which washed the base of the cliffs. As far as the eye could reach lay the deep blue waters of the Atlantic, with here and there a sail, and many a gull and cormorant busily engaged in fishing. Were it not for an occasional line of creamy spray which advanced a few feet and then retired, causing a slight murmur on the shingly shore, you would have said that the ocean was charmed into a perfect repose. But I suddenly became aware of a feeling of insecurity, unusual to me, and an unwillingness to approach the edge of the cliff ; I felt tired, and my pulse was at 120. I told my companions that I was not well. They assured me that it was nothing but the heat of the day, and unwilling to spoil their enjoyment, I said nothing more till we reached the inn. Then I told the fishing captain that I thought I was sickening for the smallpox. I could not bear the thought of bringing Froude back to nurse me, so I pushed on to Newport. As my headache did not abate, I went to bed and resigned myself with as much philosophy as I could to my fate. After two days, however, I was able to sit up, and while Froude went out fishing I made out for myself an Irish vocabulary. An assistant teacher from the school came and gave me some reading lessons in Irish. I might have mastered the language more completely had my recovery been more tardy ; but I soon regained strength. On Friday I went out, and on Saturday I went up to the Weir where I had seen plenty of salmon working their way up on the day before. In half-an-hour I had made fast a good twelve pounder. So I had the satisfaction of catching a salmon on the eighth day after being attacked with smallpox. On our return home to England we felt we were not without a reminder that ' in the midst of life we are in death,' for we had passed through one of the most dreaded forms of disease, without any of our home circle to nurse us. That certainly was a reality ; and I have often felt thankful, when visiting the sick and dying in my native land, that my friend and I, who had gone through such an ordeal, were mercifully spared to minister to others."

On returning from Ireland to Gayton, his father's living, George was called to the first real sorrow of his life, in the death of his much-loved sister, Benigna. She and another sister had typhus fever : the elder sister died, while the younger, Emily, struggled through a severe illness and recovered. He always spoke with the tenderest admiration of his sister Benigna. She was dark in complexion like himself, with bright eyes, a graceful figure, a lively manner, and a beautiful voice. He never forgot the feeling with which she used to sing Haydn's "Angels ever bright and fair." Her letters to him, which he carefully kept, indicated a friendship between brother and sister on equal terms, both being intellectual, cultivated, and high spirited.

In the autumn of 1846, and again in 1847, George Butler went with pupils to Germany. The following is a contribution of recollections from Spencer Butler, his younger brother :

" I remember very little of George personally before 1844. I was a schoolboy when he took his degree. He obtained his Fellowship while he was an undergraduate,

and stayed up at Oxford a good deal during several long
vacations to read. He invited me to join him in his
reading party to Grasmere in 1844. I remember his
taking me to tea with the poet Wordsworth ; I remember
also an ascent of Helvellyn, when we got into a mist, and
through the mist, near the top, loomed out Walrond
and Clough and Matthew Arnold, and, I think, John
Connington—all now dead.

"In 1846 George took a reading party to the Rhine,
his pupils being Sartoris, Ducane, and one or two others.
Ducane married a daughter of Lord Lyndhurst, was made
a Colonial Governor, and knighted. I think this was
George's first experience of the Continent, and he enjoyed
it greatly.

"In 1847 I was at Rugby, and George invited me to
join his second reading party. We went up the Rhine.
His pupils on this occasion were Wood and another who
became Fellow of Queen's at Oxford, and I think there
was a third. I saw Prince Albert installed as Chancellor
at Cambridge on a broiling June day, and joined George
at Dover the same evening, whence we went to Cologne.
I have a vivid recollection of my first pleasing experience
of the *al fresco* life of Cologne and Frankfort. At
Heidelberg we had some charming lodgings over a
restaurant, on the left hand of the street which ascends
to the castle, and near the entrance to the castle grounds.
Here we had a sitting-room with a grand view, looking
west over the Rhine valley and north over the Neckar
valley. George sketched a good deal, and worked hard
at German. We sometimes went to the kneip of the
Westphalian corps of students, where much beer and
tobacco were consumed ; and once, I recollect, to a great
Commers of all the students' corps at Neckar Stein. We

saw two of the students' duels one day, one of which was bloodless, and the other ending in a sliced nose, more unpleasant than serious. On the evening of one very hot day we dined with a merchant at Worms, in the cool garden of the Liebfrau Stift, and were picked up afterwards by a passing Rhine steamer and conveyed to Manheim. All this was delightful. I have mementoes of those pleasant days in two water-colour pictures, by George, of the Gesprengter Thurm of the castle and of the ascending street, with two students in brotherly embrace walking up the hill. I recollect how the airs of the opera seemed to linger in George's memory. We frequented the opera and theatres in order to learn the language.

"After six weeks of this life at Heidelberg, so new to me, the pupils left, and we two started for Dresden. We took a carriage at Frankfort and drove to Göttingen, stopping, I think, at Cassell and Gresson, where Liebig was then professor, and where there were many English students, one of whom summed up the advantages of the place by saying that there was great freedom for experiment in ·Liebig's chemical laboratory, and that you could make ' any kind of stench you liked.' I remember at Göttingen our hospitable landlord had a grand concert in the open air in the evening. Next morning we started for the Hartz mountains, and in course of time reached the top of the Brocken, where we found much mist. Then, by way of Leipsic, we reached Dresden, and went to Professor Hughes, who was Professor of English at the University. We had a delightful time there. We generally dined *al fresco* in the afternoon on the terrace overlooking the Elbe, and in time for the opera in the evening. The brothers Devrient were then acting, and Tichatchek

was the tenor. Emil Devrient was very fine in his acting
of 'Coriolanus.' It was the time of Jenny Lind's *debût*.
You can imagine that, with the great Picture Gallery and
the Museums for the day, and such music and acting as
we had in the theatres for the evening, the time slid away
pleasantly—the whole programme being over by nine
o'clock, when we joined the Hughes' supper party.
Lastly, we made a short excursion in Saxon Switzerland.
My fortnight came to an end: George remained and
perfected his German, while I joined my father and
mother on the Rhine. I recollect some shooting with
George later at Peterborough and Gayton, when his
faithful gun, which he had carried about in Germany and
paid duty for at the several frontiers as a *piece d'ordnance*,
did great execution on the game."

Among the letters which George continually wrote to
his parents during his two successive tours in Germany,
there are many pages concerning the scenery—all new
to him—which prove the freshness and vividness of the
impressions which he then received. In 1846, after
starting with his pupils from London, they stopped some
days at Bonn, where he had introductions to several
eminent professors. With Dr. Bernays he kept up afterwards a correspondence in Latin.

He writes: "We passed through some lovely scenery
between Liége and Aix la Chapelle, scenery reminding
me strongly of the Peak-country in the neighbourhood
of Matlock in Derbyshire, but still more romantic, and
better watered with streams full of trout and grayling,
and studded with villas. Some highly picturesque old
castles we passed, and churches perched on high emi-
nences, together with country houses surrounded by
beautiful gardens. An engineer as well as an artist would

be struck with admiration at seeing a line of railway across such a country. It has been compared to a needle run through a corkscrew."

During the walking tour above mentioned, with his brother through the Hartz mountains, he wrote: "The valleys of the Ocker and Ilsen were very striking, the former abounding in sharp-pointed rocky crags, jutting out at every turn of the valley from among the gigantic flinty boulders which cover the hillsides. The fir trees, which grow luxuriantly, seem to seek out the most picturesque spots, fastening their roots deep in the rocky crevices, and stretching out their withered arms far over the valley below."

After his pupils had returned to England he pursued his studies of languages and art for some time alone in Germany in both years. In one of these he visited the Eifel country, following up the Moselle from where it joins the Rhine at Coblenz.

He wrote from Trèves: "Two more delightful days I scarcely ever passed than those spent on the way hither. The country is, to my mind, much more picturesque than that through which the Rhine flows. Here in Trèves I have been very industrious in drawing. Yesterday I sketched the Porto Martis, said to have been built before ever the Romans came here—a strange old pile, with Tuscan columns; and to-day I have nearly finished a coloured sketch of the Roman baths, which are most curious, abounding in bright red colouring. I have had long walks on the banks of the river, sometimes with my books and a pocket dictionary. Occasionally I read out of doors for two or three hours together. My enjoyment would be complete if I had a congenial companion to share it with me. However, I do not object to solitude

such as I have had lately. I certainly think one is more
alive to impressions when alone, strolling through the
fields and watching the sun going down beneath the vine-
clad hills, than when surrounded by others, to whom one
feels bound to say something; and then the exertion of
calling up an idea, and expressing it, destroys that neutral
and purely passive state which is more favourable for the
reception of outward impressions."

These slight reminiscences of George Butler's early
days of travel have a peculiar interest to those who accompanied him again and again during the latter years of
his life, when the same scenes were gone over afresh, and
when he would call up recollections of his youthful days
as we drove together through the streets of Frankfort, or
sketched again the Roman ruins at Trèves, or followed
the windings of the Moselle. The country of which he
expressed so much admiration, between Cologne and
Liége, is now much changed, owing to the increase of
railway traffic and manufactures; but he was able to
make a comparison not unfavourable to the later time
during a delightful visit which we paid to M. Emile de
Laveleye, at his country house on the Meuse, in 1886,
and during our return journey to Aachen on a magnificent
summer evening, which recalled some of the incidents
described in his early letters.

During his German tour he had more than one opportunity for his favourite sport of shooting. Through the
kindness of some German Baron, possessing estates full
of game, he was able to try his good English gun, which
he did with much success, being complimented by his
host on the precision of his aim and his tireless perseverance in walking throughout the whole day. He
also occasionally met with distinguished literary men,

as for example, in Frankfort, whence he wrote to his father :

" Yesterday there was a grand dinner given by the Corporation of Frankfort. Large numbers assembled on the occasion, which was that of an annual meeting of some literary society. All, or almost all, the great literary men of Germany, whose names are known throughout Europe, were there ; and I thought myself fortunate to be able to hear speeches on subjects of national interest from the two brothers Grimm, Dahlman, Uhland the poet, Mittermaier, and a number of others, who are looked up to in Germany with a ˙respect and veneration almost amounting to idolatry. I never witnessed a more interesting scene. I could understand the speeches sufficiently to follow the argument and keep up my interest from three to nine o'clock p.m."

In 1848 he was appointed to a Tutorship at the University of Durham, which he retained for a little more than two years. It was during the latter part of his residence there that I first made his acquaintance.

In pursuing my narrative I shall continue to speak with all simplicity in the first person. To do otherwise, to assume the impersonal style, would be for me alike an effort and an affectation. A word spoken to me one day by my eldest son dwells in my mind : " Do not hesitate," he said, " to make your 'recollections' something of the character of an autobiography. You can scarcely help doing so, for my father's life and yours were so completely one." There seemed to me a guidance in these words, which indeed express the truth in regard to the united life which, beginning in 1851, continued for nearly forty years.

A few extracts from his letters, written to myself, will

best illustrate the development of his character during the next few years. In January, 1851, he wrote from St. Leonard's, where he had spent Christmas with his invalid father: "I do not wonder at your being jealous of admiration bestowed on outward accomplishments, which, however much they may charm and delight others, can never win such regard and esteem as one covets from those whose opinion is most worth having. The possession of faculties which are so much prized by the world is however a good thing, if we view it rightly. It is a gift of God, and has its rightful use. It enables its possessor to bestow pleasure of a pure and harmless kind on others; but it involves considerable responsibilities, and often leaves the mind perplexed as to what course to adopt. The difficulty is increased when there is a diversity of gifts, all calling for cultivation, and each claiming so much time and attention that it seems impossible to follow out more than one; and then comes the question, 'Which is the worthier?' and this is often not at all easy to answer. One is often tempted to envy those who have only 'one line'; they seem so contented in following it. Their circle is complete: it may be a small one, but it is complete; while the more highly gifted and ambitious often spend their lives in fruitless efforts to make the ends of their circle meet. They begin, perhaps, with a very large radius, and keep gradually contracting this till in the end they present an ill-formed spiral. However, this is not always the case. Difficulties should be spurs to a man's energy, and should never deter us from aiming at the highest that we can possibly reach. A greater danger after all is, that the exaltation which follows on success in the paths of literature or art, or any other, should beget intellectual pride."

His room at Durham was at the top of the ancient castle, which itself stood on the rock whence rises the magnificent cathedral and the university buildings, and round the foot of which runs the pretty river spanned by picturesque bridges. He was liked and respected by the students, not less by those who were inclined to be idle and noisy than by the more industrious and steady. His excellence in athletic exercises and his love for out-door pursuits were a bond of sympathy with the former which sometimes produced happy results. Their feeling was expressed on one occasion by some of their number burning with the end of a red-hot poker, on the outside of the strong oak door of his lofty apartment in the castle, the words " Butler is a brick," for which testimonial they probably got, not thanks, but a reprimand.

To Josephine Grey :

" In bad weather I work away at Plato in my lofty nest, whence I can look out to all points of the compass. Those ' heathen friends ' of mine, of whom you speak, would have been very good Christians if they had had a chance, Plato especially, whose mind was of a more believing cast than Aristotle's. *' Il gran maestro di color chi sanno '* is rather too dry and lawyer-like to please me. He is invaluable, however, as a teacher of practical wisdom. One feels the constraining force of his arguments, which are based on the common-sense of mankind. Although I do not recommend you now to take up Greek, I hope to make you acquainted some day with fragments of thought gleaned from those ancient fields which bore so rich a harvest. I have a great deal of sympathy with the old Greeks. Their literature is like their art—perfect in its kind. We have introduced elements which make our literature richer and more comprehensive, just as a Gothic cathedral is richer than a Greek temple ; but we shall never surpass, probably never equal, them in form and symmetry. I admire the old Greeks for this, and also for their versatility, for the ease with which they turned their minds from the most trivial to the most important subjects. Nothing seemed too little or too great for them. I have been reading some grand passages at the end of Plato's *Republic*, the original of Sir Thomas More's *Utopia*. The doctrine of a future state, and of rewards and chastisements being assigned to us in that state, according as our life on earth has been good or evil, is stated very clearly. It is marvellous that a doctrine on which, as Bishop Butler says, 'our hopes and fears are grounded,' should be found more fully stated in the writings of a heathen philosopher than in the Jewish Scriptures. I will make some extracts from the book when I come to Dilston. I think you will agree with me that such flowers never grew elsewhere under the cold moonlight; and that if the Sun of Righteousness had risen upon them, they would have blossomed abundantly, and been fit, so far as human reason can see, to be transplanted into Paradise."

The following, written after our engagement, shows his extreme honesty of character, while it indicates in some faint degree his just and unselfish view of what the marriage relation should be; namely, a perfectly equal union, with absolute freedom on both sides for personal initiative in thought and action and for individual development :

"I do not ask you to write oftener. I would have you follow the dictates of your own heart in this; but be always certain that whatever comes from you is thrice welcome. *I* write because I feel it to be necessary to my happiness. I have lately written to you out of the fulness of my heart, when my soul was deeply moved to strive after a higher life. But often my letters will be about trifling matters, so that you may be tempted to say, 'Why write at all?' Yet, after all, life is largely made up of trifles. Moreover, I do not wish to invest myself in borrowed plumes. I do not want you to find out later that I am much like other people, perhaps even

more commonplace than most. I would rather your eyes
were opened. at once. I cannot reproach myself with ever
having assumed a character not my own to you or to anyone.
Such impostures are always too deeply purchased by the loss
of self-respect. But I fear that you may have formed too
high an estimate of my character — one to which I can never
come up; and for your sake I would wish to remove every
veil and obstacle which might prevent your seeing me just
as I am. If I were only to write to you when my better
feelings were wrought upon, you might think me much better
than I am; so I will write to you on every subject and
in every mood. . . . Those lines which I sent to you
gave no exaggerated picture. I have often felt in a very
different spirit to that in which we should say 'Our Father.'
The praying for particular blessings, which is enjoined by the
words of the Lord Jesus, 'Ask, and ye shall receive,' has
appeared to me at times as derogatory to the Omniscient and
All-provident character of God. 'Can He,' I have thought,
'alter the smallest of His dispensations at the request of
such a weak and insignificant being as I am?' This 'vain
philosophy,' the offspring of intellectual pride, has had more
to do with blighting my faith than wilful sin or the world's
breath !

"But though I have 'wandered out of the way in the
wilderness,' I do not despair of taking possession of the
promised land. You say you can do so little for me. Will
it be little, Josephine, if, urged by your encouragement and
example, I put off the works of darkness and put on the
armour of light? Blessings from the Giver of all blessings
fall upon you for the joy you have given to me, for the new
life to which you have called me !"

I had asked him to freely give me advice as to certain
lines of conduct or action. He replied : " I should think
it undue presumption in me to suggest anything to you in
regard to your life and duties. He who has hitherto
guided your steps will continue to do so. Believe me, I

value the expression of your confidence and affection above 'pearls and precious stones'; but I must not suffer myself to be dazzled, or to fancy that I have within me that power of judging and acting aright which would alone authorise me to point out to you any path in which you ought to walk. I am more content to leave you to walk by yourself in the path you shall choose; but I know that I do not leave you alone and unsupported, for *His* arm will guide, strengthen, and protect you. I only pray, then, that you may be more and more conformed to the image of Him who set us a perfect example, and that He will dispose my heart to love and admire most those things in you which are most admirable and lovely."

He had spent several days, preparatory to leaving Durham to take up the work of a public Examiner in Oxford, in reading over and destroying or arranging a number of old letters, dating from many years back. The retrospect thus opened up appears to have awakened some deep thoughts and heart-searchings, bringing to his memory defects in duty and the absence of a sufficiently high standard in the past. The Spirit of God which at the creation moved upon the face of the waters, heralding the light which followed darkness, the order and beauty which succeeded chaos, moved now in the midst of this heart-searching in a gentle and almost imperceptible manner, and continued so to move—intermittently, it may be, as to results—but never again forsaking the soul into which it had entered with the breath of the New Life which knows no ending. The lines, written at that time by himself, to which he referred in the letter above quoted, were as follows, preceded by the words :

" ' Save me, O God ; for the waters are come in unto me, even unto my soul.'

" Oh! give me back my childhood's faith,
Drunk in upon my mother's knee ;
My love and confidence in Thee,
Lord, give me back ; oh give me faith !

" When first I learned to praise Thy name,
I had no doubt that prayer could move,
Or pity touch the God of Love :
Oh that my faith were still the same !

" Sin, and the world's ungenial breath,
Have blighted the celestial flower ;
Drooping it sinks from hour to hour,
And languishes well-nigh in death.

" Oh! send Thy Spirit from above,
And quicken me with heavenly life !
Else am I vanquished in the strife ;
Lord, give me faith ! Lord, give me love ! "

Beneath he wrote the words : " I will give thanks unto Him from whom cometh my salvation. Why art thou cast down, O my soul? and why art thou disquieted within me ? Hope thou in God; for I will yet praise Him, who is the health of my countenance and my God."

" The Castle, Durham.

" I am here amidst a wilderness of letters, which I have brought into something like order and arrangement. I read a great number last night before burning them, and this kept me till nearly three a.m. To-day I feel rather like an extinct volcano. Many letters from old friends I read—letters full of warmth, and fresh, vigorous youthful spirits, such as, I fear, some of the writers do not possess now. And there were letters from my father, some remonstrating with me for idleness and extravagance while I was at Cambridge, sometimes in a severe, but always in a kindly and parental spirit. And then I came to his later letters, in which there is nothing but a spirit of love and confidence. Then there were letters from the dead—some from dear Benigna, others from my dear friend Seymour, who died abroad. My brain reeled by the time I went to bed ; and then I read your two last dear notes, full of warm affection, and I blessed God for His present mercies, which are greater than the past—*how much* greater no words of mine can express. I felt as if I had been walking about in the Catacombs and suddenly emerged into fresh air."

To the same :

" I wish I could give you some of my stamina. I think I should be all the better if I were less robust, more sympathising with others, more considerate of weak or delicate persons. If I can help you by my strength of physique, depend upon it I will do so. In other matters I think you are more capable of giving me aid than of borrowing it.

" What Liebig says of coffee taken after dinner, is true of artistic and literary pursuits, if followed up as intently as I have followed them for the last two or three years—the one retards digestion, the other development of character. I am therefore exceedingly glad of the temporary interruption that has taken place in my favourite pursuits. Hitherto, when not engaged in my professional duties, I have devoted myself to art, literature, and society. Now, all the time I can spare from my college work and the necessary preparations for the Oxford Examinership, I dedicate to my friends and to you, under the eye of Him of whose love all human affection is but a faint image.

" You give such a gracious reception to the letters of my friends that I venture to send you more. I am sending you Ruskin's *Seven Lamps*. In the first leaf you will see a reminiscence of Ireland—an eagle's feather dropt on Slievemore in Achill—where Froude and I were together. It was a glorious day, and the blue Atlantic lay almost motionless beneath our feet, and it was wonderful to see how a pair of eagles that were wheeling in airy circles round our heads could keep on rising without any apparent motion of their wings. I can fancy even now that I hear their sharp bark as they peered down into the heather in quest of game."

CHAPTER IV.

QUESTION OF TAKING ORDERS. — HIS OBJECTIONS TO THE
SAME. — HE VISITS NORTHUMBERLAND. — DESCRIPTION
OF DILSTON, AND THE COUNTRY LIFE OF THE GREY
FAMILY.—FLODDEN FIELD AND THE BORDER COUNTRY.—
HE RETURNS TO OXFORD AS PUBLIC EXAMINER.—SAVES A
FRIEND FROM DROWNING.—EXPERIENCE AS AN EXAMINER.—
PIONEER WORK IN OXFORD.—HE GIVES LECTURES ON ART,
GEOGRAPHY, AND OTHER SUBJECTS.

DURING the years 1848–49, the Dean of
Peterborough frequently wrote to his son
expressing his desire to see him turning his
mind towards the ministry—hoping that he
would decide on taking orders. The Dean
was sincerely convinced that there was nothing which
ought to make his son hesitate to take so serious a step,
and that the duties of a clergyman would have a beneficial
effect on his character, tending to his highest good and
happiness. That, however, was far from being his son's
view of the matter. While appreciating his father's
motives in urging him in this direction, and replying in
general terms with a gentle courtesy, he seems to have
felt convinced that it was impossible for him to follow his
advice in the matter. Finally, he decided to beg his
father to let the question remain for a time in abeyance.

" I thank you, my dear father, for your welcome letter. I
think I have already told you that I have no internal call to,
no inclination for, the Church. On the contrary, I should
feel I was guilty of a wrong action if I embarked in any work
or profession for neither the theoretical nor the practical part

of which I had any taste. And if this be true of ordinary professions, is it not so in a tenfold degree in the case of the Church ? I feel, at present, no attraction towards the study of dogmatical Theology, or any branch of study in which a clergyman should be versed; and I cannot get over the scruples I have against such a step as you advise. I am at present engaged, usefully I hope, in a place of Christian education, closely connected with a Cathedral Church, with abundant opportunities of adding to my stock of knowledge in various subjects, as well as of imparting to others what I know. I do not see, at present, any necessity for planning any change in my mode of life."

His father—who only knew Durham life by hearsay— had expressed a hope that the clerical atmosphere of the place would have had an influence on his son in the way which he desired. This was a difficult matter for his son to speak of, in reply, without some appearance of harsh judgment or prejudice. He confesses that "the clerical atmosphere of the place has indeed exercised a strong influence over me;" but that influence was of another nature from that which his father imagined. He had lived at Oxford through all the fever of the Tractarian controversy. He had a great respect for some of the leaders of that movement, and had listened with deep interest and profit to their greatest preachers — John Henry Newman, Henry Manning, Dr. Pusey, and others. He had also a feeling of brotherly sympathy for some of the younger men of that school, who had come under the best influences of the Ritualistic revival, and whose early deaths he mourned: such as Matthew Morton and Hurrell Froude. But he himself had not at any time been drawn into the movement, nor allowed himself to come under the personal influence of any of its dis-tinguished leaders.

He found at Durham the same elements working, but rather as a feeble imitation than as an original movement of any depth. There was outward ritual without the inward conviction and fervour which gave it meaning and life in the cradle of its birth; and, for the most part, it was confined to the younger portion of the University. To his mind, the fashionable " Puseyism " (as it was then called) of the day frequently became "mere foppery" in a certain class of young clergymen. These tendencies were, moreover, united with a good deal of frivolity in the society at Durham, and the two combined had a repellent influence on him ; while, however, he gratefully appreciated the society of many good and kind friends in the little University.

How was it then, it may be asked, that he did actually elect to become a clergyman some six years later ? The answer is : he had gradually become convinced that the work of his life was to be educational, and the desire arose in his mind to be able to stand towards the younger men or boys who should come under his care in the position of their pastor as well as their teacher. He weighed the matter gravely for a long time before becoming a clergyman ; but after having taken the step he never repented of having done so. To the end of his life, however, his character continued to be essentially that of a layman. He never had a cure of souls. He was the Principal of a large school during a great part of his life, with occasionally, in vacation times, the choice of taking the work of some brother clergyman who desired rest or change—a choice of which he gladly availed himself. To this was added the duty, which again and again fell to him, of ministering in our large family circle in many solemn or rejoicing occasions—of sickness, burials, baptisms, and marriages. For visiting the sick and people in sorrow, he had a peculiar gift, though himself apparently unconscious of the possession of it, or of the comfort and strength imparted in times of trouble and sore need by the mere fact of his calm presence and trusting spirit.

In 1851, he wrote: "You know that I don't like parsons; but that is not to the point. If I should ever take orders, I don't mean to be a mere parson; for if I were like some of them whom I know, I should cease to be a *man.* I shall never wear straight waistcoats, long coats, and stiff collars! I think all dressing up and official manner are an affectation; while great strictness in outward observances interferes with the devotion of the heart ; and though it may indicate a pious spirit—and therefore deserves our respect,—it shows, as I think, a misconception of the relation in which we stand to God, and of the duties we owe to man. It seems to me, after all, that being a good clergyman is much the same thing as being a good man. I have a longing to be of use, and I know of no line in which I can be more useful than the educational, my whole life having been turned more or less in this direction. I regard the prejudice in favour of the clergy as educators as unreasonable ; yet to anyone who aims at gaining the hearts of his pupils, there may seem to be motives for assuming outwardly the character of a Christian teacher, with authority to speak to them as such. You have heard me speak of objections that I feel to certain portions of our Church Service. If these weighed very strongly with me, they would drive me out of the Church altogether; but when I look around, where do I see any body of Christians, any system on earth, by whomsoever instituted, which is exempt from flaws, the patient endurance of which is a part of the discipline assigned to good men here below? I am sure Mary, who sat at the feet of Jesus, would have been puzzled by the reading over to her of the Athanasian Creed, and the injunction to accept it all at the peril of the loss of her soul; but she understood what Jesus meant when He said, 'One thing is needful;' and her knowledge of Him was enough to enable her to choose the better part.

"It is a blessed office that of a teacher. With all its troubles and heart-wearyings and disappointments, yet it is full of delight to those who enter upon it with their whole heart and soul, and in reliance upon our great Teacher. I know of no occupation which more carries its present reward with it, provided that, in climbing up the ladder of learning, we subordinate all earthly knowledge to heavenly knowledge and wisdom, and strive to make our labours serve towards the highest ends."

It was in 1851 that he first visited Northumberland, the county for which he afterwards conceived an affection almost as strong and enduring as that which is felt for it by members of the family to which he was shortly to become united, and who had been rooted there for generations past. For several summers after our marriage we had not a settled home; that is to say, though living at Oxford, we had only temporary apartments, and were thus free in the long vacations to spend much time in the dear North-country home, where he was welcomed by my parents as if he had been their own son, and where, year by year, the bonds of brotherly friendship between him and the brothers and sisters of our large family were strengthened; enduring uninterruptedly to the end of his life. He was attracted from the first by the character of the Northumbrians, and by the liberal traditions and unconventional habits of life which prevailed in our family

6

and in the society around us. As an artist also, Northumberland delighted him, with its wide expanses of moorland and the rich verdant beauty of Tyneside, Tweedside, and Glendale. The character of our free outdoor life in that country may be illustrated by a a quotation from the *Memoir of John Grey, of Dilston,* my father.

" I remember," wrote one of my sisters, " our rides home with father, when the business of the day was done (which had taken us over many farms, as well as forest land), sometimes such merry, wild gallops over high grass-fields in Hexhamshire, bending our heads to the horses' manes, to receive the sharp pelting hail on our hats (the horses laying back their ears and bounding at the stinging of the hail on their flanks), and coming in with heavy clinging skirt, and veil frozen into a mask over one's face, revealing very rosy cheeks when peeled off. And then those summer evenings when we paced gently home through the soft, rich valleys, and heard the thrushes singing those notes that pierced one's heart through and through with the prophecy of all the pain that future life would bring to it, while still youth and fair imagination shed over everything that ' strange sweet light that never was on sea or shore.' '

My father wrote to a niece in 1865, from the old family home, Milfield Hill, on the Scottish borders : " We have had here a merry party of young people, enjoying them-selves to the extent that full liberty, fine weather, beautiful scenery, and gay spirits can produce. Maud and her cousins were romping from morn till dewy eve, and the Butlers, living at Ford, were meeting them daily, having the use of Lady Waterford's boat to cross the Till, which makes the walk shorter. George Butler thinks dear old

Glendale the finest country he ever saw, as I do. They were spending the summer in a house which Lady Waterford has built, commanding the purest air and finest view possible, embracing the whole of Glendale and Milfield plain, surrounded by the range of Cheviots; in front Flodden Hill, with its historic distinction; and to the north the course of the Tweed for thirty miles, from the Eildon Hills near Melrose, downward by Coldstream to near Berwick."

My father had been called to reclaim and administer wide estates in the southern part of the county, the property of the Government; and here was planted our other and later Northumbrian home, Dilston, on the banks of the Tyne. "Our home at Dilston was also a very beautiful one. Its romantic historical associations (connected with the unfortunate James, Earl of Derwentwater, an adherent of Charles Stuart), the wild, informal beauty all round its doors, the kind and hospitable character of its master and mistress, and the large family circle, made it an attractive place to many friends and guests. It was a house the door of which stood wide open, as if to welcome all comers, through the livelong summer day. It was a place where one could glide out of a lower window and be hidden in a moment, plunging straight among wild wood paths and beds of ferns, or find oneself quickly in some cool concealment, beneath slender birch trees, or by the bed of a mountain stream. It was a place where the sweet, hushing sound of waterfalls and clear streams murmuring over shallows were heard all day and night, though winter storms turned those sweet sounds into an angry roar."

In an interesting article entitled "Flodden Field and the Vale of Till," written for *The Leisure Hour*, George

6 *

Butler himself described the Border Country, and sketched some of the chief historical events connected with it, down to the tardy waking up of civilised and Christian life in this hitherto benighted region during the latter half of the last and the beginning of the present century; an awakening primarily due to the self-denying efforts of a humble evangelist, a disciple of John Wesley.

"There is no name," he wrote, "that rings with a sadder sound in a Scotsman's ear than that of Flodden. What Alba was to the Roman, Flodden Hill was to the Scot. Even English hearts—although the victory gained at Flodden by Surrey and Stanley in the absence of the king and his army may cause them to beat with natural pride—cannot but feel sorrow for the 'flowers of the forest,' the nobility, gentry, and even clergy of Scotland, who perished on that fatal day.

"Above Ford Castle, where King James, according to common belief, was lingering before the battle, stretches a long expanse of elevated moorland, in the direction of the Kyloe Crags. These basaltic rocks mark the boundary between the rough coast line and the plain of Milfield, watered by the Till. The basaltic formation is most strongly marked in the outlying promontories of Bamborough and Dunstanborough Castles and in Holy Isle. Of these, Bamborough, with its massive keep, and Holy Isle, with its small fort and low-lying Monastery of Lindisfarne, may be seen from the highest part of Ford Common. Looking northward, the eye ranges over undulating hills in the direction of the Tweed Valley, which is generally discernible by a line of silvery mist. Only at sunrise and sunset the presence of the river is further revealed by a glittering thread of gold. Beyond are the Eildon Hills, with their clearly marked outline.

BAMBOROUGH CASTLE

To the west lie the Cheviots, running towards the Scotch border; and in the middle distance, to the north-west, are the hills which rise above Glendale, Milfield, Flodden, and Branxton. Looking to the south-west, the eye ranges over a wide expanse of cultivated land, the plain of Milfield, with the river Till winding its slow course between meadows and plantations of Scotch fir and corn-fields, as far as Wooler. Further south are the rising grounds of Fenton Hall, and further still are the woods of Chillingham, with dark masses of old forest trees, between which lie green openings, where may be seen, by the aid of a good pair of eyes, and more clearly by that of a binocular, the heads of wild white cattle browsing."

In 1850, George Butler returned to Oxford, where he filled for some years the office of Public Examiner. Among many letters which he addressed to me in 1851 from there was the following:

"Ralph Lingen * has come to pay me a visit here. He and I took a long walk yesterday in the country, and bathed in a lasher about four miles above Oxford. When I was getting out, I heard Lingen cry out in distress, and on looking round I saw him in the middle of the current, evidently in trouble. He just managed to keep his head above water till I swam out to him, and then I caught hold of him and carried him to shore. He was very good, and did not try to clutch at me till just as we got to shore, when—thinking, I suppose, we were in safety—he caught me by the shoulder, and I was obliged to push him off and get clear before I attempted to land him and myself. It was a very difficult place to get out at: ground, slippery clay, bank underworn by the current, and a large heap of sedge close by, into which the current was carrying us, and where no soul could have swum. Thank God I got him out all safe; and then he nearly fainted. How-

* Now Lord Lingen.

ever, he soon recovered, and we continued our walk and talk, much to our mutual enjoyment and edification. I know you will join me in hearty thanks to God for my friend's and my own preservation. Do not mention it to anyone, unless Lingen should first do so himself. He certainly was in the greatest straits, and would, I fully believe, have been drowned if I had not got to him in time. Had he sunk, or had I been too late, I should never have forgiven myself, as I encouraged him to bathe there, although he said he was not a strong swimmer. I shall not easily forget the thrill that passed through me as I saw his struggles growing fainter and fainter, and thought that so much intellectual vigour and activity were hovering on the brink of destruction. As it is, it is an additional cause to me for thankfulness to Him in whose hands are the issues of life and death. . Our examinations are going on swimmingly (I can't get out of watery epithets), and I find my interest in my work increases ; and far from feeling more tired, I seem to get fresher towards the end of the run.

" I am sure my sisters are enjoying their visit to beautiful Dilston."

Among his books in our library stands a beautiful edition of Homer's *Iliad* and *Odyssey*, the gift of the friend whom he had the happiness of helping in his hour of peril; and in the first page of which are inscribed the words: "On the 1st June, 1851, I was bathing in the Isis with. George Butler, at the lock above Godston. I became very faint in the water, and called to him to help me. He immediately swam towards me and drew me out. I very much question whether I should have been able to regain the land had I been alone, or with a companion less brave, strong, skilful and self-possessed." In a letter accompanying the gift, he said : " One can hardly with propriety say what one feels at such times, and therefore I fear you may have thought I took very coolly the brave service you rendered. For brave, and very brave, it most certainly is when one man comes to another's help in the water ; the risk being not less great to the helper than to the helped."

A gift for saving life in the water appears, like many other gifts, to become hereditary :

From J. E. Grey.

"Dilston, Summer of 1851.

" I must tell you what a pleasant day we had yesterday with your sisters. We set off early, before the dew was off the grass, and took our ponies. Bobby was our sumpter-horse, carrying a basket of provisions and several shawls. We kept going uphill for about five miles to the south-west ; and when we had got so far we stopped to look at the view, which was most beautiful. There was broad-backed old Cheviot far off among the clouds, and Hedgehope and Simonside nearer, all old friends to us. Then we saw faintly the tops of the hills which run along towards the Solway Firth, and eastward and southward the wide stretch of Alston Moor. Down below lay Hexham, nestling in woods through which ran the sparkling waters of the Tyne. We could see where the north and south Tynes join. The sun was very bright, and there were great masses of floating clouds, which made the scene vary every moment. We could just hear the Hexham Abbey bells, which were ringing merrily for Lady Blackett's wedding. After that we got down into a deep, narrow ravine (having left the ponies at a farmhouse), and going to the very bottom of it, found the cave (Queen Margaret's cave), which was a matter of some difficulty, as it is nearly concealed. We had brought a candle, which Hatty lighted, crawling in first herself. We all followed ; the entrance is very low, but it is roomy inside. We sat on pieces of damp rock, our one candle making darkness visible, and tried to think it a pleasant, cool retreat. Cool it certainly was. We could find no traces of Queen Margaret ; no bits of ermine, or fragments of the crown with which pictures represent her scouring about these woods with the little Prince. She was, you know, the daughter of the old Troubadour King René of Anjou. We hope to take your sisters another day to the Roman Wall."

" Sunday Evening.

"The birds have been singing from early morning till sunset. The stillness and their sweet songs make one feel agreeably melancholy. The thrushes come near the window and pour forth their full-throated songs while I am playing, making a rivalry which is likely to reverse the old fable of the Lute-player and the Bird—'Music's first Martyr!'—in which the bird sang against the lute-player till her heart broke in the vain contest, and she dropped down dead upon the lute. I adjure the bird to be silent, if it would not break *my* heart; for I can never draw from ivory and wire such full, rich tones as those. There was a beautiful sunset, and all was silence except that bird's song, which seemed to fill the universe."

From G. B.
" Oxford, 1851.

" I am sure you will be glad to hear that our work is over and that I am free. We (the Examiners) could not reconcile it to our sense of duty to give any first classes; so the list presents the novel appearance of a body without a head. The few people I have spoken to about it seem rather glad of it, so I hope it will not be misconstrued or looked upon as an innovation on our part. Your last letter was brought to me while I was in the Schools. I did not do what you did with with your schoolchildren when you received mine, and say, 'Begone, rebel army; and don't kick up a row,' and then jump out of the window and run along the walk under the pine trees; because my brother Examiners would have stared, and the windows were too high. But I did something of the same kind mentally. It is now beautiful weather, and I am glad to get out of the close air of the Schools into the fields again. I sometimes go out early to Worcester College

Gardens, which are fresh and full of sweet scents and sounds ; and there I read Plato under the trees

"I had a talk with Arthur Stanley yesterday. It is quite a pleasure to see a man so fully possessed with the importance of his mission. Most people are full of their own importance or seeking after their own advancement. But here is a man who has dignities thrust upon him, and who still constantly looks to the end which he always had in view —that of doing all he can in Oxford for the good of Oxford. It was a pleasure to hear him speak of the ties that bound him to this place, of the happiness that he had experienced here, and of the pleasure it gave him to look forward to returning to his old haunts and visiting his old friends. When I told him of my intention to settle here, and of the pursuits and work I hoped to encourage here, his face brightened, and he seemed quite glad to find in me a kindred feeling to his own.

"I have had some talk with Dr. Wellesley about my lectures on Art, (he has great knowledge of Art). He said he would at any time ask the Vice-Chancellor for leave for me to deliver them publicly. Parker, the publisher, dined with me the other day, and said he would be glad to publish them. He has asked me to write a review of the four or five principal translations of Dante, which will enable me to say anything I like about the original. 'This will be a pleasant occupation for us next Christmas. We will read Dante together and talk about it, and put together the results of our conversation."

"Exeter College, Sunday Night.

"I must write to you before retiring to rest. I can imagine how beautiful the Dilston woods are looking just now. I have been reading the Gospel narrative of our Lord's ministry carefully through, and I find it more interesting and wonderful than ever. After reading the wisest of the heathen writers, and even the books of the Old Testament, one cannot fail to be struck with the surpassing beauty and perfection of Christian doctrine and life. It is not only the words of Him who 'spake as never man spake,' but every action of His life that is full of interest and inspiration. I delight in carrying back my imagination to the scenes described by the writers of the Gospel, and making every sense lend its aid to the task of realising the wondrous scenes that we read of. I wish all 'Divinity' reading were equally edifying. The history of the Church during many centuries seems to me to be made up of a mass of heterogeneous elements—here and there a bright spot appearing out of the darkness, but generally full of strife and dissensions and cavillings. One can hardly reconcile the questions on points of doctrine which agitated the Church and were discussed at the several Councils with the simplicity of Christ's own teaching."

The year following that in which no first class was given was more satisfactory. He wrote:

"We got to work yesterday afternoon, and I hope the results are considered satisfactory. To Balliol it ought to be so, as there are four Balliol first classes and as many more seconds. I am glad to have discharged the duty of Examiner, not only because it has been useful work done, I hope, but because I have derived much benefit and advantage from it myself."

He had the good fortune, a year or two later, to examine some very brilliant men, amongst whom were Charles Parker, late M.P. for Perth, who was then, and has continued to be, one of our warmest friends; one of the Coleridges, Lord Lothian, Lord Carnarvon, Mr. Fremantle, and others. I had lately an opportunity of asking one of these what he thought of his character and manner as an Examiner. He said: "It was delightful to be examined by him, if one was thoroughly prepared. He was a most kind-hearted Examiner, and had a way of drawing out what a man knew, and sparing him from any exposure of ignorance on subjects in which he was

defective. This he did on principle. He always said
he thought it only fair towards the person examined. In
my case the examination was like a delightful conversation.
He made me quite at my ease, and enabled me to do
myself full justice. He seemed to enjoy the examination
himself."

On more than one occasion it fell to his lot to examine
middle-aged men, or as they called them at Oxford "old
men." One of these was the author of an interesting
book on the Catacombs in Rome, a married man, much
past the age when it is comparatively easy to acquire
book knowledge.

His Examiner knew very well that many parts of
school knowledge are forgotten in middle life, and he did
not press the examinee on these points, but managed
expertly to bring him to the subject of Roman antiquities ;
and knowing him to be a good draughtsman, required him
to put on paper a plan or drawing of the Cloaca Maxima
and other antiquities of Rome. The result was a very
creditable examination passed.

On Christmas Eve, 1851, he returned to Northumberland ; our marriage took place on the 8th of January, 1852,
at Dilston. Shortly afterwards we settled at Oxford,
which became our home for five years.

In reviewing the work done by George Butler in the
course of his educational career, one cannot but be struck
by the fact that he was somewhat in advance of his time,
compared with many of those among whom he lived and
worked. There are men theoretically in advance of their
times, who do good service by their advocacy of progressive principles in writing or in speech. With him it was
more a matter of simple practice. He perceived that
some study useful or necessary for the future generations

and in itself worthy had scarcely an acknowledged place in the curriculum of the Schools and Universities, or that some new ground necessary to be explored was still left untrodden; and without saying much about it, without any thought of being himself a pioneer in any direction, he modestly set himself to the task of acting out his thoughts on the subject. His absolute freedom from personal vanity withheld him from proclaiming that he was about to enter on any new line, and at the same time enabled him to bear with perfect calm, if not with indifference, the criticisms, witty remarks, and sometimes serious opposition which are seldom wanting when a man or woman ventures quietly to encroach upon the established order of things in any department of life. At Oxford he was the first who brought into prominence the study of geography. His geographical lectures there were quite an innovation, creating some amusement and a good deal of wonder as to how he would succeed. It was a subject which had hitherto been relegated in an elementary form to schools for boys and girls, and was unrecognised, except by a very few persons as the grand and comprehensive scientific study which it is now acknowledged to be.

At Oxford the subject was entirely new, at least to the older members of the University, who, however, to their credit, came to the lectures, and listened with teachable minds to truths novel to them concerning the world they were living in. We drew large illustrative maps for the walls of the lecture room. I recall a day when I was drawing in a rough form an enlarged map of Europe, including the northern coast of Africa and a part of Asia Minor. It happened that several fellows and tutors of colleges called at that moment. I continued my work while they chatted with him on the curiosity of his introduction in Oxford of so elementary a study. The conversation then turned on letters we had just received from Arthur Stanley and Theodore Walrond, who were visiting Egypt. "Where is Cairo?" someone asked, turning to the map spread on the table. I put the question to an accomplished College tutor. His eye wandered hopelessly over the chart; he could not even place his hand on Egypt! I was fain to pretend that I needed to study my performance more closely, and bent down my head in order to conceal the irreverent laughter which overcame me. When our friends left the room, we—the map-makers—agreed that it was only fair that the feelings of amusement should not be monopolised by the non-geographical people. A sister who had been visiting us wrote: "How delightful that you can make some of the learned men interested in your lectures, and how varied and wide are the subjects included in that word, Geography! I have often wondered about the origin and the home of the winds. Poetry says they are chained in caves; but of course that is a joke. When Mr. Francis Palgrave meets Theodore Walrond on his return from the East, he can inquire of him where Damascus is; for you recollect when he (Palgrave) was in Oxford he was not sure that he had ever heard of such a place. There is an ancient book which has been translated into English, and can be had at most book-shops, called 'The Bible,' where I believe he could find some mention made of the place. It distresses me to think of there being anything, however insignificant, unknown to the Vice-Principal of Kneller Hall."

The *Proceedings of the Royal Geographical Society* for

April, 1890, contained the following, in an obituary notice :

" Especial regard must be shown to the valuable support given by Canon Butler to our Society in its efforts, more than twenty years ago, to improve the teaching of geography in public schools. Being himself a classical scholar of high rank, and a Head Master whose pupils attained a full measure of University success, his assertion that the liberal study of geography was a help to the classical student and not a burden, backed by the example of his own School, could not fail to influence public opinion. His pupils were among the earliest and most successful competitors for the prizes that were offered by our Society to the public schools. Year after year the words ' Liverpool College ' are attached to some of the names printed in our lists of winners of the school medals and of honourable mention. A man needs to be variously informed before he is qualified to become a good geographer, and George Butler was remarkably so. He ranked at Oxford among the very first classics of his time, and he bore a high and independent . reputation for general ability."

A Swiss geographer, writing at the same date in the *Journal du Bien Public*, says : " One can scarcely imagine to what extent young men who had passed through their *humanitarian* course of study under the pedantic régime of the old English Universities found themselves at that time (1852-3) without any recognised official means of acquiring the geographical historical knowledge so necessary in their future career as public functionaries and men of the world. England, which is called to play so grand a *rôle* in the domain of Colonisation, still continued to a great extent the slave of the pedagogic traditions of the middle ages. At the time when Mr. Butler first advanced publicly the necessity of this study in Oxford, scarcely anyone in that learned centre had yet begun to avail himself of any other geography than that of the world known to the ancients. The idea of a modern science of geography appeared to them puerile; while, on the other hand, among political geographers on the Continent a smile was sometimes raised by certain administrative errors imputed to the English Ministers of State for War and for the Colonies, arising out of pure ignorance of the maps of the vast territories under British dominion. Mr. Butler was one of the first who foresaw for geography an immense future as a branch of human knowledge, as well as from the political point of view. He broke the ice, and bravely advertised at Oxford a series of lectures on geography, which he obtained the permission of the Vice-Chancellor to announce by means of public advertisements and notices sent to the Colleges. In later years, Mr. Butler's own pupils, at the Liverpool College, were among the first who competed with the greatest success for the prizes offered by the Royal Geographical Society to the public schools, and in the printed lists of those who obtained the Society's medals appear the names of his own sons. In order to become a good geographer, a man must be highly instructed in other things. Mr. Butler fulfilled this requirement, being in the first rank among classical students in his time, as well as a proficient in modern languages and history, and a skilful draughtsman and artist."

Dr. Arnold had already 'to some extent introduced geographical description and illustrations in his historical lectures, believing geography to be an essential aid to the study of history.

George Butler was one of the first, also, who introduced and encouraged the study of Art in Oxford in a practical sense. In the winter of 1852-3 he obtained the permission of the Vice-Chancellor and Curators to give a course of lectures on Art, in the Taylor building. The Vice-Chancellor took the chair at each lecture.

These lectures were afterwards published by J. W. Parker, under the title of *Principles of Imitative Art.*

"Mr. Butler," said one of his reviewers, "very clearly defines many portions of the artist's duty, and explains briefly but intelligibly the principles of colour and perspective, of chiaroscuro, of design and composition, and conveys a large amount of information in remarkably terse and unaffected language. Moreover, he sends his hearers to the true models; to Nature first, and next to the Greek Antique as the very perfection of refinement and grandeur; while he asserts that, after all, the intense religious feeling of the very early Christian artists has produced works which in intention and expression are deeper and greater than any others in the world. We congratulate the Oxford Art Society on the possession of such a lecturer, and we conclude with a beautiful passage from the book."

The following is the passage alluded to:

"In what, then, do those early painters differ from those that have come after? Not so much in skill, nor in knowledge of the resources of art, nor in fertility of invention, nor in power of imagination; but in steadfastness of purpose, in the earnest application of a loving heart to one object; viz., the exercise of the gift of God to His honour and glory, and the edification of their fellow-men. And this is all: this intensity of purpose, this singleness of aim, this devotion, has met with its

reward—a reward not vouchsafed to others whose natural
powers far transcended those, for instance, of the humble
monk of Fiésole or Raffaell's early master.

"There is no reason to doubt that the same spirit
would be again rewarded in the same way.   Indeed, we
have had an instance of this, if the story which I am
about to relate be true, within the last few years: In
1847, a crucifix carved in ivory by a monk belonging to a
monastery near Genoa, was brought to England by some
Americans into whose hands it had fallen.   Its history was
as follows: Seven or eight years ago a monk, remarkable
only for his holy life, had a vision.   The form of our
Crucified Redeemer was presented to him in superhuman
beauty and marvellous distinctness.   A voice bade him
impress this form indelibly on his memory, for that he
was destined to work out a representation of it, for the
good of his own soul and the edification of others.

"When he awoke the vision was distinctly before
him, and he doubted not of the reality of the command
laid upon him.   He set himself diligently to work at a
model.   He had no artistic knowledge nor skill to help
him ; but he laboured to work out the similitude of the
vision.   At length he finished his model, and after working
two years executed it in ivory.

"The work is of the finest description.   It is equal, in
point of correctness and accuracy of anatomical detail, to
anything of M. Angelo or Benvenuto Cellini, and its
expression is beyond all description.   It is the suffering,
not of a man, but of a divine person.   In the upper part
of the face we see the marks of sorrow and mental
suffering, without those of bodily anguish.   The brow is
not contracted, as in severe pain, and the mouth alone
exhibits traces of corporeal suffering, which show that

the human nature is not extinct, although the divine is triumphant even in that hour of trial."

In his first idea of delivering these lectures at Oxford he was much encouraged by Dr. Wellesley, Principal of New Inn Hall, himself an artist, an able art critic, and a collector of works of art of a rare and beautiful kind. Dr. Wellesley took in hand the arrangements for the lectures, and encouraged an interest in them in every possible way. At the close of the course, he wrote:

" Dear Mr. Butler,—Everybody will be glad to hear that you are about to print your four lectures; and I cannot but feel honoured in associating my name with such able and finished performances."

" To Dilston, from J. E. B.

" Last evening, George translated to us the funeral oration which Thucydides puts into the mouth of Pericles, to which he had alluded in his last lecture on Art. His closing lecture was very successful. He wound up with some practical remarks on the pursuit of Art in Oxford, and about the use of combining the study of Greek Art with Classical learning. Several of the old people have called to tell me how much pleasure and instruction he had given them."

While promoting the study of Art in Oxford, working with pupils, and examining in the Schools, he undertook to write a series of Art criticisms for the *Morning Chronicle*, and afterwards for another paper; visiting for this purpose the Galleries and yearly Exhibitions in London. This he did for a year or two. " It was amusing," he wrote to his mother, after his first visit, in this capacity, to the Society of British Artists, " to see the ' gentlemen of the Press' (of whom I was one !) walking about, dotting down observations. I travelled up to Town with

Scott, the architect, who has engaged me to attend a meeting of his workmen, and give them an address on decorative art and the dignity of labour. Josephine and I are both engaged in copying some drawings by Turner, in the Taylor Gallery. They were originally made for the Oxford Almanac. That which I am copying is the oldest —done in 1799. They are very interesting, partly from their representing portions of Oxford which now no longer exist, or cannot be seen for the trees and buildings which have grown around them; and more so, in showing the conscientious way in which the artist worked. There is no extravagant colour or careless drawing. Everything is done with the utmost pains and accuracy."

Indefatigable in his efforts to master any subject which attracted him, he was also equally ready and anxious to impart to others any knowledge he had thus gained. He found time among his other occupations to make a very thorough study of some ancient Oscan inscriptions, with engravings of their principal monuments, which he found in the Bodleian Library. He became much interested in that portion of history—almost lost in the mists of the past—which is illustrated by the marvellous records and monuments of Oscan, Umbrian, and Etruscan life in the great Museum at Bologna. He worked at and completed, during one of the long vacations, a series of enlarged copies in sepia of the small engravings and prints of these monuments in the Bodleian. These enlargements were suitable for wall illustrations, for a set of lectures which he afterwards gave on the "Ancient Races of Italy."

"I have completed," he wrote, "several large sepia drawings from the *Monumenti Antichi* of Micali, to illustrate my lectures on the 'Ancient Races of Italy.' It is capital practice, drawing on so large a scale. I think you could help me very much in this when you come back. It works my eyes very much, poring over these old inscriptions in dead (and buried) languages, and makes me feel quite tired; but the interest of it is great."

It was very pleasant to us when we visited Florence together, some years later, to see the originals of some of the Cyclopean ruins of which we had together made large drawings, those gigantic stones of all that remains of the ancient Etruscan walls of Fiesole, up to the lovely heights of which we drove, one clear, bright winter's day, in company with Dr. Ewing, Bishop of Argyll and the Isles, whom we met in Florence.

He corresponded at this time in Latin with several foreign Savants. Among the letters I have found addressed to him in Latin by scholars on the Continent are some from Dr. F. Ritschl, Professor of Classical Literature at Bonn University; Professor Bernays, also of Bonn; Dr. Leopold Schmidt, and Dr. Philip Wagner, of Dresden.

CHAPTER V.

SOCIAL LIFE AT OXFORD.—PROFESSOR VAUGHAN'S LECTURES.—
ARTHUR STANLEY.—MUSIC.—SUMMER EVENING RIDES.—
ITALIAN STUDIES.—WATCHING THE NEW YEAR IN.—EVILS
OF A CELIBATE SOCIETY.—SCEPTICISM.—DEEP THINKING.—
VISIONS OF WOE AND OF HOPE.—DEATH OF THE DEAN
OF PETERBOROUGH.—ORDINATION OF GEORGE BUTLER.—
UNIVERSITY REFORMS.— PUBLIC EXAMINATIONS.—THE NEW
MUSEUM IN OXFORD.—PROFESSOR ROLLESTON.—UNIVER-
SITY ART GALLERIES.—A VISIT TO GERMANY FOR THE
PURPOSE OF WRITING ON ART. — SUNSET SEEN FROM
THE DRACHENFELS.

THE social side of our first years at Oxford
may be illustrated by a few extracts from
letters to my father and mother at Dilston.
Two young sisters had come to visit us,
bringing a new and lively element into
Oxford society, which at that time had a somewhat
monastic character.

"1853.—Max Müller and Mr. Thomson * of Queen's
College came in to-day with an urgent petition that, as the
day was so fine, I would allow the girls to join their party to
Newnham. It is Mr. Thomson's party, and some ladies—
friends of his—are going. He had a barge fitted up for them.
The inducement was so great that I could not refuse, and I
was amused at the children's glee, which was mixed with
commiseration for me, because I was not going. I laughed,
and told them how happy I should be at home. I hope we shall
have as magnificent a day for the picnic to Witchwood Forest,
which has been planned by Mr. Jowett, Theodore Walrond,
and Müller."

* The late Archbishop of York.

"I must tell you of our picnic. We were a large party, in open carriages and on horseback. It is a beautiful drive, and the air was pure and sweet. Walrond was the chief organiser and the life of the party. Witchwood is one of the few ancient forests belonging to the Crown which have not yet been 'disforested.' There are beautiful glades with soft turf; sometimes the branches of the tall trees met over our heads, forming a kind of vast cathedral aisle, flecked with brilliant sunshine, partly intercepted by the foliage overhead. Emmy rode on a spirited horse with other riders of the party; but changes were made occasionally, and at one time she constituted herself 'whip' in a light dogcart with a high-stepping horse, and with Mr. Jowett by her side. We did not fancy these two could have many subjects in common to furnish conversation; and after our return, we asked her how they got on. 'Oh, very well,' she replied. 'I asked him questions, and if he was long in replying I drove the dogcart over some bumps on the roadside, and this joggled the answers out of him.' It was touching to see how calmly Mr. Jowett confided himself to the guidance of a wild young girl of fifteen; but she drove well. Zoë Skene was in the same carriage with me and others. George rode. Arthur Butler drove with a friend, and George Joachim Goschen came lumbering after us on an immense horse which he had hired. His seat on horseback is not very graceful. We lunched and were very cheerful. I think I enjoyed most the drive home. The heat of the day oppressed me, but the evening was very sweet. The sun had almost set before we started to return; and wishing for a little quiet and solitude, I walked on for a good distance alone. The others seemed to have been delayed; and after an hour I felt tired, and sat down on the road by the side of a dry ditch, not very romantic, but it was pleasant—a complete solitude and silence, a very gentle evening breeze blowing, bringing sweet scents from the fields and woods, and stars coming out one by one. My ear was attentive to catch the approaching sound of wheels or horses' hoofs; but I heard none, and began to fear I might have taken a wrong road, when a solitary pedestrian loomed out from the dusk. It was Mr. Jowett, who took a seat by my side, with his feet also in the dry ditch. Then I thought 'What shall I say?' It seemed uncivil to continue my long pleasant silence. However he put me at my ease by occasional remarks, not on philosophical subjects, but on cockchafers and frogs; and then we spoke of mudlarks—the poor little boys in London who make a wretched living by diving in the mud of the Thames at low water and bringing up what they can find, chiefly things dropped from vessels. The only sound which broke the silence was the distant croaking of a frog in our ditch, complaining of the want of water. We sat there some time very contentedly, when presently the distant sound of a trotting horse on the long, white, hard road came nearer, and George drew up beside us, relieved to find me resting in such good company. He explained some delay that had occurred, but said a carriage must very soon reach us, which it did "

This gay young life was, however, only for a short period.

"Oxford is very quiet just now. We have been only to one social gathering. That was at Balliol, in honour of Mr. Hallam, author of the *History of the Middle Ages*. He is here examining in modern history. He is a dear, gentle-looking old man. He has lost all but one of eight children. George and I went into the Schools to-day, and heard Mr. Lankester being examined by Hallam on 'Hallam.' They were busy with some crisis in the mediæval history of Genoa. At the Balliol party, Goldwin Smith, George, and Professor Halford Vaughan (who is the centre of attraction here just now), had a lively discussion on the subject of Vaughan's lecture of the morning. The lecture was a powerful, poetical, and sometimes sublime oration. Six hundred people were looking fixedly at him, holding their breath, while he described the death and burial of William the Conqueror. He confessed that William was a selfish being, but a great instrument in God's hands—an instrument fearfully and wonderfully made.

Vaughan is almost too brilliant, both in conversation and in lecturing. He dazzles one. One could quite imagine one saw the dead king, looking fierce even in death, when he (Vaughan) pointed to him, as it were, and spoke of 'this corrupting hulk of majesty for which a bit of ground had to be bought in which to bury him, and which was after all thrust by hired hands, in haste and with loathing and disgust, into a hole too small to hold it, obliging them to crush up in unseemly guise the immense frame of him who had been so great.'"

"Emily bids me to tell you that Goschen is, as you suppose, partly German. He is a genius in a moderate sort of way. He has thought a great deal on some subjects, and when these happen to be started in the Union he speaks well on them. He argues well and is fluent, but is sometimes carried away by his feelings, and becomes too warm to speak well. Charles Parker then comes in with his calm temper and good head, and sorts them all up. There have been interesting debates lately, Arthur tells me. Goldwin Smith and other 'dons' go to hear them. It must be interesting to see an embryo Parliament like that, and imagine in those boys the germs of future statesmen. No doubt they often talk nonsense, as their elders do. There is to be a debate on Gladstone to-night."

"We heard a very eloquent sermon yesterday from Arthur Stanley, on the occasion of the assizes being held in Oxford. It was on the text, 'Judge not, that ye be not judged,' addressed directly to the judges, who listened with grave attentive faces. It was full of original thought. Stanley came to our drawing-room in the evening, with Mr. Jowett and Professor Wilson. He (Stanley) is a good and excellent man, not at all imposing looking, small, with pale blue eyes, which seem to be always looking at a distant horizon, and do not seem to see you even when they look at you, and an innocent mouth with an infantine expression of purity. He is cheerful, fond of society, and often quite merry; he has a quiet voice; he is most earnest and interesting when talking of anything he has at heart. What will my dear mother say when I tell her he hates music? I refrained from opening the piano. They say all his senses are imperfect—taste, smell, hearing. One would not think so from his writings. But he has imagination which makes up for the defect. He is absolutely indifferent to what kind of food he eats, with one exception—he loves buttered tea-cake. I was told so in confidence by a friend of his. So I always provide a large stack of buttered tea-cake when he comes to tea. I do not offer it to him, but I stand guard over it to see that no one else eats it, and gradually he is attracted to it, and eats layer after layer of it to the end, while we are very careful not to notice the fact."

"We have had some delightful music in the evenings when Stanley is not there. Professor Donkin is a profound musician, and plays classical music exquisitely, and Max Müller's playing is most brilliant. We were at a party in one of the colleges last week, where everybody talked at once. Müller played some wonderful things, but the noise of voices drowned the music. I sat near him and applauded him; then I took the piano, and he did the same for me— applauded warmly—and we were mutually gratified."

"George has had to be in London for some days. On Monday-evening, feeling lonely, I went into St. John's Gardens, and sat there till 9 p.m. It was nearly dark, and I enjoyed wandering alone among the trees. The tall 'Solomon's lilies' gleamed so white in the twilight, almost phosphorescent. What exquisite flowers they are, both in form and in their snowy whiteness! I am copying some of them for a design which I am attempting for the capital of one of the pillars in the new Museum. Everybody is invited to contribute. By-and-by I heard voices, and suddenly came upon Zoë and her bridesmaids, resting and cooling themselves in the evening air. It was a pretty sight. Zoë came forward and asked me to bring little Georgie to her wedding the next day, as Mr. Thomson wished him to be his ' best man.' The college gardens are perfect wildernesses of beautiful flowers now (in the summer vacation), wasting their sweetness. Georgie ánd I sometimes come home laden with bouquets which the gardeners give us."

I have many other memories of our life at Oxford— some very sweet, others grave. I recall with special pleasure our summer evening rides. During the first two years we spent there my father kindly provided me with a horse, a fine, well-bred chestnut. My husband and I explored together all the rising grounds round Oxford. Behind our own little garden there were tall trees where nightingales sang night and day for a few weeks in spring. But it was in the Bagley Woods and in Abingdon Park that those academic birds put forth all their powers. We sometimes rode from five in the afternoon, till the sun set and the dew fell, on grassy paths between thick under-growths of woods such as nightingales love to haunt, and from which issued choruses of matchless song.

Our Italian studies were another source of enjoyment. Dante Rossetti was then preparing matter for his book, *Dante and His Circle*, by carefully translating intǫ English the " Vita Nuova " and lyrical poems of Dante, together with other sonnets and poems written by some of his predecessors, such as Cavalcante, Orlandi, and Angiolieri of Siéna. Mr. Rossetti sent to us occasionally for criticism some of his translations of the exquisite sonnets of Dante, the English of which he was anxious to make as perfect as possible. We had visited Rossetti's studio at Chelsea, where he had shown us his portfolios of original sketches for his great paintings, besides many unfinished drawings and pathetic incidents expressed in artist's shorthand— slight but beautiful pencil designs. My husband's critical faculty and classical taste enabled him to return the sonnets submitted to his judgment with occasional useful comments. There was little to find fault with in them however.

Aurelio Saffi was at this time in exile, and living in Oxford. He had been associated with Mazzini and Armellini in the Triumvirate which ruled in Rome for a short period, and was Parliamentary deputy for his own native town of Forli. He was a cultivated and literary man, with a thorough knowledge of the Italian poets. As an exile his material means were at that time very slender. My husband sought his acquaintance, and invited him to give a series of evening lectures on Dante in our own drawing-room. These were attractive to some, and increased the personal interest felt in Saffi in the University. He was afterwards appointed Italian reader in connection with the Taylor Buildings. Twenty-seven years later, having returned to Italy from exile, Saffi was presiding at a great Congress in Genoa, where we were. He alluded, with much feeling, to the years he had spent in Oxford; and turning to my husband, who was near him, he said: " It is twenty-seven years to-day that, an exile from my native land, I had the happiness of being received in your house at Oxford, and I have never forgotten, and shall never forget, the hospitable and gracious reception given to me by you and your worthy companion. The times are changed; a long interval has elapsed, and it is to me a great joy to-day to greet you once more, and on my native soil."

Among our joint pursuits may be numbered the collating, in the Bodleian Library, of some old black-letter editions of Chaucer's poems, for an expurgated edition to be published by Bell and Daldy. This gave us a good many quiet hours in that venerable edifice, sitting side by side in one of the silent recesses, puzzling out the old English black letter, which was sometimes partly defaced, and transcribing it in modern characters. In everything in which I was at all competent to do so, it was my happiness to work with him.

One of our great pleasures in those early years of married life at Oxford was to receive the visits of my sister Harriet,* who had been my companion during our whole lives until I left my home in the North. We had been united from childhood in our studies and our enjoyments. On New Year's morning, 1854, 2 o'clock a.m., she wrote from the North: "A happy New Year to you! Ours has not been a *merry* Christmas here; but we have had much comfort together with trial. Do you not think we grow more truly happy as we grow older? Last New Year's Eve. I was alone at Oxford, when you had gone to join the family party around the old Dean. I sat by the fire, listening to the sweet bells ringing out so clear every quarter, under the glorious, burning, countless stars. Old Tom boomed from his dome over the desolate floods, and the other bells answered him from all the towers and spires; and I had the memory of your dear faces and my little godson's bright eyes to keep me company, though the cheerful room looked blank without you. But when the first dull dawn of 1853 broke over dear old Oxford, and I left it with my face turned to our 'ain north countrie,' my heart felt brave for the coming year. I have watched this New Year in alone too, and bade it welcome—not perhaps with a braver, but with a more trustful heart than the last. And I like being alone, for those are not the times when one feels lonely. After

* Madame Meuricoffre

conquering the first drowsiness, one's head gets so clear
in the quiet night, and it is pleasant to add up the balance
of joy and sorrow in the dying year, and to find that the
joy was most, or, at least, that what often caused us
sorrow at the time, God has since worked out to joy
for us.

> ' The slow, sweet hours that bring us all things good ;
> The slow, sad hours that bring us all things ill,
>   And all good things from evil.'

And when we have fully proved that true, we learn to
trust. My dearest love to you and George. May this
year and all your years be happy ! "

But this pleasant life at Oxford had its shadow side.
I had come from a large family circle and from free
country life to a University town—a society of celibates,
with little or no leaven of family life ; for Oxford was not
then what it is now under expanded conditions, with its
married Fellows and Tutors, its resident families, its
Ladies' colleges, and its mixed, general, social life. With the
exception of the families of a few Heads of Houses, who
lived much secluded within their college walls, there was
little or no home life, and not much freedom of intercourse between the academical portion of the community
and others. A one-sidedness of judgment is apt to be
fostered by such circumstances—an exaggeration of the
purely masculine judgment on some topics, and a con-
ventual mode of looking at things. What struck me
more than all was the surprising want of courage in
expressing, even if it were felt, any opinion differing from
that of the celibate mass around. Original thinkers there
were at Oxford who prepared, in the retirement of their
studies, works which afterwards influenced not only the
Universities, but the world. But in social intercourse

caution and timidity prevailed. · A certain scepticism on' many of the gravest questions had followed as a reaction on the era of Tractarianism, and it appeared to be very difficult for a man simply to assert his belief in anything. In some men this timidity, or self-imposed reticence, as to expressing any positive belief, or even asserting a simple fact, seemed to take the form of mental disease. If on a splendid summer morning one remarked, " It is a fine day," the man addressed would hesitate to endorse the fact,—not lest his doing so should entail consequences, but simply from a habit of holding everything in suspense; the unhappy philosopher sometimes not being sure that he himself existed. I have purposely, in these words which express the truth in an exaggerated form, recorded the impressions I received at that time.

In the frequent social gatherings in our drawing-room in the evenings there was much talk, sometimes serious and weighty, sometimes light, interesting, critical, witty, and brilliant, ranging over many subjects. It was then that I sat silent, the only woman in the company, and listened, sometimes with a sore heart; for these men would speak of things which I had already revolved deeply in my own mind, things of which I was con-vinced, which I knew, though I had no dialectics at command with which to defend their truth. A few re-marks made on those evenings stand out in my memory. They may seem slight and unimportant, but they had a significance for me, linking themselves, as they did, to long trains of thought which for some years past had been tending to form my own convictions.

A book was published at that time by Mrs. Gaskell, and was much discussed. This led to expressions of judgment which seemed to me false—fatally false. A moral lapse in a woman was spoken of as an immensely worse thing than in a man; there was no comparison to be formed between them. A pure woman, it was re-iterated, should be absolutely ignorant of a certain class of evils in the world, albeit those evils bore with murderous cruelty on other women. One young man seriously declared that he would not allow his own mother to read such a book as that under discussion—a book which seemed to me to have a very wholesome tendency, though dealing with a painful subject. Silence was thought to be the great duty of all on such subjects. On one occasion, when I was distressed by a bitter case of wrong inflicted on a very young girl, I ventured to speak to one of the wisest men—so esteemed—in the University, in the hope that he would suggest some means, not of helping her, but of bringing to a sense of his crime the man who had wronged her. The Sage, speaking kindly however, sternly advocated silence and inaction: "It could only do harm to open up in any way such a question as this; it was dangerous to arouse a sleeping lion." I left him in some amazement and dis-couragement, and for a long time there echoed in my heart the terrible prophetic words of the painter-poet Blake—rude and indelicate as he may have been judged then—whose prophecy has only been averted by a great and painful awakening:

> " The harlots' curse, from street to street,
> Shall weave old England's winding sheet."

Every instinct of womanhood within me was already in revolt against certain accepted theories in Society, and I suffered as only God and the faithful companion of my life could ever know. Incidents occurred which brought their contribution to the lessons then sinking into our hearts. A young mother was in Newgate for the murder of her infant, whose father, under cover of the death-like silence prescribed by Oxford philosophers—a silence which is in fact a permanent endorsement of injustice—had per-jured himself to her, had forsaken and forgotten her, and fallen back, with no accusing conscience, on his easy, social life, and possibly his academic honours. I wished to go and speak to her in prison of the God who saw the injustice done, and who cared for her. My husband sug-gested that we should write to the chaplain of Newgate, and ask him to send her to us when her sentence had expired. We wanted a servant, and he thought that she might be able to fill that place. She came to us. I think she was the first of the world of unhappy women of a humble class whom he welcomed to his own home. She was not the last.

A travelling circus came to the neighbourhood. A young woman who performed as an acrobat somehow conveyed to us her longing desire to leave the life in which she was then plunged, the most innocent part of which was probably her acrobatic performances. She had aspirations very far beyond what is usually ex-pected from a circus woman: she wanted to serve God. She saw a light before her, she said, and she must follow it. She went secretly to churches and chapels, and then she fled—she did not know where—but was recaptured.

It was a Sunday evening in hot summer weather. I had been sitting for some time at my open window to breathe more freely the sultry air, and it seemed to me that I heard a wailing cry somewhere among the trees in the twilight which was deepening into night. It was a woman's cry—a woman aspiring to heaven and dragged back to hell—and my heart was pierced with pain. I longed to leap from the window, and flee with her to some place of refuge. It passed. I cannot explain the nature of the impression, which remains with me to this day; but beyond that twilight, and even in the midst of the pitiful cry, there seemed to dawn a ray of light and to sound a note not wholly of despair. The light was far off, yet coming near; and the slight summer breeze in those tall trees had in them a whisper of the future. But when the day dawned it seemed to show me again more plainly than ever the great wall of prejudice, built up on a foundation of lies, which surrounded a whole world of sorrows, griefs, injustices, and crimes which must not be spoken of—no, not even in whispers—and which it seemed to me then that no human power could ever reach or remedy. And I met again the highly-educated, masculine world in our evening gatherings, more than ever resolved to hold my peace—to speak little with men, but much with God. No doubt the experience of those years influenced in some degree my maturer judgment of what is called "*educated* public opinion."

I recollect that when, with a full heart, I ventured a remark on one occasion, from the Christian point of view, on the subject of some present wrong, which would some day be set right (for so had Christ said it would be), the educated man to whom I addressed the remark looked down upon me with a smile of pity, almost of contempt, and said: "But you surely don't imagine that we regard as of any authority the grounds upon which you base your belief?" Now the things which I believed I had learned direct from God. I never sat at the feet of any man; I never sought light or guidance even from any saint, man or woman, though I dearly loved some such whom I had known, and learned much from their example; nor on churches and creeds had I ever leaned. I had already for years earnestly sought to know the truth which has sustained me through life; and, therefore, at that moment it seemed to me that the smile of contempt was directed at Him, my sole authority, in whom I believed all truth centred, and who is willing to reveal it to those who ask, knock, and seek.

Again, some painting of Raphael was being discussed and criticised. I said I found the face insipid. "Insipid! of course it must be," said a distinguished college tutor; "a woman's face when engaged in prayer could never wear any other expression than that of insipidity." "What!" I asked, "when one converses with a man of high intelligence and noble soul, if there be any answering chord in one's own mind, does one's expression immediately become insipid? Does it not rather beam with increased intelligence and exalted thought? And how much more if one converses face to face with the highest Intelligence of all! Then every faculty of the mind and emotion of the soul is called to its highest exercise." No one made any remark, and the silence seemed to rebuke my audacity. The first speaker merely accentuated his idea of prayer as a kind of sentimental, dreamy devoutness of feeling. These may seem trifling things to remember or record, but for some reason or other they stand out in the retrospect from among many similar things less defined.

In those days I thought much—too much for health, perhaps. We sometimes wished we could leave Oxford and go to the country, where life was more natural and simple; or to some provincial town, where there was a great tide of industrial life and much practical effort and conflict. Yet I should be ungrateful if I gave any evil report of the people who had received us so cordially in Oxford, and who showed us so much kindness. As I have said, it was a period of reaction. There was a tide then setting in of scepticism, of questioning concerning everything in heaven and earth, which sometimes degenerated into cynicism, or a narrow and scoffing spirit. But there were many exceptions to this; and in some of our early friends, who are still living or have lately gone to their rest, the real worth and nobleness born in them was even then maturing, to bear abundant fruit in the sequel. When the Crimean war broke out, the slaughters' of Alma, Inkerman, and Balaclava plunged many families of all ranks into sorrow. I recollect the gloom of the churches, the pulpits hung with black, and the crowd of people in mourning. About that time a vein of greater reality seemed to enter into the general conversation in the University. It might be difficult for a man in a theoretical mood to prove his own existence, but it was also difficult now to prove the *un*reality of death and bereavement.

It was well that we should have thus learned betimes what was the conventional standard at that time of justice in moral matters, even among good and true men, though the learning it may have cast a cloud over an otherwise happy springtime of life. My motive in writing these recollections is to tell what *he* was—my husband—and to show how, besides all that he was in himself and all the work he did, which was wholly and especially his own, he was of a character to be able from the first to correct the judgment and soothe the spirit of the companion of his life when "the waters had come in even unto her soul." I wish to show, also, that he was even more to me in later life than a wise and noble supporter and helper in the work which may have been called more especially my own. He had a part in the creation of it, in the formation of the first impulses towards it. Had that work been purely a product of the feminine mind, of a solitary, wounded, and revolted heart, it would certainly have lacked some elements essential to its becoming in any way useful or fruitful. But for him I should have been much more perplexed than I was. The idea of justice to women, of equality between the sexes, and of equality of responsibility of all human beings to the Moral Law, seems to have been instinctive in him. He never needed convincing. He had his convictions already from the first—straight, just, and clear. I did not at that time speak much; but whenever I spoke to him the clouds lifted. It may seem a little strange to say so, but, if I recall it truly, what helped me most of all at that time was, not so much any arguments he may have used in favour of an equal standard, but the correctness with which he measured the men and the judgments around him. I think there was even a little element of disdain in his appreciation of the one-sided judgments of some of his male friends. He used to say, " I am sorry for So-and-so," which sounded to me rather like saying, " I am sorry for Solomon," my ideas of the wisdom of learned men being perhaps a little exaggerated. He would tell me that I ought to pity them: " They know no better, poor fellows." This was a new light to me. I had thought of Oxford as the home of learning and of intellect. I thought the good and gifted men we daily met must be in some degree authorities on spiritual and moral questions. It had not occurred to me to think of them as "poor fellows!" That blessed gift of common-

sense which he possessed in so large a degree came to the
rescue, to restore for me the balance of a mind too heavily
weighted with sad thoughts of life's perplexing problems.
And then in the evenings, when our friends had gone, we
read together the words of Life, and were able to bring
many earthly notions and theories to the test of what the
Holy One and the Just said and did. Compared with
the accepted axioms of the day, and indeed of centuries
past, in regard to certain vital questions, the sayings and
actions of Jesus were, we confessed to one another,
revolutionary. George Butler was not afraid of revolution. In this sense he desired it; and we prayed together
that a holy revolution might come about, and that the
Kingdom of God might be established on the earth. And
I said to myself: "And it is a man who speaks to me
thus—an intelligent, a gifted man, a learned man too,
few more learned than he, and a man who ever speaks
the truth from his heart." So I was comforted and instructed. It was then that I began to see his portrait
given, and I see it still more clearly now as I look back
over his whole past life, in the 15th Psalm

> " Lord, who shall dwell in Thy tabernacle ?
> Or who shall rest upon Thy holy hill ?

> " Even he that leadeth an uncorrupt life,
> And doeth the thing which is right,
> And speaketh the truth from his heart.

> " He that hath used no deceit in his tongue,
> Nor done evil to his neighbour,
> And hath not slandered his neighbour.

> " He that setteth not by himself,
> But is lowly in his own eyes,
> And maketh much of them that fear the Lord.

> " He that sweareth unto his neighbour,
> And disappointeth him not,
> Even though it were to his own hindrance."

The spring of 1852 was clouded by the death of the Dean of Peterborough. His departure was sudden, but painless and happy.

From J. E. B. :—

"Peterborough, May 1st.

"Dearest Mother,—Your kind letter comforted me much. This is a most glorious spring day, and the deanery garden looks its best. As I write a rich, sweet scent reaches me from the Abbot's table in the Hall, which is covered with flowers; but the sun does not penetrate the house much, as all the blinds are down; and though the whole family are here, there is almost perfect silence. Never shall I forget while I live the sudden change that came over our merry family party. My seat was next the Dean's at luncheon. Some callers had arrived, and were lunching with us, and there was conversation and merry laughter all round. He was in good spirits; but in a moment I felt, rather than saw him throw himself back in his chair: there was a sigh, a sudden movement, and in a moment all the guests had fled. He was laid on a couch, still and motionless. He now looks quite beautiful, lying upstairs. I telegraphed to George, (all the brothers were absent), and he came off at once. I had only said that the Dean was ill. I met him at the door, and he asked: 'What account of my father?' I replied: 'Your father is gone!' I was sorry I had said it so abruptly; for he trembled and became very pale. We went out into the sunny garden, and he said: 'Oh, I wish I might have been in time to hear his last words!' and then I told him how sudden it had been, and that he had lost nothing, for there was no last word. Presently the other brothers arrived; and when they were all assembled, we went to the room where the father lay, and stood around him. They all loved him devotedly. Their presence is a great comfort to Mrs. Butler, who is very quiet, though suffering much.

"The next morning I found that George had gone up very early to his father's room with our little boy in his arms. He was kneeling by the bedside when I came in. There was a striking contrast between the little child—full of life and glee, who probably imagined his grandpapa was only asleep—and the lifeless form of the old man. I treasure the memory of some of the Dean's last words to me. Just half-an-hour before he died I had walked with him in the garden, where we had a pleasant talk. Then he sighed gently, and said: "This has been an eventful year in our family; I wonder if it will continue to be so.' And we speculated as to what might be the next event, when he suddenly stopped, and going up to a tree leaned heavily against it, breathing rather hard. I got him to come in slowly, and he said he was all right again; but I reproached myself for having perhaps walked rather fast for him. He was so polite; he would never have told me, dear old man, if it were so."

George Butler to Mr. Grey :—

" It is very consoling to us all to be assured of the regard which you entertained for my father, and for the true appreciation which you show of our loss and of his gain. It is needless for me to say how very dear he was to all of us who are nearest of kin to him, since even those who became acquainted with him recently felt towards him an attachment resembling that of kinsmen or old acquaintances. But we should be ungrateful if we only dwelt on the bitter side; we should be thankful for having been blest for so many years with the love of so tender a father, and the converse of so highly-gifted a man and so true a Christian. Though we pray to be delivered from 'sudden death,' this description does not apply to the end of one who 'died daily' to the things of the world, and always kept his lamp brightly burning."

In the following year, my husband was ordained at Oxford, by Bishop Wilberforce.

To my Mother :—

".Our gentlemen returned from Cuddesden on Saturday, whence they had a beautiful moonlight drive. I think I told you that Mr. Gorham and Mr. Hort were staying with us for the Ordination; also we saw a good deal of Arthur Gordon, son and secretary of Lord Aberdeen, who had never seen an Ordination, and came to be with his friends at the service. We went to the church at nine on Sunday morning. The service lasted nearly four hours. It was a very beautiful service. The priests and deacons were ranged in the chancel in their white robes, the bishops and other clergy around the communion table. George and I are so accustomed to do everything together, that I thought I should feel like Edith when she crept secretly to the church, and looked on while her own Harold was married to another. But I did not feel so. I quite identified myself with my Harold; and when the bishop's hands rested on his shining curls I felt as if I was being ordained too. The Bishop of Graham's-Town preached the sermon. One part of the service was very impressive, when the Bishop of Oxford said that, in order that all might draw very near in heart to God, silence should be kept in the church for a time. It was as silent as death. Both George and I were thinking (we found afterwards) during that silence of the time when all kneeling there would be in their graves; and we prayed that a voice might arise from each of those graves, saying, ' I have finished my course ; I have fought a good fight; I have kept the faith.' The silence was broken at last by the singing of the beautiful prayer, 'Come, Holy Spirit,' which beginning softly, swelled into a great chorus of manly voices. In the afternoon we went to the University Church, to hear the Bishop of Oxford preach. It was the most striking sermon I ever heard from him, and I think the impression made will not be transient. I never saw the church so crowded. The undergraduates' gallery was a sea of faces. It was interesting to observe the change after the bishop had spoken awhile. At first the men were staring about, or lounging, or fidgeting, but soon every face became serious and attentive. The bishop alluded to the many deaths there have been in Oxford, and at the end Dr. Elvey played the Dead March in ' Saul ' grandly. After the sermon we sat in New College gardens. Such a lovely day! a warm, sweet air blowing, laden with the scent of spring flowers. We felt what an apt type it is—the wind, either gentle or mighty—of the breath of the Holy Spirit, bringing life and health and joy."

We became personally acquainted with Mr. Gladstone in 1853. He and Mrs. Gladstone were invited to a breakfast at Exeter College, where we met them. Conversation was continued till late in the forenoon, as we sat together in one of the rooms looking out upon the picturesque College garden. Mr. Gladstone gave us, I recollect, a deeply interesting and graphic account of the accident to Sir Robert Peel which resulted in his death; dwelling upon his character and several of the most striking incidents in his career, and speaking in a voice and with an emotion which held us all spellbound. He afterwards entered into a correspondence with several members of the University on a subject which was then exciting great interest—that of the reform of the government of Oxford and the remodelling of some of its institutions. My husband took part in most of the debates on this subject, often finding himself opposed, naturally, to certain venerable members of the University, who were strongly conservative in this matter.

Mr. Gladstone wrote to him ·

"Downing Street, March 27th, 1855.

"I have read your inclosure with great interest. Both generally, and with reference to our University institutions in particular, I have a very strong prepossession in favour of publicity. It occurs to me that a careful report of discussions in Congregation would powerfully tend to keep Convocation quiet in the long run, as it would give them an idea of the grounds on which divisions are taken, and would thus tend to secure Congregation in the possession of power as the working legislature of the University."

The Hon. George Denman wrote :

" It was pleasant to receive your letter in the midst of attorneys' actions and other abominations, in court; though it·was not an atmosphere in which I could quietly read your speech, and answer as I wished. Your account of the proceedings in favour of University Reform is gratifying; but you greatly underrate the importance of your share in the business in which you are engaged. I go entirely with every word of your most liberal speech, and can plainly see in you·and the few who go as you do, the little leaven of liberality which is to leaven the whole lump, and make Oxford in time what she ought to be. I only wish you could be at both Univerities at the same moment."

From J. E. B. :—

" Dearest Mother,—I send you a paper, with a speech of George's in Latin; but I send you also the English. He had a kind letter from Mr. Gladstone again yesterday, concerning Oxford reform. He said he was sorry the matter was for the present made so difficult by this triumph of the Heads of Houses, but hoped that the needful reforms would be carried in the end, as half measures would do no good; adding that all this hesitation shows a great want of confidence in the University, in its power of expansion to meet the wants and exigencies of the age. It is paying her a poor compliment. He said he had read George's speech with much interest, both in Latin and English, and that the only doubt he had in reading it was in connexion with the part relating to himself (George had said if anyone could save Troy, Gladstone could). He (Mr. Gladstone) writes with an old-fashioned courtesy which I like."

Believing there was room for an experiment to be made in the direction of encouraging young men to come to Oxford for study without entering any of the colleges (an idea quite accepted now), my husband obtained permission from the University authorities to open a private

Hall. A pleasant house in St. Giles'—on the outside of the town—was taken, and was soon filled by a group of pupils disposed to work, and to take advantage of the facilities of Oxford for every kind of study. Among these was George Davies, now a Royal Academician, well known by his beautiful paintings of peaceful moorland and river scenery. He was an agreeable inmate; very modest about his proficiency, even then, in Art, of which we only accidentally became aware, by finding a half-finished painting on an easel in his bedroom. We then found he had already sent some of his efforts to the Royal Academy, and that they had been approved. He accompanied us during one vacation to Dilston, to make studies there.

The Vicar of St. Giles' required a curate at this time, and gladly accepted my husband's offered help in his church and parish. He was assiduous—during an outbreak of cholera in 1855-56, from which Oxford was not exempted—in visiting the sick. He did not let me know at the time the risks he thus ran, but took all reasonable sanitary precautions for the sake of his little family and the pupils under his roof, while putting his trust in God.

From J. E. B. :—

" George is made Examiner again for the Ireland. It is the fourth time in three years that he has been asked to examine for the University Scholarships. He is doing the work of St. Giles' parish single-handed just now, as Mr. Maule is away for a time. He loves work, and does not complain of having too much of it."

He had the pleasure of seeing his younger brother, Arthur, successful in winning the Ireland Scholarship (not, of course, in a year in which he himself was an Examiner).

He wrote: "I hope you have heard of Arthur's success. I breakfasted with him this morning, and he seemed fully aware of the advantages of position which his success has given him. He is, at the same time, very modest and unassuming; indeed, he is the old Arthur, who knows that he is not wiser than his fellows, except so far as he knows his own ignorance better."

Arthur Butler wrote to me, after taking a last farewell of his brother, in 1890: "While coming home, I went over all the past memories, in which he figured in my mind as the kindest of brothers. From the time when he took me out shooting with him as a little boy of six, carrying me when I was tired, on to those happy days when first you and he came to Oxford. To him I greatly owed the Ireland Scholarship, which I should not have tried for without his encouragement; and then and always, his cordial, hearty delight in my successes was one chief ingredient in my own pleasure."

The public examinations inaugurated by the India Board and the Office of Ordnance which led up to the fully-organised permanent examinations of the Civil Service Commission, called for the services of some of the best men of the Universities, masters of the special subjects which they professed. My husband was called to London and Woolwich in 1855, 1856, and 1857, to examine candidates for the Royal Artillery and Engineers and for the Civil Service of the old "East India Company."

In our various travels abroad in later years, it was a source of amusement to us to mark the almost inevitable incident, in any hotel in which we stayed, of some man coming forward with a word of recognition or self-introduction, beginning with, "You examined me in such a year for such a service." "Very likely," was sometimes the reply: " I am glad to meet you, but you will excuse me ; an old examiner does not always recognise the face of a former victim so readily as the victim does that of his examiner."

He was associated with Dr. (Sir Henry) Acland and others in 1852 and the succeeding year, in the efforts for the creation at Oxford of facilities for the study of the natural sciences, which resulted in the erection of the beautiful Museum in the Parks. A warm discussion had been maintained previously concerning the place which Natural Science should take in education, and its relation to, and possible dangers for, the established theological beliefs.   There were, therefore, fears and prejudices to be overcome, as well as formidable material difficulties.   The University, at that time, had not a single laboratory for students in any subject.

" Great efforts had been made by Dr. Kidd and the two brothers Duncan to light the torch of science.   Dr. Daubenay had won golden opinions by his industry and devotion to chemistry and botany.   Buckland had carried by storm some of the most intelligent residents.   He had disturbed the slumbers of many who could not open their eyes to the true genesis of the earth.   Sir Charles Lyell had led attacks on the University for its neglect of natural knowledge." *

The reaction in favour of scientific research gathered strength, and the enthusiasm in its favour sometimes caused a misconception in the minds of certain of the older men, of the real character of those who boldly expressed this enthusiasm in speech and action.   This misconception existed for a time in regard to Professor Rolleston, whom I mention here as one of our early

* *Oxford and Modern Medicine*, by Sir Henry Acland.

acquaintances in Oxford, and having become one of our most earnest seconders, twenty-five years later, in another scientific movement, on moral lines, which found little favour generally in Oxford. During the movement in favour of Physical Science studies in Oxford, some of the chief intellects were, on the one side, mainly directed to an "intense though perhaps a limited theology," while, "on the other hand," says Sir Henry Acland, "there was, probably through the usual reaction, a tendency with some of us to deify the knowledge of Nature, and a conviction, the offspring of too limited reflection, that the study of the material world necessarily led to a higher conception of spiritual life." But this was not the case with the best and strongest of the lovers of Nature in Oxford; among whom may be named Professor Donkin, one of the frequent and welcome visitors at our house, a Northumbrian born and bred, a man of sensitive and tender nature, an astronomer, a profound mathematician, a finished musician, a composer, and a fine performer on the violin, piano, and organ. He was a man of modest and retiring life and habits, and a Christian in the vital sense.

Of Professor Rolleston, Sir Henry Acland writes: "He was engaged in Biological work of the widest kind. To him Man was the crown of the whole. But Man in his material origin and descent; Man in his evolution, social, moral, and intellectual; Man of every time, character, and aspiration; man in his highest relations to his fellow-men and to his God. Nothing was amiss to him —poetry, philosophy, history. He equally revelled over the dry bones of mummies, or the dust of mounds, or the fragments of pottery. He delighted in sanitary details and hospital administration. He had been with our sick

and wounded in the Crimean war. He had been a
hospital physician. He was a fierce denouncer of slavery,
a passionate supporter of the North in the contest of the
United States. His zeal for the Temperance cause knew
no bounds." It is not surprising that such a man as this
knew how to give the right hand of fellowship to a little
knot of despised reformers who, fifteen years later, dared
to stand up for equal laws and equal social judgments in
moral matters, and that he should have repeatedly
received the messengers of the New Crusade in
his house at Oxford, in the midst of strong and
prevailing prejudice among theologians and men of
science alike.

My husband was asked to take the work of honorary
secretary to the projected new Museum. He set himself,
in the kindness of his heart, to the consideration of the
comfort of the workmen who came to be employed on the
building from various parts of the country. He observed
a want of comfort and accommodation which they suffered
from at the commencement, and, with the help of others,
succeeded in improving the condition of their sheds. He
sometimes gathered a group of them in the early morning
for prayer, and on Sundays would address them or read a
portion of the Church Service in their shed. This work
gradually became more systematic.

When the building was complete, life-size statues were
to be placed in the central part of it. It was then that
we made the acquaintance of the young sculptor,
Alexander Munro, who became a frequent inmate of our
home, after we left Oxford. Brought up among Scotch
moors, and of humble but gifted parentage, he had much
of the sweet character of a child, combined with true
artistic genius, great quickness of intellect, and a rare

enthusiasm for all that was good and noble. The task was committed to him of designing for the Museum a number of statues, representing various scientific men of past times.

Munro worked in our house, not infrequently on the clay models of portrait busts he was engaged with. He showed even then a tendency to the consumption which carried him off so early in life. He was warned by his doctor against his habit of working at night. He did not sufficiently regard the warning, and his delicate look made our hearts ache. We removed his lamp and all means of obtaining a light at night, in order to oblige him to retire to rest. One morning, however, after this severe measure had been enforced, he showed us at breakfast a lovely diminutive piece of sculpture, representing a little girl carrying a bundle of sticks, her dress blown by the wind, and a little dog at her feet; the whole carved out of a piece of slate-pencil. But how did he obtain a light? we asked. He answered meekly, but with a mischievous smile : " I went out and bought a farthing dip, and when I found I couldn't sleep, I lit it, and made this thing. Will you have it ?"

It was decided about this time by the Curators of the Taylor Gallery of Art that it was desirable to have a more complete catalogue of the valuable original drawings of Michael Angelo and Raphael which were there. With a view to supplying this deficiency, my husband proposed that he should employ a few weeks of the long vacation of 1855 in visiting Passavant and other writers on Art in Germany. From these he obtained the information which was required in order to catalogue correctly the Oxford drawings, at the same time renewing his acquaintance with some of the best works of the Old Masters.

9

He wrote to me from Bonn :

"I wished I had had time to make a sketch of Dover Castle before crossing the Channel. As you know, St. Leonard's and Dover are connected with my dear father's last years. It was at Dover that we brought him his first grandchild, and I remember how he took him in his arms and blessed him. It was at Dover, too, that I first spoke to the dear old dean of you, and soon after I brought you, as my bride, to see him. Those were happy days, when the family circle was complete, revolving like planets round the aged sun, whom we all revered so much.

"I was much pleased and surprised at Lille, where I stayed a night and part of the following day, in coming upon a number of Raphael's drawings, collected by Wicar, who left them to his native town. It is a very interesting collection. There are also drawings by Michael Angelo, Titian, and other great Italian Masters. There are also some very good drawings of Van Eyck, finished in the most wonderful way. The people at Lille seem scarcely to know of these drawings, and they have not even a catalogue of them. Professor Ritschl is not in Bonn just now—a great disappointment to me. It was a glorious afternoon when I arrived there, and I took sketching materials and drove about four miles out, then walked, crossed the Rhine in a ferry, and ascended the Drachenfels from Königswinter. When I got to the top, the view was magnificent. It was about half-an-hour before sunset, and the clouds began to be tinged with crimson and gold. On the line of blue horizon there were silvery glimpses of the distant river towards Cologne, twenty-five miles off; the cathedral standing out against the sky, like a majestic ship on the ocean. The valley of the Rhine is very rich. The Siebengebirge are very steep and rough here and there— volcanic, their sides clothed with brushwood and vines. On the right of where I stood rose up a precipitous rock, partly clothed with wood, and partly showing its warm, grey lime- stone, split in perpendicular and slanting cracks. On the · left, a smaller portion of the rock stood out in the same manner, the two making a frame for the picture, and an interesting foreground study. The glowing light upon the winding river was very bright and beautiful. The houses dotted about here and there gave a cheerful appearance to the river sides; and this was increased by the sailing boats and rafts plying on its surface.

"But the glory of the whole was the sunset. The clouds converged from the right and left towards the setting sun, and became every moment more burning and bright; and as they grew more intense in hue, they seemed to lose their consistency and to break up into those trembling bars of light which Turner loves to paint, while those in the upper region were scattered like a flock of sheep. I can give you no idea of the brightness of the tints just as the sun went down. The scarlet, crimson, and violet were of the most intense hue, and behind the clouds were spaces of a pale apple-green colour, which towards the horizon became purple, and towards the zenith blue. I had drawn an outline of the scene in a hasty manner, but I did not dare to colour, lest I should lose some of the beauty I was contemplating, and insult Nature by my poor imitation. But I shall never to my life's end forget that sunset, or my longing desire to have you with me. As I was descending I remembered that it was the anniversary of my dear sister Benigna's death, and I could not help indulging a fancy that her pure spirit had taken a delight in decking the heavens with that glorious light which is the best symbol of intense feeling and aspiration.

"So I felt cheered and delighted, and thanked God with a full heart for permitting me to enjoy so great a pleasure. It was a beautiful starlight night, and, as I waited for the steamboat and saw the stars come out one by one, many reflections passed through my mind, in which you bore the largest part. I do not like a wandering life so much as I did. I feel like the bird which had got so used to his cage that, after a day's liberty, he flew back and begged to be let in. My home is my cage; and I shall not be long in returning to it. So now, good-night, my beloved."

9 *

The day following this wonderful sunset, the news was telegraphed throughout Europe of the fall of Sebastopol. That event had taken place at the very time that the sky was decked with the crimson glory here described. He was able to make from memory a sketch in colours of the scene from the Drachenfels, which marks—as so many of his drawings do for us—some step of our journeyings through life, and recalls pleasant and affecting memories. He brought home also some sketches from the valley of the Ahr.

From Heidelberg :—

"September 20th, 1855.

"I have been made quite happy to-day by your letter, which reached me this morning at Frankfurt, and by two which were awaiting me here. It seems like too much happiness, after my long fast. I shall not leave this place without seeing Chevalier Bunsen. I had a long interview with Mr. Passavant to-day. He tells me he has made copious notes of our Oxford collection for a new edition of his *Life of Raphael*. I find my German enables me to converse very well with educated people : and on matters of Art I feel quite at home in that language. Passavant is a nice old man, and has very fine deep-blue eyes."

From Heidelberg he returned by Strasbourg and Paris to England. An article which he wrote after his return appeared in the volume of *Oxford Essays* for 1856, and is full of interesting research on matters of Art. It was a glad day when our little family was united again, after some weeks of separation.

CHAPTER VI.

FLOODS AT OXFORD, UNFAVOURABLE TO HEALTH.—CORRESPON-
DENCE.—DEEPENING OF CHARACTER AND OF SPIRITUAL LIFE.
—RESIDENCE AT CORBRIDGE.—WORK AMONG THE POOR.—
DAYS AT DILSTON.—RETURN TO OXFORD.—BAD. EFFECT OF
DAMP AND COLD.—SIR JAMES CLARKE ADVISES TO LEAVE
OXFORD.—TROUBLES AND ANXIETIES.—·LITERARY WORK.—
ARTICLES ON MICHAEL ANGELO AND RAPHAEL, AND ON THE
" DIVINA COMMEDIA."—CALLED TO THE VICE-PRINCIPAL-
SHIP OF CHELTENHAM COLLEGE.—" FRIENDS IN COUNCIL."
—ATHLETICS.—THE AMERICAN CIVIL WAR.—GARIBALDI AND
ITALY.— CATHERINE BUTLER'S MARRIAGE TO BISHOP BOWEN.
—THEIR WORK IN SIERRA LEONE.—THEIR DEATH.—VISIT
TO DILSTON.—DEATH OF MY MOTHER.

HE winter floods which so often surrounded
Oxford during the years of which I am
writing are probably remembered with a
shudder by others besides myself. The
mills and locks, and other impediments to
the free flow of the waters of the Isis, were, I believe, long
ago removed, and the malarial effect of the stagnation of
moisture around the city ceased with its cause. But at
that time Oxford in winter almost resembled Venice,
in its apparent isolation from the land, and in the appearance of its towers and spires reflected in the mirror of the
floods.

" It rained," wrote George in January, 1856, " all
yesterday, and to-day it is cold and damp. Indeed,
immediately after sunset the atmosphere of Oxford resembles that of a well, though that is scarcely so bad as

the horrible smell of the meadows when the floods are
retiring.   Then one is conscious of a miasma which only
a strong constitution can long resist."

My health failed.   I became weak, and liable to
attacks of chills and fever.

We drove out occasionally to the heights above
Oxford, to reach which we were obliged to pursue for
some distance a road which resembled a sort of high level
or causeway (as in Holland) with water on each side.
Looking back from the higher ground, the view of the
academic city sitting upon the floods, was very picturesque.
It was commonly said that Milton had in his mind that
sight, and the sound of the bell from Christchurch tower,
when he wrote the lines in the *Penseroso:*

> " Oft on a plot of rising ground,
> I hear the far-off curfew sound
> Over some wide watered shore,
> Surging slow with sullen roar."

This seems not improbable ; for he could easily have
visited these rising grounds from his father's house in
Buckinghamshire, or from that of his wife's father, who
lived at Forest Hill.   Indeed, the sound of " Great Tom "
knelling the curfew from his tower had a very musical
and solemn effect, as it came over the still waters, resembling a little in pathos the sound of a human voice, giving
warning of the approach of night ; or, like Dante's
Squilla di lontana:

> " The distant bell
> Which seems to weep the dying day."

But poetry and sentiment could not hold out against
rheumatic pains and repeated chills.

I spent several months of that year—1856, in Northumberland with our children, my husband joining us, after he had completed his engagements as a public examiner in London. His letters, during the few weeks of our separation, seemed to show a deepening of spiritual life—such as is sometimes granted in the foreshadowing of the approach of some special discipline or sorrow. He seems to have felt more deeply, during this summer, that he must not reckon on the unbroken continuance of the outward happiness which had been so richly granted to us.

To Mrs. Grey :—

" Oxford, June 6th.

" I am glad to feel that my treasures are in such good hands and life-giving air. I hope their presence at Dilston will contribute to the assurance that marriage is not a severance of family ties, but that both Josephine and I revert with the fondest attachment to old scenes and dearly loved friends at Dilston."

To his wife :—

" I am grieved to hear of your sufferings ; but you write so cheerfully, and express such a loving confidence in One who is able to heal all our sicknesses, that I dare not repine. Unbelief in God's power and will to do all that is good for us is, as St. John tells us, ' making Him a liar ; ' and however sad at heart I may sometimes feel about you, I will try to bring myself face to face with those mighty promises which are held out to those who ' rest in the Lord, and wait patiently for Him.' And then I hope we shall still be able to go hand in hand in our work on earth. I will forward your letter to dear Hatty, when I have made some extracts from it which I should be sorry to lose. Blessings on you, beloved, for all your love to me, and care for the spiritual welfare of those who are dearest to us. May your prayers be answered, and may you be spared to see the answers."

" Oxford, June 10th.

" I have been thinking of you much since we parted, and have come to the conclusion that we will go through our journey of life henceforth, if God spares us, with as few partings as may be,—for they are sore trials. The house seems very deserted ; no angel faces of wife and children — no sweet voices sounding from the garden. To-morrow will be my birthday. How much more I might have done in my life, had I sought the aid of God's Holy Spirit earlier, and tried to walk in His ways more consistently. The retrospect of years past cannot be very encouraging to many. It certainly is not to me, except that I recognise the hand of God in many events which have been mercifully directed for my good ; and this, with the consciousness of a new desire after Christ, gives me hope for the future. This morning I was reading Romans viii., and those words came to me like an assurance of favour from heaven : ' We know that all things work together for good to them that love God.'

" I received, this morning, a letter from the India Board directing me to come up to London to examine candidates for the Civil Service of the East India Company. This will enable me to finish up my Royal Artillery work also. The only drawback in accepting this further examination work is that it will keep me longer away from you. But I see in this and in every other call to remunerative employment the goodness of our God, who does not forget the temporal needs of His children. The only earthly anxiety I have is that your health may be sufficiently restored to enable you to do the work for which you are so well fitted. But, if this may not be, I must acquiesce in the decrees of Providence, and thank God for having so blessed me as to grant me almost uninterrupted intercourse with one who so lovingly helps me forward in the heavenly road. My heart yearns for you and my dear boys. You are ever in my thoughts, and it is always a refreshment to my spirit, when weary with routine work, to think of you and breathe a prayer for you at the Throne of Grace." .

"London, July, 1856.

"I enjoyed a visit to Harrow yesterday. The walk from the Hanwell Station across sweet meadows of hay was most enjoyable. I had a quiet half-hour before breakfast this morning, and I always find that when, on such occasions, I realise the presence of God, the effect is not transient, but lasts throughout the day. How easily the enemy persuades us that other things are more important than prayer. When I think of my short-comings in this and all things, I feel I can only abjure myself, flee from myself, and throw myself entirely on Christ, beseeching Him to put away from me all my sins, and renew me in His righteousness. .   I shall be delighted to give up my room at my mother's to your father when he comes to London, and sleep in the little dressing-room. Don't tell him about its being a change, but give him to understand that he has the spare room."

"July 13th.

"We were gladdened by the sight of your dear father this morning. He took a walk with me in the afternoon, in the course of which we called on Sir George Grey and General (Sir Charles) Grey. The former asked me several questions about Oxford, the climate, our Hall, and your health. He was most kind. I said we thought of trying Oxford another year. He and Lady Grey seemed delighted to see your father, and they chatted gaily about the North country. The General was not in, but we saw the children. Albert is a fine boy, of four or five, who seemed to have more military ardour than regard for his teeth, for he was holding the string of a drum, which should have gone round his neck, in his mouth,—very characteristic of a General's son. At a time when other people are turning their swords into ploughshares he is turning his ninepins into drumsticks. I had rather a wish to hear Dr. Winslow preach in the afternoon, but I felt I ought to see your father back to the house. Though his mental vigour is as great as ever, he walks a little more slowly than he used to do, and is more easily tired, dear old

man ; and he is so desirous to do everything he is expected
to do, that I feel bound to watch over his health, and see
that he is not drawn into exerting himself too much.

"I have been reading Tennyson's 'Maud,' and correcting
my review of it for *Fraser's Magazine.* Reading love stories
which end in death or separation makes me dwell the more
thankfully on my own happiness. It is no wonder that I
am sanguine in all circumstances, and that I trust the love
and care of our Almighty Father ; for has He not blessed me
far beyond my deserts, in giving me such a share of human
happiness as falls to the lot of few ? Yet He has given us
our thorn in the flesh,—in your failing health, and our uncertain prospects. But these shall never hinder our love ;
rather we will cling to that more closely, as the symbol and
earnest of the heavenly love which displayed itself in that
wondrous act—on Calvary—which the wise men of this
world may deem of as they will, but which to us will ever be
the most real of all realities, and the sure token of our
reconciliation with God.

"I think we are well fitted to help each other. No words
can express what you are to me.   On the other hand, I may
be able to cheer you in moments of sadness and despondency,
when the evils of this world press heavily upon you, and
your strength is not sufficient to enable you to rise up and *do*
anything to relieve them, as you fain would do. And by
means of possessing greater physical strength, and considerable power of getting through work, I may be enabled to
help you, in the years to come, to carry out plans which may
under His blessing do some good, and make men speak of us
with respect when we are laid in our graves ; and in the
united work of bringing up our children, may God so help us
that we may be able to say, 'Of those whom Thou gavest
us have we lost none.'"

"Sunday evening, July, 1856.

"I have spent the happiest Sunday I almost ever remember. Blessed be God for it ! For though you were not with

me, yet your dear letter has been with me all day. I have carried out your suggestion, and in doing so I have felt a purer happiness than I have ever yet experienced. I tried to represent to myself all that God has done for me through Christ, and I felt that no human love can in any way compare with this : no power with the power of Him who can make us more than conquerors over sin, and cause us to live in His presence, purified from all unrighteousness. It is long since I spent an entire day, or the largest portion of it, in direct communion with God ; and the sensation was strangely solemn to me, that I—sinner as I am, and with faltering steps—have yet this day '*walked with God.*' I had many interruptions in the morning from my own thoughts, but I tried to 'continue in prayer,' and found that my mind, instead of wearying, became more fixed on the subject I wished to dwell on. . . . . Tell me stories of my boys. ' I have no greater joy than to know that my children walk in truth.'

" With love to all at Dilston,

" I am, yours ' in the Beloved,'

GEORGE BUTLER."

While exercising much self-denial and reserve in making such extracts as the above, I give these few as affording glimpses of his inner mind and deep affection ; for his character would be very inadequately portrayed if so prominent a feature of it were concealed as that of his love for his wife, and the constant blending of that love with all his spiritual aspirations and endeavours. That love was a part of his being, becoming ever more deep and tender as the years went on. I have spoken of the strength and tenacity of his friendships. These qualities entered equally into his closest domestic relations. In the springtime of life, men dream, speak, write, and sing of love—of love's gracious birth, and beautiful -youth.

But it is not in the springtime of life that love's deepest depths can be fathomed, its vastness measured, and its endurance tested. There is a love which surmounts all trials and discipline, all the petty vexations and worries, as well as the sorrows and storms of life, and which flows on in an ever-deepening current of tenderness, enhanced by memories of the past and hopes of the future—of the eternal life towards which it is tending. It was such a love as this that dwelt and deepened in him of whom I write, to the latest moment of his earthly life,—to be perfected in the Divine presence.

On joining us at Dilston, an arrangement was made with the vicar of the parish of Corbridge (in which Dilston was situated) that he should take his duty, occupying his house for the autumn, during his absence from home. Dissent prevailed largely in the neighbourhood. But during the time that he acted as the clergyman of the parish the church was well filled. Many Wesleyans came, who had not before entered its doors, as well as several families of well-to-do and well-instructed Presbyterian farmers—shrewd people, well able to maintain their ground in a theological controversy. They were attracted, no doubt, partly by the relationship of the temporary "minister" to my father, who was so much beloved and esteemed throughout the county, and a constant worshipper in the village church, and partly by the simple Christian teaching for which they thirsted, and which they now found. There was little real poverty. We visited the people sometimes together, and their affections were strongly gained. My husband's manner with poor people was removed as far as possible from the patronising character which persons less refined in feeling are sometimes apt to adopt. He entered the humblest cottage with the same feelings with which he would make a call on an equal in social position, and treated the aged poor—and more especially women—with the same courtesy and respect which he would show to persons of gentle birth. They generally summed up their commendations of him with the words, "He is a *true gentleman.*" He did not ask questions as to their domestic concerns, or attempt to probe the state of the heart and conscience. Christian politeness seemed to him to forbid that. Yet hearts were easily opened to him, and burdened consciences sometimes found relief in voluntary confession. Our intercourse with the independent and kindly people of Tyneside was indeed very happy and long remembered on both sides. While at the Vicarage we had a visit from Dr. John Brown, of Edinburgh, with whom we had several subjects of sympathy, not the least being the love of dogs.

When I went for a few days further north to visit relations, my husband wrote : "The Vicarage is so sweet and quiet, and the children's voices are like music in my ears. We only want your presence." And later, when our rest and work there were coming to an end, "I must tell you of my last visits here. Harle is rather better ; I went to invite him to come out with me to-day. His wife said that he had been in great mental distress, 'muttering and praying from morning till night. I tell him he takes on far ower much.' This was her opinion, but not his own. He had had religious instruction early in life, but confesses to have been not only careless for many years, but to have made a mock of religion, and injured others by his scoffing tone. It is a solemn thing to see such a man crying out 'What must I do to be saved ?' Your dear father will come no doubt to see his faithful servant who has been such an able assistant in his out-door work.* "

"Dilston, October, 1856.

"After dinner, yesterday, I went down again to Corbridge to bring away a few remaining things. I first saw all the old people. T. Harle was much affected at parting. The Greenwell family were all clustered together around the fire, poor things, and listened very attentively to a short exhortation I gave them. Old Mrs. Horsfield was waiting for me when I went to see her, and seemed delighted to be able to join in prayer with me once more.

"I had so severe a headache when I awoke this morning that I begged to be allowed to ride one of the ponies to Hexham, to call on the doctor. But your father would not hear of it, and sent a boy over. As it was uncertain when the doctor would come, and I did not like to stay in on so fine a morning, I went out a little way with my gun. I found six pheasants and killed them all, and two and a half brace of partridges ; shooting decidedly well for an invalid. I got in by 3.30, and found the doctor had arrived. He has prescribed for me. They are all so kind to me here. Your father and I had some pleasant talk last night. He is sending some of the pheasants to Emmy. I remember you especially, every morning and evening, dearest, and look forward to meeting you very soon."

Our return to Oxford was not auspicious. The autumn fell damp and cold. It was decided that I should go to London to consult Sir James Clarke, on account of what seemed the development of a weakness of the lungs. I recall the tender solicitude which my husband showed for me on the journey, and also the kindness of the venerable physician. I was scarcely able to rise to greet

* A man with a native genius for engineering, who did remarkable work in correcting the waters of the Tyne, in constructing weirs and dykes, and in providing against the disastrous effects of periodical floods.

HEXHAM, AND THE TYNE VALLEY

him when he entered the room.   At the close of our
interview, he merely said : " Poor thing, poor thing !
you must take her away from Oxford."   We proposed to
return therefore at once to make necessary preparations
for the change, when he interposed : " No, she must not
return to the chilling influence of those floods, not for a
single day."   So peremptory was he, that it was decided
that, there being serious hindrances to our going abroad,
we should seek a suitable house in the sunniest part of
Clifton.

This was no light trial.   Our pleasant home must be
broken up ;   all the hopes and plans my husband had
cherished abandoned ;   the house he had taken and
furnished at some expense as a Hall for unattached
students thrown on his hands.   To carry it on alone, to
be separated for an indefinite time from each other, was
scarcely possible.   There seemed for the present no
alternative.   He accepted calmly, though not without
keen regret, what was clearly inevitable, and returned to
Oxford to make arrangements for leaving it for good.

The difficulties of our position were for a time increased by a serious reverse of fortune experienced by
my father, who had always been ready to aid, on occasion,
the different members of the family.   There had occurred
a complete collapse of a bank in which he was a large
shareholder.   The loss he sustained was great.   The
sorest part of the trial to him was the result for his
daughters, whose future he had always had in view.   The
spirit in which he bore the trial raised him still higher
in the estimation of those who already so highly válued
and admired him.

Trouble followed upon trouble for a time, and my
husband suffered all the more because of some inward

self-reproach for having failed to exercise sufficient providence and foresight in the past. His greatest anxiety was for me; but that happily was gradually lightened as time went on. His sister Catherine became for a time my loving and faithful companion at Clifton during our enforced temporary separation.

To Clifton from Oxford.

" I am very desirous to hear from you, daily, if possible. I feel a weight taken off my mind when I think that—at whatever sacrifice—you have left Oxford. I hope the warmer climate of the south-west of England may be instrumental in restoring your health. All other temporal matters seem to me of little importance compared with that. You must not attempt to go to church. You and Catherine will be able to 'take sweet counsel together,' and I trust we shall soon find some work to do for our Heavenly Master which will occupy our thoughts simultaneously and bring a blessing on us.

" People are very hospitable to me in my present forlorn state, but I do not care much for going out. I am going to meet Gladstone to-night, and will ask him for information —which I cannot get from the papers—about Neapolitan affairs. I am glad to hear of the kindness you have met with in Clifton. It seems wherever we go we find kind friends. How thankful we should be to God, who thus teaches us that He can make any place, for a time, a home to us; but that we are not to consider our real home to be on earth, seeing that He has in store for us a better home, eternal in the heavens. I heard, yesterday, a delightfully comforting sermon from Mr. Linton on Isaiah xliv. I was much comforted also by parts of the service. Now that we are so helpless we can join heart and soul in every petition to God for His providential aid, and strengthen ourselves with the promises of Scripture. He—Mr. Linton—called on me to-day, and was most encouraging about our prospects. He has such a simple, honest trust in God's care for us, that it does one good to talk to him.

"Should you at any time feel disheartened, my darling, write to me, and I will come to you. You know I count all earthly things of far less moment than contributing to your peace of mind and happiness. Speak to the dear boys of my love for them. May a blessing rest on you all on the approaching Sabbath, in which I trust we shall meet in spirit."

During the next few months, having joined me at Clifton, he supplemented our deficiency of income by his pen, finding happily some very inspiring topics for study and comment. He was asked to write a review for the *Edinburgh*, of Mr. Harford's *Life of Michael Angelo*, a very congenial subject. He wrote also for another periodical a review of the various translations of the *Divina Commedia* of Dante. He had in the previous year studied the personal character of Raphael in connection with the original drawings of that great painter in the Oxford Gallery. These formed the subject of one of the *Oxford Essays*, published in the volume for 1856. His estimate of the character of Raphael, as compared with that of Michael Angelo, is thus summed up in that Essay :—

"The age of Leo X. was a luxurious and frivolous age, unconscious alike of the dignity of Christianity and the true sphere of Art. Had Raphael not fallen in with the prevailing spirit of the age, he never would have retained his popularity as he did. Not Leo alone, but other patrons—Cardinal Bibiena, Agostino Chigi, and others— engaged the pencil of the so-called 'divine' Raphael to paint merely human subjects, or such as were furnished by Greek mythology, with its anthropomorphic and sen- suous character. He preserved his influence at the Papal Court as much by his malleable disposition as by his genius, great as that was. It is difficult to avoid instituting a comparison between Michael Angelo working in secret, at his own expense and at his own subjects, for the glory of God, and Raphael, living in splendour, and amassing riches by the practice of his art, while he ministered to the delight of a pleasure-loving age. If a further insight into the character of the two men be required, it may be sought in the works of their pen rather than their pencil,—in the sonnets in which Michael Angelo and Raphael respectively expressed their love —the one for Vittoria Colonna, the other for ' the Fornarina.' The spirit of the one is as pure as a breath from heaven ; that of the other is redolent of earth." (After giving examples of the different sonnets, he continues) : " The reader will note first the difference of style—the pure Italian and correct grammar and spelling of the former, and the Umbrian patois and inaccuracies of the other. He will then mark the transcendental purity of thought in the one, and the glowing fervour of earthly passion in the other. And then he will be fain to allow, that although Raphael may have had the sweeter temper and have been the better painter, Michael Angelo was the nobler man, animated by a higher sense of the beautiful, and gifted with more poetic power. Possibly Raphael might have been benefited by a dash of adversity in his cup of life; as it was, he was uniformly successful, everywhere beloved, and universally admired. Such a cup was too sweet to drink without danger. It was the life of Ulysses in the island of Calypso, but without any regret or thought of home."

It was a true delight to study and follow out further the character and career of this strong, stern man, Michael Angelo, as a sculptor, painter, poet, architect, citizen, soldier, and patriot; and to dwell on his noble and

affecting friendship for the peerless lady through whose
influence, added to that of the preaching of Savonarola,
he was drawn into the deeper life. "Vittoria Colonna," my
husband wrote, "had breathed a holier atmosphere. Not a
wanderer among the groves of Academus, nor those other
shades which Plato's spirit haunted—the Rucellai Gardens
—her muse had stood beside the well at Sychar, and had
held communion with Him who cried on the great day of
the feast, 'Ho! every one that thirsteth, come to the
waters l' Michael Angelo followed his heaven-sent guide
to the foot of the Cross, where alone he could realise the
hope of a better immortality than that which could
reward the colouring of plaster or the chiselling of
stone." *

He attributes to Michael Angelo a strong sense of
"the holiness of contemplation—of that earnest converse
of the soul with the divine perfection, which is represented by Dante under the figure of Rachel; the spirit
which says, 'Thou has made me glad through Thy works.'
The presence of this principle is necessary to constitute
the '*intelletto sano*' of which Michael Angelo speaks, and
to secure for man that higher enjoyment of Nature·which
the Creator has provided for His creatures, as earnests of
their immortality, and witnesses of eternal things—of
perfect purity and undying love."

For his review of the translations of Dante he had
before him, not only the four or five well-known English
translations, but several in other languages. It was a
work of intense interest to us, to compare and talk over

---

* "Nè pinger nè scolpir fia più che queti
    L'anima volta a quell'amor divino,
    Ch'aperse a prender noi in croce le braccia."
                    Sonnet to Vasari, by Michael Angelo,

together the respective merits of these attempts to render faithfully and at all adequately in other tongues the wonderful poem. The translation into German, by Philalethes (the King of Saxony) was perhaps that which pleased him most. Great and conscientious labour had been bestowed upon it. The language was particularly suitable for depicting the grotesque horrors of the Inferno. Some tender passages of human pathos in the Purgatorio were almost as beautiful, he thought, in the German as in the original Italian. But when we reached the Paradiso, then the language seemed utterly to fail, as indeed does the English also, to convey the sublime purity of thought and the celestial atmosphere of that upper region. The translation into French by Lammenais had, he thought, great merit for strict fidelity of rendering, although the poverty of the French language when applied to such imaginative and poetic subjects makes the attempt unsatisfactory.

Such reading and such literary work engaged our thoughts for many a day, enabling us to forget the immediate pressure of the anxieties connected with our temporary difficulties and the physical suffering which I often endured. The experience, moreover, of that time could not be counted as lost or useless, if it tended, as I believe it did, to deepen our sympathies with all who suffer, and in particular with those whose life is more or less an uphill struggle with poverty or insufficient means.

Through the kindness of his friend Mr. Powles, my husband was called to take temporarily the charge of a chapel at Blackheath, in the summer of this year, 1857, which gave him useful and congenial ministerial work while continuing his literary pursuits.

He had gone on in advance to arrange for our removal to Blackheath. His birthday fell on St. Barnabas day, 11th of June.

From J. E. B.—

"God bless you to-day and always, and make you a 'Son of Consolation' to many in the time to come, as you have been to me. Earthly success is no longer our aim. What I desire above all for you is the fulfilment of the promise, 'They that are wise shall shine as the light, and they that turn many to righteousness, as the stars for ever and ever.' I had an encouraging conversation yesterday with——, which fell in with the train of my thoughts regarding you and myself. She said she had seen many cases in which individual chastening had preceded a life of great usefulness, though the subject of the chastening had thought at the time that his life was passing away, wasted, or only spent in learning the lesson of submission. She thought that those to whom the discipline of life comes early rather than late ought to thank God; for it makes them better able to minister to others, and to walk humbly with their God. May that be the case with us. The little boys remembered your birthday before they were out of bed this morning, and have made an excursion to Nightingale Valley in honour of it."

Our intercourse with our kind friend Mr. Powles was among the most pleasant features of our few months' residence at Blackheath.

To Dilston :—

"July, 1857.

"At Mr. Powles' yesterday we met Froude and Kingsley. During the evening those two fell into an animated discussion on a point which to the latter, at least, seemed a matter of strong personal feeling. The dispute was kept up for some time. My sympathies went wholly with Mr. Kingsley, for— independently of the matter of the argument—he was so evidently sincere, convinced, and in earnest, becoming more hesitating in his speech as his feelings became warmer, and his arguments less articulate as his indignation increased. He got the worst of it *in appearance.* Mr. Froude kept his temper perfectly; I think because he did not care much for the principle of the question argued. It is easy to keep cool, and to smile at your opponent's agitation, if the principles in dispute are nothing to you. We had a visit the day before from Kingsley. It was a treat to talk to him, or rather to hear him talk. He is a very pleasant man, so sincere, gentle, and gracious; but he says strange outlandish things in a vehement way."

It was in the autumn of this year that my husband was invited to fill the post of Vice Principal of the Cheltenham College. He accepted the invitation, and we went to Cheltenham the same year. He here entered upon his long course of assiduous and untiring work as a schoolmaster—a work which covered a quarter of a century, beginning at Cheltenham in 1857 and continued at Liverpool, from the winter of 1865-66 until 1882. We gained much at Cheltenham in an improved climate, and in the cessation of material difficulties and anxieties. Cheltenham College ranked well among other schools at this time, under the Principal, Mr. Dobson, in the matter of classical and mathematical education. "As regards the system of classical instruction," George wrote from Blackheath to the Principal, "I have no question to ask. My experience as an Examiner satisfies me that Cheltenham stands second to no place of education in the kingdom as a school of classical scholarship, and I should be happy to take part in the working of a college which enjoys so well-deserved a reputation. The other point is, however, with me a vital one" The other point alluded to was connected with the religious teaching in the school. The

institution there of "Theological Tutors" had been allowed
almost entirely to preclude the Principal and Vice-Principal from a share in the religious teaching of the
College. This seemed to him unsatisfactory; but it
did not continue to be the case, and when Dr. Barry
succeeded to the Principalship, he at once took up
and maintained the position, in this respect, held by
the other head masters of public schools, welcoming
heartily the co-operation of his Vice-Principal in his
ministerial character.

The routine of school life here was enlivened by
occasional meetings of a social and literary kind in the
town. Our friend and family physician, Dr. Claud Kerr
of Cheltenham, lately wrote as follows in answer to a
question I asked him about the "Friends in Council,"
a club formed by himself and a few others: "Our
little club was founded nearly thirty years ago, and
it had not been in existence long before we made your
husband a member. He enjoyed the freedom of our little
Society. We fettered ourselves with no rules. We met
once a month at each other's houses, and selected our
own subjects for papers and discussion. The subjects were
almost exclusively literary, but now and then they were
scientific or social. I remember one evening well. We
met at your house, and the subject your husband gave us
was 'Modern Italian Literature.' We agreed, on going
home, that it was by far the most interesting and instructive paper we had yet heard. We said of that paper as
we said of all he wrote, that it expressed the thoughts of
one who was perfectly at home in his subject. There was
nothing laboured in it; nothing of the got-up-for-the-
occasion style: out of the abundance of his heart and
mind his words flowed, in the clearest of streams. Other

papers he gave us were very interesting ; *i.e.*, 'Shakespeare's Conception of the Character of Julius Cæsar,'—
'Michael Angelo as a Poet and Public Man,'—and one on
the 'Essays of Elia.' Of the members you are most likely
to recollect were : Macready, Dobson, Barry, James (Sir
Henry), Fenn, Barnard, Hort, Willis, Cooke, Wilson,
Ramsay. I more than once took a Tennyson (never
Alfred) to the meetings." Macready (the actor) had
retired to a house in the neighbourhood of Cheltenham.
He came to see us occasionally. At one of the meetings of
the " Friends in Council " at our house, the subject chosen
led to some discussion on the genius of Shakespeare, and
we were struck by the extreme modesty with which he
gave his opinions on a subject in which he was a master,
while every face was turned towards him. His words
were worthy of all our attention—measured, beautifully
chosen, and representing the very essence of true criticism.
He spoke in a low deep voice, which one felt was capable
of great power and modulation. He was a tall, fine-
looking old man, bowed then with years, and with a face
which resembled a tragic mask, sometimes wearing the
look of deep sadness which is depicted on the face of
the well-known portrait of him in the character of
Henry IV.

We lived in a large house in which, for some years,
we received a number of pupils. It was characteristic
that it should have supplied some of the best athletes of
the College, and many successful competitors in the school
games, in feats of strength, activity and skill. My husband
considered physical training to be an essential part of the
education of youth. This conviction he expressed in a
carefully considered address on " Gymnastics and Athletic
Games in Relation to Morals," which he gave, in French,

at Genèva in 1877, where an effort was set on foot for encouraging the students of the University and other young men in manly and athletic exercises, and to counteract the attractions of the cabarets, restaurants and billiard-rooms.

An old friend of my husband wrote to me lately : " One thing that always seemed characteristic in him was an easy combination of the natural man—(in its best sense)—of his old pursuits, literary, artistic, athletic, even sporting,—with the new spiritual life. He would dwell with such evident delight on the former things, and felt no contradiction or want of harmony between the two, while in his inner mind he kept steadily before himself and others the highest ideal ; and that not at all presumptuously, as though he had already attained, or were already perfect, but simply following after, pressing toward the mark for the prize of the high calling."

For himself, constant and even strong physical exercise was a necessity for the maintenance of health, and to enable him to continue year by year the unceasing and arduous work of teaching and study. He never gave up at any time of his life his habits of physical activity in one form or another ; and to a greater age than most men he maintained a high degree of excellence in certain exercises. This has often been remarked by his contemporaries. Mr. Froude wrote : "He was the most variously gifted man in body and mind that I ever knew ; and every gift that he had he cultivated to the utmost of his power. He was first-rate in all manly exercises. He rode, shot, skated, played cricket, and tennis. He was a fine swimmer and fencer." While a tutor at Durham, he played for his county in the county eleven, and had an excellent batting average ;

besides which he was a strong and sturdy runner with the beagles, a beautiful little pack, whose captain was an athletic young member of the University called Schiffner. At Oxford, when, in a hard frost, the wide floods of Port Meadows were frozen over, his excellence as a skater attracted many lookers-on. I was often assailed by messages in the morning in our own house, from friends at the different colleges or families in the town, asking "'at what hour will Mr. Butler skate?" in order that they might be there. There was a certain tailor of the town, whose flexibility of limb, induced, perhaps, by the oriental attitudes which tailors assume at their work, made him a curiosity of agility in cutting figures and especially in difficult backward movements. These two attracted admiring crowds; but the tailor was wanting in grace, "form," style,—in all of which his rival was perfect, in addition to his superior strength and endurance.

It was a rare treat to see him play at tennis with the famous French player and champion, Barre, who came for a time to Oxford. I do not speak of lawn tennis, but of the ancient, royal game played in a walled court, which was watched from behind a safely netted-off enclosure with breathless interest—not unmixed with a sense of danger. The strongly-built and manly figure of Barre as he followed the ball, running forward, stooping low, or springing in the air, but always with deliberate precision and ease, reminded one of sculptured athletes and discoboli of Greece and Rome. But it was a very expensive game, and not more than once, I think, did George indulge in it after our marriage.

At Cheltenham he encouraged strong and regular out-door exercise among his pupils; among whom was a well-known "Captain of the Eleven," Alan Raper (now Col.

commanding 98th Regt.), Robert Reid, and John Grey, *
my father's eldest grandson, a Northumbrian and a model
of a finely-built youth. There were many others, some of
whom were in our house, of similar tastes and of amiable
character, and who continued to correspond with us long
afterwards.

Col. Raper wrote in 1890: "I claim to share the
sorrow which must be yours, for Canon Butler was a
second father to me; he was the first out of my own
family who took me by the hand as a boy, and for
upwards of thirty years he has been my true and constant
friend."

Our summer vacations continued to be spent largely
at Dilston; we went, however, one year to Switzerland
with our eldest son. We visited Lucerne and its neighbourhood, and afterwards the Rhone Valley, Chamounix
and the great St. Bernard, passing a night at the hospice,
where we profited much by our intercourse with the
beautiful dogs, one of whom, a veteran called Bruno, the
forefather of many a noble hound, attached himself to us,
and made himself our cicerone among the rocks in the
desolate surroundings of the monastery. Another summer
excursion was, with two of our children, to the Lakes of
Killarney, including a visit to my brother, Charles Grey,
who lived then in a house of Lord Derby, at Ballykisteen
in the "golden vale" of Tipperary. In both these years
my husband brought home many sketches. The grey
rocks skirting the borders of Killarney lakes, with their

---

* After his school-cricketing days were over, Grey retained his batting
proficiency in the North in county cricket matches, and on one occasion
when an All England Eleven came on tour to Northumberland, it is
recorded in cricketing annals that his individual score was greater than
the total score of All England, against whom he was playing for the local
eleven.

richly-coloured covering of arbutus and other flowering trees and evergreens, were tempting subjects for water-colours.

The excitement of the conflict of principles in America had been increasing, and culminated in the revolt of the South and the memorable war. Feeling ran very high ; public opinion among the upper and educated classes, led by the *Times,* was almost universally in favour of the Southern party. Anyone with a contrary opinion, or rather conviction,—for that it must be in such a case,—was regarded as a person of unsound judgment, if not of low and vulgar prejudices. What Sir Charles Lyell said of himself and Lady Lyell was true also for us ; namely, that they were impelled to give up visiting, finding them-selves out of sympathy with the persons they met daily, among whom they were scarcely welcome and by whom they were looked at askance, as audacious dissenters from the verdict of that august authority, Society.

My father had been a friend of Clarkson, and a prac-tical worker in the movement for the abolition of the Slave Trade. My husband's sympathies were warmly enlisted on behalf of those who desired the emancipation of the slaves ; and he perceived that that was indeed the question—the vital question of justice—which lay at the root of all that terrible struggle. This was one of several occasions in our united life in which we found ourselves in a minority, members of a group at first so insignificant that it scarcely found a voice or a hearing anywhere, but whose position was afterwards fully justified by events. It was a good training in swimming against the tide, or at least in standing firm and letting the tide go by, and in maintaining, while doing so, a charitable attitude towards those who conscientiously differed, and towards the thousands who float contentedly down the stream of the fashionable opinion of the day. In this case, the feeling of isolation on a subject of such tragic interest was often painful: but the discipline was useful; for it was our lot again more emphatically in the future to have to accept and endure this position, for conscience' sake.

I recollect the sudden revulsion of feeling when the news was telegraphed of the assassination of President Lincoln; the extraordinary rapidity of the change of front of the "leading journal;" and the self-questionings among many whose intelligence and goodness had certainly given them the right to think for themselves, but who had not availed themselves of that right. I remember the penitence of *Punch*, who had been among the scoffers against the Abolitionists of Slavery, and who now put himself into deep mourning, and gave to the public an affecting cartoon of the British Lion bowed and weeping before the bier of Lincoln. A favourite Scripture motto of my husband's was: "Why do ye not *of yourselves judge that which is right?*" But he was not argumentative. He loved peace, and avoided every heated discussion. His silence was, perhaps, sometimes not less effectual by way of rebuke or correction of shallow judgments than speech would have been. Goldwin Smith, one of the few at Oxford who saw at that time the inner meanings of the American struggle, paid us a visit. It occurred to us, while listening to some pointed remarks he was making on the prevalent opinion of the day, to ask him to write and publish something in reply to the often-repeated assertion that the Bible itself favours slavery. "The Bible," he replied, "has been quoted in favour of every abomination that ever cursed the earth." He did not say he would write; but the idea sank into his mind, and not long after he sent us his able and exquisite little book entitled, *Does the Bible sanction Slavery ?*—a masterly and beautiful exposition of the true spirit of the Mosaic law, and of the Theocratic government and training of the ancient Hebrew people in relation to this and other questions. This book was naturally not popular at the time, and I fear that it has long been out of print. I have many a time turned to it, after reading some of his later opinions on other subjects, in order to recall the true character of that kind and valued friend of our early married life.

Among the public events which interested us most during these years was the revolution in Naples, the change of dynasty, and Garibaldi's career. Our interest was in part of a personal nature, as my sister, Madame Meuricoffre, and her husband were in the midst of these events. She had succeeded Jessie White Mario in the care of the wounded Garibaldians in the hospitals, and was personally acquainted with some of the actors in the dramatic scenes of that time. Having told her that my husband had set as a subject for a prize essay to be competed for in the College at Cheltenham, the Unification of Italy, my sister mentioned it to Garibaldi, in expressing to him our sympathy for him and his cause. He immediately wrote a few lines, signing his name at the end, to be sent, through her, to the boy who should write the best essay on the subject so near his heart. The prize was· won by Alan Raper, whose name I have mentioned as a proficient in all athletic games.

In the autumn of 1857 Catherine Butler, the third daughter of the Dean of Peterborough, had been married to John Bowen, Bishop of Sierra Leone. She had been a devoted worker among the London poor for some years when her family lived in London, working even beyond her strength. She had often spoken of the strong desire she had had for some time past for mission work, at whatever sacrifice to herself, her one idea of happiness being complete devotion to the cause of God and suffering humanity. She first saw Bishop Bowen at a missionary meeting where he was pleading for helpers to go out to the colony of which he had been ordained the chief pastor. He had set forth with faithful severity the risks to health, the hardships and difficulties which must be encountered in the climate of Sierra Leone ; he had, however, made up his mind to go there, and he now pleaded for the companionship of others who should be equally determined. Looking earnestly across the Hall, and scanning the faces of his audience, he asked : " Who will go ? Is there here anyone who is ready ?" Catherine told me afterwards that though personally a stranger to the speaker, and thinking only of the need he had set forth, her heart within her replied instantly and instinctively, "I will go ; I am ready." Her wish was fulfilled. She did go, but under circumstances which she, at that moment, had had no thought of. The Bishop made her personal acquintance shortly afterwards in her own home. The thought that he was to go to Africa alone had added greatly to the grief felt by his friends at his departure. He wrote to his sister · " Just as I had given up all hope, and submitted to God's will in what seemed to be the greatest sacrifice in going to Sierra Leone, a light has shone upon my path. The circumstances of my meeting with Catherine Butler are very providential. I had only heard of her this summer, and seen her but three times, yet I know much of her character and sentiments. I was miserable at leaving my people, but I now bless and thank God for His good gift."

Her countenance was beaming with serene happiness

on the day of her marriage. They sailed immediately, and those of their friends who accompanied them to Plymouth said that as they watched them from the shore, a dazzling line of light from the setting sun fell upon the waters, making a kind of path of glory from the shore to the vessel. The figures of the Bishop and his wife as they stood on the deck taking the last view of their friends, were almost concealed by the blaze of the setting sun from the straining eyes of those who watched them to the last. The scene appeared an emblem of their approaching end —"received into glory."

The last of my intimate intercourse with Catherine had been at Clifton. She took leave of me there, with a strong impression that she was about to be called to a more direct service than before. She knew not how. She placed under my pillow before she left me a written prayer, which summed up our united thoughts expressed in many of our conversations together. It was concluded by the words, "The Lord watch between me and thee when we are absent one from another."

The Bishop and his wife landed safely at their destination, and very happy accounts were received from them of their life, their work, and their equatorial home. These continued until April of the following year—some short four or five months. The Bishop had had two or three slight attacks of African fever, but being a man of exceedingly robust constitution, already inured to hot climates by his long residence in the East, he did not sufficiently regard these warnings, and worked incessantly. The unhealthy season began. In August, 1858, less than a year from his first acquaintance with Catherine, he wrote :—

"You will feel for me. We came into Freetown in the rainy season. Dearest Catherine was unwell yesterday. I was down again with fever. I cannot remember much about it, but on Saturday a son was born to us. I was too ill to be allowed to see her. She was in an adjoining room to mine. The next day I crawled into her room to see her. She was sweetly resigned. She said : ' It is all right !' Yet she evidently felt the death of her infant son. On Monday I was better, and sat a little while with her. Her face was heavenly. She spoke of her boy and its resting place. ' We will go and see it some day,' she said. Through the night she dozed and slept. On Tuesday I was with her, but her mind was wandering. I was told to keep quiet, and was sent to bed, but I could hear her every movement. She lay very still, making a moaning sound as she breathed. At five in the morning I heard the sound change. I went to her, and passing between the watchers I knelt by her side. In a moment my Catherine was gone."

The Bishop wrote to my husband : —

" My dear brother,—You will be surprised on getting a letter from me, but I feel forced by a dire necessity to be the messenger of my own grief—which also will be yours. God has been pleased to lay on me a heavy chastening. You know the delight with which dear Catherine looked forward to becoming a mother. It is all over now. I longed to be with her at the last, but alas ! I was unable to do so, being too ill myself. At 5.30 on August 4th her angel-spirit took its flight. My dear brother, you and your wife will pray for me. I have received and opened Josephine's and your letters to my Catherine. Alas ! how I felt what you said, and what she would have read aloud to me had she been here. Your affectionate brother

J. Sierra Leone."

He wrote later :—

' " We have laid her in the gravel—brightest of earthly treasures. When I went to take a last look at her I could only exclaim, ' She is gone, she is gone !' and kneeling by the bed where she used to lie, found relief in a flood of tears, saying again and again, ' My God ! what hast Thou done ? My God ! what hast Thou done ? "

Dr. Bowen recovered sufficiently to recommence his arduous work, sailing from place to place on the coast in a boat which he had himself built and equipped, and presented to his wife. A few short months after he again sickened.

On a Sunday morning the Captain of one of Her Majesty's ships on the coast was taking leave of him, and on shaking hands said : " My dear Bishop, let me take you out to sea with me ; it is your only chance." ˙He replied : " It is too late, thank you ; it is all over with me. Meanwhile I may as well do what I can in the way of duty.". He then rose, and preached that day his last sermon in Freetown. Early on the morning of the 23rd he signed his will. He spoke little and seemed to be in deep thought. On the evening of Saturday, the 28th, his remains were carried to the church. He was laid beside his dear wife. A sketch was sent home to us of the picturesque spot, under the burning sun of Africa, where stand the three graves of the father, the mother, and the little child.

Previously to Bishop Bowen's death two other English Bishops had been appointed to the same See ; going there full of health and hope, they had very soon fallen victims to the climate. It was earnestly impressed upon the Government by the friends of these victims that it would be desirable now to appoint to the vacant Bishopric what Canon Stowell had called, a' "real Black Bishop," there being many coloured men in Orders who would not suffer by the climate. This request was at last granted, and Bishop Crowther, educated at Oxford, and eminently qualified by his Christian character and general attainments for the post among his own countrymen, was ordained, and filled for many years the office of Bishop of the diocese.

The news of Catherine's death reached us when we were at Cheltenham. My husband excused himself from his afternoon work at the College, a thing which he very rarely did ; and we went, together with our children, for a drive into the country, alighting and spending the hours in the woods until the sunset, recalling all our memories of our dear sister, and refreshing ourselves with the exquisite beauty of the autumn scenery around us. His chief thought all day, and for many days, was for his widowed mother, mourning the death of her child in a distant land, and having had no opportunity for the practical ministering which sometimes affords a solace to the bereaved heart. He wrote of Catherine : " She was one of the most constant, true and devoted Christians I ever knew. Her heart was full of love, and she never thought of herself when a duty or a kind act was to be done."

In the autumn of 1859 I went again, with our children, including the youngest, our little daughter, to our North-country home, where their father joined us later.

From J. E. B. :—

" Dilston, August, 1859.

" The children are very well and happy. The elder ones have gone with grandpapa to see the reapers. The country looks very gay,—the harvest going on everywhere, and such fine crops. The boys are delighted with two handsome black ponies which are here, which grandpapa has selected for the Queen. They are going to Balmoral next week for the royal children to ride. They are gentle beasts, and quite unaware of the honour intended for them. Papa has also got some horses going to Windsor. General Grey trusts his choice implicitly, and the animals are always approved."

From G. B. :—

" I was glad to be able to stop a few days with my cousin Dundas Battersby at Keswick. Last night I attended, with him, a very interesting meeting for prayer. Old Mr. Hargroves, who has visited the scenes of Irish revivals, especially Belfast and Ballymena, recounted what he had seen and heard, and based upon it a very touching address. The prayers offered up had reference to the same subject, the outpouring of the Spirit on our land. It was pleasant to see ministers of many different denominations combined for one common object. I have never met with a more matured Christian than old Mr. Hargroves. I know you will regret to leave dear Dilston, with all its attractions,—now more attractive than ever, since we cannot look forward with confidence to another such meeting in an unbroken family circle. Though I feel lonely at times, yet I am always cheered by the thought that my dear ones are in safety. Absence from friends is the human counterpart to our separation from God. Perhaps there is no time when we apprehend the reality of our eternal home so vividly as during the absence of those who make our earthly home dear to us."

His thought about the uncertainty of any future meeting of an unbroken family circle in the old home, seemed prophetic ; for in the following year my mother died. Her children were summoned by telegraph, to find that she was already gone. One of them wrote :—

" May 23, 1860.

".I cannot tell you how lovely the morning was when I arrived here, after travelling all night. The light spring foliage was sparkling with dew. I found no one, as they did not expect me at that early hour. The shadows were still long and deep, but the beauty seemed to mock me, for our old home was desolated by death. Papa looks crushed ; he sits with bent head, and silent, but he loves us to talk to him about her."

To my husband :—

" We are a mournful family assembled here. I proposed in the presence of them all that you should come to the -funeral, if father wished it. There was an exclamation from the whole circle, which, though at once suppressed, showed me how much your presence is desired. They said what a blessing it would be to have one of our own people who revered and loved her as you did; but papa at once checked them, and said: ' Tell George that I should be *very* happy if he were here, but I could not think of asking him to come so far ; ' but I saw that the thought of your possibly coming was a comfort; they all know your character; and you would infuse calmness and hope even by your voice and bearing. Do come, dearest. When I look at that dear face in death, I feel as if she too would have wished it."

He came, and after his hurried night journey back to Cheltenham, wrote :—

" I did not sleep much during the journey. There was too much to think of. Kind Eliza has been very good to the children, keeping them with her at East Heyes. I thanked her in your name and my own. I have been again to see Fanny. She is sorely distressed, but not of such a deadly paleness as at first. I hope you will be able to pour comfort and consolation into the heart of your beloved father ; he will need all you can give him. May the true Comforter be with you all, bringing all things to your remembrance that are true, amiable, lovely, and of good report.   I feel refreshed by the interruption to my work, and a breath of the balmy air of Dilston. Oh, those sweet woods ! . I have just sent the children for a drive and a play in the fields. Eva looked so pretty in her white dress and black ribbon."

From J. E. B. ;—

" We have spent many hours in mamma's room, looking over letters and papers. . Oh, that locked cabinet—what revelations of our darling mother's careful love has it not

revealed ! endless relics of her dear ones which she has preserved, remembrances of John and Ellen who died, and all our letters since we were children and which she has stored up. It is very solemn thus to travel back through the past, and to learn for the first time many things about her— how she suffered, loved, and worked. And that loving heart is now still. Then there are records of family afflictions, showing how she bore her children's burdens. .'
Charles is a rock of strength to us, attending to all business matters, and then inviting us out for walks, and is in everything so genial and brotherly."

CHAPTER VII.

DEATH OF LITTLE EVA.—PERPLEXITY AND SORROW.—CONSOLA-
TION, DIVINE AND HUMAN. — LETTERS FROM FREDERIC
MAURICE AND OTHERS.—ILLNESS OF A SON.—JOURNEY TO
ITALY. — SUNRISE ON THE ALPS. — VISITS TO GENOA,
FLORENCE, AND PISA.—CALL TO THE PRINCIPALSHIP OF
THE LIVERPOOL COLLEGE.—INAUGURAL ADDRESS TO THE
PUPILS OF THE THREE SCHOOLS IN THE COLLEGE. —
DESCRIPTION OF LIVERPOOL, THE COLLEGE, AND THE
EDUCATION GIVEN THERE.—GEOGRAPHY.—MEDALS GIVEN
BY THE ROYAL GEOGRAPHICAL SOCIETY. — THE HIGHER
EDUCATION OF WOMEN. — LAST VISIT AS A FAMILY TO
LIPWOOD, IN NORTHUMBERLAND.—DEATH OF JOHN GREY, MY
FATHER.—HIS CHARACTER AND INFLUENCE.

THE summer holidays of 1862 and 1863 were delightfully spent, in part with our hospitable friends, the family of Mr. Henry Marshall, at Derwent Island, on Derwentwater Lake; at Gilsland, on the Northumbrian moors; at Ford, near our old home, Milfield Hill, on the borders of Scotland; and in part, in the latter year, at Lipwood, my father's home, on the banks of the Tyne, to which he had retired when he gave up his post and arduous work at Dilston. A few weeks also of this summer were spent at Coniston, in the house of Mr. James Marshall which he lent to us. His sister, Mrs. Myers, had been our kind and constant friend at Cheltenham. It was a beautiful summer. Mr. Marshall's house is situated on a rising ground above the lake; both the private grounds and the surrounding country affording endless fields for exploring and outdoor life.

We had returned to Cheltenham only a few days when a heavy sorrow fell upon our home;—the brightest of our little circle being suddenly snatched away from us.

The dark shadow of that cloud cannot easily be described. I quote part of a letter written some weeks after our child's death to a friend

" Cheltenham, August, 1864.

" These are but weak words. May you never know the grief which they hide rather than reveal! But God is good. He has, in mercy, at last sent me a ray of light; and low in the dust at His feet, I have thanked Him for that ray of light as I never thanked Him for any blessing in the whole of my life before. It was difficult to endure at first the shock of the suddenness of that agonising death. Little gentle spirit! the softest death for her would have seemed sad enough. Never can I lose that memory,—the fall, the sudden cry, and then the silence! It was pitiful to see her, helpless in her father's arms, her little drooping head resting on his shoulder, and her beautiful golden hair, all stained with blood, falling over his arm! Would to God that I had died that death for her! If we had been permitted, I thought, to have one look, one word of farewell, one moment of recognition! But though life flickered for an hour, she never recognised the father and mother whom she loved so dearly. We called her by her name, but there was no answer. She was our only daughter, the light and joy of our lives. She flitted in and out like a butterfly all day. She had never had a day's or an hour's illness in all her sweet life. She never gave us a moment of anxiety; her life was one flowing stream of mirth and fun and abounding love. The last morning she had said to me a little verse she had learned somewhere:

' Every morning the warm sun
　　Rises fair and bright;
But the evening cometh on,
　　And the dark cold night;
There is a bright land far away,
Where 'tis never-ending day!'

"The dark, cold night came too soon for us, for it was that same evening at seven o'clock that she fell. The last words I had with her were about a pretty caterpillar she had found; she came to my room to beg for a little box to put it in. I gave it her and said: 'Now trot away, for I am late for tea.' What would I not give now for five minutes of that sweet presence? The only discipline she ever had was an occasional conflict with her own strong feelings and will. She disliked nothing so much as her little German lessons. Fräulein Blümké had called her one day to have one. She was sitting in a low chair. She grasped the arms of it tightly, and looking very grave and determined, she replied: 'Hush! wait a bit. I am fighting!' She sat silent a few moments, and then walked quickly and firmly to have her German lesson. Fräulein asked her what she meant by saying she was fighting, and she replied: 'I was fighting with myself;' (to overcome her unwillingness to go to her books). I overheard Fräulein say to her in the midst of the lesson: 'Arbeit, Eva, arbeit!' To which Eva replied with decision, 'I *am arbeiting*, Miss Blümké, as hard as ever I can.'

"One evening last autumn, when I went to see her after she was in bed, and we were alone, she said: 'Mammy, if I go to heaven before you, when the door of heaven opens to let you in, I will run so fast to meet you; and when you put your arms round me, and we kiss each other, *all the angels will stand still to see us.*' And she raised herself up in her ardour, her face beaming and her little chest heaving with the excitement of her loving anticipation. I recall her look; not the merry, laughing look she generally had, but softened into an overflowing tenderness of soul. She lay down again, but could not rest, and raising herself once more, said, 'I would like to pray again,' (she had already said her little prayer); and we prayed again, about this meeting in heaven. I never thought for a moment that she would go first. I don't think I ever had a thought of death in connection with her; she was so full of life and energy. She was always showing her love in active ways. We used to imagine what it would be when she grew up, developing into acts of mercy and kindness. She was passionately devoted to her father; and after hugging him and heaping endearing names upon him, she would fly off and tax her poor little tender fingers by making him something—a pincushion or kettle-holder. She made him blue, pink, white, and striped pincushions and mats, for which he had not much use! But now he treasures up her poor little gifts as more precious than gold. If my head ached, she would bathe it with a sponge for an hour without tiring. Sweet Eva! well might the Saviour say, ' Of such is the Kingdom of Heaven.' She was so perfectly truthful, candid, and pure. It was a wonderful repose for me, a good gift of God—when troubled by the evils in the world or my own thoughts—to turn to the perfect innocence and purity of that little maiden. But that joy is gone now for us. I am troubled for my husband. His grief is so deep and silent; but he is very, very patient. He loves children and all young creatures, and his love for her was wonderful. Her face, as she lay in death, wore a look of sweet, calm surprise, as if she said, ' Now I see God!' We stood in awe before her. She seemed to rebuke our grief in her rapt and holy sleep. Her hair had grown very long lately, and was of a deep chestnut brown, which in the sun flashed out all golden.

> ' Hair like a golden halo lying
> Upon a pillow white;
> Parted lips that mock all sighing,
> Good-night—good-night!
> Good-night in anguish and in bitter pain;
> Good-morrow crowns another of the heavenly train.' "

This sorrow seemed to give, in a measure, a new direction to our lives and interests. There were some weeks of uncomforted grief. Her flight from earth had had the appearance of a most cruel accident. But do the words " accident " or " chance ". properly find a place in the vocabulary of those who have placed themselves and those dear to them in a special manner under the daily providential care of a loving God ? Here there entered into the heart of our grief the intellectual diffi- culty, the moral perplexity and dismay which are not the least terrifying of the phantoms which haunt the " Valley of the Shadow of Death "—that dark passage through which some toil only to emerge into a hopeless and final denial of the Divine goodness, the complete bankruptcy of faith ; and others, by the mercy of God, through a still deeper experience, into a yet firmer trust in His unfailing love.

One day, going into his study, I found my husband alone, and looking ill. His hands were cold, he had an unusual paleness in his face, and he seemed faint. I was alarmed. I kneeled beside him, and shaking myself out of my own stupor of grief, I spoke " comfortably " to him, and forced myself to talk cheerfully, even joyfully, of the happiness of our child, of the unclouded brightness of her brief life on earth, and her escape from the trials and sorrows she might have met with had she lived. He responded readily to the offered comfort, and the effort to strengthen him was helpful to myself. After this, I often went to him in the evening after school hours, when, sitting side by side, we spoke of our child in heaven, until our own loss seemed to become somewhat less bitter. One of his brothers wrote to me many years after : " I have the strongest recollection of his beautiful self-control in the midst of the deepest sorrow, when you lost your little Eva. The more that was laid upon him, the finer and purer his character came out. How different from many !" His brother Montagu, in replying to a letter from him at the time, wrote : " Your letter has indeed touched us most deeply. God grant that the spirit in which—or, shall I not rather say, the Spirit by whose help—you wrote it may abide with you even to the end. We can pray for no richer blessing."

Among several papers lying together with his Bible on his desk, I found written expressions such as he seldom uttered in speech, which showed how deeply his tender heart had been wounded : " Lord God of my salvation, hear me, Thy servant, who call day and night unto Thee ; incline Thine ear unto my cry, for my soul is full of trouble, and my life draweth nigh unto the grave. I am as a man that hath no strengh. Mine eye mourneth by reason of affliction. Lord hear me, for I call daily unto Thee. Make no long tarrying, O my God."

" Lord, Thou hast impoverished ; do Thou make rich. Thou hast taken away : do Thou give back. Thou didst require us to give to Thee our treasure ; do Thou give us now that which we ask—blessings, spiritual life, for our house and for the world. Thou hast pierced our hearts with a sharp wound. Saviour, thy own heart was pierced. Our hearts call to Thy heart. ' Deep calleth unto deep.' Sorrow came swiftly ; quick as lightning it fell upon our house. Why do Thy best gifts linger ? We pray Thee to make the advent of blessing swift as the advent of sorrow. O God, look upon the earth, its sins, its sorrows, its wrongs. The whole creation groans and travails in pain. Thou who art the Desire of the Nations, come quickly ; and give us patience to wait and to watch for the dawn of blessing, as those that watch for the morning."
—Prayer of G. B. and J. E. B., September, 1864.

We received many letters of the tenderest sympathy. Frederic Maurice wrote :

" I am afraid we are all miserable comforters. But *the Comforter* is never far from us, however He may seem to be hidden ; and He does in very wonderful ways guide us to the truth we have need of. I am not surprised that you cannot acquiesce in the notion of your own growth in goodness being the reward of separation from the child who was so dear to you. As far as my experience goes, we want to be united to each other more, to love each other better and better. The thought of our own holiness has so much to do with selfish isolation. And is not this what God designs for us? He would have us enter more into the very meaning of those bonds by which we are bound to children and to parents. He would have *them* enter more into the bonds by which they are bound to us. You cannot think that your child is really severed from you. The yearning you feel for her is the pledge and assurance that it is not so. What would her bodily presence have been to you, if that love had been away? You cannot think that she feels your love or responds to it less than heretofore, merely because the outward signs of it are withdrawn. If you ask me whether I can say that it seems reasonable to me that this love on both sides should be immortal, and that hereafter it should have all possible freedom for its expression and enjoyment, I can answer honestly, 'no *other* opinion seems to me reasonable.' I cannot present the opposite notion to myself so that it shall not clash with the belief that Jesus has died and risen again; that He has overcome separation and binds all in one, and that all shall be gathered up in Him. The renewal, or rather the preservation of every human tie, freed from the mortal accidents which have not strengthened, but enfeebled it, appears to me implied in Christ's victory over death and the grave. My words must appear to you cold and feeble. You will see that the strength is not in *them*, but in Him of whom they strive to bear witness."

Mr. Powles wrote to my husband :—" Your little Eva's image rises before me as I had last seen her, clinging round your neck and her bright hair streaming over her shoulders; and it turned my heart cold to think of your and her mother's anguish. I was pausing for courage to write when your letter came. She impressed a stranger at once. What must she have been to her parents? I could not help speaking of her when I left you—of her singular beauty and winning ways. When these little ones are taken, I always think of the words, 'Jesus called a little child unto Him.' He calls, and they go, suddenly or slowly, but in either case it is to Him."

My father recalled most lovingly her visits to Lipwood with us : "The little form is continually present with me, instinct with life, energy, and merriment. I look at the little garden which she formed and the plants which she cherished. Everything in and around·the house seems associated with her in those joyous weeks she spent here."

The following is from a brief diary of the close of that sad year : " October 30.—Last night I slept uneasily. I dreamed I had my darling in my arms, dying; that she struggled to live for my sake, lived again a moment, and then died. Just then I heard a sound, a low voice at my door, and I sprang to my feet. It was poor Stanley [our second son], scarcely awake, and in a fever. I took him in my arms, and carried him back to his bed, from which he had come to seek my help. In the morning he could not swallow, and pointed to his throat. Dr. Ker came, and said he had diphtheria. My heart sank. I wondered whether God meant to ask us to give up another child so soon."

His illness was very severe, and for some days he hovered between life and death. But we were spared the added sorrow we dreaded. When he was sufficiently recovered, it was thought better that I should go with him abroad, to escape the winter's cold, and for a change of scene from that house round which clung the memory of such a tragic sorrow. My husband and other sons came to London with us, and a pleasant and able courier was engaged, who accompanied me and my little convalescent to Genoa, where we had been invited by kind relatives living there. Before we parted, my husband kneeled by my side, and poured out his soul in a prayer which was sorrowful in tone, yet full of hope, of tenderness, and of a firm trust in God's loving guardianship in all circumstances. He wrote, on his return to Cheltenham College: "It seemed very lonely coming home last night, with only one son" (the youngest had gone to our relations at Harrow), "and no little daughter. These thoughts will return to us as long as we remain here. But I trust that we shall receive more of the light of Heaven to lighten our path, and be able to think of our child as preparing a welcome for us, and rejoicing in the service of Him who had need of her."

There was no tunnel through the Mont Cenis at that time. I wrote as often as possible on the journey, knowing how eagerly my husband would await news of us.

"Turin, November 25.

"It was well worth while to endure a little cold for the exceeding beauty which we witnessed. There had been a heavy fall of snow. In order to reach Turin at night, we had to make a very early start from St. Michel. We got up at five, and started soon after. I wish I could describe to you the strange and awful beauty of that hour. The sky was clear and brilliant with stars, and all around us there stood up sharp rocky summits, clothed with freshly-fallen snow, their unearthly whiteness piled up among the stars, as it were. It was as still as a Canadian winter; not a breath stirred the snow, which lay thickly on every branch and spray. Vicario had made the sleigh very comfortable with sheepskins and footwarmers. Then, dear husband, I saw the most beautiful sight. The sun was rising, but we did not see him; we saw only his glory on the mountains. I was not looking out at the moment; but suddenly I saw the faces of my companions flush, and Stanley cried: 'What has happened? The mountains are on fire!' I looked up. On fire indeed! But it was not like any earthly fire; it was a strange, celestial glory. Imagine all Nature in one robe of snow, cold and white, and then the heights suddenly turned to burnished gold. So pure and bright was the glory that, although very far away, its reflection made the snow on the road at our feet all one tender golden-rosy hue. It was the reflection of the reflection of the sun, which was itself still invisible. The only other transfiguration more beautiful which I ever saw was that sweet look of holy awe and wonder and peace which passed over our darling's face when she died, as if she stood face to face with God. The glory of the mountains recalled that awful sweetness, and calmed my soul. I felt God to be so great and high and calm, and that earth's longest agonies are but a moment's pain in comparison with the eternity of glory hereafter. If God made this earth so beautiful, what must His Heaven be? 'The glory of the terrestrial is one, and the glory of the celestial is another.' I wish you and my dear sons at home could have seen the mountains on fire. . . . We toiled up the ascent with seven horses, two abreast and three tandem, and two others in reserve. The snow was deep. The two sturdy guides with us were up to the waist in it more than once. We rested a short time at the top of the Pass, and then leaving all but two of the horses at the hostel, we trotted quickly down the Italian side."

" Sestri, near Genoa, November 27.

. " We arrived late at the station at Genoa. Kind Ludwig and Edith were there to meet us, and it was pleasant, after a long, dark drive, to find ourselves in her brightly-lighted drawing-room.

"To-day has been lovely. Tell my dear George and Charlie that I longed for them. It is so warm that we could sit out all day. We walked about among the orange and lemon trees, which are loaded with fruit. The scent of them is very fragrant and delicate. We have the long line of the blue Mediterranean in front, and the Maritime Alps, capped with snow, in the west. The sun is brilliant. It seems strange to me to see butterflies at this season, and to hear that hum of insects which is such a summer sound. There is sadness mixed in my enjoyment of it. It all seems to put my lost darling further off. It seems like a year since she lived among us, chasing the butterflies. But it is very good to sit out in the sun and sweet air, and to breathe freely."

"I cannot tell you," my husband wrote, "what joy your letters have given me, telling me of your safe passage over the Mont Cenis and arrival at Genoa; your descriptions are so graphic that I could follow every step of the journey. I have been taking George out for some rides. He is very companionable, and seems to be inspired by a desire to make up to me for your absence. It is an opportunity for cementing a real friendship between me and my little son. I hope to join you with him, on Christmas eve, as your kind host and hostess have expressed a wish that I should."

This hope was fulfilled. He and I went on in January to Florence. It was our first visit to that lovely city. He was so thoroughly acquainted already, by reading, with its treasures of painting, sculpture and architecture, that we required no cicerone, and scarcely a guide book to the galleries. We had lovely winter sunshine, and our pleasantest hours were spent in walking or strolling about on the hill of San Miniato, with that exquisite view at our feet, of the city with its magnificent Duomo and Giotto's tower, the Arno, spanned by bridges, winding through the town and plain beyond, and the surrounding undulating hills, with their winter covering of russet foliage, in the midst of which Florence sits.

He wrote to our youngest son from Florence:

"New Year's Eve.

"Thank you, my dearest Charlie, for your loving New Year's greeting. Yesterday evening I climbed up to the top of a high hill, and looked down all over the city. It looked so beautiful in the light of the setting sun. The Appenines in the distance were rose-coloured, and some of the churches shone like gold. When I see such glorious skies, I think of the brightness of Heaven and our darling Eva. May this New Year be a happy year to you and to your brothers."

We returned by Pisa, where we visited the Leaning Tower, the Baptistry, with the strange echoing music descending from its vaulted roof, and the Campo Santo, decorated with the weird frescoes of Orcagna. The railway was not opened then from Pisa to Genoa. We returned to the latter place, driving by the beautiful Cornice, staying one night at Spezzia. On the evening that we reached Spezzia there was a fine sunset, and I recollect my husband's pleasure at the sight of the white marble of the Carrara mountains lit up by the fading light, rose-coloured like the snowy Alps at sunset; and how he reminded me that it was from that very rent in the marble flank of the mountains before us that Michael Angelo hewed the block of marble for his colossal "David" which stands in the Piazza at Florence. We had exquisite views of the blue Mediterranean the next day from the road, which in some places was cut at a great height above the shore. We rejoined our children at Genoa, and returned to England together.

Mr. Rivière (father of Breton Rivière, R.A.), who lived at Cheltenham, had at my husband's advice gone to Oxford, where a high-class teacher in Art was desired. The move was a propitious one, and Mr. Rivière never ceased to thank my husband for the encouragement he had given him to go there, and for the friendships he there made, owing greatly, he said, to the letters of introduction which he gave him.   Having heard of the thought of our dear child concerning her future meeting with her mother in heaven, Mr. Rivière obeyed a kind instinct of his heart in designing and presenting us with a sketch representing that idea.

"The picture has arrived safely," my husband wrote. "Since I saw you last I have seen a good many frescoes (in Florence), and I often thought of your wish to draw for us a representation of heaven, with our dear child coming forth to meet her mother.   It is a beautiful idea, most tenderly and gracefully expressed in your drawing. I need not assure you that we shall prize it much.   I hope you are well, and that Art is progressing at Oxford. Alexander Munro has sent us the most perfect likeness of our dear child that marble is capable of conveying.   Both as a likeness and as a beautiful work of art, we are delighted with it."

In the winter of 1865, my husband received one day a telegraphic message from Mr. Parker, of Liverpool, asking him if he would be willing to take the Principalship of the Liverpool College, vacated by the retirement of Dr. Howson, who became Dean of Chester.   He accepted the invitation as providential, and went to Liverpool to see Mr. Parker, the Directors of the College, and others interested in the choice of a new Principal.   There was no hesitation about the matter, and he was shortly afterwards elected.   The following extracts show that it was a change in his circumstances which his friends gladly welcomed for him :

From Mr. Powles :—" I do rejoice that you are now at the head of a great educational staff, where your influence will be both powerful and direct. It is a grand thing to be at the head of a college, with nine hundred boys being educated there. Only the other day Froude and I were lamenting that you were not at the *head* of a Foundation, whatever good you might be doing as second in command. We had no idea how soon we were to rejoice in the fulfilment of our wishes."

From Dr. Thomson (late Archbishop of York) :—" I will not say that even this important post to which you have been called is equal to what your great abilities and experience might claim. . Still it is a position of great independence and influence. God give you abundant health and strength for the work."

Dr. McNeile, who was one of the Electors to the post, and whose son had been a pupil of my husband's at Cheltenham, wrote to him before he arrived in Liverpool : " I think it is a token of the great Master's will in this matter that there should be such a simultaneous coincidence of thought and feeling among us in regard to it. I have never seen any important proposal more favourably received or more cordially embraced by a public body than the proposal to offer the Principalship to you was by our Board. You will find it an arduous post, involving contact with some rough and rude characters; but you will be strengthened to meet all its requirements. Affectionately and sincerely yours, HUGH MCNEILE."

Our removal to Liverpool took place in January, 1866. My husband's first appearance before the whole assembled school, masters and pupils, was on the 27th of January.

He addressed them in the large central hall of the college building. I give a few words from that address ·

"It was my wish that my first words spoken to you officially should be from this place, in connection with the solemn act of worship with which we have inaugurated the work of the half-year.

"To some of us this is the beginning of·a new life—a life to be spent under circumstances altogether new. To all, it is the commencement of a new period, a new opportunity for doing the will of God, and consecrating to His service the faculties which He has bestowed upon us. I trust that we have all of us come here with the intention of doing our best; to offer to Him who is the author and giver of every good thing, the Lord and Governor of our lives and the bestower of all mental and bodily powers, our free and ungrudging service. We have just prayed that He will lead us into all truth, righteousness and holiness. Let us try to realise this prayer in our lives.

"And first of Truth. Let us endeavour to be faithful in our words and actions; true to God, and true to ourselves. Let nothing tempt us to speak an untrue word; and that we may attain to habits of truth, let us practise ourselves *in the intellectual habit of speaking just so as to hit the mark, neither more nor less.** We must avoid both extremes: exaggeration on the one hand, and understating the truth on the other, which is dissimulation. And, above all, let us try to act truthfully; not to contradict our professions and resolutions by our deeds, but to live true lives, as in the sight of God, and with a constant sense of His presence.

* I italicise these words, because they represent a characteristic which was very marked in the speaker himself.

" Then let us strive after Righteousness. I am sure
you will not misunderstand me in this. You have been
taught that all our doings are imperfect, more or less
stained with sin, and that we cannot offer to God any
righteousness of our own. But you have also been taught
that there is One who has fulfilled all righteousness, and
that by faith in Him you are enabled to come before the
Father as sons.

" We have just been reading of how the Jewish people
were commanded to begin their work of gathering in the
harvest. They took up a sheaf and waved it before the
Lord, and then, and not till then, they were permitted to
enjoy the fruits of the earth. So let us who have consecrated to the Lord of the intellectual harvest our powers
of mind and body by this act of worship, go to our work
in hope that He will accept our offering, and cause whatever seed is sown here to bring forth fruit abundantly, to
the praise and glory of His name, and to the good of
men, through Jesus Christ our Lord."

Liverpool is one of the largest seaports of the world.
No greater contrast could have been found than it presented to the academic, intellectual character of Oxford,
or the quiet educational and social conditions at Cheltenham. Its immense population, with a large intermingling
of foreign elements, its twelve miles of docks lined with
warehouses, its magnificent shipping, its cargoes and
foreign sailors from every part of the world and from
every nation of the earth, its varieties in the way of
creeds and places of worship, its great wealth and its
abject poverty, the perpetual movement, the coming and
going, and the clash of interests in its midst—all these
combined to make Liverpool a city of large and inter-

national character, and of plentiful opportunities for the exercise of public spirit and catholic sentiment. The College shared the characteristics of the city in the midst of which it was set. Among its eight to nine hundred pupils there were Greeks, Armenians, Jews, Negroes, Americans, French, Germans, and Spaniards, as well as Welsh, Irish, Scotch, and English. These represented many different religious persuasions. A man of narrow theological views would scarcely have found the position as head of such a school agreeable. Firmness and simplicity of faith, truth, charity, and toleration, were qualities which were needed in the administrator of such a little world of varied international and denominational elements. The principalship must be held—by the rules of the college—by a member of the Church of England, and the Directors had been happy in finding Churchmen who were willing to accept the conditions presented, and able to work well in the midst of them.

The morning's work at the college was preceded by prayer, followed by a Scripture lesson ; but no compulsion was exercised. A Jew, a Roman Catholic, or a Greek was at liberty to absent himself if he or his parents so desired ; but, as a matter of fact, this did not very often occur. As a rule, the whole school assembled for morn-ing prayers, and few difficulties arose in regard to any part of the school teaching.

There were, as pupils at the college, the sons of two half-civilised African kings, Oko Jumbo and Jah Jah. Their fathers having been old and sworn enemies, the two little fellows began their school acquaintance with many a tussle, true to the inherited instinct. They were good boys, however ; and one of them—afterwards a convinced and consistent Christian—became a missionary among his own countrymen, in spite of much opposition and even persecution, it was said, from his own father.

The College was composed of three schools under one roof, and with one principal, aided by a staff of masters for each school. Some years after my husband's entering on his duties there, the Liverpool Council of Education was formed, and scholarships were founded, by means of which boys of talent and industry were enabled to be passed on from the humbler schools in the town to the lower or middle school of the college; thence such boys would often work themselves through to the upper school, and not unfrequently from that—by winning a Scholarship or Exhibition—go up to Oxford or Cambridge. In this way it happened that several boys of humble origin passed through a brilliant career. These facilities for "rising from the ranks," educationally, had never till then, I believe, been presented in our own country so strikingly as in Liverpool, and perhaps nowhere have the successful competitors in this upward course more fully justified the system. High moral character, sound good sense and modesty—if not the polished manners of the well-born members of the older or more aristocratic schools—remarkably and, I think, invariably characterised those who climbed to the top of the educational ladder which I have described.

My husband's many and varied acquirements made him markedly suitable for his new position. It was only in the Upper School that the higher classics formed a very prominent element in the education given. A variety of "modern" subjects were taught throughout the schools; several branches of natural science—there being a laboratory attached—modern history, art, mechanics, and several modern languages, including Spanish, a useful language in commerce. While at Oxford my husband had attended the Hebrew lectures of Dr. Pusey, of which he often spoke as affording him one of the greatest delights he ever had in the way of the acquirement of knowledge. The venerable lecturer was profoundly learned, and his expositions of the Minor Prophets especially were masterly and full of deep insight. My husband had given a part of his vacations while at Cheltenham to the prosecution of his Hebrew studies, and at Liverpool he formed a Hebrew class, composed of boys intending to enter the ministry. This class was a great interest both to him and his pupils. Dr. Marks of Manchester came over on one or two occasions to examine his pupils; and Dr. Ginsburg, who lived then in Liverpool, interested himself in their proficiency. Several of them gained Hebrew prizes at Oxford and elsewhere.

Lord Derby, who was our neighbour at Knowsley, proposed some years later to give a yearly prize for Modern History. This gave a stimulus to a study which had been a good deal neglected in some of the public schools. My husband promptly added to his other labours by imposing on himself the preparation and delivery in the schools each year of a solid course of lectures on that subject. A course which he gave on the Constitutional History of England was particularly interesting. Certain experiences had brought before him, in a peculiarly practical manner, the disadvantage at which public school and University men were sometimes placed when they came to fill public positions, in Parliament, or as magistrates, governors or consuls, by their ignorance of the facts bearing on the constitution of their own country and the growth of its liberties. He wrote to Lord Derby : " If I can get a good number of boys to enter the examinations for your lordship's prizes, I venture to think that a great improvement will be made in that department of knowledge; for the unsuccessful candidates will have gained valuable information, and all will enter upon the examination with greater confidence. Boys are something like guns. What comes out of them depends a good deal on what is put into them ; and I have found during the last two years, when I have gone through periods of Greek history with the senior boys, so much improvement in their general intelligence, that I hope equally good results from a similar experiment in Modern History."

The excellence of his pupils in his favourite subject, Geography, soon came to be a matter of public notoriety.

In 1868 the Council of the Royal Geographical Society decided to adopt a suggestion made by one of its most distinguished members, Mr. Francis Galton (my husband's brother-in-law), to invite the public schools throughout the country to encourage their pupils to compete for a certain number of medals, to be given yearly by the Society, for proficiency in Physical and Political Geography.

My husband hailed the prospect of the impetus which this proposal was calculated to give to one of his favourite studies. He began at once, and continued for many years, to give (himself) geographical lectures in the college ; and his success in inspiring his pupils with enthusiasm for the subject was proved by the number of successful competitors whom he sent up, year by year, to the Society's distribution of prizes. In the first year, 1869, the gold medal for Political Geography was won by H. C. Richmond ; in 1870, for Physical Geography, by G. G.

Butler, and the bronze medal for Political Geography
the same year by J. H. Collins. At the anniversary
meeting of this year, when the awards were given, the
president, Sir Roderick Murchison, said: "The working
of this system [of the Public Schools Competition] is
due to two members of the council, Mr. Francis Galton
and Mr. George Brodrick. It is a hopeful sign of this
reform in modern education to find that a representative
of a family which gained so many successes at the Universities in purely classical studies, which has contributed
two Head Masters to Harrow and two to other great
public schools, should have competed for and won our
gold medal for Physical Geography."

In 1871 two more Liverpool College pupils, Arkle and
Collingwood, won respectively the bronze medals for
Political and Physical Geography. In 1872 W. Collingwood won the gold medal for Political and Stanley
Butler the bronze medal for Physical Geography. The
president for the year, Sir Henry Rawlinson, in presenting the medals, spoke of "the admirable system of
instruction in the Liverpool College," observing to one
of the medallists: "You are the sixth scholar educated
under a Butler who has carried off one of our geographical medals in the short space of four years, during
which we have held examinations." In 1873 Liverpool
College produced another gold medallist; and so on with
variations through the years, up to 1880, at which date
the medals gained by the pupils of my husband reached
the number of sixteen. At the presentation of medals in
1876 the Hon. George Brodrick said that " Geographical
education owed. much to Mr. Butler, who was the first
of the Head Masters of the great schools to appreciate
the importance of the study of geography." At the

anniversary meeting of 1878, Colonel Grant, one of the examiners, in introducing the medallists, said he had examined the papers of eighteen candidates, and that Newton of Liverpool College stood pre-eminent: "his answers were so lucid, so brief, and so much to the point, that he had no hesitation in saying that he surpassed all the other candidates."

The following letter, written some months after my husband's appointment to the principalship of the college, recalls certain reforms which, by patience and firmness, he was able in a short time to carry out, in spite of some difficulties such as Dr. McNeile had foretold:

"Liverpool, 1866.

"My husband has, I think, achieved most of the reforms he had set his heart on. Dr. Howson had said to him that he desired himself to see these changes, but that, foreseeing his own resignation, he left them to be brought about, as he thought might be the case, more thoroughly by his successor. The chief change is in the diminution of the work of the boys, especially the younger ones. That they have been overworked is in part the fault of some of the parents in the town, who seem to think that if their sons do not learn a great number of subjects they do not get their money's worth. This mercantile view of education grieves my husband's heart, as you may imagine: it works badly too, from a moral point of view; for whilst conscientious boys work up to eleven or twelve o'clock at night to the detriment of health, idler or less clever boys shirk or work in a slovenly way. George has sent a circular round to all the parents, and has seen and talked to many. It is necessary to gain their goodwill and co-operation, and this he is steadily doing. You understand we are not like the old public schools, isolated and autocratic. This is an immense day school, and the wishes—even the prejudices—of parents cannot be wholly ignored. Poor Agilastro, a little Greek boy, had one day last

week been loaded with far too many lessons to get up for
next day, and, seized with a fit of despair, he threw away
his books, and sat down on his locker and burst into tears.
My husband happened to overhear the little boy's lamenta-
tions, and, looking into the matter, promptly 'changed all
that.' It is a great happiness to him to 'undo the heavy
burdens,' and let the poor little oppressed fellows go free.
He will, I am sure, infuse into the work of the school in time
his own spirit of thoroughness and honesty in work."

In many other subjects, besides geography, his pupils
proved, by their success at the Universities, the thorough
nature of the teaching they had come under, as well as
their own steady devotion to work.

In writing to his mother, Mrs. Butler, at Harrow, in
1869, three years after his coming to Liverpool, he said ·
" Many thanks for your kind congratulations on our
successes. Counting Pendlebury's Scholarship at London
University, this makes our sixth Scholarship—we have
three at Oxford and two at Cambridge. We are sending
up a mathematician for Oriel next week. We are now
coming to some 'better fish than have yet been taken out
of the sea,' and I hope we shall even do more in future."
This hope was not disappointed

Among the subjects concerning which my husband
advanced with a quicker and firmer step than that of the
society around him in general stands that of the higher
education of women. It may be difficult for the present
generation to realise what an amount of dogged opposition and prejudice the pioneers of this movement had
to encounter only some twenty-five years ago. We have
made such rapid strides in the direction of women's
education that we almost forget that our ladies' colleges,
higher examinations, and the various honours for which

women compete so gallantly with men, are but of yesterday. Miss Clough called at our house in Liverpool one
day in 1867, to ascertain the state of mind of the
Principal of the Liverpool College in regard to the
beautiful schemes which were even then taking shape in
her fruitful brain for the benefit of her fellow-women. I
think she was heartily glad to find herself in a house
where not a shadow of prejudice or doubt existed, to be
argued down or patiently borne with until better days.
My husband even went a little further, I believe, than
she did at that time, in his hopes concerning the equality
to be granted in future in the matter of educational
advantages for boys and girls, men and women. But
probably Miss Clough did not speak of all that she then
hoped, or only spoke of it under her breath. An active
propagandist work was started soon after by James
Stuart, of Trinity College, Cambridge, who made Liverpool his headquarters during his first experiment in
establishing lectures for ladies, which developed into the
University Extension Scheme. It was arranged that the
first course should embrace four of the most important
towns of the north of England, constituting a sort of
circuit. It seemed desirable that a man of experience
and weight in the educational world should inaugurate
this experiment by a preliminary address or lecture, given
to mixed audiences, in each of these four towns. My
husband undertook this task. His first address was given
at Sheffield, where he was the guest of Canon Sale, who
approved heartily of the movement. Without unnecessarily conjuring up spectres of opposition in order to
dismiss them, he carefully framed his discourse so as to
meet the prejudices of which the air, at that time, was
full. It was generally imagined that a severer intellectual

training than women had hitherto received would make
them unwomanly, hard, unlovely, pedantic, and disin-
clined for domestic duties, while the dangers to physical
health were dolorously prophesied by medical men and
others. In concluding his inaugural address, my husband
said: "A community of women established purposely to
educate girls and to train teachers was not known in
Christendom till the institution of the Ursulines by Angela
dà Brescia in 1537. So unheard of at this time was any
attempt of women to organise a systematic education for
their own sex, that when Françoise de Saintange undertook to found such a school at Dijon she was hooted in
the streets, and her father called together four doctors
learned in the laws, '*pour s'assurer qu'instruire des femmes
n'était pas un œuvre du démon.*' Even after he had given
his consent, he was afraid to countenance his daughter;
and Françoise, unprotected and unaided, began her first
school in a garret. Twelve years afterwards she was
carried in triumph through the streets, with bells ringing
and flowers strewed in her path, *because she had succeeded.*
Her work lived and grew, *because it was right.* So take
courage, ladies, struggling now at this day for the right
to cultivate to their full extent the faculties and gifts
which God has bestowed upon you. You must fight your
own battles still. At all times reforms in the social position of women have been brought about by efforts of
their own, for their own sex, supplemented by men, but
always coming in the first instance from themselves."

He had it very much at heart that the social position
of head mistresses of schools should be made and recognised to be as good as that of head masters, and that the
salaries of women teachers should be equal to those of
men, the work done being equal. He corresponded. on

this subject with Mr. James Fraser, afterwards Bishop of Manchester, who had drawn up an interesting report on "Schools in America," and also with Mr. James Bryce (Professor Bryce, M.P.), who was one of our helpers at that time on the "North of England Council for the Higher Education of Women," a working council which grew out of these first efforts.

The summer of 1867 was spent by us in our dear Northumbrian haunts, chiefly at Gilsland and Lipwood; the former so called, it is believed, from a famous Border reiver called Giles. My father joined us there, and in many a pleasant excursion he was our guide,—to Lanercost Priory and over the breezy moors. This is the wild Borderland, partly Northumbrian and partly Cumbrian, close upon the Scottish Border, which is the scene of a portion of the events in Sir Walter Scott's *Talisman.* Traditions of "Meg Merrilees" still linger there. Lipwood, a little further east, was a pleasant place. The house to which my father had retired was so near the river Tyne that its musical murmurings over its wide shallow bed could be heard day and night; and the hills and moors above the house, leading up to the old Roman Wall, were breezy and healthful. This was destined to be our last visit to my father's home, though we did not know it. My husband, who had gone to examine for a Scholarship at Oxford, wrote to his little sons:

" I was glad to get your letters, my dear boys, and thank you for them. I hope you like Lipwood as well as Gilsland, and manage to find plenty of amusement. I am glad you found your gardens in good order. You will take care of dear Eva's, I am sure. I saw a little girl to-day with beautiful long, soft hair, but not so pretty as our darling's. I am proud

13

to hear you are so clever at bridge-making; but grandpapa will not commend your work if the bridges come down and duck the passengers. Mr. Rivière admired the illustration in your letter—the undergraduate and the owl. It looks like an early work of the artist! I hope to be with you soon. Meanwhile try and comfort dear mamma when she is sad."

Believing it would gratify their father to receive a classical letter, the boys each made a heroic effort in this direction, Stanley's resulting in the following. [The reader will not be too critical.]

" a Feli.*

"Care Pater,—Spero te valere. Navimus in Tyno. (Carolus non est defunctus.) Qnum se siccabamus, homo ex alto despicit nobis, cum rubra facie, nigroque 'hat,' et triste voce, ait, 'Est acqua calida?' 'Non est,' diximus. Hic plevit, abutque. Nunc plevit. Scenam monstravimus nocte postremo ad Misses Pendred. Avus noster valde bene est. Literas ab Ethel Edgarque hodie recipimus. We are all quite well. It is very fine weather. George also wrote a Latin letter to you; but the window being open, it blew away. Excuse bad Latin; I had no dictionary.

" Your loving Cat."

To this his father replied :—

" Georgius Butler, S.D.

" Carissimo filio, cui nomen Feli,—Te valere magnopere gaudeo. Quod tu et fratres tui in arte nandi profeceritis, id mihi valde jucundum est. Carolum salvum esse gaudeo. Literas a Georgio scriptas vento abreptas esse doleo.

" Cum essem Oxoniæ, vidi filiolam Doctoris Lightfoot, anuos tres natam, quae Doctorem Jacobson, Episcopum Cestrensem 'Bob' appellavit. Vidi quoque domum in qua

* A name which had clung to him since nursery times.

Georgius natus est, cum picturis, quæ in proximis ædibus servantur.

"Postea viâ ferreâ ad Londinum profectus vidi certamen inter duas Academias in Campo Domini* absolutum. Victores erant Cantabrigienses, non obstante Roberto Reid, qui se optimum gubernatorem praestitit.

"Cum Roberto Raper locutus sum. Is maxime valet. Avum tuum valere multum gaudeo. Spero vos Kesvici salvos revisurum. Si soles ex imbri sequentur, nos in limpidis Derventii lacûs aquis lavabimur.

"Matrem carissimam, avum, et amitam Franciscam saluto. Cura ut salvus sis, et cum fraterculis lotus me revisas. Vale.

"Harroviae, die iii. men Jul, A.D. mdccclxviii."

To J. E. B. :—

"I can well imagine how the house and garden must recall to your mind our angel child. May God give you comfort in the thought that she is eternally safe and happy! If at any time you feel overpowered by sad thoughts, do not hesitate to telegraph to me, and I will come to you."

My husband joined us in August, and went with us to Keswick, where his cousin, Dundas Battersby, had engaged him to undertake his pastoral duty for a few weeks, during which time we lived in that ideally-situated parsonage, St. John's, on the shores of Derwentwater Lake.

In the following winter my father died. On the 23rd of January, 1868, we were summoned by a telegraphic message from my sister, Mrs. Smyttan, who had lived with him during the last years of his life. But none of us saw him alive again. The end had been sudden, but very tranquil. "His health was excellent to the last. On

* Lord's ground.

the morning of January 23rd, as he was passing from his bedroom to his study, he sat down, feeling faint, and raising his forefinger as if to enjoin silence, or intent upon a voice calling him away, he died without a struggle, and apparently without pain, in the eighty-third year of his age." *

His loss was deeply and widely felt, both privately among his numerous descendants, and publicly in the North of England, where his influence had been so beneficent.

My husband, who had come to my father's funeral, wrote to his son George:—

"This place is full of memories of you all and of dear Eva, and now the master of the house is gone. He now lies in his coffin upstairs, and to-morrow he will be laid in the churchyard at Corbridge, side by side with grandmamma. It is very sad for all the family, but most of all for dear Aunt Fanny, who must now look for another home. It would be nice if she were to settle near us, would it not? Mamma sends her love to you all, and says that poor dog Tip goes every morning to grandpapa's room, as usual, and waits for him to come out; and when he does not appear, he goes away quite troubled and sad. Give my love to Stanley and Charlie. Think of us to-morrow at midday in the churchyard where grandpapa took you to see grandmamma's grave."

"As we passed along the vale of Tyne on our way back to Lipwood, after we had laid him in his last earthly resting-place, we were much impressed by the outward results—in the high cultivation and look of happy prosperity of the country—of a long life usefully spent. And this feeling was shared by all the dwellers there, who, equally with ourselves, could mark in all around them the

* Obituary notice in *The Times.*

impress of his mind and hand. But only those who had had the happiness of his friendship and confidence could know, with his children, how much of strength and sweetness seemed to be gone away from earth when that great heart had ceased to beat." *

My husband gave expression to his thoughts concerning my father in the following sonnets :—

> "What Spirit's warning voice called thee from earth?
>   Of years and honours full, not bent by age,
>   But active still upon this mortal stage;
> Grand patriarchal type of Northern worth
> Keen, strong, and tender, dauntless friend of truth,
>   Champion of all who suffered cruelty:
>   Of kindness full, and Christian courtesy,
> And hopeful confidence akin to youth.
> We hoped to keep thee longer, but thy life
>   Is hid in Christ—hereafter to appear,
>   When Christ Himself shall come, and every tear
> Wipe from our eyes, and end this mortal strife.
> Then shall thy dear ones own 'twas Sovereign Love
> That called thy spirit to the realms above."

> *   *   *   *

> "Well did he love the land that gave him birth;
>   Well did he serve her : from his earliest youth
>   A firm and constant advocate of truth,
> Type of Northumbria's freedom and her worth.
> To help the oppress'd, to liberate the slave,
>   To check injustice, tyranny, and wrong,—
>   Such were the tasks for which his arm was strong,
> His voice was eloquent, his counsel brave.
> The woodman's toil, the labour of the mine,
>   And busy husbandry confessed his care;
>   Cottage and farm, and school and House of Prayer,
> Rose at his bidding on the banks of Tyne.
> So lent he lustre to a noble name,
> And true Northumbria shall guard his fame."

* *Memoir of John Grey of Dilston*

CHAPTER VIII.

WORK AMONG THE POOR WOMEN OF LIVERPOOL.—FIRST EXPERI-
MENTS.—OPENING OF A "HOUSE OF REST."—AND OF AN
"INDUSTRIAL HOME."—THE SYMPATHY AND HELP OF MY
SISTERS IN THIS WORK. — CORRESPONDENCE. — M. TELL
MEURICOFFRE AND HIS FAMILY.—STORY OF MARION ; RUINED
AND SAVED ; HER PARENTS' VISITS ; HER DEATH AND
BURIAL.—CONSOLATION.—"THROUGH HOSTS AND HOSTS."
—OUR VACATION TOURS.—LOVE OF COUNTRY LIFE, AND
OUT DOOR PURSUITS.—VISIT TO SWITZERLAND, THE OBER-
LAND, GRINDELWALD, AND LA GORDANNE, IN THE CANTON
VAUD.—VISIT TO THE SCOTTISH HIGHLANDS.— TO THE WEST
OF IRELAND.—TO THE TYROL AND BAVARIAN HIGHLANDS.

 MUST go back a little way. When we
came to Liverpool in 1866, and my husband
and sons began their regular life at the
College, going there early and returning in
the evening, I was left many hours every day
alone, empty-handed and sorrowful ; the thought continually returning, " How sweet the presence of my little
daughter would have been now." Most people who have
gone through any such experience will understand me when
I speak of the ebb and flow of sorrow. The wave retires
perhaps after the first bitter weeks, and a kind of placid
acquiescence follows ; it may be only a natural giving
way of the power of prolonged resistance of pain. Then
there comes sometimes a second wave, which has been
silently gathering strength, holding back, so to speak,
in order to advance again with all its devouring force,
thundering upon the shore. But who can write the

rationale of sorrow ? and who can explain its mysteries, its apparent inconsistencies and unreasonableness, its weakness and its strength ? I suffered much during the first months in our new home. Music, art, reading, all failed as resources to alleviate or to interest. I became possessed with an irresistible desire to go forth and find some pain keener than my own—to meet with people more unhappy than myself (for I knew there were thousands of such). I did not exaggerate my own trial ; I only knew that my heart ached night and day, and that the only solace possible would seem to be to find other hearts which ached night and day, and with more reason than mine. I had no clear idea beyond that, no plan for helping others ; my sole wish was to plunge into the heart of some human misery, and to say (as I now knew I could) to afflicted people, "I understand. I, too, have suffered."

It was not difficult to find misery in Liverpool. There was an immense workhouse containing at that time, it was said, 5000 persons; a little town in itself. The general hospital for paupers included in it was blest then by the angelic presence of Agnes Jones (whose work of beneficence was recorded after her death) ; but the other departments in the great building were not so well organised as they came to be some years later. There were extensive special wards, where unhappy girls drifted like autumn leaves, when the winter approached : many of them to die of consumption, little cared for spiritually ; for over this portion of the hospital Agnes Jones was not the presiding genius. There was on the ground floor a Bridewell for women, consisting of huge cellars, bare and unfurnished, with damp stone floors ; these were called the "oakum sheds," and to these came voluntarily

creatures driven by hunger, destitution, or vice, begging
for a few nights' shelter and a piece of bread, in return
for which they picked their allotted portion of oakum.
Others were sent there as prisoners. I went down to the
oakum sheds and begged admission. I was taken into
an immense gloomy vault, filled with women and girls—
more than two hundred, probably, at that time. I sat
on the floor among them and picked oakum. They
laughed at me, and told me my fingers were of no use for
that work ; which was true. But while we laughed we
became friends. I proposed that they should learn a few
verses to say to me on my next visit. I recollect a tall,
dark, handsome girl standing up in our midst, among the
damp refuse and lumps of tarred rope, and repeating
without a mistake and in a not unmusical voice, clear
and ringing, that wonderful fourteenth chapter of St.
John's Gospel:—the words of Jesus all through, ending
with " Peace I leave with you, My peace I give unto you.
Let not your heart be troubled, neither let it be afraid."
She had selected it herself; and they listened in perfect
silence, this audience — wretched, draggled, ignorant,
criminal, some ; and wild and defiant, others. The tall,
dark-haired girl had prepared the way for me ; and I
said, " Now let us all kneel, and cry to that same Jesus
who spoke those words ;" and down on their knees they
fell, every one of them, reverently, on that damp stone
floor, some saying the words after me, others moaning
and weeping. It was a strange sound, that united wail—
continuous, pitiful, strong—like a great sigh or murmur
of vague desire and hope, issuing from the heart of
despair, piercing the gloom and murky atmosphere of
that vaulted room, and reaching to the heart of God.

But I do not want to make a long story of this. The

result of my visits to the hospital and quays and oakum sheds was to draw down upon my head an avalanche of miserable but grateful womanhood. Such a concourse gathered round our home that I had to stop to take breath, and consider some means of escape from the dilemma by providing some practical help, moral and material. There were not at that time many enlightened missions or measures in the town for dealing with the refuse of society. There was the Catholic Refuge of the Good Shepherd, some way in the country; an old-fashioned Protestant Penitentiary, rather prison-like in character; another smaller Refuge; and, best of all, a Home recently established by Mrs. Cropper. But it must not be supposed that the majority of my oakum shed friends were of a character to seek such asylums. Many of them—and especially the Irish Catholics—prided themselves on their virtue ; and well they might, considering their miserable surroundings—girls who for the most part earned a scanty living, by selling sand in the streets (for cleaning floors), or the refuse of the markets to the poorest of the population. Usually they were barefooted and bonnetless. The Lancashire women are strong and bold. The criminals of the oakum sheds and prison, sent to "do a week" or a month there, had most frequently been convicted of fighting and brawling, on the quays and docks, of theft or drunkenness. There was stuff among them to make a very powerful brigade of workers in any active good cause. But there were others—the children of intemperate and criminal parents—who were humanly speaking, useless, not quite "all there," poor, limp, fibreless human weeds. These last were the worst of all to deal with. I had the help at this time of a widowed sister who was visiting Liverpool, and who, in spite of very delicate health, threw herself heroically into the effort to help this work without a name which came upon us. We had a dry cellar in our house and a garret or two, and into these we crowded as many as possible of the most friendless girls who were anxious to make a fresh start. This became inconvenient ; and so, in time, my husband and I ventured to take a house near our own, trusting to find funds to furnish and fill it with inmates. This was the " House of Rest," which continued for many years, and developed, about the time we left Liverpool, into an Incurable Hospital, supported by the town. It was there that, a little later, women incurably ill were brought from the hospitals or their wretched homes, their beds in hospital being naturally wanted for others.

A few months later, encouraged by the help offered by a certain number of generous Liverpool merchants and other friends, we took a very large and solid house, with some ground round it, to serve as an Industrial Home, for the healthy and active, the barefooted sand girls, and other friendless waifs and strays. We had a good gathering of friends and neighbours at a service which my husband held at the opening of the Industrial Home. His " Dedication prayer " on that occasion was very touching, and full of kindness and heart-yearning towards the poor disinherited beings whom we desired to gather in. This house was very soon filled, and was successfully managed by an excellent matron, a mother. Besides the usual laundry and other work, we were able to set up a little envelope factory in one of the spacious rooms. This work called out some skill and nicety, and interested the girls very much. Several tradesmen and firms bought our envelopes at wholesale prices, and we also supplied some private friends disposed to help us. As chaplain, friend, and adviser in these two modest institutions, my husband showed the same fidelity and constancy which he did in every other seriously accepted or self-imposed duty. He often said that it was a rest and refreshment to him to visit our poor people in the evening, and more especially on Sunday. In the House of Rest were received "incurables," so called, (of whom not a few recovered). There was a very peaceful atmosphere in that house, answering to its name, a spirit of repose, contentment, and even gaiety among the young inmates, scarcely clouded even by the frequent deaths, which came generally as a happy and not unexpected release, and were regarded by the living as a series of fresh bonds between the family in heaven and that on earth.

Shortly before the creation of these two Homes, we had a visit from my sister, Madame Meuricoffre. She and her husband, with their dear little girl, Josephine, had come from Naples to England, and had paid a visit to our father in Northumberland. They had, a short time before, lost a beloved child, their little Beatrice, during an outbreak of the cholera in Naples. The surviving little girl seemed to droop after the death of her companion. She (little Josephine) took ill on the way from the North, and before they reached Liverpool this darling of her parents had gone to join her beloved sister in the presence of God. The parents came to us in deep sorrow, bringing with them the earthly remains of their child.

In 1874, when scattered efforts on behalf of the sufferers from some of the world's worst evils had expanded and developed in England into a great and wide movement for national, moral, and legislative reform, and

when appeals had been received from Continental countries for help in promoting a similar movement abroad,
my sister wrote to me, to Genoa, where my husband and
I were, on our way to other Italian towns :—

"Naples.   New Year's Eve, 1874—75, midnight.

"I want to spend this solemn hour with you.   My heart
is overflowing with gratitude to Him whose Cross you bear.
This year has finished gloriously with the carrying of the
standard of the fiery cross over the sea, and into another
land.   It must not happen that you do not get here.   With
all you have to do, it seems cruel to bring you so far; but it
would be sweet that you and dear George should once be in
Naples.   I recall all his kindness and goodness to me, since
old Oxford days, until that crowning goodness of receiving
us at Liverpool with our dead treasure, as his guests, the
pretty guest-chamber made ready for her, in spite of all the
unhealed wounds the sight must have re-opened in your
hearts.   All that comes up before us, and we long to have
you as our guests, to repay the kindness."

My brother-in-law, the Chevalier Tell Meuricoffre,
wrote to me in 1890, recalling past years :—

"I will not trouble you with many words in your great
sorrow; but I am impelled to say something of what I feel
towards the memory of my honoured and dear brother.
There have been many occasions in our lives which have
brought us together; most of them times of rest and cheerful
family gatherings, others also when death had entered our
homes.   His warm sympathy and invariable kindness have
made on me an impression which can never be effaced.
How I remember the times we have spent in your house—
at Oxford, in Cheltenham, in Liverpool, and in these last
years at Winchester.   With what a tender sympathy he
received us when we came with the mortal remains of our
dear little one, and read over them the promises of the
Resurrection.   And then the meetings in Switzerland, how
pleasant and happy they were !"

During the fluctuations of the illness of this little child while on the way to Liverpool, my husband wrote to his brother-in-law :—

"Even if your darling should sink after this revival, it must be a comfort to you to think of that look of recognition she gave you and her mother ; and her gentle whispered words will always abide with you. In good sooth, we think too much of human skill and human experience, and too little of the power of God. I cannot help praying that He who has given you a glimpse of His power to save may give you back your precious child. At all events, let us not do Him the dishonour of measuring our ideas of His power and mercy by our own feeble comprehension. Let us go to Him as to one who is all-powerful and all-pitying, and ask boldly for what we crave. And if He does not answer our prayers in the way we should choose, may He bring His power and His love home to our hearts in some other way, so that we may say : 'The Lord hath been with us even in the deep waters of affliction.'"

My sister joined me in my visits to the sick, criminal, and outcast women of Liverpool. We visited the wards of the great Hospital together. The strong sympathy of her loving nature quickly won the hearts of desolate young girls, while she greatly strengthened me in the hope that we might be able to undo some of their heavy burdens.

Among the first who came to us, to our own house, to die, was a certain Marion, who seemed to us a kind of first-fruits of the harvest in the gathering in of which we were to be allowed in after years to participate. The following account of her was written to a friend after her death :—

"I send you this brief sketch of our poor Marion, feeling that it may be good for others as well as for ourselves to bear in memory such a trophy of the goodness of God. The first

time I saw her was in a crowded room. Her face attracted
me; not beautiful in the common acceptation of the word,
but having a power greater than beauty: eyes full of intelligence and penetration, a countenance at once thoughtful and
frank, with at times a wildly *seeking* look as if her whole being
cried out: 'Who will show us any good?' She was ill, her
lungs fatally attacked. I went up to her, and with no introduction of myself said: 'Will you come with me to my home
and live with me? I had a daughter once.' She replied
with a gasp of astonishment, grasping my hand as if she
would never let it go again. I brought her home; my husband supported her upstairs, and we laid her on the couch
in the pretty little spare room looking on the garden. She
lived with us, an invalid, three months, and then died. It
was difficult to suppress the thought, 'If she had not been so
destroyed, what a brightness and blessing she might have been
in the world!' Untaught, unacquainted with the Scriptures
till she came to us, she mastered the New Testament so
thoroughly in that brief time that her acute questions and
pregnant remarks were often a subject of wonder to my
husband, who spent a portion of almost every evening with
her in her room, conversing with and instructing her. Some
of the intellectual difficulties which assail thoughtful students
occurred to her. I witnessed many a severe struggle in her
mind. She would often say: 'I will ask Mr. Butler about it
this evening.' But her questions were sometimes such as
cannot be answered, except by God Himself to the individual
soul. This she knew, and through many sleepless nights her
murmured prayers were heard by her attendant, 'preventing
the night watches.' My husband said her remarks concerning
the nature of a true faith sometimes strikingly resembled
portions of the writings of a well-known modern philosophical
thinker, which she had never read—for she had read nothing.
I speak of her intellect, but her heart was yet greater. What
capacities for noble love, for the deepest friendship, had been
trampled under foot in that dear soul!

   "A well-known divine came to visit us, and hearing of
our poor invalid, kindly offered to see and converse with her.

My husband and I agreed that we would say nothing to our friend of Marion's past life; for we thought that, saintly man though he was, he probably had not faith enough to do justice to her and to himself in the interview if he had this knowledge. (There are few men whose faith comes up to that measure.) When he joined us again downstairs his face was radiant, and he spoke—not of any teaching or comfort which he might have conveyed to her—but of the help and privilege it was to himself to have held communion during a short half-hour with a dying saint, so young, yet so en-lightened, and so near to God.

" I recall the day of her death. It was a cold snowy day in March. In the morning my husband went to see her early, before going out to his college work. She could scarcely speak, but looking earnestly at him said, as if to reward him for all his painstaking instructions, and guessing what he wished to know: ' Yes, God is with me, sir; I have perfect peace.' Her long death-struggle lasting twelve hours, joined with the peace and even joy of her spirit, were very affecting. Though it was bitterly cold, she whispered : ' Open the windows, for the love of God.' Her long black hair thrust wildly back was like the hair of a swimmer, dripping with water, so heavy were the death dews. She became blind; and her fine intelligent eyes wandered ever, with an appealing look, to whatever part of the room she thought I was in. Towards sunset she murmured: ' Oh come quickly, Lord Jesus.' During that long day she continually moved her arms like a swimmer, as if she felt herself sinking in deep waters. Then her poor little head fell forward, a long sigh escaped her parted lips, and at last I laid her down flat on her little bed. My husband and sons returned from College, and we all stood round her for a few minutes. She had become a household friend. She looked sweet and solemn then, her head drooping to one side, and with a worn-out look on the young frail face, but a look, too, of perfect peace.

" A few days before her death I telegraphed, at her request, to her father, who had had no tidings of his lost

child for five years. He was an extensive farmer, well to do
and honourable, living in a beautiful district in the midland
counties. We were surprised, on his arrival, to see a very
fine-looking country gentleman, as one would say, reminding
us, in his noble height and figure and dignified presence, a
little of my own father. He carried with him a valise and
a handsome travelling rug. We took him to her room and
retired. Their interview was best witnessed by God alone.
After two hours or so, I opened the door softly. He was
lying on a couch at the opposite side of the room from her,
in a deep sleep, tired probably more by strong emotion than
by his journey. She raised her finger for silence, and with
the look and action of a guardian angel, whispered, ' Father
is asleep.'

"After her death her poor mother came to attend her
funeral. I had filled Marion's coffin with white camelias,
banking them up all round her. With her hands crossed on
her breast, and dressed as a bride' for her Lord, she looked
quite lovely. I found the mother alone, kneeling by the
coffin, in an agony of grief and of anger. She said (her body
rocking backward and forward with emotion): ' If *that man*
could but see her now ! Can we not send for him ? ' and she
added : ' Oh what a difference there is in English gentlemen's
households ! To think that this child should have been
ruined in one and saved in another ! ' Yes, it might have
been good for ' that man ' to have been forced to step down
from his high social position and to look upon her then, and
to have known the abyss from which she had been drawn, to
the verge of which *he* had led her when she was but a child
of fifteen.

"Marion had ' prophesied ' to me, before she died, of hard
days and a sad heart which were in store for me, in con-
tending against the evil to which she had fallen a victim.
I recall her words with wonder and comfort. She would say :
' When your soul quails at the sight of the evil, which will
increase yet awhile, dear Mrs. Butler, *think of me* and take
courage. God has given me to you, that you may never
despair of any.'

"Snow lay thickly on the ground when we laid her in her grave in the cemetery. When we came back to the house I was trying to say something comforting to the mother, when she stopped me and said : ' My heart is changed about it all. The bitter anger won't come back, I think ; and what has taken it all away was the sight of Mr. Butler standing by the grave of my child, and the words he spoke. Oh madam,' she said, ' when I looked at him standing there in the snow, dressed in his linen robe as white as the snow itself, and with that look on his face, when he looked up to heaven and thanked God for my daughter now among the blessed, I could hardly refrain from falling on my knees at his feet, for he seemed to me like one of the angels of God. I felt happy then, almost proud, for my child. Oh madam, I can never tell you what it was to me to look on your husband's face then ! My heart was bursting with gratitude to God and to him.' "

There were others, about the same time, whom we took home, who died in our own house, and were laid in graves side by side in the cemetery. Of one I have a clear remembrance—a girl of seventeen only, of some natural force of character. Her death was a prolonged hard battle with pain and with bitter memories, lightened by momentary flashes of faint hope. She struggled hard. We were called to her bedside suddenly one evening. She was dying ; but with a strong effort she had raised herself to a sitting position. She drew us near to her by the appeal of her earnest eyes, and raising her right hand high, with a strangely solemn gesture, and with a look full of heroic and desperate resolve, she said : *"I will fight for my soul through hosts, and hosts, and hosts !"* Her eyes, which seemed to be now looking far off, athwart the *hosts* of which she spoke, became dim, and she spoke no more. "Poor brave child !" I cried to her, "you will find on the other shore One waiting for you who has fought *through all those hosts for you,* who will not treat you as man has treated you." I cannot explain what she meant. I have never been quite able to understand it; but her words dwelt with us—" through hosts, and hosts, and hosts !" She had been trampled under the feet of men, as the mire in the streets, had been hustled about from prison to the streets, and from the streets to prison, an orphan, unregarded by any but the vigilant police. From the first day she came to us we noticed in her, notwithstanding, an admirable self-respect mixed with the full realisation of her misery. And that sense of the dignity and worth of the true self in her—the immortal, inalienable self— found expression in that indomitable resolution of the dying girl : " I will fight for my soul though hosts, and hosts, and hosts ! "

One of the most prominent characteristics of our family life during all these years at Liverpool was that of our common enjoyment of our summer tours. There were circumstances which made our annual excursions more than the ordinary tours of some holiday-makers. In the first place, many of my own relatives were settled in different parts of the Continent, thus giving us a personal connection with those places. In order to pay a visit to the homes of some of them it was necessary to cross the Alps, while other near relatives lived in France and Switzerland. Secondly, the work on behalf of justice and morality which engaged our hearts and minds for many years came to be gradually taken up in many other countries of Europe; and in connection with it we had the happiness of coming in contact with some of the best men and women on the Continent. Some of these were persons distinguished in literature, art, jurisprudence, in political life and in the Churches. This was the bright side of a work which had its mournful aspects.

It sometimes happens that the ordinary English traveller knows little of the general life of the people among whom he travels, of the history of the country, its politics, its social condition and prospects. He is content to gather to himself enjoyment from the beauties of Switzerland or the Tyrol, or Italy, while knowing little of the dwellers in those beautiful lands. A wider and a richer field is open to those who care to seek and explore it. My husband was not content without making himself acquainted, to a considerable extent, with the contemporary history of the countries through which we passed. His aptitude for languages aided him in intercourse with people of different nationalities; so that our family relationships abroad, and our friendships with many public men as well as humble dwellers in continental countries, gave to our visits there a varied interest. These vacation tours were to us like sunlit mountain tops rising from the cloud-covered plain of our laborious life at Liverpool. Moreover, the enthusiasm which he had, and which was shared by his sons, for geographical and geological research, together with our modest artistic efforts, added greatly to the interest of our travels. It was felt to be unsatisfactory to attempt to draw mountains and rocks, without knowing something of their geological construction. During a visit which Mr. Ruskin paid us at Liverpool, he was turning over a portfolio of drawings done by my husband, and held in his hands for some time two or three sketches of the Aiguilles towering above the Mer de Glace, and other rocks and mountain buttresses in the neighbourhood of Chamounix.

He said it gave him pleasure to look at those, (he being a keen observer and student of mountain forms everywhere.) " Your outlines of these peaks, Mr. Butler," he said, " are perfectly true ; they are portraits. Very few people are able or care to represent the forms so correctly. For the most part artists are more anxious to produce an effective picture, than to give precisely what they see in nature."

Our sons inherited their father's out-door tastes. Our summer tours were therefore a source of the keenest enjoyment to us all. We saved up our money for them, worked towards them, and looked forward to them as a real happiness. The love of out-door life, of movement and exercise, and of the discovery of the new beauties and mysteries which Nature always seems to be holding in reserve to tempt one on, being so marked a characteristic in my husband, it will not be wondered at that a residence of sixteen years in Liverpool should have been to him in a certain sense a prolonged trial. Liverpool, if we except some of its central streets and fine buildings, is far from being a beautiful town ; some portions of its outskirts through which he had to pass daily on his way from our home to the College were almost squalid in appearance. Most towns have an outlet somewhere, but (as it was sometimes said) there was no country near Liverpool: it is locked in by a network of railroads, collieries, brick-fields, unsavoury manufactories and half-finished untidy-ness ; the poor hedges and trees stunted and blackened for miles. Certainly we were within a tolerably easy reach of North Wales and of Derbyshire; and our half-holidays were sometimes used up in a desperate effort to snatch a few hours of country walking between two railway journeys to and from these neighbourhoods. But for the daily enjoyment of a country walk, Liverpool offered few facilities. The new park was a relief; still it was only a park in a town. These conditions increased and intensified the longing of our whole family for a breathing space, and freedom from brick and stone walls, at least once in the year. It was our deliberate choice, therefore, to devote a portion of our time and means to this end ; and it became a conviction stronger as the years went on that it was a wise decision, in order to enable us to work on each in our department with heart and hope. We were a small enough family to be able for some years to take flight all together, and to have no anxieties or a divided heart on account of some left behind. In any memoir of George Butler these continental ramblings must therefore take a prominent place. He was then calmly, supremely happy, *at home* with beautiful Nature, and with his family around him.

In 1869 we had a delightful tour in Switzerland, in magnificent weather. Resting a few days at Lucerne, we went up towards the Devil's Bridge, and thence to Andermatt. It was early enough in the year to find those high meadows carpeted with brilliant flowers. Crossing the Furcha Pass we walked to the Grimsel, and thence by the Handeck to Meiringen and so to the Oberland.

My husband wrote to his mother, Mrs. Butler, at Harrow :—

"Bear Hotel, Grindelwald, August, 1869.

"Dear Mother,—We arrived safely here, after visiting in order, Lucerne, Hospenthal, the Grimsel and Meiringen. We did not stay long in the relaxing air of the latter place, but drove to Interlacken, and thence to this place, where the air is very fine. Even in this valley, 3,000 feet above the sea, the sun is scorching, and often the heat is excessive. I have made a few sketches, one in Lucerne, one of the Devil's Bridge, one or two at Hospenthal, and two here, which I hope to

show you. The lower glacier, with the sight of the Mettenberg, the Wetterhorn, and the Viescherhörner in the background, is a grand subject. In the forefront is the Church,
near which Julius Elliott was buried last Friday. The day
we arrived at the Grimsel his body was being carried by to
Grindelwald. On the way up here we overtook two of the
guides who had recovered the body. One was a fine, tall
fellow with an ice-axe. I thought he would at all events
know something about the accident, so I questioned him, and
learned several particulars which I had not heard before. All
the guides attribute his death to his not being roped. He
refused, I believe, on account of his weight — 15 stone —
saying he should only drag others down and not help himself.
They say he showed presence of mind when he was sliding
down the slope, making energetic efforts to drive his axe into
the ice; but the ice was too hard and slippery, and he disappeared. No mountain, not even the Finster-Aarhorn nor
the Matterhorn, looks to me more formidable than the
Schrekhorn. Tyndal, however, who is here, means to try it,
as he tried the Matterhorn after the accident of 1867.

"We left Grindelwald on Friday, and reached Lauterbrünnen in the evening. To-day the mountains, which
yesterday were enveloped in mist, are as clear as possible.
The air is invigorating; but I regret Grindelwald. The
'Bear' is an old-fashioned, comfortable hotel. I had a
balcony before my window, which looked out on the glacier
and the Wetterhorn. I finished my sketch of the church to-
day. It is an appropriate resting-place for a mountaineer.
We had a successful excursion to the Faulhorn. It was fine
going up, and the views of the glaciers winding up to the
peaks improved every half-hour as we went on. We reached
the top about twelve, and had time to look around us before
lunch. It was clear all round the horizon, and a more perfect
panorama can hardly be imagined. It is finer than that from
Pilatus or the Righi, to my mind. The sun shone on the
Lakes of Lucerne, Thun, and Brienz, bringing out delicate
colours like those of an opal—green, pink, golden. The
Jungfrau and the Blumlis Alp looked very white and pure.

Then the scene changed. A storm came rapidly up from the valley, and we were well pelted with hail before we could get into the cottage. The different effects were markedly grand. On one side deep indigo mountains beneath a level canopy of cloud, out of which burst vivid flashes of forked lightning. On another side sunshine and shadow alternated. The great peaks of the Oberland came into sight and passed out again rapidly as in a dissolving view, and a brilliant rainbow spanned the valley towards the Scheideg. We made our descent amidst showers, but thoroughly enjoyed our day."

"La Gordanne, Canton Vaud.

"We did not stay long at Murren, as it was crowded to excess with English people, and there was hardly any accommodation. It is a strange mania I think which drives crowds of English people to any one place which happens to be the fashion for the time. We came down to Lauterbrünnen, and on Thursday we had a most beautiful walk by the Wengern Alp, the rest walking about while I began a sketch of the Jungfrau and its dependencies seen through pine forests. I never saw anything more beautiful than the sunset as we returned. The hour was late, but on descending the hill I often paused to watch the tints upon the Eiger, White Monk, Jungfrau and Silverhorn, which rose out of crimson clouds into a clear blue sky, their snowy summits glowing in the rays of the setting sun. We left the place with regret, and came on to Thun, going down the lake on a fine cool evening. The three great peaks named above gradually came into view, and looked very beautiful, fresh snow having fallen. We then came on here. The Meuricoffres' carriage was awaiting us at Rolle, and we had a joyful meeting, as you may imagine. We walked to church with the family to-day and they showed us over the house afterwards. There is good accommodation, and it is very elegant and comfortable. The grounds are extensive, and reach down to the lake, where there is good bathing. There are vineyards above the house, and beyond, high grass fields, commanding extensive views of the lake and

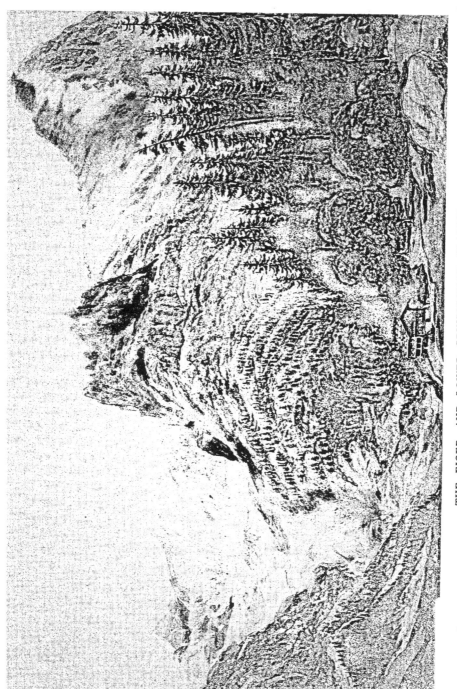

THE EIGER, AND LOWER GRINDELWALD GLACIER.

From a Water-colour Drawing by G. BUTLER.

Mont Blanc. I am glad to see once more that vast expanse of water, and I do not wonder that Gibbon chose the banks of Lake Leman for his residence while engaged on his great work. An extensive view, lovely scenery and quiet are conducive to thought and literary achievement."

The Gordanne, the Swiss home of the Meuricoffre family, was many times, in the years which followed, a meeting place for relatives and family friends from England and the South of Europe, and is to this moment full of memories of pleasant adventures and excursions on those sweet long summer days when the young people of our several families were all around us. Our Swiss tours very often concluded with a visit to this delightful home.

Two years later our summer vacation was spent in the Highlands. My husband wrote to Harrow :—

" Ballachulish, N. B., July, 1871.

" You will like to hear, my dear mother, what we are doing. We started on Monday for Callander. Finding some nice scenery in the neighbourhood, we waited there a day or two. I was sketching the Brachlinn Falls—very curious and picturesque—when James Stuart hailed us, and joined our party, to the great joy of the boys. We then went on to the Trossachs. The situation of the hotel is very good, and we had the pleasure of reading *The Lady of the Lake* under the shade of Ben Venue. Loch Achray, near which the hotel stands, is very pretty, and we enjoyed the sketching and bathing. We went on to Loch Katrine, where we spent two days, making several sketches. From there we went to Inversnaid. Had the weather been finer we should have gone up Ben Lomond. Being desirous of getting further north, we started on Wednesday for this place, fifty miles distant. The route lay through Glen Polloch, Glenorchy and the Pass of Glencoe. The weather, which was rainy at starting, cleared up, and we saw the country under every advantage. There were a number of pretty waterfalls in Glen Folloch, but we saw nothing very striking till we came to Lord Breadalbane's shooting-box at Inveroren. It stands very prettily on the banks of a lake, in the midst of beautiful grounds, covered with rock, heather, and Scotch firs. From that our route lay uphill for some miles through the deer forest of Glenorchy. We saw a large herd feeding, besides some horned sentinels standing on ridges. From the summit of the Black Mountain we saw over the moor of Bannock, with its lakes and pine woods, as far as the Grampians, the whole range of which was as visible as the Bernese Alps from the Righi. Schiehallion Peak stood out grandly. The clearness of the atmosphere and the distinct outlines of the hills reminded me of Switzerland. At the head of Glen Etive is a very singular mountain, called Buchaell Etive, reminding one, both in colour and form, of pictures of Sinai. It stands isolated, and lifts its red granite peaks proudly above the other hills.

"Then came the Pass of Glencoe, which for mountain grandeur excels all that I ever saw in the United Kingdom. The mountains are not very high, but the forms are so grand and the precipices so rugged that one can admire them even with the Swiss Alps fresh in one's memory. I made a slight sketch of the Three Sisters,—gloomy crags of very Swiss character. The next day when I went up to finish them, a matter of ten miles, the rain came on and drove me back. The view over Loch Leven, towards Morven and Ben Cruachan, is very fine, and I have been fairly successful in sketching it. This (Ballachulish) is one of the most picturesque places I ever saw. Eastward lie the mountains of Glencoe, and westward the hills of Morven and Ben Cruachan. We are well off for lodgings, with a large sitting-room, commanding a glorious view. The people are civil and attentive. We shall be sorry to leave the place, which we shall do to-morrow for Fort William. On Tuesday we shall sail up the Caledonian Canal to Inverness, and the next day go on to Balmacarra, in Ross-shire, whence we may hope to run over to Skye to see George Rainy, of Raasey, who was my pupil at

Cheltenham, and is now the owner of an island. The waste of fine situations for houses, owing to the concentration of property, strikes me very forcibly. Scotland is not more, but less densely populated now than it was formerly, excepting, of course, the manufacturing centres.

" I see the Liberal Association of Liverpool has called upon the Government to reform the House of Lords, being indignant with its interfering with the wishes of the people. I think an effective reform would be to cut off the law of entail, and to facilitate the transfer of land from these Highland lairds, who, though proud as Lucifer, are some-times poor as rats."

From Ballachulish we visited many beautiful places on the west coast of Scotland, where the arms of the sea winding inland amoung the mountains are not unlike the Fiords of Norway. We went over to the Isle of Skye, which is for the most part very barren and wild. Return-ing thence, our party separated for ten days or so—my husband with our eldest son having accepted an invitation to join his friend, Mr. Alfred Parker, in Sutherland ; from there he wrote to me :—

" Syre, by Thurso, August 11, 1871.

" Let me tell you how delighted we were by your descrip-tion of Loch Maree. It made us long to be with you. I feel a great desire to do more justice another year to the Western Highlands.

" To-day we walked six miles to a loch, called Loch Loyel, about nine miles long, with fine mountains about it, and only one house, a sheep farmer's, on the hill. I never saw anything so fine in point of colour as the blue and purple hills and the rich browns and greens of the foreground, mingled with the grey and purple, occasionally the crimson of the heather. The flower of the heather smells very sweet just now, like fresh honey, and there is a great deal of it. I hope you are enjoying a quiet Sunday as we are, and next Sunday, please

God, we shall spend together at our own home, which after all has its attractions."

"August 31.

"I wish Charlie could see some of the blue hares; they sit up in the drollest manner on their hind legs, which are longer than common hares' legs. The midges here 'beat all natur'' and make one's forehead a mass of red marks. Even the keeper winces. This is the perfection of retired solitude. You may be out for hours, hearing nothing but an occasional crow of an old cock grouse. The scenery when you get some way up the hill is very fine, open moorland with distant mountains. Yesterday we had a good walk and saw the North Sea. The Orkneys were not visible, but to-day it is clear enough for anything. We came across the tracks of deer to-day; indeed, the red deer range all over the country here, which is quite unenclosed. Tell Charlie we saw great quantities of lobelia in flower in the water, also some water lilies. Ben Clibrich, 3,165 feet, is a fine mountain with well-defined outline; Ben Loyel and Mount Hope are also very respectable. Large lakes go for nothing here. Loch Loyel is bigger than Windermere; but there is only one house on it. Oh, those Dukes!"

In the summer of 1872 my husband and his two elder sons went to the West of Ireland. He wrote:

"Waterville, August 2.

"We went out yesterday in different directions: George and Stanley fishing on the lakes, and I with the Bishop of Limerick. The scenery is very picturesque and wild. I sketched and watched the bishop fish. He is an excellent hand, and pulled the fish out of the water as fast as St. Peter could! We had met before; for he examined in mathematics while I was Examiner in classics for the East India Civil Service, in 1856. He knows all the great mathematicians—Sylvester, Cayley, and Stokes,—and is, or was, a great authority himself. Lord Ducie's yacht is expected here; so I am sending a note to Froude, who is on board with him."

"August 4.

" I was delighted to get your letter. Yesterday was fine and bright, so we went out on the bay in a capital boat, built like a whale boat, with a sail and four oars. Stanley steered, and George and I fished. Before we had gone far, he got a big fish, a pollock; and as we were going rather fast, it took some time to secure him. Soon after, he caught a larger fish, a bass, which played almost like a salmon, giving vigorous leaps and running deep. We landed him. We caught plenty of smaller fish. Towards one o'clock we made for an old abbey and castle, square and massive, which they say Cromwell battered down. They stood on a peninsula, on rocks like those at Balmacarra. There we landed, bathed, and lunched. It was the boys' first swim in the Atlantic. They astonished the boatmen by their feats in swimming. The water was cold, but clear and refreshing. One great amusement for them is to see the numberless sea fowl—ducks, puffins, gannets, divers, gulls, and cormorants. The view of the mountains about our lake was very fine, and that of the northern range still finer, with the Reeks in the distance. The day was perfect : sunny, but with plenty of clouds and every variety of effect. In a few days we go to the Knight of Kerry's, at Valencia. This is the last time, if I can help it, that I will consent to divide our party. It is so much nicer keeping together. Give my love to dear Charlie, and say I hope he will catch some trout at Rothbury."

"Valencia, August 9.

" The day before yesterday we started in a boat on an expedition to some rock caves of great size and beauty. The arches were very lofty and the echoes fine. Then we went to an old castle, once Florence M'Carthy's, where we picniced. The Knight's family are very charming. Mrs. Fitzgerald is away with her daughter, Lady Molyneux, and Miss Fitzgerald does the honours. Yesterday George and Stanley saw the Atlantic telegraph and conversed with persons unknown at Newfoundland, receiving answers as to the state of the weather."

In 1873, after a very arduous year of work, both educationally and in the cause of public morality in which we had become engaged, we had the refreshment of a very delightful tour in the Tyrol and Bavarian Highlands. Starting by the Rhine, and stopping a few days at Königswinter, in company with Mr. and Mrs. Francis Galton, and for a Sunday at Heidelberg, we went on by Basle to Shaffhausen.

I quote from a diary kept at the time :

" The Rhine between Basle and Shaffhausen is very beautiful, and of an astonishing blueness. When we arrived at Shaffhausen the moon had risen, and the coolness of the evening and the fragrant smell of the pine woods were very welcome, after a broiling hot day. The hotel windows look straight out upon the splendid ' Falls of the Rhine,' which shone white in the moonlight. The clear blueness and greenness of the river below the falls is a constant wonder and joy to contemplate. Next day my husband made a large sketch of the falls from the terrace, while our sons bathed and walked, and we all sought the coolest shade we could for refuge from the heat. After a day or two here, we went on to the Lake of Constance, getting on board an infantine-looking little *dampfboot*, suitable for the smaller size of the Rhine here. Our steam up to Constance was delightful ; a sweet air was blowing, and there were no fashionable travellers in the *dampfboot*. At first the river was narrow, with thick woods on either shore, where we saw flocks of long-legged cranes alighting upon and rising from the branches. Then it widened out into the Unter See, an expanse of shallow water, over which numberless flocks of gulls were winging and crying. The path of the *dampfboot* was marked out by fir trees planted in the shallow water, their tops showing above. At the port of Constance we changed into a larger steamer, to cross the lake to Lindau. We had a beautiful sail across. The sky and lake were all one uniform pale, pure blue, with fleecy white clouds reflected in the expanse of waters. Lindau was hot and close, and we were glad to leave it the next morning, when, starting early, we went by train as far as Immenstadt, where the railway ends. Thence we drove to Reute. The whole drive to Reute was most pleasant, and the air very refreshing when we came to ground some four thousand feet above the sea level. For several٬ hours of a most beautiful summer day we drove through high meadows completely carpeted with flowers, the sweet scent of which was carried to us by the cool mountain air. We had stopped at a wayside inn to take extra horses for the hills, and later we dined at a village in a beautiful valley. The sun was setting, and cow-bells were ringing from all the hills around. Charlie gathered a variety of gentians, from the large yellow to the small violet and blue ones. They grow plentifully there. Then we had nearly three hours' drive in the dark; and yet not without light, for there were constant flashes of summer lightning, and the road-sides were lit up by thousands of glowworms, while fire-flies flitted over our heads and darted across the road close to the horses' ears. It was a beautiful natural illumination; and when a late moon rose tardily over the horizon, we felt we scarcely wanted her. That night's drive was delightful in the cool, sweet air. When we arrived at Reute the people of the inn met us with candles in their hands. They put us up in a multitude of little wooden rooms, very primitive and scantily furnished, but clean. No English there, and scarcely a visitor except ourselves, until two days later, when the young King of Bavaria arrived. We were strolling along the road in the evening when he drove up in an ordinary carriage, with no suite. He has a handsome face, and bowed to us courteously. He was on his way to his castle, at Hohen-Schwangau, where Wagner was to meet him, they said. He stayed the night at our little inn. There seemed no particular preparation for him, except some extra biscuits with pink sugar on the top, which we saw placed on a feeble deal table outside his door. There was no fuss about him. He makes very good roads all through his kingdom; it is a delight to drive on them. They are like the smooth, well-kept roads through a great ducal park in England.

" Sunday came ; but so little was there to mark for us the different days, (frequetly we never saw an English newspaper for weeks), that we seemed all to have been oblivious of the fact. My husband got up as usual at five a.m., and went out to the river to fish. He came triumphantly back at eight, with a good basket of trout. After breakfast, recollecting the day, I proposed that we should have—as was our custom in our summer travels—a little service out of doors, 'church in a wood,' or 'church in a field,' as we called it. My husband exclaimed : 'This is not Sunday! surely not ! and I have been out fishing !' He would not believe it was Sunday till he had asked the landlord, to whom he considered it necessary to apologise, assuring him that it was not usual for English clergymen to go out fishing on Sunday (except for the souls of men). We spent this pleasant Sunday among the woods by the borders of a pretty lake—the Plan See,— which is four thousand feet above the sea. Everything looked Sabbath-like, and we could sometimes hear the ringing of mellow-sounding church bells from the valleys. The walk home in the evening was very pleasant. We had glimpses of deep indigo-coloured hills through glades of forest ; a sunset glow lingered on the highest points, and we walked by the side of herds of cows going home for the night.

" We went next to Partenkirch, a four or five hours' drive, on these well-kept Bavarian roads. The silvery-white rocky hill tops rising above dark pine forests are striking. We were pleased with the look of Partenkirch, reposing in its wide valley, with the Wetterstein and other mountains circling it round. During our stay here we had the refreshment of a little rain, which subdued the heat of this most brilliant summer. One evening we saw a remarkably fine stormy sunset. The appearance was that of a furnace of molten brass or gold somewhere up among the mountains ; bars of light lay across the deep indigo hills lower down, thereby setting them ablaze in a glory of purple and gold. We had never seen anything quite like it before.

"Friday, July 18. — We set out, again driving, for Innsbruck. The dew was still heavy on the grass, and long shadows lay across the road when we started. At the top of the long hill which leads down to the valley of the river Inn, one of the horses became restive, and the splinter-bar broke with a loud crack. We got out and walked forward while it was temporarily patched up with bits of twine. It was intensely hot in the afternoon as we descended. We crossed the river Iser, 'rolling rapidly' towards the Danube. We were well housed at Innsbruck, and much enjoyed the picturesque town and its surroundings. After resting Sunday there, we started for the far-famed Zillerthal—by train to Jenbach, and then by carriage up the peaceful valley of the Zill. It was very silent, and the scenery rather dull. We reached the pretty village of Zell, in the heart of the Ziller-thal, celebrated for the simplicity of its inhabitants and their beautiful singing. We were now in the Tyrol. There were ripening cornfields, wooded hills, and in the distance a glimpse of a snow peak or two. The Tyrolese are a very religious people. Though their creed differs, they reminded me very much (when flocking to the kirk on a Sunday especially) of Northumbrian or Scotch people. They resemble them in their simple piety, their hospitality and honesty. The old women going to church on Sunday carried in their hands a prayer-book, a pocket-handkerchief tightly folded, and a bunch of southernwood (old man), mint, and marigold, just as we used to do when we were children, and went to the Methodist meeting-house at Milfield with our nurse Naney. It made me feel quite at home in the simple Tyrolese kirks! The heads of families gather their children around them for family prayers. In more than one of the humble inns where we stayed, a number of stragglers, peasants, drivers, jägers, as well as the family, would come in to the central hall or vestibule of the inn about sundown; and after supper the master would give the signal, and all would drop on their knees, repeating aloud after him their evening prayer, which lasted about ten or fifteen minutes. Their manner was sincere and devout. The people in cottages and wayside inns also reminded me of our north-country folk. The women are modest, frank, and kindly, and invite you to come in, and set fresh milk and bread before you, for which they will take the merest trifle. They enquire your age, and if you are married, and if your father and mother are still alive; but all most respectfully. The children are shy, and hide themselves behind their mothers' gowns.

"We saw a most picturesque ceremony on Sunday—the funeral of a priest who had been much beloved by the people. A great number of gay Tyrolese costumes were crowded in and around the churchyard. The procession was headed by jägers in full dress, with their green facings, embroidered belts, feathered hats, and rifles. Then came a long line of young girls, in white, bearing torches; then priests and acolytes and peasants. The old priests seemed distressed by the burning sun on their bald pates as they stood uncovered round the grave. The ceremony was long, and the mass of people, gathered from all the mountains round, were very patient. The coffin, covered with Alpine-rose, was lowered by the Jägers, and then they sang very sweetly a parting hymn.

"A week later we started at six a.m. for the Aachen See. From Jenbach we began to mount a long hill, with eight horses. At the top we parted with most of our horses, and went at a good trot along the level to the Aachen See hof. We were more than satisfied that we had gone there. The hotel stands quite alone, on the banks of a lake of wonderful beauty. Fir woods all round give a deep shade, and at night send out an aromatic smell, which is very healthful. The foreground round the hotel is a natural garden, where masses of flowers arrange themselves in groups after their own sweet will, or festoon themselves from stumps of cut-down trees. The lake is of a deep blue, like an amethyst; not like the pale turquoise blue of Constance and Zurich. The mountain buttresses sweep down in some places almost perpendicularly into the lake. The hotel is kept by the Rainer family, famous Tyrolese musicians, who used to go round and sing at the different Courts of Europe, receiving compliments and presents of jewellery. It was a rare pleasure having such beautiful singing as we had every evening, as well as such superb weather and surroundings in the day time.

"From there we went to Salzburg; from which we visited Berchtesgaden and the beautiful König-See. Returning to Salzburg, we took the train to Gmunden. During the latter part of this journey, the railway runs through a dense forest, and the carriages are open, so that you get the full benefit of the breeze, and can clutch, if you like, at the overhanging branches of the trees as the train runs along. Gmunden is a contrast to the primitive places we had been visiting. It is a favourite summer resort of the Viennese when tired of city gaieties and business. Elegantly-dressed ladies walked under the lindens and on the terraces by the lake. It is a very pretty place, open and healthy, and many beautiful excursions can be made from it. The weather continued fine and hot, and we spent much of our time on and in the lake—our sons becoming accomplished swimmers. The lake is large, and there are some fine mountain forms around it. From here we went to Linz, on the Danube. We admired the full, powerful roll of the waters of the Danube as we drove along its shores. We then went on to Munich, where we enjoyed for a few days the famous sculpture and picture galleries. Here our party divided, my husband having to return home with our youngest son, for his college term, leaving the rest to follow more slowly."

CHAPTER IX.

THE development of the character which it is my privilege to portray cannot be fully appreciated unless the experience, both happy and sorrowful, gained by many years identification with an unpopular cause is included in this record. The trials connected with this phase of our life's work brought into relief some of the best traits in my husband's character—his unworldliness and unselfishness, his quiet and ready acceptance of real and tangible sacrifices in regard alike to earthly successes and domestic comfort, his patience and gentleness in the constant encounter with the false judgments of the world, and even in the temporary estrangement or misunderstanding of valued friends and acquaintances.

I wish it to be clearly understood by those familiar with the history of that unpopular cause to which I allude, that they need not expect here anything like a detailed account, or even an outline, of that long moral conflict. Beginning in 1869, that movement continued in vigorous action in our own country up to 1885, and is now carried forward on the Continent of Europe and in distant parts of the British Empire. Its history may one day come to be fully and worthily written. A few partial records of it exist, the most important being that written by the late Chamberlain of the City of London, Mr. Benjamin Scott, entitled *A State Iniquity*. All that I shall attempt in these pages is to indicate rather than fully to describe my husband's part in that memorable work on behalf of justice and truth. While indicating his part in it directly and personally, I must needs also speak now and again of my own share in the work, especially at times when I was obliged to be separated from him and from my home; for there is no doubt that the sorest of the trials to him in connection with this work during several years was our frequent enforced separation from each other, together with the risks and hardships to which I was often exposed when he could not be by my side. In the partial records of those times which exist mention has been made of the active persecution and ignoble treatment to which the modern reformers, like the Abolitionists in America, were at times subjected. I shall leave the record of these things to others, and any allusion to them in my husband's and my own correspondence must be understood to be made only to throw further light on the discipline of life which he was called to undergo and the fortifying of his character which that discipline induced. I have no desire either to complain of or to parade anything which we together may have had to endure, from the cold looks of friends, the scorn of persons in Office and in high life, the silence of some from whom we hoped for encouragement, the

calumnies of the Press, and occasionally the violence of
hired mobs, the creatures of persons whose shameful
interests were threatened by the reform we sought. For
it must be understood that this was the only kind of
popular opposition to which we were subjected. The
working classes were always with us; "the common
people heard us gladly." It will be easily understood
how much greater was the trial to so true and tenderhearted a man to be struck at through the wife whom he
loved and revered than to be directly and personally
insulted. But through the mercy of God the worst of
these trials were not of many years duration; bitterness
of speech and abusive violence slowly gave place, as our
movement became recognised and formidable, to a more
cautiously-expressed opposition. The tactics of the enemy
changed, although the greater outward respectfulness
continued to be combined with determined and active
hostility, and with an attempt during many years to
thwart our aims by the maintenance in the Press of a
huge conspiracy of silence.

To our old companions in arms, should they look for
any kind of adequate recognition of the worth, the sacrifices, and the labours of others besides George Butler
who were devoted to this cause, there will necessarily
appear immense blanks in these pages. It would be,
hardly possible, in so brief a space, even to record the
names of that honoured host of fellow-workers, men and
women, whose faces now rise before me. It would
certainly be a congenial task to me, were I able for it,
to sketch briefly the part which each played in this most
vital and most unpopular of modern struggles; but my
task must be limited to an imperfect representation of
the character and action of one alone of those who took

up this cross for Christ's sake. Though the outward
position of this one was less prominent than that of
many others—statesmen, men of science, or propagandist
teachers in the cause of which I speak—his influence was, .
and continues to be, a power in that direction of which
he himself was but little conscious.

At the annual meeting of our Federation, a few months
after my husband's death in 1890, the Right Hon. James
Stansfeld made the following remarks :—

" We have sustained, and our cause has sustained, a very
great loss in the death of the late Canon Butler. I have
always felt, and I have frequently publicly stated, that in my
opinion it has never been possible to over-estimate the beauty,
the simplicity, the chivalry, the modesty of his character, and
the value of his service to our cause. He has been otherwise
occupied during the most of his life, and has, so to say, only
played a secondary part in this movement ; and it is a part
of his virtue, a part of the simplicity and modesty and
chivalry of his character, that he has played that secondary
part as willingly, as enthusiastically, and with as much
determination as if he, and he alone, had been the leader of
the whole movement with which he and his wife were connected. I am sure I express, however imperfectly, the feeling
of every one in this room, and of every man and woman who
has been concerned in our long and ultimately victorious
agitation, when I say that we deeply regret his loss, and that
we feel it not merely as persons engaged in a great public
undertaking who have lost a valued friend and colleague, but
as men and women who have known in him one of the best
and purest of human kind, who have loved as well as respected him, and who deplore and deeply lament his death."

These words express very truly what all who knew
him well observed ; namely, that he appeared quite
oblivious of, or indifferent to, the position or rank

assigned to him, in a work which he believed to be needful and good: He saw his part in the work, and simply did it—did it thoroughly and conscientiously, with no thought of human recognition or appreciation of his action. He could "take the lowest seat" with as much dignity as the highest, and as humbly and earnestly perform his task in either.

Further, in consideration for some who may open this book with a fear in their minds lest it should contain painful details of some of the evils against which our efforts were for so many years directed, I will say at once that not one word shall occur in its pages which might offend the most fastidious reader.

In the gallery of the Louvre in Paris there is a well-known painting by Raphael of Ste. Marguerite trampling upon a dragon. She is generally taken to be the symbol of perfect purity: she is here represented with her un-shod, snow-white feet treading upon the hideous scales of the monster who, conquered by her, writhes and twists in his rage and torment; yet the blast of his foul breath and his cruel talons are unable to reach or hurt her; she appears unconscious of the impurity and cruelty which she has trodden down. Her steady gaze is fixed, not on heaven, but on some object straight before her—some much desired goal towards which she is advancing with steadfast purpose. No speck of impurity has soiled her virgin feet or her white attire, although these are in close contact with the slime of the vanquished monster.

I take this picture as a symbol to represent the cause which we had the honour to serve in its steady march towards victory over a hideous evil. But now we will take a brush, so to speak, and paint out the dragon. In place of that disgusting creature you shall see now only

a mist or cloud : your eyes need not be offended by looking at the evil expression of the beast, though you cannot
help knowing that he is there, behind the cloud in which
we have concealed him. It is true that you can never
fully appreciate the purity and courage of Ste. Marguerite
while her deadly foe is thus concealed from you, or while
you prefer not to recognise his existence ; but this cannot
be helped. Should any reader desire, however, with a
serious purpose, to enter more deeply into the matter,,
there are sources from which the needful information can
be derived, and these sources have been abundantly purified by the fire of the long conflict, the records of which
necessarily expose the terrible things which had to be
brought to light and destroyed.*

The appeal to take up this cause reached me first
from a group of medical men who, (all honour to them)
had for some time been making strenuous efforts to
prevent the introduction in our land of the principle of
regulation by the State of the social evil. The experience gained during their efforts had convinced them that,
in order to be successful, they must summon to their aid
forces far beyond the arguments, strong as these were,
based on physiological, scientific grounds. They recognised that the persons most insulted by the Napoleonic
system with which our legislators of that day had become
enamoured, being women, these women must find representatives of their own sex to protest against and to claim
a practical repentance from the Parliament and Government which had flung this insult in their face.

It was on landing at Dover from our delightful summer
tour, of which I have spoken, in 1869, that we first learned

* The central office of our International Federation is 36 Place du
Bourg-de-Four, Geneve.

that a small clique in Parliament had been too success- ·
fully busy over this work of darkness during the hot
August days, or rather nights, in a thin House, in which
most of those present were but vaguely cognisant of the
meaning and purpose of the proposed constitutional
change.

. During the three months which followed the receipt of
this communication I was very unhappy. I can only give
a very imperfect impression of the sufferings of that time.
The toils and conflicts of the years that followed were
light in comparison with the anguish of that first plunge
into the full realisation of the villainy there is in the
world, and the dread of being called to oppose it. Like
Jonah, when he was charged by God with a commission
which he could not endure to contemplate, " I fled from
the face of the Lord." I worked hard at other things—
good works, as I thought—with a kind of half-conscious
hope that God would accept *that* work, and not require
me to go farther, and run my heart against the naked
sword which seemed to be held out. But the hand of the
Lord was upon me : night and day the pressure increased.
From an old manuscript book in which I sometimes wrote
I quote the following :—

"September, 1869.—'Now is your hour, and the power
of darkness.' O Christ, if Thy Spirit fainted in that hour,
how can mine sustain it? It is now many weeks since I
knew that Parliament had sanctioned this great wickedness,
and I have not yet put on my armour, nor am I yet ready.
Nothing so wears me out, body and soul, as anger, fruitless
anger ; and this thing fills me with such an anger, and even
hatred, that I fear to face it. The thought of this atrocity
kills charity and hinders my prayers. But there is surely a
way of being angry without sin. I pray Thee, O God, to
give me a deep, well-governed, and lifelong hatred of all such

injustice, tyranny, and cruelty ; and, at the same time, give me that divine compassion which is willing to live and suffer long for love to souls, or to fling itself into the breach and die at once. . . . This is perhaps, after all, the very work, the very mission, I longed for years ago, and saw coming, afar off, like a bright star. But seen near, as it approaches, it is so dreadful, so difficult, so disgusting, that I tremble to look at it; and it is hard to see and know whether or not God is indeed calling me concerning it. If doubt were gone, and I felt sure He means me to rise in revolt and rebellion (for .that it must be) against men, even against our rulers, then I would do it with zeal, however repulsive to 'others may seem the task."

Appeals continued to pour in. I read all that was sent to me, and I vividly recalled all that I had learned before of this fatal system and its corrupting influence in Continental cities—the madness and despair into which it drives the most despised of society who are yet God's redeemed ones, and the blindness and hardness of heart which it begets in all who approach it in its practical administration, or in any way except in the way of uncompromising hostility. And the call seemed to come ever more clearly.

So far I had endured in silence. I could not bear the thought of making my dear companion a sharer of the pain ; yet I saw that we must needs be united in this as in everything else. I had tried to arrange to suffer alone but I could not *act* alone, if God should indeed call me to action. It seemed to me cruel to have to tell him of the call, and to say to him that I must try and stand in the breach. My heart was shaken by the foreshadowing of what I knew he would suffer. I went to him one evening when he was alone, all the household having retired to rest. I recollect the painful thoughts tha seemed to throng that passage from my room to his study. I hesitated, and leaned my cheek against his closed door; and as I leaned, I prayed. Then I went in, and gave him something I had written, and left him. I did not see him till the next day. He looked pale and troubled, and for some days was silent. But by-and-by we spoke together about it freely, and, (I do not clearly recollect how or when) we agreed together that we must move in the matter, and that an appeal must be made to the people. (Already many Members of both Houses of Parliament, Bishops, and responsible officials had been appealed to, but so far in vain.) I spoke to my husband then of all that had passed in my mind, and said: "I feel as if I must go out into the streets and *cry aloud*, or my heart will break." And that good and noble man, foreseeing what it meant for me and for himself, spoke not one word to suggest difficulty or danger or impropriety in any action which I might be called to take. He did not pause to ask, "What will the world say?" or "Is this suitable work for a woman?" He had pondered the matter, and looking *straight*, as was his wont, he saw only a great wrong, and a deep desire to redress that wrong,— a duty to be fulfilled in fidelity to that impulse, and in the cause of the victims of the wrong; and above all, he saw God, who is of "purer eyes than to behold iniquity," and whose call (whatever it be) it is man's highest honour to obey; and his whole attitude in response to my words cited above, expressed, "Go! and God be with you." I recall that attitude even at this distance of time with wonder and admiration. I think there are not many men who would have acted thus. Loving peace and hating strife, as he did, his happiness centering in his home circle and domestic life, he yet unhesitatingly recognised the call of God—a call to conflict—and respected the conviction of her who now desired to obey it.

I went forth, but not exactly into the streets, to cry aloud. I took the train to the nearest large station—Crewe—where there is a great manufactory of locomotives and a mass of workmen. I scarcely knew what I should say, and knew not at all what I should meet with. A friend acquainted with the workmen led me after work hours to their popular hall; and when I had delivered my message, a small group of leaders among the men bade me thrice welcome in the name of all there. They surprised me by saying: "We understand you perfectly. We in this group served an apprenticeship in Paris, and we have seen and know for ourselves the truth of what you say. We have said to each other that it would be the death-knell of the moral life of England were she to copy France in this matter."

From Crewe I went to Leeds, York, Sunderland, and Newcastle-on-Tyne, and then returned home. The response to our appeal from the working-classes, and from the humbler middle-class in the Northern and Midland counties and in Scotland, exceeded our utmost expectations. In less than three weeks after this first little propagandist effort, the working men of Yorkshire, recognised leaders in political and social movements, had organised mass meetings, and agreed on a programme of action, to express the adhesion of the working-classes of the North to the cause advocated. Events followed each other quickly; petitions to Parliament were largely signed, and so strong and continuous was the pressure brought to bear on the Government that it was forced to endeavour to pacify the popular indignation by appointing, as early as the following year (1871), a Royal Commission to inquire, not into the principle in dispute, but only into the "working" of a principle already condemned by the conscience of the nation—a very futile inquiry, as it subsequently proved to be

This was my first absence from home. My husband arranged a little later a meeting in Liverpool itself. Several medical men volunteered their help. It is with joy that I mention the fact. Dr. William Carter, who is now known as a distinguished physician; Dr. Birkbeck Nevins, whose scientific advocacy of our cause has, in spite of prejudice, made his name respected throughout Europe; and several other doctors of whom we retain a grateful remembrance, gathered round us from the first, and for many years gave us the most steady, strong, and practical help; while a crowd of high-class medical men, Court physicians, practitioners pecuniarily interested in the maintenance of the governmental department which we aimed at destroying, and almost the whole of the medical press, were bitterly and furiously opposed to us. Among our first and best helpers in our own town was my cousin, Charles Birrell, a Baptist minister, who had a church in Liverpool. There existed a strong friendship between him and my husband. Mr. Birrell was a gifted man, of a dignified presence, and a beautiful countenance; he was refined and cultivated, and was eloquent in speech. He was elected for six or seven successive years to be president of the Baptist Union, in which he pleaded our cause. He had been ill, but came to this meeting at Liverpool. I find in my book of scanty records—written at the time for my own use alone—the following:

"Thank God! all doubt is gone. I can never forget Charles Birrell's prophetic words at our meeting yesterday concerning the future of this work. He rose from his sick bed to speak them, and stood there, a witness for God, pale and ill, but with a holy joy in his whole countenance, seeing God rather than.the people around him, and sending us forth to our work with confidence. Then my husband's benediction! The words of those two—their prayers, their counsels—must never be forgotten. God sent them to us to dispel all lingering doubts or hesitation—kind, pure-hearted, unworldly men, messengers of hope and assurance! And now it is revolt and rebellion, a consecrated rebellion against those in authority who have established this 'accursed thing' among us. We are rebels for God's holy laws. 'What have I to do with peace' any more? It is now war to the knife. In a battle of flesh and blood, mercy may intervene and life may be spared; but principles know not the name of mercy. In the broad light of day, and under a thousand eyes, we now take up our position. We declare on whose side we fight; we make no compromise; and we are ready to meet all the powers of earth and hell combined."

At this meeting in Liverpool, which was chiefly composed of working men, with a considerable attendance of clergy of different denominations, my husband said, in the course of an earnest address: "Great moral questions do away with all considerations of sect and religious parties. I rejoice to think that the clergy of the Established Church, if they will advocate this just cause, will have the co-operation of the Wesleyans, Baptists, Friends, and other influential religious bodies. It used to be the boast of the Church of England that it was the 'poor man's church.' Let us, by our interest in this matter, show that ours is also the *poor woman's* church. Our primary duties (speaking of the clergy) are no doubt concerned with spiritual matters, and I know there is a great prejudice against 'political parsons'; but on this platform I am glad to stand side by side with brother

ministers of Christ of other churches, to advocate a great
social principle, which may eventually involve political
action. I take St. Paul's words as expressing my own
feeling: 'Who is weak, and I am not weak? Who is
offended, and I burn not?' We find the prophets of old
weeping for the daughters of their people; and our
hearts would be hard and callous indeed, if we were
insensible to the cry which has reached us from the
daughters of our people now. We should deserve to be
classed with the priest and the Levite, who, seeing a
brother fallen, robbed and wounded, passed by on the
other side."

I am sketching here my husband's and my own
individual initiative in this matter, but it must not be
imagined that there were not many others equally alive
to the momentous question. A great number of women
throughout the country—the best known for intelligence,
high character, culture, and good works—had been deeply
moved from the first moment that they heard of the
treacherous encroachment on our liberties, and the
defiance of the moral law involved in this action of the
Legislature. These ladies (among whose names stood
foremost those of Florence Nightingale, Harriet Martineau,
and Mary Carpenter) united to sign the celebrated, and
now historical Protest, published on New Year's Day,
1870, and telegraphed throughout the kingdom by astonished editors and eager newsmongers. It was like a
solitary flash of summer lightning, prophetic of the storm
which was preparing, succeeded at first by a pause and
stillness of expectation and a kind of oppression in the
air, only relieved when the first roll of thunder came and
the clouds gathered, and the purifying hurricane swept
on. The peace-loving, but combative Society of Friends

from the first furthered the cause, and the work of women in it, in their own calm, practical manner.

During this first and all my subsequent absences from home it was a habit with us to write to each other daily, or nearly so, if it were but a single line of reassurance and greeting. From the first my husband wisely determined that it should never be in the power of anyone to say that his work—the work of education—or the interests of the college, had suffered through his taking part in this cause of morality and justice. There were not a few who were on the watch to make such assertions, had he given them any excuse for doing so. He rarely absented himself from his post at the college for even a short half-hour. The large staff of masters under him testified continually to the example he set them in respect of untiring assiduity and punctuality in the performance of his duties there. Only in vacations, or on an occasional holiday, he availed himself of the opportunity of appearing with me in any conference which might be held, and of advocating the cause which he believed to be of such vital moment.

From J. E. B. :—

> "Newcastle-on-Tyne,
>
> "Last day of 1869.

"My dear Husband,—I feel rather lonely here, listening to the bells clanging out the Old Year. My heart is with you and our dear sons. How solemn this evening is! I will try to think of the great New Year of the Lord's glad appearing, when this poor old world will be renewed in righteousness. I feel deeply how good it is of you, dearest, to lend me to this work. It is God's work—most sad, but yet most holy. I am sustained continually by the thought of you. So far I have been most kindly received by the Friends and by many Nonconformist ministers. I have seen also Sir William Armstrong's head workmen ; also some of Stephenson's men and Hawthorne's engine-makers, who are all eager to help us. Mr. John Stuart Mill has written from Avignon to ask what this is all about. How he will feel when he knows, I can guess. I am sending him papers."

"January 1st, 1870.

" Your dear letters have reached me safely. Yes, I think God will grant us some years of quiet happiness together after ' these calamities are overpast,' and even in the summer of this year we will, please God, visit hills and green fields and quiet scenes together, and forget for awhile the sins and toils of earth. We have not been much apart hitherto, beloved ; and just now it is for love of those who are ' bound in misery and iron,' in the ' dark places of the earth wherein are the habitations of cruelty.' I am coming back soon, to you and to rest."

From G. B. :—

"Liverpool, December 31st, 1869.

" Your letter this morning was very welcome ; and I hope you are enjoying the same sunshine and warmth which we have been having here, this last day of the year. Now it is clouding over a little. It is not every sun that always shines ; but the Sun of God's love does, and your love does, and so we need not care for a few mists."

"January 1st, 1870.

" I see your Protest in the *Daily News* to-day, with a great number of signatures. There is no comment upon it. It is right that my first letter of the New Year should be to you, though the fact of our being apart is exceptional. You seem to be working energetically, and I hope the result will be good. Be sure to let me know if you are not well, and I will fly to you at once. What a remarkable kindling of Christian feeling seems to have arisen together with the just indignation felt at this late legislation. It was surely a bad move on the devil's part! He will find his own weapons turned against him. I have not seen Miss Harriet Martineau's letters in the *Daily News*, but will look them up at the Athenæum. I hope some church of the future will find room within its borders for such people as H. Martineau, Francis Newman, J. S. Mill, and others. They are far too good to be left out in the cold. All join in love to you, and in prayers that you may be blessed and supported in your labour of love."

We received many letters about this time from Harriet Martineau. It is not surprising that we should have received abundant sympathy in this new Abolitionist cause from one who had recorded, as she had done, the labours and sufferings of the workers in the great struggle in America for the abolition of negro slavery. Of these latter she had written: "To appreciate them fully, one must experience something of the soul-sickness caused by popular hatred. Those who are living in peace can form but a faint conception of what it is to have no respite, no prospect of rest or success, within any calculable time. Nowhere but among such people as these can an array of countenances be beheld so little lower than the angels'. Ordinary social life is spoiled to them; but another, which is far better, has grown up among them. They had more life than others to begin with, as the very fact of their enterprise shows." We had often read and spoken in our home of the labours and fortitude of the heroes of the great American conflict; and though we were never called upon to experience such a measure of suffering as they endured, it was strengthening to think of them, in connection with a movement which had so many of the essential features of the anti-slavery struggle and of other great and noble battles for principle, in past history. It was good to hold communion in spirit with the confessors of other times, who "stretched out their strong arms to bring down heaven upon our earth."

Miss Martineau wrote to my husband, early in 1870:—

"Ambleside.

"My dear Mr. Butler,—How beautiful this paper is, 'The Lovers of the Lost,' especially the opening pages. I am very thankful to you for putting me in possession of it, and I hope it will be read by as many of my friends here as are worthy of it. . . . How appalled the profligates are, and how enraged! I have heard from very high authority that it is as if the depths of hell were stirred, so fierce is the passion of certain men at the check in a career which they had supposed would be made more secure. The extraordinary violence and ill manners of the *Pall Mall Gazette* and some other papers seem to me to indicate that they think our cause is gaining ground. Their way of assuming that the whole agitation was begun and is carried on by us women—the men of all orders being left out of sight whenever possible—tells volumes, to my mind, of their dread of what we may do and are doing; and the mean way in which representations àre made, and the audacity with which falsehoods are told, make it impossible to doubt that such disturbance arises out of fear. 'Fear hath torment,' and it is a sort of torment which, in its paroxysms, betrays its origin."

Later, she wrote:—

"Mr. Mundella, while disheartened about the dreary out-look generally, is perfectly confident of *our* success, as I suppose we all are; but there is such a forest of ignorance and prejudice for us to hew our way through! The *moral interest*, however, of such a question works miracles, and opens a path for any multitude of us through the deepest woods and waters."

In April of this year I was impelled to make a tour of the towns in Kent which were actually under the operation of the new system established by Parliament. Members of the London " Midnight Mission " and of the " Rescue Society " accompanied me. My husband wrote :—

"April 11th, 1870.

" I have read your letters with deep and painful interest. How bravely you have battled on amongst those poor girls ! I am convinced that in almost all cases there is a vein of good, which only needs the touchstone of sympathy and kindness and tact to elicit it. I hope you will be able to offer some of them a shelter at our Industrial Home. Poor things, it will be a heaven for them ! I hope to be able to get to Birmingham in Easter week. We might go from there to Cheltenham. It would be nice to put a fresh wreath of immortelles on darling Eva's grave. The boys are well, and send their love to you. We do not forget to pray for you and your work. Be careful to economise your strength."

"April 13th.

" Many happy returns of your birthday. I wish I were with you in body as well as in spirit. It is hard to be long parted. May God give you strength, my dearest, to continue your labours, and grant us some years of rest and happiness before we quit this earthly scene and leave the battle to our children."

At the meeting at Birmingham, to which he here alluded, he was one of the principal speakers. A local report said· " The speech of Mr. Butler contained an exhaustive history of the first efforts of the ' Ladies' National Association,' and a statement of the reasons which induced them to turn to the working-classes and to the country generally. We think his remarks ought to be placed on permanent record." This address, full of matter, and inspired by the just and chivalrous feeling towards women in which he never failed, is too long to give here. The concluding words were as follows: "If unhappily the moral sense of Parliament should slumber; if this question should be treated with aristocratic indifference, then the industrial and working-classes must lead the way, and stir up the conscience of their rulers by just and constitutional remonstrance. This would be no new thing in the history of the nation. With great questions like Negro Emancipation, Catholic Emancipation, the Repeal of the Corn Laws, the Extension of the Franchise, and others, the movement has found most favour at first among the masses of the people; and it is thus that a nation educates itself for the enjoyment and wise use of political privileges, by mastering the great moral and social questions which from time to time arise, and which all the community have an interest in seeing settled on sound, just, and truly Christian principles."

In May, 1870, he wrote to me, on one of my absences from home:—

"You ought to know of a meeting for promoting the law we oppose which was held in London yesterday, at which the Marquis of Hamilton presided. There was much complacent talk; but it was announced that they would not seek *to extend* the measures just yet, until the country had learned to understand the advantages of them. I hope your conference in London will result in some energetic measures, such as will show the House of Commons that the country will not be trifled with. The two things that want organising, till we have got the laws repealed, are:

"1. A flying column of speakers for elections, and a resident solicitor to protect the victims of this law.

"2. When the laws are repealed, abundant hospital accommodation for the sick, and homes and refuges for all who wish to begin a new life.

" Real good can come only out of a moral awakening of the nation; but harm may be prevented, and misery and injustice lessened, by the obvious means here suggested. All success attend you!"

In June a few of us led a first attack upon Plymouth, one of the great strongholds of our opponents. The opposition was strong and bitter, and the work difficult, during a week in June of exceptional heat.

" Liverpool, June 11th.

" Many thanks, my beloved wife, for your kind congratulations on this my birthday, and for news of your success at Plymouth. It is very cheering, and shows how a good cause will, by God's help, prevail against the violence and machinations of enemies—of men, not all, of course, influenced by bad motives, but wedded to a false and vicious system, and bound to maintain it. I hope you got my telegram dissuading you from attempting to travel all night in order to reach home earlier. It would be a great pity to disappoint the Exeter people. They are very hearty, and enlightened enough to have elected Sir J. D. Coleridge as their liberal member; and the more you can do to stir up the clergy the better. I think you are taking *quite* the right line—not attacking individuals, but dealing with broad moral principles. You can very safely leave the ferreting out of abuses to the legal and other gentlemen who have espoused the cause. But speaking in the name of the women and mothers of England, who themselves enjoy immunity from these cruelties and hardships under which their outcast sisters labour, is a task which well befits you, and I bless God that you have been enabled to raise your voice with such good effect in so holy a cause. We are all well. George and Stanley are in the town for the Oxford Local Examinations. George has done well again to-day in mechanics and hydrostatics. Charlie has so got into the habit of bringing your afternoon tea that he has just brought me some, and is very loving. We look forward to your return on Monday."

In June, during our vacation, he gladly accepted an invitation, addressed to us both, to address a meeting at Chatham, a depôt at that time for recruits, and full of soldiers. A number of military officers stationed there tendered their help in arranging the meeting, and openly supported the cause we advocated. On this occasion my husband's words were thus reported :—

"He had come from a distance to be present here, for two reasons : first, to testify to the interest he took in the great question of national morality ; secondly, to show publicly how thoroughly he approved of the part taken by Mrs. Butler in visiting the different towns of England and endeavouring to arouse the conscience of their inhabitants to the reality of the evils which were coming and had come upon us. He was glad to show how completely he and she were united in spirit as regarded the work to which she had devoted herself. His engagements as the Principal of a large school seldom permitted his appearance at meetings with her at present ; but in heart he was always with her. She and her fellow-workers had been overwhelmed with abuse by a portion of the Press, but this was one of the conditions inseparable from the advocacy of any great social reform ; and he hoped that the organs of the Press which now lagged behind enlightened and Christian public opinion would in course of time follow that public opinion, and exclaim, as is their wont : ' Did we not always say so ?' "

He then spoke of the necessity of a pure life from the point of view of health, and was attentively listened to by the soldiers who were present.

The " National Association," which had been formed early in the year, and which was daily increasing in vitality and in boldness of operation, effectually prevented the further extension of the system we opposed, and by means of successful contests at bye-elections—preeminently that of Colchester, where the Government candidate, Sir Henry Storks, was defeated on this one question by over 400 votes—forced the Government to look seriously into the matter. My husband had personal friends in the Government, and on most questions he sympathised with their policy; it was the more painful, therefore, to have to maintain a prominent position personally in the perpetual attack and protest on this question. He was often reminded by cautious friends of the very distant prospect of any possible retirement from school work which he must now contemplate, so far as that retirement (or promotion of any kind) depended on the goodwill of those then in power. He perfectly understood this from the first, and his experience for many years from this time was that of an ever receding prospect in that direction. He continued to speak and write for the just cause whenever opportunity presented itself, patiently wearing his harness as a laborious schoolmaster for twelve long years after this date. Though it was a trial to him to be at variance in any way with personal friends or public men whom he regarded with esteem, yet it was not possible for him to set motives of policy or his own private interests above fidelity to a cause and a principle which he considered vital.

In March, 1871, I was called to give evidence before the Royal Commission which had been appointed. I was not fully aware until recently, when looking over his letters, how his tender solicitude for me had followed me in all my endeavours, in every varying circumstance. His duties at the Liverpool College forbade him accompanying me to London on this occasion; and even if this had not been the case, he would not have been allowed to remain with me during the examination in the House of Lords.

He had, unknown to me, written to the Chairman of the Commission, Mr. Massey, commending me to his kindly consideration. For it was a formidable ordeal, being, as I was, the only woman present before a large and august assembly of Peers, Bishops, members of Parliament, representatives of the military and naval services, doctors, and others; my questioners being in a large majority hostile, and the subject serious and difficult. On the morning before I was called, I received a number of letters, addresses of sympathy, and notices of united prayer for my support from associations of working-men in Edinburgh, Glasgow, Newcastle, Leeds, Birmingham, and many other towns.

From J. E. B. to G. B. :—

" It is over! It was even a severer ordeal than I expected. It was distressing to me, owing to the hard, harsh view which some of these men take of poor women, and of the lives of the poor generally. They had in their hands and on the table everything I have ever written on the subject, and reports of all my addresses, marked and turned down; and some of the Commissioners had carefully selected bits which they thought would damage me in examination. Frederick Maurice was not present, I am sorry to say; but Mr. Rylands, Mr. Mundella, and above all, Sir Walter James, I felt were my friends. The rest were certainly not so. To compare a very small person with a great one, I felt rather like Paul before Nero, very weak and lonely. But there was One who stood by me. I almost felt as if I heard Christ's voice bidding me not to fear. I handed to the Chairman a large packet of the letters and resolutions from working-men. He said: ' We may as well see them; for no doubt that class takes some little interest in the question.' I should think so! Let them wait till election times, and they will see! One of the Commissioners asked: 'Are these *bonâ-fide* working-men?' I replied: ' Yes, and well-known men. There is more virtue in the country than you gentlemen in high life imagine.' He then asked: 'If these laws were put in operation in the North, do you believe they would be forcibly resisted?' I replied: 'I do.'"

From G. B. :—

"Just a line to congratulate you, my dear wife. It is a good business over. I wonder how you feel after it all. I trust that your spirit will be much refreshed, and that your bodily powers have not failed you. I hope the Commission treated you well. Mr. Massey has written to me apologising for the length of your examination, and accounting for it by the extreme interest of your evidence. So I have written to thank him for the kind interest he evinced. How I wish I could have been with you! Mr. Pennington kindly telegraphed to me when you left the House of Lords, giving me Mr. Rylands' account of your examination which he said had passed triumphantly."

Mr. Massey had written :—

"Rev. and dear Sir,—I hope Mrs. Butler has not suffered from the long examination which she underwent with so much spirit and firmness on Saturday. I did what I could to shorten the proceedings, but the interest felt in her statements, and the prominent part she has taken in connection with the question, led to her detention before the Commission for a too lengthened period."

From J. E. B. :—

"I shall be so glad to get back to you, and to breathe fresher air. I am sure your prayers have been heard in regard to my evidence before the Commission. I don't think I did justice to the Commissioners in my first letter to you. I was so tired and depressed and dissatisfied with myself after the long ordeal, that I saw it all through rather a dark medium. But now I am full of thankfulness to God. I think I may quote to you what Mr. Rylands said to-day to Mr. Duncan McLaren and others: 'I am not accustomed to religious phraseology, but I cannot give you any idea of the effect produced except by saying that the influence of the Spirit of God was there. Mrs. Butler's words and manner were not what the Commission expected; and now some of them begin to take a new view of what they have hitherto called the "religious prejudice." ' He added that Lord Hardwicke came to speak to him afterwards, and that he seemed moved, and said : ' If this is a specimen of the strength of conviction in the country on moral questions, we must reconsider our ways.' I tell you all this, dear husband, that we may learn more and more to wait upon God, who hears prayer. I spent yesterday with dear Fanny in her rooms. Home to-morrow."

Lord Mount-Temple,* who, as Mr. Cowper-Temple, was a member of the Commission, wrote to me after it had closed its labours and sent out its double report :

"I drew up the reasons for dissent from the report of the majority of the Commissioners, and was much pleased to have the concurrence of those who joined with me in signing it. I think you may now be less anxious, though you will not cease from your labours. I believe firmly what you said of a crisis of choice coming to English people. The kingdom of love and purity and righteousness is coming with a new power upon the earth, and the manifestation of it depends upon hearts being ready to receive it. There are some who are looking with faith and hope to the dawn of the coming day ; but where are those whose spiritual eyes are opened to perceive how the principles of self-surrender and burden-bearing for others can be applied to the new circumstances in which we are living ? When Christianity can be extended beyond the sphere of individuals, and be thoroughly acted out by numbers of persons in co-operation and in concert, it will produce results never yet seen."

* He and Mr. Applegarth became convinced of the justice of our view of, the question by the evidence before the Commission, and the spirit of those severally who gave that evidence.

In spite of great encouragements now and again, we were from year to year forced to confess that the prospect of victory was much more distant than we at first imagined. Lóoking back over those years, we can now see the wisdom of God in allowing us to wait so long for the victory. For the mere legislative reform, or rather undoing and repairing, which was our immediate object, was but a small part of the great and vital movement which it was His design to create and maintain for the purifying of the nations; and if we had obtained a speedy triumph there would not have been that great awakening of consciences which we have witnessed, resulting in practical and lasting reforms. At times the struggle between opposing principles was very severe; and hostile criticisms, censures—public and private,—accusations, invective, and bitter words fell upon us at certain crises as thickly as the darts of Apollyon on Christian's armour at the entrance of the dark valley. Motives of the worst kind were sometimes imputed, among the most frequent being that of a lurking sympathy, not with the sinners alone, but with their most hateful sins. A certain class of our enemies thought themselves happy, it seemed, in inventing a dart which they believed would strike home in our own case; they sought diligently to spread an impression that some tragic unhappiness in our married life was the impelling force which had driven me from my home to this work; and coarse abuse was varied by hypocritical expressions of pity and sympathy.

But they were the most unworthy alone—the "lewd fellows of the baser sort" * naturally—by whom this kind of scourging was inflicted or attempted. It only had the

---

* Of the baser sort morally, though sometimes of the high aristocracy of the land.

effect of strengthening our indifference to all selfish, impure, and interested opposition, and of deepening our thankfulness for the good gifts of peace and unity of heart in our home. Such manifestations, however, taught us much of the deeper meanings of these "signs of the times." Much more serious, practically, was the opposition of honourable opponents, men of education, high character, and honesty, who in some cases had openly given their names in favour of a principle and a measure which happily many of them learned to regard later with suspicion or abhorrence. The mistaken views of such honourable men most frequently resulted from a want of courage, and a disinclination to look into the question, or from ignorance or misapprehension induced by the cunning tactics of the original promoters of this evil thing in our country; persons in constant contact and sympathy with the most unscrupulous advocates of the Napoleonic system in Paris. Among my husband's papers left to my care, I find many draft copies or outlines of letters written to such honourable opponents; long letters, full of well-attested facts, of patient argument, close reasoning, and courteous persuasions, based on every motive of justice, honour, and pity. He probably wrote these letters late at night, when he had finished his monotonous task of looking over boys' exercises, or preparing lectures or other college work; taking from hours of much-needed sleep the time he could with difficulty secure during the day, to try to bring to a right judgment on a great question of national justice men who were his friends, and whom he believed to be of a serious character or likely to influence the Legislature.

From J. E. B. to G. B. :—

" We now know something of what it must have been in the days of the first Christians, when those who espoused the despised faith found themselves in deadly opposition to lovers, friends, and brothers, as dear to them as life; and the desperate test was driven home, 'whoso loveth father, mother, wife, or children more than Me, is not worthy of Me.' And of two hearts which had been bound together in love, one now cursed what the other blessed, and blessed what the other cursed, and were consciously and deliberately rent asunder, sometimes for ever, and a man's foes were those of his own household; and from many a broken heart came the cry, 'Lover and friend hast Thou put far from me.' Days like these are, it may be, coming again. The period of indifference is past; convictions are deepening, and Satan will not let his kingdom be wrested from him in peace or quietly. And there are those among us who, if need be, *will* part with friend and lover and brother and life, and all but honour, in the battle which is to come. It is not for a creed we fight now; but for eternal principles, for justice and equity, for mercy, for liberty, for truth. It is a sifting time. The thoughts and intentions of men's hearts are revealed. My heart yearns after the former friends who now stand aloof, or who tell us face to face, 'I will work to thwart and defeat you!' But life is short, and we cannot stay to weep over withered hopes and joys."

" It may be," my husband wrote to an intimate friend, "that I have inherited from my father whatever I may have of deeper feeling, and of a predilection for the testimony of my own conscience and that of a few good men, rather than the unanimous approval of the world, which is never slow to applaud those who combine a bustling activity with worldly prudence (if these are crowned with success), and yet who never perhaps conceive or act out one great thing in their lives."

In the autumn of 1872, the Annual Church Congress was held at Nottingham. My husband had obtained per-mission to read a paper on "The duty of the Church of

England in Moral Questions." This paper was prepared with great care, while on a visit to Dilston, where my brother Charles then lived.

To J. E. B. :—

" Dilston, October.

" Here I am in your sweet old home, so full of recollections of the past as well as of natural beauty. This morning, when I looked from my window towards Hexham, there was a lovely gleam of sunshine on the upper part of the bank of trees, while the lower part lay in shadow. The grass was silvery with dew; and it looked pure and beautiful as hardly any other place in the world does. The boys and I only caught the train at Carlisle by the guard waiting a few minutes for us. It was the guard who had to swim across the Tyne when the bridge gave way in the flood, and the train floated across with the stream safely to the other bank. He was crusty at first, on account of our being behind time; but at the name of Grey he brightened up, and became very civil and sociable. I have come in for a very curious ceremony: the 'rehearsal' of all the Derwentwater coffins, seven in number. They were moved from the vault in Dilston Chapel to Hexham Abbey, except that of Lord James, who was beheaded in 1715, and was canonised as a saint. His remains are to be moved to a vault in Lord Petre's park, near Chelmsford. A son of Lord Petre came down to superintend. I must finish to-day my paper for the Church Congress. Mr. Mundella has invited us to stay with him at Nottingham. I am glad Bruce is being called to account. I hope Mr. Gladstone's constituents at Greenwich are prepared to address him firmly and respectfully on our subject. Farewell for to-day. This place is full of associations with you, and I think of you hourly."

It was at a very crowded meeting in a large hall at Nottingham that he read, or attempted to read, his paper. Copies of that paper are still in print, and in re-perusing

it after this lapse of time, it is almost impossible to imagine
how any objection could have been felt to its being read
in any assembly of adults of serious minds and purpose.
Much of it is a general advocacy of more careful moral
teaching in the Church and in schools. Where the
question is treated of influences, institutions, or public
measures unfavourable to social purity, the language is
carefully guarded, the tone is high and pure, the style
refined and scholarly, and any word which could need-
lessly bring into prominence any unpleasant association
is carefully omitted. A certain number of the clergy
present, however, had been carefully trained by evil
advisers to consider the recent legislation as an excellent
thing, and when an allusion was made to that point a
veritable tumult arose. We had heard, many times before,
rude and defiant cries and noisy opposition at crowded
meetings, but never so deep and angry a howl as now
arose from the throats of a portion of the clergy of the
National Church. These were not the majority, as we
afterwards learned by the crowd of clergymen who followed us in the street to offer sympathy, to express shame,
and to beg that they might not be reckoned among those
who could not bear to hear the truth; but the minority,
many of them being young men of "good families" put
into the Church from motives not the highest, were the
noisiest, and prevailed. I recall vividly my husband's
attitude while the tumult was prolonged. He contined to
stand upright, his paper in his hand, and his expression was one of firmness and gentleness combined.
Inwardly, I can imagine, he recognised the humorous
aspect of this burst of wrath, for he was very quick in
discerning any humorous element in the vagaries of human
beings. The President of the assembly was the Bishop

of Lincoln, Dr. Wordsworth, his former master at Harrow. The Bishop was one of the few in that rank who from the first had welcomed gladly a coming day of plainer speech, more honest teaching, and purer living.* But he was not prepared to act against what seemed to be the voice of the majority of the meeting, and after an interval of considerable hesitation on his part, and uproar on the part of the loud-voiced portion of the assembly, he requested my husband to abandon the attempt to continne his paper; and his former pupil obeyed his old friend and president, only feeling much strengthened for future war on the same ground. William Lloyd Garrison once said, during his great anti-slavery battle: "A shower of brickbats is an excellent tonic" In polite society brickbats are not in use; but hard words, shrieks, and groans supply their place pretty well as a tonic to the person at whom they are hurled. The rest shall be told in my husband's own words. He wrote to the editor of the periodical representing our cause, *The Shield,* the following:

"As some interest has been expressed about the paper I wrote for the Church Congress at Nottingham, I venture to trouble you with a line to say that, in consequence of a disinclination of a portion of the audience to listen to my recommendation that the Church Congress should protest against immoral legislation, and in deference to the wishes of the chairman, I suppressed that portion of the paper. But the entire paper is now in the printer's hands, and I will send you a copy. It is headed by a preface, which I have now added.

"During the discussion at which I was present, confes-

Among the Bishops who lent their influence from the first to the cause, were the late Bishop of Salisbury (Moberly), the late Bishop of Lichfield (Selwyn), the present Bishop of Gloucester and Bristol, and almost all—if not quite all—the Colonial Bishops.

sion to God and to his appointed ministers, was insisted
on by more than one speaker as the first step to spiritual
health. If this be true of individuals, it is also true of
the nation. A frank confession, a courageous facing of the
great social evils among us, is needful before we can attain,
as a nation to moral health. It struck me as a grave omission
on the part of the Congress that there was little, if any, reference to rescue work, and still less to the grand necessity of
repressing male vice. So long as we persevere in hiding a
deep sin, so long will our national condition be unsound. A
speaker was applauded to the echo for saying that men were
made drunkards by Act of Parliament. I was not allowed to
state that they were encouraged in vice by Act of Parliament.
Clearly, unless we get rid of the seventh commandment, this
is an inconsistency. The only speaker who approached this
part of the subject in the least degree was Mr. Leake, of
Cambridge, who hinted at the inutility of squeamishness
where grave offences had to be dealt with."

This is the Preface alluded to in the above letter:

" The following paper was written for the Church Congress
at Nottingham; the subject announced being, ' The Duty of the
Church in reference to the Moral State of Society in various
Classes at the Present Time: the causes tending to its corruption; remedies, means of improvement.' It appeared to me that
the ' great sin of great cities ' and the legislation concerning
it properly formed parts of this subject. Teetotalism and
non-teetotalism, confession and non-confession, dinners, dress,
swearing and drunkenness were fully treated of. But the
sin of unchastity and the duty of the Church in reference to
recent legislation were not dealt with except in this paper.
Every allusion to the latter subject was received so unfavourably by a portion of the audience that the chairman requested
me to omit all reference to that subject, on the ground that it
was better to avoid an appearance of dissension in a Congress
of Churchmen. My duty was obvious; I bowed to the
decision of the chairman, and read the remainder of my paper

in its eviscerated state. Having done so, I feel at liberty to say
—and I do so with the greatest respect for the Right Rev.
chairman, for whom, as my former master, I entertain a loyal
and filial attachment, and whose eminent learning and
apostolic character I greatly revere—that my opinion as to
the suitableness of the subject for a carefully-prepared paper,
to be read before a mixed audience, remains the same. I
believe it is, for the most part, ignorance of the facts which
hinders my clerical brethren from giving their attention to a
moral question of such weight; and I hold it to be of the
greatest importance that they should be awakened to a sense
of their duty.

" My readers will determine for themselves whether this
pamphlet, printed verbatim, as it was intended to be read,
contains anything improper for a public audience assembled
to hear grave subjects seriously discussed.

" God forbid that we should arrive at such a state as that
which the Roman historian describes, when we can bear
neither our vices nor their remedies. I shall gladly welcome
on the part of the clergy a recognition of their duty to look
things evil fairly in the face; and not to reject a certain class
of subjects as ' tabooed ' because their existence conveys a
reproach and a feeling of uneasiness. It is their want of
courage which has caused women to step forward and do the
work which men should have done. Meanwhile a single
voice raised in the Church Congress has been heard, though
not fully. Others will follow, and the destruction of the immoral legislation we oppose must soon take place. But then
the battle will only be commencing. Action must be organised to check the evil, and the efforts of all—clergy and laity
alike—will be required to bring good out of evil, and heal the
festering wound under which society has so long groaned.
Then will be wanted all the self-sacrifice, all the love, and all
the wisdom that the nation can produce; and above all, the
aid of Him who said to the poor sinner, 'Go, and sin no
more.' Those who are spared to take part in this good work
will be a blessing to their country and receive a blessing
themselves."

. The following is a reply which he wrote to the Archbishop of York (Dr. Thomson) who had been his intimate friend many years before, in Oxford days, and who had written to remonstrate with him for having introduced the subject of his paper into a meeting of the Church Congress. The Archbishop had not been present at the meeting, and had only heard the report of some of his clergy :

"Liverpool, November, 1871.

"My dear Lord Archbishop,—It is always a pleasure to me to hear from you, especially on moral subjects on which you are entitled to speak with so much authority, not only as a spiritual peer, but as a Christian philanthropist. I well remember a sermon which you preached at Mr. Cameron's Church at Oxford, on the text Luke vii. 39. 'This man, if he were a prophet, would have known who and what manner of woman this is that toucheth him ; for she is a sinner.' In that discourse you drew a powerful and affecting contrast between the pharisaism of the world and the divine mercy of Jesus. And I have heard you speak plainly to the people here, and read similar addresses from you elsewhere, on the sin of drunkenness and the misery which it and kindred vices entail upon society. Therefore I am bound to pay especial deference to any suggestion of your Grace's on the treatment of moral subjects, because I know you have the interest of morality so strongly at heart.

"Possibly I should have done well to submit my paper beforehand to the committee, for I certainly do not wish to incur the condemnation which your Grace pronounces on writers of pamphlets on the subject of the sin in question. I shall be truly glad when the necessity for mentioning such subjects ceases ; but until the present objectionable legislation is removed, I see no prospect of that.

"No doubt some of the writers of pamphlets may err in discretion. So do the advocates of total abstinence at times. But let us give the latter credit for wishing to repress drunkenness, and the former for the wish to purify our Statute-book. These cases are parallel in one respect, that the agitation is chiefly carried on by the middle and lower classes of society. The taking up of these subjects in a serious spirit by the clergy and laity of the Church of England would do much to divest the movement of extravagance or intolerance. Thus I am very glad to see the promotion of a National Union for the suppression of intemperance, and I rejoice to see the Bishop of Manchester boldly rebuking vice in his diocese, and speaking a word for the tender and watchful care of those poor children who are led astray before they are of age to estimate the consequences of a lapse from virtue.

"Believe me, I can feel with your Grace as a father; and I hope I have some sympathy also with the feelings of the married clergy, in the wish to keep their homes pure. But as a citizen of a free country, and a loyal subject of the Queen, I desire fervently to see all unjust and class legislation abolished, and all reasonable prejudice against Monarchical Government removed; and I, in common with others, look to the great Council of the nation assembled in Parliament to do away with that which we consider as a national blot, as unjust and immoral in its working and tendencies as it is derogatory to the character of the Sovereign. Of course the Queen's advisers are chiefly responsible for the character of the laws; but it seems to those who oppose this particular law hard that the reign of our virtuous Queen should have any moral stain attached to it, even in the estimation of the uneducated. If the measure promised by the Premier is brought forward in Parliament, I am sure that your Grace will give it the attention which it deserves. Reading the Blue Book (report of the Royal Commission) may not be pleasant, but there are some portions of the evidence which anyone may read with advantage, such as that of John Stuart Mill; and I venture to think that your Grace would not be less interested in that of my wife. No one has naturally a greater shrinking from the discussion of such subjects than she has; but she has acted from a sense of duty, and from compassion to others. I venture to send you a pamphlet of Professor Sheldon Amos. There are some remarks on page '23 on the conduct of the opponents of this legislation which I think are worth reading.

"Believe me, with much respect and regard, faithfully yours, ——."

Later in the autumn a large public meeting was held in Liverpool, the tone of which contrasted strongly with that of the Congress meeting.

My husband wrote to our eldest son, at Trinity College, Cambridge :—

"Yesterday was a hard day for your mother. She had to read her annual report to the meeting of the Ladies' National Association. Then she came to the College to meet Mr. Steinthal of Manchester and to prepare for our two o'clock meeting, at which I took the chair, and at which Professor Francis Newman read an excellent paper, cutting up the conduct of Parliament in passing bad measures in the small hours of the night. We carried our two chief resolutions and dispersed at half-past four. At eight the evening meeting began. It was very good, especially Dr. C. Bell Taylor's speech, which was really eloquent. Mr. Steinthal, Mr. Hopwood and Mr. Towers spoke effectively, but the chief feature of the evening was Applegarth's* speech. He, poor man, had been ill and was suffering from great weakness, but he made a capital speech, in the course of which he showed how utterly untrustworthy was much of the evidence on which the Royal Commissioners placed reliance, and what a contradictory and futile Report they had brought out. He also spoke of some of the causes of misery and vice ; and, his words, as those of a working man spoken to working men (of whom many were present), had great weight."

From J. E. B. to the same :—

"Applegarth's speech was very moving. There was a sharpness in his voice and an anxiety in his face, such as I have

* He had been a member of the Royal Commission.

noticed in some of those thoughtful working men, leaders of forlorn hopes, which speak of a long struggle both for bread and for principle. Father spoke excellently well. He has studied the subject thoroughly, and feels it so much. It is striking to hear such strong denunciations of injustice and selfishness coming from so gentle a man, and one so apt to think the best of people and their motives. The Liverpool press has treated us quite respectfully. (The *Daily Post* was always fair). Perhaps this change in their tone is partly owing to Dr. McNeile's letter, which was very grave and forcible. At any rate, for the moment they have forgotten to sneer ; and, besides this, two at least of the College Directors have openly joined our crusade.

" I enclose a review of the paper which father read at the Church Congress."

The following is an extract from that review, which was written by Professor Sheldon Amos :—

" The paper prepared by Mr. Butler for the Church Congress at Nottingham deserves the ·earnest attention of all those engaged in our movement. While it is decisive and uncompromising in its argument, it speaks the gentleness of the Christian as well as the instinctive taste and refinement of the scholar. The issue raised in it is the gravest possible. The position of the Church of England, as a divine society, is at stake. The competition (if such there be) between religious bodies is, in the last resort, a competition of moral forces. If the Church of England discourages dissent, and invites dissenters back to her fold, she must not lag behind them in purity of moral aim, in discrimination of moral vision, in unflinching and unresting energy of moral action. If her sublime historical antecedents, and her treasury of spiritual truths and dogmas, fail in accomplishing this for her, already is her candlestick being removed out of its place. The following passage from Mr. Butler's pamphlet is a startling and tremendous warning :—

" ' If we constantly take the wrong side, if we are found continually acting in opposition to the conscience of the mass of the people, in public questions ; if we walk in the steps of those, whether Baptists or Churchmen, Kings or Parliaments, who burnt the martyrs, drove out Wesley and Whitfield, taxed the American Colonies, upheld slavery, trafficked in Church preferments, 'supported monopolies, withstood the application of our endowments to purposes of general education, tied up land by vexatious laws, connived at drunkenness and made vice easy and professedly safe, by law,—then I think the time is not far off when the cry will come from all parts of the United Kingdom against the Church of England : "Away with it ! why cumbers it the ground ?" '

" Mr. Butler alludes to an objection frequently made that it is not the business of the Church of England to make the people discontented with the laws by keeping up such agitation. In other words, it is the business of the Church of England to encourage political indifferentism, to resist every progressive movement which involves a change in the law, and to dissociate herself and her influence from all the most ennobling and most invigorating parts of a true citizen's duty. Rather is it a part of the Church's work to refine the critical sagacity of her children, whether contemplating old laws or new ones. The single eye to moral purity is hard enough to retain, amid the distorting and blinding colours of earthly interests and occupations. It is for the Church and her ministers to be ever recalling her children to the conception of an absolute and equal standard of ideal purity and goodness.

" Mr. Butler has some excellent remarks on what may be called the religion of activity : 'What unceasing activity,' he says, ' can be kept up without weariness when the spirit is at rest ; on the other hand, what a restless spirit may exist along with practical inactivity !' He quotes from the historian of the Puritan Fathers, who says of them, speaking of a time when they were in much trouble : ' But they knew that they were strangers and pilgrims here below, and looked not much on these things, but lifted up their eyes to heaven, their dearest country, where God hath prepared for them a home (Heb. xi. 16), and therein quieted their spirits.' "

CHAPTER X.

DEATH OF NEAR RELATIVES.—CONTINUED CONNECTION WITH THE
UNIVERSITIES.—CORRESPONDENCE WITH SONS.—LECTURES
ON CONSTITUTIONAL HISTORY TO THE WORKING MEN OF
LIVERPOOL.—PROMOTION OF GEOGRAPHICAL KNOWLEDGE.—
HOLIDAY IN WALES.—MR. FROUDE, PROFESSOR STUART, SIR
JAMES STEPHEN, MR. LONGMAN.—CLASSICAL COMPOSITIONS.
— FRIENDSHIP WITH MR. FROUDE. — KINDRED TASTES.—
WILLIAM LLOYD GARRISON ; HIS VISIT TO LIVERPOOL.—
TRADES UNION CONGRESS AT LEEDS.—OPINIONS OF INDIAN
AUTHORITIES IN CONDEMNATION OF THE SYSTEM OPPOSED
BY THE NEW ABOLITIONISTS.—CLERICAL MEMORIAL ON THE
SAME SUBJECT.—DEBATES IN PARLIAMENT.

EARLY in the year 1872 my husband's mother died. He wrote from Harrow, having been summoned there by telegraph :—

" Your foreboding was true. My dear mother lived longer than they anticipated ; but she had breathed her last a quarter of an hour before I arrived. My sisters told me that she almost seemed as if she was trying to keep alive till I came. Beloved mother ! She is now at rest, and nothing can trouble or distress her more. Her hands are folded meekly across her breast. How much of tenderness and sympathy will go to the grave with her ! " ·

From J. E. B. to a sister :—

" You have heard that dear, gentle Grandmamma Butler is gone. I went with George to the funeral at Harrow. All her sons and daughters were there. The service was impressive. The Harrow schoolboys sang a Latin hymn, which was appropriate and sweet. I am told that she

mentioned me—together with many others—very affectionately before her death; and she has been so kind as to
leave me a gift to help on 'our good work.' She was the first
in the family* to write us words of sympathy concerning that
part of our work which is misunderstood by so many. Her
gentleness forbade her imputing any but the best motives to
us. It seems to add a drop of bitterness to George's grief
that he did not arrive in time to see her alive, and hear her
speak to him once more. He cannot help regretting it.

"She loved her grandchildren very much, and they
returned her affection. Her letters to them were always
welcome. We never failed to tell her of any little success or
honour gained by them at school, for it delighted her so
much; her congratulations, often accompanied by some kind
present to supplement the school prize, would generally
arrive by return of post."

We lost in the following year a dear brother and friend,
Edgar Garston (who had married one of my sisters).
They lived in the neighbourhood of Liverpool. He was
born in 1779, and went abroad when very young, spending
some years in Italy, where he made himself thoroughly
master of the language, and even of the provincial
dialects. His excellence as a linguist led to his being
asked, while still quite a youth, to act as interpreter in
Queen Caroline's trial, for which he travelled many
hundred miles on horseback on the Continent, collecting
evidence on the Queen's side. When the war in Greece
broke out he joined the Philhellenes, and was known as
"the Englishman" *par excellence.* He was tall, well-made,
and fair, with a bright, open countenance. To this he
added a pleasant address, and great skill in the use of
arms. For his services under Colocotroni he received

* We had not long to wait for the sympathy of the other members of
the family.

two decorations—the order of the Redeemer of Greece, and that of the Philhellenes. He was acquainted with several members of the Buonaparte family in Italy, especially with the eldest brother of the Emperor Napoléon III. with whom, as his partner, he once held the lists for two days, with the foils, against the best fencers of France. When he returned to England he settled as a merchant in Liverpool, and was for some years a Director of the Union Bank there. He was a type of the generous "old-fashioned merchant," a man of strict integrity and the finest sense of honour in all business relations. It was a pleasant thing to hear him at his office speaking several modern languages with equal ease and accuracy. A better friend and a kinder neighbour could not be found. His courtesy was no mere outward polish, but the genuine outcome of a tender and chivalrous spirit; and, though a thorough man of the world in the best sense, he was a sincere Christian.

M. Tell Meuricoffre wrote of him to my husband:—

"Our dear brother-in-law's departure is for me a great sorrow. He has been a friend to me for twenty-eight years. He is also to me a link with the generation which has gone before, for he had been the friend and associate of my parents in his youth. He used to remember those times at Naples so vividly, and with a kind of poetical halo about them. It was a great charm for me to hear him speak of them."

To my eldest son, at Cambridge:—

"We have just returned from the cemetery. It is a most calm and lovely day, with bright autumn sunshine. The space in front of the mortuary chapel was filled with gentle-men. It was almost like a scene on ''Change'—a crowd of merchants—but instead of talking and moving about, they were all standing still, silent, and bare-headed. There were several Greeks there, and among them the old Archimandrite. Father had gone there half-an-hour earlier. He was standing alone at the door of the chapel with a large open Bible in his hand. His face was very grave. He stood as motionless as a statue; his white robes were not stirred in the least, for there was not a breath of wind. All the other people were in shade, and he alone stood in the bright sunlight, the only white object. The sun fell full upon the white leaves of the Bible also. We followed him into the chapel, and after a part of the service out again into the sunshine. He read the rest of the service in the open air, in a voice which sounded far and clear. I was quite surprised. It was a great effort to him ; he managed to command his voice, though the tears were rolling down his face. Poor Aunt Tully stood close to the grave, looking down to where her dear husband-lay. He was laid close by the resting place of little Josephine Meuri-coffre. Many humble people came there voluntarily too, as well as merchants. When we got home I found poor father walking up and down in his study, looking troubled. I began to speak of Uncle Edgar, and he said : ' Oh, it is hard to have to bury so dear a brother ! I have seldom loved any-one, out of my own family, so much as I loved him.' "

A few weeks later my husband wrote to me when from home :—

" This is the anniversary of my dear father's death, just twenty years ago. How many more of them shall we live to see ? Let our prayer be that we may be found ready, as he was, when our time shall come ; and let us carefully cherish his memory, and all the other sacred memories of purity and devoted love in our families, as an heirloom to our children."

During the sixteen and a half years of my husband's connection with Liverpool College he kept up a constant intercourse with the Universities of Oxford and Cambridge. Having sons at both, he had a strong personal interest in doing so; but besides that, he continued occasionally to examine for the University Scholarships.

"I have just delivered," he wrote in 1878, "by appointment, a Latin sermon in the University Church at Oxford, before the authorities. I believe it is the first sermon in which the new pronunciation of Latin has been adopted." Liverpool College was, I think, the first public school in which the new pronunciation of Latin came to be used. In the recitations at the prize deliveries it certainly sounded much softer to most ears than our English manner of pronouncing it hitherto.

His letters to his sons during their University career were constant and encouraging. To a son at Oxford he wrote :—

"This will reach you just as you are going in for the *vivâ voce*, I imagine. Be sure to keep cool, and do not answer in a hurry; then I have little doubt that you will satisfy the examiners. Examinations generally assume a very different aspect when you look back upon them; it strikes one then what easy things they are, if one had only known it."

To his eldest son, at Cambridge :—

"I think you have had a good start in your University life, and I believe you will make the most use in your power of the educational advantages of your position as a Trinity man. But whatever successes may attend your efforts, I trust you will always remember this, that we are not required to do more than our powers will bear without undue strain. I think it of more importance that you should have a good education than that you should be such and such a Wrangler, or take such and such a position in the Classical Tripos. And even higher than a good education I should place the capability of *doing your work in life*, which in many cases that I have known has been interfered with by too severe or too uninterrupted study at the University. Therefore, if you should ever feel yourself growing nervous, or unable to sleep, ease off for a while, for if you do so in time it may save you from a breakdown."

Mr. Powles, in a letter of New Year's greeting to my husband, said :—

" The well-doing of your children must be a source of increasing happiness to you. It must be specially-pleasant to you to see your boys (I call them boys, as I am not speaking to them but of them) showing, all of them, aptitudes for study of one kind or another. I often think it must be a great disappointment to a studious and thoughtful father to have sons who take only the physical vigour of his character, without being able to sympathise with his higher life. I have seen several such cases. Your sons spare you this mortification, and give you a corresponding amount of happiness in their course. All success to them, and to you in them ! I have read the account of your great day at Liverpool,* and Mr. Gladstone's speech. It is to my mind the best essay spoken for many a long day. Of course, at Liverpool he can say nothing that will not be unfavourably criticised ; but the speech is a noble one. Of the solemn, earnest words in which he warns the youth of the College against unbelief one cannot speak too highly or be too thankful."

My husband corresponded with others of his pupils besides his sons. Many of them have gratefully acknowledged the value to them of his advice, urging on those who needed urging, and warning the too eager against impetuosity and overwork.

From the time of the institution of the Public Schools' Conferences he was an almost constant attendant at those gatherings. Sometimes it was his lot to introduce subjects, which were by some considered a little advanced, in connection with changes he considered desirable in the

* The Prize Distribution, December, 1872.

curricula of the Public Schools and Universities. These were, however, in general approved.

Apparently not satisfied with the amount of work he had at the College, he undertook, at the invitation of some of the working men of Liverpool, a course of lectures in the Operatives' Trades Hall, on certain important periods of English History, from the Norman Conquest to the Accession of Charles I. The Constitutional History of England, he thought, was a subject of which no class of the community with any pretensions to education should be ignorant. This course of lectures was opened in a large assembly presided over by Mr. Graves, M.P. for Liverpool.

My husband began by saying :—

"I wish in the first place to state, briefly, why I have undertaken to give a course of lectures to working men, who are fully capable of reading for themselves, and of forming intelligent opinions on the facts of history. The authors I have studied lie open to every one of you who has access to the Free Library in the William Brown Museum here. It is not because I wish to bias your judgment or lead you to adopt any peculiar views of my own about things past or present. I wish every one who hears me to read and judge for himself. But I wish to show my sympathy with the moral and intellectual movement which is taking place in this town, and to combine with my fellow townsmen for such worthy objects as you have in view. In studying the great constitutional questions which, as I take it, form the most worthy object for thoughtful students of history, we are raised above party spirit. I have no fear, however, in addressing myself to a body of intelligent men that I shall be blamed for speaking to them freely concerning moral and political principles which when rightly understood enable us to form correct opinions on past and present events. History is a study which never loses its interest nor grows old ; it links together the present and the past, and enables us to some extent to forecast the future. It deals with moral, and not only material motives of action, and exhibits for our instruction and guidance the effects on the one hand, of justice, love of truth, self-restraint and brotherly kindness; and on the other hand, those of selfishness, the absence of good faith, disregard of others, and immoral habits. In a word, it teaches us the source of a nation's strength and of a nation's weakness, leaving us to apply the lessons we have learned to ourselves and to our country."

To one of his sons he wrote :—

" I am reading Motley's *History of the Dutch Republic.* For a record of crimes, on the one hand—cruelty, hypocrisy, deceit, licentiousness,—and of patient perseverance and endurance on the other, I never read anything of deeper interest. The older I grow the more I am attracted by history. We lose a great deal by muddling so long over a small period of Greek or Roman history. William the Silent was one of the greatest men that ever lived, and I had entered upon my sixtieth year without any adequate knowledge of his life-work and character ! "

The question of the promotion of Geographical knowledge was again revived in 1879, by a suggestion from the Committee of the Geographical Society that Professorships of Geography should be founded at the old Universities. In the first month of that year the Secretary of the Society (the late Mr. Bates) wrote to my husband: " With reference to the report on Geographical education, with which you favoured our Public School Prize Committee, I am requested to say that the Committee will be obliged to you if you will draw up and send to them a separate memorandum of your views regarding Professorships of Geography at Oxford and Cambridge, giving a little more development to the description of the functions of the proposed Professor than has yet been given."

On the occasion of the awarding of the gold medals of the Royal Geographical Society in the previous year, my husband, who appeared on behalf of one of his successful pupils who was not able to attend, spoke as follows :—

"In the absence of the gold-medallist from Liverpool College, who is engaged this year in examinations, I have the honour to acknowledge the munificence of the Royal Geographical Society, and to thank the President for his complimentary reference to the former successes of the College. I am most happy as the Head Master of that School o acknowledge the stimulus and encouragement which has been given to the study of Geography by the medals, and the examinations conducted annually by men of world-wide reputation. My experience as an Oxford Examiner and Head Master of a large middle-class Public School induced me, at the request of the Committee, to lay before the Conference of Head Masters at Rugby in 1877 some suggestions relative to the more effectual teaching of Geography. Although some advance has been made in that direction, I regret that it has scarcely been commensurate with the importance of the subject ; and yet I think I am justified in stating from my own experience that the following results have been obtained :—A systematic study of Geography has promoted a more intelligent appreciation of history; it has led the way to a more thorough study of kindred sciences; it has impressed the students with a sense of the greatness of the Empire, and of the undeveloped resources of the accessible world. I may add that the students of Geography have distinguished themselves at the Universities of Oxford and Cambridge in Classics, Mathematics, and Natural Science, showing that in the development of special aptitudes afterwards they have not been hindered by devoting some of their time at school to Geography.

" If the Memorial recently addressed by this Society to'
the governing bodies at Oxford and Cambridge be adopted
by those Universities, the teaching of Geography will be
further strengthened, and England will be placed on a level
with other countries, which—with motives and advantages
less in some cases, and in no case greater than ours—have
made more ample provision for Geographical study. The
Head Masters of Public Schools who recognise the Universities as placed at the summit of the educational system will
have additional ground to be thankful to the Royal Geographical Society for helping to bring into greater harmony and
consistency the scholastic and academic systems of education in Great Britain."

From Mr. Francis Galton, to my husband :— :

" Your valuable Memorial and George's appendix and
remarks were submitted yesterday to the committee, and
discussed and referred to a sub-committee. George's list of
subjects set after the prize essays is very helpful in showing
the use of a Geographical Professor. I have kept one of
the lists to incorporate in the Memorial, which is being finally
revised."

He wrote again :—

" I had the opportunity of acknowledging publicly at the
Royal Geographical Society your help to us. I stated that
we have now sent the Memorial to the Universities, and
I added that it contained suggestions from many sources,
notably from yourself, who had for many years persistently
urged the utility of including Geography in an ordinary
education."

Professor Rolston wrote from Oxford :—

" Dear Mr. Butler,—I am sure the Council, with which
body the initiative lies, will give a most respectful reception
to a proposition pointing to the foundation of a Professorship
of *Erdkunde*. The subject has a scientific, an antiquarian,
a literary, and an imperial interest attaching to it; and

besides all this, it is a subject which is attracting and will attract diligent students henceforward for several generations. The little planet in which we live is by no means fully explored as yet, circumnavigating ships notwithstanding. I think the Universities should be most ready to have Professorships on the subject in question."

Hoping to strengthen the appeal made to the Universities, my husband wrote an exhaustive article for the *Contemporary Review*, in 1879, on the subject of Geographical Education, in its relation to many different branches of science, to practical life, to colonial and commercial enterprise, and to education generally, in its widest and fullest sense.

The years of school work at Liverpool, as I have before said, were brightened by annual excursions on the Continent or elsewhere. One of my husband's favourite holiday resorts was Rowsley, in Derbyshire, where there was some fine trout streams. It was within moderately easy reach of Liverpool. He generally stayed at a picturesque little inn, " The Peacock." He wrote of it on his first visit :—

" It is quite the ideal of an old-fashioned country inn, and is well-known by anglers and artists. It is within a mile of Haddon Hall, of which I made a sketch yesterday, while Charlie explored the country round. You must come here with me some day. It is just the place I have been seeking for some time past to spend a few days of holiday in. It has been very pleasant to meet my dear old friend Powles here. He and Mrs. Powles came here from Leamington, driving in open carriages, as we did in the Tyrol."

Others of our favourite excursions were to North Wales, and to our friends at Derwent Island on Derwentwater.

In the autumn of 1874 my husband was much con-. cerned for our friend Professor Stuart, who was attacked by severe illness at Cambridge. His own home being in the far North, he was persuaded, when well enough to be moved, to come to our house. ".I hope," my husband wrote, " we may be able to get him away from Cambridge. He should have every care with us. I would meet him at Rugby, or come up to town and bring him home from Euston. His room here is ready for him. I would do anything in my power to save so dear and valuable a life." This wish was realised, and after a few weeks of good nursing in our house, Mr. Stuart was able to go with us to North Wales, where we were the near neighbours of Mr. Froude and his family, who had taken a house for the summer at Crogan, near Corwen. " It will be a 'good joy' to me," Mr. Froude wrote to my husband, " if you and Mrs. Butler can spend your holiday so near us. I suppose I am really going on this Colonial expedition. Life is uncertain, and we must make the most of it, and lose no chance of seeing old friends." Our life in North Wales was spent chiefly out of doors, and our friend gradually regained health. At Mr. Froude's were staying Sir James Stephen, Mr. Longman, the publisher, and others. " The gentlemen play a game on the lawn called 'Badminton'." (a kind of lawn tennis), one of our party wrote. . . . " Both Fitz-James Stephen and Longman hit very wide of the mark. At the sight of one of Stephen's wildest strokes, Stuart was heard murmuring to himself—

> ' Lesbia hath a beaming eye,
>   But no one knows for whom it beameth·
> Right and left its arrows fly,
>   But what they aim at no one dreameth.'

He was called upon to repeat aloud this remark, and Mr.

Stephen was generally spoken of among us after this as Lesbia. We had some pleasant picnics on the high grass moors and to Bala lake."

My husband was not unfrequently called upon to speak, in his sermons preached before the assembled Schools in the college hall, of friends or public persons who had passed away. The death of President Garfield was one of those occasions. The American Consul in Liverpool at the time thanked him warmly for the enlightened and appreciative view he had taken, not only of Garfield's character, but of the grave circumstances and position of his country at that period. Mr. Stansfeld thus commented on another sermon on the death of a well-known citizen of our town, Mr. Cropper: "As in the few other things which I have read of yours, I recognise especially the gift of a judgment remarkable alike for candour and delicacy. It seems to me that you have taught exactly the right lesson to teach and at the right time. I shall keep it to steal from on some occasion, in the confidence that you will not mind the theft. From whom is the quotation 'without haste, but without rest'? Mazzini used to be fond of the words, and I have thought of them in connection with our movement.

He often found time for what was indeed a real recreation to him—the composing of verses in Greek or Latin, and also sometimes in English, on any incident of a pathetic or ennobling nature, private or public, which touched his heart. One of these incidents was the cruel murder of several young Englishmen on the plains of Marathon. He sent a copy of two Greek epigrams which he wrote on the subject to Lord Stratford de Redcliffe, who replied· "The copies of your two epigrams have reached me, and I lose no time in thanking you for an attention which has given me so much pleasure. I cannot presume to send you anything in return in the same un-rivalled language so ably employed by you, but you will perhaps allow me to enclose for your indulgent perusal a few couplets in our own vernacular, by which I endeavoured to express some weeks ago my feelings about the late atrocities in Greece, and the noble conduct of our. unfortunate countrymen." Lord Lingen wrote : " Arthur Helps would much like to have a copy of your verses." Lord de Grey also had written to Lord Lingen: " I am much obliged to you for sending me a copy of Mr. Butler's touching verses. The sympathy which we have met with on all hands has afforded us much comfort in our heavy sorrow. So just an apprecia-tion of the spirit in which the captives met their death as is shown in Mr. Butler's lines is most grateful to us all." He often exchanged classical and poetical compositions with Lord Coleridge and with the late Lord Lyttelton, who delighted in such literary exercises, and frequently wrote to him, not only on contemporary subjects such as educational reform and the readjustment of endowments, but on nice points of scholarship and classical questions far remote from present times.

· Occasionally my husband had the advantage (if such it be), during brief visits to London, of a plunge into the society of literary men ; but he never willingly prolonged his stay in town beyond a few days. " How I hate towns," he wrote ; " still, wherever one's work is, life is endurable."

From Mr. Fronde's house, in Onslow Gardens, he wrote on one occasion to his son Stanley :

" On Friday I met a good many men whom I have known more or less. We had a pleasant party. There were present

Alfred Tennyson and his son Hallam, Tyndal, 'James. Spedding, Browning, and others. Froude is very well. He and I were playing lawn tennis yesterday in the Square, when old Carlyle came round to take him for a drive in an omnibus, which he does about three times a week. Froude hid himself behind the bushes, and the old philosopher, unable to see him anywhere; retired, and we continued our game. Afterwards we went to see your godfather, Dean Stanley, who was glad to hear good news of you."

I sometimes used to ask myself what might be the foundation for so strong a friendship between my husband and Mr. Froude, seeing that they differed so widely. in their opinions on many important subjects, although I have so a deep a respect for friendship that I have always hesitated to approach any such bond between two human beings even with such a question as this.

We paid a visit to Mr. Froude in the autumn of 1876, on the coast of Devonshire, where he had taken a house, —The Molt, near Salcombe. There a little light came to me on the subject. I was sitting in my room in the twilight of a very hot evening, beside my open window, beneath which there was a bench, a homely "settle," on which the two friends happened to be seated. They seemed to be engaged in a deeply confidential conversation, which lasted, with brief intervals, for a very long time. I could scarcely avoid overhearing it, and I rather welcomed the chance (which I had not sought) of becoming a partaker of their intimate communications. They were talking, not about creeds or politics or science, but about *flies* for fishing. Looking down upon them quietly, I saw them with their heads bent close together, intent upon some open books they had—fishermen's books, with flannel leaves, to which innumerable artificial flies were fastened, of many beautiful colours' and different sizes. Some of these were made by my husband himself, who was very neat-handed; and the birds from which the feathers had been taken for the making of the flies were, as well as the flies, under discussion; the places and times when these birds were shot, as well as the particular flies suited for particular rivers; and all this was illustrated by fishing experiences of past and recent times. I suppose one must have the soul of a fisherman fully to understand the intensity of interest of such a subject of conversation. Clearly this was a very " out-of-door " friendship; and anyone who ardently loves external Nature must acknowledge that a community of such tastes is a very real and solid ground of friendship. To the love of outdoor pursuits was added, however, in this case, the cementing bond of many acts of kindness given and received in times of need.

J. E. B. to a son :—

"The Molt, August, 1878.

" There has been a storm here, and the wind is high and the sea roaring. Father and Mr. Froude have been out in a yacht all day, trawling. They caught a turbot, several mackerel, and many skates. They were burnt brown when they came in. Father says Froude is quite at home in a storm, and laughs wildly, rather like a sea-gull! Father bathes every morning, and gets tossed about on the rough waves like a mad Mother Carey's chicken."

In 1876 and 1877 we had two brief visits from Mr. W. Lloyd Garrison, the leader of the anti-slavery struggle in America. It was his last visit to England. He came to our house in Liverpool on landing from America. I recollect his striking and venerable appearance as he crossed the threshold of our door, and the manner in which he said, in doing so : " Peace be to this house, and to all who dwell in it." We gathered together a few friends to meet him in the evening. We were much struck by the delicacy of his physique, and even the nervousness with which he anticipated having to say a few words in a drawing-room meeting—the man who had addressed thousands, encountered hostile mobs, and undergone such violent persecution as he had met with in America !

My husband wrote to one of his sons :

" Mr. W. L. Garrison, of Boston, came here on Sunday. He is one of the most interesting men I ever saw. He speaks well, clearly and fluently, and with remarkably good taste. He is going to visit Oxford and Cambridge. We shall give him your address, and hope that you will see him."

In 1890 Mr. Frank Garrison wrote to me from Roxburgh, U.S.A. ·—

" My memory goes back to the pleasant evening which my father and I spent at your house in Liverpool, nearly thirteen years ago, to Mr. Butler's personal kindness, to the meeting in the Memorial Hall in London which my father attended, and to Mr. Butler's speech there ; again, to the farewell gathering at your house in August, and the heartfelt tribute my father paid to Mr. Butler and yourself, whose great work he fully appreciated ; and finally to the meeting last July (1889), which my brother and I were so fortunate as to reach London just in time to attend. How pleasant it is to remember the recognition then accorded to Mr. Butler ! He was indeed a Canon worthy to be canonized for his brave and unflinching devotion to the cause which you and he championed. And if, as I firmly believe, those who pass on to the next plane of life are still able to help and inspire us in the work we are left to sustain, his labours are not ended by this change, nor his interest diminished."

The meeting at our house in August here referred to was Mr. Lloyd Garrison's last farewell to England. We there presented him with an address, signed by many persons throughout the country who remembered and understood the immense importance of his great enterprise, which he lived, happily, to see crowned with success. Mr. Garrison was deeply moved on reading this address. His words to us on our own crusade strengthened the faith and revived the courage of many, and have never been forgotten.

In returning to the subject of the work for the cause with which I dealt in the last chapter, I will briefly notice the principal events connected with it in which my husband took part, up to the period when the movement experienced a new development, necessitating work on the Continent as well as in England.

The annual Trades Union Congress of British working-men was held at Leeds, in January, 1873. In the course of it a conference was held by our Society with the leaders of the working-men who were assembled from all parts of the country, followed by a great public meeting the same evening, at which George Howell (afterwards a Member of Parliament) presided. A very remarkable speech was made there by Joseph Arch, who brought to us messages from large associations of agricultural labourers. My husband spoke after him, and was followed by Henry Broadhurst (afterwards also in Parliament) and other well-known representatives of the Trades Unions, who were all determined that Parliament should ultimately undo the wrong it had enacted.

A "Northern Counties' League" had been formed—one of the many branches of our ever-widening national movement. At one of the Conferences of that League, of the Committee of which he was a member, my husband was led to speak of the establishment in India by British authority of the system we opposed. He quoted at some length the opinion of Lord Frederick Fitz-Clarence, Commander - in - Chief in 1853, saying that "if he were to rise from the dead and speak at any of our meetings as he had spoken in India we can imagine how he would have been scouted as an alarmist and maudlin sentimentalist." Lord Frederick wrote to the Governor-General of the time that, "after giving the whole subject his best attention, he concurred with his predecessors in command of the army in believing that police measures of the kind in question could not be carried out without involving the certain degradation and oppression of many innocent persons, and occasioning other evils which in his opinion would be very much greater than that which it was their object to remedy." Dr. Grierson (of the Indian Army) had said that when the natives of India saw the authorities making such careful provision for the protection of immoral persons, and at the same time doing little for the good of other classes, they were "sorely perplexed." General Jacob had said (in reporting before a Government Commission in India) ; " The proper and only wise method of dealing with this question is to improve the condition and moral well-being of the army. Coercion of every kind always increases the evil. Moral forces alone are of any value." Sir Herbert Edwardes, Sir John Lawrence, and Sir Bartle Frere had all concurred in this opinion.

My husband worked very hard during the spring of that year at a rather laborious and troublesome task, namely, the canvassing by letter of the clergy of the

Church of England with the view of getting up a clerical memorial to the Premier.

In May, 1873, this memorial was presented to Mr. Gladstone by Canon Fowle, an aged and good man, who had had the courage to preach a sermon on the subject in Salisbury Cathedral to an audience of men. I took the memorial to London. "I am thinking about poor old Canon Fowle," my husband wrote, "and praying earnestly for him. Tell him from me to remember that the influence of this memorial is not limited to the Premier alone, but will show to the public what a host of good men there are in our Church who are ready to protest against an evil and mistaken act on the part of the State." A further effort was made some years later in the same direction. A very much larger number of signatures was obtained, to the great contentment of my husband, who with the keenest sense of her faults and shortcomings, was nevertheless a loyal and attached member of the Church of England.

It was about this same date, May, 1873, that the first debate and division in Parliament took place on our question, which had been courageously and ably pioneered in the House of Commons by Mr. William Fowler, a member of the Society of Friends, and which afterwards (when Mr. Fowler lost his seat for Cambridge) was taken in hand with equal ability and courage by Sir Harcourt Johnstone. My husband congratulated me and himself heartily on the division. The majority against us was 137, yet he could rejoice! And justly so, for in counting up our probable friends in the House we had not dared to hope that we should have as many as those who actually voted for us; viz., 128.

It was on this occasion that old Mr. Henley spoke in

the House of Commons the following solemn words [Respect for his personal character caused members on both sides of the House to listen in perfect silence, a silence so great that though his voice was feeble all he said was distinctly heard.] : " It is complained," he said, " that this agitation is carried on by women ; but we cannot shut our eyes to the fact that women are most affected by this legislation. We men do not know what women suffer. Unless they tell us, we cannot know. In this matter women have placed their feet upon the ' Rock of Ages,' and nothing will force them from their position. They knew full well what a cross they would have to bear, but they resolved to take up that cross, despising the shame. It was women who followed Christ to His death, and remained with Him while others forsook Him ; and there are such women among us now."

In a division on the question of Woman's Suffrage, which occurred about this time, Mr. Henley, who had till then been opposed to granting the Parliamentary franchise to women, voted in favour of it, and spoke a few very touching words. He told me that the experience he had now had of the injustice which Parliament (not excluding the good men in Parliament) is capable of inflicting on women had convinced him that they (women) must labour for and obtain direct representation on equal terms with men.

CHAPTER XI.

CONTINUATION OF ABOLITIONIST STRUGGLE.—SUICIDE OF A
VICTIM OF THE NEW TYRANNY.—MEETING FOR PROTEST.—
SPEECHES OF GEORGE BUTLER, MR. STANSFELD, LORD
DERWENT, AND OTHERS. — A COMPROMISE OFFERED BY
GOVERNMENT, AND REFUSED. — MR. STANSFELD'S PUBLIC
ADVOCACY OF OUR CAUSE.—MISSION TO THE CONTINENT.—
—VISIT TO PARIS.—ARDUOUS WORK.—OPPOSITION AND EN-
COURAGEMENTS. — MM. JULES SIMON, JULES FAVRE, LOUIS
BLANC, ED. DE PRESSENSÉ, AND OTHERS ENCOURAGE US.—
VISIT TO ROME AND NAPLES.—CORRESPONDENCE.—MILAN,
TURIN, GENEVA.—SECOND VISIT TO PARIS.—PÉRE HYA-
CINTHE IN LONDON.—INTERVIEW WITH MR. GLADSTONE.
—DELEGATES TO AMERICA.

N the winter of 1872, Mr. Gladstone, as has
been stated, had accepted an invitation to
deliver an address at the college prize-giving
at Liverpool. It was a memorable occasion,
and our college hall, which was very capa-
cious, was probably never more crowded.

Several friends had urged me to make use of the opportunity of Mr. Gladstone's visit to speak to him on the
question of our special crusade. This advice I did not
follow, never having considered it a wise thing constantly
to introduce "in season and out of season" any subject
which may be near one's own heart. It is as often out of
season as in season that zealous advocates are led to
press their views on others, and I have never felt assured
of good being done in this way. A friend sent us shortly
after this an extract from a letter from Mr. Gladstone, as

follows: "I was about to write to you respecting Mrs. Butler, as I had not explained properly to you my reason for declining a special interview, had it been asked. When I came to reflect on it, I perceived my reason to be in the main this: There is no use in an arrangement by which a leader of any movement warmly presses his views on any member of the Government, who is already well disposed towards that movement, unless he can, which I cannot, become a propagandist of it in the Cabinet. I had a good deal of conversation with Mrs. Butler. Knowing her feelings about this special topic, I appreciated her perfect abstention."

On the 30th March, 1875, a poor young widow (Mrs. Percy) drowned herself in the Basingstoke canal—a victim of the police espionage practised under the laws which we opposed. Her husband had been confined to bed by illness for several years, and she and her young daughter, not quite sixteen, had supported him and two little brothers by singing at evening parties and taking part in private theatricals at Aldershot, where they lived. She had previously written a letter to the *Daily Telegraph*, telling simply the story of her life and the persecution to which she had been subjected from the time that her husband died. She probably hoped for some sort of response which would help her to escape; but not at once receiving any, her despair increased, and she found escape by death. A great "indignation meeting" on the subject was held in London, on the 24th May, under the presidency of Mr. Edward Backhouse, a distinguished member of the Society of Friends, a rich banker, and a munificent helper of all good works—a man whose spirit may be judged of by the following lines, written in 1873, to my husband: "I am glad that the clergy of the

Church of England are sending so many signatures to your memorial; but I am sorry the Archbishop of Canterbury had not the courage to present it to the Premier. However, I continue to hope, and we are making great preparations for the next General Election. I said I continue to hope; but in truth I feel more determined than that — something like the Old Guard at Waterloo, who, when called on to lay down their arms, replied, 'The Guards die, but do not surrender!' Whether true or not, it is well said, and so say I."

Sir Harcourt Johnstone (Lord Derwent), Mr. Stansfeld, Charles Birrell, and my husband were the chief speakers at this meeting; and though it was called an "indignation" meeting, the speeches were all characterised by great calmness, by the presentation of facts and proofs concerning the matter in question, and by a more determined spirit than ever in regard to the future work. The poor little orphan girl, Jenny Percy, had been confided to our care, and was living in our house at Liverpool, under the charge of our devoted friend and housekeeper, Jane. The little boys were taken care of by the National Association. My husband (who was at the time standing *in loco parentis* to the orphaned girl) made at this meeting the following statement :—

"The statement which I am about to read to you was drawn from little Jane Percy in the confidence of a quiet Sunday chat, after she had been a fortnight in our house, and it was written down immediately. We asked her to tell us exactly all she could recollect, if it was not too painful to her. She replied, 'I will tell you exactly what I saw and remember;' and then, speaking for the first time of the bitter trial to which she had been subjected, she said : 'They called the police, and ordered my mother to go up to the Metropolitan Police-office and bring me with her. Mamma and I went. We saw there Inspector G——. He was in his room, and mamma was first called in alone. I cannot therefore tell what passed between mamma and the inspector, because I was not there. I can only tell you this, that mamma was never the same person again after that hour. She told me that she assured Inspector G—— that she would rather sign her death-warrant than the paper he gave her to sign. I was then called in. I shall never forget the moment when I stood before Inspector G—— and he accused me. He said, " Do you know, girl, why you are here?" I replied, " No, sir, I do not." He said, " You are here because you are no better than you should be. You know what that means, I suppose?" I said, " No, sir, I do not." He laughed in a horrible way when I said this. I continued to deny that I knew what he meant; for, indeed, I did not. I knew what a bad character was: there are plenty in Aldershot; but I could not understand that he meant to accuse me and my mamma of being bad characters. He asked me if we had a " pass" into the camp. I answered, " Yes, we had always had one; for we had engagements to sing while papa was lying ill." He then shouted to someone, " See that these two women have their passes taken away from them; we will put a stop to all that!" You see mamma could not earn a living after this. It hurt me so when he called mamma and me "these two women!" Mamma said to me when we came out, " Jenny, this will be the death of me." She never looked cheerful any more. She was watched by the police wherever she went. Then she wrote that last letter to the *Daily Telegraph.* Soon after that we went away to try to get an engagement elsewhere, but could not succeed. Mamma was always crying, and we began to feel what a loss father was; for though not able to earn a penny for two years, he was a good friend. We told him of every trouble, and he would talk it over and advise us kindly. Nobody but myself knows what mamma suffered. She could never rest at night; for she said Inspector G——'s face was always before her, as she saw it when he accused her. If she fell asleep, she would wake up sobbing and in a fright. I consider that man has been the death of my mamma. He had said to her at the end, " I will not leave you alone." Well, a friend came from Aldershot to ask mamma to go back there. We went back. Friends used to say to her, "Cheer up! you will be all the more respected when this is cleared up and the truth is known." She again said she would choose death rather than do as Inspector G—— wished her to do.' *

" Jenny spoke all this in a low, quiet voice, not at all excitedly. Her visit to the police station seemed to haunt her, even more than her mother's death. She is proud of her mother, and this pride helps her to bear the loss. She said at last : 'What a law this is ! I never could believe there was such a law. Since this law was made it is not con- sidered respectable to speak to a soldier, nor have one in your house; but I can tell you that, though I have lived among soldiers ever since I was born, I never had a rough word or an insult from one in my life, and they were always respectful to my mamma. I think you will find that all those who knew her spoke well of her.'

" This ends the poor girl's evidence. Its substance may be regarded as an illustration of the results of this legislation. Probably the supporters of this legislation will deny the sufferings of Mrs. Percy, or say it sprang from a morbid imagination; but they cannot deny the fact of her death. They cannot deny that she was prevented by the Govern- ment officers from exercising her calling, through which she had found the means of supporting her family.

" What now is the practical issue to be derived from this sad experience? I presume we should all agree in saying that we do not seek to destroy the character of any official. Even if we could prove that cruelty had been exercised by twenty inspectors, we should be no nearer the great object we have in view; *i.e.* the abolition of a law the existence of which is a national disgrace. The tragic story of Mrs. Percy has already been published in foreign lands, where she is

---

* What he wished her to do was to sign her name as one of the recognised pariahs of Society, to be put *as such* under governmental regu- lation and drill.

regarded as a victim of a system which has been long known on the Continent, where they count its martyrs and victims not by twos and threes, but by hundreds. But the fact of one victim having been done to death in England will be thrown away if we do not open our eyes to the danger to which some of the weakest and most defenceless of our countrywomen are exposed. The law virtually says to every woman of a humble class: 'If your conduct is in any way open to suspicion, you must henceforward submit to a course which will justify the very worst suspicions: you must sign your name upon this register, and enter upon a life over the portals of which might be written the fatal words ·

> "*Lasciate ogni speranza, voi che entrate.*"
> ("Leave every hope behind, all ye who enter here.") '

"The narrative you have just heard is the story of a young girl, a mere child in appearance, who deeply feels the indignity of the treatment her mother received while living, and the aspersions cast on her character when dead. I may say she appears an innocent and modest girl; she is industrious, quick at learning, and desirous to obtain employment where she will be out of the way of the action of this law."

Sir Harcourt Johnstone followed with an eloquent speech, saying: "We have heard a statement from Mr. Butler, to whose philanthropy the charge of this girl has been committed, and to whom we all owe a debt of gratitude. No one can say this statement is sensational or hysterical. All on this platform have determined to avoid sensationalism, and to work in a constitutional manner for the abolition of these laws."

Mr. Birrell said:

"It has been remarked to me frequently within the last few days, by gentlemen of high station and position, that the class of persons immediately affected by these laws are not so sensitive as those in the higher ranks of society, and that therefore we need not take so much care about their feelings. I believe this to be an error. They may not be so refined in manner, but they are by no means less competent to perceive moral distinctions. Christianity began its conquests in the families of the poor ; in all the nations in which it has made a permanent dwelling the same order has been observed. The fact is that a great many things that evaporate in empty words among the higher and educated and conventional classes of Society, continue to be stern and solemn realities around the hearth of the poor man ; and there are some questions which I would rather submit to a thousand men of the employed class than to a thousand men of the class above them ; and I believe that this is one of those questions. If this poor actress pursued but an indifferent calling, was that any reason why she should be precipitated into ruin ? We have not far to look for arguments based on Christian principles to sustain us in the effort to bring these laws to an immediate conclusion."

Jane Percy continued to live with us until we found for her a good situation. In 1877 she had typhoid fever so severely that her life was despaired of. She had relapse after relapse, and was, humanly speaking, only saved by the constant attention and exceptional medical skill of our friend Dr. Carter. My husband wrote :—" I was sent for suddenly to see Jane Percy last night. She recognised me at once, and seemed much pleased to see me. After a little talk she asked me to read to her, which I did, and also prayed with and for her. Poor child ! she seemed very sensible. Her lips were black and her hands very hot. Dr. Carter comes constantly. I hope my visit so late—nearly eleven o'clock—did not disturb her night's rest, but I thought if I waited I might be too late. I shall see her again to-day." He continued to visit her constantly, in spite of his busy life at the college. She recovered, and continued to do well in every way.

In the winter of 1874–5, the Abolitionist cause entered upon a new and more extensive phase. Correspondence with continental friends had led us to foresee that the English Abolitionists were not destined to work long on a merely national scale, but that their efforts would necessarily come to be extended throughout the civilised world.

I have already said that I do not profess to give in any sense an account of our great crusade. I have omitted for the most part any record of the Parliamentary events connected with it, the most conspicuous of which were the recurring debates and divisions in the House of Commons, the appointment and report of the Royal Commission and of Parliamentary Committees of Inquiry instituted later, election contests, and, lastly, the compromise offered by the Government in the shape of a bill brought in by Lord Aberdare, and which was usually called " Bruce's Bill." This was a cleverly drawn-up bill, and no doubt it was a surprise to the Government when our Society declined to accept it.

It was impossible, however, for us to accept a measure which had at the heart of it the very principle which we had determined to get rid of, though this principle was ingeniously wrapped up in various proposals for the protection of the young and other good things. The discussion on the subject of this compromise in the heart of our own Association and the temporary division it caused were sharp and painful. There were only a few of our associates who at first perceived the danger. Some of them were at first indignant against the *intransigeant* among us, while we of the minority, on our own part, were much perplexed as to our future policy. Harriet Martineau wrote to us at that time :—

"Our cause is so strong and holy that it can bear to be sifted again and again. We shall eventually lose nothing by the half-hearted or weak ones leaving our ranks. It is better to fight with a handful of people thoroughly convinced than with numbers who are ready to accept a conclusion to the strife by shutting their eyes to the danger of an offered compromise."

At a select, and in part devotional meeting at this crisis, my husband, who presided, spoke as follows :—

. "Our faith has lately been much tried. Public meetings were never more wanted than at the present moment. It is by such public meetings and by petitions that we should probably, with God's blessing, succeed in preventing the passing of any such measure as that which the Government has prepared, and which will be simply a second edition of the law which would be repealed, slightly amended in details, but identical in principle. Humanly speaking, such an agitation carried on during the next two months would win the day. But here the discouraging fact meets us—that there is not the same zeal which was manifested last year. Many of our workers have grown weary of the unpleasant work, and the materials for promoting public meetings are difficult to obtain.

"Some of us have been sustained in this period of difficulty by the thoughts suggested by the passage which I have read (Judges vii. 2-4). How often have the Lord's people had occasion to acknowledge, 'It is nothing with Thee to save by many or by a few.' If the means to our hands seem inadequate at present, let us pray for the faith of Gideon and his three hundred. Let us go forth with the sword of the Lord—which is His Word—and not be discouraged at the odds which are against us. There is need at the same time of exertion. For although we know that God can give us this victory by the efforts of comparatively few, yet we have great reason to desire that the heart of the whole people should be stirred as the heart of one man for this object—for the overthrow of an unjust law and for the purification of our country. Therefore let us ask of God to give us access by some means to the heart of the masses of the people in this matter, and to stir up a great multitude to take part in this work ; for depend upon it, it is good to bear a hand in the removal of an oppressive law. The conflict may be bitter, but the result will be glorious and the memory sweet."

The division among us did not continue long, and our ranks closed up again.

The Liberal Parliament having been dissolved in the spring of 1874, Mr. Stansfeld, now no longer a Cabinet Minister, felt himself free to advocate openly our cause, as he had privately served it while in the Cabinet. A large meeting was held in the autumn in the Colston Hall at Bristol, at which he made his first appearance publicly as a champion of our principles.

" This was, as you know " (I wrote to my husband), " Mr. Stansfeld's first appearance publicly in our ranks, and it was a striking and pathetic appearance. He had been alone in his room almost the whole day, and looked pale and nervous when he appeared on the platform. He passed on to me a little note, on which were several memoranda—among them this; 'I am so thankful for the womens' prayers.' The newspaper report gives but little idea of the effect of his manner. An old clergyman said to me, as we were leaving the hall, ' It was like a confession of faith. He seemed to invoke the presence of the Divine Being as he stood with his hands uplifted.' This is true. It was felt to be the utterance of feelings long pent up, and was like a trumpet-blast to call us afresh to the battle, as well as the key-note of the future—full of courage and confidence. Indeed, I could not help thinking of the confessors of other times who saw before them both the cross and the crown, the glad faces of fellow-Christians and the angry lions of the circus ready to tear them to pieces. Of course, he !has shut himself out from office for a long time, and checked the success of his worldly career by this action, and he knows it; but he has cast in his lot among us, and he will not draw back. Is it not a good thing that the conspiracy of silence in the London Press has at last suddenly broken down? We have been labouring now for over five years and have not got a paragraph into the London papers; but when an ex-Cabinet Minister speaks it is thought worth while to notice the fact. The *Saturday Review* and the *Pall Mall Gazette* are mad against Mr. Stansfeld. We were rather late in retiring that night at the Priestmans'. I could not sleep after five a.m., and got up and dressed, and crept out of the house. It was exquisitely sweet on the Downs: no one astir, and only a few sheep grazing among the withered bracken; a bright sunrise, and a sweet, sharp, frosty feeling in the air. Later in the day Charlie and I took a walk together on the Downs, and had a delightful *tête-à-tête*. The trees are changing colour and the woods are gorgeous. Then he had to go back to the college."

The " conspiracy of silence " in the Press was renewed a day later, and continued almost to the hour of our victory.

In the autumn of this year the Society of Friends, members of the National Association, and others, had subscribed money and given numerous introductions for the furtherance of a tentative mission to the Continent; and I started (accompanied by one of my sons) for Paris before the conclusion of the Liverpool College term, my husband and my other sons following a week later. Our design was to do some preliminary work in Paris, to interpose a few weeks of holiday during and after Christmas to be spent in visiting friends in the South of France, and afterwards to continue our mission in Italy and elsewhere in Southern Europe. In August of the same year

I had received a letter from a person whose face I had never seen, M. Aimé Humbert, of Neuchâtel, but to whom I had sent, as to many other persons on the Continent, a brief printed circular, inquiring concerning the state of public opinion in the different countries in relation to this subject. M. Humbert wrote:—

" I accept your communication as Providential. I recall the vows and resolutions I made many years ago as to the formation of an International League against the scourge of this governmentally-regulated evil. In my opinion, it is with much tact—I should even say, with a true divination of the mysterious depths of the question—that the English Abolitionists have decided to stretch forth their hands to those persons on the Continent who sympathise with their labours. England alone can take the initiative ; but remaining alone, she would not arrive at a successful issue. Now that she is able to give the signal, her appeal will be understood
The inclemency of the season,* the difficulties of your enterprise, the disappointments which await you—what subjects for intercession to Him who has inspired your work ! You are about to confront not only the snows of winter, but the ice which binds so many hearts. Bring among us, then, the fire of that faith which can remove mountains. The breath of the Most High can break the icebergs to pieces and kindle a mighty conflagration. May we see you here in Neuchâtel in the spring, and hear from your own mouth the record of the grace and power of God."

Knowing that we should at various points of our projected tour be separated for awhile from each other, my husband, on parting, fortified my spirit by selecting and reading to me some strengthening verses from the Psalms and other parts of the Bible. When I crossed the Channel I found he had placed in an inner fold of a note-book

* It was one of the coldest winters of the century.

which he had given me, a prayer, in an envelope, on which was written, " To my dear wife ; to be used when we are separated from each other." Among the petitions included were the following :—

" Thou, O God, art the God of all the families of the earth ; on Thee we depend for protection from all dangers, for preservation from all evil. We commend ourselves especially to Thy Fatherly care during our sojourning in foreign lands. Watch, we pray Thee, over every member of our family. When scattered, reunite us. When in trouble, comfort and relieve us. Lead us by the Holy Spirit, and keep us all in faith and in hope, in purity and in holiness, and in the exercise of love one towards another. . . . Enlarge our sympathies with all orders and degrees of men. Dispose those who are high in station and influence to receive us kindly for the sake of Jesus Christ. Give Thy blessing to the efforts that shall be made to reclaim souls from error, and to free the nations from the curse of sin, and from all cruel, immoral, and unjust laws. Bless the labours of all Thy servants for the establishment of the Kingdom of Christ on earth."

I had ten days of very arduous work in Paris. My husband wrote :—

" The weather in Paris seems to be as severe as in England, and I am glad you take a carriage to go about. I am glad also to think that you have one of our sons with you. Tell my dear Stanley to be sure to look out for the best works in the Galleries of the Louvre, a list of which I herewith send ; and tell him not to do as the Parisians do while in Paris, but to do as he has always done, and so make glad the heart of his father and mother. Be sure you see Lord Lyons, and present Lord Derby's letter to him."

In certain quarters I met with the most cynical opposition ; and on visiting the Prefecture of Police, the hospitals, and the great prison of St. Lazare, my heart was ready to faint within me as I marked the horrible development and influence of that institution which poor England in her folly had recently adopted. I was watched by the police, and my movements reported. Yet we had much ground for encouragement, in the fact that the best men and women in Paris from the first seconded our efforts, although they did not as yet see much hope of the success of our enterprise. We were very kindly received by M. Frederick Passy, a well-known worker in the cause of peace; by M. Jules Favre, the eloquent advocate and member of the National Assembly; by M. Jules Simon, Victor Hugo, the Baroness de Staël, and by the whole body of the Protestant pastors and Protestant society of Paris generally. Cardinal Manning, with whom we had corresponded, and who had written a letter to my husband the same winter to be publicly read at a meeting at Liverpool, had sent me a very warm and beautiful letter of recommendation to any and all the Catholic clergy of Europe with whom we might come in contact " This lady," he said, " has undertaken a difficult and a very needful mission. I beg you to give her such assistance and encouragement as you can in her work of charity, and to recommend her to persons who may have any influence in the matter of the reform which she seeks to promote. No Catholic who fears God can refuse to give his allegiance to the sacred cause which she has espoused." *

I have an agreeable recollection of an interview with M. Jules Favre in his own study. He spoke sadly and doubtfully of the probabilities of realising so great a

---

* I quote this letter from memory, having lost the original; but the above is almost exactly the text of it.

reform in his own country, but yet resolutely as to the necessity of taking immediate steps to create an improved public opinion on the subject; and expressed his full concurrence in our views of the absolute need of an equal moral standard for men and women, rich and poor. He admitted that he had little faith in Governments, adding, " It is impossible to exaggerate the corruption of moral and national life engendered and propagated by this system. It is utterly inexcusable and an act of supreme folly to give a legal sanction to the licentiousness of one portion of the community and to the consequent enslavement of another." He further suggested that Madame Jules Simon would be glad to arrange a conference on the subject. At this conference Madame Simon, though full of sympathy with our aims, said: " I think your mission will not have any success in France, because it is too high and holy to be understood here." Ten months later, however, the same lady wrote, after receiving a copy of initial addresses on the Continent published under the title of *A Voice in the Wilderness :* " You are not under any illusion, for your voice is indeed at present but a voice in the wilderness ; but be of good courage, for those who do not understand you to - day will understand you to - morrow." M. Jules Simon, who was then First Minister of the Government, wrote: " A few years ago I could have given you practical help, but now my public position and duties prevent that. I beg to offer you, however, my most sincere sympathy and earnest wishes for your success in the cause to which you are devoted. Let me indicate to you two of my friends who would be strong helpers, M. Schœlcher (Senator) and M. Edmond de Pressensé." It is needless to say that these two became firm friends of our cause.*

M. Louis Blanc wrote, as we were leaving Paris: " If I saw you I should have a great deal to say on the subject; as it is, I must conclude this letter, which is at once too long and too short, only begging you to believe that if I cannot help you practically, it is from no want of sympathy with your motives and objects, nor of respect for the cause the triumph of which I desire."

We then went on to the Riviera, and spent some time at the Cap d'Antibes with our friends, Mrs. Close and her family. The cold had been very severe in Paris, and the fogs almost as bad as in London. This had made the conflict with gigantic evil seem even harder than it would otherwise have been. As far as Marseilles there was snow and cold, and great blocks of ice were floating on the Rhone; but when we got beyond the Esterelles, we were in another climate, and the weather· at Antibes was lovely, like the sunny crisp weather of a fine September

---

* As a member of the Senate, when no direct agitation was going on in Paris, M. de Pressensé served the cause of morality—first, by his long and ultimately successful opposition to the abominations of St. Lazare; and later, by his attacks upon impure literature The conception M. de Pressensé formed of the mission of the State, the limits and the dignity of its position and duties, was very precise.

He gave his complete adhesion to our cause as early as 1871. He publicly repeated that adhesion in 1875, when members of the British branch visited Paris In 1877 he gave a splendid address at a meeting in the Rue Roquepine, where Dr. Gustave Monod presided. The *Bulletin Continental* calls this speech a magnificent profession of faith, to which M. de Pressensé was true all his life. He subsequently joined M. Fallot in the organisation of the French League of Morality. At our conference at Lausanne, in 1887, he appeared as the chief Parisian delegate. He was then suffering from the disease which proved the cause of his death. In spite of this affliction, however, his discourse in the Great Theatre was very powerful. He was a firm adherent of the principle of legal equality of the sexes, and it is to him they owe in France the adoption of the new divorce law, which places men and women on an equal footing.

or October in England. On Christmas Eve we had a memorable picnic with the Close family. We spent the whole day in the open air, sitting on banks of sweet myrtle, overlooking the wooded landscape and the sea. From Antibes we went to Genoa, to pay a short visit to our relations, and thence (parting with our sons, who returned to Antibes) my husband and I went on to Rome, Professor Stuart accompanying us. Our limited time allowed of my only paying a week's visit to my sister in Naples. Both there and in Rome we carried on as much as possible our propagandist work. While in Naples I heard daily from my husband, who remained in Rome.

"January 15th.

"James Stuart and I," he wrote, "have just been to the Capitol, and saw the great twin brethren, Castor and Pollux, holding in their horses. I especially admired the Dying Gladiator, the Amazons, and a Diana. We then visited the Farnasina, and saw Raphael's celebrated frescoes; after which we walked to the Villa Pampilli-Doria, which is, I suppose, the finest villa of the Roman nobles. The grounds are four miles round. Garibaldi occupied it, and held it for some time against the French, who were obliged to take it before they could do anything more. The views over the Campagna are very fine, and you see St. Peter's well from the terrace where we stood. There are the finest pine trees there that I have ever seen."

"January 16th.

"I was glad to hear of your safe arrival at Naples. The shortest line from you cheers me when it assures me of your well-being. We have been again to-day to see the Capitol sculptures, and the bronzes for the first time. There was the old wolf which Cicero speaks of. He says it was struck by lightning. Well, certainly, it has a rent in its hind leg; and Cicero and I have probably looked upon the same beast!

There is a very fine bronze head of Brutus. He looks an honest man. I think it must have cost him many a sad hour before he resolved to kill Cæsar. We saw also the doves of which Pliny speaks—four drinking at one fountain. We then went into the great church Ava-Coeli, which stands on the site of the old Temple of Jupiter. It is striking both from its vast size and its marble decorations. Outside we got a good view across the Forum, with the three arches of Septimus Severus, Titus, and Constantine in perspective, and the Colosseum on the left. After lunch we went to the Lateran. There I was struck with a very fine statue of Sophocles, found at Ostrea."

"Sunday, January 17th.

"We have had a pleasant day. Stuart and I went to St. Peter's at ten, and listened to a service, where several cardinals were present, besides a number of old ecclesiastics in fur tippets. The music was beautiful, the voices entirely those of men—no boys. One tenor who sang a solo not only had a fine voice, but sang with much expression. We then called on Madame Oscar Meuricoffre, who took us for a drive to the Villa Mario, whence there is such a beautiful view. We went round St. Peter's, and gradually ascended the hill. As we rose we saw more and more of Rome and the hills surrounding it. From the gardens of the Villa you have a perfect view, with grand trees in the foreground. Don't omit, if possible, driving up there when you come to Rome. The old ilex trees are very fine, and such umbrella pines and cypresses! Oscar and Madame were very kind, and we spent a most pleasant afternoon. From the top of the Villa the view was very extensive over the Campagna and the distant hills, and after yesterday's rain the atmosphere was very clear."

"January 18th.

"Last night I went to the Montgomery Stewarts', and had a good deal of talk with the old gentleman. He asked particularly about our special work, and seemed sympathetic. He told me that we must not expect much progress to be made in Rome; at least, through the present officials. Something may come of Garibaldi's visit here. *He* will not fear to speak out.

"This morning we went to several palaces, and saw some fine Titians and Rembrandts; most of all we liked a *hare*, by Albrecht Dürer. You never saw anything so natural. There pussy sits up, with her large eyes and furry coat; and there was a fly in the air and a grasshopper on the ground, painted like life. I sketched at the Palatine in the afternoon. The sky was cloudless, and the light on the Colosseum splendid."

To his son George :—

"January 19th.

"I had made up my mind to start this evening at 9.30; but not being quite well, I thought it better to wait till to-morrow. By this change of plan I shall go by a different route, and see the Lake Trasymene, where Hannibal caught the Romans napping. I shall pass also by Perugia, Arezzo, and other towns of interest at which I wish I had time to stop. Mamma is coming here next week. She has a petition to present to the Italian Parliament, praying them to abolish the evil system of regulation in Italy. I have finished a sketch of the Colosseum, which I hope to show you."

His time having come to return to England, he wrote to me from there :—

"I had the great pleasure of meeting our three dear sons at Macon on their way from Antibes. We travelled together to London without stopping. I find your letter here on my arrival, containing your loving welcome, with news of yourself. Our dear old dog met me at the door panting with joy. He did not apparently think it strange that his old master should come home after five weeks, but looked on it as quite the right thing. He jumped up and tried to lick my face and hands, and then ran madly round the garden, flying over the fence into the next garden, and driving our neighbour's cat up to the top of a tree in no time—and all to express his joy.

"I sincerely congratulate you on the good news which your last letter contains of your work in Naples and Rome. Never was there a more striking answer to prayer. No more gratifying proof could be given you that the Lord is with you. How dear Hatty will rejoice in the progress of the good cause."

In Milan I had a particularly encouraging conference, where some weighty citizens of that business capital of Italy were present. Resolutions were unanimously passed adhering to the cause advocated.

J. E. B. to G. B. :—

"Turin, January 29th.

"I am so happy, my dear husband, to receive your two letters this morning, as I was longing for news from home. I have looked in every London paper for some notice of the Liverpool meeting, but, alas! the papers seem to have again relapsed into their old silence. Never mind, the truth will prevail. I was much struck with the eloquence of the Italian speakers at Milan. They are very artistic in attitude and expression. Guiseppe Nathan's strong convictions and genius will ensure the progress of our cause in Italy. He was the moving spirit in all the work in Rome and Milan."

I went on to Switzerland.

From my husband :—

"February 9th.

"This has been a happy day to me, as it has brought me two letters from you. I have duly received and appreciated your letters from Switzerland, and sent them on to Hatty, marked 'Very precious; to be returned.' That dear sister writes full of love and gratitude for your visit to Naples, and she is good enough to extend her gratitude to me for letting you leave me when in Rome. It would have been very 'egoiste' if I had not done so. No doubt you find a difference in the climate of Naples and Switzerland. Keep well, and may God grant you great success in all your undertakings."

In February I visited Geneva, Lausanne, Berne, Neuchâtel, and La Chaud-de-Fonds, finding in each place a prompt and hearty recognition of the message which I brought, together with, of course, all the old and expected forms of opposition and resistance from another side.

To G. B. :—

"In the train from Berne to Lausanne,

"February 10th.

"We have come to *vingt-cinq minutes d'arrête* somewhere, so I shall write to you. I am in one of those large, roomy railway carriages, with chairs and tables and a fireplace piled up with logs. It is a very hard frost, with bright sunshine. The cold is excessive in the evenings and mornings, but they have a way of fencing it out with double windows and doors and heating apparatus. It is not often that one has an opportunity of seeing Switzerland in the depth of winter. The scene, as I drove down from the Jura with Madame Humbert in a sleigh, reminded me of a picture of a winter in Canada or bear hunting in Norway. Those enormous pines which you drew in summer looked very handsome with their heavy loads of newly-fallen snow. It was intensely silent, except for the jingling of our horses' bells and the swishing sound of the sleigh through the snow. We had an excellent meeting yesterday at Berne, at which there were many honest burghers, who at once formed a committee and passed resolutions in a manly way, gravely nodding their heads at each other."

From my husband :—

"Liverpool, February 12th.

"I received your letter, dated Chaud-de-Fonds on the Jura. I was glad to hear of your success among the Swiss industrial classes. I was very glad to hear in your former letter that you had seen so many of the Deputies at Rome. I have enjoyed Mr. Stansfeld's visit here very much. We had a very good conference in the afternoon at St. George's

Hall, and a successful meeting in the evening, at which Mr. Stansfeld made a most powerful speech. I spoke a little, and chiefly about the work in France and Italy. Bishop Alford, Dr. Taylor, and others spoke.

"I have heard from George, Stanley, and Charles since we all got to our respective destinations in England. You can imagine we were all in rather ' doleful dumps ' at parting at the end of these very happy holidays, but we agreed to ' keep our pecker up.' "

From J. E. B. :—
"Paris, February 12th.

"I arrived here this evening, and found your welcome letter awaiting me. Thank you for your constant letters. I hear Froude has come home from South Africa. I wish it might lie in his way to pay us a visit. How happy we shall be when we meet again! I am quite home-sick, especially in the evenings. My visits to these towns, however, I hope may have done good. I am astonished when I see how ripe the best part of society on the Continent is to shake off the hideous incubus which is now weighing it down. The work will be a long and difficult one; but I hear men daily now asserting that they have long felt the time was approaching when this iniquity must be openly attacked. How nobly dear little Switzerland has responded, has it not? My last meeting at Lausanne was excellent; I found so many of Hatty's nice friends there. M. Humbert of Neuchâtel is travelling all night to-night, and will be here to-morrow to help me these few last days in Paris. I have sent you a most excellent speech which he made at Neuchâtel. I have been to the British Embassy. I did not see Lord Lyons, for he had a number of people with him; but he sent a young man (Lord Lytton) to talk to me. He was very affable. Lord Lyons asked me, through him, if there was anything he could do for me, and I begged him to write me a permission to see the great Lourcine Hospital, which Lecour could not give me, as it is not a Government hospital. He gave it me most willingly, with the seal of the ambassador. I had a little talk with Lord Lytton and then withdrew. We had a good conference this evening. A good many gentlemen were there who wore the order of the Legion of Honour. M. de Pressensé threw himself warmly into the question, and proposed several practical steps. He spoke admirably. M. Appia, M. Lepoids, and others spoke, and all asked affectionately after you."

" February 17th, 1875.

" I have been to see the Princess Cariati, Hatty's friend. She is a Catholic. I had to drive a long way out of Paris to see the Abbé Rogerson, who seemed delighted to talk of Dilston and old times. He told me Cardinal Manning was in Paris. I therefore ran to his hotel, but did not find him. He had given me a letter to Père Petitôt, a great preacher in Paris. I missed him also. His courteous old servant seemed much to regret that I could not see his master. I then called on M. Le Caze, also a Catholic and a member of the National Assembly, who is associated with M. de Pressensé in a commission for reporting on the prison of St. Lazare. I found M. Le Caze a true gentleman of the old school, full of goodness. He reminded me of some of our old Northumbrian Roman Catholic gentlemen of the liberal type. I like what I have seen of the Paris working-men of the Faubourg St. Antoine and the Belle-Ville quarter. I am sure some of them are honest, home-loving men. How little understood by us in England was the meaning of that noble proclamation of the Commune which puts to shame the moral attitude of many other Governments.* Such an act, I think, should

---

* The following is an extract from the Decree of the Eleventh Arrondissement of the Commune, May, 1871 : "Considering that, even before the gigantic war undertaken by North America for the abolition of slavery, the traffic in slaves was forbidden, and slave merchants severely punished ; and that the suppression of standing armies, which came into force on the day when the Communal revolution arose, ought to carry with it the odious traffic of sellers of human beings ; that in principle we cannot admit the commercial *exploitation* of human beings by other human beings : be it enacted—Art. I. The so-called Tolerated Houses shall immediately be closed in the whole of the Eleventh District, and that seals shall be placed on the doors of these establishments."

'cover a multitude of sins.' I have seen something of the misery of this Paris in coming home late in the evenings, but I dare not write of it. How do people dare to say that London is worse? I know London also. Here the road to perdition is gilded, lighted, smoothly paved, artistic—a gentle slope down which a youth may slide easily without being suddenly checked by too much offence to good taste. His initiation is so cleverly conducted; he is let down so gaily and gracefully into the inferno that his senses are confused, and he has hardly time to draw his breath before he perceives himself in the midst of all the crowning abominations ever devised by human wickedness."

From my husband :—

" I have read M. Humbert's speech which you sent me with the greatest interest and admiration for the manly spirit in which it is written, and for the eloquence of one passage in particular, where he speaks of the lowering effects of a life of vice on a young man. I never read anything which moved me more."

In the spring of 1876 several of our adherents from the Continent visited London, with the intention of attending meetings which had been arranged. Among these persons were M. Aimé Humbert, M. de Pressensé, M. George Appia (a pastor of the Church of the Augsburg Confession), and Père Hyacinthe, who had pleaded ardently for our cause at Geneva.

M. de Pressensé made at one of our meetings a very eloquent speech on the duties and functions of the State in relation to morals, a speech which has been translated into several languages and widely circulated. He had a complete mastery of his subject. He spoke in French, and very rapidly, but was well interpreted. We were disappointed at not having the presence of Père Hyacinthe at this meeting, he having been taken ill soon after his arrival in London. He pledged himself, however, not to leave England without fulfilling his engagement. We had undertaken his travelling and other expenses, as indeed we were bound to do, from Geneva, and had arranged everything for him.

To my husband :—

"London, May 24th, 1876.

"Yesterday was occupied in an interesting, but rather anxious errand. You know that Père Hyacinthe had, during the last few days, in his own mind arranged that he would speak on our question in the midst of a series of conferences which have lately been arranged for him by a committee, of which Mr. Gladstone is a member. The conferences are to be on kindred subjects, religious and moral, one of these being the Old Catholic movement. He told me that the third of the series should be on 'public morality,' and that he would speak plainly for us, and thus secure that the upper-class people who desire to attend his lectures shall hear the truth of the matter. Though suffering, he asked to see me when I called at the house of Mr. Cowper-Temple, where he is staying. We had an interesting interview. He has, you know, the nature of a child—honest, simple, and disposed to believe everything that is said to him. He was exceedingly kind to me, and as full of sympathy with us and our trials in the work as he was in Geneva. He spoke of you with much affection. But in the course of our conversation I found that this simple man of genius had no idea that everyone in London society might not be willing to hear the truth, or be glad to hear him speak of our 'holy crusade,' as he calls it. I felt at once that the persons he so simply believed in would be much annoyed, and imagine that they were taken in by us, if they were not fully warned beforehand of Père Hyacinthe's intentions. I explained to him, therefore, how opposed the upper classes in general are to us. He then agreed with me that it would be better to have his intention plainly declared in advance, and begged me at once to speak to Mr. Gladstone. Unfortunately, the persons who have formed themselves into a sort of committee for arranging these conferences are almost all strongly adverse to us, and this did not promise well for any combination. Among them are Mr. Beresford Hope and Mr. Arthur Kinnaird. I then rose, and said farewell to the *père*, and set off for Mr. Gladstone's. I said to Père Hyacinthe at parting, ' We have still much to suffer in this cause ; ' and he replied, with tears in his eyes, ' Yet the truth is with us, and God is with us.'

" I had a few minutes private interview with Mr. Gladstone. I mentioned Père Hyacinthe's idea of introducing our question—of course, in a high, pure, and unobjectionable manner — into the series of conferences proposed. Mr. Gladstone seemed startled. I had well pondered what I should say to him ; and after he had expressed himself on the unsuitableness of such a proposed combination of subjects, I told him the whole situation. I said it was not we who were taking advantage of conferences called by him and others to introduce our question, and continued : ' Père Hyacinthe came to London at our invitation and our expense, expressly to speak for us, with prearrangement of nearly a year's date, it being his own strong desire to advocate our cause in London. The religious conferences are entirely an afterthought on the part of others. I have just seen Père Hyacinthe, and I find that his one anxiety is to be faithful to the cause for which he was brought to London— to keep its advocacy before him as his first duty, and only incidentally, if he seems to be called to it, to speak on other subjects.' Mr. Gladstone quickly perceived what the situation really was. He asked if M. de Pressensé had also come to speak on our subject. I replied that he had, and that he had already spoken magnificently.

" We had a little more conversation, of which I will tell you when I see you. I believe that God is the pilot of our ship, and that some good will result even from this short interview with Mr. Gladstone. He spoke, of course, as the politician merely, and I cannot see that he appreciates the vital nature of our question, although he said cordially, ' I shall vote on your side, and you know that I adhere to your principles.' He was, I fear, however, a little bothered at this contretemps about Hyacinthe, which is of their bringing about, not ours. Before leaving the room I said : ' I should like, Mr. Gladstone, to be allowed to repeat to you the solemn words which M. de Pressensé said the other day to Lord Shaftesbury.' He asked what were those words, and I repeated slowly (in French as they were spoken) Pressensé's words : ' Listen ! If you will not accept and aid this holy revolution, you will be forced to accept one day another revolution, a social and a destructive one, which will be the bankruptcy of society; for, I tell you, this thing against which we fight is the *typical crime of the universe,* and it is now *legalised* in the midst of you.'

" Mr. Gladstone looked earnestly at me with his wonderful, deep-set eyes as I said these words. He did not speak another word ; neither did I speak another word, and I left the room. I came down from his house to St. George Street, and summoned a committee to consider the whole matter. We agreed that we must recognise the situation, and have a meeting of our own, quite independent of the religious conferences."

To the same :—

" May 23rd.

"At a meeting we had yesterday an anonymous lady sent up to me a valuable diamond ring, with a note saying that it was to be sold for our mission, and that the giver considered such jewels as worthless compared with the jewel of national purity. Her example has been followed. To-day I have received from other people—an Indian gold chain, a pair of bracelets set with pearls, a pair of Indian gold ear-rings, a gold and amethyst brooch, and a diamond brooch. I went to an old jeweller in Vigo Street who values jewellery, and he will let me know the value of each article. I go on begging for money. It is hard work.

" I am sorry to miss our dear lilies-of-the-valley ; please

send me one in a letter. M. de Pressensé called on me again to-day. He is full of faith and kindness, and sends his affectionate regards to you. , This is Ascension Day. I think of the words, 'All power is given unto Me in heaven and in earth."

From my husband :—

" May 24th.

" I have read your letters with deep interest. I hope you will speed well in your mission, and collect at least £800 before you come home. I do not see how anyone can refuse an appeal made by you. There is an American letter come to-day; I think it is from H. J. Wilson and Mr. Gledstone.* I hope they give good news of their mission. I am glad to hear you have seen Mr. Gladstone. As for the other gentlemen you mention, there would have been no advantage in your calling on them. The London fashionable religious world are capable of very shabby things, but I hope they will not deprive us entirely of Père Hyacinthe's advocacy. I am getting on as well as I can without you. Thanks to our kind friends the Parkers, my evenings are generally very pleasantly spent."

* Early in this year Mr. H J. Wilson (now M P) and the Rev. J. P. Gledstone had been appointed as delegates to America at the request of leading friends in the United States, to make a tour of the principal cities there to explain matters, and to warn American citizens against the intro duction of the system we opposed. It had been already in existence in St. Louis, where it was strongly resisted. The mission of these two gentlemen was very fruitful, and to this day any attempt to introduce the system in any part of the United States has been either wholly unsuccessful or speedily counteracted. Messrs. Wilson and Gledstone spent some hours with my husband and me at Liverpool as they passed through, and were accompanied by many good wishes and prayers as they started on their voyage across the Atlantic.

CHAPTER XII.

CONTINUATION OF OUR WORK.—MEETINGS IN BERNE.—INTENSE
HEAT.—ST. BERNARD DOGS.—LETTERS TO MADAME MEURI-
COFFRE. — THE MUNICIPAL COUNCIL OF PARIS. — OUR
EVIDENCE BEFORE IT.—SUBSEQUENT PUBLIC MEETING.—
GEORGE BUTLER ATTACKED BY THE ENGLISH PRESS FOR
HIS ACTION IN PARIS.—HIS REPLY.—CORRESPONDENCE.—
M. YVES GUYOT SENT TO PRISON.—CONGRESS AT GENEVA,
1877.—SHORT TOUR IN PROVENCE WITH MY ELDEST SON.—
VISIT TO THE RIVIERA (1878), TO GENOA, TURIN, AND LA
TOUR.—THE PEOPLE OF THE PIEDMONTESE VALLEYS
INTERESTED IN OUR WORK.—ILLNESS AND RECOVERY.—
JOURNEY HOME.—A DAY AT FONTAINBLEAU.

NO formal arrangement had been made to hold
any meetings in Switzerland during the
summer of 1876, where my husband and I
went chiefly for rest and health. Guiseppe
Nathan, from Italy, was, however, passing
through, and many of our Swiss friends desired to use
the occasion for the advancement of our cause on both
sides of the Alps, and therefore arranged among others
some meetings at Berne. We had among our supporters
there the Federal Colonel, Otto von Büren, chief magis-
trate of Berne. He presided on the occasion of a Conference held in the Abbaye des Bouchers, an ancient
building of the old, picturesque style common in Berne.
At this meeting the question was considered of the great
International Congress to be held the following year in
Geneva. This necessitated much discussion, and the
formation of an international committee. The weather

was overpoweringly hot. The windows of the hall opened upon one of the roofed stone colonnades common in that city. The atmosphere was stifling. My husband was more than once obliged to give way to the influence of sleep, as indeed several others did. It was very characteristic of him—such a lover of dogs as he was—that he found the best means of keeping himself awake to be in watching the beautiful movements or the quiet slumbers of several of those large St. Bernard dogs which are used in Berne for drawing milk carts, and which having delivered the milk, were lying outside the windows, some attached to their carts, and others loosed to stretch their weary limbs on the pavement. My husband said afterwards : " I was so thankful to those dear dogs, for they enabled me to keep awake. Their wisdom and goodness are expressed in their every movement."

As frequently happened, he was obliged to return home rather suddendy for his duties at the college. I remained a little longer.

To Madame Meuricoffre from J. E. B. :—

"Berne, August 10th, 1876.

" Our meeting at the Abbaye des Bouchers was presided over by the Stadt President, Otto von Büren, who is a remarkably good man. He is the well-known Federal Colonel who was at the head of the military forces in Switzerland during the time of the Franco-German war, and who went to Strasburg, and led out all the women and children and old men from there, and brought them to Switzerland, placing them in different Swiss towns. He was like a father to them. He is a tall, soldierly man, with extremely simple manners. Our meeting was a very useful one. I think the Swiss—especially the Bernese—like dulness, and would probable consider a meeting a failure if they did not infuse an element of dulness and slowness into it ; this they are, however, generally successful in doing. But there is great reality among them, and not a word more said than is meant. Statements were made concerning the progress of our principles on the Continent; then George was called upon. I find that his short speech made a good impression, as he himself did, which is a source of great contentment to me. Many persons have spoken to me of him since, with much reverence and affection. He spoke clearly and well, with his characteristic moderation and gentleness. The people seemed impressed by what he said about women. He expressed beautifully the conviction that men should be ready, not only to hold women as their equals, but to let those of recognised experience and goodness be at times their guides in moral and spiritual matters; for if not, they were putting from them one of the best gifts of God, and the light which God had sent them—a light without which the great question of a purer national life would never be successfully solved. He said all this in his calm and gentle manner, his hand on my chair, and standing over me like a guardian angel. They saw in his face and manner a noble honesty and humility which does not particularly characterise men of the German race in their relations to women. Many of the ladies had tears in their eyes, and there was the faintest murmur of sympathy and approbation. The Swiss seldom applaud, or betray enthusiasm; they are a matter-of-fact people. Several bankers present engaged to help us in our preparations for the Congress at Geneva next year."

Madame Meuricoffre wrote :—

" There breathes no woman on earth who would miss her husband more were he taken first—not one who depends more upon him. Next to God he is the source of strength for good in you; you stand rooted in his calm faith, and deep quiet sympathy and approval. You are as one who would plant his feet firmly on a sure rock when about to throw out a rope to save drowning creatures in the turmoil of the waters. He stands out as such a dignified figure on the few public occasions on which I have had the happiness to see him and you together,—you two, so united that either of you would seem nothing without the other."

The following letters were not intended for any eye but that of the friend of my childhood, the sister to whom they were addressed. I quote them now, however, because they express exactly what I should wish to say to-day of him who was the companion of my life for forty years. Some of the words in them read like a prophecy—the fulfilment of which I now realise :—

"Berne, August 13th, 1876.

"Much business comes upon us now, after our pleasant excursions. I feel rather sleepy and stupified, so lately down from those blazing snows. George is soon leaving for Liverpool. I am sorry to lose him, the dearest, gentlest of men. One's heart so yearns for him when he is gone. It has answered well my going to him at Zermatt, for it has been such an increase of pleasure to him ; and in my heartpangs about his returning home alone I shall have a real consolation in recollecting that our last mountain days were spent together. * He asks so little and is so grateful for every good thing. I think he was touched by my jogging quite alone on my horse all the way from Sierre in the Rhone Valley to the Riffel, where I saw him sitting on the hillside. He had given up the thought of my coming, on account of the storms and damaged roads. He was sketching. I shall never forget his face of joy when he recognised me coming up through the woods. I thought he would have broken his neck, bounding over the rocks to meet me."

"August 14th, 1876.

"I got your last welcome letter at breakfast, and left the good Bernerhof tea untasted until I had read it through. I then showed George your kind words about him. His look

* We had been all together at Grindelwald, and my husband had gone to Zermatt with some of our party, walking over the Gemmi Pass to Leucherbad, and on from there. I joined him at Zermatt.

was tender and pleased when reading it. He never draws any praise on himself, nor seems to expect it; but a little affectionate praise is well bestowed on him, for he is so grateful. I feel ridiculously much this parting from him, and every parting from him; ridiculously I mean because it is only, please God, for a short time. But about him I have the yearning of heart which one feels over an infant or an aged person, or some other holy thing which one has to let go out of one's care and sight for a time. His presence is like wholesome air. People do not notice it much perhaps, but when it is withdrawn one stretches out ones hands wearily and painfully to try and grasp again that good thing which is gone. I often wish I could describe his character, just as it is, in a poem or a book. Anyone would rise from reading it with the prayer, ' May God send us many such men upon the earth!' It is so sweet to me that *you* appreciate him, and that your keen, loving insight makes you able to see the loveliness and nobleness of his character which few quite see, and that you can understand me when I speak of the love of which God alone knows the depth and the far-reaching tenderness—a love which grows and deepens with years. Except for the pain it would give to him, I always hope I may die first. For if he were to die and leave me, I do not say I could not live or work any more, but I fear I should fall into a state of chronic heartache and longing which would make me rather useless, and perhaps a weariness to others, who would *never 'fully understand what and who I had lost.* I do not often speak of him thus, but this once I cannot help it; your tender appreciation of him makes it impossible for me not to speak. . Last night we had a lovely sunset. We saw the rose-tints on the Eiger and Jungfrau from the balcony, and I thought of you, and wished I could fly over to Grindelwald and sit on the bench beside you, and watch it with you."

In January, 1877, a few of the prominent workers in the Abolitionist cause from different countries of Europe were formally invited by the Municipal Council of Paris to give evidence on the subject, at the Palais du Luxembourg. For some months previously M. Yves Guyot,[*] himself a member of the Municipal Council, had fought a hard battle for our principles in France. He had when quite a youth promised to himself, while he still lived in his father's home in Brittany, that he would, on coming to Paris, take up the cause of the white slaves of modern times. He has nobly fulfilled his promise. He gained many of the Municipal Council to his views. The first step towards the reform that was seen to be necessary was the appointment of a Commission of Inquiry. It was before this Commission that we were summoned to state our experience. Among those called were M. Aimé Humbert and M. Sautter de Blonay from Switzerland, M. Nicolet from Belgium, M. G. Nathan from Italy, and Mr. Stansfeld, Mr. Stuart, my husband and myself from England.

We were most cordially received by the Councillors in the fine old Palais du Luxembourg. All that we had to say was listened to with great interest and courtesy, and the interview was, unlike many of that kind, a really pleasant one. A great public meeting followed. It was held in the Salle des Ecoles, in the Rue d'Arras. Some of our party felt nervous as to how we foreigners might be received by such an audience, gathered in part from the quarters inhabited by the most radical of the population. My husband, an English clergyman, some thought, must find himself a little out of place there; but this was not at all the case. He acted and spoke, as at all other times, with characteristic dignity and straightforwardness; and that Parisian audience not only listened attentively to what he said, but appeared to be personally attracted

[*] Late Minister of Public Works.

towards him in no small degree. His appearance and character were afterwards described very sympathetically in some organs of the French press. His style of speaking, in brief and epigrammatic sentences, appeared also to suit the taste of the Parisian audience. One felt in that audience that any mistake, a word spoken which might excite or irritate, would act like a spark on a powder magazine. When much pleased with anything said, the crowd of blue blouses was on its feet in a moment, and the atmosphere seemed charged with electricity !

On our return to England a violent attack was made upon my husband in the press, chiefly by the *Standard* (London) and the *Mercury* (Liverpool). Very rarely did he think it worth while to notice or answer such attacks. On this occasion, however, as his relation to the College and to education was made prominent, he thought it right to reply, by publishing in English his address, and that of one or two others who were at this meeting, adding thereto a preface. In this preface, after speaking of the summons to the Municipal Council, and the evidence given before it, he said :

"On the following day, January 25th, the delegates were invited by members of the Municipal Council to attend a meeting in the Salle des Ecoles, a room belonging to the Council. M. Laurent Pichat, a late Senator, presided, and M. Yves Guyot, a member of the Municipal Council, supported us. It is not true, as has been said in one of the Liverpool journals, that Mrs. Butler and I were deceived as to the nature of the meeting to which we were invited. We were aware that the meeting would consist of Republicans. Indeed it might be expected that under a Republican Government a Republican audience would be found. Nor had the correspondent for the *Standard* of January 28th any ground for the severe, not to say slanderous, criticism passed upon Mrs.

Butler and myself. The *Standard* referred to me as a 'Liverpool schoolmaster.' My only motive for the republication of the address delivered at the Salle des Ecoles is to show those who are interested in the welfare of the schools over which I have the honour to preside that I have neither said nor done anything derogatory to the character of an English schoolmaster. The same views which I expressed to the large popular assembly on Thursday, January 25th, were put forward in a private re-union on Wednesday, the 24th, at the Hotel Wagram in the presence of M. Herisson, President of the Municipal Council, of M. de Pressensé and other members of the Protestant community, of the Abbé Croze and other distinguished Catholics. Those who have criticised my conduct upon the representations made by Paris correspondents of the English Press will do well to compare what has been alleged with what was really said. If they will do this I have sufficient confidence in the sense of justice and the moral discrimination of Englishmen to feel convinced that whatever opinion they may form of the methods of action which I and others have adopted in the interests of morality, they will allow that we have made a conscientious effort towards an end which all must consider desirable—the raising of the moral standard in England and in the civilised world. I have printed Mrs. Butler's address also with the English version, in order that readers may judge for themselves how far the remarks of the *Standard* and other journals are justified. Full reports of the other addresses have been given elsewhere. I am, however, the only one of the speakers to whom the title of 'A Liverpool schoolmaster' applies, and therefore having the moral supervision of some eight hundred boys and young men, I feel especially called upon to give evidence that when responding to the invitation of a Municipal Body in a neighbouring capital I have done nothing prejudicial to the cause of morals, and that of education in England. It is not those who point out the flaws in our social system, and endeavour to indicate the best methods of dealing with them, who deserve reproach, but those who wilfully shut their eyes to the evils around them, and assail with invective the pioneers ·

in the way towards moral purity, constitutional liberty and equal justice to men and women. Lastly, it is not by continuing to consign these great questions to obscurity and silence that we shall strengthen the youth of England to meet the temptations of the world, but by timely warnings and sympathetic advice, in which both parents and instructors should bear their part.

"Liverpool, Feb. 26th."

One of the newspapers which taunted us stated that the situation could not have been more comical if Monsignor Dupanloup, Archbishop of Orleans, had appeared at a meeting of Communists. Now it happened that this same Archbishop of Orleans had been in communication with us, and had sent a message of the warmest sympathy with ourselves and our work.

Very different from the strictures in the English Press were some of the testimonies which came from the other side of the Channel, as to the spirit and action of my husband in this matter. A knowledge of this criticism of him had reached some of our friends on the Continent, and we learned later that the following telegram (in French) had been sent to the Directors of the Liverpool College while we were away :—

"To the Directors of the Liverpool College.

"Gentlemen,—The action of Mr. and Madame Butler in Paris has contributed to redeem, in the eyes of France, the reputation of the English for moral nobility—a reputation which had been so terribly lowered for some years past by the conduct in France of young men connected with the English aristocracy. England ought to be grateful to Mr. and Madame Butler."

An English friend coming from Algeria to London was delayed for an hour on the Quai at Marseilles, and entered into conversation with some of the sailors there. A day or two previously the reports of the meeting at the Salle des Ecoles had been reproduced in several of the provincial journals of France. The conversation turned upon these reports, and the spokesman of the group said of my husband: "He is a good man; he loves the people."

My husband had quoted with effect at the popular meeting a saying of Voltaire:—

> " Si l'homme est creé libre, il doit se gouverner;
> Si l'homme a des tyrans, il les doit détrôner;
> On ne sait que trop ces tyrans sont les vices."

J. E. B. to Madame Meuricoffre:—

"George's speech was very good. It was touching and strange to me to look at his calm face as he stood and spoke words of gentle force to a great French Republican crowd. How wonderful are God's ways! How peaceful are all holy things, though they are often the *cause* of war! I send you several journals with reports. He has gone, and I feel rather desolate, but must continue the battle a few days longer."

I remained in Paris a few days after my husband's return to England, to attend some meetings of women. Meanwhile my husband was able, on the occasion of a holiday given at the college, to attend a large meeting of the North of England Council at Leeds.

He wrote:—

"February 3rd.

"I told the meeting at Leeds about the Municipal Council of Paris. This account was specially asked for. The meeting was unanimous and enthusiastic. I fancy the promised Revised Code in France will be a tremendous bit of hypocrisy. I am very sorry that the *Droits de l'Homme***** has been suppressed. It must be rather humiliating to Jules Simon, who has always been the advocate of a free Press, to

* A journal under the direction of M Yves Guyot.

be called on by his Chief to take this course. I wonder if M. Guyot has ever read Milton's *Areopagitica.*

" I have been reading the first chapter of de Pressensé's ' *Vie de Jesus,*' and I am charmed with the tone and style of his writing. I hope to see M. Theodore Monod's speech when it is printed. I feel, as you do, very great confidence in old Dr. Monod. We owe the staff of the *Droits de l'Homme* thanks for their personal devotion to our cause, and for their loyalty in all their dealings with us. I have had a hard morning's work: first, writing out a memorial for the Cambridge Syndicate concerning the B.A. examinations, and then writing an account of our visit to Paris, down to Friday, which occupied nearly ten foolscap pages. I was asked to write it for the *Medical Inquirer,* and have sent it to Dr. Carter."

After reading my husband's address, as printed, my sister, Madame Meuricoffre, wrote to him :—

" My dear George,—I have just been reading your speech at Paris, so logical, generous, and courteous. How wonderful all this Paris affair has been ! You seem to have been able to calm those wild spirits. God knows what He is doing, does He not ? And He knows how to manage even the Parisian police !—who seem to have left you at peace this time. I am so glad you were able to be at Paris ; it was such a precious support for Josephine. She feels so much strength and rest in your presence ; but it must have cost you something to leave her behind. If other people will not be husbands and wives in the future life I am sure you two will. All these generous sacrifices and separations will be rendered back to you in some delightful union, more than to other people. At first I felt troubled about her having to work among such wild fellows, who scoff at the Master whose love inspires her ; but I think God has taken account of the generosity which actuated these men, and has just sent you English over to them to give them for the first time an insight into a better way in moral matters."

. Writing to a son at Oxford, my husband said :—

"You will have heard of our great meeting in Paris. After the latter, Mr. Stansfeld and I dined with Lord Lyons at the Embassy, and reported to him that we had not been arrested, but had had a complete success. Our Gallic neighbours have really been most kind to us ; but when I thanked the Protestant community on Friday night for all they had done, M. Appia replied enthusiastically that it was they who had to thank us for coming to them." •

To Madame Meuricoffre :—

"I sent off to your address last night a copy of the *Témoinage*, with an article by M. George Appia, which will give you some idea of the effect produced on the Christian people of Paris by Josephine's appeals. Indeed she has been under special guidance both as to her sayings and doings, and has been protected from all annoyance. Even the Police have not meddled with her during this visit. Next to the hand of a kind Providence, which has been seen so signally in this movement, we have to recognise the friendly disposition of many French men and French women of all classes. If anything could recommend Christianity to unbelievers, I think it would be the generous efforts made by a Christian lady who has no personal wrongs of her own, who has a happy home, and is loved by all around her, and who nevertheless feels for and exerts herself on behalf of her suffering sisters in foreign lands. Thank you much for your sisterly affection and sympathy with both of us. It would indeed be a strange and monstrous thing if I did not show that I valued her, and did not try to do something for the cause which she has so deeply at heart."

J. E. B. to G. B. :—

Paris, February 7th.

"I have finished my work here. Your speech at the Salle des Ecoles reads beautifully. They say good will be done by its circulation. Read it and see how carefully our gentle interpreter has corrected any error which might have come into it. I am very, very tired, and long for home. Having been united once more in the war and work for God, may we one day be united in His eternal rest."

M. Yves Guyot was one of our first martyrs, as a result of his espousal of our cause in France. On the 3rd November, 1876, he published in his paper, the *Droits de l'Homme*, an article attacking the system of the *Police des Mœurs* which caused a very considerable stir, and M. Guyot was subsequently prosecuted by the Government for having published it. The prosecution was based on the ground that the statements named in the article were "false intelligence," and of a nature to "endanger the public peace." He was sentenced to six months' imprisonment, and to a fine of three thousand francs. By arrangement with the authorities M. Guyot was allowed to postpone his imprisonment, but the money fine was promptly paid, the three thousand francs having been with alacrity subscribed by friends of the movement in London, and forwarded to M. Guyot, who in a letter of grateful thinks said he accepted the money as a proof of the solidarity which ought to exist between all members of a party of progress, without distinction of frontier, language or nationality, in all matters wherein the cause of humanity was concerned.

The matter of the imprisonment was left in abeyance for some months, but in the April following the sentence, when it became known that some of the Progressive members of the Paris Municipal Council intended paying a visit to London on a mission of inquiry, and that M. Guyot was to be one of the delegation, the Prefect of Police suddenly found out that for M. Guyot to "remain any longer at large would be a grave peril," and consequently issued an order calling upon him to surrender himself. This M. Guyot did forthwith ; he served the six months in the prison of St. Pelagie, from and after April 27th, 1877. He suffered not a little, chiefly from rheumatism, the prison being damp, and he bore the traces of this in his altered appearance for some time after his release, when his first act was to renew his attacks on the abhorred system which was now beginning to be assailed in many parts of Europe.

The great event of 1877 in connection with the Abolitionist cause was the International Congress held at Geneva in September. Representatives attended that Congress from almost every country in Europe, as well as from America and other parts of the world. The great Hall of the Reformation was crowded day by day with a concourse of people deeply interested. Two large volumes were afterwards published of the proceedings of the Congress, and its resolutions were translated into several languages and widely circulated. This is not the place in which to recapitulate the details of that great gathering, which is now a matter of history. It became a starting point for a vastly enlarged movement. I left home a little before the date of the Congress and joined my sister, Madame Meuricoffre, at Lucerne, whence we went to Hospenthal, and, making a short tour, came down eventually by the Rhone Valley to Geneva, where my husband joined us. He had written to me from Liverpool :—

" I am not sorry to be left alone for a little while just now, as it gives me time for meditation, study, and prayer on subjects which we have strongly at heart, both of a public and private nature. Still it is a comfort for me to look forward to passing next Sunday with you and our sons at Geneva. The sight of Mont Blanc will be most re-freshing.

We had sent an invitation to my cousin, Mr. Charles Birrell, to come to the Congress. He wrote :—

" I deeply regret that I am bound to the conclusion that I cannot come. It would have been a great pleasure to have taken ever so small a part in the Congress. The movement seems to expand in compass and favour, and looks very much like a new chapter in the history of Christ's recovery of the world. I will stay at home and pray that you may both be kept in near and sensible fellowship with Him, so that you may have much peace and strength. I have a strong impression that as all things which have the nature of Christ in them are compacted together in a common life, the efforts for this common object will lead many who are in-accessible to direct instruction to know and love Him."

The Congress over, my husband was compelled as usual to return quickly to his work. It gave him great pleasure, he said, to receive news of a brief tour which my eldest son and I made immediately afterwards, in a part of Provençe which seemed at that time to be little known, there being no notice either in Murray's or Baedeker's Guides, of most of the places which we visited.

We started for Grenoble.

From J. E. B. to G. B. :—

" Though we have not been long apart I must write you a letter of welcome to await you at Liverpool. The wind howled terribly on the night you were to cross the Channel, but I trust that you had a safe journey home.

" This place (Grenoble) is much warmer than Geneva. Orange trees grow in the streets, with ripening oranges upon them. It is a strongly fortified town. You may remember that Turner has some sketches of it in his *Liber Studiorum*.

It is on the river Isère; and is surrounded by mountains. It was the first city that received Napoleon after his return from Elba. Like other parts of France, it is now suffering under the blight of threatened force, and half strangled by the petty tyranny of McMahon. There are soldiers strutting about the streets to warn the people that they must all vote as the Dictator requires."

" From Grenoble we visited the Monastery of La Grande Chartreuse, which we reached by a picturesque mountain defile. We passed the *fabrique* where the famous liqueur is made. Several of the monks engaged in the manufacture were packing and carrying it away. They dress in white, with sandals, and a cord round their waist. They seem sharp-looking fellows, with bright eyes. The part of the pass which is called the Gates of the Wilderness is very fine. Our little carriage wound up slowly. By-and-by we reached the Wilderness where the monastery stands. It is no desert, however, in appearance. There are rich hanging woods, over which appear the pale grey granite or limestone mountain tops. It is a strange place, so silent, and far from the world. The monastery was founded by St. Bruno, and St. Bernard of Clairvaux retired here for study. It resembles a fine, large college, solid and picturesque, surrounded by high walls. The 'fathers' who live in it are of a very stern order. Like the *Trappistes*, they observe almost perpetual silence, each one living apart in his own dismal cell. Everything possible is done to shut out Nature and all its beauties, as well as humanity, and to remind the inmates only of sin, death, and purgatory. The impression left on the mind is more than painful—it is ghastly ! One is full of pity for the poor men who are so mistaken in their ideas of what is pleasing to God as to live such a fruitless life, or rather, a death in life. They are chiefly men of high families who retire here, and pay handsomely to the monastery. George wished to see the inside. We were of course separated then, as no woman is allowed to enter. He rang a bell at a strong, orbidding-looking gate, which slowly opened as if by an invisible hand (no one being seen), and closed again, swal- lowing up my son, and leaving me in solitude. I sat on a piece of rock and watched the scene around. The air was sweet with the scent of mountain flowers. I do not know if those high, solitary woods are haunted, but now and again there seemed to come a wailing sound of pathetic music down upon me from the wooded heights in the midst of the deep silence. At last George emerged from the melancholy place, and it was pleasant to drive quickly down the pass again in the beautiful light of the setting sun."

From here we went by rail to Pierre Latte Station, and then plunged into secluded country. We went to Valreas, Nyons, and other scantily-inhabited villages in this beautiful part of Provençe, walking a good deal, and being picked up sometimes by some modest cart or old tumble-down coach, which gave us a lift along the road. There are many ruined villages where formerly the persecuted Huguenots took refuge. Some of them are now absolutely without human life, and generally placed on the tops of little hills, white and bleached in the sun, reminding me in appearance of pictures I have seen of ruined villages in Palestine.

" Valreas, October, 1877.

" This country would delight you. It is not grand like Switzerland, but it is picturesque in the highest degree. The colouring is quite ravishing, especially in autumn, as now, and the sunlight brilliant and clear. The people are very primitive, and we pay almost nothing for our modest shelter and food in the curious old inns, which are sometimes ancient castles, half in ruins. The lower hills are covered with a short growth of sweet lavender, wild sage, and many aromatic plants which scent the air delightfully. There are no fences to the vineyards, and the purple grapes are now all fully ripe, and the vintage beginning. There are immense bunches of ripe grapes hanging over the road. I have sometimes gathered a bunch, shaken the dust off, and eaten the grapes as I walked. There seems to be no objection made to this. They are of very fine flavour. One sees them scattered about out of the wagons and baskets of the grape-gatherers, just as hay is out of the carts at home. The Provençal language spoken here is soft and musical."

In January, 1878, having been advised to try to escape the cold of the winter, I went with my husband to Cannes, where we spent together two or three weeks, again visiting, from there, Closebrook at the Cap d'Antibes the beautiful home of the Close family. Our eldest son joined us here for a few days, on his way to England from Naples. He was studying the subject of volcanoes, and while staying with the Meuricoffres had made a solitary ascent of Vesuvius for purposes of observation. The following year he visited the volcanic districts of the Eifel in Germany, and of the Auvergne in France. His letters from these places to his father were to the latter a great interest geographically and personally.

My husband and son having returned to England, I was left alone for a time, and made a solitary, slow little journey along the coast from Antibes to Genoa, stopping a day or two at Nice, Mentone, and other places. I had a sketch book with me, and the weather being very fine I spent a good deal of every day in the open air.

I reached Genoa at a time when almost the whole of Italy was visited by an extraordinary drought, followed naturally by fever and other evils. I stayed with my niece, Madame Leupold, at Sestri near Genoa. Night after night, unable to sleep, I used to step out of my bedroom door upon the marble terrace to search all over the relentless sky in the hope that some little cloud might be seen ; but the air was always the same—dry and oppressive, and the sky cloudless. It was curious to observe how many other people of the villas scattered around were doing the same thing, seeking a breath of air in the middle of the night on their housetops and terraces, and hopelessly looking out for signs of rain. Almost all the springs and streams in the neighbourhood were dried up, and every day we heard of poor workmen at the docks and on the shore, fainting and being carried to hospitals.

I fell ill, and the Genoese doctor believing it would be difficult for me to recover in that climate, advised immediate removal if it were possible. My kind friends lifted me into a carriage, and from that into the train at San Pier d'Areno, whence my niece accompanied me to Turin.

To my sons at home :—

" I am grieved to think how many of my dear people I have made anxious by falling ill. The drought was extraordinary, and malarial fever prevalent. For several days before I was obliged to go to bed I had to fight with a curious oppression of mind. Little Marie used to get me out into the Parodi Gardens, and did all she could to cheer me, and I tried to respond, but the oppression continued. I held out as long as I could, for I had determined to come home well and strong ; but at last there came on a burning pain in my temples, and fever which lasted many days and nights. Edith is a perfect nurse ; she sat up with me night after night. I do not know how I can ever repay her. Ludwig was also most kind. The doctor sent me away. Edith left Catarina with me at Turin, and I had everything I required. Unluckily, at Turin I became worse instead of better, and next day could not even ask for what I required. Catarina ran for a doctor. It was two hours before he came. She was not very useful, for she only sat down on the floor and wept."

My illness was so serious that they telegraphed to my husband, who was then paying a visit to Professor Stuart at Cambridge. The message reached him late in the evening after a very pleasant party which Mr. Stuart had given in honour of Mr. Welsh, the American Minister, and at which were present Professors Cayley and Adams. My husband lost no time in coming to me. I recovered sufficiently to be taken in a short time to Pinerolo, from there to Torre Pellice, and thence to La Tour in the Waldensian valleys. The change was delightful.

To my sons :—

March, 1878.

" Edith met father at the station at Turin to revive his courage. He was not the worse for his long journey, and kind James Stuart had insisted on accompanying him. I must tell you about Torre Pellice. It was the cradle of the Waldensian Church, whose history, you know, is a romantic one. The Italian people of the reformed faith took refuge in these valleys, on the eastern side of that spur of the Alps, as the Huguenots did in the valleys where stand Nyons and Remuzat on the western side, where George and I were last autumn. They were a numerous sect, and fought well and died hard for liberty of conscience, until the dragonnades of Louis XIV. reduced them to less than one-third of their original number. It is a healthy and attractive place. If you look on the map you will see Pinerolo on the one side, and Sisteron on the other side of the spur of the Maritime Alps running down to Grasse and Antibes. There is only a rocky pass between the two for foot-passengers. The most striking object from the heights here is Monte Viso, which is very prominent and white. Father and Mr. Stuart took long walks, and were delighted with the views and fine air. I stayed at a little pension kept by a friend of Edith's, a Madame Canton-Durand, the widow of a Swiss pastor. I was much pleased to find myself in a clean Swiss room, with a wooden floor and no carpets, and the bright sunshine pouring in. When about to leave the place we asked Madame Canton-Durand for her account. She said in a very decided tone, that she had no account, and would not accept anything. She added that the Waldensians owed so great a debt of gratitude to Cromwell that she could not think of charging us anything. I reminded her how much trouble I had given, and said I was not responsible for gathering in debts due to Cromwell. She did not reply, but waved her hand and left the room. They have strong traditions of hospitality in these valleys. Father and Mr. Stuart stayed at a little hotel near, but were constantly at Madame Durand's during the day, and she insisted on having several little dinner parties for them. She told father that many people had been calling, asking for information about our work and mission on the Continent (this valley had sent a delegate to the Geneva Congress), so we sought out all the French and Italian papers we had and distributed them. Some of those who came to inquire had walked long distances over the hills. They one and all said that the Church of the Valleys much needed stirring up; that like other churches it had become formal and sleepy, since the days of persecution ended, and that if the valleys could only become *enthousiasmé* with the love of a great cause it would be good for them. So true it is that spiritual life can hardly be kept up in the churches except on condition of constant actual conflict with external evils. They said that if we had remained longer they would have had great meetings among the workers in the silk and cotton *fabriques*. At their first little dinner party Madame Durand had invited to meet them a venerable gentleman, M. Charbonnier, the Moderator of the Church of the Valleys, who looked like an old Covenantor,—a strong man. He was of an old Italian family, who were driven to the valleys by the persecutions, and who finding a little vein of coal, worked it, and sold the coal to the poor refugees to make a living. This got them the name of Charbonnier. Many families changed their names at that time.

"The next day Madame Durand invited the two M——s and an old Professor of the College who is learned and humorous. I heard from the open window of my room after dinner, a loud, shouted conversation between the two M——s (father and son), and perceived that it was concerning our work, which had been explained to them over their wine and dessert. I do not for a moment mean that the M——s were the worse for wine !—but the son was rather crude and opinionated, and the father put him down with vehemence. The son soon saw he had better hold his peace. The old Professor struck the table with his fist in his ardour, till the glasses rang again, saying : ' The valleys must take part in this holy war ! ' ' But what can we do ? ' said M——, junior. ' Do ? ' said the old Professor. ' We can all help to do the most simple work of all ; that is, to root up the old, false traditions ! ' M. Pons and some others came next day. Nothing could exceed the kindness of these people. A man who had driven us up in a two-horse carriage from Pinerolo, about ten miles, disappeared, and never could be found to be paid. It seemed that he had received a hint not to ask for anything. We certainly must have these Waldensians for our allies.

"Father is such a kind nurse. His trusting heart and calmness make it delightful to have him near one when there is any real trouble. He is never excited and never exaggerates, and is always full of thankfulness to God for every improvement and any relief."

We travelled slowly homewards, stopping for rest a day at Aix, another at Fontainbleau, and again at Amiens, Professor Stuart having returned to Cambridge without pause by the way

From G. B. to his son Stanley :—

"Amiens.

" I wished for you at Fontainbleau. You have no idea what a nice place it is—planted in the midst of a great forest. The Château is one of the finest in France. Our hotel looked upon the court where ' Les Adieux ' took place.

I saw Napoleon's bath-rooms, and the table where he signed his abdication ; 'a very *ornary* table, with no *pints* about it,' as Mark Twain would say. The rooms are large, numerous, and splendidly furnished. The clocks are kept going, and everything in readiness for a new King or Emperor ! The paths and glades in the forest seem most delightful, and would tempt one to walk on, making fresh discoveries all day."

CHAPTER XIII.

VISIT TO THE EIFEL DISTRICT IN GERMANY. — TO TRÈVES, ELZ, AND THE VOSGES.—CONFERENCE AT LIÉGE.—CARDINAL MANNING.—THE CATHOLIC PRESS ON OUR WORK.—DEPUTATIONS TO CANDIDATES FOR PARLIAMENT.—CONGRESS AT GENOA.—ITALIAN WORKING MEN'S SOCIETIES.—VISIT TO GARIBALDI.—SPIRITUAL CONFLICT.—A CLOUDED SKY.—FIRMNESS OF CHARACTER AND OF FAITH IN MY LIPE'S COMPANION.—STRONG HELP GIVEN IN TIME OF NEED.—A SUNDAY MORNING'S INCIDENT IN WINCHESTER CATHEDRAL; AN ALLEGORY.

 N the following year (1879) we had an interesting tour in a part of Germany and Alsace-Lorraine, most of which was new to us. We went by the Rhine to Bonn, where our son Charles was then residing. My husband called on one or two of the Professors of the University whom he had known many years before; with Professor Bernays he renewed many old associations. We also saw Professor Christlieb, a good and learned man.

To my sisters :—

"July, 1879.

"From Bonn we went to Coblenz, whence we made an excursion up the valley of the Ahr to Ahrweiler and Altenahr.

"We then made a push to visit the Laacher See, which we had long wished to see. Charles came with us (from Bonn), walking almost everywhere, while we drove. This lake is supposed by Humboldt and other geologists to have been the centre of the volcanic action of the Eifel country, and we had heard of its beauty. We went by train to the foot of the ascent, and thence by another little train, which

crawled at the rate of four miles an hour, uphill to Nieder-
mendig. The land here lies high, and the air was most fresh
and healthy. We found an old open carriage, and drove in
it from there to the lake, some four miles further, with a pair
of loosely-made but active and willing horses, tied with ropes
to the carriage. We passed under some volcanic-looking
hills, one of which has two craters at the top, and an old,
wide lava bed down its side. The Laacher See is about two
miles wide, a completely round basin of lovely turquoise
colour, and of a great depth for its size. They say the lake
was not itself a crater, but must have been formed by
volcanic action. There is a jet of carbonic acid gas coming
out of the ground at a spot near it, showing some infernal
process going on below. We reached the top of the hill,
whence we saw the blue lake lying below us, surrounded,
much like a Roman amphitheatre, with a great gallery of
woods; low wooded hills and trees rising all round it, except
on one side, where in a level spot stands the beautiful old
Abbey of Santa Maria Laach, and a newly-built, simple
hotel, scarcely yet known by English travellers. It is a most
secluded place—no dwellings in sight : it has a monotonous,
peaceful beauty, with low sounds as of whisperings coming
round mysteriously; for the wooded amphitheatre is like a
whispering gallery, and you hear echoes of forest voices in
your ears from the other side.

" Opposite the hotel, across the lake, is a deserted convent
or college, built by the Jesuits for retirement and study ; but
now, since the Emperor drove out the Jesuits from Germany,
it is, like many other abbeys and monasteries, forsaken and
empty. They say the Government is about to turn this
Jesuit College into barracks or a beer brewery! My husband
went at once to sketch the Abbey. He found it inside a fine
Gothic building. This abbey is also quite deserted, and some
of the Protestant German soldiers seem to have painted the
handsome Gothic pillars with gaudy stripes and epaulets, to
imitate a hussar's uniform. There were smudges also over
some of the pictures of the saints. The acoustics of the
building are wonderful. If you speak or sing you hear, as it

22 *.

were, angels in the roof echoing it all back in soft, distant tones. Then we came back and sat on a stone balcony of the hotel, overlooking the lake, drinking our coffee. For the first time since we left home we had a perfectly calm, sunny evening, and we enjoyed it thankfully.

" This abbey was inhabited, not by Jesuits, but by Benedictines, who were good engineers, for in the 12th century heavy rains deluged the lake and threatened to undermine the monastery, and they made a sluice with pipes from the lake to the little river Nette, which since then has always carried off the superfluous water from the lake; there is no river running from the lake. All round are beds of lava, tufa, and basalt. The tufa is dug out in squares, and much of it is sent to Holland; it hardens under water, so that it is much used in making dykes. Bonn Cathedral is partly built of it."

" July 16.

" We have come on to Metz. My husband has gone out to look over the melancholy battle-fields of the Franco-German war, until our evening train starts for Nancy. I must tell you of our visit to Moselkirn, a place about half-way between Coblenz and Trèves. We could not go up the Moselle by steamer, as I had so much wished, for they only go three times a week, and we should have had to wait. The rains have been so heavy that the ' blue Moselle ' was of a deep brown, and overflowing its banks. At the little station of Moselkirn we asked a man to show us the hotel of the place. He took us to a very dirty village, consisting of one long, narrow street, where we plunged through mud to the tops of our boots, to a miserable tavern. He pushed open the door. It was dark, dirty, full of tobacco smoke and of men in a state of semi-intoxication, shouting and singing. We asked if we could have a room. They took us up a sort of little hen-ladder, which they called stairs, to a dark, low-roofed room, in which were two little straw mattresses in a corner. I never slept on anything so hard in my life. They were simply coarse sacks filled with straw, and flung on the top of the stone floor. However we made the best of it, and managed to laugh at everything.

" In the morning we were told that the famous Castle Schloss-Elz, which we wished to visit, was three miles off, and almost inaccessible from Moselkirn. For a wonder, the sun shone that morning beautifully. Oh, blessed sun ! what a new world it seemed, and what hope and life came back to me when he showed his face again ! Determined to see the castle, my husband got a man who had an ox-waggon, and hired him to take us to it. The only road by which the waggon could go was by the bed of the river Elz, which flows into the Moselle. It was a curious new experience for me in travelling. The waggon was one of those which no doubt you will remember, drawn by oxen, and made simply of two trunks of trees, with rough wooden ladders placed at the sides, looking like a trough or hayrack. They put a sack with some straw for me to sit upon. The jolting you can hardly imagine. We were often obliged to hold on hard by the sides in order not to be pitched out. But the drive was curiously beautiful. The little Elz, which in hot summer weather is nearly dry, was unusually full from the heavy rains. The sun shone gloriously on the water, through the wild, uncultivated woods, which sometimes arched over it so low that we had to stoop down in the cart to avoid the branches. There were beautiful shadows and lights, dancing and gleaming and changing upon the water, through the leafy roof overhead. Every now and then a sky-blue king-fisher would dart from its nest, startled by our noisy intrusion and by the water splashing right and left from the wheels of our cart, and would flit across and across the river before us, as if to ascertain what business we had there ; and the trout wagged their tails and scuttled out of our watery path, while green and blue dragon-flies chased each other before us.

" Now and then we left the river and crossed a little meadow, shut in all round, like the Valley of Racelas at Dilston, with high wooded banks, silent and secluded, and carpeted with a mass of brilliant flowers, purple and blue and

pink. Then down again we went towards the stream at a horrible trot, jolting over the rocky shingle and into the river again with a plunge. Then again we would come out upon a dry terrace of rock and small boulders, over which the jolting was worse than ever ; it was too wet under foot for me to get out and walk, though we did so whenever we could. Then back again into the river, and the driver would wait on the edge till we scrambled into the waggon again, which my husband sometimes did so recklessly that he found his heels higher than his head ! But he had no time to re-arrange himself before our driver, uttering an emphatic '*so*,' would plunge us into the middle of the stream again with a bubbling, gushing sound, alarming more kingfishers and trout.

"At last we stopped at the foot of a great strong rock and alighted, leaving our waggon below. We were well rewarded when we got up to the castle, for it is indeed a wonderful place, so unlike anything modern, and like a dream of the middle ages. It stands alone on its rock, its bastions rising up like a continuation of the rock, crowned with a number of picturesque, irregular, mediæval roofs and towers, other towers stuck on to the walls, and latticed windows high up in little lantern towers built on to the larger towers ; and there are so many of these that it is like a little village rather than a single castle. And though it is so ancient and weather-beaten, and in some places ruinous, yet it has a strong charm in the fact of its being still the home of the descendants of the great family of Elz. In those latticed windows there were glimpses of crimson velvet cushions and fluttering white muslin curtains, and there were tame white doves and pigeons, which looked like pets, fed by a lady's hand. The rock on which the castle stands slopes steeply down on all sides, except where there is a road leading over a stone bridge to the great gateway. The Elz runs murmuring round the foot of the rock ; and all round the outside of the river is an amphitheatre of high woods—woods upon woods, nothing but woods,—no view beyond, no dwelling-house in sight, so that the castle is in fact completely hidden until you come suddenly upon it from the woods. And then it bursts upon you as a surprise, standing up, ancient, tall, and strong, in its melancholy and secluded grandeur. In the brilliant sunshine it looked most beautiful, but it must be a sad place to live in.

"My husband took his seat on the road leading to the gates to make a sketch, and I wandered up to the castle, and through a sort of stone gallery, which led me to an inner court open to the sky. Then I came to another gate leading to the castle. I was looking about me in this silence like death when I heard the step of a man come to the door, which opened at the same time. A tall gentleman came out, dressed in Lincoln green, with high Hessian boots, and several decorations—quite an old-fashioned dress;—and his face and head also had a mediæval look. He resembled a picture by Rembrandt; a thin, weather-beaten, but refined face, high forehead, and long red beard. He did not look at me, but gave to the man, who bowed low, an immense bunch of keys on a great iron ring, each key about six inches long. Then he closed the door and disappeared. I returned to where George was sitting, and throwing a rug on the road I sat down and fell fast asleep. When I awoke it was with a bewildered feeling, scarcely knowing where I was. I seemed to have been hearing forest-talk all around me in my dreams; voices seemed to echo from one wood back to another. There seemed no life left at all, either inside or outside the castle, after the gigantic keys had been given to the custodian.

"I walked up again to the castle gate, and saw an apparition standing just above me on the rock; the largest and blackest pointer I ever saw,—a lovely beast, black as night, and shining like satin. He bayed and barked at me most furiously, that being the duty which had been taught him—to defend the castle. I don't like angry dogs, but I flattered him in a kindly voice, and happening to have a bit of bread in my pocket which I had reserved for my own lunch, I broke some off and offered it to him. He was young, foolish, and amiable, so he forgot about defending the castle and accepted the bread, and we quickly became great friends. I gave him more bread, and he said all sorts of polite things to me; and when I sat down on the stone steps he sat at my feet, his back to me and his face to the world; every now and then looking round with an amiable smile, which seemed to say: 'Now you belong to the castle, what can I do to prove my loyalty to you?' Suddenly a bright idea flashed across him, as he caught sight of my husband's sketching umbrella, and himself sitting under it, some way off. I heard angry distant thunder in his chest, and then he seemed to say to himself: 'Oh, I will show my loyalty by attacking this intruder; I will defend you from this man.' He looked up into my face with a knowing, affectionate expression, and then darted off, barking vigorously to warn the stranger off the premises. I watched him going nearer and nearer, his bark becoming fiercer and fiercer, till at length he stopped, with the stiff-legged look of a defiant dog, and I could see that my husband was coaxing him with the same result as myself, for the good-natured creature presently began to wag his tail and say polite things. Then he ran back to me with a look as if he would say, 'The man will not hurt you, he is a harmless person;' and again he sat down at my feet, his back to me and his face to the world. This dog would get a prize anywhere; his gums and the roof of his mouth were as black as the rest of him, and not a spot of tawny or white anywhere. He had blue eyes, and was really a great beauty.

" We started again on the river drive home, and I began to suffer a good deal from the jolting and the fatigue. We nevertheless, after some refreshment, took the four o'clock train to Trèves. It was still fine, and by keeping a good look-out all the way we saw much of the beauty of the winding river and its banks, with the bright towns and villages at intervals. We have now followed the Moselle from its junction with the Rhine up to its cradle, which is in one of the Vosges valleys. We went by the side of it all the way to Metz and Nancy, and then up to Bruyères, where it is quite infantine.

" We were delighted with Trèves. The interest of it as a 'little Rome' is very great. The first morning we visited the old Roman amphitheatre, some little way out of the city. My husband, you know, had been at Trèves many years before, and could tell me everything concerning its ancient history. The theatre is immense; we drove into the middle of it. We tried to imagine what it would be to be a solitary martyr standing there, with a vast multitude sitting around. The circle of seats round held fifty-three thousand spectators, about double the present population of Trèves. All round those galleries there are now only grass and sweet wild flowers —blue-bells nodding their innocent heads where once the cruel audience turned down their fifty-three thousand thumbs as a signal that the poor gladiator or martyr was to receive his death-blow, while they shouted their applause. All round, at intervals lower down, are the mouths of the caves or cellars where the wild beasts were kept to fight with men and tear in pieces the Christians. There were subterranean passages for the beasts and victims to be brought up by, as in the Colosseum at Rome.

"We then went to the Roman baths, which, to my mind, are much the most picturesque of the Roman ruins of that kind which I have ever seen ; much more so than the baths of Caracalla, at Rome. The bricks at Trèves are of such a lovely colour—not brick-colour, but crimson and rose,—and fitted in so prettily round the arches, mixed with other material, and now partly overgrown with flowers and wild ferns; so you may think how picturesque they look. Here and there is a prostrate column of white marble, or a portion of a brick arch just appearing above the ground, around which have been carefully planted and trained cluster roses. The ruins are lofty, rising up like a great cathedral. What fellows these Romans were for washing! There are the ruins of old terraces and rooms, and a whole system for heating water; a great furnace, and brickwork conduits to convey the water from it all over the place. You may remember my husband's drawing of these baths at home, which he made thirty-three years ago.

"We next visited the Church of St. Paulinus. The only thing that interested us much was, that in the crypt, into which we were taken, were placed some ancient sarcophagi of granite and marble, not very long ago discovered; and in them lay the bones of six noble Senators of Trèves, who all died for their faith. The provincial Governor of Trèves was formerly the greatest potentate among all the provincial Roman Governors. There was no history of these Senators, nor could the custodian tell us anything about them. We felt attracted by their silent witness. There was exactly the same inscription on each, in Latin, as follows:

Alexander,	Rufus,	Felix,
Senator of Trèves,	Senator of Trèves,	Senator of Trèves,
Martyr.	Martyr.	Martyr.

And so on through the six. We wondered about them all day. Their memory seemed to connect so closely the Roman and Christian memorials of Trèves, and to show how the Christian faith had penetrated that solid mass of heathenism. exciting deadly hatred and persecution, but at last triumphing,

"On our last day we spent part of the forenoon in the ancient Library—a curious place. In some things, certain functionaries resemble each other very much in all parts of the world. The Librarian was a dignified old scholar, who spoke perfectly English, German, and French, as well as Latin; and said he would very much like to see Oxford and the Bodleian Library some day, but he was too busy to travel. His ways, the look of the Library, and his politeness in getting one books, all reminded us of old Oxford days. My husband told him we were anxious to know about the six Senators, martyrs, and he immediately delved away among the oldest and mustiest books you ever saw, with the dust of centuries upon them. He brought us several, laying them out on the desks before us. He is a true gentleman, and seemed really interested in our research. We learned that they were martyred in the reign of Diocletian. He had given over the government of Gaul entirely to his old friend and schoolfellow, Maximian. The latter was a brutal man, a Croat by birth, gigantic of stature, with flaming red hair and beard, and a coarse, cruel nature. These Senators and most of the martyrs of Gaul died by crucifixion; their hands and feet bear the marks of it, and generally the iron nails are found lying in their coffins beside them. It was supposed to add to the indignity of their death to make them die like the God they worshipped, and to fling the very nails after them to take with them to the other world! Some of these poor martyrs were crucified by enormous nails driven through their shoulder blades. We saw some seven or eight inches long. It seems that Maximian had no difficulty in getting leave from Rome to crucify a Senator, however influential a man he was, if he was a Christian.

"From Trèves we came to Metz, where we only halted for a few hours. The corn seems to grow well over these horrid battle-helds. We went on to Nancy, where we spent the night. It is a beautiful city, and we enjoyed walking through it in the bright, sunny evening, after a heavy shower. Next day we started for Gerardmer, in the Vosges.

"Later we went further to explore the country of Pastor Oberlin, the Ban de la Roche, in the Vosges. It is a very picturesque but rather bleak country. We found there some of Oberlin's descendants still living, and the place was full of memories of him."

"My last to you was written from Gerardmer. We left there early one fine morning, in a carriage with two strong horses, to come over into Germany by the little Schlucht Pass. It is really one of the finest passes I have seen which is not a snow pass. From it you drop down straight upon Münster. My husband walked the greater part of the way, through exten-sive forests of the finest silver firs of enormous size. From the heights we had a picturesque view looking back over the little lakes Retournemer and Longemer and the valleys. We got to the highest point about twelve o'clock, and were rewarded beyond all our expectations. There is a little hotel there, where we alighted to dine. Walking forwards about fifty yards, a beautiful view burst upon us. In front of us lay the winding, rocky terrace-road which descends on the German side, with fine bits of granite rock towering up; beyond this, waving lines of forest-covered hills sloping down to the plain;

then the wide plain, with lower hills dotted over it, like waves in the sea. In this plain lay Münster, a bright speck of a city far off, with many spires and towers. Beyond the plain was a line of hazy light, which marked the course of the Rhine; beyond that again a delicate, undulating line of cobalt blue, which were the hills of the Black Forest on the further side of the Rhine.

"There was not, of course, the majestic beauty of snow peaks, but it was very open and lovely, and we were the more struck by it because we had not expected anything so fine. We had coffee on the terrace of the hotel, and my husband quickly sketched an outline of the view, to fill up at home. We came down to Münster on a beautiful evening, and thence to Colmar."

On our journey back to the Rhine we paid a second visit to the Laacher See, where our eldest son joined us.

From Königswinter, on the Rhine, I wrote to my husband, who had returned to England:—

"August, 1879.

" You judged very well to send back a card by your driver to tell us to go by steamer from Brohl. George and I drove down through the Brohl-Thal from the Laacher See, and enjoyed it all the more because you had just driven down before us. What quarries of tufa and trass there are, with all their caves and galleries. George has been to-day to the top of the Volkenberg, geologising, and Charlie took me for a short row on the river. There was a beautiful sunset. He went back to Bonn after dark. I must now do my duty in going to Liége to the Conference, which will be over in a few days, and allow me to return home."

"Liége, August 20th.

" I awoke this morning remembering that it was the anniversary of Eva's translation to a better world, and I thought of you and of her, and found your letter as I came down to breakfast.

" You remember that I called on Cardinal Manning shortly before leaving home, and told him of the proposed Congress to be held by us next year at Genoa. I asked him if he could use his influence in our favour in Italy. Now, see what the good man has done! The Catholic Press is already announcing the proposed Congress at Genoa, and all the Catholic journals of Rome have declared themselves in favour of the principles of our Federation. This would seem to be by an order from the Vatican. From the *Voce della Verita*, the more popular journal, to the *Unita Cattolica*, the most Ultramontane, all have spoken against the system we combat. Mr. Humbert is convinced that it is Cardinal Manning's doing. He (the Cardinal) told me when I saw him that he was just starting for Rome, and would see the ' Holy Father.' He promised me to speak to him, and this is the result. Will you kindly write and mention to him this news, which was printed in the Belgian Catholic Press to-day, and say how grateful we feel to him? He asked me, in London, if I could tell him exactly what part Pius IX. had taken in the matter when the Italian Government first introduced this legislation, under Cavour. At that moment I could not, but am going to find out.* We

* The following extract from a speech made by Signor Tommasi-Crudeli in the Italian Parliament, in 1888, throws some light on the history of our movement in Italy, before and since the Congress at Genoa in 1880: " We have been reproached," he said, " with yielding in this matter to the Radical party. This is not just. The movement against the immoral regulations was taken up in every part of the Chamber. From Dr. Bertani, who sat on the extreme left, and de Renzis on the left centre, to Guidici on the extreme right, all contributed to the preliminary efforts, until Signor Crispi called them to work with him. Outside Parliament it has been the same. Men of all parties rose up in rebellion against a degrading system which has no argument to rest upon. The protest of the conscience continued all along the line, until it reached Pope Pius IX. (Sensation.) Yes, it is true! The late Pontiff, shortly before the system was introduced in Rome, when his conscience as a Christian had silenced all his political prejudices, wrote a letter to King Victor Emmanuel, protesting against the crime about to be perpetrated by the establishment of a patented merchandise in human beings in the Holy City." Cardinal Manning obtained full possession of these facts concerning Pius IX. soon after his visit to Rome above mentioned.

are to have meetings at Seraing, where there are great foundries, at Verviers, and other industrial centres."

From G. B. :—

" You seem to have begun your work at Liége under very auspicious circumstances.· I will write to Cardinal Manning. George's letters from the Auvergne are very interesting. His swims in those clear pools in their volcanic basins, and the large trout make my mouth water. He seems to have done a great deal, and will carry away much useful knowledge."

It was impossible for my husband not to continue to take a keen interest in politics, in spite of the reserve he felt obliged to exercise on account of his position as a schoolmaster. When a question came forward of some great social or moral reform, he felt himself at liberty to take part, like anyone else, in deputations to candidates for Parliament. In the contested election of the early part of the year 1880, in Liverpool, he made strenuous efforts for the cause for which he and I worked.

He headed deputations to Mr. Whitley and Lord Ramsay, the rival candidates, accompanied by our friendly physicians and by leading working-men of Liverpool.

" I hope that you will enter upon your campaign at Woolwich," he wrote to me, " with health, strength, and spiritual power : of the latter I have no doubt. I read with increasing interest Mr. Gladstone's speeches, which have a true liberal ring about them. Oh that he would look our question fairly in the face, and speak of it according to his convictions ! What these convictions must be when he has gone into the subject I cannot for a moment doubt."

From Mr. Stansfeld :—

" February, 1880.

" Dear Mr. Butler,—Your handwriting is always ' gude for sair een,' in my case at least ; and it was especially so this morning, amidst the fog. Thank you for your account of the Liverpool candidates and our question. I cannot say much for 'a good heart' in again buckling to this question: but, heart or no heart, I shall certainly go on to the end of it, or of me; and I think that we shall win, and that before long. In all probability we shall have a dissolution before the Committee of Inquiry is in a position to report."

A public Conference was held by our Association every year, and every third year a Congress,—more important and of larger dimensions. In 1880 Genoa was chosen as the seat of our Congress. Through the labours and genius of our gifted friend Giuseppe Nathan, the whole of the Liberal and Mazzinian working-men's Asociations of Italy had already given their adhesion to our cause. The gathering in Genoa was therefore very large and very striking. The Congress was held in the Hall of the Municipal Council and in the great Carlo Felice Theatre. Previous to starting for Genoa, my husband wrote : " I am working hard at my address. I am appointed to represent the working-men of England, whose Secretary has sent me an address from them to the Italian work-men. It is short and weighty. Londini is putting it into good Italian for me."

To his son Stanley, who was unable to accompany us to Genoa :—

" Hotel Isotta, Genoa, September, 1880.

" The Congress is over, and has been a great success. I wish you could have been present yesterday to see the great mass meeting in the square outside the Carlo Felice Theatre, addressed by several Italian Deputies. All made themselves audible to a great distance, as your mother and I found by descending from the balcony and mixing with the crowd. I returned thanks to the Italian Committee, and spoke of Saffi's excellent presidency of the Congress. Also this morning I wished much for you. Garibaldi drove by our hotel in an open carriage, just under our window. The carriage stopped a moment, and he looked up, evidently aware that a good many of us were staying here. He is very like his portraits; only he looks very feeble, and goes about wrapped up and swathed in white and red robes. He suffers badly from rheumatism. We are to go to-morrow to visit him, at 10 a.m."

From J. E. B. to the same :—

"On Sunday a great public meeting was held in the square. The people were very orderly. All the Ligurian Operative Societies had marched past from the country with bands and banners, in order to show their complete acceptance of our principles, and halted in the square. . . . It was touching to see Garibaldi, so infirm and aged. He is more popular in Genoa, perhaps, than anywhere. The sight was striking from our hotel window as he passed in an open carriage with two horses, which were led, proceeding slowly on account of the dense crowd in the street. Not only was the street crowded, but every window was filled with faces, and even the housetops were covered with people, cheering him most enthusiastically. I must tell you of our visit to him. He is staying with his daughter, and he had expressed a desire to see privately some of the members of the Congress. Saffii introduced us. At the door of his room hung a heavy curtain, and this was held back as we entered by his devoted body-servant, who lifts his poor master about and does everything for him. This man is immensely tall and well made, and so dark that I should imagine he is of African descent. He looked very picturesque in his scarlet jersey, holding back this curtain. Inside the room lay the old soldier in bed, with a counterpane of snowy whiteness over him, contrasting with his own scarlet shirt. His daughter had made him look very pretty with bouquets of fresh flowers laid upon his bed. It is a very sweet, benevolent face, and his blue eyes express intelligence and goodness combined.

23

He had an appropriate word for each of us. He said to me (in Italian, of course): ' Remember this, that though we pass away, and the leaders of a cause fall one by one, principles never die; they are eternal, world-wide, and unchangeable.' Mrs. Lucas, a sister of John Bright, conversed with him some time. We did not stay too long, lest we should tire him. It has been so pleasant having George and Charles and the Meuricoffres here, and so many other dear relations."

My husband was, as usual, obliged to return home quickly. From Turin he wrote: " The events of the last few days have passed somewhat like a dream, especially our visit to Garibaldi. That sweet-looking, benevolent face and kindly smile and kindling eye are things which I shall never forget. Probably this is our only chance of seeing the old hero." (It was so, as his death occurred not long after.)

To J. E. B., from Liverpool :—

" I see the Roman journals gave a good account of our closing meeting. I will take care of all the papers which come, such as the *Epoca;* and will keep all letters for you. Mr. Stansfeld has written from Halifax to say that they feel sure now of having a strong Liberal Government. Whether he will be in the Cabinet he cannot tell. Possibly his decided opinions on our question which would not allow him to be put off with a hope, may keep him out. He sends me his best wishes for some preferment, which he thinks would have come my way but for what they will call ' my crotchet.' It may be so; but it does not matter."

I interrupt for a moment the record of incidents or events in order to express, as well as I can, what I owed to my husband for help and support in a time of mental conflict during our prolonged crusade.

We read in the Gospels that the disciples of Christ

found themselves one dark evening separated from the Master, "in the midst of the sea;" that He saw them from the shore "toiling in rowing," for "the wind was contrary." Such is sometimes the position, spiritually and morally, of one who has up to a certain point "fought a good fight and kept the faith," but against whom arise contrary winds and buffeting waves; one for whom "fightings without and fears within" have proved too severe, and who is now "toiling in rowing," with faint heart and gloomy outlook,—the presence of the Master no longer realised to reassure and guide. "Old Satan is too strong for young Melancthon," said one of the Reformers of the XVIth century; and the same enemy has proved many a time since then too strong for much humbler workers. The problems of life at times appear so perplexing as to be incapable of any solution: the lines of good and evil, of right and wrong, light and darkness, appear blurred; and the weak and burdened spirit loses the hold it had retained hitherto of the highest standard, fidelity to which alone can bring us again out of darkness and trouble into light and hope.

Moses, for the hardness of the people's hearts, allowed a relaxation of the severity of the original Law given from on high, and so suffered the moral standard to be lowered in some of the most important relations of life. There was a time when it seemed to me that hearts are harder now than even in the old days, and when the stern ethics of Christ—the divine standard—seemed to become impossible as a matter of practical enforcement. Horribly perplexed, I was tempted to give up the perfect ideal. It is in this way, I think, *through lack of faith*, that compromises creep in among us; compromises with error, with sin, with wrong-doing—unbelief taking root first in the individual soul, and then gradually spreading, until a lower standard is accepted in family life, in society, in legislation, and in Government. And at last, as even in our own land, we may see publicly endorsed and signed what the Hebrew prophet calls "a covenant with death" and "an agreement with hell." Such an acceptance and public endorsement of a compromise with evil proclaims the failure of faith of a whole nation, and the beginning of a "down-grade" in which virtue is regarded as no longer possible for man.

To speak of clouded moments of one's own life involves no small effort. But in justice both to my husband and to the movement I have tried to serve, I am impelled to do so. There are some people who, if they remember at all that moral uprising against national unrighteousness in which we took part, still regard it as an illusion, and its advocacy as a "fad," or even as a blot on an otherwise inoffensive career—something which must always require explanation or apology. But there are others who understood from the first its true meaning and far-reaching issues, and who have perhaps imagined that an unbroken consistency of action, based on an immovable strength of conviction, must at all times have characterised any man or woman destined to take a representative part in it. A sense of justice forces me to confess that the fact (in regard to myself) was not always as they imagined; for there was a time when I resembled the faint-hearted though loyal disciple, who when venturing to walk on the waters, in an evil moment looked away from Christ and around upon the weltering, unstable floor on which he stood, and immediately began to sink. When, moreover, the sense of justice of which I speak regards one who was and is dear to me as my own soul, then I am doubly forced to speak, and to give " honour to whom honour is due," by telling of the wisdom which God gave him in encouraging and supporting through a few troubled years the tried and wavering advocate of a cause in which both faith and courage were put to a severe test.*

A deeply-rooted faith—a personal and not merely a traditional faith—in the central truths of Christ, and moral strength, the fruit of that faith, were in him united with other qualities which were needful for the task he so well fulfilled. Others whom I have known—teachers and fathers in God—have had this moral and spiritual faith in a high degree, together with an eloquence and power in argument to which he had no pretension. But few—it seemed to me at least—possessed such patience as he had, such long-suffering, such a power of silent waiting, such a dignified reserve, and such a strong respect for individuality as to forbid all probing of inner wounds or questioning of motive or action, even in the case of one so near to him as myself. He had great delicacy and refinement in dealing with the bitterness or petulance of a soul in trouble. He had great faith in his fellow-creatures. And these, together with his unfailing love, like the sun in the heavens surmounting the hours of cold and darkness, gradually overcame the mists which had wrapped themselves round the heart and obscured the spiritual vision of her for whom he never ceased to pray.

At this time his voice, when simply reading the words

---

* I would have it clearly understood that concerning the wickedness of the unjust and unequal laws against which we contended, I never had the shadow of a doubt. It was as clear to me as a geometrical fact; I never could waver in my conviction that two and two do not make five, or believe that three and two can be proved to make four.

of Christ at family prayers, used to sound in my ears with
a strange and wonderful pathos, which pierced the depths
of rebellious or despairing thought.   At times his attitude
—probably unconsciously to himself—assumed in my
eyes an unaccustomed and almost awful sternness.   Sometimes my unrest of mind found vent in words of bitterness (which, however, only skimmed the surface of the
inward trouble), and I waited for him to speak.   Then he
seemed to rise before me to a stature far above my level,
above that of other men, and even above his own at other
times, while he gently led me back to great first principles
and to the Source of all Truth, presenting to me in a way
which I could sometimes hardly bear the perfection and
severity of the Law of God, and our own duty in patient
obedience and perseverance, even when the ascent is
steepest and the road darkest and longest.   He very
seldom gave me direct personal advice or warning.   He
simply stood there before me in the light of God, truthful,
upright, single-minded ; and all that had been distorted
or wrong in me was rebuked by that attitude alone ; and a
kind of prophetic sense of returning peace, rather than
actual peace, entered my soul, and my heart replied,—
" Where you stand now, beloved, I shall also stand again
one day—perhaps soon,—on firm ground, and in the light
of God ; " and my soul bowed in reverence before him ;
although never could he bear any outward expression of
that reverence.   It seemed to hurt him.   He would gently
turn away from it.   He spoke firmly when he differed
from any doubtful sentiment expressed or argument
used.   His simple " No," or " I think you are wrong,"
were at times more powerful to me than the most
awful pulpit denunciation or argumentative demon-
stration of my error could have been ; and then,

even if he condemned, his love and reverence never failed.

He knew the Psalms almost by heart, and the inspired words which he always had so ready were more potent for me, when spoken by him, than any other thing. His religion and his method of consoling were not of a subtle or philosophical kind; and he was all the better a comforter to me because he did not, perhaps could not, easily enter into and follow all the windings of my confused thinkings and doubtings and revolted feelings. Strong swimmer as he was, I felt in my half-drowned state his firm grasp and his powerful stroke upon the waters as we neared the land; and when, by his aid, my feet stood once more upon the solid rock, I understood the full force of the grateful acknowledgment of the Psalmist, "Thou hast kept my feet from falling, and mine eyes from tears."

I have not, up till now, dwelt upon the wrongs and sorrows which we were forced deliberately to look upon and measure; nor shall I do so, for I promised my readers that I would not. Could I do so, they would not wonder at any suffering or distress of brain caused by such a subject of contemplation. Dante tells us that when, in his dream, he entered the Inferno and met its sights and sounds, he fell prone, "as one dead." I once replied to a friend who complained of my using strong expressions, and asked the meaning of them, as follows: "Hell hath opened her mouth. I stand in the near presence of the powers of evil: what I see and hear are the smoke of the pit, the violence of the torture inflicted by man on his fellows, the cries of lost spirits, the wail of the murdered innocents, and the laughter of demons." But these, it will be said, are mere figures of speech. So they are,

used purposely to cover—for no words can adequately
express—the reality which they symbolise. But the reality
is there, not in any dream or poetic vision of woe, but
present on this earth ; hidden away for the most part from
the virtuous and the happy, but not from the eyes of God.
Turning from the contemplation of such unspeakable woes
and depths of moral turpitude, it was a strength and comfort beyond description, through the years of strife, to
look upon the calm face of my best earthly friend. It was
a peace-imparting influence. And now that I walk alone
and look only at his portrait, even that seems to take me
into the presence of God, where he now dwells among the
" spirits of just men made perfect," and to whisper hope
of the approaching solution of the great mystery of sin
and pain.

I often recall an incident which occurred at Winchester,
in the Cathedral ; a trifle in itself, but which dwells in my
memory as an illustration of the help he gave to me
spiritually in time of need. It was during the service on
Sunday. I suddenly felt faint, the effect of a week of
unusual effort and hard work. Wishing not to disturb
anyone or make a scene, I took the opportunity when all
heads were bowed in prayer to creep down from the stalls
as silently as possible, past the tomb of William Rufus,
and down the choir, holding on when possible by the
carved woodwork of the seats. A moment more and I
should have dropped. I could scarcely steady my steps,
and my sight failed, when suddenly there passed a flash of
light, as it seemed, before my eyes, something as white as
snow and as soft as an angel's wing ; it enveloped me, and
I felt myself held up by a strong, loving arm, and supported through the nave to the west door, where the cool
summer breeze quickly restored me. It was my husband.

He was in his own seat near the entrance to the nave, and his quick ear had caught the sound of my footstep. Quite noiselessly he left his seat, and took me in his arms, unobserved by anyone. The flash of light (the angel's wing) was the quick movement of the wide sleeve of his fine linen surplice, upon which the sun shone as he drew me towards him.

CHAPTER XIV.

FATIGUE OF BODY AND MIND, THROUGH PROLONGED WORK.—
WISH TO RETIRE. — HOPE DEFERRED. — VISIT TO THE
ENGADINE.—MORTERATSCH AND ROSEG GLACIERS.—LAND-
SLIP. — RENEWED HEALTH. — ANNOUNCEMENT OF RETIRE-
MENT FROM THE LIVERPOOL COLLEGE. — OPINIONS OF
FRIENDS ON THE SUBJECT.—APPOINTMENT TO A CANONRY
AT WINCHESTER. — FAREWELL ADDRESS, AND PARTING
WORDS OF FRIENDS AND COLLEAGUES.

E observed, in the spring and summer of
1881, an increasing weariness in my husband,
with, sometimes, depression of spirits. He
was coming near the end of his twenty-five
years of school work ; but he did not know
it, and the prospect of any retirement seemed as far off as
ever. Work increased, partly owing to the establishment
in Liverpool of the " University College," the formation
of which involved frequent attendance at meetings and
extra correspondence on his part. It was often late before
he returned home, when he would speak of feeling *very*
tired—an unusual thing for him.

Even for some years before this he used to say that
after a long day in school, he found it very difficult to
continue his work up till midnight or later, correcting
school exercises and preparing lectures. On going into
his study late, I sometimes found him with a pile of papers
before him, leaning his head on his hand, asleep. He
told me he found it not easy to concentrate his thoughts
for prayer after these long days of work ; sleep overcame
him in the effort. He adopted a plan, then, of simply—

if I may so express it—"writing a letter to God." He would write out slowly, lifting up his heart all the time, petitions and thanksgivings, and special requests for himself, his family and friends ; just as one would pour out one's heart to a friend in writing, to whom one could not speak face to face. He knew he could at all times speak face to face with our Father in Heaven, but he found the mechanical act of writing enabled him to keep awake and also to define his thoughts as he could not otherwise do when mentally fatigued. I believe others besides himself have tried "writing letters to God," and found it helpful. Most certainly such letters never fail to reach their destination, when the heart that dictates them is true.

The duty of arranging his papers and letters, since he was taken from us, has brought to me a knowledge which I possessed less completely before, of the constancy with which he held converse with God in this way. His writings of this kind are very numerous and meet me on every hand, as witnesses to his habit of seeking light and help from God on all occasions. Sometimes, also, when we had agreed together to inquire of God on any particular matter, a record was made of it in writing. The following was written about the time of which I am speaking :—

"O Lord, we believe that Thou carest for us, and that every event is overuled by Thee. We cease from all appeals to man, and turn to make our appeal alone to Thee. We ask Thee to provide for our future and to direct our path, that we may serve Thee in peace and without anxiety. We remember Thy promise, 'Behold I have set before Thee an open door, and no man can shut it.' Open now a door for us, we beseech Thee, O our God, and make our path plain before us. We leave our request with Thee."

He was not ambitious. Never did he pray for earthly success or honours. He never thought of any exalted Church preferment. A Canonry he may have thought possible; but his ideal I think was a country Living, with opportunity for useful work both among his parishioners and in connection with public movements. " I will not forget," he wrote to me on one occasion, "your prayer before parting. If the appeal to our friends comes to nothing, we have a higher authority in whom to trust, and this I never lose sight of."

He was not, strictly speaking, much of a theologian, I suppose. He had little taste for controversial writings, but his Bible was his constant companion. Even in railway journeys—especially in his later years—he almost invariably carried a Bible in his little handbag, and would take it out to read during the journey. "I find," he wrote, "that Biblical criticism is too apt to take the place of profitable reading. When I want to derive food and sustenance from the Word of God, I take no commentary, but shut myself up with the plain Word, and meditate on that. I had a delightful hour on Saturday in thinking upon that passage in 1 John iii. That expression 'seeing Christ as He is' suggests a volume of thoughts. Seeing Him as He went about on the earth doing good, was much; seeing Him by the eye of faith as He now is, is more; but seeing Him as we shall see Him, and as He shall be hereafter, is a thought which expands the mind and fills the heart to overflowing, yet without our ever arriving at the fulness of the truth." . . . "The more I read the Scriptures, the more convinced I am that it is intended that God's people should have no doubt whatever that they are God's people. This conscious assurance may be accompanied by the deepest humility and sense of our own sinfulness, but should not admit of any doubt of the gracious intentions of God towards us. On the contrary, a knowledge of what our Redemption has cost, and of the awful nature and effects of sin, from which it has saved us, should fill us with a trembling anxiety lest by any carelessness we should offend our Saviour and Judge : and so the most unbounded confidence may co-exist with the greatest distrust of ourselves ; and while we feel 'I can do all things through Christ which strengtheneth me,' we realise the truth of that which Jesus said, 'Without Me ye can do nothing.' "

We had never visited the Engadine, and had heard much of its life-giving air. My husband applied successfully for the summer Chaplaincy of Samaden, which he was to occupy for six weeks, and he and I went together early in July.

The journey out was in itself restful, especially when, after leaving the train at Chur, we took a carriage over the Albula Pass. He had the pleasure of watching several beautiful chamois flying from the sight of our carriage, in couples, over the rocks. We seemed to be almost the only travellers of the season as yet. There was still much snow, and the scenery was wild and even wintery, but very beautiful. He enjoyed much the charge of the little church, which is built on the hillside just above Samaden.

A week or two later we were joined by two of our sons, and later again by James Stuart. Our son Charles was then in Greece, and the letters which we received from him, as well as others which he wrote as a press correspondent, and which were published, were very interesting to his father. Never having been able to visit Greece, which he often desired to do, it was some compensation to be able to follow his son in imagination in his visits to far-famed historical and classic spots.

To my sons in England :—

"July 11th, 1881.

"We are longing for you to be here; but you will come soon, I hope. The air will give you new life. We went yesterday to the Morteratsch Glacier. I had never yet seen such a mass of snow. Father and I found a seat on a slope all crimson-coloured with Alpine-rose in full flower, with such a view before us, rising height above height over the glacier; —unbroken fields of snow. Of course, you have seen far wider snow fields in your great 'ascensions;' but for a person who cannot climb, it is a great thing to find a defile high enough to command such an expanse of snow. It had been cloudy all day; but about four o'clock (when we were there) the sun shone out, and rolled up the soft white clouds from the mountains, like a curtain drawn up; and when all was cleared, the snow seemed illuminated from within by ten thousand celestial fires, surmounted by pure white and golden-tinted spires and domes. There was one grand broad dome of snow, part of the Piz Bernina; and the Piz Pallü was one vast sheet of glory. We were told that these were parts never yet trodden by the foot of man, the routes for ascending being on the other side.

"The plain in which Samaden lies is flat and uninteresting, but we are within easy reach of many beautiful places— Silva Plana and Sils Maria, the lake and woods about St. Moritz, Pontresina, the Bernina Pass into Italy and the picturesque Beversthal on our southern side. The latter is called the Paradise of botanists. We have good rooms. In front, immediately under our windows there is a lively stream, a mill wheel, ducks, and washerwomen; and in the distance a magnificent panorama of snow mountains. At first I could scarcely look at the snow with my tired, smoke-blinded eyes from Liverpool, but I soon felt stronger, and it is a great happiness on getting up very early every morning to throw the windows wide open and see again that blaze of pure snow and light, with lovely shadows."·

When the rest of our party arrived, we were very happy, and the more so because we saw my husband gradually regaining his elastic step, and power of enjoyment of Nature and outdoor life. He made many sketches.

To my son Charles at Athens :—

" We went one day to the Roseg Glacier. It looked rather dark and stormy as we got near the hut. We carried our luncheon basket up nearer the glacier until we found a large granite boulder humping up its shoulder against the cold wind which swept down from the ice, and which had a soft carpet of grass and flowers at its foot on the sheltered side ; just the place for our dining-room. Previous to luncheon we had had large views about going on the glacier ; but a little later we saw it to be undesirable, for a storm came swirling down from those (at that time) awful, stern-looking mountain giants which rise above it. I was glad, however, once to see it in that wild weather. It is the largest glacier I have yet seen ; the two wide rivers of solid ice sweeping down in magnificent curves and then converging are very grand. I recalled your account of your ascent of the Piz Sella the year before from the hut where we had halted. After lunch I was gathering flowers, when I heard a strange deep noise, and a shout from the gentlemen calling me to come quickly and look out. There was a sight which I had never seen, though one often sees after traces of the phenomenon. Looking across the valley to the steep barren mountain to the left as you face the glacier, we saw what seemed to be the mountain-side moving downwards, slowly and quiveringly, with a noise like several heavily-laden goods trains roaring among the mountain echoes, with occasional explosions and thunder. This grating angry noise lasted several minutes, while the movement went on. It was a landslip. There is no road at the foot of that mountain slope, and evidently it is a place which

people avoid.   What we saw was a mass of stones and earth
pushing downward, the movement being continuous.   It was
like a long thick snake quivering its body from the top to the
bottom of the mountain.   It went slowly, but with an appearance of irresistible power.   Some way off from it was a
shepherd with a flock of sheep.   They all stood still—so still
that you could have fancied them carved in stone—and continued so till the movement ceased.   I fancy they were afraid
of flying stones.   This sight gave me some slight idea of what
a really great landslip must be, and seemed a very small
miniature of that dreadful scene at Chio in the earthquake,
where the whole village—you told us – seemed to come slowly
quivering down the mountain side.   The storm came soon,
with pitiless rain, and we hurried home as fast as possible.
As we went across the valley to Samaden, the clouds suddenly
cleared off and the broad valley was spanned by a brilliant
rainbow, while smaller rainbows encircled some of the lower
hilltops like crowns studded with jewels."

When the time came for my husband's return to England, I accompanied him over the Julier Pass to Thusis,
at which picturesque place we stayed a day or two.   Our
windows looked direct up the entrance to the Via Mala,
and from the balcony he made a bold drawing of the
towering rocks which form a natural gateway to the Pass.
From here he turned homeward, while I went back to
Samaden to spend ten days longer with my sons.

"It seemed strange coming back without you," I wrote
to him.   "When I awake I look out as before at that beautiful
group of mountains in the fresh morning light.   The cheerful
little mill keeps dashing its waters as it did, and the guinea
fowl constantly repeats 'Come back, come back,' as if it knew
my thoughts.   I think, however, with gratitude, of these most
happy weeks we have had together, the very memory of which
will continue to be refreshing to us for a long time.   You are
now putting on your harness again.   May God strengthen

you, and grant to us a very clear direction as to our future life, assigning to you some work less arduous than you have at present."

In the spring of the following year, 1882, my husband carried into practice a resolution which he had made some time before, by announcing to the Directors and Council of the Liverpool College his desire to resign his post there, which he had held for more than sixteen years. The following is a portion of the circular in which he made that announcement :—

" My Lords and Gentlemen,—

" It is now upwards of sixteen years since I received and accepted an invitation from the Council to undertake the duties of the Principalship about to be vacated by my predecessor, Dr. Howson, now Dean of Chester. I have endeavoured during that time to fulfil, to the best of my ability, the various duties committed to my charge. I was especially instructed by my predecessor to pay attention to the higher education of the pupils, and more particularly to those in the Upper School. This instruction I endeavoured to carry out by a more complete system of examination than had prevailed hitherto, and by taking upon myself an in-creased amount of actual teaching, including the greater part of the Composition of the First Class, and lectures in Geography, History and Art.

" The list of University Honours gained by the pupils from the foundation of the college to the present day shows that these endeavours on my part, aided by the loyal sup-port and trained ability of my colleagues, have been successful. Liverpool College is now known no less at Oxford than at Cambridge, and few schools can boast of a better average of honours in proportion to the numbers they send to the Universities.

" In the useful and popular study of Geography the college has gained higher honours than any of the public schools in Great Britain; and while our attention has been given to the higher subjects of education, such as Theology, the ancient Classical Languages and Literature, and Mathematics, we have by no means neglected more modern studies, such as Modern History, French and German, Chemistry and Natural Science, Drawing, and all that is included in an English education.

"We are enabled to point to a large and increasing number of old college pupils who are filling useful and responsible positions in commerce and various departments of trade. Three of these, of an earlier generation, have recently filled with marked and recognised ability the office of Mayor of Liverpool. So that it cannot be justly laid at the door of the college that its high University distinctions have been purchased by the neglect of humbler but more necessary studies.

"I have now entered upon what is considered the last decade of ordinary human life, and I may be pardoned if I act upon a long-cherished desire to devote such years as remain to me of this life to ministerial rather than scholastic work.

"I have, therefore, the honour, my Lords and Gentlemen, to announce to you my wish to resign at Midsummer next the Principalship of Liverpool College.. And in making that announcement I have to offer you my unfeigned and hearty thanks for the confidence with which you have for so long a time honoured me. I hope and believe that I am consulting not only my own wishes, but the best interests of the College, in making way for a younger man. And I take this early opportunity of making known to you my wishes, in order that you may have more time and greater facilities for the appointment of my successor.

"Liverpool, 2nd March, 1882."

Some extracts from letters of friends who had received this circular will show how this step was generally regarded.

" Many thanks," Mr. Powles wrote, "for the circular of to-day. I am glad that it is accompanied by the list of honours obtained by the pupils of Liverpool College, so that the results of your work may be apparent. I do earnestly hope that something may be offered you—a Canonry or a Deanery—by the Queen. Public work such as yours ought to have public acknowledgment. Such results as you have personally brought about in Classics and Geography are— I do not think I deceive myself in saying—unique."

From his brother, Montagu Butler :—

" *Quad felix faustenque sit* is my first feeling on reading your most interesting circular, and hearing of the very important step you have decided to take. It must be indeed plain to everyone that you leave the College in the highest state of prosperity and distinction, and that your devoted labours during these more than fifteen years have been richly fruitful."

One of the large staff of masters who worked with him at the college expressed more or less the feeling of all in the following words :—

" The announcement of your resignation has caused us a shock of unpleasant surprise and regret, and if you will forgive it I must yield to an impulse to say so to you at once. Some fitting occasion will, I trust, be found in which the entire body of masters can unite in giving formal and public expression to the strong sense of mingled respect, admiration, and affectionate feeling we all entertain towards you. Meanwhile, I confine myself to the confession that I have all along known it to be a very great boon and privilege to be associated with you in the common work, and to be the recipient of that extreme kindness and sympathy which you have invariably shown to me. I trust that no feeling of impaired energy or health has led to this step we deplore."

I had some years before written to him during an absence from home :—

" I know how much you rejoice on every occasion of any of our friends being promoted or rewarded in earthly matters. I cannot help praying for you daily that, if it please God, all earth's rewards shall not pass you by. I scarcely like to express to yourself all I feel about you, but God is witness to the loving care of my heart concerning all that concerns you. I believe that His ear is open to me when I beg His favour for you in the things of this life as well as of the next. He has marked your faithfulness to duty, your untiring diligence, your unselfishness, your absolute freedom from envy when others have again and again distanced you in this world's race; and He is just. You shall have your reward. What you have given will be measured back to you again, in ' full measure, pressed down, and running over.' But His rewards are not always according to our devising."

He wrote to me :—

" Thank you, dearest, for your loving sympathy with me in my worldly career. I have no doubt that I shall eventually get as much in the way of worldly honours as I deserve. We must be patient, and recollect how much worse it would be to be promoted to a place for which one is not fit than to miss the promotion one deserves."

From Madame Meuricoffre ·—

" My dear George,—I do not much like to enter on the subject of your being kept waiting so long for preferment. It makes me feel rather angry. I should be sorry to say hard things, but I fancy I see that there is something more than chance in it, when men of much less real worth climb up fortune's tree far before you. It is perhaps from a giving in to a feeling which is natural to men in whose eyes this world fills too large a place. One reads of some of the most worthy men whose lives have been, not really overlooked, but left out, because they were a reproof to many; but it is precisely these men whose memories are honoured as they' themselves never were outwardly during their lives. The persons who succeed the best in this world are frequently the mediocre persons who are not too great or good to be understood and appreciated in their own generation, and who excite no distrust, no jealousy by being somewhat ahead of their time. There is greatness as God sees greatness, the gift of wisdom, the spirit enlightened by God's Spirit, the life that does not only preach about Christ but copies His life, the clearsightedness which knows how to separate the sin from the sinner, the willingness to suffer and to wait. The great ones of this world do not understand all this ; they are rather afraid of it, and think it is safer not to have to do with the romotion of such an one. I express myself badly, I fear, but I cannot help thinking that they have a feeling like this,— ' He believes so thoroughly in God ; then let God help him, and we will help men who do not aim at so high a standard, and men who can on occasions serve two masters.' "

From Mr. Meuricoffre :—

" I have read with interest your dignified letter to the Council of Liverpool College. They must feel indebted to you for the high position to which you have brought the institution, and its taking rank with the oldest and most renowned schools in respect to University honours. As a commercial community, I think they must feel particularly grateful for the special importance and strong impulse you have given to the study of Geography. It is a branch of knowledge of the highest importance for men who are expected to direct a commerce that extends to every part of the globe."

Dr. Fraser, Bishop of Manchester, wrote :—

" I am almost sorry to see the announcement of your resignation. Your letter to the Council is very graceful, and almost pathetic. I wish you might be soon placed in a position adequate to your claims."

Mr. Gladstone had previously acknowledged the efficiency of the work done at Liverpool College, in writing from Hawarden at Christmas :—

"Of those who took an interest in the foundation of the college the survivors are now but few. I have read with sincere interest and much gratification in the *Liverpool Daily Post* the report of the proceedings at the Distribution of Prizes. It affords a striking testimonial to your powers and your successes. The excellent address of Professor Stuart seems to have been worthy of the occasion. It is really difficult sometimes to keep one's temper with the 'men of science,' many of whom, or of whose retainers, show their narrow training by their narrow minds. Professor Stuart dealt well with these in telling them some needful and un-palatable truths. Wishing you all a happy Christmas."

Three months after his resignation of the Principal-ship, in June, 1882, my husband received the following from Mr. Gladstone :—

"Dear Mr. Butler,—I have much pleasure in proposing to you, with Her Majesty's sanction, that you should be appointed to the Canonry of Winchester, to be vacated by the Rev. E. Wilberforce."

He received this in a spirit characteristic of him, with quiet thankfulness, as from the hand of God. It relieved us all of anxiety concerning the future. On writing to me a little later he said :—

"How faithfully God answers prayer ! This certainly came at the last rather unexpectedly to me, perhaps not so to you, as the answer to prayers offered up by you, as I know, for long, that our Heavenly Father might smooth the way before us, and allow me to end my days in a less laborious calling."

Lord Lingen wrote :—

" *Sero sed serio* is the motto of some noble house—that of the Cecils, I think. The Canonry is a moderate recognition of long years of work for public ends, and if one feels that it might have been greater, it is some satisfaction to feel that no one can say that it ought to have been less. It is my own strong opinion that if one has enough with which to live one's own life, all addition to such sufficiency is in this country undesirable. There is no pleasure in putting on six great-coats on the top of the one which keeps you warm enough ; and if one looks at the life of most rich people in England, the cumbersomeness of their existence is much the same as such a mode of dressing. The Cathedral Close with its Dean and Chapter will be something like going home to you, and at Winchester the Capitular element has its younger academical neighbour in the Masters of the School; I should think it altogether a very pleasant society. The services of a great Cathedral are something to have at hand as one grows older. Altogether, I hope you feel in calm sunshine with the glass at ' fair.' "

The sister above quoted wrote on this occasion from Naples :—

" I am deeply thankful for your news. Winchester is a very pretty place ; and I think your artistic taste will feel at home with the Cathedral architecture and its surroundings. I think it cheers the spirits of persons with a really artistic nature to come home to something pretty, and two of your former homes—Durham and Oxford—have much outward beauty. When I first received the news I must confess to you that I burst into tears, and Conrad, who was sitting near me, feared there was some bad news ; but I soon reassured him. I did not quite realise till then how heavily has been lying on my heart the apparent non - recognition of your merits ; but perhaps I had exaggerated what I took for slight. I had however been fretting over it, and the reaction was delightful. You will look back on these last seventeen years with satisfaction, I am sure. What good work they cover! I do not allude only to what you did, but to what you were. Many will feel pulled upward by the remembrance of you. I hope you may be able to pay us a visit at the Gordanne before you have to settle in your new home. My heart goes travelling back now to all the past occasions when you have been so kind to me. Those delicious early months at Oxford I look back upon as a poem introduced into the story of my life; and do you recollect when I came to you as a bride, and you showed me the handsome little wardrobe you had got to hold my wedding finery? Then later on, when we came to Oxford on a bleak, frosty December night, with my little baby in a white lace robe! Then at Cheltenham we came again, and I recollect beautiful little Eva flying about the garden, and stopping to kiss the flowers like a radiant butterfly!"

The formal farewell took place on June 23rd. My husband's address in the great hall of the college, which was crowded to excess, is much too long to insert here *in extenso.*

"It is now sixteen years and a half," he said, "since my predecessor, Dean Howson, made his farewell speech, and introduced me to the representatives of the college."

He then went on to refer to his friends and supporters of 1865 who had passed away; viz., Rector Campbell, Dr. McNeill (afterwards Dean of Ripon), Mr. Parker, "to whose constant and active interest in the college all will bear witness, and to whose friendship, perpetuated in his descendants, I owe more than I can express. Another life-governor, dear to me by more than one tie, Mr. Garston, was a man qualified to shine in Court or Camp, whose chivalrous bearing we all remember. I must add to these the names of Mr. Edward Moon and Gilbert Sandbach, both great friends of the college."

He then alluded to some of the more distinguished pupils whom the college had sent forth into the world. Then he touched on the larger questions; the cause of Education in Liverpool itself, the founding of the new University College there, and other matters. " I have felt on occasions very grateful to the local press of Liverpool for the prominence and publicity kindly given to utterances here on subjects of interest, too often of late subjects of deep sorrow, and this has made me feel somewhat less the want of a chapel attached to the college, which I have sought to obtain, but have not been permitted to realise."

In conclusion he said :—

" I must offer to your chairman, as representative of the Council, my sincere thanks for the confidence that Council have reposed in me for the last sixteen and a half years. I felt it an honour to be invited here from Cheltenham, and I · regard it as a privilege that I have been permitted to assist at my own obsequies. When I announced my wish to retire three months ago, some kind friends in Liverpool expressed the earnest wish that I might obtain some recognition in the way of church preferment. This has come to pass sooner than I could have expected by the offer of a Canonry at Winchester by the Premier. This is naturally a source of great satisfaction to Mrs. Butler and me, as it is precisely the kind of preferment I should have selected had I been able to choose ; and it comes at a time which makes it most acceptable. There is no place which has a greater air of antiquity than Winchester, and it is perhaps appropriate that before going there I should have grown grey in the service of this college. Many proofs of friendship have been shown to me lately, and among them one from the University of Durham, where I spent three years of my life as Tutor, and which has offered to confer on me the degree of Doctor of Divinity. In taking leave of my colleagues I am happy to think that as I have not any single unkind feeling towards any one, so, as I was assured by them yesterday, they entertain feelings of kindness and regard towards me. They have been so generous as to present Mrs. Butler and me with a memorial, which we shall always cherish among our most valuable possessions.

"As one advances in years there are few things which one values more than the affection of the young; and I wish to express to the boys of the Upper, Middle, and Lower Schools my sense of the kindness which prompted them also to offer to us marks of their sympathy and regard, feelings which we cordially reciprocate. I am conscious of many shortcomings, of infirmities of temper, and lack of patience, for which I am responsible, as I am for errors of judgment— which have been, however, involuntary. As one gets older, one does not find sight or hearing to improve, or that capacity for work increases; and all these are necessary qualifications for a Head Master. I therefore thought it my duty to resign my office even before I had any prospect of preferment."

Mr. Alfred Parker spoke as follows :—

"I cannot resist availing myself of the opportunity of saying a few words on the subject which is nearest all our hearts to-day; I mean that this is the last time when we shall see Mr. Butler occupying his chair as Principal of this college.

"Although I am one of Mr. Butler's oldest friends resident here, I do not wish to speak on grounds of private friendship, but rather as a citizen of Liverpool.

"It is difficult to realise that some seventeen years have sped their course since the Dean of Chester resigned the Headmastership of this school to his successor. The name of Butler was one of good augury. It had a classical ring about it. At Cambridge it told of Senior Wranglers, of Senior Classics, and of Fellows of Trinity. At Oxford it told of first classes, of Fellowships, of Ireland and Hertford Scholarships, the latter (the blue ribbon of Oxford Latin

Scholarships) won by Mr. Butler in a good year, against many brilliant competitors.

"But it is not by their University achievements, brilliant though they may be, but as teachers of youth that the name of Butler will go down to posterity. I do not know of any other instance of almost an entire family devoting itself in the strength of its manhood to the cause of Education. Let Rugby, and Haileybury, and Harrow, and Cheltenham, and Liverpool College each tell its tale.

"A Latin poet has compared the Roman schoolboy to the soft and plastic clay, easy to be fashioned by the potter's wheel. Think how many generations of English schoolboys have been sent forth into the world with the genuine stamp of ' Butler ' upon them—a stamp which does not tell alone of the highest scholarship, but which tells of purity, of honour, of manliness, of all those qualifications which English parents most desire their sons to possess.

"I venture to think that few acts of Mr. Gladstone—who is Vice-President of this College—have been more grateful to his native city than the gift of a Canonry at Winchester to one who has worked so long and faithfully for Liverpool.

"What amount of leisure this preferment admits of I do not know, but to one who can converse in several modern languages with the same facility that he can write Greek Iambics or Latin Elegiacs, to one who has written on Art, and whose paintbrush is seldom idle, and who knows how to appreciate the river and the loch, the hill and the moor, the difficulty will only lie in the choice of occupation."

CHAPTER XV.

MIGRATION TO WINCHESTER.—VISIT TO CORNHILL-ON-TWEED.—
FISHING AND SHOOTING.—LAST EXPERIENCE OF THE MOORS.
— GEORGE BUTLER'S OUTDOOR TASTES, AND LOVE OF
ANIMALS.—OUR DOGS.— SUMMER VISIT TO SWITZERLAND
(1882).—DESCRIPTION OF OUR HOME AT WINCHESTER.—
THE CATHEDRAL, AND ITS SERVICES.—VISIT TO SWITZERLAND
(1883). — STORM ON THE LAKE OF BIENNE. — ROSENLAUI,
A HAUNT OF ARTISTS.—LAUTERBRUNNEN.—GRINDELWALD.
—FAMILY GATHERING AT THE "BEAR."—CONGRESS AT THE
HAGUE.—FRIENDLY RECEPTION.—THE PICTURE GALLERIES.

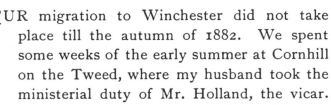

UR migration to Winchester did not take place till the autumn of 1882. We spent some weeks of the early summer at Cornhill on the Tweed, where my husband took the ministerial duty of Mr. Holland, the vicar. We were here in the near neighbourhood of my old home on the Cheviot Hills, and among many old and dear associations. Naturally, we paid many visits to my brother, George Grey, of Milfield Hill (my early home).

J. E. B. to a sister :—

" My husband is quite pleased with his success in fishing this year, and was perfectly happy standing up to his middle in the Tweed, in a cold east wind. The gillie who was with him said, ' Ye winna catch muckle fush the day, sir ; there's a must on the hull ' (a mist on the hill) ; but at the end of the day he changed his opinion, and said, ' Ye 're a real dab, sir ; ye beat Mr. Gregson a' to sticks ! ' "

From Cornhill my husband went to his friend's, Alfred Parker, at Syre, in Sutherlandshire. This was his last experience of the moors. It was not on account of advancing years that he decided that it should be the last, but from the wish to devote his time more exclusively to the duties of his new sphere. "What refreshment you must find" (his brother Montagu wrote to him) "in so pleasant a return to grouse days, and in the discovery that your eye is not dim nor your natural force abated! May it continue so for many years, whatever the poor grouse may have to say as *advocati diaboli* against your canonisation!"

Arthur Butler wrote to me after his brother's death :—

"How sadly short life is! We lose dear friends and relatives long before their time, as it seems to us, and with their powers, all but the one essential power of life, still so fresh and unexhausted. So it was with dear George. His heart was as fresh at seventy as a young man's, and his interest in all the simple pleasures of Nature wholly unabated. To us younger ones in old times he was 'the Squire,' a term first used of him by the farmers at Gayton. It expressed somewhat our views of him in his earlier days—a mixture of dignity, country tastes, and general superiority. His later days were beautiful beyond words."

Those who knew my husband only in his last years can scarcely realise his marked character as an out-of-door man and the keenest of sportsmen. That character was strong in him to the end. I have sometimes been unable to suppress a smile in some solemn public meeting when he occupied a prominent place on the platform. I have seen, (I used to hope that others did not see it—at least, if they were unappreciative), the furtive movement of his right hand, the graceful turn from side to side of the wrist, and the far-off look in his eyes. He was fishing in imagination! He was in spirit in dear Glendale, casting for trout in the Till or the College Burn, among banks of birchen trees and sweet clear pools, wherein his quick eye followed

> " Here and there a lusty trout,
> And here and there a grayling."

And thus he would beguile the time through some uninteresting argument, or long drawn-out peroration, such as sometimes intervene to vary the monotonous enthusiasm of public demonstrations.

I recall the days long ago at Dilston, when, standing at the front door of my father's house and looking down on the Tyne valley, I could see him pacing the stubbles with his dogs in the plain below, and could hear through the clear, frosty September air the almost plaintive voice of the keeper who was with him, " Mr. Butler, sir! wait a bit, sir!" The keeper was a stout walker, yet he had a difficulty in keeping up with my husband's pace through a whole day's walking, and hence this occasional remonstrance. Arthur Butler told me that one day, when he himself was about to take aim at some partridges rising in front of him, he heard a double report from behind, and saw two of the birds before him fall right and left. He turned to see the unerring shot: it was his brother George.

In his last years at Winchester, when he had to a great extent lost his elastic step and vigorous movements, he would still instinctively raise his walking-stick to his eye, in the old attitude of the "crack-shot" of former days, if a bird flew over his head or a rabbit skipped across the meadow. Then in a moment he was erect, and his hand seemed to regain firmness and his eyes brightness as he would recall some memories of old sporting days. Mlle. Humbert, who lived with us for many years as our friend and helper in our work, studied in her walks with him to gain a good sight for the river; for, as she remarked, "the Canon has a bad opinion of anyone who cannot see a fish in the river when it is there, so I have practised seeing them, and I see them beautifully now."

He hated *battues*, and never was present at one; his natural kindness made him shrink from inflicting pain, and he took care therefore never merely to wound a bird, but to kill it dead. Nor was he ever keen to make up a large bag. It was the fresh air, the exercise, and the needful skill which attracted him.

After his retirement to Winchester he kept up to some extent his fishing practice. It was not without charm to him that he had come to the haunts of Isaac Walton, who has immortalised "the troutful streams" of Hampshire, and whose tomb is in the cathedral. He did not, however, so much enjoy the slow, smooth-flowing rivers of the South as the more lively ones of the North.

In 1884 he fished for some days at Ringwood. He wrote :—

"I slept eight hours without waking last night after fishing, and no doubt I shall do the same to-night. Yesterday I jumped over a great many ditches, and didn't slip once. It is some good having had experience in the fen country at Peterboro. I caught a splendid salmon of about twenty pounds; so I am not such an old man after all! My boy was much excited about this fish."

Not only the boy, but also our dear brother canons seemed much interested in this fish. Several of them came to admire the said salmon, rather reminding one, except for the difference of dress and countenance, of pictures of " Bolton Abbey in the olden time," when the monks gathered round to admire the fishing results of one of their brethren.

He wrote from the Duke of Bedford's seat at Chenies to his son Stanley :—

" May 17th, 1884.

" This is the anniversary of your birth ; and though I am absent from you in the body, I wish to assure you that I am with you in the spirit, and pray for every blessing on you. The sun is shining brightly, too brightly for fishing, and the cuckoo is making itself heard. Sir James Stephen came down to meet Froude here, and we found Matthew Arnold and his son, so we have had some pleasant conversation. It is a beautiful river here, and much improved, like the Lathgill, by little weirs which form streams."

In order to give a complete idea of my husband's kindliness of nature, and to fill in some characteristic touches of his home life, I must speak of our affectionate companions—our dogs.

It seems to me sometimes that the world is divided by rather a sharp line into people who love dogs and people who do not love them, or are indifferent to them and to the animal creation in general. Anyone of the latter category who may happen to have read thus far, had better just pass over the next few pages, as probably the spirit of them may appear to him puerile. At the same time he may usefully reflect that God made these creatures, only a little lower than man, as man himself is only " a little lower than the angels." Individuals among them, it must be acknowledged, have excelled in certain virtues—Christian graces, one might almost say, in which men are too often wanting—such as patience, long-

suffering, forgivingness, and fidelity, even to death. Mrs.
Barret Browning wrote of her dog :—

> " Tears are in my eyes to feel
>   Thou art made so straightly,
> Blessing needs must straighten too ;
> Little canst thou joy or do,
>   Thou who *lovest greatly*."

But are we so sure of the limitations to which these,
our fellow-creatures, endowed with such strong affections,
are subjected ? Is it given to us in our wisdom exactly
to measure those limitations, or to affirm dogmatically
that so divine a thing as love in any creature—love which
is capable of outliving unkindness and neglect, which
endures every test, and becomes more and more perfect
to the end—is destined to perish everlastingly ? In some
of the nobler animals, under favourable circumstances,
especially dogs, there is distinct development and perfecting of character as they grow older. To what end is
this perfecting ? St. Francis of Assisi acknowledged
brotherhood with all the creatures of God's hand. He
reverenced and loved them. The love that was in him,
the legend says, overcame the ferocity even of the wolfish
nature. He sought one day in the forest a savage wolf,
the terror of the villages and the murderer of flocks:
" Brother wolf," he said, " if thou wilt now repent and
change thy manner of life, give me thy hand in token
thereof;" and the gaunt beast wheedled up to him, fawning,
and sweeping the ground with its tail, and holding out
to him its right paw. Following him home, it became his
docile companion from that time forward. A pretty
legend, you say; yet only one of many such legends of
the animal-loving saint, which prove how strong a bond
of sympathy may exist between a Christian man and

25

God's dumb creation, down to the humblest being which has life. " Thou shalt be in league with the stones of the field, and the beasts of the field shall be at peace with thee." (Job v.) St. Francis accepted these words as of literal purport, and such they became to him.

The attraction which animals had towards my husband was notable. Our dogs would hardly look at any of us if he was present. Little children were in the same way attracted to him. I have seen little girls, strangers to him, run to him in the road, and, looking up in his face, eagerly impart to him some childish confidence. Babies whom he christened seemed to feel safe with him. Being pillowed on his arm induced composure and sleep, even if they had been fractious a moment before.

Visitors to Switzerland know that every Swiss peasant keeps a cat, on account of the cheeses and consequent mice. We were often amused to see these Swiss cats leave their hunting of mice and lizards in the meadows and run to the footpath which we were treading, making straight for this lover of animals, and rubbing themselves, tails erect, against his ankles, as if instinctively conscious of his liking for them, and sure of a caress. A cat of his own would follow him out of doors like a dog, answering to his whistle.

Our first dog friend was Bunty; (the origin of the name is obscure). He lived with us many years at Liverpool, and came with us to Winchester. He was a dog of excellent parts; not of pure breed, chiefly otter-hound. He had beautiful eyes, full of human expression. He had a strong sense of humour. It is generally said that dogs hate to be laughed at. This was not the case with Bunty. He could bear to be laughed at, would enter into the joke, and, so to speak, turn the laugh against himself,

by behaving in a manner which he well knew would excite
laughter. He shared many pleasant holidays with us.
He was a strong swimmer and diver, and was of a most
social and genial temper. Like most well brought up
dogs, he was very honourable. When his dinner was
set before him, and his master pronounced the word
"creditum," he would not touch it, but rushed for it as
soon as he heard the word "absolutum." [It was cur-
rently reported among the younger boys at Liverpool
College that he knew a little Greek as well as Latin.] He
was once shut into a room alone, very hungry, with a
delicious plate of meat on the floor. After some time we
went in. The good dog was standing as still as a statue
beside the plate, but with his face averted and his eyes
steadily fixed on the opposite wall, that he might not be
tempted; wiser than some Christians, for whom the
discipline would have been too severe of not even looking
upon a forbidden thing. He died in 1883. "I am very
sorry," my husband wrote, "to hear your account of our
faithful dog's illness. I have written to his doctor about
him; and having done what, according to our light, is
best for the dear dog, we must leave him to the Providence which watches over sparrows and will not overlook
faithful dogs." I was not at home when he died. "I
gave dear old Bunty his last cup of tea this afternoon,"
wrote his master, "and a piece of bread and butter. He
took both from my hand, but did not come out of his
kennel; he is evidently dying. The gardener is digging
his grave, and he will be interred with all respect, and
leave behind him precious memories." My husband had
the free hand of a sculptor. A few things which he
carved in stone were worthy of preservation; among
them a perfect likeness in stone of this good dog, in an

attitude of watchful repose. Beneath, he carved the words ·—

ΑΡΙΣΤΟΥ . ΚΥΝΟΣ . ΣΗΜΑ.

"Some of my friends," he wrote, "find a difficulty in believing that I carved Bunty's likeness in stone. Froude says, some centuries hence, when the monument is disinterred and its inscription discovered, some Dryasdust will start a theory that a Greek colony once inhabited the Close. Every-one seems to be in a state of alarm just now about mad dogs. The 'curare' poison appears to be the old 'wourali' poison discovered among the North-American Indians by Waterton. I hope people will learn to treat dogs more sensibly and naturally, and then they won't go mad. The *Lancet* recom-mends everyone to be inoculated for hydrophobia. Let the editors begin, and the sub-editors tell us how they died."

Bunty's successor was Carlo, (he died the other day), a handsome thorough-bred retriever, quite black, with shining curls—a sensible, gentlemanlike dog, excellent in his own special art of retrieving birds, and an uncompromising guard and watchdog. His attach-ment to his master, whom he outlived for two years, was profound. This poor dog was very wretched and melancholy when his master left his home for the last time and returned no more. He would seek him in every corner of the house, and along the riverside where he had been accustomed to walk with him or watch him fishing; and returning, would rest his chin on the arm of his master's empty study chair, as if waiting for the familiar hand to pat his head. His dumb grief was very touching. I must mention also a later treasure, a splendid St. Bernard—Eiger—the gift of Emil Boss, of Grindelwald.

Our Winchester home not being yet ready for us, we

went to Switzerland in 1882. I went on in advance, direct to my sister's home, the Gordanne.

To G. B. :—

"La Gordanne, August 6th.

"I got safely here last night. I had never before had the misfortune to travel in the height of the season, when London passenger-birds are on the wing. The crowds and rush for places were very great. Our train was of such exceptional length that I, being in the last carriage, had to alight among the pine woods outside Rolle. The Meuricoffres' carriage was waiting for me. It was quite dark. As I came up the drive here I saw a cheerful sight—Tell, Hatty, Thekla, and the two little boys all waiting at the door with lamps or candles in their hands, like a family of glowworms. And then such a forest of loving hands held out to greet me. They had arrived from the mountains only three hours before. The place looks lovely this morning—great masses of splendid geraniums and hydrangeas!—the lawns so pretty, and the fountains. They will all be so glad to see you here."

"August 8th.

"Last evening was very beautiful. I sat alone for an hour under the large linden tree up above the vineyards, whence one sees the whole of the lake below. Mont Blanc rose, a mass of spotless snow, into a cloudless sky, and then majestically and slowly folded broader and broader shadows across his huge white shoulders as the sun lowered, and the portion of his snows which was still in the light became first golden and then ruby-coloured. Such a sight makes one think what must be the beauty of Him who creates, when His creation is so beautiful."

I went on with two of my sons to the Diablerets, and from there, where my husband joined us, to Champery, at the foot of the Dent du Midi, whence we made some pleasant excursions.

We finally settled in our new home before Christmas. How can I describe the charm which that new home had for us?—the beautiful old house, with its thick walls, its picturesque gables, its antiquity (dating from the time of St. Swithin, Chancellor to Alfred the Great), its ample accommodation, which enabled us to receive many friends and relatives, and its surroundings of fine ancestral trees and flowering shrubs, gorgeous in spring! We enjoyed especially our secluded garden at the back of the house, which served in summer as a kind of out-door drawing-room. Many memories cling round that little garden. There were trees which gave shade in summer, under which in later years played our little grandchildren, or lay asleep on the soft grass among rugs and shawls, our large dogs guarding them,—a sight which the grandfather loved. In that garden also, many social gatherings were held. People of various nationalities paid us visits at different times—French, Swiss, Italians, Germans, and Dutch. Freedom and privacy were pleasantly combined within the precincts. The well-fed thrush's song, the gentle breeze among the trees, and the periodical sleepy chimes of the cathedral clock, or of its bells calling to prayer, were often the only sounds to be heard in the stillness. The quietness in the evening after the gates of the Close were shut was very soothing. In the closing years of a very busy life, nothing could have been sweeter. To crown the pleasantness of it, there was a strong feeling of brotherhood in the society of the Close, which increased amongst us as time went on. Dean Bramston was dean when we first went there. He was succeeded by Dean Kitchin, between whom and my husband a very strong friendship grew up. The places of four of the canons

whom we found there when we went were vacated during·
the first six years of my husband's residence. The death
of the Venerable Archdeacon Jacob at a ripe age was
followed by those of Bishop McDougal and Archdeacon
Atkinson. Canon Carus retired. In my husband's later
years, Canon Warburton showed him much kindness,
invariably offering to take his place in the Cathedral when
his strength began to fail, as he had himself done for
others while able.

On first coming to Winchester we felt the change in
the social atmosphere from that of the North of England
to be rather abrupt. The society of Winchester is largely
ecclesiastical and military, there being a military depôt
there. Two sounds in the air which were periodically
alternated proclaimed the principal elements in the social
life of Winchester; viz., those of church clocks and bells
and of the bugle at the barracks, echoed from the opposite
hills. There seemed to be less breathing space, so to
speak, socially and politically, if not intellectually: yet
expansion to a great extent was possible within so easy a
reach of London, and with so much coming and going.
It was often remarked that the society of the Close itself
was less conventional and more liberal, in the best sense,
than that of the city outside.

I recall my husband's love for the noble cathedral,
which grew gradually to be to him as a friend. Its august
mass of stone-work formed for us in the Close a wide and
solid screen against the north wind. Internally it was a
place of repose to which one could resort at any and all
hours for moments of silence and rest, or for the enjoyment of its inspiring music and services, which do not
become monotonous to a soul accustomed to offer real and
spiritual prayer and praise; though to those who are not

so accustomed, it may, I can imagine, become fatally mechanical and deadening.

My husband disliked all littleness and formality in religious observances. I visited once with him a pretty church about a day's journey from Winchester, where the ritualistic element prevailed. A very gentle and courteous young curate showed us the beauties of the place, detaining us a long time especially to display before us one after another a collection of altar cloths exquisitely embroidered. There seemed to be one for each holy-day of the Christian year, as well as for each month. My husband spoke kindly to our young host, but after a time whispered to me, " Do let us get away from this, and into the fresh air ;" and we left the church. As we walked through the meadows he was silent for some time, and then spoke kindly of this young clergyman, at the same time saying: " I wonder if he really thinks that all this prettiness is acceptable to God ? Poor young man ! We need a revival of spiritual life in our Church, and an awakened sense of the great truths which we have to defend, and of the spiritual warfare in the world around us. There is so little reality in all this kind of thing !"

But our fine old cathedral at Winchester was as far as possible removed from all littleness ; grave and grand, a monument of ancient times, and laden with historic memories of the deepest interest. When he lost his health it became a real rest and help to my husband, physically as well as spiritually, to take his part in the services there. It seemed to withdraw him from the anxieties of the world, to lift him in some measure even above bodily pain and weariness, and to enable him simply to contemplate the eternal realities and the " rest which remaineth for the people of God."

In 1883 we again visited Switzerland.

J. E. B. to a son :—

"Neuchâtel, July, 1883.

" At the little conferences we have had the stone-throwers were kept quiet, but yesterday father and I had a narrow escape from 'a watery grave.' It is dangerous to make excursions in such weather. There is splendid sunshine and great heat ; but once in every twenty-four hours there comes a storm of such violence that people rush to fasten doors and windows, and anchor their boats in the lakes. It sweeps down from the Jura with great rapidity. First there comes on a moaning, tearing wind, breaking the trees ; and then hailstones and coals of fire, forked lightning of many colours dashing about. Then follows a roaring of thunder, as if the gods were amusing themselves by emptying out cartloads of iron bars from the clouds. This has lasted nearly three weeks. Yesterday, however, seemed more settled, with a breeze from the north ; so we started early, taking our dinner with us, and went to a village in the canton of Berne, on the border of the Lake of Bienne. We went across the lake to the island of St. Pierre, a beautifully wooded little island, standing isolated. It is where J. Jacques Rousseau retired to live, and where he wrote his famous *Contrat Social.* The row across was pleasant, and the weather beautiful. A man and his wife rowed, as there are no steamers, and they remained to take us back. We wandered about the beautiful woods, and then had our repast on the grass, and some coffee at a little châlet, from which we had a splendid panorama of the snow mountains. The Finsterarhorn came out the most distinctly, and then the whole family of the peaks which you know so well. We visited Rousseau's room, a dismal stone apartment, with one very little window, but commanding a view of the Bernese snow-giants. There is a trap-door in the floor, through which he used to escape when visitors came whom he wished to avoid. In the evening we walked back to our landing-place to take our boat, and all seemed serene except a very small black streak to the south-west. We rowed through the calm lake, admiring the evening glow. It was about a quarter to six. The black streak came nearer and nearer, followed by a whistling sound in the air. We had still more than a mile to row. We were not so far, however, from the actual shore; but that shore presented no landing-place, only rocks and *débris*. The Miss Humberts begged that we should make straight for the rocks, but the boatman said there was no fear, and bade us be calm. He had hardly spoken the words when his wife, a much taller and more muscular person than her husband, gave a wild shriek, and called to her husband in her loud, rough Bernois: 'To the shore! There's not a moment to lose!' Her husband obeyed, and they strained themselves to the utmost. The perspiration rolled down her brown, weather-beaten face, and her hair was flowing loosely back. We had not reached the shore when there swept over us a horrid darkness, and we were in a cloud, in the midst of a howling wind, so strong that no boat could have stood it. Lightning hissed into the lake like sticks and bars of fire, and the water which had been so calm a moment before was torn up into furious waves with foaming crests. I never saw anything so sudden. Everything was soon blotted out of sight except a piece of the wet rock jutting out where we wished to land. The boatwoman was the first to jump into the foaming water, and with her strong arms to seize the chain and haul the prow of the boat to a little point of the rock. We all jumped out and scrambled up to the top of the rock as best we could, but even when landed we could scarcely stand. There was a fishing-boat, the only object visible, near, which we watched as it whirled round and round before the blast, tossed about like a withered leaf in autumn. Happily it was empty. Our boat soon filled with water, as the rain was now falling in bucketsful, or rather in waterspouts. We reached the railway, and walked along it to the nearest station, of course very wet, but thankful to be alive."

From Neuchâtel we went to Rosenlaüi.

To Amélie Humbert :—

" We came here from Meiringen yesterday, my husband walking and I riding. The porter had put our portmanteaus and all our belongings on one rather weak-looking horse, and on the steepest part of the ascent the strap broke, and all my husband's sketching things and our rugs were rolling down the hill on their way back to Meiringen. We were trying to rescue them in a drenching rain, when a head appeared above the bank, on a level with our feet, and a strong man jumped up and said in German : 'Ah! I see. I am a Meiringen guide; my name is Andreas, and I will help you. Six francs and trinkgeld.' Andreas himself carried two heavy portmanteaus, and the rest was replaced on the horse. He made many jokes on the way to cheer us, and so we arrived at Rosenlaui, very wet, in the cold of the evening, which was rather severe. There were many English in the little, slightly-built wooden hotel ; so every window was of course wide open. This the English call bracing. I felt it to be cruel. I certainly love best the more tender scenery of Switzerland, with the snow mountains at a little distance. Then they look indeed like heaven's sentinels and strong watchmen. Here we are too much just under them, half buried by their monstrous bulk ; we can hardly see the sky from our windows. I like a wider horizon. To-day, how-ever, the sun came out, and we went to a little open plain some way off, where we spent the whole day among pine trees, on a dry slope of fine grass, facing a magnificent view of the Rosenlaui glacier, with its hummocks of sky-blue ice ; and of theWellhorn, Wetterhorn, and Engelhörner."

To a son :—

" Meiringen.

"After a week at Rosenlaui I came down here alone, by father's advice, as it was so cold. I was just in time, for the first thing I heard this morning was that the road was broken down in the night by the heavy rains, and is now impassable. Yesterday, as I passed the insecure part, it struck me that it must give way before long. There were holes in the road, like trapdoors, through which you could look down a steep bank to the glacier river. My guide kept very close to the inside bank, away from the holes. It seems strange to be separated in this way from dear father; but I am sure he is congratulating himself that I got safely down. I sent him back word to that effect by two gentlemen who were walking up before the accident occurred. He is not without society. The place is a great haunt of artists, like North Wales, where 'you can't throw a stone anywhere without hitting an artist.' Sir Robert Collier is there, painting one of his great Royal Academy pictures of the Rosenlaui glacier. He said father had selected exactly the best spot for the view. Mr. Severn also is there, and M. Berthoud, President of the Swiss Academy of Painting, whose large Alpine pictures you have seen, and who is a very pleasant companion."

From G. B.:—

"Rosenlaui.

"I shall only stay to finish my afternoon sketch, which Sir Robert Collier approves of, and advises me to stay another day to finish. The artists are getting on well. Sir Robert is making a beautiful picture. Mr. Severn is doing a large water-colour drawing just below the little bridge which we went over. M. Berthoud also has been very busy. We are a very pleasant society, if only you were here. Your approval of my drawings is worth more than anyone's to me."

From J. E. B.:—

"I am glad that you are a pupil under two such distinguished painters as Berthoud and Sir Robert Collier. They have all sorts of tricks, those painters, whereby they produce their fine effects and avoid many painful struggles through which we humble imitators go. I see there is more snow than ever on the Wellhorn to-day. What an extraordinary year! There is as much snow as they generally have in April or May. I am going on to Berne, where we shall all meet, please God."

" Berne.

" It seems very strange to be here alone. I have been thinking much of the old days of our united family party in our travels, and the cheerful companionship of our sons; and the old scenes come before me. I have been to the famous ice and cake shop here for a cup of tea, and it recalled the merry parties which used to meet there. We shall be less and less able in future to go about all together. I have a telegram from Hatty (Mme. Mauricoffre). She cannot get away for some time. Her duties to the dying and wounded keep her. She had friends and acquaintances at Casamicciola, some of whom are buried in the ruins, others rescued with difficulty. I have been reading a terribly interesting letter from her about the earthquake. She has also taken charge of a number of little orphaned children who have been dug out from the ruins of villages in other parts of Ischia, and are gathered together in her house and courtyard. What scenes she has witnessed ! "

Two of our sons having come out from England, we went together to Lauterbrunnen.

To a niece at Seelisberg :—

" Lauterbrunnen.

" Dearest Constance,—Yesterday our gentlemen walked down from the Wengern Schiedeg. They had sent word to me not to join them, for it was too cold. To-day (Sunday) is a lovely day. Your uncle and George have gone up to Mürren to see Dr. Montagu Butler and the church which he got built there. Stanley remains with me, and we are going out to spend our Sunday somewhere in the meadows, in view of the Silverhorn, which this morning is like an angel of light, basking in the sunshine of God's presence. George and Stanley amused me by their account of their father's doings at the Wengern Schiedeg. He has become so strong and hardy since he came to Switzerland, that he ventures on rather bold things. One morning he went out in a thick rolling mist at 7 a.m. to sketch, and sat down on a wet, slippery rock (at an elevation, as you know, of some 7,000 feet) to make the portrait of a fine old Alpine cedar, at least whenever it appeared through a rent in the mist. After a while, he said, ' I was up early, I think I will take a nap;' and off he went into a sound sleep, wrapped in a blanket of icy-cold cloud, and sitting on a wet rock ! He was rather annoyed when they woke him up after a while; but he was none the worse. Yesterday, when coming down through the forest, he said he believed there was a 'shorter cut' to Lauterbrunnen, and he at least would try it. His sons, though convinced that there was none, let him go; but as he was long away, they began to get uneasy, and followed. He had gone over some horribly rough ground, and was just advancing through thick brush to the edge of a very high rock, which comes straight down upon the valley. ' Mother would think it a very short cut indeed,' they said to him, ' if she saw you coming down there through the sky.' He laughed, and merely remarked : ' It's rather rougher than I thought. I've been down once or twice, but am none the worse.' They arrived safely, and we had tea together; and I read to them Aunt Hatty's letters about Ischia. To-morrow your uncle means to mount his eagle's nest again, to sketch on wet rocks. I go to Grindelwald, where we shall all meet. I hope Aunt Hatty and Thekla will also come there, to our old home, the ' Bear.' How it will remind us of old days, our talks and walks, and the dogs and the horses and the guides ! George tells me there is a family of twelve St. Bernard pups, all the grand-children of old Sultan. He says they have blue, puzzled eyes, and look rather sad, as if they knew they were born into a world of sin and sorrow ! ' "

This hope was realised of a family gathering once more at Grindelwald, after which my husband returned to Winchester for Chapter business. · He wrote to me :

" Winchester, September 3rd.

" I arrived here after a successful journey. No words could describe the extreme beauty of the mountains after I left you. As we drove into Berne, we got ·the cathedral and public buildings in full relief against the range of mountains, which were clearer than I ever saw them. I hope dear Stanley has made a successful ascent of the Schreckhorn. It looked lovely from the lake of Thun, with two caps of fresh snow, one on the tip of each horn. What a pleasant time we have had !"

"September 8th.

" I received your deeply-interesting letter, giving me an account of your meeting with the poor hunted girls* at the Château Gingins. What a state of slavery the Genevese have imposed upon themselves ! I hope you will be able to state the case in a way to stir up any feelings which Lord Granville has similar to those which Lord Palmerston expressed when he quoted 'Civis Romanus sum.' I trust Miss Booth will reach home in safety. Perhaps she will come and take a rest with us in the quiet of the Close."†

The third triennial Congress of our Abolitionist Federation was held this year at the Hague. Our principles had made great advance during the last three years on the Continent.

J. E. B. to a sister ·—

" The Hague, Holland, September 17th.

" Our opening meeting was held with great solemnity in the historical Trèves-Zaal, where Ministers of State meet in Council, close to the House of Parliament. This beautiful hall was lent to us by the Government. The town was very gay, for the King opened Parliament in this hall on the morning of our opening meeting. As soon as this ceremony was over, we entered, amidst decorations of flowers and banners, and with the sound of the retiring military bands in our ears. Our President, M. Emile de Laveleye, made a very striking

* Catherine Booth and Maud Charlesworth.

† Catherine Booth did come to rest with us for a few days. She enjoyed much the quiet and my husband's sketches of Swiss scenes.

inaugural address. Then the Baron von Schimmelpenninck pronounced a cordial welcome to the Congress in the name of his country. That evening the Mayor of the Hague gave us a brilliant reception, at which about three hundred members of the Congress were present. Our daily séances have been held in the large Hall of Arts and Sciences. On Wednesday, my husband read a paper on 'The Corporate Action of the Religious Bodies in England' in regard to our question, in which he remarked that that action had formed one of the main elements in the campaign which terminated in the victory of April 20th of this year. The mention of religious liberty would be nowhere, he said, better received than at the Hague, in the heart of a people whose heroic struggle for national independence and freedom of worship formed one of the noblest features of modern history. He then gave an account of the adhesion to our cause of the Nonconformist Churches, who 'stood like a wall of stone,' and to the gradual coming round to our side of many thousands of Anglican clergy, who 'in general had some class prejudices to get over before they could look fairly at any movement of and for the people,' but who were now largely won.

"Mr. Modderman, late Minister of Justice, sent in his adhesion to the Federation, and the poor Prince of Orange, who is confined to his room, asked our Continental Secretary to go and see him and tell him all about us. He read eagerly the papers given to him, and expressed his sympathy with the movement. A few of us went as a deputation to the Minister of the Interior on Wednesday, and the next day to the Minister of Justice, one of the Ministers sending his large carriage to the hall to be at our disposal. It is pleasant; when we think how any allusion to our work is still avoided and disliked in England, to find such a cordial welcome here, and so much respect and kindness from members of the Legislature and of the King's household, as well as from the people generally. M. Pierson preached a magnificent sermon in Dutch, in allusion to our work, in the great cathedral, on the Sunday before our opening meeting. The Queen was present.

M. Casembroot, Admiral of the Fleet, gave his adhesion publicly at one of our meetings, saying he saw the immense difficulties before us, but adding : ' I should be unworthy to be a sailor if I hesitated in the presence of difficulties. We must brave the tempest, and, if needful, die to save the ship.' Baron von Schimmelpenninck invited some of us to a dinner, or banquet, in a large room of one of the hotels. There were there almost all the Ministers of State. Speeches were made, not at the end of dinner, as in England, but between each course. Lastly, the Count and Countess von Hogendorp gave us a reception in their rooms, at which we made our farewells to our friends.

"We have enjoyed the picture galleries very much. Paul Potter's bull and the portrait of William the Silent are, on the whole, the most striking paintings. What a noble face the Silent's is, and what a noble character it was ! And now we are about to start homewards. We came here by the Rhine as far as Cologne, and met on the steamer the American delegates and the Mayor of Colmar, on their way also to the Congress. My husband came from Winchester with George, and met us here the day before the opening of the Congress. He made the farewell complimentary speech, in which he alluded to the historical names and inheritance of renown of some of the Dutch families who had shown us so much kindness. Tell Meuricoffre's introductions here have been most valuable."

CHAPTER XVI.

CONTINUANCE OF PUBLIC WORK.—ELECTION OF M. EMILE DE
LAVELEYE AS PRESIDENT OF OUR SOCIETY.—CORRESPON-
DENCE —DEBATES IN PARLIAMENT.—VICTORY.—WE WERE
"LIKE UNTO THEM THAT DREAM."—VISIT TO ZERMATT.—
THE MATTERHORN.—MEETING AT BALE, 1884.—THE CHURCH
AT GRINDELWALD.—VISIT TO CHAMOUNIX, 1885.—CONFER-
ENCE AT ANTWERP.—VISIT TO BARON PRISSE AT ST. NICOLAS.
—TRIAL OF MR. STEAD.—CRIMINAL LAW AMENDMENT ACT.—
DEATH OF A BROTHER.—JOURNEY TO THE SOUTH OF FRANCE.
—-AVIGNON.—CANNES.—GENOA.

GO back a little way to continue the record of our part in the movement in which we worked for many years.

In the spring of 1882 I was called to give evidence before the Parliamentary Committee which had been sitting for some years, and which, when closed, did not throw much more light upon the question than the Royal Commission had done, although it elicited a very powerful expression of opinion from the country and from the churches, which had had time to mature their convictions. My husband was still working closely at Liverpool. He wrote to me in London: "To-morrow you will have your grand fight in the Committee, in which I prophesy that you will be victorious and aid the good cause greatly. May God be with you."

To my husband ·—

"May 5th.

"I find it hard work mastering all the details to which I may have to answer to-morrow. When you get this I shall be before the Committee. I know you will be praying for me. My brief is rather a full one. Political affairs are indeed start-ling. Some of the ladies I have seen very much desire to be allowed to have your paper printed. They have taken up the question of Protective Laws for Girls, and ask your leave to cut your paper into two, making it into two leaflets. I said I felt sure you would consent to this. Lady Selborne is inter-ested in the matter, and Mrs. Gladstone. But I think these ladies are much in need of better information on the whole subject. They are, of course, in a position of influence, and as they desire now to help against the great evil, we must thank God for it."

From my husband :—

" I hope your examination is drawing to a successful close. I walked out alone this afternoon, and as I walked I prayed that you might be sustained by our Heavenly Father, and deliver your evidence without fear or faltering, and without suffering from the exertion. If you find it necessary to rest to-morrow, pray do so. Though I long for your presence I can endure a brief spell of waiting. I hope you have called on our dear friend Mr. Thomasson. When you do, pray say to him and Mrs. Thomasson all that is kind from me."

In the course of our visit to Switzerland of which I have spoken, in 1882, we attended the annual Conference of the Federation, which was held at Neuchâtel. At that meeting M. Emile de Laveleye was elected as our Presi-dent. My husband, speaking for his friend Lord Derwent, our late President, said :—

" Lord Derwent is prevented by illness from presiding on this occasion. He has rendered valuable service to our cause. I am sure that all who remember the dignity, courtesy and ability with which he presided at the Conference in London last year, must regret his absence on public as well as private grounds. In fulfilling the duties of his position he has united

the firmness of a judge with the courtesy of a high bred gen.
tleman and the *savoir'faire* of an old member of the House of
Commons. We are now compelled to seek another President.
No one unites so many high qualifications as M. Emile de
Laveleye, who is not only one of the most distinguished
literary men in Europe, but who stands at the head of modern
writers on political economy. We owe him much for his
past great services. He is not one whom we have had to
convert to our views. His keen intellectual insight at once
made it clear to him that under no circumstances is it per-
missible to make a compromise with vice."

A resolution condemning the legislation we opposed
was brought in towards the end of April, 1883, by Mr. C.
H. Hopwood, but was, unfortunately, "crowded out."
The occasion was not, however, lost either upon the
Legislature or the country, as may be judged by the
following : *

To my son Stanley. :—

"Winchester, March 3rd, 1883.

"We have had some hard work lately. Father and I
went to Cambridge for a quiet Sunday. It was bright and
pleasant there, and the Fellows' garden was beginning to put
on its spring clothing. Then we came up to London to
prepare for the coming on of our question in the House. A
Member of Parliament whom we met at Cambridge told us
that the amount of pressure brought to bear at this moment by
the country was, he thought, ' unprecedented in the history of
any agitation.' Our friends are active in every nook and
corner of the country; even from remote villages petitions
come pouring in. Also many single petitions, such as from
Cardinal Manning and the Moderator of the Free Church of
Scotland. Mr. Hopwood told us that several M.P.'s came to
him yesterday and said they must vote with us, though before

The actual abolition of this legislation took place only two years
later.

they had been hostile. 'It is a strange thing,' said one, 'that ·
people care so much about this question. All my leading
constituents have urged me to vote with you.' One of our
strongest opponents, a military man, said to him: ' Well ! you
have had extraordinary support from the country; it is evident
that yours is the winning side.' I was in the lobby two days
ago, and saw a petition lying in someone's hand, on the back
of which was written : ' Petition from 1553 inhabitants of
West Ham.' You know that these are poor working fathers
and mothers, some of whom have lately had their children
stolen. They have had less than a week to collect these
names. These silent figures are eloquent. There is a distinct change of tone in the House, and your father and I
believe that it dates from the time that we came forward
publicly to confess God as our Leader. Our cause was
openly baptized, so to speak, in the name of Christ, and our
advance has been steady ever since. Also, I thought I saw
what I never observed before in the sceptical and worldly
atmosphere of Parliament—*i.e.* signs of a consciousness of
a spiritual strife going on. Some members spoke to us of
the spiritual power in our movement ; while on the other
hand there is a seething and boiling of unworthy passions
such as would appal one if one did not remember that it was
when the great Incarnation of purity drew near to the ' possessed ' man, of old, that the 'unclean spirits' cried out.

" To return to my story. Some of our friends in Parliament telegraphed to us at Cambridge that no debate would
come on, on account of the arrears of talk on the Address.
This is disappointing. Mr. W. E. Forster's management of
Irish affairs necessitates much discussion.

" We have arranged for a great meeting for prayer. We
shall hold it close to the House of Commons during the whole
debate if there is one, and all night if the debate lasts all
night. We have invited about twenty of our best friends in
the House to join us. This meeting has been advertised in
the *Times*, the *Standard* and *Daily News*. Some of our parliamentary friends counselled this course, saying that it was
well that all the world should know with what weapons and

in whose name we make war, even if they scoff at the idea, as of course many do."

March 4th.

" We went to the House at four o'clock yesterday. Justin McCarthy was speaking. There was still to the last a chance of Mr. Hopwood's resolution coming on, but perhaps not till midnight. I did not remain in the Ladies' Gallery, but came and went from the Prayer Meeting to the Lobby of the House. We saw John Morley take the oath and his seat. The first thing he did after taking the oath was to sit down by Mr. Hopwood and say : ' Now tell me what I can do to help you to-night, for the thing our Newcastle electors were most persistent about was that I should oppose this legislation.' I then went to the Westminster Palace Hotel, where we had taken a large room for our devotional meeting. There were well-dressed ladies—some even of high rank—kneeling together (almost side by side) with the poorest, and some of the outcast women of the purlieus of Westminster. Many were weeping, but when I first went in they were singing ; and I never heard a sweeter sound. There were some cultivated voices amongst them, and the hymns were well chosen. I felt ready to cry, but I did not ; for I long ago rejected the old ideal of the ' division of labour,' that ' men must work and women must weep.' A venerable lady from America rose and said : ' Tears are good, prayers are better ; but we should get on better if behind every tear there was a vote at the ballot-box.' Every soul in that room responded to that sentiment. I never saw a meeting more moved. The occasion and the circumstances were certainly pathetic. As we continued to pray, we all felt, I think, a great pity come into our hearts for those men who were at that moment in the House, so near to us, who wield so great a responsibility, and so many of whom will have a sad account to give of their use of it.

" Charles Parker told me next day that at that time several M.P.'s were walking about the Lobby, and that two young men, not long in Parliament, said to him : ' Have you heard, Parker, that the ladies were to hold a prayer meeting

to-night to pray for us ? But I suppose it is given up, as this
debate is to be postponed.' Mr. Parker, better informed,
said : ' On the contrary, that is just what they are doing now,
praying for us. It throws a great responsibility on *us*.' The
young men, he said, looked very grave. Father had to return
home ; I went back to the House, while other women remained
and continued their intercessions. All Westminster was
wrapped in a haze, out of which glared only the great light
on the Clock Tower. I walked through the mist, feeling
rather sad, and wondering how much longer this horrible
yoke would remain fastened on the neck of a people who
wish to get rid of it, and how long women will be refused
a voice in the representation of the country. I climbed up
the wearisome gallery stairs, and from the grating saw a
crowd of our gentlemen friends from the country sitting in the
Strangers' Gallery opposite. How patiently they sat through
those long hours ! Some of them had come even from Scotland
for the purpose. Father had gone home ; but just above the
clock I saw George, and tried to catch his eye, but he, believing that I was at the other meeting, did not look towards
our gallery or see me. I sat on till midnight for the chance
of our resolution coming on. By-and-by Mr. Hopwood asked
the Speaker's leave to make a statement. He then made a
very good speech, explaining, rather to the country than to
the House, how it was he was prevented from bringing on
his resolution, and saying that Parliament and the Government should have no peace on the question, for the country
was aroused and nothing could lessen their present determination. He called them to witness to the needless waste of
time there had been in talking and recriminations before midnight. Mr. Trevelyan told me he thought our opponents
had purposely prolonged the debate on the Address.

" I must tell you that just in the second hour of our
prayers your telegram was handed to me. I thought it was
some business, and was pleasantly surprised when I saw it
was from St. Andrews—so far off,—and yet it brought you
so near, and just at a moment when it was peculiarly
precious to me.

"After another half hour at the meeting I returned once more to the Lobby of the House and found some of our friends waiting about. They took me out on to the terrace along the river front. The fog had cleared away, and it was very calm under the starlit sky. All the bustle of the city was stilled, and the only sound was that of the dark water lapping against the buttresses of the broad stone terrace—the water into which so many despairing women have flung themselves.

"I forgot to tell you that before the debate began I ventured into the circular hall or lobby next to the House itself, having caught sight of the venerable face of old Mr. Whitwell. He remembered me and shook hands. I stood near him in a corner, as if he had taken me under his protection. The first word he said to me was: 'Has it ever struck you that there is no one thing in the whole of Christ's discourses to which He has given such emphasis as that of the certainty of prayer being answered? Now you may be sure our persevering prayers will be answered in this matter.' I saw several other friends, among them your member, Mr. Williamson, who said: 'Tell your son that I have presented his petition from St. Andrews, and that I support the prayer of it with all my heart.' I am glad to tell you Albert Grey and Robert Reid, father's old pupil at Cheltenham, are with us on the question. I met Cardinal Manning in the Lobby and had a pleasant talk with him. He is much in earnest about all good movements. He has been ill, and looked even thinner than a spider! He said he would do all he could for us, through his influence on the Irish Catholic vote."

In April of the same year we obtained what we considered our real victory in the House of Commons, in the suspension of the legislation we opposed. We knew that if once suspended, the hateful system would never again be permitted to be restored so long as public opinion was alive to the question; at the same time we were quite aware of the danger of leaving the written laws on the statute book, making it possible to revive them if at any future time our watchers might be off their guard. A continuous effort therefore was made during the next three years to obtain their actual repeal, although the triumph of 1883 was practically the death-blow to the system.

To my sister in Naples :—

Winchester, April, 1883.

"Someday I trust I shall be able to tell you in detail of the events of the last few days. I longed for your presence during the debate; it was for us a very solemn time. All day long, groups had met for prayer—some in the houses of M.P.'s, some in churches, some in halls, where the poorest people came. Meetings were being held also all over the kingdom, and telegraphic messages of sympathy came to us continually from Scotland and Ireland, France and Switzerland and Italy. There was something in the air like the approach of victory. As men and women prayed they suddenly burst forth into praise, thanking God for the answer as if it had already been granted. It was a long debate. The tone of the speeches, both for and against, was remarkably purified, and, with one exception, they were altogether on a higher plane than in former debates. Many of us ladies sat through the whole evening till after midnight ; then came the division. A few minutes previously Mr. Gerard, the steward of the Ladies' Gallery, crept quietly in and whispered to me, ' I think you are going to win !' That reserved official, of course, never betrays sympathy with any party; nevertheless, I could see the irrepressible pleasure in his face when he said this.

"Never can I forget the expression on the faces of our M.P.'s in the House when they all streamed back from the division lobby. The interval during their absence had seemed very long, and we could hear each others' breathing, so deep was the silence. We did not require to wait to hear the announcement of the division by the tellers : the faces of our

friends told the tale. Slowly and steadily they pressed in;
headed by Mr. Stansfeld and Mr. Hopwood, the tellers on
our side. Mr. Fowler's face was beaming with joy and a
kind of humble triumph. I thought of the words, ' Say into
Jerusalem that her warfare is accomplished.' It was a victory
of righteousness over gross selfishness, injustice, and deceit,
and for the moment we were all elevated by it. When the
figures were given out a long-continued cheer arose, which
sounded like a psalm of praise. Then we ran quickly down
from the gallery, and met a number of our friends coming
out from Westminster Hall.

"It was half-past one in the morning, and the stars were
shining in a clear sky. I felt at that silent hour in the morning in the spirit of the Psalmist, who said, ' When the Lord
turned the captivity of Zion we were like unto them that
dream.' It almost seemed like a dream. When Mr. Cavendish
Bentinck was speaking against us I noticed an expression of
pain on Mr. Gladstone's face. He seemed to be pretending
to read a letter; but at last passed his hand over his eyes
and left the House. He returned before Mr. Stansfeld made
his noble speech, to which he listened attentively."

The actual repeal of the laws was retarded, and we
began to feel in 1885 that we must make strenuous
efforts. There had been on several occasions solemn
meetings of a devotional character on the question,
notably one which lasted several days, and where all the
churches were represented. This was promoted by the
Society of Friends.

An " all-day of prayer " was called in February, 1885.
A paper was issued in advance, giving the subjects to
which each succeeding hour would especially be devoted.
One of these was as follows :—" For the Prime Minister :
that God will incline his heart now to desire and determine to give a practical response to the persistent appeal
which has been made to him by the churches and the

people of this country ; that he may now discern clearly his responsibility in the matter, and may be moved to use his great influence to rid us of this law before he retires from office."

A different president was appointed for each hour in the day. It fell to the hour of my husband's presidency to mention especially the attitude of the Prime Minister in this matter—a subject which he had very deeply at heart, having all his life felt a loyal attachment to Mr. Gladstone personally. His voice betrayed strong emotion as he prayed in the following words, which were taken down at the time :—

". . . . Especially for Thy servant the Prime Minister of this country. Thou, O Lord, hast given him many excellent gifts, and the will and the power to use these for the glory of Thy name and the welfare of mankind. But inasmuch as no one can do the good that he would without Thy enlightening and support, do Thou give him grace and courage now to deal with the momentous question which has brought us here together this day. May he see clearly the danger of permitting the continuance of laws which were framed in an evil hour for an unworthy purpose. Lord, inspire him in this matter with that burning eloquence which has so often fallen from his lips, and may his example and influence lead his followers to choose the right course, to restore the balance of justice, and to act as becomes the representatives of a Christian country."

During the year which followed this meeting James Stuart worked with all his heart and might in Parliament for the success of our cause. I believe that the Cabinet were rather surprised when a petition was presented to them by him, signed by two hundred members of Parliament on both sides of the House, adjuring the Government to give immediate attention to this question, as the patience of the people of England had been sufficiently tried.

The actual repeal of this legislation was carried in April, 1886. .My husband and I were at that time staying with my sister in Naples. It was a great joy to us to receive a telegram on the 13th of April, signed by Mr. Stuart and Mr. Stansfeld, saying: "The Royal assent has this day been given to the Repeal Bill." I thanked God at that moment that Queen Victoria had washed her hands of a stain which she had unconsciously contracted in the first endorsement of this legislation.

Among the many affectionate congratulations we received in our absence, none were so welcome to us as those from our sons. They had all along manifested the most loyal sympathy in our work, and at times had given us good practical help.

Mrs. McLaren of Edinburgh (a sister of the late John Bright) wrote to me out of the fulness of her heart ·—

"I was in London at the last meeting of our Association, and there I missed you, and marked how, in the inscrutable providence of God, you were not with us in the time of victory. I knew you were passing through some anxiety of a domestic kind, but that you were with your husband, whose rejoicing in the marvellous work to which he and you were called has been mingled with a self-denial that gave to his countenance and bearing that look of holy meekness and patience which characterises but few of those who profess to be followers of the Cross of Christ, but which are eminent in him. I thought then of your prayer long ago: you did no ask for triumph, or earthly praise or glory; you asked to be allowed to bear the Cross of Christ, if so be you might help the fallen and forlorn. I have often felt how this prayer has been answered; and now, in the hour of success and victory, you have been absent, and under the shadow of personal anxiety."

Our old and tried friend, Mr. Powles, wrote :—

"How thankful you must be for the success of Mr. Stansfeld's motion on Tuesday! It was a truly marvellous work for you and your fellow-workers to have achieved. Who could have supposed but a few years back that the time of victory would so soon arrive? It is, indeed, not often that self-sacrificing devotion is allowed to see so much fruit of its labours."

And yet to us those seventeen years often seemed very long.

In our annual summer visit to Switzerland in 1884 we went first to St. Beatenberg, a plâteau commanding an extensive view of the lake of Thun, and across the valley to the mountains of the Bernese Oberland. Some of my husband's best sketches were made during this summer. He spent the whole of the days out of doors at Beatenberg, taking early morning and evening views of the mountains. From there we went to Zermatt. Here he again made some good drawings. He was often out sketching on the Riffel Alp as early as six o'clock in the morning, when for most people the keen, frosty air would have been rather too severe. I have seen him established on a rocky platform, surrounded by a group of inquisitive little mountain bulls, sniffing at his paint-box, standing between him and the view, or looking over his shoulder with quite a human expression to see how he was getting on with his work. Though so fond of animals, his patience was sometimes tried by their familiarities, and he would stop his work in order to throw a clod of earth at the leader, which would send them all floundering down the mountain.

It was late in the season when two of our sons, who had joined us, made the ascent of the Matterhorn. The icy covering of the upper part of that mountain gave it the appearance of having recently clothed its gaunt shoulders with a shining coat of mail, and fresh snow was lying upon its flanks. Our sons took Taugwalder as their guide. The ascent was made very successfully. The descent down, however, was much more difficult, owing to the lateness of the season and the state of the snow. They described to us the strength, precision, and ease with which Taugwalder swung himself down from rock to rock—they following. Not until they had reached the bottom did their guide speak, and then only two words in a tone of relief, "*C'est fini.*". It was the last ascent of that season. My husband had accompanied our sons as far as the stream spanned by a little wooden bridge familiar to visitors at Zermatt. He parted from them with words of blessing and confidence, commending them to Him who "will hold up your goings in His paths, that your footsteps slip not." During several hours of that day he was making a sketch of the Matterhorn. He knew that during part of that time his sons were on the summit. From that spot, near the bridge, the mountain wears a defiant aspect, and looks almost perpendicular. His thoughts were much engaged concerning them while still he diligently sketched. He kept this drawing afterwards as a memento of the occasion. The only interruption during these hours of solitude was a brief conversation with the late Mr. Donkin, who passed over the little bridge carrying his photographic apparatus.

The annual Conference of the Federation was held this year at Bâle. We interrupted our holidays for a week in order to attend it. M. Emile de Laveleye, our president, was prevented by illness from coming to it, and my husband took his place. On the morning of his opening speech he got up very early and refreshed himself by a swim in the lively waters of the Rhine; after which he walked in the hotel gardens, thoughtfully rehearsing the subject matter of his opening address. That address was by many felt to be really eloquent in its strength of conviction, its high and generous tone, and its hopefulness for the future.

In the spring of 1885 several events occurred both of public and private interest for him. Among these was the appointment of his brother, Montagu Butler, to the Deanery of Gloucester.

Two years previously it had entered into my husband's mind that a church was required at Grindelwald for the yearly increasing number of visitors who went there, and he set himself to promote the building of one. In April, Emil Boss, the famous mountaineer, who from the first had taken a great interest in my husband's design, paid us a visit at Winchester. He was much attached to my husband. It was pleasant to see those two together. The simple and generous character of Boss attracted the affectionate regard of my husband. Emil, in turn, confided in him with an almost childlike confidence. He would follow him to the cathedral, and sit by him during the service,—an experience new to the mountaineer. He was quite as much at his ease in the midst of us at Winchester as he was at Grindelwald. He generally brought some of his large St. Bernard dogs with him to England, to whom we were glad to show hospitality as well as to their master. He used to speak of a dream in which he indulged of building a châlet in a choice situation at Grindelwald, which my husband should inhabit (when, as he hoped, he should become permanent chaplain of the new church), and of taking him out chamois hunting! He assured us that he could "smooth over every difficulty for Canon Butler," and that he should kill his chamois without undue fatigue or risk. And, indeed, he was quite capable of fulfilling his promise.

Many friends from the Continent visited us during the spring of 1885. We were never at a loss at Winchester in the matter of the entertainment of strangers; for the Cathedral and its history, the old Court House where the first English Parliament was held, and all the other romantic and ancient associations of the place, afforded quite enough interest for several days for any intelligent visitor.

Among the events of public interest occurring at this time was that of the movement promoted by the editor of the *Pall Mall Gazette,* which led to the passing of the Criminal Law Amendment Act.

In July we again started—a larger party of us than usual—for Switzerland. First to Chamounix, whence my husband wrote :—

" We are in most comfortable quarters here. Rhoda and Dulcie Carter are delighted with everything. They have gone out for a long walk with George, leaving Mrs. Butler and me to enjoy the grand view from the front of the house. The air to me is delightful. I feel exhilarated by the mountain air as soon as I come to Switzerland."

We again visited Grindelwald, where we had the joy of meeting once more the Meuricoffre family. We had magnificent weather, favourable to mountain and glacier excursions. The nights were especially beautiful towards September, when there was a fine display of autumn meteors. It was my turn on this occasion to be obliged to hurry home, leaving my husband for a little longer enjoyment of the mountains. I was called home in order

MONT BLANC AND THE GLACIER DE BOSSONS.

to advise in the matter of the action of our poor *protegée*,
Rebecca Jarrett, who had been engaged by Mr. Stead to
help him in his difficult researches.   Two years previously
we had opened at Winchester, as we had done at Liverpool, a little House of Rest, which served as a shelter for
poor girls and young women who were recognised failures,
morally and physically.   Some were sick, rejected by
hospitals as incurable; others friendless, betrayed and
ruined, judged for one reason or another not quite suitable for other homes or refuges.   We also took into the
House of Rest, however, a few persons of more mature
age, not invalids, who had fallen into trouble and misfortune, and who sometimes became excellent helpers in
our work.   Among these latter was the woman I have
mentioned, who had put behind her and abjured her
miserable past, and who showed much intelligence and
tenderness as our aid in the work of rescue.   The task,
however, to which she was invited in London was of a
different kind, and too heavy a responsibility for her.
Hence the summons I received to come home and support her, and also in part to answer for her conduct, as
she had been living with us.   This little House of Rest
was at a short distance from our own house. My husband
held there services of an informal character every Sunday
evening.   The poor inmates looked forward all the week
to his visits and delighted in them.

He wrote to me after I had left Switzerland :—

" I found your telegram from Calais on my return from a
walk, and was thankful to hear you had prospered so far.
This morning I went to church at the Alt Catholische Kirche,
next to the Rathaus, which is now used by our church
attendants.   The sermon was very uninteresting, but I comforted myself with the psalms and prayers, which I could

read. I thought Psalms xxx. and xxxi. were full of en-·couragement for poor Rebecca. Tell her from me to read them, and also that I feel sure that the promises contained in them will be realised by her and by all who are now suffering for taking part in the cause of rescuing the victims of rich and unprincipled men. As I came out I rejoiced to think that little Grindelwald can show a better congregation than Berne. After luncheon I sat out on the balcony, looking at the mountains. Of course I went down to see the bears, from respect to the national *culte*. There was a cub who played like a kitten on the branches of a tree. I expected him to come a cropper, but he didn't. Then I walked across the Aar by the new bridge, which is very fine, and saw a man down below fishing in a gravel-bed, just like a Scot at Melrose. So I have spent the day as pleasantly as I could in your absence. May God bless you, and give you strength to deliver your witness faithfully and convincingly. My prayers are with you and the others in this case."

Our annual Abolitionist Conference was held at Antwerp late in September. M. de Laveleye presided, and it fell to my husband's lot to present the international report for the year, which covered much ground, including accounts of progress made in France, Switzerland, Italy, Spain, the Northern countries of Europe, and Russia, in which latter country some prominent medical men had ably defended our cause.

"The result of these communications," he said, "will be sufficient to show that the work of the Federation will never languish so long as the evils against which we contend remain." He then went on to speak of "the contemporary movement in England, promoted chiefly by the efforts of the *Pall Mall Gazette*, and by those of Mr. Scott, Chamberlain of the City of London. Public opinion," he said, "has received an impetus in favour of social purity, the like of which I have never known. It is owing to the facts published by Mr. Stead that the Criminal Law Amendment Act has been carried through its varied stages, and has become law. A mass meeting took place in Hyde Park, at which chosen representatives of numberless interests addressed audiences assembled around the different platforms. The character of this meeting was very serious and earnest, expressive of national shame at the crimes revealed, and of firm purpose to bring them to an end. It is evident that our crusade in England is assuming more of a religious, though not of a sectarian character. Those who are fighting on our side represent all the denominations. While preserving our liberty of conscience, and welcoming all who unite in a desire to see the moral standard of our common humanity elevated, we feel we are engaged in one work, and with a profound conviction that it is God's work."

The Conference over, we spent a very pleasant Sunday at St. Nicolas, at the house of Baron Prisse, the brother of Madame de Laveleye. "A large party of us went at his invitation to his home at St. Nicolas, including M. and Madame de Laveleye and their sons and daughter. He first took us across the Scheldt in his own private steamer, and then by train. The Baron is the only Protestant gentleman in St. Nicolas, and there is no church except the great Catholic cathedral; so on Sunday forenoon we had a private devotional service in the house, conducted by Baron Prisse and my husband. The former read first, in French, from the Bible, and spoke a few words. My husband then took one of the Psalms, in English. We had very good singing. . The de Laveleyes are all musical. The family are charming, cultivated, witty, and merry. During a pleasant walk on Sunday afternoon, Baron Prisse described to us the manner in which the carrier-pigeons are trained. This town is one of the great pigeon-training places of Europe. The houses have flat roofs, and when there are competitions between the birds, the owners will lie for hours together on their backs on the roofs looking up at the sky for the first re-appearance of the dear little messengers. I am afraid there is a good deal of betting. It is wonderful to see the excitement, the Baron told us, when the competing birds are coming back, sometimes having been as far as Madrid! Then there is great rejoicing over the winner, who, however, does not himself enjoy it so much, as he is carried in triumph through the streets, tied to a stick, poor bird!"

In the late autumn the trial, which is now historic, of Mr. Stead and some of his fellow-workers took place. My husband wrote to me in London, from Winchester:—

"I was delighted to get your telegram, and to hear that you will be back so soon. We had a beautiful anthem of Mendelssohn's to-day in the cathedral, from the ninety-first Psalm, about ministering angels and protection. I was applying it to you and turning it into a prayer, and quite forgot that I had to supplement Canon Carus in part of the service. However all went right. I shall be so glad to welcome you home. Tell Mr. Stead, if you have an opportunity, to read Ecclesiasticus ii."

In January, 1886, my eldest brother, then the head of our family, died at his home, Milfield Hill. My husband, at the earnest desire of his widow, hastened to the North. It was in the depth of winter. "The weather was very bad," he wrote, "with snow on the ground. The old church at Kirknewton was full, and people came from great distances to attend the funeral of their old friend and neighbour. His loss is much felt by his family and friends. He was a good father, husband and neighbour; and as high an example as could be found of an English country gentleman. I am glad to have had George and Charles here with me."

My brother was well known as a great rider; some of his exploits have been recorded in *The Field*, and celebrated in other ways, both in prose and verse. This boldest of riders was one of the gentlest of men, most tenderhearted and kind, and in manner very refined and quiet. We all loved him dearly.

Shortly after this my husband and I went to the South of France.

We had an interesting journey. Starting from Paris early in February, we made a halt at Avignon.

From my journal :—

" It was quite dark when we arrived at the station. Everything here was very different from Paris or London · indeed the moment we entered the antiquated yard of the hotel—once a monastery—it seemed as if we had gone back into the middle ages. Naturally all the picturesque incidents of the visit to Avignon of Catherine of Siena came before our memories. Also we thought of Daudet's mule who kicked the Pope's wicked legate into space !

" Next morning we engaged a tumble-down trap, and set off to see the antiquities. My husband said he thought the vehicle might have come down from the thirteenth century. Our driver was a poor ragged old man with bright blue eyes, rosy cheeks, and very delicate features, and with a sweet, gentlemanly deportment. He had much old-world politeness, though he was ragged and poor like his cab. It was the best cab in the place, however, and had the privilege of a stand near the hotel. We drove up to the enormous and imposing Palace of the Popes, and passing this huge mass of masonry, which itself stands on the high rock, we ascended higher still to the top of the Rocher des Doms. This rock rises abrupt and solitary from the plain, and has a wonderful reach of view. It is not barren, but on the contrary planted with luxuriant trees, some already loaded with blossom. The maritime' pines are the finest I ever saw. There were magnolias, and palms, and acacias, and every kind of lovely foliage. The top of the Rocher is a tolerably wide level, around which we walked to see the views, thinking how the Popes and Troubadours, Cardinals, Court ladies and Ambassadors, must have often commented upon it. Avignon is a walled city; the walls cease on the western side, just where the Rocher des Doms rises, forming part of the defence. You look down, therefore, on the whole city eastward, and beyond it over the plain of Vaucluse, bounded by a line of blue mountains, and through this plain dances the beautiful river Durance, which joins the Rhone about a mile south of Avignon. It is very unlike the Rhone, and resembles rather the North Tyne, spreading over a wide gravelly bed and sparkling over shallows. The Rhone is deep and swift, with curling eddies of deep green and blue, and sometimes a pink hue on its heavy roll of waters. To the north-east rises in solitary beauty Mont Ventoux, with snow on the top. But the view looking west and south-west is the most striking. First you look straight down the edge of the rock as from a precipice to the white road running round its foot, on which the mules and people creeping along look very small indeed. On the other side of this road flows the Rhone, winding grandly round that part of Avignon; at the first view one is quite startled, and inclined to ask how many rivers there are. The plain, as far as you can see, is flashing with bright waters, as if three or four beautiful rivers were winding about, parting and meeting again, making the landscape brilliantly alive. This apparent multiplication is caused by the Rhone dividing twice around two large islands and meeting again. These islands are covered with woods, vineyards, and farmhouses. We recalled the accounts we had read of the visit of Catherine of Siena. She was conducted to the presence of the Pope through rooms of untold splendour to the great Hall of the Consistory. Gregory XI. had called her there to address the Cardinals in conclave. The great rooms of the palace were described as decorated with everything most rare and gorgeous from all lands, perfumed with spices from the East, furnished with tapestry of beautifully blended colours, statuary, softly-cushioned divans, and lovely flowers. Troubadours were there making sweet music, and the windows and balconies opened upon the views which I have tried to describe. It is no wonder that Catherine felt as she walked through the palace that she must close her eyes and pray, lest the scenes around her should have an enervating effect on her soul, set on a stern and holy purpose.

" We descended, and drove in our thirteenth-century cab all round the walls, quite a long drive. Next morning we started at eight o'clock on our further journey. There was a sweet spring smell in the air, and we soon came into the land of olives and of almond trees in full flower. As the train flew on it seemed at moments as if the rocky hillsides were suddenly lit up with a lovely rose colour, so entirely clothed were they with the delicately pink blossom ; and when the deep blue of the Mediterranean came in sight, first through the arches of a Roman aqueduct, the contrast of colour was quite startling, though harmonious.. My husband seemed interested in every part of the way. We passed through that curious flat plain called the Plain de la Crau, which was simmering with heat in the sunny air. It must certainly be the moraine of some vast glacier. Between the thousands of small boulders with which it is covered there grew dwarf plants of lavender. The scent from this wilderness is very sweet. I can imagine that when the south wind blew softly, the noses of the courtiers on the Rocher des Doms at Avignon may have been greeted with the most ravishing scent from this great plain of lavender."

"Cannes, February 18th.

" It seems strange to be sitting here at the open window, with the sun shining, and to hear the hum of bees and flies, and smell the sweet scent of summer flowers. We see the deep blue of the sea through the feathery branches of large palm trees, and there is an abundance of the brightest flowers. I feel a little sad at being so far from you all, and am constantly wishing you could enjoy this beautiful climate. Mr. and Mrs. Thomasson are here and have shown us great kindness."

G. B. to a son :—

" The Esterelles are looking beautiful this morning, and there are some fine pines and olives near, which seem to be saying: ' Come and sketch us.'. I have been to lunch with Lord Derwent, and enjoyed a quiet conversation. I hear that poor Lord Mount Temple is very ill. I hope he will pull through. He and Lady Mount Temple are two of the kindest and best people I know. I am grieved also to see, to-day, announced the death of Principal Tulloch, whose removal from Scottish education and theological life will make a great blank."

Journal continued :—

" To-day the Prince of Wales laid the foundation stone of the Memorial Church in memory of his brother Leopold. My husband had a ticket given him to go to the ceremony. I walked down to Cannes to buy flowers. The streets seemed to become suddenly more and more alive. It was all the population flocking to see the ceremony. There were carriages of every kind, from elegant Russian and Austrian vehicles with high-stepping horses decked with plumes and silver trappings to little pony-phaetons driven by healthy-looking English girls. Crowds of people also on foot, hurrying along, with bouquets of flowers and chatter of expectation. In about half-an-hour I walked slowly home-ward through the almost deserted streets, and met my dear Canon just leaving the hotel, looking as if he had just made a careful *toilette*. I said: ' You will be very late, as all the world has gone long ago.' He replied: ' I shall be soon enough.' I found afterwards that he had purposely delayed, as he did not care to be wedged into the crowd. In a very short time he came back, saying: 'I have done the civil thing.' He had stood outside the crowd for a moment ! Very characteristic of him ! He does not much like functions."

We went on to Genoa.

" This morning I walked down to the harbour," my husband wrote to his son George, " and recalled the last time I was here at a Congress, in 1880, and remembered seeing Charles take a header into the sea off a ship which was refitting. We have come in for the Carnival—a gay sight. We contented ourselves with looking down from our windows at the carriages full of masqueraders. There were a good many laughable incidents, and some good-humoured scrimmages. We had a beautiful journey here, looking out at all the picturesque places *en route*. The most so are Alassio and Albenga. Albenga has six or seven towers, a fine bridge, and a magnificent background of snow-capped mountains. I should like to stay there and sketch for a few days. All our Genoa nephews and nieces have been full of kindness to us."

CHAPTER XVII.

FROM GENOA TO ROME AND NAPLES.—DEDICATION OF WORK-
MEN'S REST AT POZZUOLI.—VISITS TO CASTELLAMARE AND
SORRENTO.—HOMEWARD JOURNEY.—BOLOGNA.—VERONA.—
MILAN.—LUCERNE.—ILLNESS AT WINCHESTER.—PARTIAL
RECOVERY.—HOMBURG AND AIX LA CHAPELLE.—SWITZER-
LAND. — RENEWED ILLNESS AT BERNE. — RIPENING OF
CHARACTER. — PERFECTING IN PATIENCE. — REMOVAL TO
TERRITET.—RECOVERY AND RETURN HOME.

EXTRACTS from journal and letters:—

"Naples, April, 1886.

"We travelled through the night from Genoa
to Rome. As we got near Rome in the
cold, early morning, the Maremma had a
steamy mist resting over it. All along we passed shep-
herds, standing still like statues, watching their flocks
in the cold, grey morning, with their ragged cloaks and
clouted legs and sheepskins about them. Their yellow
skins and hollow eyes showed what a fever-stricken place it
is. Things brightened as we got near Rome. Then long
rows of grey aqueducts came in view, and soon we passed
close by them, the ruins thickening as we went. We were
glad to get into the hotel and have a warm breakfast. My
husband was pleased to meet a Mr. Forbes, who has been
exploring, and has found some new facts concerning old
Roman life. He told him one story which was new to us.
The Emperor Commodus, it seems, was an excellent shot
with the javelin. He took a bet one day that he would kill
a hundred lions with a hundred javelins, without missing
one. All Rome came to look on. He did it, and the poor
animals were laid all round the Colosseum, each with a
javelin in his heart, to the great delight of the spectators.

There are narrow stone passages, inclined planes, leading from the arena on every side, down which the corpses of men, women, and beasts were slid, and so got easily out of the way. A few days after this famous battue of the Emperor he engaged in single combat in the arena, and was beaten by his opponent. His helmet fell off and rolled down one of these inclined planes, slippery with the blood of his dumb victims. He had been becoming unpopular, and the people groaned, saying it was an evil omen. Some of his rivals quietly made it turn out to be so by assassinating him. My husband remarked: ' Serve him right for killing so many captive lions.'

" We started on Saturday for Naples. My husband had never been on this line before ; and as the name of every station brought up to him some classical and historical association, he became more and more interested and happy,— so lively, indeed, that I could not, even if I had wished it, take a nap for five minutes ; but I did not wish it.

" After scudding over the wide open campagna, with its fascinating monotony of miles of aqueducts and other ruins, we entered the wide valley between the two lines of mountains which continues nearly the whole way to Naples. We passed Signi, an old Tuscan town, anciently called Signium. My husband gave some lectures about it long ago at Oxford, when I drew for him a large, rough picture of the Cyclopean architecture of this very place. What mysterious people these Oscans were—so civilised and artistic, and yet we know so little about them. We passed Aquinum, where Juvenal was born, and stopped a good while at the stations of Capua and Caserta. The country from here to Naples is like a continuous garden of fruit crops and flowers, and gives one a pleasant feeling of great industry. The people are, in fact, very industrious. The ancient name of this wide tract of land, the campagna of Naples, is the Terra di Lavoro. The soil is volcanic, and so productive that they gather crop after crop in one year.

" Then old Vesuvius hove in sight, in his silvery-grey robes, lazily puffing off a graceful pine-tree-shaped volume of smoke. On the other side Ischia came into view for a moment—ethereal and blue—sitting on the sea, with the neighbouring little island of Procida, the two looking like a little boat in the tow of a great man-of-war. Arrived at the station, we saw at once Thekla's smiling face, followed by Laura, Tell, and the others who had come to meet us."

From G. B. to his sons at home :—

"Naples, March 15th.

"To-day I spent some hours in making sketches near Virgil's tomb. There is a fine view over the bay, with Vesuvius and all the towns lying at its foot glittering in the sun, the blue water below, and heavy clouds rolling up from Vesuvius into the clear sky. Near me were some large pines, a bay tree or two, and vine props with the vines tied to them. Add to these some small sailing vessels with latteen sails, and you have the picture. I went yesterday with Tell to the Villa Meuricoffre. It is a beautiful house and garden; the trees are splendid. They have the largest magnolia in Europe, besides some very fine umbrella pines. Camelias grow freely, and there are flowers of every kind. The house is very spacious. There is a loggia, or small circular gallery, outside the library, from which there is a splendid view over the bay and islands. We then walked through the gardens of the Royal Palace, close by, and saw the collection of paintings and sculpture inside. I must keep my description of Pompeii for another day. I went there with Mr. Rolfe, a friend of Fronde's, a very pleasant companion and the best of cicerones."

"March 22nd.

"I have just been to the Aquarium and seen wonderful creatures. There were some beautiful loligos, who could go backwards and forwards like river steamers; then there were some creatures of a bright red colour, which looked like old women in red cloaks. There was a large octopus, whom the other fishes teased and insulted just as small birds combine to bully a hawk, sometimes paying the penalty. The octopus waved his feelers round to try to catch one of his tormentors, but did not succeed. There were lampreys which had a very bad expression of countenance. They hid themselves in pieces of old crockery, put there on purpose, and looked out with their wicked little eyes. There was a fish called Angelus, but not at all like an angel; I should have thought a better name was Diabolus. Then there was every kind of anemone, and other creatures half-way between animal and vegetable. One fish called a peacock had a beautiful iridescent hue. The occupants of the tanks took little notice of the visitors, nor were they alarmed by the boom of the cannons from the Castell dell Uovo, which runs out into the sea."

" I wish you had been with me to-day. I could not finish my sketch of Virgil's tomb, so I went on to Pozzuoli, where I saw several good points of view, and made a little sketch looking towards Capo di Miseno. On the way back I visited the Temple of Serapis, with its large worm-eaten columns, and many smaller ones. The columns are about 20 feet high and very massive. The perforations made by the marine animals are deeper than one's finger can reach. They must have had very sharp incisors. There are the priests' cells all round the quadrangular enclosure. It must have been a very large temple; but its chief interest lies, as you very well know, in the evidence which it affords of the change of elevation of the land. The temple was first above the sea level, then below it, and now is some 40 feet above it. There is much to be seen in the museum, which I have greatly enjoyed."

J. E. B. to a friend :—

"April 10th.

" Last Sunday we had a delightful day at Pozzuoli, where Sir William Armstrong is establishing great ironworks for making ironclads for the Italian Government. He has sent out from England some forty or fifty picked men ; they are all Northumbrians, and choice men in every respect for bodily strength and high character. They are also tried and skilled workmen. Mr. Stephen Burrowes, my sister's helper in her work for the sailors, suggested that a Workmen's Rest or Home for our English workmen and others should be established at once at Pozzuoli. Our party went in five or six open carriages to Pozzuoli—all the Meuricoffre family and others of the Swiss and Protestant community of Naples. Our dedicatory service presented a curious combination of associations of different centuries and various countries. The spot where we assembled was close to the ruined Temple of Serapis. It was also in the near neighbourhood of the large Roman amphitheatre of the times of Tiberius. Before us was the sea, its gentle waves beating on the shore—the shore, as you know, where St. Paul first landed in Europe, a prisoner, on his way to Rome. Opposite was Baiæ, where Nero held his infernal court—itself lovely and peaceful in appearance—and Capri, the sharp outline of whose steep rock, whence Tiberius used to fling his slaves headlong into the sea as an after-dinner amusement, stood clear against the pure blue sky. This whole neighbourhood has all its old entrancing charm still, and that wonderful beauty which made it of old the last resort of people satiated with every other form of luxury. It was the ideal of a summer Sabbath evening. My husband offered up a dedicatory prayer, invoking the blessing of God on the design which we had come to inaugurate, on every workman who should work there, and on the dear Meuricoffres and all who work with them for the good of the people around them. He alluded in his prayer to the advent in that very place of the great apostle of the Gentiles, charged with the precious gift for Europe—the gospel of our salvation. Then we sang hymns, some of the old favourites of the English workmen. It was strange to hear those familiar songs, pronounced with the strong Northumbrian guttural, ascending from the ruins of the Temple of Serapis—a blending of associations, past and present, heathen and Christian, ancient and modern.

When the men found out that my sister and I were Northumbrians they could scarcely suppress their joy; and after that, whenever she or I made a remark, however trivial, they cheered. Most of them come from Blyth and Morpeth. They were chiefly Wesleyans, and, politically, supporters of Thomas Burt, M.P.

"Our drive home in the evening was delicious beyond description. It was perfectly calm, with a lovely sunset, the trees already flashing into their summer tints, and the air full of that most delightful scent of the early orange and lemon blossom which comes out while the trees are still covered with their golden fruit. It was a memorable day for us, as a pleasant family gathering, and full of Christian hope."

We spent another pleasant long day at the Capo di Miseno. I shall never forget the feelings which my husband expressed, now and again, during the day, as we looked from that high and isolated rock, around upon the sea and land and islands. He seemed to be completely transported into the old Greek world. It was not the Latin and Roman associations which attracted him just then; for the most part these are not so attractive, poisoned as they are by memories of the corrupt decadence of Imperial Rome. It was the spirits of the old Greeks which hovered round him there; all the most poetic associations being connected with the Greek colonisation of this part of Italy. We looked over to Cumæ, the most ancient of the Greek colonies of Italy, and across the Phlegræan Fields, and could trace the path by which the Sibyl's cave was reached, and the hollow in which stagnates the Lake Avernus, and many other spots immortalised in ancient song or history. It was the words of Pindar rather than those of Virgil of Pliny which came to my husband's mind, and of which his memory was at all times tenacious. The whole scene was for him peopled with the shades of the classic past. The sun made everything radiantly beautiful, and the woods of the royal hunting grounds, fringing the coast from where we stood to Cumæ, were stirred by a gentle breeze, which seemed to bring on its wings echoes of the lament for Adonis. Wild boars and deer still roam in these forests, and slake their thirst in the "small lakes covered with waterlilies." Towards sunset we drove by the Lake of Fusaro, where we rested awhile, returning to Naples by the light of the beautiful moon.

We went from Naples to Castellamare. My husband having gone first to Sorrento, whence he wrote to his sons :—

"I came here for a little change of air ; the doctor thought it would help me to throw off the remains of a feverish attack I had last week. Your mother and Thekla started to-day from Santa Lucia, and steamed for Capri, where I joined them. We saw the blue grotto, and I made a sketch of the famous rock, and got back about four o'clock."

"Castellamare.

"The Galtons are here. I went up Vesuvius with Uncle Frank. We did it in the easiest way, as I am not yet quite strong—driving to the foot of the mountain, then riding till we came to the steep ascent up an ash slope and over lava streams. I could not have done the ashes. You sink in five or six inches and slip back a foot at every step. So first I, and then all the party, took a ropeman, who goes in front with a noose, which you take hold of, and he hauls you up. In this way we reached the edge of the crater, and there I sat down. There were showers of stones flying about. I did not much fancy being hit on the head by one of them. They were quite hot, and some fell very near us. The most interesting sights to me were the streams of lava, which assume very fantastic forms. Some are like slag out of a furnace; others are twisted like coils of rope or maccaroni. These looked metallic and black, but had some orange-coloured bits among them. The most curious sight was that of the sulphur fumaroles near the top. The heat was considerable and the colouring lovely, varying from pale primrose to the deepest orange and scarlet

"We came down in much less time than we went up, and had lunch on some of the twisted lava rocks. We have nice rooms here in the Hotel Quisisana (here one gets well). We have a large terrace with great sketching privileges. Mamma went on to the terrace last evening to watch Vesuvius erupting. It looked very pretty to see the crimson glow on the summit of the mountain, and the stars looking down upon it and a young crescent moon over Capri; but it gave her a shivering fit. This is certainly rather a dangerous climate."

On our way homeward he wrote :—

"Bologna, April 20th.

"We arrived here from Florence, admiring much the views from the summit of the Appenines over Pistoia. Coming down the side of the Appenines we were reminded of Cumberland. There were clear streams flowing over rocky beds. We had a good morning yesterday at the Picture Galleries here, the gem of which is Raphael's 'St. Cecilia.' We also went to the Museum, where there is a most interesting collection of Umbrian and Etruscan remains. We went next to the Archigymnasis, or University, where there is a large library, and busts of Mezzofanti, the great linguist, and of Laura Bassi, who was Professor of Metaphysics and Astronomy. She has a beautiful face, gentle and dignified. In the afternoon we went to St. Luca, a church on an eminence, three miles off. There is a magnificent view: you see from the Alps to the Adriatic, and a long range of the Appenines with various cities of the plain. There is an arcade running all the way up the hill, and another to the Campo Santo, some three miles off. It is a peculiarity of Bologna that you hardly ever need an umbrella; there are arcades everywhere. We have met one or two pleasant people here. Mr. —— talked a good deal, and told us he was an agnostic, which was very kind of him, as we did not ask him about his creed."

We spent two or three delightful days at Verona. The monuments of that beautiful city are easily seen, the city itself being small. We had bright sunshine, and my husband's artistic eye was much attracted by the warm colouring of the marble monuments, churches, and doorways of old houses, the white of the marble being burnt by the sun in some places to an exquisite rose colour. On our way to Milan the Lago di Garda looked very lovely, sleeping in the sunshine; and as our train was not a rapid one, my husband was able to make a slight sketch of the lake from the carriage window.

" Lucerne, Easter Sunday, 1886.

" We arrived last night after a most beautiful journey over the St. Gothard. We stood outside almost all the eight hours on the platform of the carriage. The views are wonderful and varied, and then there is the constant surprise of the marvellous engineering in the spiral tunnels and turnings and windings of the line. It was very beautiful going round and across the Lake of Lugano, and we had picturesque glimpses of the Lakes Como and Maggiore. We ran through meadows full of asphodel, white narcissus, blue hepaticas, and purple anemones. At Milan we had a pleasant visit from Charles, just down from the Maloja. On Good Friday we visited a number of churches, and saw Leonardo da Vinci's great work."

My husband started from Lucerne direct for Winchester. I remained a few days for work in Switzerland.

To my husband :—

"Berne, April 27th.

" I think of you every moment. I was glad you were able to travel home with Mr. Jackson, who seemed so kind, and interested in taking care of you. The memory of the last few days are to me most delightful, especially that ideal Sabbath day which we spent together on those flower-scented meadows sloping to the Lake of Lucerne."

"Neuchâtel, April 28th.

" Here is another lovely day. I see they are establishing quarantine in Italy on account of the cholera ; I hope Charles may return to the mountains before it gets worse, and that the beloved people at Naples may be spared a repetition of that scourge. How completely they took us into their hearts and home, even giving up their rooms to us ! God be praised for all His mercy to us, and for the delightful memories we have brought away of our tour in Italy."

"Boulogne, June 1st.

" I am waiting here for a few hours in hopes that the sea will be more calm. Amelie Humbert came with me through the Val de Travers to the highest part of the Jura. It is a new line, boldly cut through that gorge, and was brilliant with spring foliage. I had a third-class carriage entirely to myself from Neuchâtel to Dijon, and was able to see the views well. I spent a day after you left with dear Adela at Le Ried on the Jura. She was rather better, and was reclining on a sofa in the garden, soft showers of white cherry blossom falling on her when the warm sweet-scented breezes blew now and then. I saw again M. Paul Roberts' design for his great painting for the new museum at Neuchâtel. It is very fine. His studio, which he built himself, is a charming place, with every possible facility for painting."

I found, to my great grief, on my return home that my husband had become rather seriously ill. His illness developed into rheumatic fever, which lasted several weeks during the summer. It was on Whitsuntide in this year that his beloved little church at Grindelwald was opened. He had hoped to be there himself. His place was taken by the Bishop of Ripon. The Precentor of the Cathedral of Winchester, our friend Mr. Crowdy, who was acting then as chaplain at Grindelwald, wrote many letters to my husband, knowing how much he cared to hear of his church.

J. E. B. to Madame Meuricoffre :—

"June 17th.

"There is no change yet. We have called in Dr. McLean for consultation with our Winchester doctor. Everyone is very kind, and many are praying for him. Canon Crowdy writes frequently from Grindelwald, whence we have news also of Charles. They received your kind telegram which you sent to Grindelwald on Whit Sunday, thinking George was there. I read it to him : 'A thousand Pentecostal blessings on your church, dear brother.' He smiled and said : 'Dear, kind Hatty!' We hear that the Bishop of Ripon preached an impressive sermon on 'Christ's treatment and the World's treatment of weakness and failure'—' He shall not break the bruised reed, nor quench the smoking flax.' The Boss's are all delighted with the church, but grieved that 'their own Canon,' as they call him, cannot be there.

"Our brotherhood of the Close show us great kindness. Archdeacon Atkinson, now in residence, comes in unfailingly every evening after the Cathedral service is over, and it is a solace to my husband when he reads and prays with him in his sympathetic manner."

Our neighbour at Broadlands, Lord Mount Temple, who had himself lately recovered from a severe illness, and who was a good deal senior to my husband, wrote to me :—"Your telegram was indeed a godsend to us this morning, encouraging us to believe that our blessed Lord has still some of His gracious work to be executed by the most excellent and beloved canon." Lord Mount Temple came himself shortly afterwards, humbly asking if he could be of any use, or might see my husband. I took him at once to his room, where the venerable man knelt down by the bedside of his friend, and having recited to him the facts of his own recent recovery in answer, as he believed, to the prayers of friends, he himself prayed earnestly that the same healing power might be exerted for my husband. His strength and simplicity of faith were fortifying to us both, and my husband never forgot the kindness of that visit.

Lord Mount Temple wrote sometime afterwards :—

" My dear Canon,—I can hardly give expression to the delight and thankfulness which your bright letter gave me [a dictated note]. I greatly value the privilege of having been instrumental in some slight degree for the opening of the channel of the Divine grace of healing being proved in your case. I do rejoice intensely at your partial recovery, and feel confident that it will be carried on to completion if you are watchful to observe all the rules of prudence and caution. I am myself gradually advancing, step by step, to better general health than I had for some years before my failure. In your present weakness you have the immense comfort of thinking how earnestly you and yours have striven to set wrong things right amidst almost insurmountable difficulties."

Mr. William Shaen, who had for many years been one of our best and wisest advisers in our public work, came to Winchester with several other friends for some committee business in connection with that work. In order to leave the house quiet, we held our committee in our shaded and secluded garden. Mr. Shaen wrote to my husband from London :—

" Dear Friend,—You were much missed and much wanted at our Congress, which is just over, in London.* In spite of all difficulties and drawbacks, it was a most useful and encouraging gathering, giving promise of renewed and unceasing vigour in the future. It was a great disappointment to me not to be able to see you for a few minutes when we had our meeting of the executive in your garden; but I had the pleasure of making the acquaintance of your charming house and garden and your magnificent dogs."

Mr. Shaen came a little later to pay my husband a visit, which the latter much desired. It was a touching interview between the two old fellow-workers. We little dreamed that Mr. Shaen would be the first to be called away. He died very suddenly in the following spring.

Mr. Powles wrote, during my husband's illness :—

" Your doctor's verdict you have accepted, as one might have been sure you would. Hitherto your life has been one of self-denying activity, laborious for others; now, if it pleases God, that your self-denial should be exerted in patience and comparative inactivity, I know you will fulfil His pleasure in perfecting this grace also. Your inactivity, too, will be as fruitful of good as the active labours of many a strong man. You are continually in my thoughts and prayers, and many besides myself are thinking of you with loving anxiety."

* Many distinguished persons were present at this International Congress of our Federation They accepted an invitation from Mr. Barnett to a party at Toynbee Hall in Whitechapel. There were about a hundred present. M. de Laveleye gave an interesting address to a large gathering of working men and their wives, frequenters of the lectures at Toynbee Hall, who had been invited. This visit and the work done by the members of Toynbee Hall left a strong impression on M. de Laveleye's mind. He frequently alluded to it in after years.

My brother, Charles Grey, wrote from Ireland :—

"I trust we may have dear George restored ere long to his usual health. I know he must be a very patient and un-complaining invalid. The more I have seen of him the more lovable I have thought his character. He is always so un-controversial in discussing any subjects, and with all his learning so very unassuming. My constant prayer will be for his steady recovery, and that God will support you in your trouble."

He did recover slowly, and we were then advised to try the baths at Homburg. Before leaving Winchester he wrote a circular, to be distributed among his friends in the Close and elsewhere :—

"After a long and trying illness, from which I· am now recovering, my first duty is to offer my humble thanks to God not only for raising me up from sickness, but for making a time of bodily inactivity a season of spiritual comfort and communion. Secondly, I desire to offer my sincere acknow-ledgments to the congregation from which I have been so long unwillingly absent, and for the comfort afforded me by the knowledge that the prayers of the Church were daily offered up for my recovery. In the next place, I wish to record my grateful sense of the kindness and sympathy of friends, more especially of the Dean and my brothers of the Chapter, for their sympathy and unremitting kindness in calling to make inquiries. From some other quarters this sympathy has been quite unexpected, and deserves more than a passing acknowledgment. It is my earnest prayer that I may be spared to return in some way the kindness which friends have shown me. I hope to be able in the autumn to again take my part in the duty of the Cathedral, from which I have been so long debarred by illness. Praying that the Divine blessing may attend our renewed intercourse,

"I am, sincerely and gratefully."

We accomplished, not without difficulty, the journey to Homburg.

To my sons :—

"Homburg, August, 1886.

"Father is very much affected by the death of his old friend, Henry Nethercote. He sat in deep meditation for some time after hearing the news. They were born in the same year, went to Harrow on the same day, and have been friends ever since. You recollect how merry H. Nethercote was when he last visited us at Winchester.

"We had a very pleasant visit yesterday to Frankfort. We took an open carriage and drove round the town. Father pointed out to me his old lodgings where he lived forty years ago. Then we went to the Kaisar Saal, a very ancient building in the midst of old Frankfort, parts of which are very picturesque and rather mouldy. We wished for you and your photographic apparatus. The sun was so bright, casting deep shadows in which were clear reflected lights."

G. B. to his son Stanley :—

"Aix la Chapelle, August.

"My doctor at Homburg advised me to come on here for a few weeks. The weather is intensely hot, with severe thunderstorms occasionally. It is too hot for walking. We drive out every afternoon for a couple of hours, and enjoy the air. The country is a good deal like England. We drove yesterday through a large property a few miles from here with red deer in the park.

"I am so glad that you and Rhoda are at the Close, and that you regard it as your home. Certainly it is as pleasant a home as anyone could desire. Comparing Winchester with other places, it cannot be called bracing; but one can take drives over the downs, where there is plenty of good air. We took our drive to-day here through beautiful woods, where the bracken was just changing colour. We spent, last week, two days with the de Laveleyes at their country house at Hermalle, near Argenteau on the Meuse. It has a fine old fashioned garden, with rare trees and shrubs, and such fruit trees! The peaches and pears were quite a wonder; evidently they have an excellent gardener. . The peach trees are trained upon trellis-work—light wooden laths placed at right angles. I wonder if this keeps off the slugs! We had a long wait at the station at Mastrecht, so we took a carriage and drove all round that ancient town. The afternoon sun was pouring down upon us, setting off the architecture of the old churches and towers. There is a long drive from Argenteau station to the de Laveleye's house, where we arrived some time after dark. We could not see anything; but we heard at the entrance, almost before our carriage stopped, the cheery greetings of our kind hosts; M. de Laveleye's above all, calling out his most kindly welcome in his remarkably musical voice. They are indeed a delightful family. The following morning we sat for some time on the terrace opening from the drawing-room on the ground floor, fenced from the sun by flowering plants. The Meuse is an extremely pretty river. It flows round the foot of the garden, with picturesque rocks rising on the other side. They have a boat on the river, and live a free, out-of-door life. I hope to go on from here to Grindelwald for a few days. The doctor here says he thinks the more bracing air will be good after this heat, provided I take precautions. I want much to see the Boss's and the church before returning."

The first days at Grindelwald, early in September, were health giving. "The weather is fine," my husband wrote, "and the mountain air very refreshing. I hope to recover my walking powers. The Boss family gave me a most hearty greeting." After a few days the weather changed. He wrote later: "I preached in our little church yesterday and administered the Holy Communion, taking most of the service. I felt rather tired in the afternoon; it is wet, and my limbs ache, but I am taking every precaution." We thought it best to return at once to Berne. Extracts from letters and journals will best describe what followed.

To my sons at home :—

"Berne, September 24th.

"I am much grieved to have to tell you that we are stranded here by father's having become more rheumatic. I got Professor Demme to come this morning. He says that the increase of rheumatism might have come on anywhere, owing to the change of weather."

"September 28th.

"It goes to my heart to have to report that father's fever and pains are worse. Dr. Demme found it so this morning: He said: 'Now, poor Canon, you will need much patience; but you *have* patience. I cannot cut the fever short, but God can; and it must be as He wills.' Dr. Demme is a distinguished physician, is very kind, and has a decided and reassuring manner. He told me, when alone, that we could not safely move for a fortnight, perhaps a month, and perhaps two months. When I went back to father I found him depressed as I never saw him in all his illness at Winchester. There were two large tears rolling down each side of his face, as he lay with his head on the pillow. He said: 'Will you write to the Dean and to my kind brother canons and to our dear sons?' That was all he said. Later, in the evening, he said: 'It may have been an error of judgment going to Grindelwald, but I thought it was for the best;' and then a little later, as if the thought was weighing on his mind: 'It was not for any selfish purpose that I came to Switzerland: I thought it was right to take a service in the church on Sunday, and I felt happy in doing so.' I have seldom seen him look so sad. He hoped to gladden you all by coming home well. But you know how open he is to comfort of the best kind. He asked me to read to him. I read that beautiful hymn of Wesley's which he likes so much, in which are the words—

'Through waves and clouds and storms
He gently clears the way:
Wait thou His time; so shall this night
Soon end in joyous day.'"

A little later our doctor counselled a move from the town to a Pension in a village near his own country house.

" Muri, October 1st.

" I am so happy to send you a better account to-day. The air and quiet here are delicious; no noisy traffic, only herds of cows and goats passing with their musical bells. The woods are beginning to be gorgeously coloured, and above their flashing autumn tints rise the pure white Alps. The weather is magnificent. Yesterday, when we moved him, was an anxious time. He had no more fever, but the pain has been sharp and constant, and his dear face bears traces of much suffering. He cannot use his hands; he can only look on while we do everything for him. The dressing and moving were painful; a cold perspiration covered his face from weakness. We brought him here in a large open carriage, with two good horses. Charles was very helpful to us, arranging pillows and rugs so as to make a comfortable recline in the carriage. Just as we left the door of the Bernerhof Aunt Hatty drove up, her face full of the tenderest sympathy. She did not speak, but signed to us that she would follow us in her carriage to Muri. The drive was quite exquisite. There was not a breath of wind, but a crisp autumn feeling in the air. As we left the river and ascended, there lay before us the whole line of snowy Alps. I felt it must do father good. He was silent, but after a time he drew a long breath, and said, ' How wonderfully beautiful!' He recovered his spirits as we drove along. Before going to his room he sat nearly an hour in the porch of this house, and slept better after. But alas for the sudden changes of temperature in beautiful Switzerland!"

To Madame Meuricoffre :—

" October 11th.

"Again a relapse, and this time the saddest of all. Last night he seemed doing well, and I left him about midnight in the care of the nurse, as I needed a few hours' sleep. About four in the morning I awoke with a troubled impression. The weather had changed, and a cold wind was blowing and rattling the shutters. I went to him, and found him with insufficient covering and feeling cold. The nurse had, I fear, fallen asleep. I brought a soft light covering, and did everything to restore warmth; but the mischief was done. He signed to me to send the nurse away and to remain with him. I did so, and continued to apply warmth; but as he lay back a look came over his face which I shall never forget. He gasped, 'Oh, I cannot! I cannot!' It was a spasm of the heart. At last he fell asleep and awoke relieved, but remembering with a shudder how cold he had been. These small hours of the morning are deadly hours, when a chill seems to come over the whole world. Dr. Demme came, and after an examination said: 'Your heart is affected, which I had hoped to avoid. You have taken a chill.' He stayed with us some time, and cheered us with hopes of recovery. I determined never again to leave my dear patient at night, and last night I sat by him. I do not know how I resisted sleep, but God strengthened me. I prayed earnestly for his dear life. He also tried to pray, but his memory and voice failed. Several times in the night he whispered, 'Into Thy hands I commend my spirit.' Towards morning he slept quietly."

Our son Stanley came to us from England. Our eldest son, George, was about to start for India, and had taken his passage, but postponed his visit in order to come out later to his father. Professor Stuart also came from England, under the impression that it might be to take leave of his dear friend for whom he had had so strong an affection for many years.

To my eldest son:—

"We are sorry, dear George, that you should have to give up your Indian journey; but I knew well that you would not go if your father seemed to be sinking. Dr. Demme has called in a second physician, Professor Lichtenstein. They were here yesterday, in a storm of wind and rain which shook the house, and hardly allowed them to hear each other speak. After a long examination and consultation, they told me, looking very sorrowful, that father's heart is seriously affected. He may be cured, but only by a slow course of extreme care. Any chill or accident might be fatal. They said we must give up all thought of home, or even going to the Gordanne (as we had hoped). It was a heavy blow. Stanley and Charles are deeply grieved. But father himself became our best comforter. When the doctors told him how ill he is (he wished to know the truth), he begged to be raised on his pillow, in order that he might make them a little speech. There was all his own sweet courtesy and some old-fashioned formality in the way in which he addressed them. ' I thank you, gentlemen,' he said, ' for telling me the truth, and for all your kindness and consideration towards me. I cannot deny that this is a heavy blow to me; but we are all in the hands of a Power and a Love which are infinite; and I believe I can say that I accept all that God sends, knowing that He designs it for our good.' Having made this dear little speech, his head fell back, and he was long silent. He looked very pale. In the night I heard him praying, and it was such a calm, submissive, and noble prayer, that I felt ashamed to be less courageous than he. He said at one time yesterday: ' If I die, you will all be scattered to the winds, poor dears. No more pleasant home at Winchester.' But in his prayer he said: ' Lord, wherever Thou art is now my home, and Thou wilt be a Father to the fatherless.' Stanley must leave on Sunday, and then you will come out, dear George. This small house is shaken by storms, and seems rather comfort- less now, without carpets and fireless, though so agreeable in the fine weather. However, his room gets the sun. God does comfort us. Our Saviour is always swift to the rescue when His people are in straits. Everyone is kind. Paul Robert, the painter, came all the way from his home on the Jura to-day, just to inquire about father, and to ask if he could be of any use. Charles had brought us some engravings of the beautiful birds he (Paul) had painted, and father had expressed a wish to see him. He came and talked a little about sketching, and then kneeled down and prayed for him briefly and in a tone of great hopefulness, and then went away. Father is thankful for everything, and never complains of any discomfort. He always says, when I give him anything to eat or drink : 'Thank you, that is so good,' even when it is *not* quite so good as I should wish it to be. He sometimes talks of you all in his sleep, and speaks of your affection for him "

By our doctor's advice we took advantage of the earliest day of sunshine to convey my husband carefully back to Berne, where we found a large, well-warmed apartment awaiting us. As the autumn was advancing, we were glad of the added comforts. The expense necessarily entailed by hotel life would have been a cause of anxiety had it not been for the kindness of several friends, who in many ways contributed to lighten our burden. In this my husband constantly recognised the hand of God.

In a few days he again rallied. We begged Dr. Demme to tell us more particularly concerning the case. He did so ; addressing father very gently, he said : "Canon, you have been face to face with death. Dr. Lichtenstein agrees with me that you have been brought back from the borders of the grave. The half of what you have had would have killed most men. God has been very good to you. Your illness has been extremely severe, and you are not yet out of danger."

To Mme. Meuricoffre :—

" It seems to me he has been held in life because so many have been praying for him. In almost all the Protestant churches of Berne earnest prayer has been made for him, and also in many circles of friends both at home and on the Continent. I have now determined to remain with him every night. It is the time when he most needs mental and spiritual help, and I love those quiet hours in his room. He is sometimes gently delirious. Last night the moonlight came full into the room. At times he slept calmly, and then would awake with a perplexed look, and wandering in speech. But he always knows me, and smiles when I bring my face close to his.

" His fancies in his delirium are all gentle, and sometimes even sweet and pleasant. He thinks he is walking in the fields, and calls his dog : 'Carlo, dear old dog, come along!' or he imagines a friend has been to see him, and awakes me when I am dosing with such remarks as : 'Dear wife, will you see Canon Sumner downstairs? he has been to see me.' Then he will become suddenly quite reasonable again. He said last night : 'I did not know I had been so near death. We wish to have a few more years, do we not, dear, to work and to glorify God ? If I can never serve in the cathedral again, I should like to write some hymns.'

" I have very great comfort in the beautiful ripening of his character in patience and in all holy virtues. In these silent nights there is such a sense of peace surrounding us : the 'God of Peace and of all Consolation' is here. It is very instructive to behold such a picture of a tried and humble Christian. He rejoices in the thought of his first grandchild, and likes to think she was born at our dear home in the Close. He thanks God that he has been permitted to be 'a link in the generations.' He almost always becomes wakeful about two hours after midnight. I then relight the fire and make the wood burn cheerfully; I draw his arm-chair to his bed and manage to move him gently into it, and then wheel it to the fire, where he sits with plenty of wraps, drinking the cup of tea which I prepare for him, with a great deal of good Swiss milk. This seems to refresh him, and he sleeps better after it. At those hours he always likes me to read some short passage of God's word and then talk over it. His face becomes then quite illumined and his mind clear, and he appears filled with joy. New light seems to be granted to him on many parts of the Gospel narrative, and when he prays his heart seems full to overflowing with tenderness and strong desire. It is when the love of God and the beauty of holiness are more clearly revealed to us that the truest and tenderest repentance springs up in the heart. We then see how far we have fallen below the ideal standard, and we are filled with sorrow. The tears often course down his face as he prays or is rapt in contemplation, scarcely conscious even of *my* presence; but there is no bitterness in this tender sorrow, and not the shadow of a doubt of God's fatherly love and care for him. He realises the ' strong consolation ' which is granted to those who have ' fled for refuge to lay hold of the hope set before them ' in Christ Jesus. What a precious memory for me will be these ' after-midnight teas ' and these wonderful moments of communion—heaven's gate being open when the world's is shut."

He dictated letters home occasionally.

To his daughter-in-law, the mother of that first little grandchild, he wrote

" I wonder if you would be so very kind as to send me a photograph of baby, and I should so much like a very small lock of its hair, which shall be treated with due honour. I will have a locket made for it. George has gone over the Alps with the Meuricoffres, and will visit Venice and Verona. He means to take some photographs. I am glad that, as he gave up his Indian visit on my account, he should have some such practice, which will bear fruit another year among the cities and moutains of India. Tell the dear Dean, Bishop McDougall, and other kind friends how much I value their sympathy, though I cannot yet myself write to them."

To the same :—

" November 18th.

" The news which has just reached us of Bishop McDougall's death has, you may be sure, grieved us very much. For Mildred and his other children it is very sad. If there is still time, get a wreath for me, dear Rhoda ; and

let it be placed on his coffin, with the affectionate remembrance
of a brother canon and friend. He was one of the kindest
of men. I was much touched by his generous wish, some
weeks ago, to come out and nurse me. For him the change
is a blessed one.

"Last Sunday morning, at seven o'clock, the mountains
were deep blue, and the sky was covered with horizontal
barred clouds of a glowing crimson, such as Turner alone
could paint. This was a presage of bad weather. Dr
Demme is very anxious we should get to Territet, where it is
warm and sheltered."

Winter was coming down in clouds and snow over the
Alps. I rejoiced with trembling over the slow but, as I
trusted, sure progress of my dear patient, and hoped
against hope that my own strength would hold out through
the arduous nights and days. But a further trial of faith
was awaiting us. Again a relapse, more severe and less
anticipated than any that had gone before. The fever
increased, and the heart weakness was alarming.

I must now record a passage of my own personal
experience at this crisis, which will be variously interpreted by any who may read it, but which I shall state
with all simplicity for the encouragement at least of those
who believe and know that there is a "God in heaven
who heareth prayer." I had passed a sleepless night, in
vain attempts to soothe the sufferings and allay the fever
of my dear invalid, myself weak and exhausted, and now
full of pain. The night was long, dark, and cold, both
spiritually and materially. Towards morning he fell into a
troubled sleep. I went softly into a little ante-room, leaving
the door open between. A feeling of despair came over
me. My own strength was failing, and he was worse.
Who would now minister to him, I asked ; and was there

to be no end to these repeated and heartbreaking disappointments? When Elijah fled into the wilderness, and gave himself up to bitter thoughts in the depths of his discouragement, the voice came to him, questioning, "What doest thou here, Elijah?" bidding him arise out of his depression. So to me it seemed at that moment that a voice came—or rather, I would say, a light shone—into the very heart of my darkness and despair. The promises of God in the Scriptures with which I had been familiar all my life came to me as if I had heard them for the first time. I fell on my knees and kept silence, to hear what the Lord would say to me; for, for my own part, I had nothing to say. My trouble was too heavy for speech.

"The prayer of faith shall save the sick." "Call upon Me in the time of trouble, and I will deliver thee."

"Is this true?" I exclaimed. Yes, I knew it was true. It seemed to become a very simple matter, and grace was given to me, in my pain and weakness, to say only, "Lord, I believe." The burden was removed. I returned to my husband's room, and sat silent for a while until he moved, and the day broke. I brought him his breakfast, and said to him confidently: "You are going to be better to-day, beloved." He smiled, but did not speak. Two hours later our kind doctor came. He took his temperature and felt his pulse, and with a sigh of relief he said: "Well, dear Canon, a wonderful thing has happened. A great change has come. You are much better. Now I know the signs of the skies—I see that dark line over the mountains, which means an approaching snowstorm. Is it possible for you to be ready for the mid-day train for Territet? You shall be carried to the station and every care taken of you. If you do not escape our severe Bernese winter now, you may be imprisoned here for weeks." My husband smiled again, and said, "All right." With the ready help of our son Charles and a friend, preparations were completed in an hour or two. The invalid carriage from Bâle which we had kept waiting at the station for fifteen days, in the hope each day of being able to leave, had been sent away when the last relapse took place; and now we had to take what we could get. The north wind was keen; but our invalid was carried by strong and willing porters, and placed in a large second-class carriage, in which we were alone with a good stove and every appliance for arranging a couch. In spite of the strength which had been given me in that cold "hour before the dawn" of that day, I felt very anxious as I looked at him. We proposed to him to recline on the wraps we had arranged, but he preferred to sit up. He continued to look out at the views, admiring the woods, which had fragments of richly-tinted foliage still lingering here and there. We reached our destination in the evening, and felt the relief of the milder air. A comfortable room was prepared for him in the Hotel des Alpes. Dr. Demme had said to me emphatically: " Necessarily he will be much exhausted when he reaches Territet. Get him to bed at once, and do not be alarmed if fever returns; for this I fear is inevitable." The gently recalcitrant mood of our patient was quite delightful to me. He had no idea of going to bed at once, but would have a little conversation with Mr. Chessex, and "look about him." I left him with his attendant, to go and make some arrangements. When I came back he had gone to bed. I kneeled beside him, rejoicing to see his expression of relief and quiet enjoyment. Both temperature and pulse were normal! He took my hand in his, which was now quite cool, and said impressively: "Dear wife, we must never—never forget this." (I had related to him during the journey my experience of the early morning.) He fell into a sound and refreshing sleep, with his hands clasped, in the act of giving thanks to God. Next morning he came to the *salle à manger* to breakfast at nine o'clock.

To Madame Meuricoffre ·

"December 8th, 1886.

"That wonderful act of Divine love on the day we came here has been followed by a steady progress. There has never been the smallest approach to fever or high pulse. I think we may safely go home next week. Last Sunday afternoon George started for England. My husband wished me to go for an hour or two to see some friends at Vevey. When I came back I found him resting on his couch, looking very happy. He said: 'I have been very clever. I first walked with George to the station and saw him off. Then I went to evening church, and then came in and got some tea, and here I am all right.' He had kept some tea hot for me, on the stove. Never did tea seem to me so good."

A lady told me later that at a party of friends in Berne, Dr. Demme had spoken of this recovery, and said that it had been very remarkable,—a "Divine interposition" in answer, as he believed, to prayer: he added that my husband had had inflammation of both lungs and pleurisy, as well as the serious heart attack; adding, "any one of which was enough to kill most men."

The Dean of Winchester wrote ·

"Do not come back too hastily; for I rather dread the Close for you in damp cold weather. I don't at all like writ-

ing this, for I shall be so heartily glad to see you back ; it
will be like 'life from the dead.' I am full of thankfulness
that our merciful Lord has spared you for, I hope, a good
spell of fresh work for Him and among us."

We reached home for Christmas. "Home is home,"
my husband wrote; "and this is a very warm and
pleasant home, and we are delighted to be back."

CHAPTER XVIII.

THE RIVIERA EARTHQUAKE.—RESIDENCE AT WINCHESTER, 1887.
—RENEWED HEALTH.—VISIT TO RHEIMS, COMBALLAZ, AND
VEVEY.—CONFERENCE AT LAUSANNE.—ELISÉ RECLUS.—
VISIT TO THE CHURCH AT GRINDELWALD, IN MAY, 1888.—
RENEWED INTERCOURSE WITH OLD FRIENDS.—VISIT TO
COPENHAGEN. — BEGINNING OF LAST ILLNESS. — FAMILY
GATHERING AT CHRISTMAS.—ESCAPE FROM THE WINTER'S
COLD TO THE RIVIERA.—RETURN HOME BY TERRITET AND
DIJON.—RESIDENCE AT WINCHESTER, JUNE, 1889.—HIS
LAST APPEARANCE IN THE CATHEDRAL.—INVITATION TO
CAPO DI MONTE.

T was in February, 1887, that the Riviera was
visited by a severe earthquake. Our son
Charles happened to be at Turin when the
first shock was felt. He had intended to
return to Switzerland on his way homewards, but wrote from Turin ·—

"I am just starting for Savona to put myself at the disposal of the Prefect there, to whom the Prefect of Turin gives
me a letter, with the view of helping the people if possible.
Most people seem to be flying from the Riviera just now."

He had with him a friend, a young Irishman of very
loyal and generous character, who had helped to wait on
my husband during his recovery and who afterwards came
to us in Winchester. He was one of those excellent
servants who could make himself useful in a hundred
different ways. He accompanied my son, to whom he
was much attached, in his visits to the ruined towns of
the Riviera.

"I am rather disappointed," my son wrote from Savona, "with the local authorities. I presented my letter from the Prefect of Turin. Many speeches were made, but little was done. What I wanted was a word to several Syndics or military officers, to enable us to distribute provisions and blankets, and to excavate; but they were so slow in doing what I wished that I went direct to Diano Marina; but there the chief official refused to allow us to go among the ruins and to help. Without a permit every one is kept away by the sentinels. We saw bodies being dug out. The whole town is in ruins. Finding it hopeless to get official permits, we went to Mentone in order to buy bread ourselves. But we found there a great panic, all the shops shut and no bread to be had. We therefore returned to Savona, after spending a very cold night at the railway station at Mentone. Yesterday, however, with difficulty I contrived to buy about sixty kilogrammes of bread, some sausages and marsala. We brought them ourselves, as in some of the villages the people are starving. We are going from here to Bussana, Baiardo and San Remo."

"Charles has been working hard," his father wrote, "among the poor and starving people on the Riviera. He and Michael Walsh seems to have seen terrible sights. At Diano Marina almost the whole population was killed by the falling in of a church in which they had taken refuge. We are collecting money to send out to him, as he cannot help people without it. Besides those who were killed at once, a great many were dug out in a terrible state, dying as soon as they were brought into the air. At Diano Castello some ninety were killed and seventy wounded. At Baiardo about two hundred and fifty killed; and at many other villages higher up the hills the loss of life has not been computed, but it seems to have been considerable. There were also odd houses all along the sides of the mountains where damage has been done. Charles and Michael have gone about distributing provisions, which are much needed. They both seem well, sleeping in the open air like the poor people who are without shelter. The relief seems to have been well timed. They had two asses laden with provisions, and went to some quaint remote places where Government help had not yet arrived. The people blessed them fervently wherever they went. The Mayor of Bussana seems to have been the only person saved out of his large family. He gave Charles a rosary which his dead wife had worn, and thanked him. It was all he had left of his ruined property. Michael says that many of the people have gone mad, through despair, having lost their all, the fruits, probably, of their hard labours for years past."

During the spring of this year my husband kept his usual term of residence, rejoicing much in the restored power of taking up his duties in the Cathedral. He also wrote several articles for reviews, one being a very full and careful review of M. Gambier Parry's "Ministry of the Fine Arts," for the *Edinburgh*. He wrote besides some articles for *Longman's Magazine*. Wishing to attend our Annual Federation Conference, which was held this year at Lausanne, we started from home in August and stayed a couple of days *en route* at Rheims.

"To-day," he wrote to a son, "we have done justice to Rheims. We have paid several visits to the Cathedral. I will not say that it is the finest Cathedral I have ever seen, but I must allow that it is hard to beat. One sees from the entrance the whole extent of the Cathedral, four hundred and sixty-six feet. The great height of the nave and choir, the beauty of the clustered pillars and the coloured windows, also the works in sculpture and painting, including some *Gobelin* tapestries which go right up and down the side aisles, are all very striking features. Outside, the proportions and massive-ness of the architecture, the richness of the decorations and the height of the two western towers are the chief features. The doorways full of sculptured figures struck me especially, and we wished for you to photograph them. We drove round the Boulevards, and saw from an elevation which we climbed the great champagne 'caves' of Veuve Pommery, who seems to be a benefactor to the whole neighbourhood. She had built schools, cottages and playgrounds, and done much for the people. We saw also a large gathering of young gymnasts from the military school of St. Cyr ; in fact Rheims was *en fête.* It is a clean and prosperous city ; I am very glad we stayed here. To-morrow we shall go to the Bernerhof, Bern, where I know a cordial welcome from Mr. Kraft will await us."

"Berne, August 16th.

" Here we are, after a long but pleasant journey, having started at five in the morning. We came by a new day express which no one seems as yet inclined to use, as we were the only people in it. The guard came into our carriage occasionally and chatted pleasantly. The country between Belfort and Berne one seldom sees, because hitherto the expresses have only gone in the night. It is a very pretty country. We can recommed to you our route to Switzerland by Rheims, and to anyone who can appreciate fine architecture. The Cathedral has left an impression on my mind which I shall never forget. Belfort is a fine place, and interesting, after its sufferings in the Franco-German war. It certainly deserves its name, as it is, like Peschiera, ' *Bello et forte arnese.*' Your mother was interested in seeing an old book in the library at Rheims, of the times of Joan of Arc, in which it is recorded that the village of Domremy shall be henceforward for ever freed from all taxes '*à cause de la Pucelle.*' Your visit to India will, I hope, this year come off without hindrance. We shall look forward with great interest to your letters from the east."

"Comballaz, September 2nd.

" There is good sketching to be had here at Comballaz. You see the Dent du Midi very well, and still better from Les Mosses, which is the watershed of this part of the country. The Diablerets mountains are visible from a short distance from here ; they look fine, especially at sunset. We shall be sorry to leave this place on Saturday for Lausanne, where we must go for the Conference. Town life and poly-glotistic talk are not so agreeable as mountain air and arca-dian life. The moon was full last night; it rose over the mountains in front of us and looked its best."

The Conference was a very crowded one, the great theatre at Lausanne being filled at our meetings from the gallery to the floor. Our best orators were M. de Pressensé and Mr. Reveillaud, from Paris; the address of the latter sparkled with French wit and brilliant thought. We spent part of September, after the Conference was ended, at Vevey and its neighbourhood.

From G. B. :—

"Vevey, September, 1887.

" The air is now not so hot, but clear and bracing. We shall leave this place with regret; the views are very picturesque, and the Couvreu family, the principal people in this place, are most hospitable and kind. They are now at one of their country houses, near Clarens. Mr. Couvreu is of an old Walloon family, a handsome old man; and his family are all intelligent and kind."

From J. E. B. :—

" Yesterday we visited Elisé Reclus, the great geographer, in his little cottage at Clarens. He was condemned, you know, to be shot in Paris, after the Commune, and one of his brothers was actually executed; but he, Elisé, was saved at the last moment (after the manner of romances), the reason given for sparing his life being that the French nation could not afford to lose a man of such high scientific reputation. He is not only a Communist, but a professed Anarchist; one of the most delightful men, nevertheless, that I ever conversed with. The expression of his countenance is open and clear, like that of a child. He is fair, with blue eyes; his manner is vivacious and his interest in everything has the freshness and intensity of ardent youth, though he cannot be very young. He works continually at his great book—never returns to his own country, from which he is exiled, but occasionally comes to the British Museum for research. We had a long and pleasant conversation. He is quite familiar with English politics, up to the latest news of the day. In parting from him at the door of his cottage my husband asked him if he would pay us a visit at Winchester next time he went to the British Museum? He replied eagerly: Certainly, I will.' We reminded him that we live under the shadow of a great cathedral, and asked how would he feel in regard to our ecclesiastical surroundings. He smiled, and said: 'Oh, I shall not mind that—I shall enjoy it very much.'"

He very soon carried out his intention, by visiting us the same autumn, on which occasion I wrote to my son George:—

" Mr. Arthur Shadwell and two or three clergymen were coming to dine with us yesterday, when who should arrive an hour earlier but Elisé Reclus, on his way back to Switzerland. We had no opportunity of telling our other guests beforehand who he was, and that besides being a scientific man he was an exiled French revolutionary and anarchist. However, everyone was delighted with him. , He is a very sincere, unaffected and modest man, full of enthusiasm, and with an intellect like a razor. Mr. ——, you know, is a strong conservative and high churchman. We found him engaged in a most animated *tête-a-tête* with Elisé Reclus before dinner. They seemed to be disputing warmly; but we discovered that it was concerning a no more burning question than the comparative antiquity of Welsh and Breton poetry l Reclus gave us a picturesque description of the Aigue Morte and the Tower of Constance on the South coast of France. His picture of them was full of vivid personal as well as geographical interest. He expressed sympathy with the persecuted Hugenots, some of whom were confined for thirty or forty years in that hideous Tower of Constance. We had been speaking of the present distress in London ; he seemed penetrated with pity for the unemployed, the sufferings of some of whom he had witnessed. I was struck by the expression of his face and the flash of his eye when he said : ' It is wrong, Madam—it is wrong. This is not what was intended by the Creator of men. There will be a change. It will not come quickly in England, but it will come—a complete change.' "

My husband often expressed his thankfulness during this year for the amount of health and strength which had been restored to him after the severe experience of the year before. He was able to take some part in social and political movements during the year. He was an earnest supporter of the Home Rule movement. As a historian, he had become convinced of the great debt England owes to Ireland, on account of justice denied to that country for centuries past.

This good health was continued to him during the spring and summer of 1888. He enjoyed extremely a visit to Grindelwald in May, accompanied by his son Stanley. It was in the interest of his little church that he spent a short time there.

" We had an excellent journey here," he wrote ; "Switzerland looks beautiful—such foliage, and masses of flowers ! As it was fine, we did not stay at Berne or Thun, but telegraphed to Boss for a carriage to meet us at Därlingen. It was quite hot as we drove up. All the dogs seemed to recognise me, and made a tremendous fuss. Eiger's mother found her way at once up to my bedroom, and laid herself down on the mat, and as I write a young St. Bernard pup comes in for a pat,—a younger brother of Eiger's probably."

A few days later ·—

" We had an early communion service at the church, and evening service at 5.30. I found the church very dry and comfortable. In the middle of the day Stanley and I took a walk to a point beyond the stream which comes down from the Muhlbach, where we got a good view of the upper glacier, and saw avalanches falling from the Eiger and the Mettenberg. I am not at all tired and feel very well.

"The weather is warm and delightful, and the trees are coming out into fuller foliage daily. The people here are very kind to us; and with Stanley as a companion I get on well, though not without constant thoughts of home. The dogs share in the affectionate feelings of their masters, especially Eiger's mother 'Avalanche.'"*

During the summer and autumn my husband paid several visits to old friends; he visited Mr. Froude in Devonshire, his old friends on Tweedside, and in August his friend the Lord Chief Justice in London.

"I reached Lord Coleridge's," he wrote, "at five, and we had a nice chat. There was a pleasant dinner party to meet Mr. Gladstone. Besides Mr. Gladstone, there were Mr. and Mrs. Phelps, an American Judge, Lord and Lady Hobhouse, Lord Justice and Lady Bowen, Mr. John Morley, Sir Charles Forster, and several others. It is a pleasure to me to stay with my old friend Coleridge. . . . I am very glad to have been permitted to see dear Fanny at Richmond once more, and to have the hope that my visit may have been of some comfort to her. When very weak and ill one feels consoled by every proof of affection on the part of friends."

After my husband's serious illness in 1886, I had resolved in my own mind never again to be absent from him for more than a few hours, if possible, during our united lives. I refused all invitations to attend meetings,

---

* I was correcting the proofs of these *Recollections* at Grindelwald when the disastrous fire (August, 1892) broke out, which destroyed half of that pleasant village, including this church, for which my husband worked so earnestly. I had the pain of witnessing its complete destruction.

NORHAM CASTLE, ON THE TWEED.
From a Water-Colour Drawing by G. Butler.

in London or elsewhere,—sometimes, I fear, to the surprise as well as regret of my fellow workers in public matters. My choice was, however, deliberate, and I have never had cause to regret it. He had, I thought, sufficiently suffered by my frequent absences from home during many years of our married life, while engaged in opposing a great social wrong; and he had borne this trial without a murmur. He was now advanced in years, and less strong, and these things seemed to me to constitute a most sacred claim to my personal and constant devotion to him. Never, except for a day or two during the serious illness of a dear sister, did I consent to be separated from him. Even on that occasion I was told by those at home that he seemed to feel my absence sadly, and that at the sound of a footstep or wheels on the drive, he would go to the window to see if by any chance it was his wife who had returned, though he knew that it was scarcely possible.

He sometimes expressed his loving thoughts towards me in pure and beautiful verse. The following, translated from the German, he wrote during one of my absences from home. The tenderness and refinement of feeling expressed in it increased and deepened with every added year of his life —

"And art thou gone? I look around me,
  And vainly hope to see thee near:
Some strong delusion, Love, hath bound me;
  Thine voice sounds ever in mine ear.

"So when the lark at morn is singing,
  In vain we seek him in the sky;
His music in our ears is ringing,
  His form eludes our searching eye.

"In vain, at dawn of day awaking,
  I look with eager glance for thee:
Still sounds my voice, the silence breaking,
  'O come, beloved, back to me!'"

How often does the echo of those words sound now in the silence of my own heart :—

"O come, beloved, back to me!"

Our Annual International Conference took place at Copenhagen in the autumn of 1888. My husband had planned to write an article on the famous Thorwaldsen sculptures in Copenhagen, which the editor of the *Contemporary Review* had agreed to take for his paper. He enjoyed very much the brilliant ten or twelve days we spent in Denmark. The weather was fine, the air exhilarating, and our reception by Danish friends cordial and kind. We had the good fortune to meet on the journey there my brother-in-law, Mr. Meuricoffre. He and my husband visited the galleries together, the latter making very full and careful notes for his projected article.

To Madame Meuricoffre :—

"We came here through Jutland, crossing the Little Belt to the island of Fyen, and then the great Belt to the Island of Jutland. This was in order to avoid the nine hours of sea from Kiel. To-morrow we go by steamer to Malmö, in Sweden, for a meeting. Then our work will be over, and we shall come home. James Stuart has gone off with Mr. Thomasson to Norway ; they mean to sail about the fjords for a few days. Yesterday my husband and I gave ourselves the whole day to see the Thorwaldsen sculptures thoroughly. They are well worth seeing. Especially grand is the 'Risen Christ.' He stands on an elevated pedestal, with his hands spread out, and his head slightly bent forward as if waiting to gather the whole world into his arms. The words are written below in Danish, 'Kommen til Mig' ('Come unto Me'). The figure is colossal and stands high in the apse of the church. It is exceedingly striking as you enter at the west end."

30

The article on the Thorwaldsen's sculptures lies among my husband's papers still in its unfinished state. What there is of it exhibits the same careful, conscientious spirit which he threw into all his literary work. It would have been valuable, if finished, as a commentary upon the works in those famous galleries.

One of the brightest episodes in this visit to Denmark was a long day spent at Elsinore, at the home of the parents of Mrs. Kitchen, wife of the Dean of Winchester, who with the Dean was then staying there. We visited, of course, the Castle, and other scenes of the story of Hamlet. The day was bright, the sea sparkling, and the air so clear that we could see every object, even men, women and children walking about on the opposite shores of Sweden.

Though we had had brilliant sunshine in Denmark we encountered cold and stormy weather in re-crossing the sea. My husband remained on deck the whole time, pacing up and down ; but the air was keen and the vessel rolled very much. When we landed I observed that he was much chilled. From that day he never was quite well again. He had been, perhaps, over-fatigued by his researches in Copenhagen, and the sudden change to cold weather was consequently the more dangerous for him.

It was in the autumn of this year that the illness developed which at last prevailed over his wonderful natural vitality and strength of constitution. It was a bitter moment to us when the London physician whom we consulted, and whose reputation in respect to that form of illness gave authority to his decision, pronounced him to be very ill, adding that he might live a few weeks or perhaps months, but that, being in his seventieth year, no hope of ultimate recovery could be entertained. His changed appearance seemed only too strongly to confirm this verdict. But God had much mercy still in store for him and us; his life was prolonged beyond the short period predicted, and that prolonged life was enriched by much real and pure enjoyment; thanks, in a great measure, to the extraordinary patience with which he was endowed.

I speak of extraordinary patience; for such it was, manifestly to all. I have before alluded to his naturally quick temper. He possessed the artistic temperament, and a finely-strung nervous system, which had been no a little tried by many years of close work as a schoolmaster. He evidently had at times a severe conflict with his natural tendency to irritability. He would speak quickly or with a touch of irony; but so great, at the same time, was his tenderness of conscience and gentle courtesy of disposition, that in a moment regret took the place of every other emotion, and it was touching to see how he would at once apply himself to soothe any wounded feeling which his quick word might have produced. Generally he would frankly express his regret; and in any case he would take the first opportunity of doing some special act of kindness or speaking some very gentle word to the person whom he thought he might have hurt. In regard to this failing he had gained a great mastery over himself in the course of years, before this illness came upon him. It is a form of illness which is commonly said to be of all others the most depressing and the most liable to produce irritation of feeling. Friends constantly wrote: "Of course he must be very low-spirited." "Do not be distressed if you find him very irritable. That symptom always accompanies jaundice." But what were the facts?

. Surely there is no more beautiful subject of contempla-

30 *

tion in this life than that of the work of the Spirit of God in a human heart, correcting, educating, and perfecting. And it is such a work that I have to record; and I speak now not only in praise of him who was the subject of that marvellous grace, but in praise of God who granted that grace, and who elected to show forth in this soul what His power and love can do. For certainly in him "patience had her perfect work."

Before the illness had declared itself, there was a very short period of depression — a feeling of misery and unrest. He blamed himself for this, and there was some inward conflict, more severe than I knew at the time. I do not know exactly in what manner the cloud passed away; but it seemed to me that he had manfully faced the situation and submitted himself to the will of God, and that *the victory was gained once for all* after those first few weeks of mental discomfort. For he never went back after this, but always forward; always becoming more patient, more cheerful and more courageous to the end. He retained to the last, in a remarkable degree, the power of pleasant companionship, and his conversation, when not actually subdued by pain or weariness, was observed by many to be, even in the last weeks of his life, full of energy and interest; his memory continued to be remarkable, when speaking of literary or historical subjects, of passing events, or incidents of our life and those of his friends.

He had great joy in the birth of his first grandson at Winchester, in September, 1888, just as his health began to fail. Madame Meuricoffre, who had paid us a visit in that month, wrote to the father of the little child

"I have always in my memory a vivid and sunny picture of that last Sunday afternoon, the day of little Bob's birth.

We went to the cathedral, and sat in the nave and listened to the beautiful notes of the anthem ascending to the roof; and when we came back, you and your mother were waiting for us in the porch of your father's house, in that amber afternoon sunlight. Then you came forward, and passed beyond me to meet your father, who was coming along the other side of the Close; and when you met, he looked up, and you clasped hands, his face beaming with loving emotion at the news of the birth of his first grandson. Then many kind friends came round the garden gate to congratulate you. Your father was even then very ill; but.our visit did not at all leave .the impression with us of having been with a sick person, but rather of a joyous time, and of him as a courtly, charming, and lovely presence—something that made one want to put on one's best dress and do one's best to be courtly to. And with this there was a growing peacefulness surrounding him which kept moving one further and further from the small and mean things of this world. What a distinguished circle of friends he had! and he took such pains to keep friendship fresh, never failing in any of the sweet courtesies of life."

To Naples. From J. E. B. :—

" December 30th.

" Our dear Charlie arrived suddenly from South Africa on Christmas morning, to his father's surprise and joy; and so our little family was complete on this, probably the last Christmas in which we shall all be together. On hearing of his father's serious illness, he said, he could not help coming straight home to see him. Even if his father recovers, this substantial sign of affection will be always remembered by him with loving tenderness; and if he should not recover, Charles will be glad, when he goes back to the Transvaal, that he saw him once more.

" Last night, at prayers, my husband read that beautiful chapter in the Revelations : 'And there shall be no more death, neither sorrow nor crying, neither shall there be any more pain ;' and then he prayed for us all. It might have been a farewell prayer. It was very calm, and full of hope. He is so happy with his three sons and Rhoda and our two grandchildren around us. He said to me: 'What a happy Christmas this has been ;' although he has scarcely had a day without pain. Therefore, when you think of us in your loving sympathy, you can praise God too."

Soon after the New Year we started for Cannes, in order to avoid the cold and damp.

From J. E. B. :—

"Cannes, January 14th.

"We were glad to get across the Channel. It was a bleak sight to see the dark, weltering sea, almost lost to view in the fog and the driving snow. George came across with us, to his father's great comfort. He saw us into our carriage *de luxe* at Calais. His hand was like ice (with the cold) when we bade him good-bye, though he was most cheering, and watched us till the train started. By the time he would be returning the fog was flat down to the ground, like a huge blanket, blotting out heaven and earth.

"We travelled here without a pause, my husband sleeping pretty well in his *coupé-lit.* At Marseilles the sun was shining brightly ; everything so different from dear, foggy England. This morning, it was wonderful to be awakened by the brilliant rising sun shining over the sea and into our windows. After breakfast, we went out on the terrace. The sun was so hot that we were obliged to seek a shaded place ! There are roses blowing, and jonquils and heliotropes and geraniums in flower, and the bees humming at midday. My husband kept thanking God continually. He said : 'Even if I have but a short time to live, this is a blessed alleviation of the discomforts of my illness.'"

From G. B. :—

"January 21st.

"We were very glad, dear George, to hear of your safe arrival at home after your act of devotion to us. We have had splendid weather ever since our arrival. Tell our Winchester friends, when you see them, that the wish most in our minds is how we could send them some sunshine and pure air. The view from our rooms here is worth a great deal, looking over the bay towards St. Marguerite and the Esterels. I hope you took no harm from your exposure to cold and the tossing on board the steamer. Your presence made all the difference to us."

As the spring came on, he had much enjoyment, in spite of some days of pain and langour, in exploring the country around us, in our drives and walks in the woods, in sketching, and, not least, in the society of some dear friends in the same hotel. I give a few extracts from letters and journals.

Madame Meuricoffre, who, with her husband, had paid us a visit from Naples, wrote :—

"We have been talking of you and the dearest Canon, and those bright days at Le Cannet ; particularly of that lovely drive to Mougins, where we sat on the high-walled terrace and made tea, and looked across the lovely country towards Grasse and the snowy Alps beyond. How lovely it was, and how our dear one enjoyed it ! Tell was much struck with his great and happy enjoyment of beautiful Nature ; perhaps to him it was a purer and more impersonal enjoyment than if he had been strong. What a blesing that love of God's nature is ; it outlasts all !

"I shall not forget Easter Sunday, when he administered the Communion in the large salôn of Mrs. Renton to a number of invalids, himself looking as ill as any. How touching it was to see him in that quiet room, with the afternoon sunshine ; so delicate, and yet so upheld by the familiar holy service. His voice sounded so sweet and full of feeling. He was not at all spent afterwards, but was very bright and cheerful when we returned to your own salôn and had tea together."

To Madame Meuricoffre, from J. E. B. :—

" Hotel Grande Bretagne, Le Cannet, Cannes,

"April 28th.

" This is our last day here, and I am thinking of all the mercies and happiness of the past three months and a half that we have been here, of our excursions to the Hermitage, the Observatory, Vallouris, and other sunny places. One evening lately I was alarmed about my dear one; he had an attack of shivering and fever, with great weakness. Sir Mark and Lady Collett and others of our kind friends observed his paleness in the evening, and were very tender in their inquiries and sympathy. I kept the door open between his room and mine till past midnight and went in often, and I tried to cast my burden on the Lord. In a few hours the fever became less, and at last he fell into a sound and quiet sleep, and I retired. Just as I was falling asleep I had such a pleasant sensation. I thought I was lying flat, with a restful feeling, on a smooth, still sea —a boundless ocean, with no limit or shore on any side. It was strong, and held me up, and there was light and sunshine all round me. And then I dreamed I heard a voice say : ' Such is the Grace of God. Like this ocean are His love, His power, His goodwill—boundless, endless. He is never weary of blessing.' I took it to mean that I was to rest in God, and expect all good things from Him."

While we were at Cannes, Catherine Booth-Clibborn and her husband were endeavouring to hold a few drawing-room meetings in aid of their beautiful mission among the poorest people of the South of France. Hearing that there was much prejudice to overcome, and that they were not, so far, very successful in Cannes, and also that Catherine Booth had been very ill, my husband determined to attend one of her meetings. They met at the door of the house where she was to speak. Both were greatly changed in appearance since her visit to us at Winchester.

"Dear Canon, you are very ill!" she said, clasping his hand and looking wistfully at him; while he marked with equally tender sympathy the suffering look in her refined and spiritual face. She said afterwards that his presence at the meeting (which cost him some effort physically) had done good both to herself and her cause, the latter being regarded with scornful indifference for the most part by the English society at Cannes, not less by the religious than by the worldly portion of it,—with some marked exceptions.

"Territet, Switzerland, April 29th.

"We journeyed from Cannes to Grenoble through the night. It is a picturesque line of railroad. He was very tired when we reached Geneva the next forenoon, but the following day well enough to enjoy a beautiful sail up the lake to Territet. The Mont Blanc range of mountains was dazzlingly beautiful, the lake and sky calm and blue, and the air very sweet. We found at the Hotel des Alpes M. and Madame Vaissier, who had been with us at Le Cannet, the former in a dying state, though a few weeks before he had looked strong and well. My husband's sympathies are deeply moved for them both, and his prayers for them are pathetic and earnest. They are an attractive couple—she a noble and accomplished woman. Their country home is near Dijon."

To a sister :—

"Territet, Sunday Morning, May 5th, 1889.

".This is a lovely morning. I am sitting at my window looking over the lake, in which the mountains are reflected as in a polished mirror. Albeit the air is sharp, the sunshine is lovely; it is an ideal Sabbath morning. The fine, deep-toned bells of the old church on the hill are rolling their echoes over the lake, and my husband has just been reading to me the first sermon of Jesus in the Synagogue at Gallilee, when He

'.closed the book,' and the ' eyes of all were fastened on Him '
If. .we could keep our eyes always fastened on that face, then
no anxieties would visit us."

A meeting of magistrates, pastors, and other citizens
of the Canton de Vaud was called at Montreux to consider
the progress made and the further measures required in
Switzerland in regard to the international movement for
higher morality and reform of the laws. It was convened
in our near neighbourhood, in the hope that we might be
able to be present. My husband wished to go. It was
not intended that he should attempt to speak, and friends
had courteously arranged for him an easy seat in a corner,
where he could hear all that passed. His frail appearance was evidently affecting to those there who had seen him
in years past in full health. In the midst of a silence at
the commencement of the meeting, M. Buscarlet, of
Lausanne, gently suggested that he should offer prayer.
My husband stood up (after the manner of the Swiss in
public prayer), and in a few solemn words prayed for the
outpouring of the Spirit of God on all present. I marked
his words, and recall some of them now: " In such a
cause as this, O God, in which the welfare and strength
of nations are at stake, we may not rely on any force other
than Thy inspiring and sustaining power. . . . ¯Lord,
keep ever before our eyes the hope of the heavenly vision
promised by Jesus Christ to the pure in heart. Thou
knowest how much of impurity and injustice there is in
every land. But we come not here to arraign others; we
come to make our own confession and request. We know
that we must all stand before Thy Judgment Seat, to give
account, not only of the things done in the flesh, but of
the use made of opportunities of saving others from the
evils of the world. . . . Give us, Lord, the zeal which

was conspicuous in Thy servants the prophets and in the great reformers of later days, and breathe into us Thy Spirit, that this zeal may be tempered with the gentleness and purity of Him who was the friend of sinners, Himself the only blameless one, our Lord and Saviour Jesus Christ."

We travelled home by Pontarlier, staying a day and night at Dijon. This route was chosen by my husband because of his strong wish to hear again of M. Vaissier, and possibly to see him and his wife. We drove to their house, and found Madame Vaissier still hopeful, although her husband was worse. The end was near, for we heard of his death soon after our arrival in England. Madame Vaissier (with her husband, a Catholic) spoke of the spiritual help and impulse they had both derived from intercourse with the English with whom they had formed grave and pleasant friendships at Le Cannet.

Soon after our return to Winchester, my husband entered once more on his residence. It was the last.

"He says" I wrote to a sister, "that he believes God will give him strength just to get through his duties; and if he believes this, I am sure he will have the strength. Just before these duties began, he wished to spend a day in London for some business. I went with him. We got home for afternoon tea. He was, of course, tired, but not much so. We actually made a show of going to the Royal Academy! It was not quite successful, for he got tired after going through two or three rooms, and often sat down. Some acquaintances whom we met did not recognise him (with his complexion, as he said cheerfully, of the 'colour of autumn leaves'), but that did not matter. He enjoys immensely the fact that he has been to the Royal Academy!"

To a sister :—

"July, 1889.

"You who know what his 'pluck' is will not be surprised to hear of his going bravely through the cathedral services, although he suffers a good deal in the effort. I think many are learning from him how good a thing is humility in a character. The vergers in the cathedral sometimes look across at me with a sympathetic look, as much as to say, The dear canon is getting on.' Our good Dean says : 'Yes, he is the *dear* canon to us all.' He preached his last sermon last Sunday. He looked very ill, and walked slowly to the pulpit. I think some people were nervous about him, but God helped him to the end. He spoke clearly, though low and slowly; with a pathos that went to our hearts. Canon Warburton and others spoke most lovingly about it to me as we walked home. He had a good deal of fever in the night and his mind wandered a little, showing how much weaker he is physically, though so strong in patience and in resolve to do his duty."

"August 4th.

"This is our last Sunday in our peaceful home here. James Stuart has been to spend a last day with us. I went with him to the garden gate as he was leaving, and he turned back with a face full of feeling, and paused awhile. He said : 'I now fully realise for the first time that my dear, dear friend must leave us before long.' He is much affected by the change in my husband in the last three weeks, and is full of admiration of his unselfishness and courage, keeping up, though so weak, all the old politeness and pleasant conversation and hospitality."

During the summer many old friends and relations came to see him. He dearly valued this proof of their affection. His brothers Spencer, Arthur, and Montagu (Master of Trinity College, Cambridge), his sisters, and my sister, Mrs. Garston, who had for many years hospitably received him in her London house whenever he went to Town, were among those who visited us. His servants who stayed any time with us, always became strongly attached to him. One of these, Jane Taylor, a faithful friend as well as servant, had been with us for twenty-five years, at Cheltenham and at Liverpool. She had been our helper in the work we were called to do on behalf of the miserable and sinful. Without Jane's help, we could not easily have received such into our house as we did. Her prudent reserve, her magnanimous judgment, and common sense well fitted her to second all such efforts, and she did so with constancy and perseverance. She came to Winchester to see her " dear master " once more, and remained with us some time.

We were advised, as the autumn drew on, to go for a few weeks to Scarborough. Dr. Teale, who visited my husband while there, was impressed, as other medical men had been, by the strength of his character in illness. A brother wrote, some months later: " I have just seen Dr. Teale in Scotland. He spoke most strongly of the impression George had made upon him by his high courage, his bright and cheerful spirit and his patient submission. He had always taken a very serious view of his case, but the brightness of the patient himself led him at times to be more hopeful." We found ourselves again amidst kind friends at Scarborough, among whom were the Rowntree family, and that of Mr. J. E. Ellis, M.P.

We returned to Winchester only to take leave of friends and to prepare for going to Italy. M. Tell Meuricoffre had written to ask my husband to accept the use of his beautiful country house at Capo di Monte during the late autumn, although he and my sister would be absent from Naples during the greater part of that time. . .. .

CHAPTER XIX.

RESIDENCE AT CAPO -DI MONTE.—BRIGHT SURROUNDINGS AND
RENEWED HOPE.—AMALFI.—OUT-OF-DOOR LIFE.—TEMPORARY
IMPROVEMENT IN HEALTH.—CHANGE OF WEATHER.—STORMS.
INFLUENZA.—RETURN TO NAPLES.—JOURNEY NORTHWARD.
—ROME.— GENOA.— CANNES.— INCREASING WEAKNESS.—
SAD THOUGHTS.—SUBMISSION.—KINDNESS OF FRIENDS AND
MEDICAL ATTENDANT.— SUNSET HOURS.— PREPARATIONS
FOR THE JOURNEY HOME.— BOULOGNE.— LONDON.— THE
END.—WINCHESTER.—THE CATHEDRAL SERVICE.— TESTI-
MONIES OF FRIENDS, AND OF SONS.

THE long journey to Naples was accomplished with as little fatigue as possible. We rested three days at Lucerne, two days at Milan, and again three at Florence.

From Lucerne my husband wrote to his son Stanley: "I wore my new fur coat, George's present to me, on the journey. I saw several fur coats on the way, but none so handsome as mine; which I think will last my time, and be a constant reminder of its donor." Every proof of affection from his sons and other near relatives seemed now to be doubly valued by him. His sons' and daughter-in-law's letters he always kept in a bound packet within reach of his hand, placing them at night on his table by the side of his Bible, and often opening and re-reading them. I found the precious packet sometimes locked in his hand while he was sleeping.

At Florence he was well enough to drive with me in an open carriage to our favourite haunts on the hills around, and even to walk through the galleries of the Uffizzi.

We arrived in Rome on a Saturday evening. The following Sunday was a day of warm and brilliant sunshine. He had a desire to go out early; and we went to the Colosseum, where we found ourselves quite alone. We sat some time on the fragments of ruins in a blaze of sunshine, and in a complete stillness and silence, realising vividly some of the wonderful historic memories which haunt the place. There we held our quiet morning service of prayer and praise, and the streets were only beginning to show signs of busy life when we returned to our hotel.

From G. B. :—

"Villa Meuricoffre, Capo di Monte, Naples,

"November 3rd, 1889.

"This afternoon we took a short drive round the Royal Park, and saw more picturesque subjects than we have seen yet. The ground is of great natural beauty, and the owners of the villas have added to this by cultivating their pine trees in the best way. As yet the foliage of the deciduous trees is hardly touched by the cold, only warmed by not infrequent tinges of yellow and orange. There were some large masses of cloud in the sky, and Vesuvius was a deep indigo, the distant clouds (strata cumulus) being finely grouped, and allowing Capri and the Sorrento coast to be clearly seen. This is a beautiful house, and the view from the terrace, looking towards the bay, is magnificent. The Meuricoffres' servants treat us with the greatest kindness, having imbibed, it would seem, the generous and hospitable spirit of their master and mistress."

I wrote to our sons later in November :—

"Our first beautiful month here is coming to a close. Everything predicts that 'the family' is coming home—

gardeners bringing in pots of splendid flowers and ferns to decorate the rooms, and others brushing up the walks and terraces, and altogether a 'movement' as of some coming event. It was a beautiful idea of Tell and Hatty to lend us this lovely house. Last Sunday father and I sat for an hour in the King's Garden, close at hand, and it was so hot that we had to seek the shade of some evergreen oaks. Naples was simmering in the heat far below and the sea glittering. There were roses in full flower, and the scent from the orange-blossom was very sweet. But the next day there came a change—a thunderstorm—and now it is quite cool. The mountains at sunset have a colour which no painter could give—a deep rich purple—over which there seems to be drawn a veil of golden gauze, if you can imagine that. Father has decidedly improved; he says he feels much better.

"Our dear people have come home from Switzerland, and we are very happy. Yesterday the Swiss pastor, M. Tissot, called on father, and we had a pleasant little service in the library, after which father conversed with him in German. God's Spirit gives insight, and M. Tissot prayed as if he knew what was passing in all our hearts; and especially beautiful were his thoughts and requests for father. He also mentioned you all in prayer (having heard of you from Aunt Hatty), and Conrad at Buenos Ayres and Charles in Africa. He is a man very well fitted for holding up evangelic truth in this strangely mixed population. While he was speaking and praying father's face wore an expression which was truly saint-like. He has been all along very patient and gentle, as you know; and now he seems to have more joy, and is full of thankfulness for everything."

"December 1st.

"A young Irish lady, who is studying music as a profession, came last evening. She sang 'The Wearing of the Green' with so much pathos in her beautiful voice that she stirred all our sympathies, which are already deeply moved for poor Ireland. Then she sang some of the music of Orfeo very well, and father got out his little classical library and translated to us the sad poetic story of Orpheus and his Eurydice. Tell led him on to give us some other classical fragments, and was charmed with the living interest which his own realisation of the different scenes described gave to it all."

As the winter set in, and the time came for our friends to return to their house in town, we decided to go to Amalfi for greater warmth. Here we were able to be out almost all day in the sunshine. A wonderful improvement became manifest in my husband. Week after week he continued to regain a little strength, and continually said that he felt better. Hope dies hard in a loving heart; and though I had had such clear warnings concerning the improbability of his ultimate recovery, I began again to hope that he might yet be spared to us. So much strength was restored to him that he was able often to walk a mile before breakfast on the rocky terrace, gay with flowers, and flooded with the unfailing sunshine with which we were blessed for the first few weeks. He would afterwards sit for an hour or two sketching, and in the evening walk with me down to the beach. We were staying at the Capuchin Monastery, which is turned into a hotel—a most picturesque ancient building, which seems to cling like a marten's nest to the cliff high above the sea, and to which you ascend by a long series of steps cut in the rock. This ascent, after our evening walk, often taxed my own powers of breathing and climbing, while it delighted and astonished me to see the sturdy manner in which he ascended, slowly but without pause till he reached the top. It was an endless delight to us to watch from the stone balcony of our rooms the varying and exquisite colours of the Gulf of Salerno, especially at sunset. Along the opposite shore runs a spur of beautiful mountains, at the foot of which, on a clear day, the sunburnt marbles of the ruins of Pæstum can be discerned.

> "December 4th.

"The beauty of this place is wonderful: lines of indescribable colours on the sea, the soft, distant mountains tipped with snow, and the rocks burning into flame towards sunset. Yesterday we drove to Ravello, on the top of the rocks, a good stiff climb from here; a delightful place, though I imagine it may be cold at night. We sat an hour or two on the terrace of the Pension Palumbo, anciently the archbishop's house. The silence was like that of a Scotch moor on a hot July day—not a leaf stirring, and now and then the soft hum of a passing bee. We saw the celebrated Ambo in the church, and went over Mr. Reid's house and grounds. Everywhere there are traces of the Saracens in the picturesque ruins."

My husband wrote to his sons on Christmas Eve:—

"Accept our affectionate Christmas greetings, and the assurance how much we desire the advent of every blessing to you. I am getting better every day, thank God! and have much better nights."

J. E. B. to Madame Meuricoffre:—

> "Christmas Eve.

"My husband prayed so earnestly for you and yours last night. It seems to me that the whole of the Christian's onward path is one which must necessarily lead to greater and more perfect *simplicity*, and this goal he certainly is reaching. His prayers are those of one who has become 'as a little child' before God, absolutely simple, confiding, and faithful. He thanked God for all the useful presents you

have sent us here, and prayed for the two Mesdames S——
in their trouble, saying, 'Lord, we do not know them very
well; but they are friends of our dear sister and brother,
whose every interest we would wish to make our own when
we come with our requests before Thee;' and he prayed for
M. Tissot and for all your friends, and for you especially.
Don Francesco took us yesterday for a beautiful walk above
the Monastery, and showed us his cows. It was rather a
scramble, but George came in not at all tired. The soft
coolness of the evening and the 'sweet breath of kine' reminded us of a meadow walk in England on a summer
evening."

But a change came over this fair scene. The influenza
swept over Southern Italy with great force, Prince
Amedeo being one of its first victims. The sun was
darkened by clouds, and the sea was lashed by violent
storms. A great depression of spirits fell on the inhabitants of the village, and several deaths occurred. It was
no longer possible to live out of doors. The extraordinary
revival of health and strength granted to my husband,
and which had justified some hope that his fine constitution would at last prevail over the disease, was suddenly
arrested, and he became feverish and ill. It would,
indeed, have been a wonder if that mysterious blighting
influence, which seldom spares those with already impaired health, had left him entirely unscathed. From
that time he never rallied again. I had a slight attack of
influenza which kept me to my room. The sun shone
out for a brief interval one day, and he went out for a
short stroll alone, (while well I always went with him).
He was rather long in returning; and while I was
anxiously watching his room door, it was opened in order
that he might be carried in on a chair by two porters.
He had gone up a little path to a spot a few paces from

31 *

the terrace, where I had begun a sketch, in the desire to see again that exquisite view which we had chosen together as a subject for drawing some weeks before. The storms had partly broken down the path. He slipped and fell, spraining his ankle severely. He looked very pale when brought in; but in a short time made me smile by telling me how he had amused himself when lying on the ground in pain, and unable to rise for some time before help came. He called to some men who were pruning the lemon trees on the terraces above, but they did not hear. Having tried them in Italian, he then called to them in French and German, then in Spanish, and finally in Greek and Latin,—characteristically philosophical in making the best of the situation!

He suffered much pain for several days; but nothing daunted him. That very evening, as I kneeled by his chair, he said: "Now let us thank God! it might have been much worse. We have many mercies to record, and we will think of the brighter days which are coming."

My sister wrote:—"Oh that accident, and this influenza! It is very pathetic to see that Christian warrior labouring bravely on, but with ever decreasing strength. I have seen many sudden deaths,—when the victim was hurried away, and those who loved him stood overwhelmed and incredulous,—but seldom such a pathetic journey as this; you holding his hand and stepping down and down, still with patience and hope, and accompanying him to the verge of the river."

G. B. to a son:—

"Hotel dei Capuccini, Amalfi,

"January, 1890.

"It makes me sad to think of your being laid up with influenza, and of Charles with a broken wrist in the

Transvaal. Here there is a great panic about influenza. We have very stormy weather, and I am advised to keep to my room. There are some magnificent effects of sea and sky,* but these do not compensate for human suffering."

To Stanley:—

"Your mother is not well yet, and we have not heard from George for some time. I kept awaking during the watches of the night, and thinking of him and also of Charlie so far away. As the patriarch Jacob said, 'If I am bereaved of my children, I *am* bereaved.'"

It was seldom that he expressed so much sadness as these few words imply; it was difficult wholly to resist at that time the oppressive influences, material and moral, which seemed to sweep down upon the fair earth and cloud our hopes. A telegram having arrived with better news from England, he wrote:—"Many thanks for your good news telegraphed. However it may be in some families, in ours, thank God, distance does not cool affection; and I trust that this tradition will always be preserved in the family long after we elders have gone to our rest."

We returned to Naples, driving in an easy carriage to La Cava, where we rested a couple of days. A fortnight later we began our northward journey to Cannes. Our first stage was to Rome.

To my sister at Naples:—

"Rome, February 13th, 1890.

"I regretted our hurried parting, through our getting to the station rather late. Will you say to Tell how deeply

* Among these was the marvellous sight of five gigantic waterspouts stalking one after the other from the South across the Gulf of Salerno— huge pillars of water, with cloudy pine-like tops, menacing the shore, and awaited with anxiety and horror by the inhabitants, who stood ready to break them with strident voices before they could reach the land.

affected I have been by his considerate kindness and tenderness all along to my dear George. I shall never forget the sight of him guiding my dear one's slow steps along the platform, and his face when we parted, full of anxious sympathy. My husband called as loud as he could from the Pullman car, 'Good-bye, Tell! may God reward you for all your kindness;' but I fear he did not make himself heard. At four o'clock we thought of you having afternoon tea, and my heart was very full in thinking of our dear teas together and all your love for us. The setting sun on the snowy Appenines was very lovely, but it was all a little sad to me. When we reached our hotel he was overcome with weariness. While sitting over the fire, he said in his quaint way: 'St. Paul must have been very tired coming all the way from Pozzuoli to Rome. No wonder he called at the three taverns to refresh!'"

To my sons :—

"Genoa, February 15th.

"We came here by the day express. We had bright sunshine. When we reached Pisa, the Baptistry, Cathedral, and Leaning Tower looked very picturesque in the evening sun, which made them look pink and gold-coloured against the purple hills. We had the carriage to ourselves, and father reclined for several hours and slept. On arriving at the station we were greeted by the kind face of Frank Budd, who gave us prompt help in getting to our hotel. All our relations here have been to see father. It was a great effort for Aunt Eliza to come all the way from the Coronata, and he felt very much touched by her kindness."

"Hotel de Paradis, Cannes,

"March 3rd.

"Though he has got over the fatigue of the journey, I fear he is going down in strength. He has lost his appetite and is weaker. It is evident that this great wave of sickness which has passed over Europe, and has prostrated so many strong people, has seized upon him—not exactly in the form of influenza, but taking all the little strength out of him. He talks in his sleep, and sometimes imagines he sees one of you come into the room, and greets you gladly; and on awaking looks disappointed. Then I go and talk to him about you all, which comforts him. In the afternoon and evening, however, he generally becomes as bright as possible, and converses in the most interesting way. Comparative strangers are quite struck with him: he is so nobly patient and cheerful, and so full of interest in everything. There never was a truer heart—'An Israelite indeed in whom is no guile.' He has such a straightforward, honourable faith in God. He believes that it is as impossible for God to deceive him as for himself to deceive one of his own children, and so he rests with the greatest calm on the eternal promise."

To Madame Meuricoffre :—

" Dr. Frank came and stayed a long time. He is one of the kindest of men; and my husband enjoys his visits and conversation. Wishing to know what to say to the Dean of Winchester concerning arrangements for the terms of residence among the canons, my husband had asked me to write to Dr. Frank for his verdict as to his being able again to enter on his duties there. The doctor told him very gently that he must not now look forward to being able ever again to minister in the cathedral. He received the announcement in silence, and his eyes were filled with tears. When I took his hand it was very cold, and he seemed to shiver. Dr. Frank spoke most tenderly to him. He said: 'Canon, you will go home, and your very presence in the Close will be a benediction. You will preach more effectually in your illness than you could have done in the pulpit.' After Dr. Frank had gone he remained perfectly still for some time, with a sadness in his face which I seldom see now. I guessed there was some inward trouble, and got him into conversation. He was grieving because, he said, he had done so little for God, had ministered so short a time even in Winchester, and now all was ended. I reminded him of Aunt Hatty's kind words about the testimony of character, apart from all our doings or not doings. He took it gratefully, and said: 'Yes; it is not what we have done which avails, but what Christ has done.'. Still he seemed to be thinking mournfully, and I could only silently ask God to speak to him. He has been so hopeful all along that I think the realisation that he could never again take up his ministerial duties was very bitter to him, and for a few short hours a cloud rested upon him—the cloud into which the sons of God are all baptised sooner or later. He appeared at last to fall asleep; but soon after I heard him whisper, with clasped hands;

> ' Nothing in my hand I bring,
> Simply to Thy cross I cling,'

repeating the rest of the lines. Before retiring to bed he prayed aloud, and gave himself up to God in perfect submission to His will. ·

"Dr. Agnes McLaren has been most constant in her kindness, calling and helping us practically in many ways. She is much trusted by Dr. Frank, and had asked him privately what he thought of the Canon. When I asked her what he said, she replied : ' Well, he considers him the most wonderful man he ever saw.' ' Of course,' I answered, ' but what next ? ' ' He does not think there will be any sudden change, but advises that as soon as it is a little warmer you should get him home. It is his own wish to go home, and his wish should now be your guide.'"

Some months later Dr. Frank wrote to me in England :—

"I prize it as a great privilege to have known Canon Butler, and to have possessed his friendly and indulgent confidence. I most sincerely concur in what has been said about the extraordinary courage and cheerfulness and reverential resignation, which, thanks to most exceptional endowments, enabled him to place himself so entirely above his illness."

"Clear as crystal," was Dr. Frank's expression at another time, in speaking of his character. "What more can be said? No special testimony can add to the knowledge of a character the bearing and manifestation of which, under circumstances of such trying stress' and strain, were open to all."

In answer to an affectionate letter from Tell Meuricoffre, my husband replied from Cannes:—

"It is a great pleasure to Josephine and me to look back on the time we spent under your hospitable roof at Villa Meuricoffre, and again at Naples, not to speak of Amalfi— that lovely sun-visited spot which did us both so much good, until the sirocco came and obscured the heavens, and we saw the ships driven by the storms, and successive waterspouts causing alarm to mariners on the sea and landsmen on the shore. We are chiefly bound to Naples as your home, and as the centre from which you and Hatty dispense in every direction kindness and hospitality, and fulfil so admirably the duties of citizens—duties in which your sons are now also taking an important part. We are very quiet here. Our old friends at the Grande Bretagne come to see us—Sir Mark and Lady Collet, Lady Maria Brodie, and Mr. and Mrs. Renton. George von Bunsen also comes to see me."

During these last weeks his delight in the Scriptures and his fervency in prayer were ever more manifest, in spite of additional physical weakness. And the amount of energy he possessed till nearly the end is a subject of wonder even in the retrospect. It is a fact surprising to many that until two days before his death he unfailingly rose at half-past seven or eight o'clock in the morning, and after having his bath and dressing, with the help of his attendant, he joined me at breakfast, always with the same cheerful morning greetings and pleasant conversation on a variety of subjects. "Those sweet *tête-à-tête*

breakfasts," I wrote to a sister, " were like heaven to me.
Often my nights were long and dark, when I lay awake
thinking what it would be for me when he was no longer
on earth; but when the morning came, his bright ' Good
morning, darling! I am pretty well. How are you?' used
to dispel all clouds, and I could again rejoice, seeing his
manly fortitude and cheerful spirit." After breakfast we
read together. The evenings, when watching the beautiful
sunsets over the sea, were generally very happy times.
Sometimes at the sunset hour he would say suddenly,
" Shall we pray?" not liking to delay our evening devotions till he became too tired. When he prayed at that
hour I was often struck with the eloquence of his speech.
It was quite unconscious eloquence; for he never thought
of his words in the least. He was consciously in the
presence of God, and in that presence all hesitation of
speech, all weariness and weakness, seemed to disappear;
and sometimes, when I thought he had ceased, he would
after a pause renew his prayers and praises. His devotions were often simple ascriptions of praise and affirma-
tions of his trust in God, and of God's greatness, power,
and love.

Extracts from diary :—

" February 25th.—We sat near our window watching the
sunset glow over the Esterels, the sea, and the woods, and
talked long of dear friends. Arthur had written to him
when about to start to England from Valescure: 'This is a
beautiful place; but when once one has turned one's face
homeward, one ceases to regret the things one is leaving
behind.' My husband said: 'If this is the case in respect
to our earthly home, how much more is it so when we have
turned our faces to go to our heavenly home.' He watched
the landscape till the rose-colour on the hills faded away;
and then, leaning back in his chair, with clasped hands, he

poured out his soul in an earnest and affectionate prayer for all whom he loves most, and whom he may soon be called to leave—our sons and our little grandchildren, his brothers and sisters and mine, and then for his brother canons and the Dean at Winchester. He pleaded in a sustained and pathetic manner, concluding: 'Thou Lord hast promised that whatsoever things we shall ask in Thy name Thou wilt give us. Now, therefore, in humble confidence, I ask that Thou wilt pour out Thy Holy Spirit on all these.'"

"February 27th.—Again a beautiful sunset and pleasant talk. We were speaking of the different attributes of Christ, and he said: 'I like to think of Him as our Interpreter.' I asked him to explain, in what sense. He replied: 'I feel that He takes our inarticulate wishes and interprets them to the Father. I imagine the Lord Jesus saying to God, "Here is a poor, sinful man" (indicating himself); "he wants to feel rightly; he does not know how to attain to greater sorrow for sin and greater love for God, nor can he pray as he desires; he neither feels nor speaks as he would. But now I bring him to Thee, O Father. I present him to Thee; I am here his Interpreter—to interpret his heart's longings to Thee, and to express to Thee, for him, all his poor wishes and prayers."' It seemed to me a beautiful thought."

"March 2nd.—He was up early, in spite of his weakness; and while waiting for breakfast he read aloud, in a firm voice and with deep feeling, the 27th Psalm, (it had never seemed to me so beautiful as then): 'The Lord is my light and my salvation; whom shall I fear? The Lord is the strength of my life; of whom shall I be afraid? . . . For in the time of trouble He shall hide me in His pavilion: in the secret of His tabernacle shall He hide me; He shall set me upon a rock. Wait on the Lord: be of good courage, and He shall strengthen thine heart: wait, I say, on the Lord.' I referred later to the impression which that 27th Psalm had made on me in the morning as he read it, and he said: 'It is so sometimes; words with which we have been familiar all our lives come to us with an entirely new meaning and power. It is because God speaks to us through them.'"

"March 3rd.—He has almost laid aside his little collection of favourite classics, which we brought from home, and turns constantly to the Bible. He occasionally translated to me, at Naples and Amalfi, lines of Pindar and Theocritus, especially when we still had the hope of going to Sicily, which would have made up to him in some small degree for never having visited Greece. The classical associations of the neighbourhood of Naples were very pleasant to him however. To-day he read for a long time a number of his favourite hymns."

Our eldest son came out to us to make all arrangements for his father's homeward journey, and to accompany us.

"March 9th.—He is very happy because George has come, and is not the least anxious about the difficult journey before us. Lady Molyneux called yesterday and left this message: 'Tell him his courage is helping many. It is a fresh testimony to his Master.' When I told him it, he said, with tears in his eyes, 'God bless her for saying it.' She called again to-day. As I went out of his room with her she paused in the passage outside his closed door, and said, 'this place seems to me like the gate of Heaven.' In the evening we spoke of the journey home, and he said: 'We have not wilfully decided to go home; we have put the whole matter in God's hands.' Though very weak, he would have our usual evening devotions, in the course of which he prayed: 'Lord Jesus Christ, go before us in everything, and everywhere."

"March 11th.—A most glorious evening as we travelled along that beautiful coast to Marseilles. Everything was flooded with sunshine. As he lay on his couch in the railway carriage, we pointed out to him the different beautiful places, Mont St. Cassien (the Hermitage), Grasse, and the Islands, where we had sketched together, and then the ruins of Fréjus. He was too much exhausted to speak, but greeted the different familiar views with a tired smile of farewell. He whispered once, 'What a beautiful world this is!' and 'I shall never sketch again.'"

" March 13th.—Boulogne.—His strength is failing fast, but his calmness is wonderful; he leans on George, and has the quiet spirit of a little child; never at all agitated by the difficulties of the long journey in his helpless state. He was dressed in his fur coat and ready to be taken down to the steamer, and as there were a few minutes to spare, I said, 'You are not strong enough to-day, dearest, for our usual morning prayer; we will rest in silence.' He replied, 'O yes, O yes, I am quite strong enough;' and he began to speak with God. It was not petition. It was all praise, from first to last—grateful thanksgiving and adoration,—for spiritual blessings first, for the gift of eternal life, then for the kindness of friends, the love and loyalty of his sons, and for the fine weather and bright sunshine on that day. All praise—till at last his voice failed and ceased, and gradually he fell into a half sleep, to be roused up in a few moments for the departure. If the atmosphere of heaven is one of constant praise, then this, his last articulate prayer, was an anticipation of heaven, —of the life to which he was hastening. There seemed to me reason enough to pray, to cry for help and for pity, so great was his weakness—so pathetic the situation. But it seemed not to occur to him to ask anything then, but only to thank God for everything.

" When he had been carried to the vessel and was lying quietly in the cabin with closed eyes, and a look of peace and content, I bent over him and said, ' We have a beautiful day dear, and a perfectly calm sea.' Without opening his eyes, he said in a low voice, ' How kind God is to us !' "

" Evening of March 13th.—We reached the hotel in London. His exhaustion was extreme. I kneeled by his bedside, and he asked, ' Whose house is this ? Where are we now?' I answered 'In London, dear, and *home to-morrow*.' He was contented, and smiled. He had beckoned me to him with his thin right hand; I came very near, but he only whispered very softly, 'I shall be so glad to sleep.'"

"I remained with him through the night. Towards morning I lay down in an anteroom for half an hour's rest. I slept a little, and awaking suddenly, I went quickly to his room, and greeted him. There was no response, no sound, no recognition. For the first time in all the years of our life together his sweet 'Good-morning' was not spoken; and a sense of great desolation came over me. Once or twice during the day, however, he seemed to know my voice, and about four o'clock in the afternoon, just before the end, appearing to feel that he was starting on a long journey, he turned his head to me and took my hand, and said rather anxiously, 'You will go with me, beloved, will you not? you will go with me?' The appeal went to my heart; I saw his mind wandered a little. I answered without hesitation, 'Yes I will! *I will go with you*.' For I knew that my heart would follow him whither he was going, and would dwell with him there."

J. E. B. to my sisters. March 23rd. :—

"You already know the sad story of our 'coming home.' We must try not to dwell on those sorrowful incidents, but rather on the character of him who is gone, and on all the sunshine which was permitted to fall on our path, up to almost the end. Several persons have thought that the journey home might have accelerated the last symptoms. But we are comforted in that matter. He was on a waterbed, in a reserved carriage, sleeping profoundly almost all the way from Marseilles to Paris. At Paris we were met by an agent of Sir Edward Watkin who came to offer his services, and at Boulonge the Superintendent of St. John's Ambulance Association himself came to us from London, a quiet, skilful man, who arranged for getting on board and for his journey to London in a manner to make it as easy as possible. Nothing struck us more than the way in which my dear one surrendered himself to the care of others (he, accustomed all his life to be so independent of help). As George said, ' he showed such perfect trust in us, that we would not jar or hurt him, and that we would do everything that was right, answering us slowly and gently, and in short sentences, like a child.' Through the kindness of Sir E. Watkin a large invalid compartment was waiting for us at Folkestone. My husband's patient face seemed to attract everyone, and call out all that was best in them. A man ran after us on the platform and held up to the carriage window a tempting cup of tea, saying he thought perhaps the ' dear gentleman ' might like to take it. We reached the London hotel at about 7.30. No doubt, in spite of all our care, the journey must have tired him ; but the end was coming, and coming fast, even before we left Cannes. Dr. Frank thought then, however, that his wonderful constitution might serve him a longer time, and that he would reach his home and live some short time there. The end seemed to us sudden, even after so long a discipline of preparation. All his brothers, and his sister, Mrs. Galton, came to us in London, just to look on his dear face once more. He was dimly conscious, I think, of their presence, and grateful. During the last sad hour none were with him except the two sons and myself. The moment after his spirit had fled, and the dear venerable head rested on the pillow, and the familiar calm, benevolent look settled down on his face, the setting sun pierced the clouds and fog, and its rays happening just to fall on his pillow and silvery hair, made a complete aureole around his head. One of my sons said he was reminded at that moment of some beautiful *Pietà* he had seen. . And, indeed, there was an extraordinary beauty of expression in the beloved face, of *suffering past*, and of *the love which never dies !* "

He was laid to rest in the cemetery at Winchester. The service in the cathedral was very affecting. Our friend Charles Parker, who was present with many others, wrote ·—

"His funeral was the brightest and the most beautiful I have ever seen. With his love of art, I thought he would have liked to see it as it was. Then the hymn 'Now the labourer's task is o'er;' * I never before heard it so beautifully sung. I kept fearing it would end before we reached the west door, but there were more verses than I knew of; and nothing could be more touching than the passing of the procession, between the lines of his fellow labourers and the choristers, out of that fine Cathedral Church (now more than ever associated with his memory), as the last strains died away. I am thankful to have been there, and to have seen you once more in what was your last home with him. When we were shown into his study how touching it was to see his large dog lying outside the window, looking wistfully in, as if searching for his master among us.

"My thoughts go back over nearly all your married life, and all my long friendship with him, in pleasing remembrance of his unfailing kindness and loyal affection. I rejoice in the work he has done, and in the work God has done in, as well as by him."

On the following Sunday, Canon Durst alluded very beautifully to the sad journeying homeward, likening the closing scene to that of a vessel arrived in port and within sight of home, which is wrecked as it reaches the shore. He spoke of the growing weakness, which made the last painful journey a race with the Angel of Death · the arrival while yet alive upon his native shores, to lie

---

* Now the labourer's task is o'er;
    Now the battle day is past;
  Now upon the farther shore
    Lands the voyager at last.
 FATHER, in Thy gracious keeping
 Leave we now Thy servant sleeping.

down and die in London; "and so, after this painful travelling, so sad for him, so sad for those whose loving hands were bearing him, he has indeed come home and found rest."

> "Safe home, safe home in port!
> Rent cordage, shattered deck;
> Torn sails, provisions short,
> And only not a wreck;
> But oh! the joy upon that shore
> To tell our voyage perils o'er!"

From the many letters and testimonies received I give a few extracts, and my task is done.

First some fragments from the letters of my sister in Naples, with whom we had so lately been, and who loved him so much:

"Naples, March 18th.

"We have been sitting together talking of you and of all that has passed. And now you are again at Winchester. And the dear master! he has come back to the loved home he longed to enter once again; come back, but not as you hoped. You took him home—your lover, your husband, your own true-hearted. We picture that home-coming, pathethic beyond words.

"It is sweet to have this house so filled with the memory of his presence; something more than memory, an actual lingering sense. He was so quiet and unobtrusive: he made no noise; but what an individuality he had, to leave behind him as he does, such a vivid sense of his presence! I recall the lovely moments when you and I sat in the corner of the library here, and Miss M—— sang to us from 'Orfeo,' and he translated the Greek story to us in his soft voice, which even in his running translation had a stately rhythm; and the time I saw him resting on my little couch (when you had come back to Naples from Amalfi) in the blaze of the afternoon sunshine. He was sleeping, and I turned and looked and looked again at that fine, delicate profile, and printed it on my heart.

32

" How wonderful is the unmistakable impress of God's Spirit on a human face ! I feel that to have seen him and lived near him as I have done this winter, should be, and is, a consecration for the rest of my term on earth. The peace of God shone in his face and through his dear and wasted form, with such Christ-like meekness, and noble fortitude. He was always expressing gratitude for every trifling thing, and under circumstances in which most persons would have had every excuse for being rather irritable or depressed. When sleeping that Sunday afternoon on my couch, he seemed to me as if his soul was already looking on the face of God. He often had that look lately.

" How he loved Nature ! I don't believe he noticed the fog when you reached London, for the heavenly horizon was beginning to light up for him. And now he is amongst those beauties which eye hath not seen, nor the imagination of man conceived, but which God has prepared for those who love Him, as he did.

" In looking back, how plainly one sees how all your work was based, established, strengthened (next to God) on his dear love and sympathy ; and how you were able to form (through him) an ideal of justice and purity in man. I daresay you would often have been carried away without the anchor of his unfailing wisdom and sound judgment—for you had always the sense of these as a kind of invisible tribunal, influencing you even when never brought to the test of discussion."

Some months later, Lord Coleridge wrote to me from Winchester ; (the place reminded him of his visits to us there in past years) :

" Royal Court of Justice, Winchester.

" I am constantly reminded of your husband by some turn of thought, some quaint story, some remark of delicate and refined observation put into pure and happy language ; but, as I have often said, he was a man more remarkable in himself than anything he ever did or wrote : a man so perfect in character, so full and varied in accomplishments, in whom the absence of angularities makes it difficult to describe him in a way which would vividly impress others. He was an admirable scholar, but he seldom talked scholarship; a fine artist, both in judgment and in execution, but he seldom discoursed on it; a very considerable linguist, which one found out almost by accident; full of fun, but never giving way to ' inconvenient ' jesting; an athlete quite unboastful, a sportsman silent about his exploits. It is not easy to draw the character of such a man, who effaced himself all his life : who took a position below his merits without a jealous or repining thought, and saw men every way his inferiors pass him in the race of life without one word of satire or of depreciation. How little I can say ! almost the dream of a shadow, yet a shadow suffused with gentle light, and a dream happy, soothing, elevating."

Margaret Parker, sister of our friend Charles Parker, wrote, in July, 1890 :

" I must tell you what thoughts came to me as I returned the other day from Harrow. I drove along the well-remembered road *alone*. The scent of the hay wafted by the sweet evening breeze, the wild roses still in the hedges, the blue summer sky with floating clouds, brought up vivid memories which cannot be described : most of all, my mother's delight each year in that drive to Harrow. In 1887, Canon Butler drove with her and me back from the Harrow Speeches, and told us many of his recollections of Harrow, and recalled memories of those who were gone. I remember thinking how he seemed to draw out sweetness rather than sadness from past years, content to feel that they had yielded joys which he would always treasure. There was no bitterness, no mourning in his tone, but a gentle acquiescence in all the passing away. . . . He was one who never sought the highest place, nor even seemed to think what his place was, but only what his duty in the highest sense was. And as to his place in his friends' estimation, it seemed as if he did not think of that either, but rather of the bonds of affection between them and him, and of their gifts and graces."

Mlle. Amélié Humbert wrote in the summer:

" We have been to Grindelwald. All the way I seemed to see you and dear Canon Butler; all seemed so full of memories of. beautiful days gone by. It was the loveliest day of the summer: no cloud, the brightest sunshine and the most exquisite view of the everlasting hills, from which there was a constant falling of avalanches. I took a solitary walk to the dear church in memory of Canon Butler. It was open and empty, and I walked up the aisle. All was so silent, and the bright sunshine shone through the open windows, and I praised God in thinking of the joy and bliss of him whom we should have loved to see in that pulpit, but who is now among the ransomed throng, waiting for you."

Dean Kitchin, writing to one of my sisters from Winchester, said:

" I shall always continue to miss the dear Canon here. It was an object-lesson in all the nobler qualities of life to watch him under the burden of his long and depressing illness.* I never saw in anyone a more complete and beautiful triumph of spirit over the weakness of the flesh."

The following testimony from associated ladies of the West of England is one of many such received from fellow-workers at home and abroad:—

" The memory of all Canon Butler's devotion to the cause in which you both laboured, becomes more precious to us as the days go on. He not only shared in the work, but his love and sympathy relieved you of half the suffering that might otherwise almost have overwhelmed you when the weight of the sin and misery in the world lay heavily upon your heart, and (for a season) friends and acquaintances ' forsook you and fled.'

·" Surely only a very noble and self-sacrificing nature, and a soul full of the highest and purest aspirations could have borne such a lofty and yet humble testimony to the truth, under circumstances like these; and the remembrance must be very precious to you and to your children, as it is to all women who understand what he and you did and suffered for them and for the love of God."

The impression his character made on the minds of those nearest of kin to him may be imperfectly guessed by the following:

From my son George:—

"You need never have any fear, dearest mother, that father's memory will ever grow dim to us. I shall remember many incidents of his life and many of his sayings as long as my own life lasts. One thing especially I shall never forget,—his sweetness to me during those last few precious days I was with him. Your sorrow for him is beyond that of anyone; but next to yours comes that of his sons. We too mourn him deeply; and around and beyond the small circle of mother and sons is a wider circle of less near relatives and many dear friends who feel his loss, as you know. It is like the ever-widening ripple on water: we cannot tell where it ends. It will be our first duty to keep his memory ever fresh, and to prevent our love for his dear character ever growing less."

From my son Stanley (written a few days before his father's death) ·

" Father's last letter to us was as cheerful and bright as ever. I can imagine that he longs to be at home again. He used to say long ago that he always hoped to die in harness. Still the last few months spent at Naples and Amalfi must have been full of beauty and peace, partly from the scenery and sunshine, but more from his own state of mind; and this we must be very thankful for. There is something very beautiful and grand in his calm faith and courage, and in his utter freedom from selfishness; and though it is sad to see our dearest earthly friend failing in strength of body, yet the strength of his mind and the purity of his heart are a solace to us now, and will be a guide and example to us in all our future life."

Numberless beautiful wreaths and flowers were laid upon that grave in the cemetery at Winchester. In a few short days all were faded; but there remains one there to this day still unfaded, a wreath of purest white and silvery *immortelles* gathered on the Veldt by our youngest son, and bearing the inscription, " From South Africa.'

My husband translated into Latin, in 1864 (the year of the departure of our little Eva), the following lines by Horatius Bonar, expressing the desire of a dying saint that his friends should rejoice rather than mourn for him. I believe that it was in this spirit that he would have wished us to regard his own departure:

"Ad vitam hinc abeo, non loca Tartari,
  Nativum e tenebris æthera consequor,
  Immortale viget libera qua Salus
    A morbo atque doloribus.

Muto divitiis pauperiem meam,
  Et pannos nivea cælicolum stola;
  Pallentem maciem corporis exuens
    Sanctorum decus induo.

Libertas vocat: en! vincula desero;
  Rumpentur celeri turbine compedes;
  Campos Elysios, arva fragrantia
    Læto sole, premam pede.

Pro nisu veniet laurigero quies;
  Pro mæstis aquilæ penna laboribus;
  Ipse et perpetuis a scatebris bibens
    Restinguam assiduam sitim.

Ergo absint lacrymæ digredientibus;
Non me vana decet lacryma nec dolor:
Festiva niteat nostra dies nota
    Quando annos agitis novos."

" I go to life and not to death,
    From darkness to life's native sky;
I go from sickness and from pain
    To health and immortality.

I go from poverty to wealth,
    From rags to raiment angel-fair,
From the pale leanness of the flesh
    To beauty such as saints shall wear.

I go from chains to liberty,
    These fetters will be broken soon;
Forth over Eden's fragrant fields
    I walk beneath a glorious noon.

For toil there comes the crowned rest;
    Instead of burdens, eagle's wings;
And I, even I, this life-long thirst
    Shall quench at everlasting springs.

Let our farewell then be tearless,
    Since I bid farewell to tears;
Write this day of my departure
    Festive in your coming years."

J. W. Arrowsmith, Printer, Quay Street, Bristol.

DO NOT
REMOVE
THE
CARD
FROM
THIS
POCKET

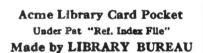